HISTORY OF WOMEN IN THE UNITED STATES

HISTORY OF WOMEN IN THE UNITED STATES

Historical Articles on Women's Lives and Activities

Edited by Nancy F. Cott

Series ISBN 3-598-41454-4

1. Theory and Method in Women's History
   ISBN 3-598-41455-2 Part 1
   ISBN 3-598-41477-3 Part 2

2. Household Constitution and Family Relationships
   ISBN 3-598-41456-0

3. Domestic Relations and Law
   ISBN 3-598-41457-9

4. Domestic Ideology and Domestic Work
   ISBN 3-598-41458-7 Part 1
   ISBN 3-598-41475-7 Part 2

5. The Intersection of Work and Family Life
   ISBN 3-598-41459-5 Part 1
   ISBN 3-598-41476-5 Part 2

6. Working on the Land
   ISBN 3-598-41460-9

7. Industrial Wage Work
   ISBN 3-598-41461-7 Part 1
   ISBN 3-598-41693-8 Part 2

8. Professional and White-Collar Employments
   ISBN 3-598-41462-5 Part 1
   ISBN 3-598-41694-6 Part 2

9. Prostitution
   ISBN 3-598-41463-3

10. Sexuality and Sexual Behavior
    ISBN 3-598-41464-1

11. Women's Bodies: Health and Childbirth
    ISBN 3-598-41465-X

12. Education
    ISBN 3-598-41466-8

13. Religion
    ISBN 3-598-41467-6

14. Intercultural and Interracial Relations
    ISBN 3-598-41468-4

15. Women and War
    ISBN 3-598-41469-2

16. Women Together: Organizational Life
    ISBN 3-598-41470-6

17. Social and Moral Reform
    ISBN 3-598-41471-4 Part 1
    ISBN 3-598-41695-4 Part 2

18. Women and Politics
    ISBN 3-598-41472-2 Part 1
    ISBN 3-598-41697-0 Part 2

19. Woman Suffrage
    ISBN 3-598-41473-0 Part 1
    ISBN 3-598-41696-2 Part 2

20. Feminist Struggles for Sex Equality
    ISBN 3-598-41474-9

HISTORY OF WOMEN IN THE UNITED STATES

Historical Articles on Women's Lives and Activities

2. Household Constitution and Family Relationships

Edited with an Introduction by

Nancy F. Cott
Yale University

K · G · Saur
Munich · London · New York · Paris 1992

Publisher's Note

The articles and chapters which comprise this collection originally appeared in a wide variety of publications and are reproduced here in facsimile from the highest quality offprints and photocopies available. The reader will notice some occasional marginal shading and text-curl common to photocopying from tightly bound volumes. Every attempt has been made to correct or minimize this effect.

Library of Congress Cataloging-in-Publication Data

History of women in the United States : historical articles on women's lives and activities / edited with an introduction by Nancy F. Cott.

p. cm.

Includes bibliographical references and indexes.

Contents: 1. Theory and method in women's history -- 2. Household constitution and family relationships -- 3. Domestic relations and law -- 4. Domestic ideology and domestic work -- 5. The intersection of work and family life -- 6. Working on the land -- 7. Industrial wage work -- 8. Professional and white-collar employments -- 9. Prostitution -- 10. Sexuality and sexual behavior -- 11. Women's bodies -- 12. Education -- 13. Religion -- 14. Intercultural and interracial relations -- 15. Women and war -- 16. Women together -- 17. Social and moral reform -- 18. Women and politics -- 19. Women suffrage -- 20. Feminist struggles for sex equality.

ISBN 3-598-41454-4 (set)

1. Women--United States--History. 2. Women--United States--Social conditions. I. Cott, Nancy F.

HQ1410.H57 1992

305.4'0973--dc20 92-16765

CIP

Die Deutsche Bibliothek - CIP - Einheitsaufnahme

History of women in the United States: historical articles on women's lives and activities / ed. with an introd. by Nancy F. Cott. - Munich ; London ; New York ; Paris : Saur.

ISBN 3-598-41454-4

NE: Cott, Nancy F. (Hrsg.)

Vol. 2. Household constitution and family relationships. - 1992

ISBN 3-598-41456-0

Printed on acid-free paper/Gedruckt auf säurefreiem Papier

A Reed Reference Publishing Company

Printed in the United States of America

Printed/Bound by Edwards Brothers Incorporated, Ann Arbor

ISBN 3-598-41456-0 (vol. 2)

ISBN 3-598-41454-4 (series)

Contents

Series Preface

In the space of one generation, women's history has become the fastest-growing area of scholarship in U.S. history. Since the resurgence of feminism in the late 1960s and 1970s, insistent questions about the historical meanings of "woman's place" have sowed and reaped a garden of scholarship. Where scholarly works used to be bare of mention of women, academic enterprise has now produced a vigorous growth of books and articles, bringing to light diverse women of every region, race, class and age. This research is marked by a renovating intent that refuses to accept as "human" history a history of men. Interest is lively and debate is stimulating and sought after: attendance at the Berkshire Conference on the History of Women rivals the size of the annual convention of the American Historical Association.

While books in women's history are daily increasing in numbers and strength, as in any fast-developing field the scholarly literature in the form of articles is most expansive and up-to-the-minute. All the history journals now publish articles on women's work, domestic settings, family relations, household matters, female politics and organizations and so forth, and new journals have sprung into being to concentrate on such topics. Women's historians publish in numerous regional and thematic history journals as well as in feminist outlets and in journals of other social science disciplines. This series brings together a collection of outstanding articles from the field, almost all written in the past twenty years and more than half published during the 1980s. It brings together, in volumes organized by topic, essays otherwise widely dispersed. These volumes reprint only articles that originally appeared in journals, not chapters of books; review articles are not included. Articles have been chosen for overall quality and for range. Each one was chosen for one or more of the following reasons: because it is the standard authority on its subject matter; represents an important statement on a topic by a recognized scholar; presages an important book to come; provides a first look at new evidence or new methods; or opens an untapped area or new controversy. Older articles have been reprinted if their data or interpretation have not been surpassed or if they marked an important stage in the historiography, even if since superseded.

The historical coverage of the series extends from the Revolutionary era to the 1960s. The articles themselves are dated from the 1940s through 1988. Volumes are organized by topic rather than time period. Within each volume, the articles are ordered chronologically (with respect to substance), so that the whole can be read as an historical overview. The only exception to this ordering principle is volume 1, on Theory and Method, in which the contents are arranged in order of publication. Within each volume there is an attempt to include articles on as diverse kinds of women as possible. None of the volume topics is regionally or racially defined; rather, all volumes are topically designed so as to afford views of women's work, family lives, and public activities which cut across races and regions. Any volume in the series stands on its own, supplying as full a treatment of a designated subject matter as the scholarly literature will provide. Several groupings of volumes also make sense; that is, volumes 2 through 5 all center around domestic and family matters; volumes 5 through 9 consider other varieties of women's work; volumes 9 through 11 concern uses and abuses of women's bodies; volumes 12 through 14 look at major aspects of socialization; and volumes 15 through 20 include organizational and political efforts of many sorts.

As a whole, the series displays in all its range the vitality of the field of women's history. Aside from imbuing U.S. history with new vision, scholarship in this area has informed, and should continue to inform, current public debate on issues from parental leave to the nuclear freeze. By bringing historical articles together under topical headings, these volumes both represent accurately the shape of historical controversy (or consensus) on given issues and make historians' findings most conveniently available for current reference.

Introduction

The emergence of the current field of women's history was contemporaneous with the rise of interest in family history and demographic history. While these fields are separable because of their differing emphases and because of differing practitioners' goals or interests, their subject matters often overlap. Analysis and interpretation of women's domestic lives has required investigation into the same data of household structure and family relationships over time that family and demographic history explore. This volume includes signal early articles in the history of the family, which helped to inform the emerging field of women's history. It represents also the continuing stream of articles focusing on women by looking at marital and parent-child relationships and the nonconforming instance of the single woman in different regions and among several ethnic and racial groups in the U.S.

Significant continuities and major changes both can be said to characterize household constitution and family relationships from the eighteenth through the twentieth centuries. A nuclear family pattern--that is, co-residence of parents and their children, without grandparents or lateral kin--has been most characteristic in the U.S. since the nation's beginning: this is the single most significant continuity. Nor has age at first marriage varied a great deal over two hundred years, generally averaging in the early twenties for women and the mid-twenties for men, except for somewhat higher averages at the close of the nineteenth century and somewhat lower averages in the decade or two following World War II. From the period of the American Revolution onward, young men and women have exercised considerable autonomy from parental control in choosing their mates--this trend was certainly increased in the nineteenth and even more after the turn of the twentieth century, but it began as early as the Revolutionary era.

On the other hand, a modern commentator is perhaps more likely to notice the changes than the continuities in family life. The size of families and of households has dropped dramatically. This is in part because there are so many fewer children born to each married woman--the average number has dropped from about seven in 1800 to fewer than two, now--and also because households now rarely include live-in domestic servants, apprentices, or visiting kin, as they often used to. In the late eighteenth century there were virtually no places to live outside family households (except army encampments during war).

Today there are many non-family sites in which people live, such as hotels, schools and colleges, old age homes, prisons, hospitals, and other institutions; more important, it is an accepted and feasible thing for a single adult to make a "home" alone, or for unrelated groups of adults to live together. The shift in this direction, beginning in the early nineteenth century and still continuing, was made possible through economic change which also was fundamentally familial: that is, the move away from an agricultural/artisanal society in which households were the locus of economic production and members of families worked together to produce a "living." In modern urban commercial and industrial society, factories, offices, shops, banks and other non-household institutions are the sites of economic production, and individuals earn wages or salaries as individuals, whatever their family status. The shift toward more various definitions of households was only possible when a "living" could be attained by individuals, rather than requiring family cooperation.

If, as commentators have noticed for at least a hundred years, the American family over time has left off being a productive unit and instead become a unit for consumption of goods, it has not "lost" its economic function (as some would lament), but transformed that function. As the productive work of families and households as such has declined, the relative weight of affective or emotional tasks within the family also has grown. Nuclear families have been the site for rearing and socializing children over the whole of U.S. history, but that work of "social reproduction" has become more prominent as other forms of production no longer take place within the home's four walls. While the number of children per family has declined, the amount of care to be lavished on each has increased. Individuals' expectations of the affection to be sustained between husband and wife have also, it seems, grown. If marriages have been sought for reasons of love and emotional support for hundreds of years, nonetheless the emotional reasons for marrying or staying married assume much more weight in a modern age of individual wage-earning, since the economic urgency for marriage is diminished.

These themes of continuity and change play through the articles in this volume. The articles not only generalize about developments over time in households and families but also illustrate regional, racial and ethnic variation--most emphatically in black families, slave and free, as compared to white families. "American" norms of household constitution and family relationships have been, in fact, race-specific--i.e., derived from white behavior. Almost any question one would raise about family structures and roles--for instance, about family formation, courtship, sex roles, the sexual division of labor, childrearing--will find the experience of blacks, whose lives were shaped by coercion into slavery, differing from that of whites. Exploration of structures and roles within black families requires, often, a different set of questions.

The articles selected here shed particular light on women who are both in households and families or purposively out of them. The ways that historians of the family have pursued their inquiries have not always illuminated women's roles as daughters, mothers, sisters, or wives, but these articles focus on both the values and the constraints that have shaped women's experiences. Studies of women who created exceptions from the nuclear family "norm"--whether by declining to marry, or by following the Mormon path of plural marriage, or by migrating on their own, or by becoming (willfully or not) single mothers--clarify both the norm and the range of the possible. This fuller portrayal of the past helps us understand and evaluate alternative family forms developing in our own day.

Household Constitution and Family Relationships

The American Family in Past Time

JOHN DEMOS

TO STUDY THE HISTORY OF THE AMERICAN FAMILY is to conduct a rescue mission into the dreamland of our national self-concept. No subject is more closely bound up with our sense of a difficult present—and our nostalgia for a happier past. How often, in reference to contemporary problems, does the diagnostic finger point in the direction of family life. Significantly, this emphasis comes from both the right and the left. Conservatives detect a loosening of the bonds of family, a poisonous infiltration of permissiveness. Time was, they contend, when domestic life established sound patterns of authority that served to guarantee an orderly society. On the other side, counterculture spokesmen decry a damaging trend toward rigid—and alienating—nuclear households. It is their aim to recapture the spirit, if not the exact forms, of an "extended-family" system allegedly typical of the premodern era. These perspectives differ greatly as to substance, but there is a common pejorative thrust. In both cases the story of the family through time is a story of decline and decay.

But the *reality* of family life in the past is something else again. To capture that reality is an extraordinarily difficult task. Source materials are scattered and fragmentary. The pertinent methodologies are highly complex. And, in truth, professional historians have only recently become concerned with such seemingly private and personal subjects. For precisely the same reasons, however, the field presents a fascinating challenge to scholars. Moreover, since there is such an overlay of myth and misconception here,

○ JOHN DEMOS, professor of history at Brandeis University, has been a fellow at the Center for Psychosocial Studies in Chicago during this academic year. He is the author of various books and articles on the history of American family life. This essay will also appear in a volume to be published by Little, Brown and Company, tentatively entitled *Marriage*, and edited by Henry Grunebaum, M.D. and Jacob Christ, M.D.

the outcome may have some sociological importance. If the family in contemporary America warrants special consideration—perhaps even a major overhaul—then this must be based insofar as possible on an accurate understanding of its previous history.

The first Americans were, of course, post-Elizabethan Englishmen and heirs of a traditional culture with roots far back in the medieval past. This culture was imported whole when they crossed the ocean to begin the settlement of a new world. Prominent among their mental baggage were deeply held beliefs and values about family life—its proper shape and substance, and its place in that larger scheme of things that has sometimes been characterized as the "great chain of being."

There was, to begin with, the unquestioned assumption of a tight link between the family and the community at large. The individual household was the basic unit of everyday living, the irreducible cell from which all human society was fashioned. It formed, indeed, the model for every larger structure of authority; as one seventeenth-century author declared, "a family is a little church, and a little commonwealth . . . a school, wherein the first principles and grounds of government and subjection are learned, whereby men are fitted to greater matters in church or commonwealth." Or—to reverse the metaphor—religious and political communities were only families writ large. The head of the family, normally the father, was also an agent of the state. In fact, the principle of fatherhood lay right at the heart of most political thinking in this period. The higher ranks of men—gentry, noblemen, bishops—were all pictured as fathers to those who fell within their various jurisdictions. The king was simply the grandest and most powerful of these patriarchal figures. Of course, the Puritans—prominent among the colonial settlers—came to exclude the king from their scheme of authority, but this was a substantive, not a structural, difference. Like all men of their time, they assumed the fusion of family and community in the preservation of order.

But what did this mean in detail? It meant, first of all, that a man was not free to do entirely as he pleased within his own family. The larger community—the state—felt concerned in all his behavior toward his wife and children, and acted accordingly. Thus, for example, a disobedient child was not only punished with a thrashing at the hands of his father; he was also liable to action by the courts. Or—another example—colonial magistrates might remove a child from the care of "unseemly" parents and place it in some other family. Or, again, a local court could order the reunion of a husband and wife who had decided to live apart. Occasionally, this obliged a man (or a woman) to leave the colonies altogether, in order to search for a long-lost spouse in England. In general, individuals who lived by themselves were regarded as potential sources of disorder, and court records are full of directives to such people to find families in which to locate themselves. In all these ways the state might interfere in the sphere of family life. The word "interfere" expresses, of course, our own view of the matter, and the point is that people in the seventeenth century felt quite differently. They regarded such activity as a natural and vital prerogative of the state.

This pattern seemed appropriate because the premodern family performed a wide range of practical functions—both for its own members and for society at large. The household was, for example, the primary unit of economic production and exchange. The vast majority of the American colonists were farmers, and, as in most agricultural communities, there was ample work for everyone, right down to the very young. These families possessed a kind of occupational cohesion not even approximated in our own day. Moreover, the family was also the chief agency of education in colonial America. Schools were limited both in their number and in the character of their facilities, and colleges were for the wealthy few. It was, therefore, from parents that most children learned what they knew of the three Rs. And it was parents (or parental surrogates) who transmitted the vocational skills that would be essential to adult life, whether in farming or (less often) in some one of the skilled trades. In this connection the apprenticeship system precisely epitomized the larger significance of family life.

The family also provided a variety of social services that are now the prerogatives of other institutions. It was the usual place of recourse for sick persons and the elderly. (Old people no longer able to care for themselves would sometimes move in with the family of a grown son, in exchange for a gift of money or land.) Orphans and the indigent were "placed," by local magistrates, in particular households. Even criminals were occasionally handled in this way—implying the effectiveness of the family both as an agency of restraint and as a setting for personal reform.

This range of activity and function, so different from that which obtains today, has encouraged the belief that the colonial family was different in its *composition* as well. Scholars have long thought that premodern society was organized into "extended households"—large kin-groups, including several conjugal pairs, and spanning three or four generations. A corollary assumption has connected our own "nuclear" pattern with the coming of the Industrial Revolution little more than a century ago. But recent demographic research has shown these notions to be quite unfounded. It is now clear that nuclear households have been the norm in America since the time of the first settlements, and in England for as far back as evidence survives. The fundamental unit, then as now, was husband, wife, and their natural children. Occasionally, to be sure, this group was modified through the temporary residence of an elderly grandparent (as mentioned above), or of an apprentice, or of some charge on the community; but such arrangements were of limited impact overall.

The most compelling evidence of this nuclear orientation relates to the process of marriage-making. It was the firm expectation of all concerned that a newly wed couple would establish their own separate *ménage*. The families of both bride and groom joined together to provide the necessary means, contributing land, housing, money and personal effects in amounts stipulated by formal "deeds of gift." Usually such agreements involved painstaking discussion—and often some rather tough bargaining. The fathers of the intended exercised a powerful hand here, by virtue of their control over property; but it should not be thought that these were arranged marriages in some total sense. Affection took precedence—in the literal sense of coming first in time—and practical considerations followed. Life in these communities presented regular opportunities for courtship, and some for sexual dalliance (witness the long sequence of "fornication" cases in the court records). In practice, the range of potential partners was limited by factors of geography and social class. Most colonial settlements were small (less than one hundred families), and there was little chance for courting between towns. Moreover, it was expected that a man and woman planning marriage would evince an overall equality of material—and spiritual—estate. But love must be present, to begin with, and would remain strong, it was hoped, as the couple waxed in years. The letters of John and Margaret Winthrop are a moving testimony to marital devotion ("I kiss my sweet wife, and think of thee long. Farewell, thy John"), and it seems reasonable to infer similar feelings among humbler folk who did not leave written records behind.

As in all societies, however, some marriages worked less well than others. In a few cases, a *very* few, the local courts might sanction divorce. The acceptable grounds were limited to desertion (for a period of no less than seven years), adultery and impotence. (The third of these grounds reflects the important assumption that marriage should provide sexual companionship and yield children.) Incompatibility was recognized as a significant problem—an occasion sometimes for outside intervention, but not for divorce. Legal records reveal a variety of domestic troubles in frequently pungent detail: a man punished for "abusing his wife by kicking her off from a stool into the fire"; a woman charged with "beating and reviling her husband, and egging her children to help her, bidding them knock him in the head, and wishing his victuals might choke him"; a couple "severely reproved for their most ungodly living in contention with the other." In all such cases the courts stood ready to declare their interest—and to exert their authority.

For the colonists, as for people everywhere, family life was influenced by profound beliefs as to differences of age and gender. Concerning women, the thinking of this period was clear enough: in virtually every important respect theirs was the weaker, the inferior, sex. Their position in marriage was distinctly subordinate, their chief duty being obedience to their husbands. Their mental and moral capacities were rated well below those of men. Governor Winthrop's journal records the sad tale of a lady who went insane "by giving herself largely to reading and writing"; in short, intellectual activities were simply unsuited to women's character. There is one other element in the colonial view of women that is hard to specify and even harder to analyze: an implicit, but unmistakable, undercurrent of suspicion and fear. Femininity was linked to deep and mysterious dangers—a special potentiality for evil and corruption. There was a sense that women were less than trustworthy. Thus one finds in legal and personal documents a comment like the following: "If you would believe a woman, believe me. . . ." Thus, too, witchcraft was attributed far more often to women than to men. (There are cultures where the reverse is true.) Still, one must not overemphasize these alleged sex-differences. Colonial women were never truly set apart. Women's lives and characters overlapped with men's at many points; a whole world of thought and feeling and practical circumstance was effectively shared. Their experience from day to day was too similar, their partnership too profound, to support the more radical forms of sex typing that would develop in a later era.

And what of the young in colonial America? There remain from the period various books and essays on the proper deportment of children, which convey some impression at least of what was expected. A central theme in these works—especially, but not exclusively, in the writings of the Puritans—is the need to impose strict discipline on the child virtually from the beginning of life. Here is the advice of the Reverend John Robinson, a leading preacher among the Pilgrims just prior to their departure for America: "Surely there is in all children . . . a stubborness and stoutness of mind arising from natural pride which must in the first place be broken and beaten down, that so the foundation of their education being laid in humility and tractableness, other virtues may in their time be built thereon." The key terms are "broken" and "beaten down." The child was regarded as coming into the world with an inherently corrupted and selfish nature, and this created *the* central problem for parents. Another urgent concern was the inculcation of religious principles—again, from an extremely early age. Cotton Mather's diary contains the following description of a conference with his four-year-old daughter:

> I took my little daughter Katy into my study and then I told my child I am to die shortly and she must, when I am dead, remember everything I now said unto her. I set before her the sinful condition of her nature, and charged her to pray in secret places every day that God for the sake of Jesus Christ would give her a new heart. I gave her to understand that when I am taken from her she must look to meet with more humbling afflictions than she does now [that] she has a tender father to care for her.

A tender father indeed! This passage startles us; the calculated appeal to fear affronts our sense of the needs and sensibilities of children. But there is a vital issue of context here. *Colonial society barely recognized childhood as we know and understand it today.* Consider, for example, the matter of dress: in virtually all seventeenth-century portraiture, children appear in the same sort of clothing that was normal for adults. In fact, this accords nicely with what we know of other aspects of the child's life. His work, much of his recreation, and his closest personal contacts were encompassed within the world of adults. From the age of six or seven he was set to a regular round of tasks about the house or farm (or, in the case of a craftsman's family, the shop or store). When the family went to church, or when they went visiting, he went along. In short, from his earliest years he was expected to be—or to try to be—a miniature adult.

This description has blurred somewhat the distinction between theory and practice, between norms and actual behavior, in the settlers' approach to family life. It is necessary, therefore, to consider more directly the ways in which their ideals and expectations were modified, and in some cases transformed, by various factors inherent in the American environment.

There was, first of all, the simple factor of space. Most of the colonists assumed that the proper way to live was in compact, little village-communities, such as their forebears in England had known for centuries. But in the New World, of course, the ecological context was wildly different. Out beyond the fringes of settlement there was land for the taking, seemingly limitless in extent and empty of "civilized" use or habitation. (Thus was the presence of Indians discounted.) For many people this presented an overpowering temptation—to move, and to live for and by oneself. Thus, by the early eighteenth century, the typical pattern of settlement was not a checkerboard of well-spaced villages, but rather a straggling, jumbled mosaic with houses strung out willy-nilly into the wilderness.

But the lure of empty land fragmented not only villages; families, too, were significantly affected. Movement away from the older centers of settlement was often accomplished in terms of successive generations. Young people, as they approached adulthood, began to consider the possibilities of settling new land near the frontier. The usual alternative was to accept a "portion" in their home village, that would come from their parents on the occasion of marriage, but often this portion was simply much *less* than what they could hope to gain for themselves elsewhere. And so they would leave. There is a passage in William Bradford's famous history of Plymouth that vividly lays bare this dimension of colonial experience. Bradford deplored the process whereby settlers moved steadily away from Plymouth to take up new lands elsewhere, leaving the original site "like an ancient mother grown old and forsaken of her children, though not in their affections, yet in regard of their bodily presence and personal helpfulness; her ancient members being most of them worn away by death, and she like a widow left only to trust in God." The metaphor is poignant enough in its own right, but it must have rung doubly true to many of Bradford's readers. For it was part of the New World experience that families should be continually divided, and that at least some elderly people should be left behind to fend for themselves after their children had moved on.

This altered balance between men and their environment would, in the long run, affect authority relations within the family. There are many scraps of evidence to suggest that the position of the young was measurably strengthened. If a child—an older child—felt unduly constrained by his family situation, he could simply leave. Better still, he could use the threat of leaving as leverage in struggles or quarrels that might arise with his parents. There was also the fact that younger persons were often the most flexible and resourceful in meeting the challenges of the new land. Here, indeed, is the start of a central theme in the lives of immigrant families through the whole course of American history: parental authority is progressively undermined as the child discovers that he is more *effective* in the new setting than his foreign-born father and mother.

It also seems evident that the American environment worked to improve significantly the status of women. This process is most easily traced with respect to a woman's legal standing; her right to hold property, for instance, was extended well beyond the traditional limits of the Old World. Moreover, by the eighteenth century many women were active in business and professional pursuits. They ran inns and taverns; they managed a wide variety of stores and shops; and, at least occasionally, they worked in careers like publishing, journalism and medicine. More broadly, they seem to have interacted easily and informally with men, in all sorts of everyday encounters. There are, in the records of colonial America, no grounds for inferring a pervasive system of deference based on sex.

And what accounts for this rise in woman's status? First, there was her sheer functional necessity, given the special circumstances of colonial life. Her area of responsibility included those basic domestic chores with which we are still familiar today, and much, much more. The average household was also a miniature factory—producing clothing, furniture, bedding, candles and other such accessories—and in all this the woman's role was central. There were some occasions when she joined the menfolk for work in the fields. Finally, it was very much to her advantage that she was relatively scarce. Recent studies suggest that men outnumbered women by a ratio of roughly three-to-two during most of the colonial period.

One more topic, highly germane to family life, deserves special mention here—namely, the prevalent attitudes and behavior in regard to sexuality. The traditional view is tediously familiar:

Puritans were nothing if not "puritannical"; thus colonial culture was characterized by sexual repressiveness of an extreme kind, and the trend ever since has been slowly but steadily in the direction of greater freedom. But this picture is seriously misleading, for the reason (among others) that it obscures important changes even within the colonial period. It is true enough that the earliest settlers, especially in New England, maintained a firm moral code, which proscribed all sexual contacts outside of marriage. However, this code was directly violated by at least some individuals from the very start, and in the eighteenth century it was widely compromised. Gradually "fornication" ceased to be a crime that was taken into court; instead, legal dockets became filled with cases of "bastardy." In short, there was a growing tolerance for premarital sexual experience; the main problem was the disposition of those illegitimate children brought into the world as a result of this tolerance. There is other evidence bearing out the same trends. It is possible, for example, to obtain rates of bridal pregnancy by comparing the dates on which given couples were married with the dates of birth of their first children. (A "positive" case is recorded whenever the interval is eight months or less.) The results for colonial America are most interesting. Positive cases appear only rarely until the very end of the seventeenth century. In the early eighteenth century, however, the rate rises markedly. And by 1750 as many as one-third to one-half of the brides in some communities were going to the altar pregnant.

By the end of the eighteenth century it was clear that American family life had been considerably transformed. Some elements of the transformation have been sketched in the preceding pages: the break in the tight web of connections between the family and the larger community; the dispersion of the household group, with the young increasingly inclined to seek their fortune in a new setting; the improvement in the status of women; the erosion of parental authority; and a growing permissiveness in the area of sex. These changes were experienced by many people at the time as a kind of decline, and there is a nonpejorative sense, too, in which they represented a loosening of old commitments and standards. It is important to see the tendency whole, because the early nineteenth century marks a crucial transition point in the history of American family life—which, to some extent, entailed an effort to turn back the clock. This does not mean that the pattern of the settlement era was revived in any specific terms, but, broadly speaking, some of the trends discussed above were now reversed. Thus, for example, women's status began to decline again in certain respects; new attempts were made to subject children to stern discipline; and sexual mores swung back into a more restrictive mold. Above all, there developed a powerful movement to endow the family *as such* with new and deeper meaning.

The process was evident, first of all, in the growth after 1800 of a new literary genre, extolling the blessings of home and hearth in rapturous detail. Books of "domestic advice" fairly gushed from the presses, and their readership expanded dramatically. Trite and sentimental as they seem today, one can hardly doubt their salience for their own time. Their simple message, endlessly repeated, was the transcendent importance of family life as the fount of all the tender virtues in life. Love, kindliness, altruism, self-sacrifice, peace, harmony, good order: all reposed here behind the sacred portals of home. Here, and nowhere else—for it was widely agreed that the same virtues were severely threatened in the world at large. Indeed, if the home should give way, human life would be reduced to the level of the jungle. We should note well this assumed disjunction between home and the life of the individual family on the one hand, and the "outside world" on the other, for it was truly fundamental to many aspects of nineteenth-century culture. Hitherto perceived as complementary to one another, the two spheres were increasingly presented in the light of adversaries.

All this was related to a new, anxious and dichotomous view of the present quality and future prospects of American society. There was a mood of expansiveness abroad in the country, a sense of unlimited opportunities for individual enterprise, an impatience with institutions, a readiness to challenge all forms of traditional restraint. Americans of every sort believed that they were carrying out a uniquely wonderful experiment in human improvement, which would one day yield "perfectionist"—not to say, "millennial"—results. But there was also a darker side. Careful analysis of the popular culture of this period reveals deep undercurrents of fear, a sense that all meaningful bearings were slipping away.

Right here the family would play a pivotal role. The vision of worldly gain, the cultivation of the "go-ahead" spirit (a favorite period phrase), was enormously invigorating, to be sure; but it also raised a specter of chaos, of individual men devouring each other in the struggle for success. Somewhere, the old values—especially the *social* values—had to be safely enshrined. One needed some traditional moorings, some emblem of softness and selflessness to counter the intense thrust of personal striving that characterized the age. There had to be a place to come in out of the storm occasionally, a place that assured both repose and renewal. That place, lavishly affirmed from all sides, was Home.

Rooted at the center of Home stood the highly sentimentalized figure of Woman. It was she who represented and maintained the tender virtues. Men, of course, had to be out in the world, getting their hands dirty in all sorts of ways; indeed, it was precisely because of this that their women must remain free of contamination. The literature of the time shows a consistent preoccupation with the career of the well-meaning but sorely pressed male, deeply involved in the work of the world, yet holding ever before his eyes the saintly image of the lady in his life. It was she—to quote from a popular sermon—"who, like a guardian angel, watches over his interests, warns him against dangers, comforts him under trial; and by her pious, assiduous, and attractive deportment, constantly endeavors to render him more virtuous, more useful, more honourable, and more happy." Such a creature was "a pearl beyond price," a fit centerpiece in what has been called "the cult of True Womanhood."

This posture of admiration—almost of reverence—contrasts sharply with the imputations of deviousness and inconstancy found in most earlier assessments of women. But it would be quite erroneous to infer from such flattering rhetoric any genuine improvement in women's status. In fact, the nineteeth-century American woman, when compared to her grandmothers in colonial times, had given up a great deal. For example, women could no longer be permitted to work outside the home (except among the poorest classes where the issue was simple survival). Their position in life was defined in terms of a purity directly opposed to everything characteristic of the larger world. Thus the domestic hearth was both their altar, and, from another perspective, their prison. As one scholar has aptly written, nineteenth-century American woman was "a hostage to the old values held so dear and treated so lightly . . . the hostage in the home." And, like all hostages, she was not free to come and go as she pleased.

But there is more still. Even within the home her influence was sharply circumscribed. A husband's authority was supposed to be absolute in all major family decisions. By contrast, a wife's authority was exerted entirely by way of symbolism. Indeed, her great virtue was submissiveness and obedience to the will of her spouse, and her central role was that of comforter. (Here is a random sampling of titles of contemporary essays on the subject: "Woman, Man's Best Friend," "Woman, the Greatest Social Benefit," "Woman, a Being to Come Home To," "The Wife, Source of Comfort and Spring of Joy.") In all this one absolutely basic assumption seems clear: women would not live for themselves. Their function was to provide moral uplift for everyone else with whom they came in contact—chiefly their husbands and children. Meanwhile no one wished to consider what they might do on their own account and for their own reasons.

There was a single exception to the rule that women must not be active outside their homes. The churches of this era had launched a vast program of humanitarian reforms, and looked to their female membership for day-to-day support. Few people could object when women involved themselves in distributing Bibles or encouraging missionary work or planning orphanages and almshouses, for here was a plausible extension of their inherent moral role and influence. But problems arose when they crossed a critical boundary and began to participate in more patently political branches of reform.

It was one thing for women to go about their neighborhoods raising money to send clergymen to convert the heathen in India or Africa; it was quite another thing to have them making speeches before antislavery conventions. The latter was too much a public activity; it was verging on the "outside world" that could only sully a woman's purity. Yet for some women, the lines drawn between these various forms of humanitarian work did not seem altogether clear. And, for at least a few of them, there were disturbing parallels between the slavery of the Negro and the position of their own sex. It was no coincidence that the first important advocates for women's rights were closely associated with abolitionism.

In its beginnings organized feminism was very much a nineteenth-century phenomenon; and its end, of course, is not yet in sight. This complex and important movement cannot be described here, but certain of its general characteristics deserve at least brief notice. It was not, at first, primarily about the right to vote; it was much more centrally about the right of women to work outside the home. The early feminists despised all the adoring rhetoric on woman-in-the-home; they sought to expose this myth of domesticity for what it really was. But so entrenched was the pattern against which they fought that it was many years before they could make significant headway. Thus the initial phases of feminism are best seen not as a sign of improving status for women, but rather as a cry of protest against intolerable confinement. It is a striking symbol of all this that the so-called "bloomer" fashion was a matter of some importance in the eyes of the early feminists. Their attempt to free women from the literally suffocating network of stays, corsets and hoop skirts that formed the conventional dress of the time directly paralleled their attack on the figuratively suffocating environment of Home.

And yet the relation of feminism to the cult of true womanhood was not entirely antipodal. In fact, in some ways cultural stereotypes nourished the growth of the movement. The idea of feminine purity was distinctly two-edged; in the hands of conventional moralists, it helped to rationalize the confinement of women to a domestic role, but it could also serve an opposite purpose. If women were inherently more virtuous than men, should they not use their influence to purify politics, business, the world of public affairs? This question was resolved, for particular individuals, on a variety of different grounds; much depended on one's view of politics, reform, religion and history. Here lay the origins of a dilemma that has pervaded the growth of feminism ever since. Are women to have equal status because they are similar to men (in all essential particulars), or because they are generically different (and in some ways superior)? Is their full participation in public life to be justified on the basis of a humanity shared with men, or of some sex-defined "specialness" (that might enable them to contribute to society in distinctive ways)? Many of the early feminists were logically tied to the former position, but emotionally inclined toward the latter. To this extent, one can regard them as True Women—dressed in bloomers.

The True Woman of the nineteenth century was only one-half of the most thoroughgoing system of sex-role differentiation ever seen in American history. It goes without saying that men, too, were typed to the point of caricature. As previously mentioned, they belonged preeminently to the world of affairs. And if this was their sphere, it called forth an appropriate character, which included strength, cunning, inventiveness, endurance—a whole range of traits henceforth defined as exclusively "masculine." The impact of these definitions on family life was truly profound. The man of the family now became the breadwinner in a special sense. Each day he went away to work; each night he returned. His place of work no longer bore any relation to his home environment. What he did at work was something of which other family members knew little or nothing. His position as husband and father was altered, if not compromised; he was now a more distant, less nurturant figure, but he had special authority, too, because he performed those mysterious activities that maintained the entire household.

Among their other attributes, American men of the nineteenth century were saddled with a heavy burden of libido. Sexual desire was regarded as an exclusively male, and mostly unfortunate, phenomenon. Women, in their purity, were supposed to be passionless—not merely chaste, but literally devoid of sexual feelings. This complex of ideas was an invention of the age, with massive behavioral consequences.

The whole subject of sex was enveloped in a pervasive hush, which remained virtually unbroken until our own century. Polite conversation was protected from "stain" by the use of well-chosen euphemisms: legs, for example, now became "limbs," and pregnancy itself was mentioned only as "a delicate condition." Clothing was designed to cover all parts of the body except the face and hands; and even statues in museums were discreetly draped if their sculptors had failed to provide for "decent attire." Women were examined by male doctors, indeed babies were delivered, behind sheets and blankets—which, by totally blocking vision, ensured virtue but impeded sound medicine. Coitus was sanctioned only within marriage, and only for the purpose of procreation; even then it was viewed as a necessary evil. (Marriage manuals advised that frequent "congress" might lead to poor health, and recommended once a month as a reasonable standard.) Masturbation became *the* phobia of the times; to practice this secret sin was to risk intemperance, insanity and death. Adolescent boys went to sleep strapped in elaborate devices intended to stifle even involuntary desire, and dozens of patent medicines offered a similar promise of "relief."

Still, there was general agreement that male sexuality was finally irrepressible. Although everywhere resisted by polite society, it would continue to flourish in a thousand dark corners. And so it did—witness the growth, in the middle of the nineteenth century, of a vast industry of prostitution. (Regrettable as this was, it preserved certain fundamental distinctions: men indulged their "lowest" instincts with women from the lowest social class.) For many women, of every status, the situation was more tortured still. Recent research on the history of gynecology has uncovered a demand, in an astonishing number of cases, for the surgical procedure of clitoridectomy. Evidently this was the last resort of women who, contrary to expectation, found themselves afflicted with "sensual" wishes.

Given all these conventions, it is hard to imagine that many married couples were gratified in their most intimate relations. But sex was merely an extreme case of a pattern that affected every sort of contact between men and women. When their appropriate spheres were so rigorously separated, when character itself appeared to be so gender-specific, what was the likelihood of meaningful communication? Gone was that sense of instinctive sharing, that implicit sexual symmetry, which had suffused the full range of experience in premodern society. Instead there was a new mode of partnership—formal, self-conscious, contrived. Men and women came together from opposite directions, as uncertain allies. Understandably, many of the alliances so formed did not survive. Divorce rates, which rose steadily after mid-century, barely hinted at the true dimensions of the problem. For every marriage that was ended in court, unrecorded others dissolved through tacit agreement between the parties themselves or through simple desertion of one by the other. It is worth noticing, in this connection, the development of the notorious "tramp" phenomenon. Demoralized and destitute wanderers, their numbers mounting into the hundreds of thousands, tramps can be fairly characterized as men who had run away from their wives. (They had, of course, run away from much else besides.) Their presence was mute testimony to the strains that tugged at the very core of American family life.

Many observers noted that the tramps had created a virtual society of their own, based on a principle of single-sex companionship. But in this they followed an important trend in the culture at large. The early decades of the nineteenth century witnessed an extraordinary proliferation of "voluntary associations"—clubs, lodges, unions, "circles" and the like. Men and women, even boys and girls, joined with groups of their peers for reasons that ran a wide gamut from frivolity, to self-improvement, to social reform. In a great many instances, membership was restricted to one sex or the other. The Elks, the Mothers' Association, the volunteer firemen, the Women's Christian Temperance Union, all shared this same characteristic: quite apart from their specific activities, they offered companionship with one's own (sexual) kind. Increasingly, such companionship seemed preferable to what could be found at home. The growth of these organizations was, then, another sign of a deficit in family life, and particularly in the relations of men and women.

Sex-role differentiation was paralleled by an increasing sensitivity to differences of age. And of all such differences those pertaining to childhood received the greatest attention. Now, for the first time in Western history, the child stood out as a creature inherently different from adults—someone with his own needs, talents and character. This did not, of course, happen all at once, but from a long view the change was unmistakable. Around 1800, for example, children began to appear in clothing that was distinctively their own. They were also spending more and more time at play among groups of their peers. Of similar import was the development, toward mid-century, of a system of Sunday schools. (Here was explicit recognition that the religious needs of the child were special and different, and that it was quite inappropriate to have him sit through regular church services with his parents.)

But perhaps the most telling evidence of this trend was the astonishing growth, and distinctive content, of popular literature on child rearing. To be sure, there had always been some books of this type in circulation, but they were mostly imports from England or France, and were decidedly casual in tone. Their chief concern was manners—how children should behave in a variety of social situations. The nineteenth-century literature, by contrast, dealt with the development of the child's character in a much deeper sense. Moreover, it was an exclusively native production; foreign models no longer seemed appropriate to the American scene. In part, this expressed a new spirit of truculent nationalism, but it was something else as well. For one feels in these works a note of extreme urgency—a reflection, presumably, of the fright and puzzlement of many parents faced with the task of raising children in the brave new world of nineteenth-century America.

What was it that gave to childhood both a more distinctive and a more worrisome aspect than for several generations before? There was, first of all, the factor of massive social and economic change. The nineteenth century spanned the transition from an agrarian, small-town social order to one that was characterized by large-scale industrialism and urbanization. But the view of the child that made him virtually a miniature adult was particularly appropriate—perhaps *only* appropriate—in an agrarian setting.

On the farm he could, and did, take part in the work of the place from his earliest years; most likely, too, he would grow up to be a farmer himself. Thus it made sense to regard him as a scaled-down version of his father. Consider, by way of contrast, the position of a city-child in the mid-nineteenth century. His father works in an office or factory on the other side of town; the child himself knows hardly any of the details. He has no economic function in the household whatsoever. Moreover, his own future course—including his adult vocation—is shrouded in uncertainty. The diversified economy of the city opens up many possibilities, and there is no reason to assume that what he eventually does will bear any relation at all to what his father presently does. In short, circumstances seem to isolate the child in a profound way, and to create a gulf between the generations that had not been there before.

But there were other reasons, too, for the heightened concern with child rearing. The weakening of traditional institutions appeared to leave the individual family very much on its own. If people failed in their duty as parents, there would be no one else to do the job for them. Everything depends on the child's home environment: this was the message of all the authorities on the subject. Yet on so much else these authorities spoke with a divided voice. What, for example, should be the long-range goals of child rearing? What type of character would a model home foster? Certainly there was much concern with the development of qualities like independence and resourcefulness—a readiness to assert one's own claims and interests. Because America had become an egalitarian society, open to talent, the child should be encouraged in a certain style of expressiveness, which would help him to realize his inner potentialities. It was this that led foreign visitors to regard nineteenth-century American families as unduly child-centered. There was, however, another side. The same writers on child rearing gave great emphasis to the values of order, discipline, control. Children must be hedged about with moral precept from an early age, and must learn implicit obedience to legitimate authority. Thus, and only thus, would they develop the "sound conscience" and "steadfast principles" so necessary to ensure a straight course in the face of all the pitfalls they would encounter in later life. These two main criteria of development—expressiveness and control—were logically at odds with one another, and attempts to apply them simultaneously were bound to end in confusion.

This was, moreover, a time of widespread reassessment of the moral standing of children. To some extent old notions of infant depravity were revived, and parents were once again urged to concentrate on "breaking the will" of the very young. But such views never regained overall dominance, and by the middle of the century various countertrends were plainly in evidence. At one extreme was a new and highly idealized picture of childish innocence and inborn purity—as with Little Eva in *Uncle Tom's Cabin*. But while many people would have recognized Little Eva as at least a symbolic possibility, their expectations for their own offspring were considerably more modest. Increasingly, the child was viewed as a *neutral* quantity—with potentialities for either good or evil.

If there was one outcome toward which all of the above trends seemed to point, it was a deep intensification of the parent-child bond—or, to be more precise, of the mother-child bond. The careful rearing of children was, after all, the most important activity of the True Woman. From virtuous homes came preachers, philanthropists, presidents ("All that I am I owe to my angel mother"—a favorite period cliché); from disorderly ones came thieves and drunkards. There was no doubting either the impressionable nature of the young or the decisive impact of the domestic environment. Yet if children were so deeply subject to the influence of their parents, there was also an opposite effect. A familiar character in novels from the period was the "errant" or "ungrateful" child. Although raised by solicitous parents in a morally scrupulous home, he yielded in later life to worldly temptation, and filled his days with crime and debauchery. When reports of his conduct filtered back, his parents were stricken with grief, and one (or both) took ill and died. This plot-line lays bare an innermost nerve of family life in nineteenth-century America. Father, mother and children were locked in a circle of mutual responsibility, and the stakes were literally life-and-death.

Anxiety reached a peak at the moment when a child left home to make his way in the outside world. Here was a test both of his personal integrity and of the family in which he had grown up. Most young men took this momentous step in their late teens or early twenties; for women of about the same age there was a comparable shift—into marriage. Increasingly, as time passed, these events were joined to significant psychological changes, involving nothing less than the shape of the developmental process. Indeed, one can ascribe to this period the addition of a generically new stage of development between childhood and maturity—the stage known ever since as "adolescence." Before the nineteenth century adolescence was not recognized, and, from all indications, was rarely experienced in the forms so familiar today. By 1850 shrewd observers detected new patterns of behavior, and "special problems," among some of the nation's youth; by 1900 these were so widespread as to command an organized social response. (It was then, incidentally, that the term "adolescence" entered into common discourse.)

The sources of this change were variable and complex, but much depended on the widening gap between the generations. When childhood and adulthood had been defined in such sharply different ways, it was harder to move from one to the other. Growth itself came to seem disjunctive and problematic—no longer a smooth ascent gradually accomplished, but a jolting succession of leaps and bumps. Adolescent behavior expressed the reluctance and doubt of young people about to undertake that last and longest leap of all, into adult life and responsibility. From a psychological standpoint, the critical issue was (and remains) "identity." Always, in premodern society, youth had received an adult identity in the natural course of things. The decisive change, in more recent times, has been the presence of so many alternatives—of career, of life-style, of moral and philosophical belief. In ever-growing numbers young people have faced demanding choices, which greatly complicate the preadult years. Thus, as one recent scholar has written, adolescence is "like a waiting period . . . a temporary stopover in which one can muster strength for the next harrowing stage of the trip."

It was the plan of this essay to carry the story of American family life forward to about the year 1900. There is no space here to deal with our own century, and perhaps that is better left to other branches of social science anyway. Obviously we have witnessed striking changes even within the last two or three decades: the renewed activity of the women's movement and the so-called sexual revolution come readily to mind. At the same time there are profound continuities. Much of what we expect from family life bears the stamp of an earlier time—repose, comfort, a place of refuge from the rigors of the wider social environment. But all this is beyond the scope of the present inquiry.

So, too, are many earlier events and trends that, while highly interesting in themselves, lie outside the historical middle. From the early nineteenth century onward immigrants have flowed in a vast tide to America from all parts of Europe. Differing widely in language, religion and custom, these groups have also presented special variants of family life. (Thus, for example, immigrant families have tended toward more frequent extension than native American ones.) Blacks have played an equally significant role. Black families have, of course, been subject to the most extraordinary pressures—first, of slavery; later, of massive social prejudice and exploitation. (Recent studies have uncovered evidence of great resiliency in the response to these pressures, far more than the fashionable myth of black matriarchy would suggest.) Still another area of special interest is the long and variegated history of utopian communities. Most of these have proposed radical alterations in family structure, ranging from the celibacy of the Shakers, to the polygamy of the early Mormons, to the "complex marriage" of the Oneida Community. (Americans have long believed that the preservation of social order depends on "sound" family life; the utopians simply stood this idea on its head.)

Immigrants, blacks, reformers: here are major sources of the diversity that has attended American life for the past two centuries. Yet there is, after all, a powerful mainstream tradition. The chief minority groups have themselves acknowledged as much, by gradually approximating the cultural norm with the passage of succeeding generations. The alternative models of the utopians have been either forcibly suppressed by governmental fiat (for example, the Mormons) or fatally weakened by attrition (for example, the Shakers). Thus a scholar may still claim to speak of "American family life" in general, as if such a thing has actually existed!

The same type of intellectual license is needed to underwrite a set of conclusions about the meaning of the past for the current and future course of the American family. History never provides clear-cut "lessons," except for those who must have them at any price (including truth); but it does lay down the boundaries within which events are likely to develop. Perhaps this is particularly true in the present case, since the family is such a deeply conservative institution—so slow to change, so powerfully interwoven in our personal and collective roots.

First, and definitely foremost: there is no golden age of the family gleaming at us from far back in the historical past. And there is no good reason to construe recent trends in terms of decline and decay. To every point alleged as an adverse reflection on modern family life, one can offer a direct rejoinder. Consider, for example, the matter of divorce. We all know that the rate of legal divorce has been rising enormously in recent years. (In fact, the trend is more than one hundred years old.) But what does this tell us about marital failure? In earlier times countless marriages were ended by simple, and legally unrecognized, desertion. Hence the figures in question are partly an artifact of legal history—a more general access to the courts, and so forth. Even without this effect, troublesome problems of interpretation would remain. Perhaps we seek more from marriage than did our forebears—more intimacy, more openness, more deep-down emotional support.

But surely these comparative judgments, which purport to make one period better than another, are beside the point anyway. Far more important is the effort to understand how family life relates to larger historical processes. For the family continually interacts with other cultural institutions and, more especially, with the variable circumstances of its membership. There is a sense in which every historical era gets the family system it needs and deserves. Thus, in colonial America, the norm was a stable "peasant" household, gradually evolving toward looser internal forms to permit full exploitation of a novel environment. Thus, too, the nineteenth-century family experienced a wrenching transformation under the multiple impact of industrialization, urban growth, egalitarian ideology and demographic change. It is hard, in fact, to avoid seeing the nineteenth century as a time of troubles —not to say tragedy—in the history of the family. Sex-role typing, the generation gap, a guilt-laden sense of domestic responsibility, tortured attitudes toward sexuality—the total situation was hardly a benevolent one. And yet we should remember that massive social change always exacts a high price in human suffering. The period from about 1820 to 1920 encompassed a veritable revolution in American life and culture, and the pressures on the family were necessarily extreme. Surely the vast majority of people who experienced all this found something immensely valuable in their domestic life. Perhaps, indeed, it was Home that kept the toll of misery from rising far higher. Who can say that any alternative pattern would have worked better?

But this, in turn, raises further questions. Is the notion of "alternatives" meaningful in any sense? Is the family amenable to planned social intervention? In short, can we hope to influence the shape of our domestic life—let alone to change it? Surely, in individual cases, the answer may be affirmative; but what about larger schemes, for redesigning the family *system*? On this, history enters a caution. As noted previously, Americans have always assigned a primary causal role to family life: good homes will create a good society (or—from the standpoint of reform—change the family, and you will change everything else). To be sure, there is a certain logical plausibility here. But, in practice, it is much easier to trace those processes that move the other way—that is, *from* the society at large, *to* the family in particular. On the checkerboard of social institutions, the family seems to display a markedly reactive character. Time and again, it receives influences from without, rebuffs them, modifies them, adapts to them. There are dynamic and reciprocal aspects in all this; but even so the openings presented to human agents, bent on "social engineering," are extremely small.

Can we, then, realistically expect a widespread trend toward extended families, as advocated by some critics of contemporary society? Impossible! For nothing has been more durable in the long history of Western family life than its nuclear character. Will we see a new era of restrictive child-rearing, in protest against cultural permissiveness? Most unlikely, for developmental norms depend on much else besides household structure. Careful study of these and related points may suggest the limits within which the family is likely to develop. For the most part, they are modest limits—some will say, confining ones. But this need not be received as a counsel of despair. For if the current patterns of family life are the only ones we have, they are nonetheless variable enough and flexible enough to yield many different outcomes in immediate human terms. *The* family, considered as a species, is molded by history and thus lies beyond our power to control. Not so those *particular* families to which we personally belong. The past lives in us always; but what we make of it, individually, is up to ourselves.

Parental Power and Marriage Patterns: An Analysis of Historical Trends in Hingham, Massachusetts

DANIEL SCOTT SMITH
Department of History,
University of Connecticut, Storrs

Few of the changes in the family suggested by modernization theory have been empirically documented with historical evidence. Through a reconstitution analysis of the families of Hingham, Massachusetts, from the mid-seventeenth through the mid-nineteenth century, important changes, consistent with theoretical expectations, in the extent of parental control over marriage formation are documented and analyzed. Changes are apparent in measures which reflect the structuring of marriage on both the individual and social level. The shift from the centrality of the family of orientation to the dominance of the family of procreation was not linear but concentrated in the late eighteenth and early nineteenth centuries.

Perhaps the central conceptual issue in the sociology of the family is the relationship of modernization to family structure. Paradoxically the theoretical significance of this problem has not engendered an empirical preoccupation with the details of the transition from "traditional" to "modern" family structure. For sociologists, as Abrams (1972:28) puts it, "the point after all was not to know the past but to establish an idea of the past which could be used as a comparative base for the understanding of the present." While historians often implicitly use a conception of the modern family as a baseline for their researches into the past, formally at least they attempt to relate the family to the culture and other institutions of an historical period. Only rarely have either group of scholars actually measured the dimensions of change by analyzing data over a long time interval. Thus the element of change in family structure has been more usually assumed or inferred from casual comparisons of past and present than consciously measured and analyzed. A great chasm persists between the theoretical perspective on the family and moderization (see Smelser, 1966:115-117, for a concise summary) and a limited body of empirical evidence more often qualifying or denying these relationships (for example, Furstenberg, 1966; Lantz *et al.*, 1968; and Laslett and Wall, 1972) than supporting or extending them.

The problem of the connections between modernization and family structure may be conveniently divided into three analytically distinct areas—the relevance of the family for the structuring of other institutions, the role of the family in shaping individual lives, and finally the significance to the individual of the family he is born into (family of orientation) for the one he creates by marriage (family of procreation). Since the historical trends in the first two areas have presumably seemed so obvious, systematic empirical data have not been collected and analyzed to establish the precise dimensions and timing of change. In the first instance the modern family is not as quantitatively important for the organization of other structures—economic, political, and social.[1] What influence the modern family

[1] While it is undoubtedly true, for example, that more members of the Virginia House of Burgesses in 1773 had fathers who served in that body than United States Congressmen of 1973 whose fathers were also congressmen, no quantitative evidence exists to determine the magnitude of these changes. Perhaps more importantly, it is not certain how family status "worked" to get men into office in the colonial period—whether through deference to the family name or through arrangement by the class of elite families. Nor has the relative importance of wealth and family status in political recruitment been determined. Determination of the timing of the shift away from family domination of office would be of considerable historical importance. Trends in this area are not necessarily linear. Harvard students, for example, were ranked by their ability in the seventeenth century, but their family status counted in the eighteenth (Shipton, 1954). The fathers of 16 per cent of the U.S. Senators of 1820 had held political office, 8 per cent in 1860, 12 per cent in 1900 and 19 per cent in 1940 (Hoogenbloom, 1968:60). Although the numbers involved are very small to be sure, perhaps the final phase of the system in which office was a concomitant of social prestige and the emergence of politics as a specialized profession is reflected in this cycle. In the

exerts in these areas is indirect, exerted either through early socialization and personality formation or mediated by intervening institutions. Male occupational status in modern America, for example, is related to the family of orientation mainly through the provision of education, not by direct parental placement. Few families today control jobs which can be given to their children (Blau and Duncan, 1967:131-133). Having less of an instrumental role, the family is now a specialized institution providing nurture and affection for both children and adults. Perhaps the best historical study of the transformation in this second area is the impressionistic classic of Aries (1962) which delineates the social separation of the family from the community and the emergence of the psychological centrality of the child in the conjugal family. Since this interpretation now rests on changes in ideals and lacks adequate behavioral support, more historical analysis is required to determine the extent of this shift. It is possible, for example, that emotional or expressive ties between parents and children have been essentially invariant over the course of American history. These affective relationships may appear to have increased historically only because of the separation of instrumental activities from the family.

Although not necessarily more significant than the changes in the first two areas, the relationship between the family of orientation and the family of procreation has often been considered to be the central issue in the modernization of the family. Davis (1949:414-418), in fact, has argued that this distinction is the most adequate key to understanding other variations in family structure. If the family newly created by marriage is dominated by pre-existing families of birth, then households are more likely to be extended in structure, marriages are more likely to be arranged and will take place at earlier ages, intrafamilial relationships will tend to be authoritarian, etc. Despite Parsons later disclaimer that his well-known analysis (Parsons, 1943) was mainly concerned with the isolation of the family from other social structures and his acceptance of the Litwack-Seeman critique as complementary not contradictory, he was not deterred from elaborating his earlier argument. The substance of the debate on extended kinship in modern American society continues precisely on the quantity and nature of interaction between married couples and their parents (Parson, 1965). Historians as well have concentrated on this question, usually employing the classic extended-nuclear dichotomy to summarize their findings. Greven (1970) has argued that by withholding land fathers in seventeenth century Andover, Massachusetts, were able to exercise considerable power over their adult sons. Once land had become relatively scarce in the early eighteenth century, they found it more difficult or less desirable to do so. More recently an entire volume of papers has been devoted to crushing the proposition that extended *households* ever were a significant element in western society, at least since the middle ages (Laslett and Wall, 1972).[2]

THE HISTORICAL PROBLEM

In a decade review of research on modern American kinship, Adams (1970) has suggested that the most recent work is moving beyond debate and description to the more significant tasks of specification, interrelation, and comparison. This change of emphasis is as important for historical as for contemporary studies, even though an adequate, empirically based, systematic description of the historical evolution of the relationship between the family of orientation and the family of procreation does not presently exist. Despite the fact that it is always easier to decry than to remedy scholarly failures, this absence should be a challenge rather than an obstacle for historians. Much of the critical evidence regarding the extent and kind of interaction between parents and adult children is, of course, unwritten. Despite their interest in the same substantive issues, historians inevitably are forced to employ different methods than sociologists. Yet there are serious problems in the interpretation of historical evidence on the family. While a body of literary comment on ideal family relationships does exist, it becomes progressively more biased toward higher social strata as one moves farther back into the past (Berkner, 1973). Furthermore, the relating of historical information about ideals to actual behavior is not easily

economic area nineteenth century entrepreneurial capitalism may be closer in terms of the linkage between family and property to medieval feudalism than to twentieth century corporate capitalism (Bell, 1961:39-45).

[2] The relevance of household composition data to the nuclear-extended dichotomy pertains only to three-generation households. Although servants were an important addition to pre-industrial western households and lodgers to nineteenth century urban-industrial households, these nonkin additions were *in* but not *of* the family. Other kin also resided in households but their presence is probably chiefly due to demographic failure elsewhere—orphanhood, widowhood, and spinsterhood.

accomplished (Goode, 1968:311-313). Since literary sources are available, relatively inexpensive to exploit, and suggestive concerning the more subtle aspects of family interaction, it would be foolish to dismiss them as biased and unreliable. It would be equally risky to base the entire history of the American family on these sources. What appears to be crucial at this point for a reliable descriptive history of the American family is the development of series of quantitative indicators for various aspects of family behavior.

On both theoretical and historical grounds the idea that a shift from the centrality of the family of orientation to the family of procreation has occurred within the time span of American history may be questioned. American history, it is often argued, lacks a "traditional" or "premodern" period. If modernization and the transformation of the family from extended to nuclear are related, one would not expect to find evidence for it within the three and one-half centuries of American history. The classic polarities of sociological theory are often used by historians to contrast America with England or as a literary device to highlight rather small shifts over time. Still, the dominant theme in American historiography is "uniqueness" and this peculiar quality of the American experience is linked to the various characteristics of modernity. Ideal types, of course, describe no particular empirical realities. Since these classic dichotomies emerged from the attempt to understand the transformation of western society in the nineteenth century, their empirical relevance surely ought to be as much in the analysis of the history of western development as in the explanation of cross-cultural differences. If the discussion of historical change in the family is to progress, the selection of terms is less important than the precise specification of the extent of change along the theoretical continuum.

Some important aspects of the nuclear, conjugal, or family-of-procreation-dominant family system such as neolocal residence, undoubtedly have been dominant since the earliest American settlement in the seventeenth century (Goode, 1970a:xvi). Other significant historical continuities such as the priority given to nuclear as against extended kin (Demos, 1970:181) may also be present. If change is to be detected in an area of known continuity, a specific, well-defined problem and subtle and discriminating measures of change are required. The relative centrality of the family of orientation versus the family of procreation can be examined from various angles. Marriage formation, however, is probably the most crucial since it is the point of transition for the individual. Transitions involving decisions are inevitably problematic. Furthermore, marriages produce records for nearly the entire population, not just for atypical elites. Thus a substantial data base exists for historical analysis. If the American family has undergone substantial historical change, it should be reflected in the conditions of marriage formation. Were, in fact, the marriages of a significant segment of the American population ever controlled by parents at any point in our history? Parents today are, of course, not irrelevant in the courtship and marriage formation process. The earlier, "traditional," pattern of control should be direct rather than indirect, involve material rather than psychological relationships, and involve power exercised by parents in their own interest at the expense of the children.

A shift in the control of marriage formation is clearly to be expected by the sociological theory of family modernization.[3] Confident, if vague, statements exist describing the emergence of a non-parentally controlled, participant-run courtship system within the time span encompassed by American history (Reiss, 1964:57-58; Stone, 1964:181-182).[4] Yet Reiss presumably relies on literary evidence in his broad summary and Stone on the decidedly atypical experience of the English aristocracy. Furthermore, the shift specified is subtle–from a parental choice, child veto system in the seventeenth century to its converse by the late nineteenth or early twentieth century. Given the particularistic relationship between parents and children, choosing and vetoing choices may not be a constitutional system but instead an ongoing process of action and reaction.

METHOD AND SAMPLE

The dead, of course, cannot be subjected to

[3] According to Smelser (1966:117), for example, "In many traditional settings, marriage is closely regulated by elders; the tastes and sentiments of the couple to be married are relatively unimportant . . . . With the decay of extended kinship ties and the redefinition of parental authority, youth becomes emancipated with respect to choosing a spouse."

[4] The necessary imprecision of Reiss' succinct summary reflects the dearth of hard historical evidence: "The seventeenth century saw the working out of a solution. Romantic love had spread to much of the populace (but) almost exclusively among couples who were engaged. . . . The parents were still choosing mates. . . . By the eighteenth century the revolt had secured many adherents and was increasingly successful, so that by the end of the nineteenth century, in many parts of Europe and especially in America, young people were choosing their own mates and love was a key basis for marriage. The revolution had been won!" (Reiss, 1964:57-58).

surveys. The extent of parental power in courtship and marriage formation cannot be directly measured. Inherently the concept has a certain diffuseness and multidimensionality. Parents, for example, could determine the actual choice of spouse, they could determine the age at marriage but not name the partner, or they could merely structure indirectly the range of acceptable spouses. The actual process of decision making and bargaining is forever lost to the historian of ordinary people. If the dead cannot be interviewed, they can be made to answer questions if various consequences of the larger issue of parental control over marriage can be explicitly formulated. This is possible through the construction of long-term series of indices which are logically associated with the operational existence of parental control. Unlike the possibilities available in direct interaction with respondents, these indices inevitably lack meaning in an absolute, substantive sense. Conclusions must rest not just on one measure but on the conformity of various indicators to some pattern. Quantitative measures, whatever their limitations, have the great advantage of providing consistent information about change over time—the great question in the sociological history of the family and the most severe limitation of literary source materials.

Since the expected transition to a participant-run courtship system allegedly occurred between the seventeenth and late nineteenth century, either comparable data sets separated by more than a century or a long continuous series seem appropriate. For sociological purposes the former would be sufficient since a test of the change is all that is required. For historical analysis the time-series approach is better suited since the timing and pace of the transition are equally interesting. If the change did occur, was it gradual or concentrated in a few decades as a result, say, of the American revolution or the inception of rapid economic growth.

The larger study from which the ensuing data derive covers the social and demographic experience of the population of one Massachusetts town over a quarter-millienium (Smith, 1973). Economically, this period—1635 to 1880—encompasses the shift, mainly after 1800, from agriculture to commerce and industry. Demographically, it includes the transition from a fertility level which was high by west European standards to the below replacement reproduction rates of the mid-nineteenth century (Smith, 1972a; Uhlenberg, 1969). The basic methodological technique of the larger study was family reconstitution—essentially statistical genealogy (Wrigley, 1966). Records of births, deaths, intentions to marry, marriages, and wealth data from tax lists were combined into family units for analysis. Various series of comparable data extending over the two centuries were constructed to measure change in demographic, familial, and social behavior. By examining differences in the timing of changes in these indicators, the history of the evolution of the population and social structure can be interpreted (Furet, 1971). Every decision about research design necessarily involves a price. Although long-term trends and change can be studied by this approach, the conclusions strictly must be limited to the population of the town of Hingham. Furthermore, primarily because of migration, nearly one-half of the families could not be fully reconstituted. Although wealth is inversely related to outmigration after marriage, this distortion only marginally affects most indictors. Since the wealth-bias is fairly consistent over time, trends are affected to a lesser degree than levels for any particular cohort.

EVIDENCE

In early New England, as in the pre-industrial West generally, marriage was intimately linked to economic independence (Wrigley, 1969:117-118). As a result, age at marriage and proportions never-marrying were higher in western Europe than in other cultural areas (Hajnal, 1965). Since the late marriage pattern tended to reduce fertility, European societies had less of a dependency burden from non-productive children; the easy mobility of the young, unmarried adult population may also have facilitated the transition to modern economic growth. Arguing in theoretical terms, one historical demographer has suggested that mortality level was also an important mechanism in the determination of marriage age. Higher mortality would open up opportunities for sons who then could marry earlier than if their fathers survived longer. The growth of population was thus controlled by the countervailing forces of mortality and marriage age (Ohlin, 1961).

These central demographic characteristics of west European societies can be used to formulate a test of the extent of paternal economic power. Since newly married sons were not incorporated into the paternal economic or living unit, marriage meant a definite transfer of power intergenerationally. The transfer might be eased by custom, limited by paternal retention of formal title to the land, and

TABLE 1. DIFFERENTIAL IN MARRIAGE AGE OF SONS BY AGE AT DEATH OF FATHERS

Period of Fathers' Marriage Cohort	Age at marriage of sons by age at death of fathers: Under 60	60 and over	Difference
1641-1700	26.8 (64)	28.4 (142)	+1.6
1701-1720	24.3 (30)	25.9 (130)	+1.6
1721-1740	24.7 (38)	26.7 (104)	+2.0
1741-1760	26.1 (43)	26.5 (145)	+0.4
1761-1780	25.7 (42)	26.8 (143)	+1.1
1781-1800	26.0 (71)	25.8 (150)	−0.2
1801-1820	25.7 (93)	26.5 (190)	+0.8
1821-1840	26.0 (42)	25.9 (126)	−0.1
1641-1780	25.73(217)	26.89(664)	+1.16
1781-1840	25.86(206)	26.11(466)	+0.25

Note: Sample size of sons whose marriage ages are known in parentheses.

moderated by continuing relations along non-instrumental lines. However, fathers inevitably had something to lose–either economic resources or unpaid labor services–by the early marriage of their sons.[5] One might expect, therefore, that sons of men who die early would be able to marry before sons of men who survive into old age. By law male orphans inherited at age twenty-one and were thus economically free to marry. On the other hand, if fathers either could not or would not exercise such control, no differential in marriage age should exist between these two groups of sons.

Over two centuries of the study 60 years was the approximate mean age of fathers at the time of marriage of their sons. For the three cohorts of sons born to marriages up to 1740, Table 1 shows a differential of 1.6, 1.6, and 2.0 years in the predicted direction between sons whose fathers died before age 60 and sons whose fathers survived that age. For sons born to marriages formed after 1740 and especially after 1780, the "paternal power" effect is greatly diminished. While one and one-half to two years may appear to be a small difference, this gap is wider than that between the marriage ages of first and younger sons or between sons of wealthy and less wealthy parents (Smith, 1973). Nor should an extreme differential be expected. Fathers had a cultural obligation to see their children married although it was not in their short-run self-interest. The most meaningful interpretation of the magnitude of the differential depends on comparison with results obtained from reconstitution studies of English population samples..

Since the meaning of this differential is inferential, this index cannot by itself confirm the argument that parents significantly controlled the marriage of their sons. An additional aspect of the relative centrality of the family of orientation in a society is a concern for the preservation of the line at the expense of a coexistent desire to provide for all children in the family. Inasmuch as the number and sex composition of surviving children are not completely certain and economic circumstances are not perfectly forecast, this tension is essentially insoluble for individual families (Goode, 1970b:125-126). By favoring only one son, families could help to maintain the social continuity of the family line. Although strict primogeniture did not obtain in Massachusetts, the eldest son was granted a double share in intestacy cases before the egalitarian modification of the law in 1789. Fathers, however, were not legally required to favor the eldest son. They had a free choice between an emphasis on the lineage or giving each child an equal start in life. If common, this limited form of primogeniture should have an influence on the social origins of the spouses of first and younger sons. Having more resources eldest sons should be able, on the average, to marry daughters of wealthier men. In seventeenth century marriage contracts the wife's parents provided half as much as the husband's for launching the couple into marriage (Morgan, 1966:82). In order to test the influence of birth order on marriage chances, Table 2 compares the quintile wealth status of fathers and fathers-in-law who were living in Hingham at the earlier date to men who were taxed by the town at the later date. While these nonmigratory requirements limit

[5] John Winthrop, the leader of the great Puritan migration of 1630, was partially influenced to leave England by his declining economic status resulting from launching three of his sons with substantial gifts of land that cut his own holdings in half (Morgan, 1958:43).

TABLE 2. RELATIONSHIP OF WEALTH STATUS OF FATHERS AND FATHERS-IN-LAW OF FIRST AND YOUNGER SONS

Tax list date for: Fathers and fathers-in-law — Sons	Same quintile as father: 1st	Same quintile as father: younger	Higher quintile than father: 1st	Higher quintile than father: younger	Lower quintile than father: 1st	Lower quintile than father: younger	N
	%	%	%	%	%	%	
1647--1680	25	29	58	29	17	43	26
1749--1779	30	33	44	26	25	41	94
1779--1810	26	30	55	27	18	43	117
1810--1830	36	27	30	36	34	37	139
1830--1860	34	35	34	30	32	34	138

Percentage of men whose fathers-in-law were in the columns shown.

and perhaps bias the sample, the differences are quite dramatic. First sons taxed on the 1680, 1779, and 1810 property lists were roughly twice as likely as younger sons to have a father-in-law who was in a higher wealth quintile than their own father. They were similarly only half as likely as younger sons to have a father-in-law who was poorer than their own father. Birth order was thus an important determinant of the economic status of the future spouse and influential in determining the life chances of men during the colonial period.[6]

A radical change is apparent for men on the town tax lists of 1830 and 1860. Birth order in the nineteenth century exerted no significant effect on the relationship between the relative wealth of father and father-in-law. Instead of a gradual dimunition in paternal power, as was apparent in the effect of father's survival on the marriage age of sons, a decisive break is apparent.[7] While the measure in Table 1 involves the operation of paternal power on the individual level, primogeniture reflected in Table 2 is more a social constraint on the "freeness" of marriage choice. Apparently it was easier for all fathers to discriminate automatically against younger sons than it was for individual fathers, after the middle of the eighteenth century, to postpone the age at marriage of their own sons. The change evident in both indicators relating to the marriage process of sons is consistent with the larger hypothesis of a shift away from the dominance of the family of orientation in the family system.

The distinction between individual and social aspects of parental control is also apparent for daughters as well as sons. Traditionally in western society women have been more subject than men to parental control, particularly in the area of sexual behavior. Although penalties for premarital fornication were assessed equally against both parties, colonial New England did not escape this patriarchal bias. As a symbolic example geographically-mixed marriages usually occurred in the hometown of the bride, suggesting that the husband had to receive his wife from her father. Post-marital residence in these cases, however, was more often in the husband's town. Although the Puritan conception of marriage as a free act allowed women veto power over the parental choice of the husband, marriages in the upper social strata were arranged through extensive negotiations by the parents (Morgan, 1966:79-86). In short the existing evidence points to a pattern intermediate between total control of young women by their parents and substantive premarital autonomy for women. The historical question, once again, is not either-or but how much? Were women, in fact, "married off," and was there any change over time in the incidence of this practice? Direct evidence does not exist to chart a trend, but a hypothetical pattern

[6] This empirical conclusion contradicts the conventional interpretation of the social insignificance of primogeniture in colonial America (Bailyn, 1962:345; Keim, 1968:545-586). Earlier studies, however, have only shown that all sons generally got some property, not *how much* each one actually received. Wills lack a monetary value for the bequests making direct measurement impossible. In Virginia younger sons often received land in less-developed (and presumably land of less value) frontier areas while first sons got the home plantation. More generally historians who have analyzed inequality in colonial America have thought in terms of industrial society and have thus ignored sources of *intrafamilial* inequality. No published studies exist comparing the actual life experiences of first and younger sons in early America. In England, of course, the differential treatment accorded to first and younger sons was of considerable economic, social, and political importance (Thirsk, 1969).

[7] The use of primogeniture may actually have increased in the early and mid-eighteenth century as the supply of land within settled areas declined. This trend has been documented for the town of Andover, Massachusetts (Greven, 1970:131-132), and on a broader cross-cultural basis the relationship between land scarcity and impartible inheritance has been suggested (Goldschmidt and Kunkel, 1971).

may be suggested. If parents did decide when their daughters could and should marry, one might expect them to procede on the basis of the eldest first and so on. Passing over a daughter to allow a younger sister to marry first might advertise some deficiency in the elder and consequently make it more difficult for the parents to find a suitable husband for her. If, on the other hand, women decided on the basis of personal considerations when (and perhaps who) they should marry, more irregularity in the sequence of sisters' marriages should be expected.

Table 3 demonstrates a marked increase in the proportions of daughters who fail to marry in order of sibling position after the middle of the eighteenth century. Because of the age difference among sisters most will marry in order of birth. Since women may remain single for reasons independent of parental choice, *e.g.*, the unfavorable sex ratio in eastern Massachusetts in the second half of the eighteenth century, the measure which omits these cases (left column of Table 3) is a more precise indicator of the trend. However, the increasing tendency in the eighteenth and particularly the nineteenth century for women to remain permanently single is certainly consistent with an increasing absence of strong parental involvement in the marriage process of their

TABLE 3. PERCENTAGE OF DAUGHTERS NOT MARRYING IN BIRTH ORDER IN RELATIONSHIP TO THOSE AT RISK

Periods when daughters are marriageable	Spinsters excluded		Spinsters included	
	%	N	%	N
1651-1650 to 1691-1710	8.1	86	11.2	89
1701-1720 to 1731-1750	11.6	138	18.4	147
1741-1760 to 1771-1790	18.2	176	25.1	191
1781-1800 to 1811-1830	14.9	214	24.9	245
1821-1840 to 1861-1880	18.4	298	24.7	320

Note: In a family with n known adult sisters, there are n-1 possibilities for not marrying in birth order, *e.g.*, an only daughter cannot marry out of birth order, two daughters can marry out of order in only one way, etc. The interpretation of this measure is dependent, of course, on the assumption (true until the early nineteenth century) that the mean interval separating living sisters remains constant. With the fall in marital fertility during the nineteenth century, the gap between sisters increases. Since daughters who never marry obviously do not marry in order of birth, the left column excludes and right column includes these women.

children. More and more women in the late eighteenth and early nineteenth century were obviously not being "married off." Suggesting the obvious point that their marriages were controlled more indirectly through the power fathers had over economic resources, a similar index of sons marrying out of birth order shows no secular trend.

Just as primogeniture relates to the intergenerational transmission of economic resources, so too does the relationship of parental wealth to the marriage age of daughters. If wealth transmission by marriage were important in the society, than parents obviously would have greater direct control over their daughters than if women were expected to provide no resources to their future husbands. If daughters brought economic resources to the marriage, then one would expect that daughters of wealthier men would naturally be sought after by other families as being the more desirable marriage partners for their sons. The higher level of demand should mean that daughters of the wealthier would marry at a younger age than daughters of the less wealthy. If, on the contrary, property transfer and marriage were not intimately connected, then the class pattern of female marriage age would conform to male class career patterns. Market conditions rather than the behavior of individual actors can be assessed by examining the differential by wealth in the female age at first marriage. For daughters born to marriages formed in Hingham between 1721 and 1780 there is a perfect inverse relationship between paternal wealth and marriage age. Once more there is evidence for a significant role of the family of orientation in structuring marriage patterns. This wealth pattern is dramatically reversed for daughters born to marriages between 1781 and 1840. The stability in the mean marriage age (bottom row of Table 4) masks the divergent class trends. Daughters of the wealthy married later in the nineteenth century, while daughters of the less wealthy married at a younger age than before.[8] The slight positive relationship between wealth and male marriage age becomes much stronger during the nineteenth century as well. Nothing could be more suggestive of the severing of direct property considerations from marriage.

[8] Although the data are unreliable because of an absence of information on the marital status of many daughters, the shame shift occurred in the class incidence of permanent spinsterhood. In the eighteenth century the daughters of the wealthier strata were most likely to marry; in the 1781-1840 period, daughters of the wealthier were most likely to remain spinsters.

TABLE 4. AGE AT MARRIAGE OF DAUGHTERS BY WEALTH QUINTILE OF FATHERS

	Daughters born to marriages of				
	1721-1780		1781-1840		
Wealth quintile class of father	Age	N	Age	N	Change in mean age
Richest 20 per cent	23.3	99	24.5	114	+1.31
Upper-middle 20 per cent	23.5	98	24.4	179	+0.96
Middle 20 per cent	23.6	110	22.1	172	–1.47
Lower-middle 20 per cent	24.5	92	23.1	159	–1.37
Poorest 20 per cent	24.5	57	22.9	135	–1.63
Fathers not present on extant tax list	22.7	37	23.0	96	+0.30
Totals	23.7	493	23.3	855	–0.37

During the nineteenth century, then, daughters were not property exchanged between families. Nineteenth century marriage, in contrast to the preceeding two centuries, was between individuals rather than families. Parents, of course, continue to play an important role in structuring the premarital environment of their children (Sussman, 1953). Their role today is presumably more indirect and their influence is more psychological than instrumental. What may be conceded in principle may be denied in practice. The extent of parental resources and the age of the children are key determinants of the efficacy of parental power. One could argue that the historical shift has been not the disappearance of parental power but its limitation to the earlier phases of the life cycle of the child. On the symbolic-ideological level the shift, albeit incomplete, toward the recognition of the child's independence from his family of orientation is apparent in child-naming patterns.[9]

The decline of parental involvement in marriage formation is also suggested by the decrease in the proportion of marriages involving couples who were both residents of the town. One may presume that parents were more knowledgeable about, and hence more influential in, marriages to children of other families in the town. Between 59.6 per cent and 71.8 per cent of all marriages in decades between 1701-1710 and 1791-1800 involved two residents of Hingham; by 1850-1853, only 48.2 per cent of all marriages, by 1900-1902 only 32.0 per cent and finally by 1950-1954, a mere 25.8 per cent were both residents of the town. Improved transportation and communication in the nineteenth and twentieth centuries, of course, modify the magnitude of this trend. Once again, the shift is in the predicted direction and it occurs at the time—the first half of the nineteenth century—consistent with changes in the other indices.

CONCLUSIONS

At least in the area of parental control over marriage, significant, documentable historical change has occurred in American family behavior. There are difficulties, of course, in extending the findings of a local study to the entire American population. The trend in the family parameter which has been best-documented on the national level, fertility, is consistent with the more detailed evidence on the families of Hingham. From the early nineteenth century onward American marital fertility has been declining. With a level of fertility lower than the national average in 1800, New England was the leader in the American fertility transition (Grabill *et al.*, 1958:14-16; Yasuba, 1962:50-69). What the sequence of change in the Hingham indicators suggests is an erosion and collapse of traditional family patterns in the middle and late eighteenth century *before* the sharp decline in marital fertility began. In the seventeenth and early eighteenth century there existed a stable, parental-run marriage system, in the nineteenth century a stable, participant-run system. Separating these two eras of stability was a period of change and crisis, manifested most notably in the American Revolution itself—a political upheaval not un-

[9] Some 94.4 per cent of families formed before 1700 with three or more sons and 98.5 per cent with three or more daughters named a child for the parent of the same sex. For families formed between 1841 and 1880 with the same number of boys or girls (to control for declining fertility), the respective figures are 67.8 per cent and 53.2 per cent. The decline in parent-child name sharing and especially the more rapid decrease in mother-daughter name sharing reflects the symbolic fact of the ultimate separation of children, especially girls, from their family of birth. The persistence of kin-naming in the nineteenth and twentieth centuries simultaneously confirms the continuing importance of kinship in modern American society (Rossi, 1966; Smith, 1972b).

connected to the family (Burrows and Wallace, 1972).[10]

Articles which begin with a capsule or caricature of a theoretical perspective and then procede to a narrow body of empirical evidence typically conclude that the theory fails to explain the data adequately. Only criticism and revisionism represent *real* scholarly contributions. Only covertly does this study follow that format. Substantively, the empirical measures presented above for the population of Hingham, Massachusetts, confirm, if more precisely define and elaborate, the conclusions and interpretations of Smelser, Goode, Reiss, and Stone. It is perhaps revisionist in the sense that the current state of the field is confused because of the great gap separating a bold and sweeping theory of change and the evidence which would support it. A systematic history of the American family can be reconstructed if sociological theory, long-run series of quantitative data, and historical imagination in devising subtle measures of change are combined. The vulgar notion of a drastic shift from "extended" to "nuclear" families had to be exposed and rejected in order to generate historical research. The equally simple-minded opposite extreme of the historical continuity of the conjugal family is just as fallacious both on historical as well as the better-known sociological grounds. American *households* may always have been overwhelmingly nuclear in structure, but household composition is a measure of family structure—not the structure of the family itself. Historians love complexity—the tension between change and continuity over time. Unravelling this complexity is the particularly challenging task for scholars working in the history of the family.

REFERENCES

Abrams, Philip
1972 "The sense of the past and the origins of sociology." Past and Present 55 (May): 18-32.

Adams, Bert N.
1970 "Isolation, function, and beyond: American kinship in the 1960's." Journal of Marriage and the Family 32 (November):575-597.

Aries, Phillipe
1962 Centuries of Childhood. A Social History of Family Life. Tr. by Robert Baldwick. New York:Knopf.

[10] Trends in premarital pregnancy—very low mid-seventeenth and mid-nineteenth century levels, high mid- and late eighteenth century rates—support this periodization of family change (Smith and Hindus, 1971).

Bailyn, Bernard
1962 "Political experience and enlightenment ideas in eighteenth-century America." American Historical Review 67 (January): 339-351.

Bell, Daniel
1961 "The breakup of family capitalism: on changes of class in America." Pp. 39-45 in Daniel Bell, The End of Ideology. New York:Collier.

Berkner, Lutz K.
1973 "Recent research on the history of the family in Western Europe." Journal of Marriage and the Family 35 (August).

Blau, Peter and Otis Dudley Duncan
1967 The American Occupational Structure. New York:Wiley.

Burrows, Edwin G. and Michael Wallace
1972 "The American Revolution: the ideology and practice of national liberation." Perspectives in American History 6:167-306.

Davis, Kingsley
1949 Human Society. New York:Macmillan.

Demos, John
1970 A Little Commonwealth: Family Life in Plymouth Colony. New York:Oxford.

Furet, Francois
1971 "Quantitative history." Daedalus 100 (Winter):151-167.

Furstenberg, Frank F., Jr.
1966 "Industrialization and the American family: a look backward." American Sociological Review 31 (June):326-337.

Goldschmidt, Walter and Evalyn Jacobson Kunkel
1971 "The structure of the peasant family." American Anthropologist 73 (October): 1058-1076.

Goode, William J.
1968 "The theory and measurement of family change." Pp. 295-348 in Eleanor Bernert Sheldon and Wilbert E. Moore (eds.), Indicators of Social Change. New York:Russell Sage Foundation.
1970a World Revolution and Family Patterns. New York:Free Press Paperback.
1970b "Family systems and social mobility." Pp. 120-136 in Reuben Hill and Rene Konig (eds.), Families in East and West. Paris: Mouton.

Grabill, Wilson H., Clyde V. Kiser, and Pascal K. Whelpton
1958 The Fertility of American Women. New York:Wiley.

Greven, Philip J., Jr.
1970 Four Generations: Population, Land, and Family in Colonial Andover, Massachusetts. Ithaca:Cornell.

Hajnal, J.
1965 "European marriage patterns in perspective." Pp. 101-143 in D. V. Glass and D. E. C. Eversley (eds.), Population in History. London:Edward Arnold.

Hoogenbloom, Ari
1968 "Industrialism and political leadership: a

case study of the United States Senate." Pp. 49-78 in Frederic Cople Jaher (ed.), The Age of Industrialism in America. New York:Free Press.

Keim, C. Ray
1968 "Primogeniture and entail in colonial Virginia." William and Mary Quarterly 25 (October):545-586.

Lantz, Herman R., Margaret Britton, Raymond Schmitt, and Eloise C. Snyder
1968 "Pre-industrial patterns in the colonial family in America: a content analysis of colonial magazines." American Sociological Review 33 (June):413-426.

Laslett, Peter and Richard Wall (eds.)
1972 Household and Family in Past Time. Cambridge:Cambridge University Press.

Morgan, Edmund S.
1958 The Puritan Dilemma: The Story of John Winthrop. Boston:Little, Brown.
1966 The Puritan Family: New York:Harper Torchbooks.

Ohlin, G.
1961 "Mortality, marriage, and growth in preindustrial populations." Population Studies 14 (March):190-197.

Parsons, Talcott
1943 "The kinship system of the contemporary United States." American Anthropologist 45 (January-March):22-38.
1965 "The normal American family." Pp. 31-50 in Seymour Farber, Piero Mustacchi, and Roger H. Wilson (eds.), Man and Civilization: The Family's Search for Survival. New York:McGraw-Hill.

Reiss, Ira L.
1964 Premarital Sexual Standards in America. New York:Free Press Paperback.

Rossi, Alice S.
1965 "Naming children in middle class families." American Sociological Review 30 (August): 499-513.

Shipton, Clifford K.
1954 "Ye mystery of ye ages solved, or, how placing worked at colonial Harvard and Yale." Harvard Alumni Bulletin 57 (December 11): 258-263.

Smelser, Neil J.
1966 "The modernization of social relations." Pp. 110-122 in Myron Weiner (ed.), Modernization: The Dynamics of Growth. New York: Basic Books.

Smith, Daniel Scott
1972a "The demographic history of colonial New England." Journal of Economic History 32 (March):165-183.
1972b "Child-naming patterns and family structure change: Hingham, Massachusetts, 1640-1880." Unpublished paper presented at the Clark University conference on the family, social structure, and social change.
1973 "Population, family and society in Hingham, Massachusetts, 1635-1880." Unpublished Ph. D. dissertation, University of California.

Smith, Daniel Scott and Michael S. Hindus
1971 "Premarital pregnancy in America, 1640-1966: an overview and interpretation." Unpublished paper presented at the annual meeting of the American Historical Association.

Stone, Lawrence
1964 "Marriage among the English nobility." Pp. 153-183 in Rose Laub Coser (ed.), The Family: Its Structure and Functions. New York:St. Martin's Press.

Sussman, M. B.
1953 "Parental participation in mate selection and its effects upon family continuity." Social Forces 32 (October):76-81.

Thirsk, Joan
1969 "Younger sons in the seventeenth century." History 54 (October):358-377.

Uhlenberg, Peter R.
1969 "A study of cohort life cycles: cohorts of native born Massachusetts women, 1830-1920." Population Studies 23 (November):407-420.

Wrigley, E. A.
1966 "Family reconstitution." Pp. 96-159 in E. A. Wrigley (ed.), An Introduction to English Historical Demography. New York:Basic Books.
1969 Population and History. New York: McGraw-Hill.

Yasuba, Yasukichi
1962 Birth Rates of the White Population of the United States, 1800-1860. Baltimore:Johns Hopkins.

FAMILY HISTORY AND DEMOGRAPHIC TRANSITION

Robert V. Wells

In recent years, the family has emerged as a major subject of historical inquiry.[1] Numerous books and articles have appeared describing, among other things, the composition, kinship, and other interpersonal relationships, economic functions, and political importance of families.[2] In addition, other works have dealt with values and attitudes toward the family and its members.[3] Venturous scholars have even tried to relate family matters to such subjects as the Salem witchcraft trials, the development of a revolutionary milieu in eighteenth-century New England, and the nature of British politics in the seventeenth and eighteenth centuries, or in the case of the *Annales* school, to the total environment of a locality.[4]

Characterized by a wide range of approaches, these efforts have produced an extraordinary number of interesting findings. However, on the surface at least, historical research on the family has lacked unity and a common sense of direction. Not only have individual scholars often pursued answers to their own idiosyncratic questions, using their own definitions, but the appearance of disunity also has been fostered by the wide temporal and geographic distribution of work on the family. Thus, while our knowledge about families in the past has been increasing rapidly, it has generally been difficult to relate the results of one investigation to conclusions reached in other studies.[5]

Certainly this broad attack on the history of the family is to be encouraged. To study only one aspect of the family or families of only one time or place would be unnecessarily limiting. Furthermore, it is important to recognize that current methodologies available to historians of the family tend to focus on the details of the lives of relatively few persons. In such a situation generalization becomes possible only after a reasonably large number of similar studies have been done. Nonetheless, it seems desirable that historians of the family, of whatever persuasion, try to approach their work with at least some reference to a broader picture.

It is easy to call for some organizing theme to give unity and direction to work on families of the past; it is more difficult to suggest what such a theme should be. At the risk of being presumptuous, however, my purpose here is to do exactly that.

Perhaps the most popular theory among demographers today is the theory of Demographic Transition, which describes (and often attempts to explain) the historic decline of both death and birth rates in the industrialized nations of the world.[6] However, in the light of recent work on the history of the family, this theory (which we will consider in more detail shortly) needs to be recast if it is to make any sense. When I attempted to do this, it became apparent that not only could history help to reshape the theory of Demographic Transition, but that the altered version of the theory also gave coherence to many of the hitherto remotely connected studies in the history of the family.

Thus, the purpose of this paper is fourfold. First, I want to offer a critique of the theory of Demographic Transition as it currently stands. Second, I want to suggest in abstract how the theory might be reformulated to account for the historical evidence which challenges the current model. Third, by surveying families in American history, I will try to relate the revised theory to the facts of the past. I will conclude by indicating some areas of research in family history which appear to be worth further study. In so doing, I hope to show how closely integrated much of the research in family history has been in the past, and how unified it can be in the future.

Because my own special area of competence happens to be American history, I shall rely heavily on evidence from this country, especially in testing the revised hypothesis. However, I shall attempt to indicate how data from other countries also seem to fit the new model. If the evidence appears scattered sometimes, that is in part the result of my own knowledge (or lack thereof), but is more the result of the sizeable gaps in our knowledge of the relevant areas of history. In any case, it should be emphasized that I am putting forth this model of the Demographic Transition with the awareness that future research will probably revise it. My main concerns, then, involve both the accuracy of the theory as revised here and a hope that this paper will serve to give a greater sense of common purpose to students of family history.

The theory of Demographic Transition can be usefully divided into two parts for purposes of analysis and criticism. The first area which we will consider *describes* the general decline in birth and death rates in industrialized countries. The second part deals with *attempts to explain* why the change occurred.

In the past, according to Transition theory, all populations were characterized by birth and death rates which were much higher than those found in industrialized countries today. Although these rates might vary over the short term, over a long period of time they tended to be rather closely balanced, with the result that natural increase was small and population growth was slow. Starting in France, and possibly Scandinavia, in the late eighteenth and early nineteenth centuries the death rate began to decline noticeably. Since the birth rate did not fall until later, there was a transitional period (hence the name of the theory) of rapid population growth as births exceeded deaths by a considerable margin. However, in the long run the birth and death rates once again came into rather close balance, though at much lower levels than before, and rapid growth ceased. While France was the first nation to experience this transition, other nations (all industrialized) have followed much the same path, although the timing of the change, the rate of decline of fertility and mortality, and the extent to which the transition has been completed vary considerably from one nation to another. Much of the current interest in this theory stems from the fact that in many of the non-industrialized countries of the world, death rates have fallen remarkably since World War II, leading to rather rapid transitional growth at the present. Obviously, demographers are interested if and when fertility will fall in these parts of the world, slowing the growth rate and bringing the birth and death rates into balance at a relatively low level.

In the light of recent historical investigations, about the only parts of this theory which are clearly beyond question are that rapid growth occurred during the demographic transition, and that birth and death rates are now lower in some parts of the world than they ever have been for any extended period in the past. The assumption that relatively slow growth was universal before the transition began needs to be qualified in light of recent findings suggesting rather remarkable oscillations of population in Egypt between about 700 B.C. and the present, the depopulation of Europe during the plague of the fourteenth century and its ultimate recovery, and the rather remarkable short-term variations found in the populations of some British colonies in America around 1700.[7]

Interestingly, when most demographers and historians deal with the demographic transition, they make remarkably few clearcut statements about the cause of the change. Almost all demographers note carefully that the decline in mortality and fertility always is well under way wherever literacy is high, over half the labor force is employed in nonagricultural pursuits, and the majority of the people live in urban areas. Although few specify the exact relationships, it seems to be a common assumption that these trends (whether called development, industrialization, or modernization) have caused both mortality and fertility to decline.

The explanation for why death rates might have fallen in such a situation is quite plausible. It seems safe to say that the changes noted above were generally accompanied by better and more available medical aid. In addition, standards of living tended to improve as well, producing better diets and more healthful environments.

The reasons why the birth rate should have declined as well are less obvious. Perhaps the best summary of the possible causes behind falling fertility have been given by David Heer in his article, "Economic Development and the Fertility Transition."[8] Heer notes first that the decline in infant mortality accompanying rising living standards may reduce the need for parents to have large numbers of children in order to have a few reach maturity. The change from agriculture to industry, and from rural to urban, also may have led to reduced childbearing according to Heer, simply because children were no longer economically valuable in a new environment. Closely related to these factors was the emergence of governmental care for the aged, which meant that parents no longer needed children to care for them when they grew old. Finally, social attitudes stressing education and achievement in an industrial society and recognizing birth control as acceptable may also have fostered decreased fertility. Put simply, Heer and others stress the fact that in an urban, industrial environment children are no longer benefits, but may actually be detrimental to parental aspirations, and hence fertilty declines.

In spite of the plausibility of the theory, historical evidence suggests that these causal relationships may not have existed. One assumption which seems common to most advocates of Transition theory is that urbanization and industrialization occurred *before* fertility began to decline. Yet, we have evidence of family limitation being practiced by English and Genevans in the seventeenth century, and by some French, American, and Japanese people in the eighteenth and early nineteenth centuries.[9] In every case, these fertility declines predated any significant industrial development. Ironically, in England and possibly elsewhere as well, the move to industry and the cities was associated with an *increase* in the birth rate, quite in contrast to what Transition theory would lead us to expect.[10] Finally, the baby boom which followed World War II is an extraordinarily puzzling phenomena from the perspective of the theory of Demographic Transition. The explanations cited by Heer implicitly assume that once the birth rate declined it would probably stay low. Certainly it should not increase during times of rising prosperity and movement into cities. In fact, so inconsistent was behavior with theory that the prosperous United States had a much greater surge in fertility than did Europe, where war devastation might presumably have led to a reversion to early patterns of reproduction.

Two questions thus arise. The first is, why did fertility fall in the historical change known as the Demographic Transition? The second is, does any connection remain between this decline and the processes known as industrialization or modernization?

In order to answer these two questions we should look at four possible models which might explain a widespread decline in fertility. First of all, it is possible for birth rates to drop for unintended reasons. Changes in health, sexual customs, or marriage patterns all can depress fertility, even though reduced childbearing may not have been the purpose of the initial change. It is clear, however, that the demographic transition involved a deliberate reduction in fertility, and so we must concentrate on conscious efforts to reduce the birth rate. The second model (and first one positing a conscious effort to control reproduction) assumes that when the birth rate was high, there was neither the knowledge of how to limit families nor any desire to do so. Within this framework, the demographic transition is seen as the result of new environments which lead to pressures to control childbearing for the first time, as well as make available the knowledge which allows these desires to be put into effect. Once again, however, the historical evidence makes it difficult to accept this possibility. We noted above that several populations in various parts of the world seem to have practiced family limitation well before industrialization and urbanization introduced new life styles which might have altered the desires of parents to have children. In addition, this evidence and the extraordinary study by Norman Himes on the *Medical History of Contraception* make it clear that knowledge that births could be limited was reasonably widespread before industrial societies began to emerge.[11]

The third model of why fertility falls is a variation of the second. In this case, the assumption is that people wanted to limit their families, but could not because they did not know how to. The appeal of this explanation is that it offers some reason why the educated upper classes generally controlled their fertility before the less knowledgeable lower classes. Likewise, it would also seem to explain why highly literate nations generally have much lower fertility than nations where the educational level is low. However, the evidence suggests that this model too may be invalid. In England in the seventeenth century, both peers and the peasants of Colyton were limiting the size of their families.[12] While their motives may have been different than those of the peers, the residents of Colyton did not have to wait until the industrial revolution to share in the knowledge that births could be limited. Furthermore, among the Colyton residents and the Quakers of the middle colonies whom I have studied, the onset of family limitation was rapid.[13] The speed at which family size fell seems to preclude any slow spread of the knowledge of birth control. I have found no evidence suggesting that the Quakers either gradually or suddenly became aware of methods of limiting births. In fact, the only specific mention of family limitation I have found suggested the adoption of an old method of restricting births (nursing) to a woman who had had a difficult pregnancy and wanted to avoid another.[14] Regardless of the effectiveness of nursing as a long-term means of family limitation, the important point is that, in this instance, it was motivation for and not knowledge about birth control which changed.

The fourth model is very closely connected to the experience of the Quaker wife cited above. It assumes that most populations have at least some notions of how to control fertility (if not by contraception, then certainly by practicing abortion, infanticide, or abstention). Thus, fertility declines occur primarily because the motivation is strong enough for a people to practice one or more of these methods, rather than because they suddenly learn some new technique. Given the rapidity of change in Colyton and among the Quakers, and the fact that major declines in fertility had occurred long before rubber condoms or diaphragms (let alone pills or IUDs) became available, there can be little doubt that at least the initial stages of the demographic transition occurred because people began frequent use of traditional forms of family limitation.[15] It is of interest to note here, incidentally, that Kingsley Davis, a prominent demographer, has issued a telling criticism of current birth-control programs, stressing that they are failing not because of lack of knowledge or techniques, but rather because people see no reason to reduce their fertility.[16]

Emphasizing the importance of motivation in the reduction of fertility is certainly not in conflict with the theory of Demographic Transition. Where this paper does differ from the theory is in the suggestion that motivation to have few children did not result from the economic and social changes accompanying industrialization. Rather, I wish to hypothesize that fertility fell for reasons which *also* produced a decline in the death rate as well as changes in family structure and interpersonal relations and in economic development. Thus, industrialization and the demographic transition continue to be associated, but as two effects of the same cause, rather than one causing the other.

Central to this hypothesis is the assumption that human beings have sets of values which are generally well integrated.[17] If this is true, then the demographic transition may be seen as only one manifestation of a major change in value orientation, a change which can conveniently be typified as the shift from a traditional to a modern world view.[18]

The nature of this change in values has been portrayed effectively in an article by Laila El-Hamamsy entitled, "Belief Systems and Family Planning in Peasant Societies."[19] In an analysis of peasant cultures in both Egypt and Latin America, El-Hamamsy found that persons in such societies were generally characterized by a sense of powerlessness over their own lives and over the world around them. Both nature and human affairs were seen as capricious, hard, and uncontrollable. God had ordered the world according to some mysterious laws, and it was not within the province of men to interfere. As a result, most peasants either do not think about the future or else feel that the future will be the same as the past. Fear, fatalism, and a sense that contentment with the status quo is desirable to avoid disappointed ambitions have led most peasants to conclude that they can do little to alter the course of their lives. Within this framework, there is no apparent reason why few children would be preferable to many (in fact, interfering with conception might anger God), just as there is no apparent reason for altering any other social or economic traditions.

These views are strikingly different from attitudes (which we shall call modern here) which have emerged in Western European society since the sixteenth century. According to E. A. Wrigley, the best way to sum up modern attitudes is with the concept of rationality.[20] Wrigley defines a modern society as one in which recruitment to roles is done on the basis of achievement rather than birth, social roles are more clearly and narrowly defined, and where the rule of law is substituted for arbitrary and capricious behavior. Furthermore, self-interest (or, at most, interest in the nuclear family) is seen as replacing any willingness by individuals to submit to broader social or institutional needs. Thus, in contrast to the traditional view, persons with modern values believe not only that the world is knowable and controllable, but that it is also to an individual's advantage to plan his or her life and attend to the future, as well as to the present and past. To merely avoid trouble is no longer enough (as it was in traditional society) for the modern individual; such a person wants to advance, and often measures advancement in terms of his or her material well-being.

It is easy to see how at least some demographic patterns and forms of family structure might readily have been altered once modern attitudes began to prevail. The reduction of mortality, for example, may well have resulted from the emergence of attitudes that misery did not have to be accepted after all. Such notions would have been conducive to both medical experimentation and the acceptance of new techniques. Similarly, in situations where children came to be seen as burdens, modern values might permit and promote the use of family limitation to protect or enhance one's position in the world. Likewise, the movement into cities, frequently seen as a cause of falling fertility, may actually only be another manifestation of modern attitudes. Urban immigrants may well have been those people who first came to believe that by individual actions (such as migration, or learning industrial skills) it was possible for a person to improve his lot. As we shall see shortly, attitudes toward both women and children changed during the course of the demographic transition, reflecting perhaps a modern emphasis on the worth of the individual and a denial of the unchangeable order of the world. Finally, industrialization and economic development may well be related to the demographic transition. But, instead of one causing the other, the habits of saving, investment, and experimentation and the adoption of new technology necessary to industrial society may have been a response to the sense that the future could be controlled, much as family limitation may have been a different reaction to the same concern for the future.

Certainly the relationships outlined here are plausible. The historical evidence that we have tends to support this line of argument. But before we turn to the data, one last point needs to be made. It is obvious that my argument rests on the assumption that values help to shape the decisions that individuals make. It is not, however, my contention that a shift in values alone will be sufficient to change behavior. Thus, while the hypothesis advanced here asserts that the demographic transition (and related phenomena) could only occur after modern attitudes appear, it does not imply that such changes would have been an automatic result of the adoption of new ideas.

Having put forth a new hypothesis, it is now necessary to begin to test its merits. I shall attempt to do this by drawing on historical evidence for families in America. As was noted earlier, this focus on America is primarily because my expertise lies there. However, as I shall indicate from time to time, evidence from other countries also appears to fit the hypothesis advanced above.

The obvious place to begin is to show that modern ideas were emerging in America before the demographic transition or any of its economic or social correlates were apparent. Although some would say that the emergence of modern attitudes began as early as the sixteenth century, it is clear that at least some of the first colonists had attitudes which were similar to those found in the peasant societies discussed earlier. Edmund Morgan has found a remarkable fatalism and willingness to accept misery among the early settlers of Virginia.[21] The Puritans who settled in New England also shared many traditional attitudes. Nature was seen as mysterious and fearful. Any deviance from the proper path could bring God's wrath upon individuals or a whole people. A theology which stressed predestination and order was certainly not conducive to notions of the individual improving himself. In fact, residents of Massachusetts Bay who were so bold as to advance ideas of human equality, the rule of the law, or the capacity of people to improve themselves were often accused of heresy and driven from the colony.[22] To the extent that the early settlers worried about the future, they were concerned with the next world rather than this one. Life on earth was merely a brief prelude to an eternity in heaven or hell.

In some ways, the surprising thing about colonial society is how quickly modern attitudes began to appear. Richard Brown has recently shown that such values were clearly present in America by the end of the seventeenth century.[23] By the time of the American Revolution, modern attitudes seem to have been quite prevalent in the colonies. According to E. A. Wrigley, "a government which . . . levies large extractions arbitrarily and without due notice . . . is incompatible" with modern, rational attitudes toward life.[24] Thus, the American resistance to Parliamentary interference stands as partial proof of the presence of modern values in society. The colonists were asserting not only constitutional principles, but also an attitude that life was controllable and misfortune need not be passively accepted. Anyone who reads the biographies of the Hancock or Otis families in Massachusetts, the Browns of Providence, Rhode Island, or the Beekmans in New York will certainly be struck by the fact that these people were concerned with this world and with controlling as much of their lives as possible.[25] A man like Benjamin Franklin may have expressed the new ideas better than most of his contemporaries, but the values he articulated were shared by many others.

According to the hypothesis advanced earlier, the emergence of new attitudes should have had an effect on population in general and on the family in particular. Perhaps the earliest evidence of modern ideas affecting population trends in America was the adoption of smallpox inoculation in Boston and elsewhere in the colonies during the eighteenth century.[26] It is possible to debate at length the motives and scientific attitudes which led Dr. Boylston and Cotton Mather to introduce inoculation in Boston in 1721. Nonetheless, the careful tabulation of statistics regarding the effectiveness of the treatment and the wholehearted adoption of inoculation after 1750 seems to be indicative of an attitude that disease could be understood and controlled, and that death need not be always accepted passively.[27] In fact, the last quarter of the eighteenth century saw considerable interest in the scientific study of the patterns and causes of death.[28] Richard Shryock has shown how professionalism, education, and scientific attitudes began to characterize the medical profession by the late eighteenth century.[29] Although these changes did not have a significant impact on health until the nineteenth century, when accurate findings finally began to accumulate, they too reflect a modern outlook on the world.

As with the death rate, the Americans' growing sense of an individual's worth and his influence over his life may have affected family size and structure well before industrialization and urbanization played a prominent role in our society. About the time of the American Revolution, at least some Quaker couples living in the middle colonies began to limit their families deliberately.[30] Although we cannot be sure, it seems plausible that these Friends were responding to the dislocations of wartime by postponing some of the births they might otherwise have had. At present we do not know why individual Quaker couples decided to limit their childbearing. We can suggest, however, that the military campaigns in the middle colonies, the pressure of being pacifists in a time of conflict, severe inflation, and the withdrawal of Quakers from political affairs after 1750 may have made the future uncertain for many Friends. In such a milieu, a reduction of childbearing would make good sense. It is of interest to note here that times of severe crisis seem also to have produced a similar response in Colyton, England, in the 1640s, in France at the time of her Revolution, and in Japan following World War II.[31] It would be wrong, however, to assume on the basis of this evidence that catastrophies generally lead to a durable reduction of fertility. Without modern attitudes to give people the feeling that they need not passively accept their fate, and without a clear sense that a smaller family would improve prospects for the future, such change would not be likely to occur.

While the American Revolution may have triggered the adoption of family limitation among the Quakers, a crisis which evolved more slowly may have led other parts of the American population to reduce their fertility. In the early years of settlement, land had been abundantly available. But, by the middle of the eighteenth century, at least some of the older settlements were beginning to feel the pressure of population on natural resources. As a result, fertility began to change. Kenneth Lockridge has shown that overpopulation was becoming a legitimate concern in New England by the second half of the eighteenth century.[32] Thus, it is of considerable interest to find that the proportion of children in the total population in New England in 1790 was generally lower than in the other states.[33] The age distribution indicates clearly that childbearing was lower there than in any of the other colonies.

Increasing population density and declining economic opportunities may have led to reduced fertility in New England first. But by the early nineteenth century, the same phenomenon was appearing elsewhere. A recent book by Colin Forster and G. S. L. Tucker, *Economic Opportunity and White American Fertility Ratios,* has shown that between 1800 and 1860 substantial reductions in fertility occurred wherever farmland became scarce.[34] This was true from one section of the United States to another. It was also true as a given region became more densely populated over time. Yet density alone may not have produced the change. Evidence from the present indicates that population density does not necessarily cause a decline in the birth rate. Thus, if my hypothesis is correct, it was not only greater density which mattered, but also the perception that reduced fertility would aid individuals in either protecting or advancing their economic well-being.[35]

The ways by which fertility was controlled, at least in these early stages of the transition from high to low birth rates, are not certain. We do know that deliberate family limitation was practiced by at least one part of the American population by 1800. There is no reason why other groups were not capable of the same behavior given proper motivation. There can be little doubt that family limitation within marriage became widespread during the nineteenth century, but it is also possible that part of the reduction in the birth rate from about 50 per 1,000 in 1800 to 28.5 per 1,000 in 1900 was the result of altered marriage patterns.[36] Etienne van de Walle has shown that in nineteenth-century France, both late marriage and family limitation within marriage were used to control childbearing, though generally only one method or the other was used in a particular locality.[37] Thus, it is plausible that both marriage patterns and marital fertility could have been altered by residents of the United States to ensure their future well-being by limiting births. Unfortunately, our knowledge of nineteenth-century marriage patterns does not allow us to determine which means of control was more prevalent at that time. Suffice it to say that both may be rational responses to a perceived problem and hence either means of control would fit the hypothesis as stated earlier.

The decline in the birth rate which began around 1800 (if not before) continued until 1933 when it leveled off. After several years of minor fluctuation, the birth rate began to climb slowly after 1938, and spurted upwards between 1940 and 1947. Had it not been for peculiarities in the age composition, the birth rate would have continued to climb until 1957, at which point it once again would have declined.[38] This baby boom, which occurred primarily after World War II, has been extremely difficult for Transition theory to explain. At a time when America was more urbanized and industrialized than ever before, fertility should have decreased rather than risen. As the theory has been reformulated here, however, the baby boom makes more sense. Often reduced fertility involves the postponement of children who might be desired if circumstances permitted. In such a situation, any favorable change in the environment might lead to a sudden surge in fertility. As Richard Easterlin has suggested, this seems to be exactly what happened after World War II.[39] For a variety of reasons, persons in the prime childbearing years were unusually prosperous. This alone might well have increased the birth rate, for the same reaction may have occurred in England in the late eighteenth and early nineteenth centuries as rising incomes were accompanied briefly by rising births, much to Malthus' dismay.[40] However, the perception of well-being in post-World War II America must certainly have been accentuated by the contrast with the decade of the 1930s, a recent and vivid memory to those who had the boom babies. Why the boom came to an end is not clear, though we can surmise that a decade of high fertility was enough once again to emphasize the high costs of children, even in times of prosperity.

So far we have seen how the modified version of Transition theory can help to explain variations in fertility patterns in American history which were inconsistent with the earlier theory. It is now time to turn our attention to the way in which the hypothesis advanced above may help to connect demographic change with altered kinship relationships and attitudes toward women and children.

Recall that traditional societies place an emphasis on order and stability. Everyone has a place in society, and is expected to stay there until death. Human dignity and individual development are not considered important in such societies. In contrast, modern values place an emphasis on achievement (often monetary) and equality before the law. Although the evidence is scarce, it is possible to suggest that as modern values replaced traditional ones in America, attitudes toward family, women, and children altered significantly.

It is convenient to look first at the studies of colonial families in Andover and Dedham, Massachusetts done by Philip Greven and Kenneth Lockridge respectively.[41] Both these works show that in the seventeenth century, families were well ordered and controlled. The ideals described by Edmund Morgan in *The Puritan Family* were being practiced there.[42] Perhaps the most remarkable finding was the extraordinary authority exercised by parents over their older children. Of course, the desire to inherit the farm may have had some influence on keeping sons dutiful, but in a land of abundant acreage, it seems implausible that such control could have worked without a system of values which encouraged duty and suppressed any thoughts of individual advancement. Interestingly enough, in both Dedham and Andover control broke down in the eighteenth century, precisely the time when newer attitudes were emerging. John Demos' study of Plymouth indicates a rather high degree of mobility there, suggesting that modern attitudes may have emerged slightly earlier among the Separatists than among the Puritans.[43] However, even among the Plymouth inhabitants authority within the family was important.

I have argued elsewhere that attitudes regarding the family had changed noticeably by the time of the American Revolution.[44] No longer were marriage and life in a family deemed necessary for all individuals. Alternative roles and alternative living arrangements became more acceptable by the end of the eighteenth century. By the nineteenth century, family ties seem to have loosened even further. Mobility was common as a series of recent community studies have shown.[45] No longer did individuals wait at home to inherit the family farm. Rather, Americans set out to improve their lot. And, if the evidence is to be believed, they kept on moving until they established themselves economically. Clearly, attitudes by this time favored individual advancement rather than passive acceptance of fate – a plot made famous by Horatio Alger. One hardly need add that migration for personal betterment is still a prominent feature of American life.

When we look at the actual structure of families, the evidence appears somewhat confusing as to whether nuclear or extended families prevailed. On the one hand, we find nuclear families common before 1800; on the other hand, kinship ties today are still important to many groups in our society. In the end, this debate over whether extended or nuclear families prevailed may miss the point. Instead of worrying over whether an individual had only immediate relatives or a large family to associate with, perhaps we should concern ourselves with the quality of those relationships. Michael Anderson has shown, for example, that in nineteenth-century Lancashire, extended families existed in towns, but on the basis of mutual aid and for calculated advantage.[46] Families were to be used for protection and advancement. They were not designed to control an individual and keep him in his place. The kinship ties among various American ethnic groups seem remarkably similar to this pattern, encouraging rather than restricting individual advancement.[47] However typical the Andover families of the seventeenth century may have been at that time, such relationships seem to have dissolved as modern values became more prevalent.

As traditional values gave way to modern, we might expect parental attitudes toward children to shift – and that they did. Studies of both Puritan and Quaker attitudes toward children show that before the middle of the eighteenth century, parents felt their main duties were controlling the child until he was responsible and trying to protect the state of his soul.[48] Little emphasis was placed on the development of individuality; life after death was considered more important than life on earth. Gradually, these attitudes changed. Parents began to respect, rather than fear, the unique qualities of their children. Discipline remained important, but by the first half of the nineteenth century it was important to insure success in this world rather than the next. Parents came to feel that they had a significant role to play in shaping their children's future; not all had been predestined or would be decided by fate.[49] The childrearing literature of the early twentieth century was much like that found a hundred years before, with one exception. In addition to being taught that they could influence a child's success, parents were told they could shape his health as well. In the 1830s death was still only partly predictable and controllable; by the 1930s disease was something to be prevented or cured, not endured.[50] Thus, rather than viewing attitudes toward children as either cause or effect of variations in fertility or infant mortality, or as the result of an urban-industrial society, it seems more useful to see lower fertility, attempts to improve health, and notions of a child's unique qualities all as recognitions that the future on earth has some promise, especially if people work at improving it.

The role of women also seems to have evolved as modern values came to replace traditional attitudes. In the seventeenth century legal and social pressures combined to limit women's roles outside of marriage. By the time of the Revolution, however, legal changes began to indicate a recognition that women had equal rights before the law as property holders, an essential characteristic of modern society.[51] Furthermore, attitudes toward marriage changed at the same time. No longer were unwed women oddities; those who married were able to choose a husband more on the basis of love, rather than for economic considerations. Individual happiness increasingly played a part in a woman's choices – in fact, women had choices by 1800 in a way they had not apparently had a century earlier.[52]

The nineteenth century was a time of paradox for women in America. On the one hand, women joined in various reform movements as never before, expressing, it seems to me, the notion that the future could be improved. On the other hand, women were seen as the unchanging repositories of purity and virtue, who, among other things, suffered with great patience.[53] This latter attitude sounds remarkably traditional, but given the extent of reform activity on the part of nineteenth-century women, it is hard to believe that they felt no chance to alter the future. Rather, I would suggest, many of the notions of purity and suffering were related to sex. Women were not supposed to enjoy sex, while at the same time they were to understand the animal drives of their husbands and sons, especially when they strayed to prostitutes. While these attitudes may seem strangely out of place today, they may have made good sense in the nineteenth century. At a time when people wanted to limit births but had only crude means available, it may have been useful to deny a woman's interest in sex. *Coitus interruptus* could not have been terribly satisfying to many women. Likewise, prostitution, whatever its evils, served as one means of reducing the risk of pregnancy for wives.

It is of interest to note that the admission that women, like men, have a sexual side corresponds nicely to the development of more efficient and less obtrusive forms of birth control.[54] The twentieth century has seen a greater concern for the development of a woman's full personality than ever before. It may well be that this has happened not only as a result of modern attitudes, but also because more effective birth-control methods have allowed these attitudes to prevail, whereas in the nineteenth century the desire to control fertility worked at cross purposes to any tendency to liberate women.

One last point deserves mention, before we examine what future research on the family should entail. Not all parts of the American population have experienced changes in mortality and fertility at the same rate. Undoubtedly some of the variations can be explained by different preferences for the ideal family size, by different promises for the future, and by different access to the best birth-control methods. At the same time, at least parts of the population may simply have maintained traditional attitudes much longer than others. Blacks, for example, seem to have had levels of fertility and mortality in the late nineteenth century which were unchanged from the colonial period, when their experience was much the same as the whites.[55] Undoubtedly some of this can be explained by the denial of medical services to blacks, but we should not overlook the possibility that under slavery and the Jim Crow laws there was little reason to hope for the future. For many blacks, the world was uncontrollable and uncertain, much as it is for many peasant cultures today. Interestingly, once blacks began to move out of the South (an action which in itself is indicative of a sense that the future can be improved) and into the cities, the demographic differences between the races narrowed noticeably.[56] Although differences still exist, the trends since the 1930s have been remarkably similar, suggesting that many of the factors which determine fertility and mortality are color blind, even if much of the rest of our society is not.

In contrast to the black experience, the Hutterites, a religious group in the northern plains states, continue to have children at a rate that only the colonists could match.[57] This is noteworthy because the religious values of this group are extremely conservative and very traditional. Order, discipline, and the submission of the individual are important values to these people. While they are aware that the future can be controlled, they are more concerned with the success of the group than with the development of the individual. Unlike immigrant groups who fostered kinship ties to protect and advance the individual, the Hutterites use kinship ties to subordinate individual success to the good of the whole, a very traditional attitude.[58]

As projected here, the new version of the theory of Demographic Transition appears to make better sense of the historical facts of fertility and mortality changes. In addition, the emphasis on a revolution in values serves to integrate many of the disparate approaches to the study of families in the past. Nonetheless, what I have said here is only an hypothesis, and as such must be tested and presumably revised. It is my hope that historians of the family will find this task worthwhile, not only because it has some significance in a world faced with problems of implementing large-scale reductions in fertility, but also because this hypothesis can provide some unity to research on the family.

What needs to be done? First, we need to know more precisely when fertility, mortality, and migration patterns changed in the past. These patterns must be connected with the revolution in values I have assumed to have occurred. If modern attitudes do not predate or at least overlap with new forms of demographic behavior, then the whole hypothesis falls. Likewise, it is important to determine how the changes occurred. In part this is important because we need to know which changes were deliberate and controlled and which were accidental results of other changes in behavior. In the case of fertility, it is useful to know, for example, that a falling birth rate came from birth control rather than new marriage patterns, because the attitudes toward women and children and the future trends of childbearing may be determined by which method is used.

Of considerable interest here are comparative studies. Such comparisons would be cross-national, cross-cultural, or based on socioeconomic differences within a society. The theory, as outlined here, seems to fit the American experience. But does it hold in Europe or Japan? Furthermore, do regions which have still to experience the demographic transition all have traditional attitudes? Have recent declines in mortality been the result of the acceptance of modern attitudes, or have they been imposed from above by an imported medical technology?

Obviously most students of family history will continue to have more interest in one aspect of the family than another. This is understandable, and is probably the most practical approach to the immediate problem of finding out what families in the past have been like. At the same time, I would hope that no longer would one definition of or approach toward the family be considered the only appropriate one. Studies of the family should no longer focus exclusively on kinship, *or* fertility rates, *or* childrearing practices, *or* the role of women. Rather, they should seek to incorporate all relevant changes in values and behavior which may have affected the family. We must accept the idea that as a subject, the family is a complex, but highly interrelated entity. A satisfactory approach to the history of the family must involve a study of all aspects of behavior within the family setting, as well as recognizing that family patterns are closely related to more general attitudes and behavior patterns of the society under study.[58]

Union College

FOOTNOTES

1. Several older studies do exist. One of the first was Arthur W. Calhoun, *A Social History of the American Family*, 3 vols. (Cleveland, 1917). More useful are the works by Philippe Ariès, *Centuries of Childhood* (New York, 1965); and Edmund S. Morgan, *The Puritan Family*, rev. ed. (New York, 1966).

2. See, for example, Bernard Bailyn, *The New England Merchants in the Seventeenth Century* (New York, 1964); John Demos, "Families in Colonial Bristol, Rhode Island: An Exercise in Historical Demography," *William and Mary Quarterly* 25 (1968): 40-57; Philip Greven, *Four Generations* (Ithaca, 1970); and Leonard Labaree, *Conservatism in Early America* (Ithaca, 1948), pp. 1-31. At least two journals have devoted whole issues to the family in history; see *Journal of Interdisciplinary History* 2 (1971), and *Journal of Marriage and the Family*, Vol. 35 (1973).

3. Mary S. Benson, *Women in Eighteenth Century America* (New York, 1935); Edward Shorter, "Female Emancipation, Birth Control, and Fertility in European History," *American Historical Review* 78 (1973): 605-640; Bernard Wishy, *The Child and the Republic* (Philadelphia, 1968).

4. John Demos, "Underlying Themes in the Witchcraft of Seventeenth Century New England," *American Historical Review* 75 (1970): 1311-1326; Pierre Goubert, *Beauvais et la Beauvaisis de 1600 à 1730* (Paris[?], 1960); Kenneth Lockridge, *A New England Town* (New York, 1970); Lewis Namier, *The Structure of Politics at the Accession of George III*, 2nd ed. (London, 1957); Lawrence Stone, *The Crisis of the Aristocracy* (Oxford, 1965), pp. 589-671.

5. The studies published in *Annales: Economies, Sociétés, Civilisations* and under the auspices of L'Institut national d'études démographiques are clear exceptions as the French scholars quite clearly build on each others' work.

6. Reference to the demographic transition appears in virtually all major texts on population; see, for example, Donald Bogue, *Principles of Demography* (New York, 1969) or William Petersen, *Population*, 2nd ed. (London, 1969). It also plays a prominent role in such recent studies as Ita I. Ekanem, "A Further Note on the Relation between Economic Development and Fertility," *Demography* 9 (1972): 383-398; H. J. Habakkuk, *Population Growth and Economic Development Since 1750* (New York, 1971); Donnella H. Meadows et al., *The Limits to Growth* (New York, 1972); and E. A. Wrigley, *Population and History* (New York, 1969).

7. T. H. Hollingsworth, *Historical Demography* (Ithaca, 1969), pp. 307-311, 355-388. The data on growth rates in the British colonies are contained in Robert V. Wells, *The*

Population of the British Colonies in America Before 1776: A Survey of Census Data (Princeton, 1975).

8. Published in D. V. Glass and Roger Revelle, eds., *Population and Social Change* (New York, 1972), pp. 99-114. Many of the articles in this book first appeared in *Daedalus* 97 (1968), an issue of the journal devoted to historical population studies.

9. Jean Ganiage, *Trois Villages de l'Ile-de-France* (Paris, 1963); Akira Hayami, "The Demographic Analysis of a Village in Tokugawa Japan," *Keio Economic Studies* 5 (1967-1968): 50-88; Louis Henry, *Anciennes Familles Genevoises* (Paris, 1956); T. H. Hollingsworth, *The Demography of the British Peerage,* supplement to *Population Studies* 18 (1964); R. V. Wells, "Family Size and Fertility Control in Eighteenth Century America," *Population Studies* 25 (1971): 73-82; E. A. Wrigley, "Family Limitation in Pre-industrial England," *Economic History Review,* 2nd Ser., 19 (1966): 82-109.

10. Wrigley, *Population and History,* pp. 179-184.

11. First published in 1936 in Baltimore. Himes argues that birth-control knowledge was not widespread, and that fertility fell because it was diffused. His evidence seems to me to support the contrary position just as well, if not better.

12. Hollingsworth, *British Peerage;* Wrigley, "Family Limitation."

13. Wells, "Family Size and Fertility Control."

14. Cecil K. Drinker, *Not So Long Ago* (New York, 1937), pp. 55, 59.

15. Himes, *Medical History of Contraception,* pp. 201-206.

16. Kingsley Davis, "Population Policy: Will Current Programs Succeed?" *Science* 158 (1967): 730-739.

17. Several studies from various parts of the world deal not only with this issue, but also show that values play an important role in determining demographic behavior. See J. A. Banks, *Prosperity and Parenthood* (London, 1954); J. A. and Olive Banks, *Feminism and Family Planning in Victorian England* (New York, 1964); William B. Clifford, II, "Modern and Traditional Value Orientations and Fertility Behavior," *Demography* 8 (1971): 37-48; Eva Mueller, "Economic Motives for Family Limitation: A Study Conducted in Taiwan," *Population Studies* 26 (1972): 383-403; and Shorter, "Female Emancipation."

18. After considerable thought I have decided to use the terms "traditional" and "modern" here. There is an immense literature on these terms, much of it reflecting the peculiar interests of the authors. Hopefully my use of these terms will be made clear in the definitions which follow.

19. Included in Harrison Brown and Edward Hutchings, Jr., eds., *Are Our Descendants Doomed?* (New York, 1970), pp. 335-357.

20. E. A. Wrigley, "The Process of Modernization and the Industrial Revolution in England," *Journal of Interdisciplinary History* 3 (1972): 225-259.

21. Edmund S. Morgan, "The Labor Problem at Jamestown, 1607-1618," *American Historical Review* 76 (1971): 595-611.

22. Perry Miller's two volumes on *The New England Mind* (Cambridge, Mass., 1953) are the obvious place to begin an understanding of Puritan attitudes. But Edmund S. Morgan, *The Puritan Dilemma* (Boston, 1962) offers an excellent, short introduction.

23. Richard D. Brown, "Modernization and the Modern Personality in Early America, 1600-1865: A Sketch of a Synthesis," *Journal of Interdisciplinary History* 2 (1972): 201-228. Richard Dunn's study of the Winthrop family, *Puritans and Yankees* (Princeton, 1962) offers an interesting illustration of this change occurring within one family.

24. Wrigley, "Process of Modernization," p. 230.

25. W. T. Baxter, *The House of Hancock* (Cambridge, Mass., 1945); James B. Hedges, *The Browns of Providence Plantations,* vol. 1 (Cambridge, Mass., 1952); John J. Waters, Jr., *The Otis Family in Provincial and Revolutionary Massachusetts* (Chapel Hill, N.C., 1968); Philip L. White, *The Beekmans of New York in Politics and Commerce, 1647-1877* (New York, 1956).

26. John Duffy, *Epidemics in Colonial America* (Baton Rouge, La., 1953), pp. 16-106.

27. Otho T. Beall, Jr., "Cotton Mather, the First Significant Figure in American Medicine," *Bulletin of the History of Medicine* 26 (1952): 103-116, discusses some of Mather's motives; the statistics produced during the eighteenth century may be found in Massachusetts Historical Society, *Collections,* 1st Ser., vol. 3 (1794), p. 292.

28. Two of the notable results of this interest are Edward Wigglesworth, "A Table Showing the Probability of the Duration, the Decrement, and the Expectation of Life in the States of Massachusetts and New Hampshire, formed from sixty-two Bills of Mortality on the Files of the American Academy of Arts and Sciences in the year 1789," *Memoirs* of the American Academy of Arts and Sciences, vol. 2, pt. 1 (1791): 131-135; and Joseph McKean, "Synopsis of Several Bills of Mortality," *Memoirs*, A. A. A. S., vol. 2, pt. 2 (1804): 62-65.

29. Richard H. Shryock, *Medicine and Society in America, 1660-1860* (New York, 1960).

30. Wells, "Family Size and Fertility Control."

31. Wrigley, "Family Limitation;" Ganiage, *Trois Villages;* Menoru Muramateu, "Changing Attitudes Toward Population Growth in Japan," in Brown and Hutchings, eds., *Are Our Descendants Doomed?*, pp. 266-277.

32. Kenneth Lockridge, "Land, Population, and the Evolution of New England Society, 1630-1790," *Past and Present* no. 39 (1968): 62-80. This pattern is also apparent in Charles Grant, *Democracy in the Connecticut Frontier Town of Kent* (New York, 1961), especially pp. 83-103; and Greven, *Four Generations.*

33. U. S. Bureau of the Census, *A Century of Population Growth* (Washington, 1909), pp. 96, 100.

34. Published in New Haven in 1972, this work elaborates on Yasukichi Yasuba, *Birth Rates of the White Population in the United States, 1800-1860* (Baltimore, 1962).

35. In addition to Banks, *Prosperity and Parenthood*; and Mueller, "Economic Motives;" see David M. Kennedy, *Birth Control in America* (New Haven, 1970), pp. 45-50 for evidence that fertility is often controlled for economic reasons.

36. Estimates of the birth rate vary. This author has used those in Ansley J. Coale and Melvin Zelnik, *New Estimates of Fertility and Population in the United States* (Princeton, 1963), pp. 21-22, 34. The only major study of marriage patterns, Thomas P. Monahan, *The Pattern of Age at Marriage in the United States* (Philadelphia, 1951) offers little help on this subject.

37. Etienne van de Walle, "Marriage and Marital Fertility," in Glass and Revelle, eds., *Population and Social Change*, pp. 137-151.

38. Coale and Zelnik, *New Estimates*, pp. 23, 36.

39. Richard Easterlin, *The American Baby Boom in Historical Perspective* (New York, 1962).

40. This change is rather complex as is evident in Wrigley, "Modernization," pp. 250-256. Malthus' reaction to these phenomena is, of course, to be found in T. R. Malthus, *An Essay on the Principle of Population, as It Affects the Future Improvement of Society* (London, 1798; reprinted with the 7th edition, New York, 1960).

41. Greven, *Four Generations;* Lockridge, *A New England Town*.

42. See note 1.

43. John Demos, *A Little Commonwealth* (New York, 1970).

44. Robert V. Wells, "Quaker Marriage Patterns in a Colonial Perspective," *William and Mary Quarterly* 29 (1972): 436-439.

45. There are a number of such studies; among the most prominent are Merle Curti, *The Making of an American Community* (Stanford, 1959); Richard J. Hopkins, "Occupational and Geographic Mobility in Atlanta, 1870-1896," *Journal of Southern History* 34 (1968): 200-213; and Stephan Thernstrom and Peter R. Knights, "Men in Motion: Some Data and Speculations about Urban Population Mobility in Nineteenth-Century America," in Tamara Hareven, ed., *Anonymous Americans* (Englewood Cliffs, N.J., 1971), pp. 17-47.

46. Michael Anderson, *Family Structure in Nineteenth Century Lancashire* (Cambridge, Eng., 1971).

47. The literature on immigrants is immense, but among the most helpful places to start is Philip Taylor, *The Distant Magnet* (New York, 1971), especially chapters 9-12. Two other works of some interest are John J. Appel, ed., *The New Immigration* (New York, 1971); and, of course, Oscar Handlin, *The Uprooted* (Boston, 1951).

48. Sandford Fleming, *Children and Puritanism* (New Haven, 1933); Jerry W. Frost, "As the Twig is Bent: Quaker Ideas of Childhood," *Bulletin* of the Friends Historical Association (Autumn, 1971): 67-87; Walter J. Homan, *Children and Quakerism* (Berkeley, 1939).

49. For evidence that these changes occurred in other groups, see David J. Rothman, *The Discovery of the Asylum* (Boston, 1971), chs. 2, 3, 9; and Wishy, *Child and the Republic*.

50. Compare, for example, John S. C. Abbott, *The Mother at Home* (London, 1834), or Lydia Child, *The Mother's Book* (Boston, 1831), with *The Child Rearing Literature of Twentieth Century America* (New York, 1972), compiled and published by Arno Press.

51. Richard B. Morris, *Studies in the History of American Law* (New York, 1930), ch. 3, "Women's Rights in Early American Law."

52. Herman R. Lantz et al., "Pre-Industrial Patterns in the Colonial Family in America," *American Sociological Review* 33 (1968): 413-426; Wells, "Quaker Marriage Patterns," pp. 428-439.

53. The clearest statement of this position is Barbara Welter, "The Cult of True Womanhood: 1820-1860," *American Quarterly* 18 (1966): 151-174. A more complex view is given in Charles E. Rosenberg, "Sexuality, Class and Role in 19th-Century America," *American Quarterly* 25 (1973): 131-153.

54. Kennedy, *Birth Control in America*, pp. 36-135; Page Smith, *Daughters of the Promised Land* (Boston, 1970), pp. 227-252.

55. Reynolds Farley, "The Demographic Rates and Social Institutions of the Nineteenth-Century Negro Population," *Demography* 2 (1965): 386-398.

56. The movement into the cities and the motives behind this migration are presented clearly in Clyde Kiser, *Sea Island to City* (New York, 1932); for recent trends in fertility and mortality see Irene B. and Conrad Taeuber, *People of the United States in the 20th Century* (Washington, 1971, a census monograph), pp. 443-453, 500-517.

57. J. W. Eaton and A. J. Mayer, "The Social Biology of Very High Fertility among the Hutterites," *Human Biology* 25 (1953): 206-264.

58. Since this article was written, a number of works on various aspects of family history have appeared. Because the original notation was illustrative rather than exhaustive I have chosen not to revise the manuscript to include the more recent examples. More important, my ongoing reading has only reenforced my belief in the hypothesis offered above.

Naming, Kinship, and Estate Dispersal: Notes on Slave Family Life on a South Carolina Plantation, 1786 to 1833

Cheryll Ann Cody

THE structure of slave families and kinship ties has become the central issue for historians concerned with the long-term impact of slavery on the social experiences of Afro-Americans. Recently Herbert G. Gutman has suggested that the pattern used by slave parents in naming their children reveals the importance of both paternal and maternal kinship in defining the place of the child in slave society.[1] If, as Gutman supposes, the names for children were selected to preserve symbolically kinship ties, then the system that developed must be viewed as a response by slaves to the threats and realities of separation imposed by their owners. In a critique of Gutman, Stephen Gudeman points out that definition of the "internal system" used by slaves to reckon their position in society is critical to understanding this response.[2] Of equal importance is definition of the rules used by owners to govern their own behavior. Gudeman emphasizes the juridical ties, but it is useful to observe that owners viewed the slave family as a functional unit as well. In addition to its reproductive function, the family or household served as the basic structure for the distribution of food and clothing to slaves. Furthermore, Robert William Fogel and Stanley L. Engerman have suggested that owners encouraged family life as a deterrent to running away and other forms of resistance.[3]

The business records of Peter Gaillard, which span his career as a South Carolina cotton planter from 1782 to 1833, provide an unusual opportunity to examine both the values of slaves and the behavior of owners.[4]

Ms. Cody is a graduate student in the Department of History at the University of Minnesota. She wishes to thank Robert McCaa, Russell Menard, Edward Tebbenhoff, John Campbell, Allan Kulikoff, Stuart Schwartz, John Howe, John Modell, Carla Phillips, and George Terry for helpful discussion of the research problem and comments on an earlier draft of this essay.

[1] Gutman, *The Black Family in Slavery and Freedom, 1750-1925* (New York, 1976), 113-114, 185-215.

[2] Gudeman, "Herbert Gutman's *The Black Family in Slavery and Freedom, 1750-1925*: An Anthropologist's View," *Social Science History*, III (1979), 59-62.

[3] Fogel and Engerman, *Time on the Cross: The Economics of American Negro Slavery*, I (Boston, 1974), 127.

[4] Peter Gaillard Plantation Accounts and Memoranda Book, 1783-1832; Gail-

Gaillard's plantation, The Rocks, located in Upper St. John's Berkeley Parish about fifty miles from Charleston, was one of the first in the region to produce short-staple cotton. His slaves provided the labor for the cotton fields of The Rocks and also served as the basis of marriage gifts to his sons and daughters. Gaillard acquired slaves, once his estate was well established in the 1790s, primarily to give his sons their economic start rather than to expand his own labor force.

As this study reveals, slaves held a very different view of their families from that of their owners. The names of their children suggest that slaves conceived of their families in a broad sense, including extended kin. Owners, in contrast, saw the nuclear family as the primary unit, perhaps because of its reproductive function, and established rules to maintain this unit when dividing their estates, without regard to preserving the larger net of kinship. The family history of Nero and Binah illustrates the tensions between the cultural view of the family held by slaves and the functional one applied by their owners.

Nero, Binah, and their two young daughters, Hannah and Little Mary, were inherited by Gaillard from his father in 1782. A third child, named for Nero, was born in 1785. Hannah and Little Mary survived to maturity and each produced nine children. (Nero died at age fifteen and presumably fathered no children.) The names selected for the grandchildren and great-grandchildren of Nero and Binah reflect the familial values held by the children's parents and provide insight into the rules governing naming as applied by slaves. (See Figure 1.) Family names were frequently repeated, with both female and male names being selected from paternal and maternal kin. Thus Hannah and Little Mary each named daughters for their mother. Little Mary's Binah was born after the death of her cousin, and both were named before the death of their maternal grandmother. Neither woman named a son for her father, Nero, whose name had been shared by their long-dead brother. Each sister named a daughter for the other.

The names selected by the descendants of Nero and Binah for their children suggest several hypotheses on the familial values of slaves which

---

lard Family Plantation Book, 1825-1847; Peter Gaillard Planting Book, 1803-1825; all at South Carolina Historical Society, Charleston, S.C. The business records of Gaillard, which include inheritance and purchase lists and a birth register for The Rocks, have been used to reconstitute 127 nuclear families and multigenerational kinship networks. Each entry of an individual slave to the records includes name and birth date, as well as death date, sale date, or date and name of the Gaillard child to whom the slave was given. The inheritance and purchase lists are structured by family with lines demarking each unit and include the date of acquisition for the entire group. The birth register is organized chronologically and includes the name of the mother of each child. The fathers of particular children can frequently be determined from the inheritance and purchase lists and from a partial 1825 inventory made of the dispersal of slaves in which families are delimited. Unless otherwise stated, these sources provide the data for this essay.

FIGURE 1
FAMILY HISTORY OF NERO AND BINAH

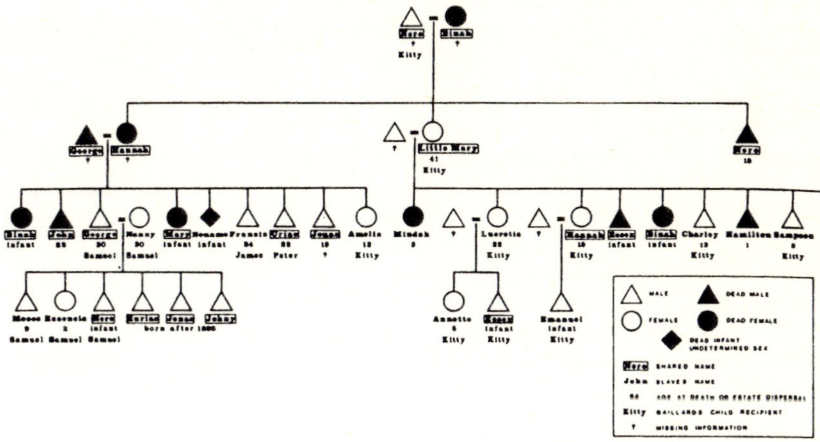

are tested in this essay. (1) The frequent naming of children for parents and extended kin indicates how important these ties were and that slaves traced their lineage bilaterally. (2) Siblings named their children for one another, particularly brothers for brothers and sisters for sisters, suggesting the strength of same-sex sibling ties. (3) Frequently broken paternal and fraternal ties were symbolically mended through naming practices.

In 1822 and 1825 Gaillard made gifts of slaves to his children that splintered the family of Nero and Binah. The decisions he made reflect his assessment of the critical familial relationships based, no doubt, on the function kin served in the daily lives of slaves. Gaillard's practice reflected three basic rules. (1) Husbands and wives and their young children remained together. (2) Daughters were more likely to remain with parents and extended kin than were sons of the same age. They were also more likely to remain with siblings because young children stayed with parents. Conversely, sons were frequently separated from siblings, partly because they were more frequently separated from parents. (3) The extended family was a functional unit that cared for the elderly and orphans, perhaps creating a matrifocal system.

Old Binah died in 1816, George in 1815, and Hannah in 1821. The fates of the elderly widowed father, Nero, and the five orphaned children of George and Hannah provide insight into slave family structure as well as the function of extended kin. In 1822 Nero and his only surviving child, Little Mary, were given to Kitty Gaillard Porcher and moved to her husband's plantation approximately twelve miles from The Rocks. With them went Little Mary's five children, aged six to twenty-two, and the three children of her two oldest daughters.

The orphaned children of George and Hannah did not fare as well. Thirty-year-old George, his wife Nanny, and their three children were given to Gaillard's son Samuel and remained at The Rocks. None of George's brothers or his sister stayed with him. Twenty-four-year-old Francis and twenty-two-year-old Urias were given to two other Gaillard sons, James and Peter, both of whom lived on neighboring plantations. The ultimate fate of nineteen-year-old Jonas is unknown; he may have been a runaway. The youngest child of George and Hannah, thirteen-year-old Amelia, was separated from her immediate family. Her oldest brother, George, who had an established family including a son eight years younger than Amelia, could have provided a home for her. Instead, less than a year after her mother's death Amelia was moved with her maternal grandfather, aunt, and cousins. Amelia's inclusion in this group suggests that she was part of the functional household headed by Little Mary. Clearly, the sons of George and Hannah were all of an age where they could care for themselves. Little Mary's sons, aged thirteen and eight, were younger and remained with their mother. Little Mary's grown daughters, Lucretia (with her two small children) and Hannah (with her infant son), also stayed together. The physical durability of slave families thus depended on the functional view of the family held by the owner and his desire to maintain kinship bonds.

Acquisition and Dispersal

Gaillard acquired his slaves by both inheritance and purchase. Between 1782 and 1789 he inherited a total of 134 slaves composed primarily of family groups. Most of the slaves came from the estates of Gaillard's father (58) and father-in-law (48). The remainder were inherited from his mother, mother-in-law, a sister-in-law, and a cousin. In the first six years of the nineteenth century Gaillard made four purchases of slaves totaling 123, nearly one-third as individuals and the others in family groups. One large purchase in 1806 of 88 slaves from John Peyre consisted primarily of nuclear families with only 13 listed individually. From several sources he also bought 23 individuals in the years 1803 and 1808, all but one of whom were males, and none of whom was related by kinship to any other. The approximate birth dates listed by Gaillard indicate that all of these young men were between fourteen and twenty-five years of age. When buying individuals, Gaillard demonstrated a strong preference for young male slaves that indicates both a supply and a market for unattached youths.

Family groups predominated among inherited and purchased slaves. (See Table I.) Nearly 80 percent came with their spouse or consanguineal kin. Slaves who were inherited were more likely to be acquired with other members of their family than were those who were purchased. Only one of every eight inherited slaves was not a member of a nuclear unit, while more than one of every four purchased slaves arrived at The Rocks apparently without kin. The higher proportion of families among inherited slaves probably reflected the attitudes of Gaillard's father, Theodore, who ordered in his 1782 will that "the Negroes . . . are not to be parted from

TABLE I
FAMILY STRUCTURES OF INHERITED AND PURCHASED SLAVES

	Inherited			Purchased		
Familial Groups	*Individuals*	*Families*	*Family Size*	*Individuals*	*Families*	*Family Size*
Father/Mother/Children	71	16	4.5	60	10	6.0
Mother/Children	37	12	3.1	19	5	3.8
Father/Children	2	1	2.0	0	0	—
Husband/Wife	8	4	2.0	10	5	2.0
Totals	118	33	3.6	89	20	4.4
Individuals	16			34		
Totals	134			123		

their father or mother under the age of fourteen years."[5] In the legacies that Peter Gaillard received, the nuclear units remained intact: husbands and wives were not separated, and young children remained with their parents. However, it cannot be determined whether older children had been previously removed from their families and given to heirs or sold.

The data on the familial structures of inherited and purchased slaves reveal several interesting patterns. Two-parent nuclear families were predominant among both groups. When those couples who had no children are included in the count, families with both husband and wife present outnumber those with only one parent present by two to one. Nonetheless, a substantial number of families fell in the latter class: seventeen were headed by a mother without her husband, and one by a single father. Age differences between husbands and wives offer a partial explanation for this imbalance. For twelve of fourteen partners born between 1750 and 1790 the husband was older than the wife. The median age difference was four years and the mean seven years. Two husbands were more than fifteen years older than their spouses. Mother-headed families occurred with greater frequency among slaves who were inherited than among slaves who were purchased. There were fewer children in mother-headed families (mean = 2.3) than in those with two parents (mean = 3.0). This variance may capture a life-cycle difference between the two groups. Women who appeared on the list as single parents may have been younger and might not yet have established a stable relationship with a man, or they may have been older widows only part of whose families remained with them. The relatively high frequency of couples with no recorded children, nearly 20 percent, indicates that the birth of a child was not a prerequisite to the forming of a stable union, in the eyes of either slaves or owners.

Peter Gaillard used slaves and land to underwrite the economic security of his sons—Peter, James, Thomas, David, and Samuel—and daughters—Betsy (Elizabeth), Lydia, and Kitty (Catherine). The gifts, which by 1825 had redistributed almost all his slaves in groups of near-equal size, were made to each of his sons at the time of marriage, when the young man set up his own plantation carved from the father's holdings (or, in Samuel's case, took over management of The Rocks), and to his daughters at that time or thereafter.[6] Thus the eighty-eight slaves Gaillard bought in 1807 were used to provide two of his sons with shares equal to that of their elder brother.[7] His daughters fared as well as their brothers in the number

[5] Will of Theodore Gaillard, Charleston District Will Book (1780-1783), vol. 19, 128, South Carolina Department of History and Archives, Columbia, S.C.

[6] Accounts and Memoranda Book, 1783-1832; Dorothy Kelly MacDowell, *Gaillard Genealogy: Descendants of Joachim Gaillard and Esther Paparel* (Aiken, S.C., 1974).

[7] Peter Gaillard II received 53 slaves, as did his brothers James and David. Tom Gaillard was given 52 slaves and Samuel 54. In addition, David and Samuel purchased slaves from their father.

of slaves but not in the timing. At her marriage in 1805, Betsy received four slaves, probably personal servants, but she was not given a substantial endowment until twenty years later. Similarly, her sisters received household servants at their marriages and most of their share in 1822 and 1825.[8]

Names and Values

To assess the impact of dispersal on slave families requires some sense of slave family structure as perceived by the slaves. Although kinship networks reveal consanguineal and matrimonial bonds, they cannot demonstrate what these ties meant to slaves or how extended kin functioned. Names have been used by historians to examine two interrelated aspects of New World slave life—the persistence of African culture and the familial values held by slaves.[9] Because Africans named their children to chronicle events occurring at the time of a child's birth, the day, or the season, the continued use of this type of name (day-names) among native-born slaves has been seen as evidence of the persistence of African culture in the New World.[10] Gutman finds the pattern of names used by the slaves on the plantations he studied more revealing than the names themselves.[11] Though kinship groups in the New World did not influence economic and political life as they had in West Africa, he suggests that such groups may have continued to influence community life and personal relationships.[12]

The naming practices of the Gaillard slaves indicate that, although the records were maintained by owner and overseers, the parents or the extended family of a child chose the name. Evidence supporting this assertion is twofold. First, among the Gaillard slaves the names of biblical

[8] Thirty slaves were sold by Gaillard between 1789 and 1819 in groups composed of individuals, nuclear families, and more complex kinship units. The largest number sold at one time was 17 in Jan. 1817, including several families. One slave was sold away from The Rocks and shipped to New Orleans.

[9] Peter H. Wood, *Black Majority: Negroes in Colonial South Carolina from 1670 through the Stono Rebellion* (New York, 1974), 181-186; Gutman, *Black Family,* 185-213; Sidney Mintz and Richard Price, "An Anthropological Approach to the Afro-American Past: A Caribbean Perspective" (Institute for the Study of Human Issues Occasional Papers in Social Change, No. 2, 1976).

[10] Wood, *Black Majority,* 181-186. Wood argues that although African day-names frequently were modified by owners to produce a phonetic derivation of the original or were translated into English, they persisted with high frequency in 18th-century South Carolina. Gutman finds that the 15 most common slave names at emancipation were conventional Anglo-American names (*Black Family,* 186). See also P. Robert Paustian, "The Evolution of Personal Naming Practices among American Blacks," *Names,* XXVI (1978), 177-191; Newbell Niles Puckett, "Names of American Negro Slaves," in George Peter Murdock, ed., *Studies in the Science of Society: Presented to Albert Galloway Keller . . .* (New Haven, Conn., 1937), 471-494; J. L. Dillard, *Black English: Its History and Usage in the United States* (New York, 1972); and Melville J. Herskovits, *The Myth of the Negro Past* (New York, 1941).

[11] Gutman, *Black Family,* 197-201.

[12] *Ibid.,* 209.

characters and legendary heroes of classical antiquity, as well as derogatory nicknames, were decidedly absent. When these names did occur, they frequently bore some immediate familial significance. The persistence of these types of names may reflect the pattern of names given to slaves when they first arrived in America and subsequently transmitted for generations by parents to their children.[13] Second, the complexity of the genealogical knowledge needed to select the children's names was less likely to have been held by Gaillard than by the child's parents and kin. In assessing the significance of the repeated appearance of names in a family, it is necessary to consider the absolute frequency of the name among the whole population of the slaves who lived at The Rocks. (See Table II.)

In 1825 George and Nanny named their second son Nero, the name shared by the child's maternal great-grandfather, who was still living, and maternal great-uncle, who had been dead for twenty-five years. The division of the estate in 1825 separated George from his younger brothers Urias and Jonas. His next two sons, born in 1827 and 1829, were named for their paternal uncles and shared the biblical names. The names Urias and Jonas were only used twice at The Rocks, once for George's brothers and once for his sons. A fourth son, Johnny, was also named for his father's brother, John. The name John was fairly common at The Rocks: five slaves in addition to George's brother and son carried it. (See Figure 1 and Table II.)[14]

The extensive genealogical knowledge used in selecting a child's name is revealed in the names given to Billy and Caty's offspring. Of the ten children born to Billy and Caty between 1792 and 1819 all four sons and three of six daughters bore the name of a known kinsman or kinswoman. The first son was named William for his father, and the fifth daughter was named Caty for her mother. The other three sons were named for their paternal grandfather, Jim; for a paternal uncle, Winter, who had died three years before the child's birth; and for their maternal grandfather, Thomas, twelve years deceased. The first daughter, who was possibly named for a kinswoman, Jenny, shared the name of her paternal grandmother, who was still living at the time of the child's birth. Since the name Jenny appeared with great frequency—twelve times among Gaillard slaves—its repeated use may have little significance. Billy and Caty's youngest daughter, Molly, shared the name of her maternal grandmother. (See Table II.)

The use of kin names was continued and perhaps intensified after the division of Gaillard's slaves in 1825 had demonstrated the vulnerability of

[13] Mintz and Price, "Anthropological Approach to the Afro-American Past," 32-42.

[14] Gudeman, "Gutman's *Black Family*," *Soc. Sci. Hist.*, III (1979), 61. Gudeman's assertion that slaves practiced a plantation exogamy of names—in other words, that first names were repeated only when an individual was named for a relative—is not supported by the Gaillard data. One hundred sixty male names and 145 female names were listed for the 836 individuals who lived at The Rocks. Several names were repeated with frequency. See Table II.

TABLE II
NAMES SELECTED FOR THE CHILDREN OF THREE NUCLEAR FAMILIES AT THE ROCKS

Parents' Names and Birth Year of Child	*Name*	*Parity*	*Sex*	*Relationship of Kin Sharing Name*	*Survival Status of Kin*	*Age at Death*	*Time since Death*	*Frequency*[a]
George and Nanny:								
1817	Moses	1	M	no apparent				4
1823	Essencia	1	F	no apparent				1
1825	Nero	2	M	father's maternal grandfather	alive			4
				father's maternal uncle	dead	15 yrs.	25 yrs.	5
1827	Eurias	3	M	paternal uncle	alive			2
1829	Jonas	4	M	paternal uncle	?			2
1832	Johnny	5	M	paternal uncle	dead	23 yrs.	16 yrs.	7[b]
Billy and Caty:								
1792	Charlotte	1	F	no apparent				5
1794	Martha	2	F	no apparent				3
1797	Jenny	3	F	maternal grandmother	living			12
1798	William	1	M	father	living			12[c]
1800	Jim	2	M	paternal grandfather, paternal uncle	living living			6[d]
1802	Beckey	4	F	no apparent				4
1811	Winter	3	M	paternal uncle	dead	?	3 yrs.	5
1813	Caty	5	F	mother	living			9
1816	Molly	6	F	paternal grandmother	living			9
1819	Thomas	4	M	maternal grandfather	dead		12 yrs.	9
				maternal uncle	living			

Winter and Peggy:								
1836	Amy	1	F	maternal aunt	dead	9 mos.	14 yrs.	6
1837	Dorcas	2	F	father's paternal aunt	living			5
1839	Martha	3	F	paternal aunt	living			3
1840s	No name[e]							
1840s	Murry	1	M	father's paternal uncle	dead	27 yrs.	20 yrs.	2
1840s	Ellen	4	F	father's paternal aunt	unknown			4
1840s	Samuel	2	M	maternal grandfather	living			10
				maternal uncle	living			
1840s	Jenny	5	F	mother's maternal aunt	dead	3 mos.	50 yrs.	12
1840s	Rachel	6	F	maternal aunt	dead	8 yrs.	40 yrs.	8

[a] One hundred sixty male names and 145 female names were used by the 836 individuals who lived at The Rocks.
[b] John, Johnny.
[c] William, Bill, Billy.
[d] Jim, Jimmy, James.
[e] Dead infant.

extended kin networks. Billy and Caty's son Winter, who was inherited by Samuel Gaillard, remained at The Rocks and began his family with Peggy in 1836. Their eight children who survived early infancy all received the name of an extended kin member, and none was named for a parent. (See Table II.)[15]

Phonetic derivations and direct English translations of African day-names, as well as the names of months and seasons, were used for slave children born at The Rocks.[16] However, simple observation of the appearance of African-naming practices provides a less than full understanding of the significance of these names. Evidence of the names chosen for native-born Gaillard slaves suggests that kinship and the preservation of familial ties were more important in the selection than conformity to African naming rules. In fact, adherence to familial rules produced some absurdities. On August 1, 1811, Billy and Caty's third son was born. Despite the season of his birth, they named the boy Winter after his father's younger brother who had recently died.

The names reflected a strong recognition of the individual identity of each child. As Gudeman has suggested, "the first name, above all, provided the slave with an individual *persona*."[17] Infants were not named until several days after birth and sometimes not until more than a month.[18] The reluctance to name a child who was sickly or whose chances of survival were slight showed parental concern for the individuality of the child.[19] The high mortality rate among infants, particularly in the first month of life, contributed to this concern.[20]

[15] This change is reflected in the decline in the use of paternal names after 1825. See Table III.

[16] Phonetic derivations of African names present a problem of analysis for historians. If day-names persist because they sound close to English common names, it is questionable if the purpose of the name was preserved.

[17] Gudeman, "Gutman's *Black Family*," *Soc. Sci. Hist.*, III (1979), 60.

[18] Gutman, *Black Family*, 193; Eugene D. Genovese, *Roll, Jordan, Roll: The World the Slaves Made* (New York, 1974), 449. It is difficult to determine if the delay represents a failure of the owner to record the name or an actual practice by slaves. Infants who died in the first week after birth frequently had no name recorded.

[19] Daniel Scott Smith, "Child-Naming Patterns and Family Structure Change: Hingham, Massachusetts, 1640-1880" (Newberry Papers in Family and Community History, No. 76-5, Jan. 1977), 4-8.

[20] Richard H. Steckel, "Slave Mortality: Analysis of Evidence from Plantation Records," *Soc. Sci. Hist.*, III (1979), 86-114. See also Steckel, "Economics of U. S. Slave and Southern White Fertility" (Ph.D. diss., University of Chicago, 1977), 88-89, 91; Jack Ericson Eblen, "New Estimates of the Vital Rates of the United States Black Population during the Nineteenth Century," *Demography*, XI (1974), 301-309. Cheryll Ann Cody, "Slave Demography and Family Formation: A Community Study of the Ball Family Plantations, 1710 to 1896" (research in progress). Evidence on mortality suggests variations in levels depending on disease environment, duration of settlement, population density, and medical care. On determinants of early mortality see Kenneth F. Kiple and Virginia H. Kiple, "Slave

Further evidence of the importance attached to the individuality of each child can be seen in the almost complete absence of necronymic naming.[21] Only one instance of naming a child for a deceased sibling was observed in fifty-one opportunities. Further, again with but a single exception, even when the deceased child shared the name of a parent or one of his or her extended kin, parents did not give a subsequent child that name. Thus, for example, Hector, first-born son of Charles and Daphne, shared the name of his father's paternal grandfather, who had died some eight years before his birth, and the name of his paternal uncle, who was two years older than Hector's father and was separated from the family by the estate division. In spite of Hector's death at six months and the birth of two more sons to Charles and Daphne, his name was not reused. The near absence of necronymic naming contrasts to a degree with the naming practices of Peter Gaillard, who, after his son, four-year-old Samuel, died, named his next son Samuel.[22] Little is yet known about southern white naming practices. (Evidence presented by Daniel Scott Smith for Hingham, Massachusetts, indicates that the practice of necronymic naming had significantly declined there by about 1800.)[23] It is evident, however, that slave parents did not adopt the practice of their owners in selecting names for their children.

Gutman has argued that slaves more frequently named their children for their father and paternal kin than for their mother and maternal kin, because the paternal kin ties were more easily broken. He further notes that slave daughters were rarely named for their mothers, owing, he surmises, to a "taboo of unknown origins and meaning."[24] Gudeman has offered a more satisfying explanation for this pattern. He suggests that because the kinship relationship of mother to offspring was recognized in law by the masters and the patrifilial relationship was not, one function of naming a child for his father or paternal kin was to assert the child's place in slave society, a place which was determined bilaterally, through both mother and father.[25] Evidence from the Gaillard plantation offers some clarification of Gudeman's explanation.

Preservation of the father's name through his sons occurred with high frequency. As seen in Table III, among families inherited or purchased by Gaillard and families begun at The Rocks between 1786 and 1825, over half of those with three or more sons had one son named for the father. By contrast, daughters were seldom named for their mothers—less than one

Child Mortality: Some Nutritional Answers to a Perennial Puzzle," *Journal of Social History*, X (1977), 284-309. On the critical first month of life see Louis Henry, *Population: Analysis and Models*, trans. Etienne van de Walle and Elise F. Jones (New York, 1976), 148-151.

[21] Gutman argues that slave use of necronymic naming was imitative of that of their white owners (*Black Family*, 192-194).

[22] MacDowell, *Gaillard Genealogy*.

[23] Smith, "Child-Naming Patterns," 6-8, 28.

[24] Gutman, *Black Family*, 190-191.

[25] Gudeman, "Gutman's *Black Family*," *Soc. Sci. Hist.*, III (1979), 61.

TABLE III
FAMILIES WITH CHILD NAMED FOR PARENT,
BY NUMBER OF CHILDREN OF SPECIFIED SEX

	Number of Sons in Family						*Number of Daughters in Family*					
	1 or 2		*3 or More*		*All*		*1 or 2*		*3 or More*		*All*	
	%	N	%	N	%	N	%	N	%	N	%	N
Families Purchased or Inherited	11.1	18	57.1	7	24	25	0	21	5	20	2.4	41
Born 1786-1825	0	2	57.1	7	44.4	9	3	33	7.4	27	5	60
Born 1826-1854	0	10	20	10	10	20	0	19	10	10	5.3	29

instance in every ten families with three or more daughters. For families that were inherited or purchased, estimates of the frequency with which children were named for parents must be considered a lower limit. Because parents did not give necronymic names to children, a child named for a parent who died before the family came to The Rocks would not be counted.

After 1825 the number of families in which sons were named for fathers declined dramatically from 44 to 10 percent. This change reflects the increased use of extended kin names and especially an invigorated practice of fraternal reciprocity—brothers naming their sons for one another.[26]

While parents were far more likely to name their sons for fathers than their daughters for mothers, paternal kin and maternal kin contributed nearly equally to the names selected. In the twenty-five families for which at least two-generational kinship networks can be constructed, 152 children lived to receive names. Six sons were named for their fathers and one daughter for her mother. Male children received the name of a kinsman more frequently than females, by about 54 to 47 percent. Seventy children received the name of a kinsman other than a parent. Thirty-six were named for paternal kin and thirty-four for maternal kin. (See Table IV.)

First-born children were frequently named for paternal and maternal grandparents, and in nearly equal numbers. Six males shared the name of their paternal grandfather and five that of their maternal grandfather. Similarly, eight females were named for their paternal grandmother and eleven for their maternal grandmother.

The large numbers of sons named for paternal uncles, and daughters named for maternal aunts, indicate the strength of same-sex sibling ties. Table IV shows that parents were nearly six times as likely to follow this pattern as to select the name of the father's sister or mother's brother. Male children were named twice as frequently for their father's brother as for their mother's brother. The pattern of fraternal reciprocity can be seen in the example of the three sons of George and Nanny: Urias, Jonas, and Johnny all shared the names of their father's brothers. Female children were three times more likely to bear the name of a sister of their mother than that of a sister of their father. Nero and Binah's daughters (see Figure 1) each named a daughter for their mother. Hannah's daughter Little Mary shared the name of her mother's sister, and Little Mary reciprocated by naming a daughter Hannah. This preference for naming children for parent's siblings of the same sex may well reflect a functional reciprocity in daily life—for example, the care of small children or the performance of household chores—as well as a desire to assure continued ties to the siblings of each parent in case of the parents' death.[27]

[26] Gutman, *Black Family*, 200-201. Smith argues that fraternal reciprocity was rarely practiced because boys who shared the forename of a paternal uncle would also share the surname, thus producing social confusion ("Child-Naming Patterns," 12).

[27] Gutman, *Black Family*, 198-201, 209. See also Mintz and Price, "Anthropological Approach to the Afro-American Past," 32-42.

TABLE IV
FREQUENCY OF PATERNAL AND MATERNAL
KIN NAMES BY RELATIONSHIP

	Grandfather	*Grandmother*	*Uncle*	*Aunt*	*Other Kin*	*Totals*
Paternal	6	8	11	3	8	36
Maternal	5	11	6	10	2	34
All	11	19	17	13	10	70

$X^2 = 13.29$; df = 4; P = .01. Where both a grandparent and an aunt or uncle shared a name, the relationship is recorded only as the grandparental tie.

Although paternal and maternal names occurred with near-equal frequency, paternal names were preferred and were frequently used for the first children of a union, while maternal names were used for subsequent children. Winter and Peggy produced eight children who lived to be named. Their first daughter, Amy, was named for her mother's dead sister. The next four children were named for paternal relations, including, somewhat distantly, the father's paternal uncle and aunt. Their last three were named for maternal kin, including Samuel for his mother's father. (See Table II.) Such ordering reflected the priorities parents felt in preserving kin names and demonstrating affective ties. Further evidence on paternal priority can be found in the frequent appearance of the names of extended kin other than uncles and aunts and grandparents. The father's extended kin were four times more likely than the mother's to provide a name for a child.

The naming practices of the Gaillard slaves reveal the high value placed on children and on the extended family. The delay in naming weak infants and the virtual absence of necronymic naming suggest that parents respected the individual identity of their children. Parents frequently named their sons for fathers but rarely named daughters for mothers, perhaps because, as Gutman argues, owners recognized only uterine ties and the paternal relationship was more vulnerable, though Gutman's supposition of a taboo seems untenable. After the divisions of the 1820s demonstrated that fathers were not separated from their families, the frequency of naming a son for his father was reduced, an indication that slaves adapted their naming practices to reinforce threatened or broken relationships. The most interesting pattern is the use of nonparental kin names. The names of paternal and maternal relations appeared with near-equal frequency; however, the order of name usage suggests a preference for preservation of paternal ties. The strength of same-sex sibling ties is revealed by the practice of naming sons for their father's brothers and daughters for their mother's sisters. The importance of these bonds may have reflected a functional relationship, as in the example of Little Mary, who cared for her deceased sister's young daughter.

Durability of Families

The dispersal of Gaillard's estate to his sons and daughters had a profound effect on the slave families at The Rocks. It is evident that Gaillard tried to preserve families as he defined them. He respected the nuclear unit and showed some understanding of the functions of extended kin. However, the view of the family he held was not the same as that held by his slaves.

Evidence of the durability or vulnerability of slave families will be analyzed here for three nuclear relationships—husbands and wives, parents and children, and brothers and sisters. By examining the frequency with which adults remained on the same plantation with their elderly parents, and the proportion of adult siblings who remained together after the estate division, some conclusions can be drawn on the effects of estate division on the extended family.

The structure of Gaillard's records makes it difficult to determine the survival of marital ties,[28] but it appears that couples were rarely separated—only once in twenty-eight cases. Fifty-six-year-old James and his fifty-year-old wife Rachel were purchased in 1806 with their four children. Six years later, James and his twenty-four-year-old son Kirkham were given to Tom Gaillard, while Rachel and the other three children—thirty-one-year-old Dowa, thirty-year-old George, and twenty-year-old Mirtilla—went to James Gaillard, whose plantation lay some twenty miles from his brother's.

Only a few young children were separated from their parents. Table V shows that no children under age ten were so separated, but about 5 percent of those between ten and fourteen were parted from their mothers, and about 10 percent of the girls aged ten to fourteen from their fathers. About 10 percent of boys aged fifteen to nineteen were divided from their parents; no girls of that age group were separated from their mothers. The most dramatic decline in the number of children who lived after the division on the same plantation as their parents occurred among those aged twenty to twenty-nine. Only 40 percent of all slave men in this age bracket whose mothers are known to have still been alive were kept together with their mothers, and a similar pattern can be found for sons and fathers. Over 60 percent of women aged twenty to twenty-four remained with their mothers when the estate was divided, as did nearly 90 percent of those aged twenty-five to twenty-nine. Daughters were twice as likely as sons to stay with their mothers. The fathers of women in their

[28] Because Gaillard recorded only the mother of the children born at The Rocks, evidence on paternity must be gleaned from other sources. The inheritance and purchase records were organized by family and provide the husband's name for families that were established before they were acquired. Lists of families at the final dispersal of the estate in 1825 were similarly structured. The regularity of births to the mother preceding 1825 has been used as evidence of the steady nature of the union before that date. Unions that were begun at The Rocks and not included in the 1825 lists cannot be examined.

TABLE V
CHILDREN WITH PARENTS ON SAME PLANTATION AFTER ESTATE DIVISION, BY AGE, SEX, RELATIONSHIP, AND SURVIVAL STATUS OF PARENT

	Mother				*Father*			
	Known Alive		*All*		*Known Alive*		*All*	
	N	%	N	%	N	%	N	%
Sons								
0-4	21	100.0	21	100.0	6	100.0	6	100.0
5-9	24	100.0	24	100.0	13	100.0	13	100.0
10-14	23	95.7	26	84.6	9	100.0	9	100.0
15-19	10	90.0	13	69.2	4	100.0	5	80.0
20-24	15	40.0	18	33.3	10	50.0	11	45.5
25-29	7	42.9	9	33.3	5	40.0	5	40.0
30-39	10	60.0	12	50.0	5	20.0	8	12.5
40+	3	66.7	15	13.3	1	100.0	11	9.1
Daughters								
0-4	26	100.0	26	100.0	5	100.0	5	100.0
5-9	18	100.0	20	100.0	8	100.0	8	100.0
10-14	28	96.4	31	87.1	11	90.9	13	76.9
15-19	21	100.0	23	91.3	7	100.0	8	87.5
20-24	13	61.5	19	42.1	8	62.5	12	41.7
25-29	9	88.9	9	88.9	3	100.0	6	50.0
30-39	9	46.7	17	35.3	2	50.0	13	7.7
40+	3	100.0	13	23.1	1	100.0	13	7.7

twenties were also more likely to remain with their daughters than with their sons. The number of cases is quite small, but the same pattern emerges. The higher proportion of parents who continued to live on the same plantation with their daughters suggests that the care of elderly parents was entrusted more frequently to daughters than to sons.

Thirteen of the sixteen women who stayed with one or both parents had begun families of their own when the estate was divided.[29] Because so many women with children were entrusted with the care of elderly parents, the resultant pattern reinforced the maternal kinship ties and tended to produce three-generational matrifocal families. The matrifocality of slave families was further reinforced by Gaillard's willingness to separate boys and young men from parents and siblings. Girls and young

[29] The median age of first birth was 17.9 years for the 14 women who eventually produced children. One woman died childless at age 25, and another moved to a plantation without surviving records. See also Fogel and Engerman, *Time on the Cross*, 137-138; Gutman, *Black Family*, 50, 171; Cody, "A Note on Changing Patterns of Slave Fertility in the South Carolina Rice District, 1735-1865," *Southern Studies*, XVI (1977), 457-463; and Cody, "Slave Demography and Family Formation."

women were more likely to remain with parents and siblings, particularly with their sisters.

In order to examine systematically the durability of sibling ties, the proportion of siblings who were kept together after the division has been determined for each individual. For example, Beckey, twenty-three-year-old daughter of Billy and Caty, had four surviving brothers and three sisters when the estate was dispersed. Beckey, her parents, her younger brothers, Winter and Thomas, and her younger sisters, Caty and Molly, all were given to Samuel and remained at The Rocks. Her two older brothers, William and Jim, went to Peter and David, respectively. Martha, Beckey's thirty-one-year-old sister, was given to Betsy and Lydia. Two of Beckey's four brothers thus remained at The Rocks, as did two of her three sisters. Like calculations for each individual sibling are summarized in Table VI.

Children under age fifteen usually were given to the same owner as their parents and with most of their siblings. Although for no age group did all children remain with all siblings, more than 90 percent of the siblings of children under age five were not separated from the family. Table VI shows that the chances of being parted from siblings increased with age but without regard to sex—until about age twenty. Thereafter, young men were markedly more likely than their sisters to experience separation. It is not surprising that during the years twenty through twenty-nine, when young men and women were beginning their own families, the new families would be recognized by the owner as primary.

The strength of sisterly bonds becomes apparent after women reached age twenty. Women of twenty to twenty-four years of age were twice as likely as young men of the same age group to have a sister with them after the estate was divided. They were also more likely to have a brother with them. For the age cohorts thirty to thirty-nine and forty-plus, the influences of parental ties and younger children in the family can be removed and the persistence of sisterly ties can be measured most clearly. Few women over thirty had brothers and sisters under age fifteen, who were unlikely to have been separated from parents. Women in their thirties were more than twice as likely to remain on the same estate with sisters as with brothers, and women aged forty or beyond were four times more likely to have sisters with them than brothers.

Gaillard's definition of crucial, and perhaps functional, family bonds governed the dispersal of his estate. He preserved the nuclear unit of father, mother, and children under age fifteen. His treatment of young male and female slaves suggests he drew a clear distinction between the familial needs and functions of the two sexes.[30] Beyond age fifteen, sons were frequently separated from their parents and their younger siblings, while daughters more frequently remained with them. Daughters were also more likely to stay with their sisters than were their brothers. This

[30] Genovese raises several interesting questions about the sexual division of labor within slave families (*Roll, Jordan, Roll,* 486-487, 489-490).

TABLE VI
SIBLINGS ON THE SAME PLANTATION AFTER THE ESTATE DIVISION, BY SEX, AGE, AND RELATIONSHIP

	Brothers		*Sisters*		*All Siblings*	
	N	*%*	*N*	*%*	*N*	*%*
Males by Age						
0-4	46	91.3	44	97.7	90	94.4
5-9	53	84.9	51	92.2	104	88.5
10-14	65	83.1	68	82.4	133	82.7
15-19	49	69.4	47	68.1	96	68.8
20-24	75	34.7	44	25.0	119	31.1
25-29	29	37.9	24	41.7	53	39.6
30-39	25	32.0	25	44.0	50	38.0
40+	3	33.3	17	23.5	20	25.0
All	345	64.1	320	66.9	665	65.4
Females by Age						
0-4	27	92.6	43	90.7	70	91.4
5-9	59	83.1	55	87.3	114	85.1
10-14	70	68.6	80	73.8	150	71.3
15-19	65	84.6	52	82.7	117	83.8
20-24	36	50.0	35	57.1	71	53.5
25-29	23	65.2	20	65.0	43	65.1
30-39	20	25.0	29	55.2	49	42.9
40+	10	10.0	15	40.0	25	28.0
All	310	69.7	329	74.2	639	72.0

pattern of dispersal resulted in a family structure in which matrifocality was reinforced.

To slaves, separation from kin was an ever-present threat. The names they selected for their children reveal both the importance and the fragility of kinship bonds. The Gaillard slaves frequently named children for both paternal and maternal kin, indicating recognition of bilateral descent. At the same time, the priorities of naming suggest that slaves were more concerned to preserve paternal and fraternal ties, which they perceived as most vulnerable to separation. After the estate division had demonstrated the durability of paternal ties, this practice was modified as parents attempted to mend broken bonds symbolically. Naming patterns also suggest that the bonds between siblings of the same sex were highly valued and that the reciprocity of naming may have represented a functional reciprocity as well.

The rules Gaillard used in dividing his estate reflected his definition of slave families. The two-parent nuclear family was preserved as a unit of reproduction and child-rearing, but older children were frequently separated from their parents. The maintenance of parent-daughter ties and sisterly ties suggests that Gaillard viewed these relationships as more critical than the bonds of sons to their parents and brothers. The division thus contributed to complex family structures organized around maternal and sisterly ties. The differing views of the family held by slaves and their owners meant that even under the best of circumstances the division of estates was not accomplished without pain.

"THE *THING* NOT ITS VISION": A WOMAN'S COURTSHIP AND HER SPHERE IN THE SOUTHERN PLANTER CLASS

STEVEN M. STOWE

Historians generally acknowledge that the doctrine of "woman's sphere" was the central tenet of the ideology of gender in mid-nineteenth-century America. In particular, women in the middle and upper classes were supposed to occupy a realm of personal beauty, domestic competence, and social influence that belonged to them alone. This doctrine of separate spheres served to anchor women in female networks which supported collective work and companionship. But the distinctness of woman's realm, and the intensity of the homosocial bonds it fostered, coexisted with the strong social claims of marriage and the family. Ideally, woman's sphere was to intersect with the world of men in an harmonious bond. Yet this coexistence between intense female friendships and the claims of marriage generated tension that many antebellum women had to confront as they matured. The aim of this paper is to explore this tension at a moment in the female life cycle when it became particularly acute, that is, as a young woman contemplated leaving the largely female world of her childhood and adolescence to marry. By looking at the courtship letters of one young woman, Bessie Lacy of Raleigh, North Carolina, I hope to suggest what it was like to inhabit the woman's sphere at this particular juncture. I also hope to suggest ways in which courtship correspondence is a valuable text in studying the culture of women's experience.[1]

Born in 1832 to Drury and Williana Lacy, a moderately well-to-do couple of the planter class, Bessie was the oldest child and only daughter in a family of five children. The broad pattern of her youth was typical of her time and class. As the eldest, she was expected to help look after her young brothers; as a girl, she was largely in the care of her mother, an articulate woman who skill-

Feminist Studies 9, no. 1 (Spring 1983).

fully introduced Bessie to the many ways women were expected to be mild, loving, and beautiful. Until she left for boarding school at age thirteen, Bessie remained at home most of the time where she did what a young girl could to help her mother attend to the household, manage the domestic slaves, and participate in the local activities of women. Drury Lacy, in addition to his planting interests, was also a Presbyterian minister in both Raleigh and New Bern, and Williana's duties and Bessie's early experience, therefore, were shaped by the attitudes toward the role of women in a minister's family and by the domestic reach of the church. The Lacys were also strong supporters of southern sectionalism and later of the Confederacy. If not a part of the southern upper class in terms of wealth and kinship, the Lacys were certainly part of the elite in that they bolstered the dominant values of slave-owning whites. Thus Bessie grew up in a household that stressed not only the values of Christian womanhood and romantic notions of what a lady should be, but which also emphasized the crucial role that white women played in maintaining racial hierarchy. A true woman was ornamental; yet she was also central to the slave system that stretched far beyond the home. A mild temperament had somehow to reside in a firm, watchful mistress.[2]

Between the ages of thirteen and seventeen, Bessie Lacy left her family to attend a female academy where (it was hoped by her parents) her commitment to feminine responsibilities would be sealed. But academy life also gave her the experience of a wholly female world where the close emotional ties she forged with other young women became her measure of intimacy and satisfaction. The first section of this paper is concerned with the sisterhood that Bessie found in the academy. The second major section explores her sense of the courtship relation that followed, a relation which was a counterpoint to her homosocial friendships and which marked out the shrinking boundaries of woman's sphere.[3]

Bessie Lacy joined the Edgeworth Female Seminary near Greensboro, North Carolina, in the autumn of 1845. She probably supposed, as her parents certainly did, that she would emerge four years later with the attributes of a mature woman. She was expected to become a scholar and a lady, and her progress toward both goals would be measured by the seminary's routine of classes, constant female company, and walled-in seclusion from the outside world and from men. Increasingly since the early

1800s, the social tempering of young southern elites, most of them away from home for the first time, occurred in such academies. It was at Edgeworth that Bessie settled down to learn moral philosophy, history, drawing, and guitar playing. But here, too, she formed close relationships with her female peers which informally shaped her expectations of womanhood. In her first letters home, Bessie almost never mentioned her course of study or other requirements of school life. Instead, she wrote about the other girls, of their disagreements and play, and of her own homesickness. She and the approximately fifty other students boarded for the entire five-month term. Visits home were not allowed in most cases, and parents were assigned only a single day each week for their calls. At first, Bessie resented the closeness of group life at Edgeworth. She complained about the need to adjust to the habits and personalities of her schoolmates. She worried that she would not be accepted into a group of friends and that she was not as good-looking as some others.[4]

Neither Bessie nor her parents foresaw that the informal social life of Edgeworth women would become the school's most lasting reward, although Williana was anxious, recalling her own school days, lest Bessie fall in with "evil companions" and form "hasty friendships." Instead of being drawn to evil, however, Bessie began to form strong ties to other "good" girls. As the months passed, the young women gave each other a sense of intimacy: an intense feeling of similar identity and shared convictions. In her letters home, especially after 1846, Bessie began to comment frequently on individual friends, outings, the "attic where we all sleep," and the "*heap* of fun" on trips to town. The seclusion of Edgeworth began to seem safe rather than isolated. The teachers, for the most part young women themselves, also found a place in Bessie's growing delight in a female realm. "Miss Julie lets me come and lay my head on her shoulder and cry whenever I want to," Bessie wrote of one teacher. Of another, northern, teacher she wrote disapprovingly, "Miss Brown's manners are so frigid that she does not easily win the hearts of the warm-hearted Southerners." Bessie immersed herself in this warm, comfortable world. She kept her affectionate, dutiful ties to her family, but also learned ways to love others; and she learned a language of intimacy.[5]

This is nowhere better seen than in Bessie's relationship with one sister-student, Maggie Morgan. The two young women were close friends for at least three years, from the time Bessie was sixteen years old. Maggie was apparently a year younger; but she and Bessie were known as one of the academy's couples, sharing clothes and a bed as well as studies, hopes, and stories. Through her strong friendship with Maggie, Bessie learned to expect a kind of intimacy from a well-loved person, an intimacy which would become an emotional standard for her later relationships. At first, however, Bessie wrote about the future as if it would be no different from Edgeworth. Of herself and Maggie she wrote to her father: "Our hearts are impenetrable to the keenest arrows of Cupid. Consequently we have concluded to spend our days in single blessedness, or to use a homely phrase, we will be *old maids.*" They would be single together. Bessie wrote confidently of herself and Maggie living in a "snug little room" where they would paint, make music, and cook for each other.[6]

The two women continued to share images of a happy life together even after Bessie graduated. In content and form, their letters to each other were love letters, carefully written on embossed paper in the best, finished hand. They used endearments common to courtship letters between women and men, addressing each other as "Darling" and "Dearest," and many letters began with no salutation at all, a conscious epistolary practice reserved only for one's closest intimates. Maggie's letters also combined themes of future happiness, domesticity, and work with images from a shared past. She conjured visions of Bessie, often mixing the second and third person voice in a jumble of feeling: "[I] sit and think of Bessie, fancy her by me with that little sweet hand in mine and her soft cheek laid close by mine and then I . . . hear your sweet voice." Maggie saw a future time when the two would "get a great big mahogony bedstead, where we will sleep like *we* always do."[7]

Their many letters in 1848-49 fashioned an intimate discourse that went to the heart of identity.

> I do wish you were here this winter to sit by me in church. You used to keep my hands so warm under your cloak. I miss you amazingly . . . . Don't you remember how I used to whip you and make you go and wash your face to put you in a good humor? I think my whippings used to do you a heap of good . . . . The reason I love you darling is that I can't help it and the reason I can't help it is that you are the strangest little being I ever saw, one minute a little bundle of temper, the next a little bundle of perfection.[8]

Maggie's voice in these letters is at once caring and seductive, parental and loverlike. Hoping to keep Bessie's emotions attached to their school community after Bessie had left it, she frequently wrote of life at Edgeworth. "You wanted to know who I slept with, who I loved most, who is my Bessie now-a-days. Well, I sleep with, I love, the sweetest girl in school—Flax Reid. She is so like and yet unlike you . . . . [You are] a strange, perverse little bundle of humanity—a wild wicked saint and withal a most loveable creature."[9]

Maggie expressed her love by showing that she *knew* Bessie, knew her well enough to see the contradictions of her temperament and love them. Drawing upon the language of romantic fiction, Maggie saw Bessie as the beloved paradox, the "wicked saint." But she also mixed memory into images of a future with Bessie. At times the language of both women seems too ripe for modern sensibilities, but there is no mistaking the intensity of their feelings nor the ease with which they expressed it. The female world of the academy had fostered this experience as surely as it taught its other lessons, and, as Bessie's subsequent experience suggests, intimacy once achieved could not be lightly given up. Women who found trusting, warm relationships wanted to carry them beyond the academy into the outside world. Planter society, however, did not make this easy, as Bessie discovered by 1848. When the time came for women to leave the academy, the continuity of the homosocial world was broken—at least until it could be reestablished in different form after marriage. Bessie graduated from Edgeworth when she was seventeen years old, and although she apparently continued her schooling in Virginia, it must have come as a considerable shock to leave a place where she had spent four contented years. For Bessie and other young women, the daily feminine routine and rituals, the round of study, the safety of the cloistered seminary were exchanged for a return to parents, the childhood home, and, usually, the social isolation of the plantation.

By 1848, Bessie's family life had changed in a drastic way, for her mother had died of tuberculosis two years earlier. Returning from Edgeworth, Bessie was expected to be mistress of her father's household, putting to immediate use the domestic and ornamental skills she had acquired. Interrupted only by intermittent trips to Virginia, she did this devotedly and to her father's satisfaction. But the demands of her new role, coupled with the loss of the academy world, led Bessie to cast about for a place to anchor her need for intimacy. For a while she settled on the males of her family. She was explicitly domestic, for example, in letters to Horace, the oldest of her three brothers. "Soon you'll go to college," Bessie wrote. "And then come home and frisk about awhile and get married. Don't you want me to come and keep house for you? . . . ." She again referred to herself, approvingly, as an "old maid," suggesting to Horace that she be a kind of temporary spouse, and then a companion to his future wife. With her father, too, Bessie spoke of a kind of domestic relationship. She acknowledged that she often had been a "harum-scarum daughter," but promised that she could become "a good economist [and] a good housekeeper . . . ." She told him: "I will make your coffee just as strong, your tea just as sweet as you like. I will bathe your head when it aches and comb your hair as long as you like. I will cry when you are sad, laugh when you are merry, read poetry and sing songs."[10] What begins here as a statement about her maturity changes into a proposal for a shared intimacy that sounds like a re-creation of Edgeworth.

Had her father remained unmarried, Bessie might have continued in her role as mistress of his house; many unmarried daughters did so. But Drury Lacy remarried in 1849. Although Bessie seems to have liked her stepmother, she now was excluded from the intimacy she had proposed to find in her father's home; she was once more a marriageable daughter. She passed through a religious crisis in 1849-50, apparently joining her father's church. This was also the year of her most intense correspondence with Maggie Morgan. In sum, Bessie began to experience a dislocation that came with the end of adolescence and the growing constriction of a proper female life. Although the widespread availability of female networks in the nineteenth century has been assumed, Bessie, by 1850, seems to have been without one. She was neither schoolgirl nor wife, and her prospective network was located in a shifting, problematic group of marriageable, unmarried women. Given dominant heterosexual values, this placed her in a kind of social limbo.

As for men, Bessie appears to have been quite removed from them before 1850, except in rather formal social activities. Her academy years had given her restricted contact with men at outings and balls, and she had taken part in gossip, romantic tales and fantasies, and in the rumors of love that circulated among the young women.[11] But actually encountering strange men—seeing them on a daily basis at close range—was not in her experience. It is no wonder that upon graduation from Edgeworth Bessie did not look to a man for happiness. She knew certain of her needs and interests by the time she was eighteen years old, for her academy days had allowed her to discover them. Her courtship would show her some of the limits and complexities of her changing sphere.

Bessie began a courtship with Thomas Webber Dewey in 1851. How she met him and why she accepted him as a suitor, can only be guessed. Thomas was a brother of one of Bessie's friends at Edgeworth, and it is probable that they had met during her years there. Although living at home at the beginning of the courtship, Bessie traveled to Hampton-Sidney, Virginia, in early 1852 to study and live with her grandfather. Her move to Virginia meant that the first year of her courtship with Thomas had to be carried on almost entirely by letter. This was not at all unusual and illuminates a key feature of courtship in the planter class. Courtship was an epistolary affair, and the language of letters carried a heavy freight of meaning for women and men. In many instances it is not too much to say that letters were the stuff of the relationship, not simply a piece of it. During this first year Thomas, the son of an established planter, attended to the duties of a single young man: he traveled about the countryside making political contacts and learning more about financial and planting prospects near Raleigh. His doings are not as important here as Bessie's perceptions, but the scant evidence from 1851 shows Thomas to have been a conscientious young man making a place for himself in the male sphere.

Bessie's letters to Thomas at this time record changes in the way she wrote about her intimate life—a discourse, as we have seen, that began at Edgeworth. Her letters provide a rich example of conventional courtship rhetoric and also constitute a kind of literary work of Bessie's own creation. As such, the letters reflect both the broad social values implicit in courtship and Bessie's own self-perception. Changes in these letters followed important shifts in her perception of her emotional life during this crucial time, and these shifts in turn suggest her emerging sense of woman's sphere. Changes in the form and content of the correspondence reveal three different periods in her courtship. The early period is marked by highly stylized letters and Bessie's emotional aloofness and extended from late 1851 until the spring of 1852. At this point, her letters became notably more personal and introspective, a period which lasted until her formal engagement in November 1852. The third period, characterized by sudden shifts in her voice, lasted from late 1852 until her marriage in October 1853.

Bessie's early courtship letters appear strikingly different from other letters she wrote during this period. It is not even necessary, at first, to read the courtship letters to sense their comparative aloofness and propriety. Bessie followed certain formal conventions which suggest that courtship mapped a potentially dangerous emotional terrain, at variance with everyday life. These letters are invariably brief, never more than seven sentences, a fact in itself remarkable in view of her long, colorful, and unrestrained letters to friends and family. She always used elegant—and expensive—stationery and envelopes in her letters to Thomas, rather than the large sheets of thin, lined paper and the usual sealing wax. Although small in size, the courtship letters have an unmistakable heft to them. Moreover, it is clear that Bessie must have written at least a first draft of these letters, so perfect is the handwriting. Her letters to her father, by comparison, often include crossed-out words, misspellings, and now and then an incomplete sentence. Thus, even in the form and physical appearance of the letters it is clear that Bessie was closely following a set of conventions that made her letters akin to letters of application or introduction. They were written with an eye toward their outward appearance, as if Bessie herself were on display, and their very form emphasized ladylike qualities: brevity, mildness, elegance. Thomas, as a man, was expected to judge and admire their form, to see it as a kind of proof rather than as incidental to the letter's content. It was evidence that Bessie knew and observed the opening moves of courtship and wished it to continue. These early letters were also signs of the social nature of courtship; that is, romantic love was not simply a matter of personal preference, but was shaped by conventions which allowed two people to reach a mutual perception of an otherwise confusing experience. By following the conventions, Bessie furthered her courtship and also showed her adherence to the social values of ladyhood.

The content of Bessie's early courtship letters complements their formal characteristics. A single example will suffice.

> Thank you, Mr. Dewey, for your beautiful present. I will always think of you when I read it. But with far deeper interest will I remember you when my eyes fall on the pages of the Book of Life . . . . I beg you *permit me*, as your *sincere friend* to ask you once more to give your careful and prayerful attention to your soul . . . . If you *really are my friend* have regard to what I now ask, even if you have no desire to be a child of God . . . pray to God to give you that desire . . . .[12]

Several things happen here. Bessie accepts a gift—a book—from Thomas, a sign that his courtship is welcome and can continue. Yet she deftly shifts the focus from her acceptance of his gift to the state of his soul. It is likely that Bessie was concerned about Thomas's spiritual well-being, although she did not protest when he later decided against the ministry. But it is certain, too, that by showing her concern Bessie was following a lover's convention, deflecting in an appropriately feminine way, the emotional potential of his gift and of her response to it. She was at once allowing herself to be courted and yet keeping him at a distance, for what man could deny that the state of his soul was of overriding importance? He was meant to be held at bay—yet attracted—by her implacable spirituality. Her voice is correctly aloof yet intense.

Compared with her casual, often humorous letters to her father and brothers, this letter is low-keyed and tight. Bessie further distances Thomas as "Mr. Dewey" and stresses her sincerity rather than her pleasure or warmth. She defers ("I beg you *permit me*") in a way that was certain to elicit protest from a man, for women were not supposed to be supplicants. Moreover, she twice emphasizes that he is a "friend," a sign that their relationship was neither less nor more than correct. The coolness of this voice, this deliberately aloof voice which Bessie assumed only in letters to Thomas, underscores the self-conscious, studied quality of her letters' physical form. As with her handwriting, the self of her early letters was in an important sense anonymous and apart; indeed, she sometimes referred to herself in the third person. There was, moreover, distinct power in this. Abstracted from the whims and peculiarities of a single personality, her letters took on a formal weightiness. They were a social act, a message from woman's sphere. Relying on this, Bessie could express her intentions all the more forcefully.

But continuity and meaning early in courtship were thus purchased by setting aside the intimate discourse of family and close female friends. Courtship conventions served to make sense of Bessie's intentions—and made her desirable—at least in part by obscuring her personality. Her adherence to the motifs of the conventional love letter, that is, made her an object of love and obscured her intimate and personal qualities. In this way, letters that served as a test of a lover's suitability for courtship also helped to shape a love relationship built on the social and sexual alienation between the sexes. Women and men retained their perceptions of each other as removed and mysterious even during the founding of what was meant to be a lasting union.[13]

It is significant, then, that Bessie's letters began to change by the spring of 1852, suggesting a second period in the courtship. Part of the value of studying courtship conventions in the context of a single individual's life lies in discovering the ways in which a person could bend conventional themes to fit her own needs and thereby confront tensions in her life. One sign of the change in Bessie's experience is that by 1852 her letters to Thomas are different in appearance. Increasingly, she began to write on ordinary note paper, in a large, hasty hand, not correcting handwriting errors. It is no longer possible to leaf through her correspondence and find courtship letters by their appearance alone. The physical style of her letters to Thomas became familiar and functional, having less to do with formal signs.

For the first time, Bessie attempted to connect her relationship with Thomas in a meaningful way to the rest of her life. She began to write of her daily routine, her relatives in Hampton-Sidney, and her studies. She no longer relied on "topics" such as Thomas's religious faith, and she abandoned referring to herself in the third person. Yet it is fascinating to see how her letters still trace the boundary between convention and personal need, between what might be considered the strategies of courtship and her willingness to share herself. "I wish I had a name for you," she wrote Thomas in May 1852. "Tom sounds very desrespectful. Mr. Dewey sounds as if I did not love you—it sounds icy. 'Old Tom' suits when I can say it with my lips . . . but I can't write it." In seeking to give him a fitting name, and thus possess him as romantic tradition promised, Bessie also sought to define an intimate attitude toward him: "You know, Mr. Dewey, that no icy words could make my heart cold—and you know '"Old Tom"' that for you I have a respect so high and pure that it almost amounts to reverence and you know Tom that there is a love within me which I pray may never grow into idolatry."[14] Which name suits him best, she cannot decide. And in this letter her playful voice turns somber; she fears that love might slip into idolatry, that the absence of her lover would be filled by her imagination of him. In letters of this sort, Bessie used a courtship convention ("naming" a lover) and yet also expressed her awakening fears about its particular meaning for her.

Increasingly, her letters pursued intimacy, and she began to rely less on formal courtship conventions and more on self-revelation. Her letters, for example, reveal her attempt to share with Thomas her struggle to shape an identity apart from the seminary, apart from her childhood, and apart even from whatever it was he had to offer her. The change is striking: Bessie began sharing self-doubts by stripping away much of her "ladylike" self; or, rather, by complementing it and filling it out. She confessed, for instance, a dislike for the necessity of a woman's "*behaving* all the time." Like many elite women in her situation, Bessie began to understand that the ornamental aspect of woman's sphere created a screen, "but while I am sitting up straight and knitting my thoughts take long jaunts in dreamland."[15]

She began giving Thomas glimpses of her woman's life and its shape. Dreaming, she implied in more than one letter, was an important inner counterpoint to a woman's outward decorum. As a young elite woman living in her father's home, she confessed that there were luminous June days when she sat in an orchard under thick trees and a soft sky, "just the day to . . . let your whole mind sleep but imagination and, giving loose reins to that, be bourne wherever it chooses to wander . . . ." She continued, "I always wake up from a tour of this sort vowing against soul-excursions and seeing fully the unprofitableness of such journeyings. But there is a fascination in such a set of thoughts . . . . There never was a poor child born with such a wandering spirit as I have and were I not a woman I believe this moment I'd be in Africa or Japan in some almost inaccessible place . . . ."[16] Correct rhetoric had vanished and Bessie's reserve along with it. She tried to make her life accessible to this man even as she wished to be transported out of it. She wondered about herself and wanted to tell Thomas about her wondering. She gave him a picture of herself similar to that which Maggie Morgan had given her as a bundle of contradictions, "I wonder what sort of nature I have. Everybody thinks it is so happy and joyous and full of glee. Well so it is. But I always love mournful music most and still, dark pictures and books wild and mysterious." Then she confessed that "I'm half afraid yet you would not love me if you knew me very well—if you knew what a strange sort of head I have with nothing developed but ideality, and what strange visions come to me, and pictures; and what music sometimes whirls and rushes through my brain. Do all these things trouble your head as they do mine? And do you sometimes almost grow afraid of yourself as I do?"[17] In another letter she asked, suddenly, in a postscript:

"Do you dream away your life?"[18]

In reaching out to know Thomas's intimate life, and at the same time revealing something of her own, Bessie was seeking a kind of emotional reciprocity belied by courtship rhetoric and the rituals of romantic love. No advice manual for young ladies would have suggested that she write so freely of her dreams and "strangeness." And neither Bessie's frankness about her life nor her eager curiosity about Thomas's feelings partook of the coyness and subterfuge of romantic fiction. At this period in the courtship, Bessie was drawing on a previous experience of intimacy, seeking to define it and live it as she had at Edgeworth. She had shared her wishes and her changing identity with Maggie; now she sought to break through courtship conventions and similarly share them with Thomas. She wanted to impose homosocial standards and expectations onto her heterosexual relationship.

But her efforts at intimacy were limited by the social and emotional realities of her courtship and young womanhood. Edgeworth was out of her life by mid 1852. Knitting and "behaving," or sitting under the trees in the hot orchard, left Bessie alone with the contradictions of woman's sphere. Though there was nothing else to do but put her domestic and ornamental accomplishments to work, there was as yet no home and nothing to ornament. As she told Thomas, she had learned the unprofitableness of dreaming. But the social situation of a courted young woman without family or household of her own was all too ripe for dreams. Thomas, moreover, had a different set of needs. Although only a few of his letters remain, it is clear that he was deeply involved in acquiring political and business ties, matters of which Bessie knew little. He seems to have become fully caught up in the difficulties of establishing his character and connections while apart from Bessie, and courted her without often seeing her. Whatever the pressures of a man's sphere, Thomas did not write to Bessie for days at a time during the spring of 1852, leaving her bereft and puzzled, unable to do much but project upon him her image of a lover. "Why didn't you write," she asked him. "I will not believe that you love me any the less—for I judge thee by myself and such a thought is treason."[19] He told her only what he knew best as a man: leave off dreaming, avoid "morbidness," become your schooled, ladylike self. She wrote, in response: "I will stop dreaming. I am getting over my almost frantic love for music. I can do anything *for your sake,* and you must tell me always when

I do or say or write anything that you disapprove. I am yours now and you can mould me as you please. You must mould me."[20] There is an unmistakable edge of desperation in her voice. If Thomas could neither give her intimacy, nor love her as a bundle of contradictions, she might take what he did have to offer: authority.

By the end of 1852, Bessie and Thomas began to struggle with the significance of their attachment, and their future began to spill over the confines of their correspondence. Bessie started to express anxiety about marriage. She pulled back somewhat from her past open expression even as she was drawn closer to marriage through the momentum of courtship: she had exchanged many letters with Thomas for more than a year; a strong commitment had been established. But Bessie increasingly refrained from asking about Thomas's feelings and instead began mentioning, with increasing urgency, the need to have her father's sanction. In the early months, she was content when Thomas deflected her doubts. "I wonder if it is right for you and me to love each other as we do and write to each other without telling Father," she wrote Thomas on one occasion. "My conscience hurts me on that question sometimes. Tell me your views—do you wonder too." At another time she linked her doubts to the feeling that "I am beginning to have in my heart the deep, true love and a sincere respect that a child ought always to have for a parent."[21] When Thomas further procrastinated, Bessie became more thoughtful about her wishes and duties as a daughter and a woman. "Sometimes . . . there is to me a drawing back from marriage . . . . It is a hard thing to leave Father and Ma and all that the heart has treasured since childhood . . . .It is removing myself from my Father's immediate love that I dread. I owe him such an immense load of gratitude. . . ." She concluded by giving Thomas a pledge and a direction: "You have won me. Win Father and I am thine whenever you claim me." Although she admitted that she had previously "thought more of loving you than of marrying you," she gave Thomas a choice and allowed her future to rest on an encounter between him and her father.[22]

Drury Lacy consented to his daughter's formal engagement. But before the marriage took place in October 1853, Bessie went through a final period of her courtship marked by intense emotional fluctuations. Given the first two periods, it might be expected that the third would reflect intimacy either attained or denied. In fact, however, Bessie's closing courtship letters are characterized by a new voice, one that drew upon her previous rhetoric, but not in any measured or predictable way. In the six months after her engagement, Bessie's letters are marked by startling variations in language and tone. Formal engagement, of course, opened to friends and kin an attachment that had been personal, if not altogether secret. The new "public" responsibilities of betrothal were unsettling and doubtless contributed to Bessie's new voice. There were other events in her life that amplified the disquiet. A month after the engagement, Bessie's seventeen-year-old brother, Horace, died after a sudden illness and her old religious doubts seem to have been stirred. About the same time, Bessie returned from Virginia to live once more at home. Not only did this place her in the context of her childhood, it also allowed her to see Thomas face-to-face on a regular basis for the first time in more than a year. Finally, Bessie's friend Maggie Morgan was married, an event certain to have affected Bessie in mixed ways.

However these events shaped Bessie's emotional life in the spring of 1853, it is clear that the courtship was unsteady and less candid. Sometimes her doubts were explicit: she feared that the formal betrothal masked Thomas's true feelings. She felt that she could not rely on what he said and did in company. Bessie worried that Thomas might feel obliged by his engagement to conceal changes in his feelings toward her, and told him to "never let a strict and high sense of honor cause you to profess what you do not feel."[23] Her letters assumed a stern, directive tone. For example, she criticized Thomas for having one of his "curious fits" during a walk with her. Her terms were not uncertain. "I will expect you tonight in one of your best humours; if you look as solemn and cross as you did last night I will make you go right straight home again, so you had better practice a smile all day . . . . I would write a great deal more but this pen and ink say I won't."[24]

More than once Bessie challenged Thomas to object to her assertive voice. She suggested that he might want to consider her letters (and herself) to be "very bold, forward" and "too severe and . . . too punctilious," qualities unbecoming in a lady.[25] She began to address him as "friend," resurrecting the earliest period of their courtship. When he protested she wrote, "Let me say *friend.* It does not come from a *cold heart* and is not a freezing word as you would have it. I mean as much as if I said *dearest.* And that I can't say—it wouldn't be right in me. But it is *your duty* to say *dearest* and feel dearest, too."[26] In these letters Bessie began to instruct Thomas about his duties as a man and hers as a woman. A sense of dual sexual spheres began to shade into her language. Slowly she abandoned her search for intimacy, unanswered by Thomas, and settled for an attempt to secure a set of terms for her marriage. She wanted to clarify his responsibilities and establish certain of her rights. She wanted a position of strength from which she could have some control over what he was to give her.

It was a difficult shift of feeling, however. Bessie's assertive letters were counterpointed by ones of a strikingly different kind. These other letters, fewer in number, give her language the quality of having been written by more than one person. Suddenly, in the midst of her authoritative mode, the rhetoric of a submissive and imploring child appears. In one such letter, she asked that Thomas "forgive Bessie for all she does wrong, that you will ever bear long and patiently with the wicked child." She wished him to "say 'live'" to her, adding, "Think of her as your Bessie, think of her as loving you so entirely that you have the power of moulding her yourself. Think of the poor little child as stealing off from all and dreaming fond dreams of you—saying to herself words you have said to her, counting days and hours for your letter, and love her. For her whole heart is yours, she is your Bessie alone, your Bessie entirely and forever. *I plead for her*."[27] Here she returns to speaking of herself in the third person, distant and alone. And although she once again refers to her dreaming, there is nothing in this letter to suggest that she wants her lover to share her world. Shifting from an authoritative voice to an imploring one, Bessie passed through the final struggle of courtship. Although her engagement to Thomas nearly foundered in the summer of 1853, the two were married that fall. In her courtship, she had moved from an early period where order and correct epistolary expression were foremost into a second period where she openly and passionately sought an intimacy she had known in her family and in the academy. Failing in these efforts to gain intimacy and yet not giving up on the intensity of her relation to Thomas and her image of him, Bessie supplanted her quest for intimacy with a confused yet potent combination of demands and entreaties, one that might sustain her in marriage.[28]

Any assessment of the wider social meaning of Bessie Lacy's letters must be tentative. But it is helpful to recall that ethnographers view language as evidence of both individual perception and cultural forms. The conventions of a language, as Bessie's letters show, provide a kind of cultural framework that both supports and restrains an individual's personal voice. In one sense, Bessie used the rhetoric of courtship to establish herself as a lover and to act as a lover should. But when her expectations of intimacy led her to push love's rhetoric to its limits, she encountered the restraints that courtship imposed and came up against new boundaries of woman's sphere. At this crucial juncture in Bessie's life, her seminary identity, her vanished childhood, and the social pressures on her to marry all became condensed into a paradox: she was supposed to find everlasting bliss with a stranger. The reliance on courtship-by-letter made distance between women and men the proper course for heterosexual love. The very language of courtship strengthened the paradox through its shifting themes of intimacy and estrangement. Such language validated the ideology of sexual spheres by making the social division between the sexes appear to rest on temperamental differences inherent in sexuality. In this way, women—and men—came to have a sense of their separate sphere as part of a natural and inescapable reality.[29]

Amid the tensions of courtship, marriage could appear as a haven from the passions of romantic love. Courtship, as Bessie's experience suggests, served to partly exorcise intimacy from a relationship while preserving marriage—an emotionally trimmed, functional marriage—as the goal. Convinced of their temperamental differences, lovers sought refuge by becoming socially responsible spouses. Accepting the sexual spheres as reality, women placed sentiment in perspective and gained strength in being wary of men. A sober, wry Maggie Morgan had learned this by the eve of her own marriage, writing Bessie, "I think I shall not be unhappy. I am not looking for *bliss*."[30] Bessie could no longer expect her to write about happy youthful days, Maggie said. The new realities of being the wife of a Raleigh planter awaited her; "I must grapple now with the *thing* not its vision."

NOTES

1. This paper is part of a larger study of the family life and social values of the antebellum southern planters. Historical discussion of woman's sphere in the nineteenth century is ever-growing. For a sampling, see Nancy Cott, *The Bonds of Womanhood: "Woman's Sphere" in New England, 1780-1835* (New Haven: Yale Univer-

sity Press, 1977), especially 197-206; Mary Beth Norton, "The Paradox of 'Women's Sphere'," in *Women of America*, ed. Carol R. Berkin and Mary Beth Norton, (Boston: Houghton Mifflin Co., 1979), 139-49; Mary P. Ryan, *Cradle of the Middle Class: The Family in Oneida County, New York, 1790-1865* (Cambridge: Cambridge University Press, 1981), chaps. 3 and 5; and John Mack Faragher, *Women and Men on the Overland Trail* (New Haven: Yale University Press, 1979), chaps. 4 and 5.

2. This information was compiled from a reading of the Drury Lacy Family Papers, Southern Historical Collection, University of North Carolina, Chapel Hill, North Carolina. All references to the Lacy correspondence are from this collection. An accessible work that gives the flavor of such family correspondence is Robert M. Myers, ed., *The Children of Pride: A True Story of Georgia and the Civil War* (New Haven: Yale University Press, 1972). For general views of Southern women, see Anne Firor Scott, *The Southern Lady: From Pedestal to Politics, 1830-1930* (Chicago: University of Chicago Press, 1970); and Julia C. Spruill, *Women's Life and Work in the Southern Colonies* (1938; reprint, New York: Norton, 1972). I have also benefited from discussions with Catherine Clinton; see her *The Plantation Mistress: Woman's World in the Old South* (New York: Pantheon Books, 1982).

3. The extent to which Bessie Lacy's courtship was distinctively upper class and southern, with respect to other classes and regions, cannot be demonstrated in this paper. Suffice it to say that courtship among southern elites was by the nineteenth century comparatively elaborate, self-conscious, and ritualized. There is no full scholarly study of the history of courtship in the United States, although a forthcoming book by Ellen K. Rothman promises to fill the gap. See her "Intimate Acquaintance: Courtship and the Transition to Marriage in America, 1770-1900" (Ph.D. diss., Brandeis University, 1981). I am indebted to Rothman for discussions of North-South differences. For a range of nineteenth-century views, see William A. Alcott, *Moral Philosophy of Courtship* (Boston, 1859); Susan Petigru King, *Crimes Which the Law Does Not Reach* (New York, 1859); Caroline Howard Gilman, *Recollections of a Southern Matron* (New York, 1838), chap. 31; and "Husband Hunting," [North Carolina University] *Magazine* 7 (1857-58): 41-49.

4. Williana Lacy to Bessie Lacy, 10 July 1845; Drury Lacy to Bessie Lacy, 10 Jan. 1845, 13 June 1845. The literature on southern women's academies is not extensive. For one recent view see Frances Griffin, *Less Time for Meddling: A History of Salem Academy and College, 1772-1866* (Winston-Salem, N.C., 1979); for a typical description and statement of purpose, see St. Mary's School, *Manual of St. Mary's School, Raleigh, N.C.* (Raleigh, 1857).

5. Williana Lacy to Bessie Lacy, 26 Nov. 1845, 30 Aug. 1845 (see also Williana's letters to Bessie, 2 Jan. 1846, 23 Feb. 1846); Bessie Lacy to Drury Lacy, 12 Jan. 1847, 27 Jan. 1848, and 21 Sept. 1847 (see also Bessie Lacy to Drury Lacy, n.d., [probably 1847]). Carroll Smith-Rosenberg, "The Female World of Love and Ritual: Relations between Women in Nineteenth-Century America," *Signs* 1 (Autumn 1975): 1-29, is the watershed paper on the importance of emotional bonds among nineteenth-century women.

6. Bessie Lacy to Drury Lacy, 11 Feb. 1847.

7. Maggie Morgan to Bessie Lacy, 12 Jan. 1849.

8. Ibid., 13 Jan. 1849.

9. Ibid., 15 Sept. 1849.

10. Bessie Lacy to Horace Lacy, 15 Aug. 1847; Bessie Lacy to Drury Lacy, 27 Jan. 1848.

11. See, for example, Bessie Lacy to Drury Lacy, December 1846.

12. Bessie Lacy to Thomas Dewey, "Christmas," 1851.

13. Other courtship rituals, such as the prohibition of unchaperoned meetings and the

emphasis on conquest and surrender, also kept women and men personally alien to each other even as they brought them together as a social couple. For a southern woman's novel built upon such rituals, yet critical of them, see Susan Petigru King, *Lily* (New York, 1855). A self-consciously male point of view is expressed by William Porcher Miles, "American Literature and Charleston Society," *Southern Quarterly Review* 7 (April 1853): 380-421; Miles laments "stiff" and alien relations between the sexes, attributing it to women's social exile on plantations.

14. Bessie Lacy to Thomas Dewey, 10 May 1852.

15. Ibid.

16. Ibid., 30 June 1852.

17. Ibid., 7 May 1852.

18. Ibid., 22 Feb. 1853.

19. Ibid., 7 May 1852.

20. Ibid., May 1852.

21. Ibid., May 1852; 30 June 1852.

22. Ibid., 26 July 1852. In a letter written to Bessie's father in November 1852, Thomas wrote that his "attachment [to Bessie] only requires a father's sanction, a father's approbation, to be fully returned as I could desire . . . ."

23. Bessie Lacy to Thomas Dewey, n.d., [late 1852]. There is some evidence, too, that Bessie and Thomas enjoyed times of emotional closeness as well, but these seem to have added to her uncertainty. See, for example, Bessie Lacy to Thomas Dewey, 19 Jan. 1853, 8 Feb. 1853, and [October or November] 1854.

24. Ibid., [1853], see also 4 Feb. 1853.

25. Ibid., n.d., [late 1852].

26. Ibid., 4 March 1853.

27. Ibid., 1853.

28. As their marriage drew near, Bessie's and Thomas's doubts involved their family and friends in some rather partisan arguments about whether the wedding should take place. See Mary R. Lacy to Thomas Dewey, 1853; Mary Dewey to Thomas Dewey, 11 July 1853; Alexander McPheeters to Thomas Dewey, 26 July 1853; Sarah Dewey to Thomas Dewey, 29 Aug. 1853, and 1 Oct. 1853. The courtship crisis having passed, however, Bessie and Thomas lived out their married lives together, raised a family, and survived the Civil War as Thomas pursued a banking career and Bessie worked in women's associations.

29. For useful introductions to ethnography, see Rhys Isaac, "Ethnographic Method in History," *Historical Methods* 13 (Winter 1980): 43-61; Dell Hymes, *Foundations in Sociolinguistics: An Ethnographic Approach* (Philadelphia: University of Pennsylvania Press, 1974); *Language Acquisition and Communicative Choice: Essays by Susan M. Erwin-Tripp* (Stanford: Stanford University Press, 1973); Basil Bernstein, "A Public Language: Some Sociological Implications of a Linguistic Form," *British Journal of Sociology* 10 (1959): 450-64; and *Selected Writings of Edward Sapir in Culture, Language, and Personality*, ed. David G. Mandelbaum (Berkeley: University of California Press, 1949).

30. Maggie Morgan to Bessie Lacy, 4 Feb. 1853.

A SLAVE FAMILY IN THE ANTE BELLUM SOUTH

LOREN SCHWENINGER

Twentieth century scholars of Afro-American history have offered two basically different interpretations concerning the effect of slavery on the black family. In his famous 1932 study *The Negro Family in the United States*, Negro sociologist E. Franklin Frazier asserted that slavery destroyed the black family. Fundamental economic forces and material interests, he said, shattered even the toughest bonds of black familial sentiments and parental love.[1] Supporting Frazier in the 1959 comparative analysis, *Slavery: A Problem in American Intellectual and Institutional Life*, white historian Stanley M. Elkins listed four reasons for the destruction of the black slave family: sexual exploitation, separation, miscegenation, and restrictive legal codes. "The law could permit no aspect of the slave's conjugal state to have an independent legal existence."[2] In an examination of the urban South, historian Richard C. Wade likewise concluded that "For a slave, no matter where he resided, a house was never a home. Families could scarcely exist in bondage. The law recognized no marriage."[3] And Daniel P. Moynihan, in his 1965 report, re-iterated that slavery had an extremely negative effect on the black family.[4]

Recently, three writers have put forth a far more optimistic view of the black family in bondage. Herbert Gutman, Robert Abzug and John Blassingame contend that strong family loyalties developed among slaves. Admitting the obvious institutional barriers, they argue that bondsmen used the family as a shelter against the brutalities of the Southern slave system. "Although it was weak, although it was frequently broken," Professor Blassingame writes in *The Slave Com-*

Loren Schweninger is an Assistant Professor of History at the University of North Carolina at Greensboro.

[1]E. Franklin Frazier, *The Negro Family in the United States* (Chicago: University of Chicago Press, 1939), pp. 40, 41; "The Negro Slave Family," *Journal of Negro History XV* (April, 1930), pp. 198-259.

[2]Stanley M. Elkins, *Slavery: A Problem in American Institutional and Intellectual Life* (Chicago: University of Chicago Press, 1959), pp. 53, 54.

[3]Richard C. Wade, *Slavery in the Cities: The South, 1820-1860* (New York: Oxford University Press, 1964), pp. 117-121.

[4]Lee Rainwater and William L. Yancey, *The Moynihan Report and the Politics of Controversy* (Cambridge, Massachusetts: The Massachusetts Institute of Technology Press, 1967), pp. 61, 62, 414, 415.

munity, a psychological study of Blacks in bondage, "the family provided an important buffer, a refuge from the rigors of slavery."[5] Thus, though asking the same basic question of the way in which the institution of slavery affected the black family, scholars have advanced two fundamentally different interpretations.

An investigation of one slave family will not end the controversy. In a limited sense it can only tell us about *a* family, and one that was in many respects very fortunate.[6] The members of the Thomas-Rapier slave family received an education; achieved a degree of economic independence; and eventually became free or at least "quasi-free." Moreover, they belonged to extremely permissive and beneficent masters. They lived in an urban environment (as did only 10% of the South's slave population), and hired out, though it was against the law. But, like many other Blacks in the ante bellum South, they too suffered the pains of separation (living in Alabama, Tennessee, and Canada); sexual exploitation (the slave mother bore three sons by three different white men); and the legal denial of the slave family. Yet, in spite of these institutional barriers or perhaps because of them, the members of the Thomas-Rapier family maintained their integrity. Indeed, as seen in a rare collection of slave letters, notes, and autobiographical reminiscences, they preserved a cohesive family unit for three generations. In a larger sense, then, an investigation of one slave family can perhaps shed some light on the family experiences of many slaves in the ante bellum South.

Born in Albemarle County, Virginia, about 1790, the black slave, Sally, grew up on the 1500-acre tobacco plantation of Charles S. Thomas, a friend and neighbor of Thomas Jefferson.[7] At a young age

---

[5]Herbert Gutman is working on a book length study of the black family. See: Tamara K. Hareven, editor, *Anonymous Americans: Explorations in Nineteenth-Century Social History* (Englewood Cliffs, N.J.: Prentice-Hall, Inc., 1971), p. 209; Robert H. Abzug, "The Black Family During Reconstruction," in Nathan I. Huggins, Martin Kilson and Daniel M. Fox, *Key Issues in the Afro-American Experience* (New York: Harcourt Brace Jovanovich, Inc., 1971), pp. 26-41; John W. Blassingame, *The Slave Community: Plantation Life in the Ante-Bellum South* (New York: Oxford University Press, 1971), chapter III.

[6]It is not the purpose of this paper to enter the contemporary sociological debate on the origins of the "black matriarchy." As it happened, the central figure in this slave family was a woman. All three of her slave children, however, became dominant fathers, maintaining their marriages for twenty-six, forty-two, and thirty years respectively. In addition, it is not the purpose of this essay to differentiate between the family attitudes of the mother, who remained in bondage, and her children, who eventually gained their freedom. Their family attitudes were for the most part the same.

[7]"The Autobiographical Reminiscences of James P. Thomas," Moorland-Spingarn Collection, Howard University, Washington, D.C., [1911], p. 1; hereafter "Thomas Autobiography." In the original manuscript many of the pages are out of place and

she was sent to the fields. Working from sun-up to sundown, season to season, and year to year, she (along with forty-one other slaves on the "big gang"), prepared beds, planted seeds, transplanted shoots, "wormed and topped" young plants, hung, and then stripped, sorted and bundled the final product. When she was about eighteen, Sally suffered (or accepted) the sexual advances of a white man, (probably John Thomas, the owner's eldest son); and in September 1808, she gave birth to a mulatto boy, John. Some years later she gave birth to a second mulatto child, Henry.[8] As Virginia law required that progeny take the status of the mother, both children were born in bondage, but as part of the Thomas Trust Estate, they were protected against sale or separation.[9] Consequently, when one of the heirs of the estate (again probably John) joined the westward movement of slaveholders across the Appalachians into the Cumberland river valley about 1818, Sally, John and Henry were transported to the fast growing town of Nashville, Tennessee.[10]

The city offered many opportunities. With the master's permission, Sally hired out as a cleaning lady, a practice common among urban slaves, and secured an agreement to retain a portion of her earnings. She then rented a two-story frame house on the corner of Deaderick and Cherry Streets in the central business district. Converting the front room into a laundry, and manufacturing her own soap (blending fats, oils, alkali and salt in a small vat in the front room), she established a business of cleaning clothes. She soon built up a thriving trade.[11] At the same time Sally arranged for her eldest son, John, to hire out as a waiter and poll boy to river barge Captain Richard Rapier,[12] who was

---

un-numbered. Thus the page numbers cited are only approximate; Albemarle County Probate Records, Deed Books, Book XXXII (January 2, 1835), p. 89; *Ibid.*, Book VI (July 14, 1814), p. 26; *ibid.*, Book IX (November 17, 1825), p. 260; The Genealogy of a Slave Family.

[8]"Thomas Autobiography," pp. 2-7; U.S. Census Office, Sixth Census of the United States, "Population Schedules for Lauderdale County, Alabama," Vol. IV, 1840, p. 104.

[9]Winthrop Jordan, *White Over Black: American Attitudes Toward the Negro, 1550-1812* (Chapel Hill: University of North Carolina Press, 1968), p. 76; Albemarle County Probate Records, Deed Books, Book XXXII (January 2, 1835), pp. 89, 90.

[10]"Thomas Autobiography," pp. 3-6.

[11]*Ibid.*; *The Nashville Business Directory* (Nashville: Printed by John P. Campbell, 1855), *passim*; "Miscellaneous Notes of James P. Thomas," Moorland-Spingarn Collection, Howard University, Washington, D.C., n.p.

[12]Richard Rapier, described as "a large fleshy man weighing over 200 pounds," settled in Nashville about 1799. Soon he was transporting large quantities of tobacco to New Orleans and returning with sugar, teas and coffee. In 1806 he formed a "copartnership" with Lemuel T. Turner and James Jackson.

plying the Cumberland-Tennessee-Mississippi river trade, between Nashville, Florence (Alabama), and New Orleans;[13] and arranged for Henry to hire out as an errand boy to various "white gentlemen" around Nashville. Part of their earnings, along with her own, she saved in a tea cannister, which she hid in the loft, hoping someday to be able to purchase "free papers" for the children. "However, that might cost as much as $2000!" Undeterred, she conscientiously set aside part of her earnings every month, and by early 1826, she had saved over $300.[14]

Though thirty-six years old, Sally was still an attractive woman. In October 1827, in the house on Deaderick Street she gave birth to a third mulatto son, James.[15] The father was the famous ante bellum Judge John Catron, but according to the state law, which, like the law in Virginia, assigned progeny the status of the mother, James was born in bondage. "Now my own father presided over the supreme court of Tennessee [and served as a justice on the United States Supreme Court]," James later recalled, "[but] he had no time to give me a thought. He gave me 25 cents once, [and] if I [were] correctly informed, that is all he ever did for me."[16] With three children, John nineteen, Henry about sixteen, and James, Sally despaired that she might not be able to save enough to free her family.

But her despair soon turned to joy. She received word in 1829 that her eldest son had been emancipated. "I bequeath one thousand dollars to my executors for the purpose of purchasing the freedom of the mulatto boy, John, who now waits on me, and belongs to the Estate of Thomas," Richard Rapier stipulated in his will, and the Alabama General Assembly, the only legal emancipator of slaves in the state, passed a law freeing "a certain male slave by the name of John H. Rapier."[17] Then, she saw an opportunity to free Henry. With the final

[13]Davidson County Probate Records, Minutes, Vol. C. (July 1801), p. 405; *The Tennessee Gazette and Metro District Advertiser Repository*, March 29, 1898; *The Clarion*, September 27, 1808; *The Imperial Review and Cumberland Repository*, May 5, 1808; *The Democratic Clarion and Tennessee Gazette*, May 19, 1812, May 31, 1814.

[14]"Thomas Autobiography," chapter 1; "Miscellaneous Notes of James P. Thomas," Moorland-Spingarn Collection, Howard University, Washington, D.C., n.p. (See page 33)

[15]"Thomas Autobiography," p. 7.

[16]*Ibid.*, chapter 1; *Acts Passed at the First and Second Session of the Nineteenth General Assembly of the State of Tennessee* (Nashville: Allen Hall and A. S. Heiskel, Printers to the State, 1832), pp. 167-170.

[17]Lauderdale County Probate Records, Wills, Vol. VI (June 3, 1824), p. 117; *Acts of the Eleventh Annual Session of the General Assembly of the State of Alabama* (Tuscaloosa: McGuire, Henry and Walker, 1830), p. 36; Richard Rapier, Auburn, California, to James P. Thomas, December 14, 1877, Rapier Papers, Moorland-Spingarn Collection, Howard University, Washington, D.C., hereafter Rapier Papers.

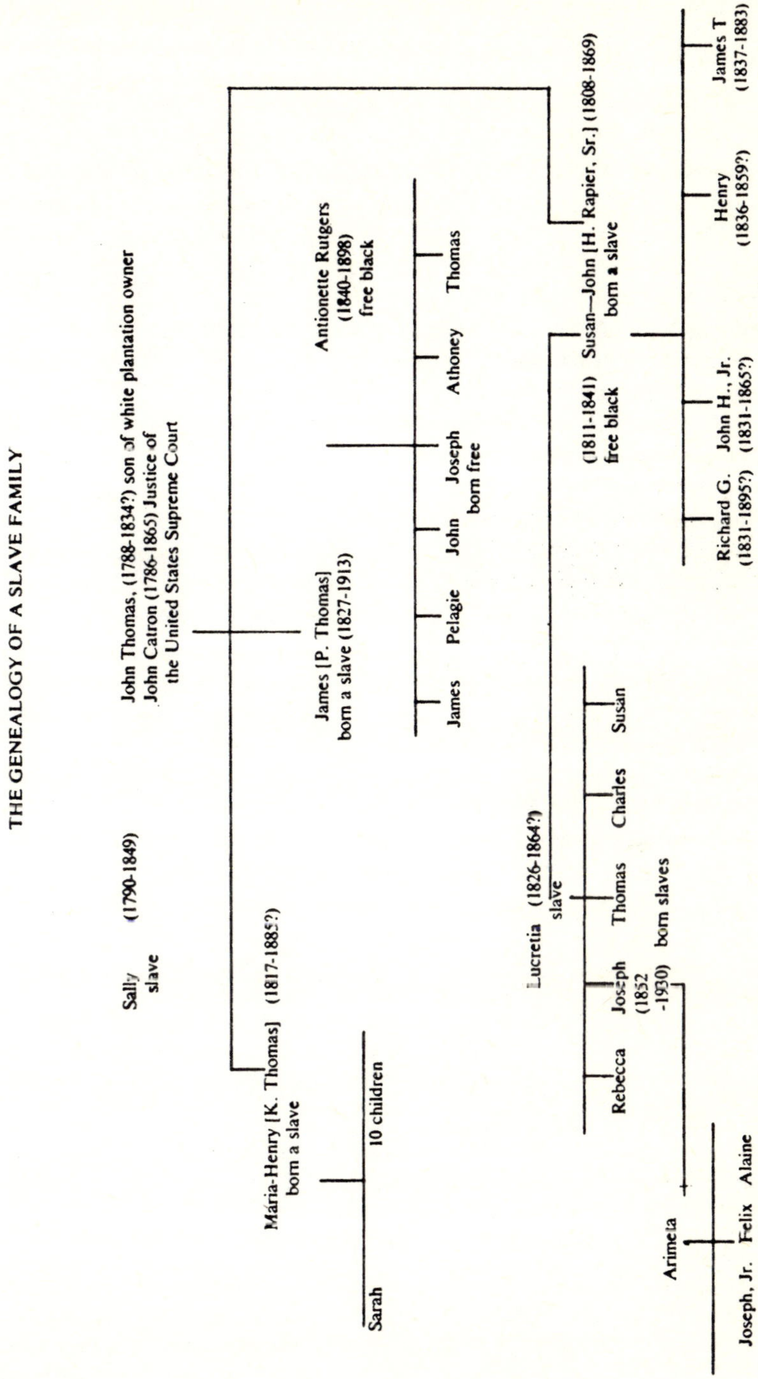
THE GENEALOGY OF A SLAVE FAMILY
Sally (1790-1849)
slave
John Thomas, (1788-1834?) son of white plantation owner
John Catron (1786-1865) Justice of the United States Supreme Court
Maria-Henry [K. Thomas] (1817-1885?)
born a slave
Sarah
10 children
James [P. Thomas]
born a slave (1827-1913)
Antionette Rutgers
(1840-1898)
free black
James
Pelagie
John
Joseph
Athoney
Thomas
born free
Lucretia (1826-1864?)
slave
Rebecca
Joseph (1852 -1930)
Thomas
Charles
Susan
born slaves
Arimeta
Joseph, Jr.
Felix
Alaine
born free
(1811-1841)
free black
Susan—John [H. Rapier, Sr.] (1808-1869)
born a slave
Richard G. (1831-1895?)
John H., Jr. (1831-1865?)
Henry (1836-1859?)
James T (1837-1883)
born free

settlement of the Thomas Estate in 1834, "Sally and the two mulatto boys," reverted to one John Martin, an affable young man who wanted to sell a part of his inheritance for a quick profit. Fearing that her children would be sold "down river to Mississippi," Sally urged Henry to escape. Heeding his mother's advice, Henry fled through upper Tennessee and Kentucky but was captured near Louisville and confined to a guard house. He managed to work off his leg-chains one night, however, steal down to the Ohio River, untie a boat, and drift into the current. "The night was cold," Henry wrote afterwards. "I headed the yawl downstream, sculled over the falls and made for the Indiana shore. There I found a man who freed my hands."[18] Taking the surname Thomas, he travelled to Buffalo, New York, where he opened a barber shop.[19]

Shortly after Henry's escape, Sally went to Ephraim H. Foster, a prominent Tennessee lawyer, and asked for assistance in putting James out of Martin's reach. "Will you talk with him [Martin] and see what he will take for the boy," she asked. "Very well, Aunt Sally," Foster replied, "I will see him and let you know what can be done." A few days later Foster told her that Martin wanted $400. "I have saved only $350," Sally explained, but quickly added: "Now if you, Col. Foster, will pay the fifty and make it four hundred, have the bill of sale made to yourself, you can hold James in trust until I return [the] money. I want you to be his protector." Foster agreed and the bargain was sealed. A short time later, she paid off the debt and received a bill of sale, "free papers," for six-year-old James.[19] Even then, however, he was not free. The law required emancipated Blacks to secure a manumission deed from the county court, and "thereupon immediately leave Tennessee."[20] Thus, despite having "free papers," James was still legally a slave.

---

[18]"Thomas Autobiography," chapter 1; "Miscellaneous Notes of James P. Thomas," Moorland-Spingarn Collection, Howard University, Washington, D.C., n.p.; John H. Rapier, Sr., Florence, Alabama, to Henry K. Thomas, Buffalo, New York, February 28, 1843, Rapier Papers; A. M. Simmons, Cincinnati, Ohio, to Henry K. Thomas, Buffalo, New York, May 26, 1836, *ibid.*; *Buffalo City Directory* (Buffalo: Horatio N. Walker, Publisher, 1844), p. 213.

[19]"Thomas Autobiography," pp. 1-6.

[20]*Acts Passed at the First and Second Session of the Nineteenth General Assembly of the State of Tennessee* (Nashville: Allen Hall and A. S. Heiskel, Printers to the State, 1832), p. 167; Robert William Fogel and Stanley L. Engerman in their statistical study *Time on the Cross: The Economics of American Negro Slavery* (Boston, 1974) also conclude that the slave family was a viable institution, but they, like most historians concerned with the peculiar institution, emphasize the role and attitudes of whites. They suggest that the Negro family survived for three basic reasons: the desire of planters to promote family stability (to increase the output of contented slaves); the extreme reluctance of owners to break up family units; and the Victorian attitudes among the planting

But neither the law nor slavery seemed to curtail his activities. As a young boy, he performed a variety of chores for his mother: keeping salt in the hopper for making soap, cutting wood for the fire place, cleaning up around the house, and delivering clothes to customers. He also enrolled in the Nashville school for Blacks. Thomas recalled sitting on splintery benches, in a drafty one-room school house and listening to ill-prepared lessons on such basic subjects as "the fundamentals of reading." In addition, he remembered that the school remained open only a few months each year, the pupils, or "scholars," had to pay a very high $4 tuition fee, and that free Blacks Rufus Conrad, Daniel Watkins and Samuel Lowery taught at the school from time to time. "But often," he said, "there was no school because there was no teacher." In 1836, for instance, a black teacher, described as "a fine scholar," was taken out by whites and whipped nearly to death. "Tennesseans generally opposed educating blacks," he recalled, "they might want the same as whites." But young James had an intense desire to learn and quickly mastered the basics of mathematics, reading and writing.[21]

Having secured a rudimentary education, James hired out as an apprentice barber. Working with bondsman Frank Parrish, who had earlier established a barber shop on Public Square, he quickly learned the trade.[22] "James [is] still with Frank Parrish and has the character of a good barber, So a Gentleman told me," his brother, John Rapier, observed in 1843. "He is well thought of by the Gentlemen. James has

---

class, which made miscegenation extremely rare, resulting in a miniscule percent of mulattoes in the ante bellum South (7.7 in 1850 and 10.4 in 1860). Besides the impressionistic evidence used by the two cliometricians to support their contentions, the dubious relationship between the extent of sexual exploitation and the percent of mulattoes in the South in a given year (which is itself upon question), and the mis-interpretation of the quantified evidence concerning the break up of families on the New Orleans auction block between 1804-1862 (the authors suggest 84 percent of the sales involved unmarried individuals, but failed to reveal that the slave's familial status was generally not recorded), the greatest weakness of the study is the obvious inadequacy of quantification methods in evaluating the slave family. Statistical evidence does not reveal the feelings of interdependence, unity, and cohesiveness that black family members in bondage felt for one another. Robert William Fogel and Stanley L. Engerman, *Time on the Cross: The Economics of American Negro Slavery* (Boston, 1974), pp. 126-144.

[21]"Thomas Autobiography," chapters 1, 2; "Miscellaneous Notes of James P. Thomas," Moorland-Spingarn Collection, Howard University, Washington, D.C.; James P. Thomas, Nashville, Tennessee, to John H. Rapier, Jr., St. Paul, Minnesota Territory, October 3, 1856.

[22]The Nashville *Republican*, April 21, 1836; The Nashville *Daily Republican Banner*, April 9, 1841; Davidson County Probate Records, Minutes, Book E (October 4, 1853), pp. 563-564. Many times, as in this instance, probate court cases included biographical material about Blacks to illustrate their "good character." Davidson County Probate Records, Wills and Inventories, Vol. 16 (November 28, 1854), pp.429-430.

manners to please almost anyone who does not let their prejudice go far on account of color."[23] Two years later James was still with Parrish, earned $12 a month, and at the same time had begun violin lessons with one Gordan McGowan. "James will make a man of musick I think. He seems to be very fond of it."[24] Having served a five-year apprenticeship, in 1846, he opened his own barber shop. The nineteen-year-old slave established his shop in the house where he had grown up (and where his mother still operated her cleaning business), at 10 Deaderick Street. The location was ideal. Within a few steps of several banking houses, newspapers, and law firms, as well as the county court house, Market Square, and the Capitol, "the place on Deaderick," he explained, "was convenient to bankers, merchants, lawyers, politicians, and professional men." He counted among his customers six famous Tennesseans: William Carroll, one time governor; E. S. (Squire) Hall, an important businessman; General William Harding, owner of Bellemeade Estate; Ephraim Foster, a Whig political leader; and William G. (Parson) Brownlow, the Civil War governor.[25] Francis Fogg, the well-known Davidson County lawyer, visited the Thomas shop daily. "He returns to us in the evening," Mrs. Fogg noted approvingly, "with face smooth and curls nicely arranged."[26]

While attending to his duties as a barber, James listened attentively to conversations that took place among his customers. "They had time to talk in the barber shop. Nobody seemed in a great hurry. Everything was discussed—social, commercial, political and financial." He remembered conversations about the abolitionists, the advancement of cotton on the Liverpool market, the magnetism and sporting pro-

---

[23]John H. Rapier, Sr., Florence, Alabama, to Henry K. Thomas, Buffalo, New York, February 28, 1843, Rapier Papers.

[24]John H. Rapier, Sr., Florence, Alabama, to Richard Rapier, Buffalo, New York, April 8, 1845, Rapier Papers.

[25]"Thomas Autobiography," chapters 1, 2, 3; *The Nashville General Business Directory* (Nashville: The Daily American Book and Job Printing Office, 1853), 1-20; For the early business and financial activities of E. S. Hall in Nashville, see: John Claybrooke Papers, Manuscript Division, State Library and Archives, Nashville, Tennessee; For the activities of the other whites mentioned, see: Philip Hamer, *Tennessee: A History*, Vol. I (New York: American Historical Society, 1935), pp. 282, 370, 381, 475; "Leadership in Nashville: Biographical Sketches of 116 of the Most Prominent Citizens in Nashville," Catherine Pilcher Avery Papers, Manuscript Division, State Library and Archives, Nashville, Tennessee; "Old Days in Nashville, Tennessee: Reminiscences by Jane Thomas," (no relation to James Thomas), reprints from the Nashville *Daily American*, 1895-1896 in Jane Thomas Papers, Manuscript Division, State Library and Archives, Nashville, Tennessee; *The Official Political Manual of the State of Tennessee* (Nashville, Tennessee: Marshall and Bruce, 1890), p. 180.

[26]Ellen S. Fogg, Nashville, Tennessee, to E. H. Foster, Louisville, Kentucky, February 15, 1849, Ephraim Foster Papers, Manuscript Division, State Library and Archives, Nashville, Tennessee.

clivities of Andrew Jackson, plantation acreage along the Mississippi, and fugitive slaves. Once, he recalled being sharply questioned about runaway Blacks. "You have a brother living in Buffalo, New York, I believe," General Harding asked pointedly. "Yes," was the reply. "Well he treated me in a gruff manner. I went to ask him if he knew anything about a boy who ran off from me. I told him I only wanted to see him. I had come to Buffalo for that purpose. I received a very cold and indifferent reply." James could do little but apologize for his brother's "rudeness." Though he usually remained silent when the conversation turned to such controversial issues; at times he ventured an opinion on the slavery question. Once, for example, while shaving a young Virginia lawyer, he defended the Wilmot Proviso, a proposal to prohibit slavery in the newly acquired Mexican territories. "The set back I got caused me to be careful in the future. Among other things he told me I had no right to listen to a gentleman's conversation."[27] Despite such "set backs," James built up a flourishing business. Charging 25 cents for a haircut, 15 cents for a shave, and $1 for occasionally extracting teeth, he operated one of the most prosperous "tonsorial establishments" in Nashville. In the city's first business directory (published in 1853), he advertised in large boldface print: "JAS. THOMAS, BARBER SHOP, 10 Deaderick St."[28]

Meanwhile, Sally's other two children, freedman John H. Rapier and fugitive Henry Thomas, were also prospering as barbers. Rapier opened a shop in Florence, Alabama, soon saved over $500, purchased a white frame house on Court Street in the downtown district, and like James, converted the house into a place of business as well as a residence. In 1831, he married Susan, a free Black from Baltimore, Maryland, and in the next decade the couple had four children: Richard, John Jr., Henry and James.[29] After his wife's death in childbirth at the age of twenty-nine, he purchased a sixteen-year-old slave, Lucretia,

[27]"Thomas Autobiography," chapter 2.

[28]*Nashville Business Directory* (Nashville: Daily American Book and Job Printing Office, 1853), p. 68.

[29]Richard Rapier, Auburn, California, to James P. Thomas, December 14, 1877, Rapier Papers; In this letter Richard, John Rapier's eldest son, refers to his date and place of birth. In the "Diary and Notes of John H. Rapier, Jr.," March 10, 1857, Rapier Papers; John, Rapier's third son, likewise refers to his birth date; U.S. Census Office, Sixth Census of the United States, "Population Schedules for Lauderdale County, Alabama," Vol. IV, (1840), p. 104; James T. Rapier, Florence, Alabama to John H. Rapier, Jr., St. Paul, Minnesota Territory, September 27, 1858, Rapier Papers, "Thomas Autobiography," p. 73; *Alabama State Sentinel*, November 25, 1867; The inscription on Susan Rapier's tombstone reads: "Sacred to the memory of Susan Rapier. Born in Baltimore, Md. 25 of December 1811 departed this life at Florence Alabama 10 of March 1841—also her two infant children Jackson and Alexander—Depart my friends and dry up your tears for I must lie hear [sic] till Christ appears."

and between 1848 and 1861, they had five slave children, the youngest named Susan.[30] During the ante bellum period Rapier acquired real estate holdings in Alabama, the Minnesota Territory, and Canada, purchased valuable railroad stock, and saved $2000 in cash. By 1860, he was one of the wealthiest free Blacks in Alabama, with about $10,000.[31]

Henry Thomas also opened a barber shop. Locating in the basement of Buffalo's elegant hotel Niagara, he too built up a lucrative trade. About 1835, he married a black woman, Maria, and they had eleven children, ten boys and a girl, Sarah.[32] In 1852, to avoid apprehension by slave catchers (who were encouraged by the 1850 Fugitive Slave Law), he moved to the black community of Buxton, Canada West. With resources he had saved as a barber, he purchased one hundred acres of wilderness land, built a log house, cleared the trees, and put in a crop of corn, wheat and barley.[33] "The settlement improves slowly, but prospects are good for its success," he noted in 1856. "The lumber mill is making improvements for the neighborhood. Soon the railroad will pass through. The school is flourishing. I have six acres in wheat and 2 in barley."[34] Thus, using one of the few profitable occupations open to ante bellum Blacks, James, John and Henry were all able to achieve a degree of financial independence.

---

[30] U.S. Census Bureau, Sixth Census of the United States, Population Schedules for Lauderdale County, Alabama," Vol. IV, (1840), p. 104; United States Census Bureau, Seventh Census of the United States, Populations Schedules for Lauderdale County, Alabama," Vol. I, (1850), p. 293; United States Census Bureau, Eighth Census of the United States, Vol. VI (1860), p. 39.

[31] John H. Rapier, Sr., Florence, Alabama, to Richard Rapier, Buffalo, New York, April 8, 1845, Rapier Papers; John H. Rapier, Sr., Florence, Alabama, to John H. Rapier, Jr., St. Paul, Minnesota Territory, September 16, 1857, Rapier Pape ,; Lauderdale County Probate Records, Wills and Inventories, Vol. B (September 13, 1869), pp. 78-80, Land Deeds, Book II (May 3, 1844), p. 78; Book XVI (August 7, 1858), p. 324; The Florence *Gazette*, March 5, 1862; Loren Schweninger, "John H. Rapier, Sr.: A Slave and Freedman in the Antebellum South," *Civil War History*/Vol. 20, (March 1974), p. 31.

[32] A.-M. Simmons, Cincinnati, Ohio, to Henry K. Thomas, Buffalo, New York, May 26, 1836, Rapier Papers; *Buffalo City Directory* (Buffalo: Horatio N. Walker, Publisher, 1844), p. 213; John H. Rapier, Sr., Florence, Alabama, to Henry K. Thomas, Buffalo, New York, February 28, 1843, Rapier Papers; "Thomas Autobiography," chapter 1; *Buffalo City Directory* (Buffalo: Jewett, Thomas and Company, Commercial Advertiser Office, 1847-48), p. 158.

[33] Henry K. Thomas, Buxton, Canada West, to John H. Rapier, Sr., Florence, Alabama, October 27, 1856, Rapier Papers; James T. Rapier, Buxton, Canada West, to John H. Rapier, Jr., St. Paul, Minnesota Territory, June 26, 1857, Rapier Papers; "Thomas Autobiography," chapter 1.

[34] Henry K. Thomas, Buxton, Canada West, to John H. Rapier, Sr., Florence, Alabama, October 27, 1856, Rapier Papers.

The members of the slave family were also successful at maintaining close family ties. Though separated by hundreds, even thousands of miles, though forbidden to travel in certain regions, and though denied postal privileges, they kept in close touch. As a slave and also when he was a free Black, John Rapier Sr. frequently visited Nashville. And between 1838 and 1846, he arranged for all four of his children to attend school in the Tennessee capital and to stay with their slave uncle and slave grandmother. "John and James are so [well] pleased with their grandmother [and school], he noted in 1843, "that they do not want to come home, so James writes."[35] A couple of years later he added: "My two sons that are with mother are well when I last hear[d] from them. I entend to go up to Nashville in the course of ten or twelve days and See them all." On that occasion Rapier confessed that he had not been to Tennessee in nearly a year. "I am extremely anxious to See the family again," he said, promising to deliver a letter from his brother, which had been smuggled into the South from the North. After a visit to the Tennessee capital, he wrote to "Brother Henry": "Mother looks as young as she did 8 years ago and works as hard and hardly takes time to talk to you." Forwarding other family news, he said that "Brother James" was doing extremely well as a barber; and of his sons, he proudly observed that Richard wrote in an excellent hand; Henry wanted to continue his education; James read extremely well "for a little boy of his age [6] and training;" and "John has wrote me two letter and writes very plain for a boy of eight, . . . and has as much taste for reading as any child I know off and is very good in arithmetic."[36] Rapier not only journeyed to Tennessee often, but about once a year, he travelled to New York or Canada.[37] After one such sojourn, he expressed concern for Brother Henry's future in the North. "I told him to buy [more] land in that country and to pay the taxes. [But] I am fearful that Brother Henry will come to want in [Canada] as I am of the opinion that [it] is poor farming country."[38] For their parts, Henry and James also expressed a deep concern for the welfare of the slave family. Henry usually concluded his letters

[35]John H. Rapier, Sr., Florence, Alabama, to Henry K. Thomas, Buffalo, New York, February 28, 1843, Rapier Papers.

[36]John H. Rapier, Sr., Florence, Alabama, to Richard Rapier, Buffalo, New York, April 8, 1845, Rapier Papers.

[37]"The Autobiography of William King," (1890), p. 255, King Papers, Public Archives of Canada, Ottawa, Ontario; King, who founded Buxton, reminisced about Rapier's frequent visits to Toronto and Buxton during the 1850's; John H. Rapier, Sr., Florence, Alabama, to John H. Rapier, Jr., Minnesota Territory, September 16, 1857, Rapier Papers.

[38]John H. Rapier, Sr., Florence, Alabama, to John H. Rapier, Jr., Minnesota Territory, September 15, 1856, Rapier Papers.

with the simple, but significant, line: "All the family is well and wishes to be remembered to you."[39] And James Thomas wrote: "A letter from your hands [John Rapier Jr.] offers me a great deal of pleasure to say nothing of the family news it imparts."[40] It seems that separation, an inherent part of the institution of slavery, had little effect on the spiritual unity of the slave family.

There was also a solidarity among the members of the Rapier family. Deeply concerned about the welfare of his children, John Rapier offered them advice on everything from economic matters to questions of morality: "Settle your debts," "Save your money," "Stay away from liquor," he admonished "The Four Boys." "Stick closer to work and Say nothing and do nothing but what is right and you will do well my sons."[41] In 1845 he wrote Richard, who was attending school in Buffalo and living with Henry Thomas: "Study your books so I can hold you up as an example to your lettle Brothers. You are blessed if you will look at your situation. You have kind relations who are anctious to see you grow up an ornament to society."[42] Perhaps the best expression of the spiritual unity of the Rapier family was written by James Thomas Rapier, James P. Thomas's namesake and one of Sally's twenty-six grandchildren. Also living with fugitive Henry Thomas, and attending school in Buxton, he wrote:

> In our boyhood . . . all four of us boys were together. We all breathed as one. [Now] we are scattered abroad on the face of the Earth. Do you ever expect to see us all together again? I do not. Just look where we are . . . John in [Minnesota]. Myself in the north. Henry and Dick in California. Father in Alabama. Did you ever think how small our family is?[43]

Among the Rapiers, as well as the Thomases, there was an almost

---

[39]Henry K. Thomas, Buxton, Canada West, to John H. Rapier, Sr., October 27, 1856, Rapier Papers; March 13, 1857; Henry's only daughter Sarah wrote to John Rapier, Jr.: "Through Papa and James I would like to give you some news . . . Mama and Papa are well as is the rest of the family and they sent their compliments. We shall all feel very much pleased if you make a visit to this place." Sarah Thomas, Buxton, Canada West, to John H. Rapier, Jr., Minnesota Territory, March 10, 1857, Rapier Papers.

[40]James P. Thomas, St. Louis, Missouri, to John H. Rapier, Jr., Minnesota Territory, June 17, 1858, Rapier Papers.

[41]John H. Rapier, Sr., Florence, Alabama to John H. Rapier, Jr., Minnesota Territory, September 15, 1856, Rapier Papers; John H. Rapier, Sr., Florence, Alabama to John H. Rapier, Jr., Benton County, Minnesota Territory, December 13, 1856, Rapier Papers.

[42]John H. Rapier, Sr., Florence, Alabama, to Richard Rapier, Buffalo, New York, April 8, 1845, Rapier Papers.

[43]James Rapier, Buxton, Canada West to John H. Rapier, Jr., Little Falls, Minnesota Territory, January 27, 1857, Rapier Papers.

religious devotion to the institution of the family.

The ability of the slave family to remain so close seems all the more remarkable in the face of the legal restrictions placed on Blacks. Statutes forbade a free Black from either visiting with slaves, or travelling from one state to another, both on penalty of being sold into slavery. Laws prohibited slaves from owning personal property, renting real estate, earning money, or securing an education. "No person shall hire to any slave," one Tennessee code pronounced, "the time of said slave."[44] Lawmakers prescribed a ten year prison sentence to anyone helping a slave to escape, forging a pass for a slave, harboring a runaway or inciting a Black to defy a white; and laid down the death penalty for Blacks convicted of assaulting or molesting a white woman, maliciously setting fire to a barn, preparing any poison, or conspiring to revolt. "A ring leader or Chief Instigator of any plot to rebel or murder any white," one law stated, "may be lawfully killed [on sight], if it is not practicable, otherwise, to arrest and secure him."[45] Nash-

[44]*Acts Passed at the First Session of the Fourteenth General Assembly of the State of Tennessee* (Knoxville: Heiskell and Brown, Public Printers to the State, 1821), p. 34; *Acts Passed at the Second Session of the Fourteenth General Assembly of the State of Tennessee* (Knoxville: Heiskell and Brown, Printers to the State, 1822), p. 22; *Acts Passed at the First Session of the Fifteenth General Assembly of the State of Tennessee* (Murfreesborough: J. Norvell and G. A. and A. C. Sablett, 1823), p. 76; *Acts Passed at the Extra Session of the Sixteenth General Assembly of the State of Tennessee* (Knoxville: Heiskell and Brown, 1927), 31-33; *Acts Passed at the First and Second Session of the Nineteenth General Assembly of the State of Tennessee* (Nashville: Allen A. Hall and A. S. Heiskell, Printers to the State, 1932), pp. 165-170.

[45]*Private Acts Passed at the Called Session of the Nineteenth General Assembly of the State of Tennessee* (Nashville: Allen A. Hall and F. S. Heiskell, Printers, 1832), pp. 5, 6; *Public Acts Passed at the First Session of the Twentieth General Assembly of the State of Tennessee* (Nashville: Allen A. Hall and F. S. Heiskell, Printers to the State, 1833), pp. 2, 3, 75, 76, 14, 87, 94, 99, 100, 215, 216; *Public Acts Passed at the First Session of the Twenty-first General Assembly of the State of Tennessee* (Nashville: S. Nye and Co., Printers, 1836), pp. 92, 145, 146, 167; *Acts Passed at the First Session of the Twenty-third General Assembly of the State of Tennessee* (Nashville: J. Geo. Harris, Printer to the State, 1840), pp. 82, 83; *Acts Passed by the First Session of the Twenty-fourth General Assembly of the State of Tennessee* (Murfreesborough: Cameron and Company, Printers to the State, 1842), pp. 229, 230; *Acts of the State of Tennessee Passed at the First Session of the Twenty-sixth General Assembly* (Knoxville: James C. Moses, 1846), p. 278; *Acts of the State of Tennessee Passed at the First Session of the Twenty-eighth General Assembly* (Nashville: McKennie and Watterson, Printers to the State, 1850), p. 30; *Acts of the State of Tennessee Passed at the First Session of the Twenty-eighth General Assembly* (Nashville: McKennie and Watterson, Printers to the State, 1850), p. 304; *Acts Passed at the First Session of the Twenty-ninth General Assembly* (Nashville: McKennie Printers, 1852), pp. 120, 521; *Acts of the State of Tennessee Passed at the First Session of the Thirtieth General Assembly* (Nashville: McKennie and Brown, Book and Job Printers, 1854), pp. 121, 122, 157; *Acts of the State of Tennessee Passed at the First Session of the Thirty-first General Assembly* (Nashville: Printed by G. C. Torbett and Company, 1856), pp. 71, 77; William Imes, "The Legal Status of Free Negroes and Slaves in Tennessee," *Journal of Negro History*, IV (July 1919), pp. 260, 261.

ville ordinances required free Blacks to pay a capitation (head) tax of $1 or $2, register at the court house, and "carry free papers on their person at all times." Blacks without such papers were to be treated as slaves. Moreover, Negroes were not permitted to walk the streets after dark, enter tippling houses, make weird noises, or gather within the city limits for any purpose, except public worship, and Blacks attending church were to be supervised by whites.[46]

But the slave family disregarded the elaborate code governing Blacks. Sally hired out, earned money, rented a house, and operated a business. "Mother lived so long at the corner of Deaderick and Cherry Streets," James Thomas remarked later, "that the people of Nashville thought she [was free] and owned the property." She moved about the city with little hindrance, boarded her grandchildren as they attended school, and secretly advised Henry to escape to the North.[47] In a similar manner James Thomas hired out, earned money and established a business. He eventually accumulated a large amount of personal property—furniture, mirrors, clothes, and about $1000 in cash, and while still a slave, became the manager of one of the largest barbering establishments in Nashville. He travelled to various parts of the city without a pass, entertained free Blacks in his home, and attended black church meetings. At one such gathering he recalled the black congregation, mostly slaves, singing until 12 o'clock at night. "The owners," he wrote, "seemed to care very little how much religion their servants got. They seemed to encourage it."[48] In much the same way John Rapier and Henry Thomas acquired personal property, hired out, earned as much as $50 a month, and, despite the laws against the movement of Blacks, travelled throughout the South, North, and Canada. Rapier even assisted a slave, Sam Ragland, to escape on one occasion.[49] In short, the slave family was not in the least constrained by the restrictive black codes.

Sally's dream that all of her children secure their freedom finally

---

[46]*Revised Laws of the City of Nashville* (Nashville: Union and American Steam Press, 1854), pp. 147, 154-58; *Revised Laws of the City of Nashville* (Nashville: Harvey M. Watterson Printers, 1850), pp. 124-26; *Acts Passed at the First Session of the Twenty-fifth General Assembly of the State of Tennessee* (Nashville: L. Gifford and E. G. Eastman, Printers, 1844), p. 18.

[47]"Thomas Autobiography," chapter 1.

[48]*Ibid.*; "Miscellaneous Notes of James P. Thomas," Moorland-Spingarn Collection, Howard University, Washington, D.C., n.d.; James P. Thomas, Louisville, Kentucky, to John H. Rapier, Jr., St. Paul, Minnesota Territory, March 1, 1856, Rapier Papers; James P. Thomas, Nashville, Tennessee, to John H. Rapier, Jr., Minnesota Territory, October 3, 1856, Rapier Papers.

[49]Loren Schweninger, "John H. Rapier, Sr.: A Slave and Freedman in the Antebellum South," Vol. 20, *Civil War History* (March 1974), *passim*.

came true in 1851, when her youngest son, James, asked Ephraim Foster to present a manumission petition to the Davidson County court. The slave and his master appeared at the courthouse in Nashville on March 6. "James has always maintained an exemplary character," Foster told the nine-judge panel hearing the case. "He has been industrious, honest, moral, humble, polite and had conducted himself as to gain the confidence and respect of whites. He is a man of great worth in his place." The testimony of such an eminent Tennessean swayed the magistrates and, after a short deliberation, they ordered "the slave James, otherwise called James [P.] Thomas, emancipated and forever set free." Thomas now addressed the court himself. He requested immunity from the 1831 law requiring manumitted Blacks to leave Tennessee. "I have deported myself in a manner requiring the confidence of whites. I have always earned a good living. I would be greatly damaged having to Start anew in some Strange Country." The judges, after receiving the required $500 good behavior bond, granted the immunity. James P. Thomas thus became the first black man in the county, perhaps the state, under the stringent emigration law of 1831, to gain legally both freedom and residency.[50]

A short time before James gained his freedom, however, Sally died of cholera.[51] A woman of great drive and dedication, she had devoted her life to freeing her children. She had hired out, started a business, and gladly put up her life savings to purchase "free papers" for James. She had also assisted Henry in his quest for freedom. Due in part to her unwavering efforts, the slaves John H. Rapier, Sr., Henry K. Thomas, and James P. Thomas, all gained free status before the Civil War. In addition, the Thomases and Rapiers all found great strength in the slave family. Members of these families were quite successful: John entered politics during Reconstruction; Henry farmed hundreds of acres in Canada; and James acquired property in St. Louis valued at $250,000;[52] while Sarah Thomas became a school teacher, James T. Rapier a Congressman, and John Rapier, Jr. a surgeon, stemmed from

---

[50]"Thomas Autobiography," pp. 1-8; Davidson County Probate Records, Minute Book E (March 6, 1851), pp. 134, 135.

[51]"Thomas Autobiography," p. 1; James Thomas said that his mother died in a cholera epidemic in 1850, but it was probably in the spring of 1849, when hundreds of Nashvillians died from the dreaded disease.

[52]The Florence *Journal*, September 18, 1869; Assessors Records, City of St. Louis, Plate 1874-1876, number B65, Blk 300, 301, 691; Assessors Records, City of St. Louis, Tax Books for 1871, Book 17 (1871), pp. 20-21; Probate Records of the City of St. Louis, Warranty Deeds, Book 452 (August 13, 1872), pp. 470, 471; "Autobiography of William King," pp. 355-360.

the security they found in the slave family.[53] It seems that for the black slave Sally, sexual exploitation, miscegenation, separation, and legal restrictions—the very forces designed, in part, to destroy the black family—gave impetus, *not* to disintegration and disunity, but to an extraordinary feeling of family loyalty, unity, and love. For Sally, her children, and her grandchildren, the slave family was indeed "a refuge from the rigors of slavery."

---

[53]James T. Rapier, Montgomery, Alabama, to William King, Buxton, Ontario, July 7, 1872, King Papers; Loren Schweninger, "James Rapier and Reconstruction," (PH.D. dissertation, Chicago, 1972), *passim*.

Antebellum Southern Households:

A New Perspective on a Familiar Question

Elizabeth Fox-Genovese

In recent years, the term "household" has enjoyed a growing popularity among students of early American history. Frequently associated with such terms as "*mentalité*" and "peasantry", it apparently reflects both the prestige of the English demographic and the French Annales schools and the attempt to portray early Americans as something other than capitalist entrepreneurs (Henretta, 1978; Clark, 1979; Waters, 1976). As part of this general project, we have even been offered a "household mode of production", which despite some sparkle proves analytically to be of little value (Merrill, 1977). Household, in fact, offers historians an invaluable analytic tool, but only on condition that they exercise some care in defining it as a unit, pay attention to its internal dynamics, and carefully establish its relation to the dominant mode of production (e.g., Medick, 1976).[1] From African chiefdoms, to

1. Michael Merrill provided an important shift in emphasis in calling attention to the importance of households in eighteenth- and early nineteenth-century America.

the Greek *oikos*, to the peasantry of medieval France, to the Italian city-states, to the early modern English countryside and beyond, various productive systems, like various political relations, have been anchored in households. Thus, the early French attempts at systematic taxation assessed obligations by *feux*—hearths or households. One can sympathize with those harrassed royal officials: The fledgling state they represented could not begin to keep track of family members, who had disconcerting tendencies to die or to migrate temporarily. But one could identify households as what we might call objective units of residence, and probably production, the members of which owed the crown a certain tax. It was left to the members to figure out the principles that governed the contribution to the common obligation.

In fact, the contemporary use of the term "household" probably derives from anthropology and, especially, from West Indian fieldwork, although not only there. The anthropologists who elaborated the concept probably had much the same concerns as the early French tax collectors. They wanted to account for units or groups of people who did not seem to conform to what ethnocentric Western scholars regarded as normative, or even normal organzation: so-called co-resident

---

But he weakens his genuine contribution in claiming to identify a "household mode of production". As an analytic tool, the concept will not wash and flattens all the significant distinctions between capitalist and precapitalist modes of production. In fact, it drains the concept of mode of production of all historical precision and interest. Households constitute ubiquitous features of historical development, and the decisive questions turn not on identifying their presence, but on exploring their internal dynamics and specific relations to modes of production. Nonetheless, precedents for Merrill's line of argument can be found in Marx, who distinguished a social system based on households (which he called the Germanic type) from the Asiatic system and the ancient system, based on the city. According to Marx, the household system was charactertized by each separate household's forming "an independent centre of production," with each separate household's being more or less loosely linked with others ("provided they belong to the same tribe")," 'for war, religion, the settlement of legal disputes, etc.' or for the use by the individually self-sufficient households—of communal pastures, hunting, territory, etc." For the foregoing citations, and for discussion of Marx's early use of this concept, see Marx (1964). The pitfalls of the "household mode of production" emerge clearly from the controversy surrounding the work of A. V. Chayanov (1966).

nuclear families (see Gonzalez, 1969).[2] Household offers one way of studying basic social units without becoming embroiled in the complexities of kin relations. And household frequently offers the seductive mirage of precision, for the element of co-residence suggests that households are simply objective categories, sub-units of a territory or state. Unfortunately, life resists pigeon-holes, and therefore so must scholars: Household members need not reside in their households, although to be called members they must, presumably, return occasionally, contribute income, or in some other way identify themselves with the unit. But problems of membership do not exhaust the complexities of the household as a unit of analysis for historians.

Historians cannot afford to postulate transhistorical households. For historians, the very nature of the household depends upon its relations to the larger systems in which it is embedded. That dominant political, social, and economic systems influence households does not mean that households do not influence the systems. Obviously they do. But political and legal institutions, the complexity, nature, and availability of markets, and the social relations of production, among other factors, shape the ways in which households develop. If we are willing to consider households as the primary mediating units between the individual and society, as genuinely pivotal institutions, we must nonetheless learn to describe scrupulously the specific character and activities of different households in interaction with different social systems. Households may, to take but a few examples, include more or less production, rely more or less heavily on kin relations for their self-definition, include more or fewer members, or be more or less permeated by the principles of commodity production and the wage relation. Households may, in short, incorporate more or less of the business of society within themselves. Households may vary from a single room (to which a single individual returns to

2. I am indebted, here and elsewhere, to personal correspondence with Sidney Mintz concerning the anthropological view of household.

sleep), to a self-sufficient family farm, to, conceivably, a big compound of nobility in some West African society.

Despite interest in households in the northern North American colonies and states, there has been less attention to the role of households as households in the development of the antebellum American slave society. The lively and occasionally acrimonious debates over the nature of that society have focused largely on aggregate characteristics. There have been, to be sure, numerous and sometimes excellent studies of individual plantations or farms. But, as a rule, southern historians have not explored slave society in particular, or antebellum southern society in general, from the perspective of the household. The existing studies of plantations and farms can, in some measure, be adapted to the study of the household, but they were not undertaken primarily to elucidate the role of the household as a unit. Rather, they have focused on such questions as the developmental possibilities of the slave economy, the profitability of slavery, the strength of the black family, the role of scientific farming in southern agriculture, the self-sufficiency or staple-dependency of southern farms, and, more generally, the capitalist or precapitalist character of slave society. The studies—drawing upon specific sets of plantation records to document in detail theses that have accompanied the general questions that have emerged from the debate over the nature of antebellum southern society—provide invaluable insights on and specific illustrations of the questions to which they respond. In so doing, they can demonstrate the ways in which analyses derived from aggregate data obscure the specific variations within slave society, but they cannot be expected to correct the general analyses simply through the accumulation of case studies.

There is some irony in the dearth of household studies for the antebellum South, for it is peculiarly appropriate to describe antebellum southern society precisely as a network of households and thereby to recast the debate more fruitfully. Scholars who interpret southern slave society as essentially capitalist, like those who interpret it as manifesting decisive precapitalist features, converge in their descriptions of plantations or farms. They differ in their interpretation of the social and economic characteristics of relations among households, in their assessment of the principles that informed household organization, and, especially, in their estimates of the permeability of household boundaries. They do not disagree over the capitalist character of the world market within which southern households were embedded; they do not disagree over the importance of chattel slavery as against free wage labor in the larger units of production; but they do disagree sharply over the implications of chattel slavery for the political economy, the political culture, the developmental possibilities, and the world-view of antebellum southern society.

At one extreme, scholars from Lewis C. Gray (1932) to Kenneth Stampp (1956) to Robert Fogel and Stanley Engerman (1974) have emphasized the compatibility of chattel slavery and capitalist development. This tendency in the debate emphasizes the planters' similarity to any other rational capitalist entrepreneurs. In a recent contribution, James Oakes (1982) has attempted to assimilate southern farmers to northern farmers in a single category of aggressive, middle-class men-on-the-make, but his impressionistic account suffers from internal contradictions that gravely weaken his general interpretation of southern political economy and detract from a specific discussion of households. Fogel and Engerman (1974), acutely sensitive to the tie between labor relations and political economy as a whole, drive the captialist interpretation to its logical conclusion and insist upon the similarities between slave labor and capitalist wage labor. The opposing school, which insists upon the special character of slave labor and its implications for the general political economy of the society, consists primarily of Marxists such as Eugene D. Genovese (1965; 1975), Harold D. Woodman (1968; 1972), and, most recently, Mark V. Tushnet (1981), but its general conclusions are compatible with some of the views of such conservatives as M. E. Bradford (1979), despite the very different formulations. Others, such as Ulrich B. Phillips (1929; 1969), remain ambiguous on the main theoretical point.

Gavin Wright, who has made decisive contributions to the discussion of political economy and who emphasizes the duality of the southern economy, curiously avoids the interpretation that would seem logically to flow from his own work, namely that decisive political and ideological differences evolved from slaveholding or non-slave-holding (1978). All adherents of the various general interpretations of slave society have turned to the plantation to illustrate and buttress their interpretations, but none have systematically examined plantations or farms as households that pooled incomes.

Scholars primarily interested in small slaveholders and yeomen have naturally emphasized the farm rather than the plantation as the characteristic southern agricultural unit (Owsley, 1949; Clark, 1942; Weaver, 1945). Recognition of the ubiquity of small and medium-sized farms throughout the antebellum South has tempted some (most recently, James Oakes) to argue that the real life of southern society consisted in the life of its plain folk (1982). The demographic predominance of the yeomanry and small planters is not in doubt, but the most fruitful way to interpret their experience is. Steven Howard Hahn has recently developed Wright's view of the dual economy within an explicitly Marxist context and demonstrated that the character of the Georgia yeomanry differed dramatically from that of their northern farmer counterparts, despite superficial similarities (1979). Although Hahn does not rely explicity on the household as a unit of analysis, his work suggests the rich potential of the household as a prism through which to view not merely the discrete units that constituted southern society, but the nature and force of the ties that bound those units to each other.

Since households exist in such a wide variety of societies, and since until the full development of industrial capitalism so much production occurred within households, it is essential to locate households with respect to the predominant characteristics of the societies to which they belonged. The households of the antebellum South, like those of the North, were initially spawned by merchant capital. The divergence in the historical development of northern and southern households still requires a full explantion, but by the late eighteenth century, the two societies were committed to fundamentally different systems of property and labor relations. Southern households persisted and multiplied as distinct social formations within merchant capital; northern households persisted and multiplied as units of petty commodity production, also within the tentacles of merchant capital; but the predominance of free labor in the North provided the foundations for an industrial capitalism that would, in time, subsume merchant capital to itself, whereas the predominance of slave labor in the South committed southern society to persisting dependence upon merchant capital. Over time, the two societies would diverge markedly with respect to the amount of production of —not merely subsistence, which is a special and variable case—but the social surplus that occurred within the household without. If one considers households as units that pool income, with careful attention to the sources and kinds of income, the distinction between the two networks of households acquires a new significance.

Even a preliminary investigation of the southern households must suffer from the constraints imposed by the dearth of appropriate data in the secondary literature, but it can reconstruct general models of southern households of various types. I shall consider only agricultural households, for the principal wealth of the region overwhelmingly derived from agriculture throughout the antebellum period. I shall also follow the conventional classification of large planters as those holding 10-15 slaves, and yeoman slaveholders as those holding 10 slaves or fewer.

The household constitutes an indispensible unit of analysis for southern society, but the nature, composition, and boundaries of the household cannot be assumed a priori. To study southern society as a network of households also requires that the investigation yield, if not a definition, at least a working model of the household and its dynamics. In some measure, southern households challenge neat categorization. Donald Bender has suggested that any analysis of households recognize three theoretically distinct, if practically overlapping, categories of kin (consanguineal and affinal relations), propinquity (co-residence), and domestic functions (1967). His proposal appropriately calls attention to the fallacies of reducing households to family or co-residence, even if family or co-residence may in any specific situation constitute important sources of household membership and self-representation. The caution is especially important for southern plantation society in which master and slave households interlocked in a complex web of interdependency.

A working definition of households as units that pool income implicitly respects Bender's objection to equating them arbitrarily with families or co-residence, but it does not necessarily solve all problems. As a hypothesis, income-pooling emphasizes the material bases of any household. But, for the historian, it must take account of the changes in forms of income and the changing social relations that generate income. It also requires precise reference to how the boundaries of the household should be drawn and how criteria for household membership should be established. For, unmodified, income-pooling implicitly distracts attention from the relations of dependency and power between genders, generations, and possible classes with respect to the income of the unit. Households, however we define their boundaries, presumably pool income in the interests of consumption, reproduction, or possibly production. In each of these activities, members of the household differ in their contributions to and control over the common fund. Differential contributions and rewards constitute a significant problem and a possible source of latent or manifest conflict in all households. But the nature and substance of those conflicts also differ according to the relations between specific households and the dominant mode of production.

Harriet Friedmann (1980) has provocatively argued that peasant households do not embody the principles that characterize the captialist markets in which they sell their products. She sharply differentiates peasant households from households engaged in petty commodity production, for, in her view, petty commodity producers can move to full "commoditisation" by a simple intensification of the relations and process in which they are engaged, whereas peasant households must undergo a thorough transformation in order to be assimilated fully to capitalist social formations. To embody the logic of the capitalist wage relation, peasant households must, in her word, "decompose" before they can reconstitute themselves as units fully integrated into the logic of the capitalist mode of production Friedmann does not discuss the antebellum southern household *per se*, but she suggestively distinguishes between the hacienda and postbellum southern share-cropping units as respectively precapitalist and capitalist social formations. In her judgment, the hacienda, in its various forms, remains logically tied to its roots in the *encomienda* ("which conferred the right to the labour of specific indigenous peoples") and the *mercedes de tierras* ("which granted lands to colonists for military service"). It thus remains closely bound to the manorial forms that predominated in Medieval Europe. Share-cropping, by contrast, rests upon contractual relations, even though it may coexist with independent household production. As Eugene D. Genovese and I have argued elsewhere, the specific social formations of antebellum southern plantations cannot be assimilated directly to the hacienda—in part because of their discrete origins—but did rest upon unfree labor relations that distinguished them sharply from fully capitalist agricultural units (Fox-Genovese, 1975; Fox-Genovese & Genovese, 1983). Thus, with respect to antebellum southern households, Friedmann's argument can be assimilated to the view that southern slave society developed as an offshoot of merchant capital and did not shed its hybrid character until the Civil War.

The antebellum South, as a whole, remained dependent on a capitalist world market, the principles of which were not embodied in its dominant labor system. Unlike northern farms, which can most usefully be understood as agricultural versions of petty commodity production, southern plantations depended on slavery that was radically distinct from the capitalist wage relation. As M. I. Finley has insisted, human societies have manifested a range of partially unfree labor systems that form a continuum with respect to degrees and forms of unfreedom, but slavery constitutes a radical break with them all (1980). In the antebellum South, slavery's domination of the economy shaped even the development of non-slaveholding farms; the arguments are well known. But if the emphasis on merchant capital as the constituting force of southern households helps to delineate the specific structure of southern political economy, the emphasis on southern households as the embodiment of one tendency within merchant capital reveals the specific nature of southern society as a distinct social formation.

The plantation South would never have existed, much less expanded, had it not been for the capitalist world market. From its origins in the tobacco economy of the Chesapeake in the seventeenth century until the development of the cotton belt of the Deep South in the nineteenth, the plantation system grew apace with the development of and demand for staple crops exchanged in the world market. The process of change over time is critical. Expansion of the South entailed the extension of slaveholding into the newly opened territories. Yet some of the older areas, while remaining slaveholding, practically withdrew from the market in favor of greater self-sufficiency. The profitability of slavery is not at issue. Although individual planters might withstand downturns in the market by virtue of credit extended by merchants or kin, the system as a whole required profits to survive and expand. At issue remains the nature of the social formation and the characteristic productive relations that produced the staple. The most telling characteristic of southern political economy may well be that the decisive social relations of production were contained within the household rather than outside it, for the household constituted the dominant unit of production throughout the antebellum South. Although not all southern households were plantations or even farms; although not all southern households included slaves; and although not all slaveholding southern households followed the same economic strategies, the slave system and household reinforced each other in such a way as to discourage capitalist development.

The debate over the character of the southern economy and its potential for growth has generated a massive investigation of the aggregate indicators of southern economic performance. Although the aggregate statistics permit a variety of interpretations, ultimately the most telling of them point to the role of world demand in establishing the level of profits, the low rate of urbanization and industrialization, the high level of regional self-sufficiency in conjunction with the low level of development of internal markets, the disinclination of planters to invest in industry despite its potentially high profits, and, especially, the underdeveloped market in free labor power.[3] Recently, work on the law (such as Tushnet, 1980) has demonstrated the ways in which the legal implications of the master-slave relation permeated the legal institutions of the whole region. And, from the perspective of gender relations, the institution of chattel slavery decisively shaped the experience and possibilities of southern women. It remains beyond dispute that the defense of slavery penetrated every element of southern ideology, reshaping national political, economic, and religious discourses into characteristically southern patterns.[4]

It has become a commonplace that households—or families—reproduce the dominant social relations and ideologies of the social formations to which they belong. But, aside from its heuristic, commensensical value, the proposition leaves much to be desired. Like any tautology, it fails to account for change and, for our purposes more important, it fails to

3. Wright (1978) and Genovese (1965) concur on the general picture, especially the dependence on the world market, despite persisting disagreements about the fundamental dynamics of the system. Even Fogel and Engerman agree on many of the general features although their interpretation of the dynamics, especially the internal dynamism of the system, diverges sharply from that of others (1974). Fred Bateman and Thomas Weiss argue that slaveholders chose not to invest in industry although the returns would have been higher than the returns from farming (1981); see also Elizabeth Fox-Genovese and Eugene D. Genovese (1983: Chs. 5, 6).

4. See, among many, Frances Anne Kemble (1975), Clement Eaton (1964), Donald G. Mathews (1977), Anne C. Loveland (1980), Wiliam Freehling (1965), Allen Kaufman (1982), and Drew Gilpin Faust (1981).

account for the wide variation in the material foundations of households and thus for the wide variation in the possibilities for households to ensure the compliance of their members. In this perspective the specific nature of specific types of households to ensure the compliance of their members. In this perspective the specific nature of specific types of households as income-pooling units becomes decisive, especially if one pays close attention to the sources of income as structural relations between the household and the larger economy and society.

The separation of labor from the land and the emergence of capitalist ground rent in Great Britain—the emergence of a market in labor-power and in land—exercised a decisive influence on the establishment of southern households. The southern colonies of North America rapidly manifested a demand for labor that was met, especially during the mid-and late-seventeenth century, by the surplus labor generated by the internal transformation of the English economy (Menard, 1980). But the special problems in the supply of productive resources, with land abundant and labor scarce, governed the internal constitution of the southern households that would shape southern political economy as a whole. The migration of white landless labor initially provided a pool of dependent labor—indentured servants—for early southern settlers. But the easy availability of land encouraged such laborers, at the end of their term of service, to establish their own households based on the ownership and exploitation of land. The relation between indentured servants and their masters, as in the Chesapeake, may plausibly be interpreted as a special and qualified case of the wage relation; but with the conclusion of the terms of service, the laborers invariably sought to escape from the wage relation as a source of income. Their formation of households was closely tied to the settlement of land. The demographic characteristics of the first generations of settlers, at least through the middle of the seventeenth century, precluded rapid expansion—and even reproduction—of households, but the independent household remained the dominant model, despite the difficulties for many of ensuring its survival. But, with the consolidation of settlements and demographic adaptation, the opportunity for landownership seriously undermined the supply of wage labor. By the third quarter of the seventeenth century, the basic patterns of a slaveholding society had been established. The difficulty of securing a long-term, stable agricultural wage-labor force led successful planters to turn to the use of slaves. But the introduction of slavery did not modify the structure of the settlements as a network of households; it reinforced it. The world market simultaneoulsy strengthened the dependence of the colonies on the metropolis and widened the divergent social systems of the two.[5]

From the seventeenth century until the collapse of southern slave society, southern household formation followed a variety of patterns according to crop, region, and level of income. But throughout the period, southern society grew as a proliferation of households. Although in this respect southern expansion did not necessarily differ from northern expansion, the early introduction of slavery as the foundation for the cultivation of staple crops decisively influenced the character of the dominant form of southern households. In particular, it established distinct limitations to the penetration of market relations into the interstices of southern households.

Students of antebellum southern economy and society have regarded the degree of self-sufficiency as a principal indicator of the character of southern slave society. The debate remains confused with respect to both argument and evidence. In no instance should self-sufficiency be taken to mean autarchy. Carole Shammas (1982) has recently argued for a highly qualified interpretation of the putative self-sufficiency of northern farms. Preliminary evidence suggests that many southern households engaged in more household manufacture

5. These conclusions emerge from the work of the splendid group of historians of the Chesapeake in the seventeenth and early eighteenth centuries; see Land et al., (1977), and Tate and Ammerman (1977). See also Morgan (1975), Wood (1974), Mullin (1972), and Kulikoff's splendid manuscript (forthcoming). The decisive work on the development of the tobacco trade in the context of the Atlantic economy remains Price (1973).

and produced more of their own food-stuffs, especially pork, than did their northern counterparts; but the caution is well taken. With respect to the antebellum South, those who view it as essentially capitalist, like those who view it as essentially precapitalist, have defended and attacked the position that antebellum southern households were largely self-sufficient. Those who take the antebellum South to have been essentially capitalist and antebellum plantations to have been essentially self-sufficient apparently wish to demonstrate the rationality of the planters as entrepreneurs, the flexibility of slave labor, and the existence of economies of scale in southern agriculture. Those who take the antebellum South to have been essentially precapitalist and antebellum plantations to have been essentially dependent on food purchase, apparently wish to demonstrate the irrationality of the planters, the limitations imposed by the use of slave labor, and the dependency of the region as a whole.[6] In fact, the readily available evidence does not permit a clear determination of the issue. The most recent general study by Samuel Hilliard (1972) demonstrates that the South as a whole was more self-sufficient—that is, less deeply engaged in market exchange—than were the Northeast or the Old Northwest. Hilliard also demonstrates that discrete areas within the South, notably those with the highest concentration of large plantations and slaves and adjacent to large waterways and ports, were heavily engaged in market transactions for the basic food stuffs and other supplies. Since his work relies on aggregate statistics, it cannot answer questions about the behavior of specific households, which can only be determined through the study of individual records. But it does suggest an interesting paradox, namely that the behavior of the largest plantation households, which established the general character

6. In fact, there is no necessary relation between a particular scholar's position on the capitalist or precaptialist nature of North American slave society and on the self-sufficient or food-importing status of plantations. Both self-sufficiency and food importation would be compatible with the high level of southern profits or the underdevelopment of internal southern markets. But scholarship on both sides of the debate has paid insufficient attention to the centralization of aggregate demand in the hands of a few.

of the slave society, differed significantly from the behavior of the smaller households, which felt the constraints of slave society most acutely.

The specific form of the debate over self-sufficiency has partially obscured the most serious consequences of southern slavery for southern economic development. The preference of individual planters for household production or for purchase of food and basic goods may have had significant consequences for the economic success of the planter. A planter who speculated unwisely on the possible price of cotton only to face a collapse in cotton prices at the moment at which he had committed his household to heavy dependence upon the purchase of food could incur unhealthy indebtedness or even the forced sale of some of his slaves—in short, capital losses. But, however portentous these choices in individual cases, they had little effect on the general structure of southern households, or the large planters who purchased food and other consumer goods purchased in the aggregate. As a general rule, they depended for their purchased provisions on the same merchants or factors on whom they depended for sale of their cotton or the extension of credit (House, 1954; Woodman, 1968). Their demand reinforced the dependence of their region on merchant capital and external capitalist social formations; it did not contribute to the capitalist development of their region. Their behavior thus strengthened the tendency of smaller households to turn to cotton, or some other staple, as the first cash crop, and to turn to the purchase of slaves for any increase in their labor force (Gray, 1933; Genovese, 1965). The aggregate statistics for household production fall into roughly the same pattern as those for food purchase. The per capita value of household manufactures remained higher throughout much of the South than it did for the rest of the nation. The southern counties in which the per capita value of household manufactures was negligible are the same as those in which the value of purchased foodstuffs was highest. But this information only confirms that the regions surrounding New Orleans, Charleston, Mobile, and other ports constituted variants of the classic plantation economies that had been generated by merchant capital at least since the early colonization of the Azores (Tryon, 1917; Verlinden, 1970)

The debate over the self-sufficiency or market dependence of southern farms underscores the importance of southern households as a basic unit of analysis for southern society. Lewis C. Gray, in what remains the classic study of southern agriculture, actually proposed differentiating yeoman farmers from small planters according to their choice of diversification or staple cultivation (Gray, 1933: Vol. I). In fact, his distinction between those who diversified and those who cultivated the staple probably applies to all categories of southern households as defined by numbers of slaves. In this respect, it could be said that the proportion of land that any farmer gave to diversification and staple cultivation reflects a choice on the part of the farmer in any particular category of household, but not the determining characteristics of the household. Yet the location of the household, its access to transportation, and the suitability of its soil and climate for staple cultivation all influenced the choices made by farmers. Regions such as northern Virginia early tended toward the diversification and self-sufficiency that characterized the region by the late eighteenth century and the Tidewater by the early nineteenth century (Isaac, 1982). But even those regions most given over to general cultivation and in which the households most resembled units of petty commodity production remained tied to the slave system as a whole—in part because of political connections and in part because the path to economic growth lay through the acquisition of slave labor rather than through the kinds of capital intensivity normal in the process of industrial capitalist development.

The multiple ties that bound the yeomanry to the larger slave society have been outlined (Hahn, 1979; Fox-Genovese & Genovese, 1983), but the full history of the yeomanry still awaits adequate local studies. Understanding the nature of those households—their specific relations to the other households of their locality in particular and southern slave society as a whole—will be indispensible to an assessment of the household as a unit of analysis for southern political economy and social relations. Much of the expansion of southern society occurred through the proliferation of such households, which constituted the numerical preponderance throughout much of the South, especially the Upper South. But it is not fruitful to consider those households simply as discrete units; they must be related to the vicissitudes of the slave society as a whole. For various reasons, it is safe to assume provisionally that the nature of that society encouraged regionally specific forms of production and reproduction as well as a sharp distinction between the internal dynamics of the household and the capitalist world market; but this hypothesis ultimately depends upon our assessment of the character of southern slavery and of its dominance in the region as a whole. We can best grasp the distinct structure of southern households as a product and a manifestation of a specific social formation through a closer look at the households of middling and large planters, although planter households will also inescapably force a reconsideration of the nature of slave households.

The essential unit of income-pooling for slaves and masters was the plantation or farm. Co-residence and division of domestic functions normally defined the unit. There were exeptions in the case of very large planters who might own more than one plantation or who might divide a single plantation into quarters (see Dunn, 1977). But throughout much of the South, the empirically self-evident unit of the contiguous farm or plantation was coterminous with the boundaries of the household. For both Whites and Blacks, the planter provided the central link with the outside world, and the central authority within the plantation itself. Katherine Du Pre Lumpkin recalled: "Grandfather was a heavily burdened man. There can be no doubt it meant this to be a resident cotton planter, whose plantation was a community and business rolled into one" (1971). This household, like others, included not merely the big house, but "slave quarters, stables, and springhouse, and the work radiating out into the fields from this hub of activity" (Lumpkin, 1971: 44). Grandfather William Lumpkin figured as a large planter with his one thousand-odd acres and his fifty-odd slaves. But from the 1830's to the outbreak of the War Between the States, his life centered on his working household in Oglethorpe County, Georgia. His granddaughter retained a vivid picture of the complex life contained within the boundaries of that household.

The buildings referred to as "stables" housed horses and cattle when they were not in pasture; carriages and other conveyances; farm wagons and ox-carts; the harness and gear for all these vehicles; plows and farm implements; the smoke-house; the blacksmith's quarters; and carpenter shop; threshers; and all other equipment necessary to the independent functioning of a large and complex plantation. "As nearly as possible Grandfather made his plantation provide for all his needs. On a place of this size he had to do so if he were to have any net cash income" (Lumpkin, 1971). Accordingly, the plantation household grew and processed all basic foodstuffs, including corn and wheat, vegetables, pork for the slaves, and beef, lamb, mutton, pork, hams, bacon, chickens, turkey, and geese for the big house. Clothing the throng of people for which grandfather was responsible (he had five children by his first wife and sixteen by his second) required additional efforts on the part of the members of the household.

> To clothe the slaves, great bolts of goods must be hauled in from Athens or Augusta. The garments then had to be made for men, women, and children .... There was the mending also. Altogether the sewing could probably keep a few women busy practically all of every day (Lumpkin, 1971: 26).

With land cheap and slaves dear and getting dearer, the health and increase of the slave labor force constituted the primary challenge to the planter. The responsibilities of production and reproduction of and for the household intertwined in a complex web at the center of which stood the planter. His responsibilities were enormous and his ability to meet them sucessfully determined the life and safety of those dependent on him and his own standing in his community: The life of the household and its economic efficiency could not be separated. The planter would look on every natural and human-made feature of his property as a part of himself, as familiar to him as "the palm of his hand." He would expect to know every detail of every agricultural operation and every human problem within his household.

> Above all, he would know his slaves, each by name, and each for his good points and his foibles, most of them being inherited, or the children of those who had been handed down. He would expect constantly to guide and discipline and keep them contented by skillful handling. First and last, he would know that every plan, every decision, every quandry nagging his mind, save those of marketing his cotton and purchasing supplies from the outside, resolved itself into human problem, if it could be so called: the problem of managing his black dependents. He would know he was master in all things on his plantation, everything, nothing excepted, including the life of his slaves. With it he would know that his station was secure as a southern gentleman (Lumpkin, 1971: 22).

The Lumpkin plantation may be considered as something of an ideal type. The variations on this type were considerable. Depending upon region, date of settlement, access to markets, kinds of crops, and success of the planter, the size and character of plantation households would vary. But the variations did not amount to radical departures from the basic model. For large or small, new or old, plantations related to the market as units under the direction of a single individual: The principles of market relations governed the marketing of the surplus and some purchases for the unit as a whole; they did not penetrate the relations within the household. With the exception of the overseer, who frequently did not belong to the plantation household in the way that the slaves did, members of the plantation as a productive unit normally did not receive wages. In addition to the overseer, large planters might also employ a male or female tutor for the white children (Mathis, 1979; Fithian, 1957). In addition to a payment in cash, the tutor would receive board and lodging and would function as a member of the plantation household during his or her tenure. The planter might also pay a yearly contract to a physician upon whom he would call in the case of serious illness in the household. Finally, he might hire specialized slaves or even extra field hands, or occasional free labor, White or Black, but the principal income of the plantation derived from, and the principal expenses were met by, the sale of the staple crop, supplemented by household production of goods and services.

The life cycle of the plantation household began with the purchase or inheritance of the plantation itself. The formation of a plantation household required a considerable initial capital outlay. A young southerner might inherit a plantation with slaves; he might inherit or be ceded land, and his wife might bring a dowry or inheritance of slaves; he might marry an heiress with land and slaves; or he might accumulate some capital to invest in land and slaves. In some instances, he might even begin by renting a plantation or hiring slaves (Bleser, 1981; Mathis, 1979; Jordan, 1948). In the settled regions of the Upper South, the odds were great that, however the plantation was acquired, it would already be an operating unit, whereas in the Lower South, throughout the first half of the nineteenth century, planters actively participated in founding new plantations.

The careers of John Horry Dent and Hugh Davis of Alabama both illustrate this process (Mathis, 1979; Jordan, 1948). In particular, Mathis's study of Dent makes it possible to study the plantation as an income-pooling unit. Dent began his career with no land, but with his wife's inheritance of 45 slaves. The young couple moved from South Carolina to Alabama with their slaves. Dent bought land on credit and began planting. In the first year of planting, 1838, the crop yielded an income of only $800. By the next year, the income from cotton had risen to $2,000; by the year after that to $3,500. During these early years, Dent also had his slaves clearing land and building cabins for his family and themselves. The plantation produced most of the subsistence of its members, and Dent managed to hold plantation expenses down to $800 per year. This ratio between income and expense permitted him to retire his debt. By the 1840's, he was himself lending money to others. Between 1838 and 1860, he changed plantations three times, buying and selling on each occasion. By 1860, he had joined the less than 1% of southern planters who owned more than 100 slaves. Between 1850 and 1860, his income from cotton ranged between $4,500 and $9,000 per year and was significantly augmented by his income from loans. By the mid-1850's, after his second marriage, he was spending as much as $3,500 a year on plantation expenses.

Throughout his career, Dent's income was composed primarily of the income from the sale of cotton, but also of basic foodstuffs; significant income in kind from the household production of subsistence goods; occasional rents from the hiring-out of slaves and interest from loans; and occasional transfer payments, in particular his wife's inherited slaves and his own inheritance of seventeen slaves from his mother. All of the income was under his direct control, but he used it to provide for the survival and comfort of his entire household. His increased expenses in the mid-1850's reflect the tastes and demands of his second wife and concern for the education of his adolescent children, as well as his increased prosperity. Income-pooling on the Dent plantation was governed first by the needs of cotton and basic food production, and secondly by the prevailing gender and generational relations within the family.

Both of Dent's wives clearly contributed significantly to plantation management, although the precise nature of their activities remains unclear. We know considerably more about their expenditures. Dent's second wife in particular had strong views on consumption. She regularly engaged in shopping in the neighboring town, Eufaula. She also insisted on purchasing a cook stove in the North. The records of these expenditures, like those on the education of the children, as well as surviving journals and correspondence reveal Dent to have been a devoted family man who saw "home" as the center of his existence (Mathis, 1979). But he apparently never doubted his absolute right to direct the income-pooling of the Black and White members of his household, and he invariably subordinated their individual needs and desires to the success of the household as a viable unit of production and reproduction.

Hugh Davis of Alabama began his planting career in 1848 with sixteen slaves. The son and grandson of planters, he had begun his adult life as a lawyer. While practicing law, he had begun to acquire slaves—some through purchase, some as gifts from his father, some from his wife's relatives, and some in lieu of fees. Even before he began planting, he had hired out some of his slaves as a source of income. After he started his own plantation, he continued to hire out some of his slaves. He also continued to purchase slaves so that by 1853, he owned 31 slaves and, at his death in 1862, he owned 78. Although he systematically attempted to maintain an equal balance between male and female slaves, he did not always buy slaves who were married to each other. He did, on occasion, make a special effort to acquire a spouse for one of the slaves he already owned. His biographer maintains that he did favor strengthening slave families when possible. Yet, throughout his planting career, only sixteen slaves were born on his plantation; the increase in his slave force derived overwhelmingly from purchase. The income from his staple crop cultivation largely accounted for his ability to increase the size of his household. He also drew income from his continuing practice of hiring out slaves (Jordan, 1948).

In a general way, the sources and distribution of Davis's income much resemble those of Dent's, although Dent lent less money and received less income in interest. Throughout the South, planters drew income from the cultivation of staple crops and distributed it among the White and Black members of their households. It would be possible to explore the variations on this pattern in detail for different regions at different times, but the variations in detail would not significantly alter the general model of the southern plantation household. The principal lesson of adopting the household as a unit of analysis for antebellum southern society is precisely to underscore the significance of the household as a unit of production, reproduction, co-residence, domestic division of labor, and income-pooling.[7]

The boundaries of the southern household were normally coterminous with the boundaries of a single plantation or

7. The yeoman households of the Up Country differed from Low County and Black Belt plantations in many respects, notably in number of slaves and size of cash crops. But the structure of these households with respect to boundaries between

farm, but the basic principle of those boundaries was the planting activity of the single adult, white, male planter. Thus, it is appropriate to consider the multiple quarters or dwellings of a single planter as part of a single household. Whether a planter maintained a summer residence or a town house, or presided over the farming of several quarters, the income from the component units of his household was centralized in his hands and could easily be transferred from one unit to another. It was also possible for a woman, as a daughter or widow, to inherit a plantation, and even to run it herself. But normally, regular, sustained operation of a plantation household was taken to require the presence of a family that included both an adult man and an adult woman. The principal exception to this rule of the nuclear family as the core of white membership in the plantation household occurred when an older white widow or widower operated a plantation in conjunction with one of her or his adult children and perhaps the child's own legitimate family of procreation.[8] Plantations also could include individual relatives, especially single females, without plantations of their own.

For white families, the boundaries of the plantation household circumscribed basic kin relations, co-residence, and domestic functions. The availability of land made it possible, and even encouraged each generation, to re-form its own plantation household. The dependent members of the family resided on the plantation and shared domestic functions. The income for the unit as a whole was centralized in the hands of the planter, who directed its distribution and organized the productive relations that produced it in the first place.

---

household and market closely resembled each other. It will require further study to understand fully the extent to which yeoman farms might resemble unit of petty commodity production as did northern farms, but it seems likely that the general political economy and social relations of the antebellum South led to recognizable differences between the experience of southern yeomen and their northern counterparts. The work of Steven Hahn suggests that slavery and the ethos of a slave society had a significant influence ven on households that did not own slaves (1979).

8. A man like John Henry Hammond could try to keep his grown sons within his own household and to oversee their direction of one of his plantations. His attempt did not meet with great success (Bleser, 1981).

Members of the planter's family contributed in a variety of ways to the management of the slave force that produced the basic source of income but rarely, if ever, contributed monetary income derived from activities external to the plantation. The transfer payments, normally inheritances of slaves, contributed by wives and other kin themselves derived from other plantations. As in the case of Hugh Davis, a potential planter might earn the initial income to start planting but, once established as a planter, he would devote his principal attention to the management of his plantation, and derive his principal income from it.

Plantations as households or as domestic formations emerge as remarkably self-contained units. Their relations with the larger economy were centralized in the hands of the owner. The relations of the master to the market reflected the principles of capitalism that informed the market, but the relations of the master to his household reflected the principles of the slave labor that dominated the production of the staple crop and the reproduction of the labor force. Other kinds of households have, historically, embodied this unusually sharp differentiation between the internal life of the household and the external economy. In many instances, households engaged in petty commodity production resembled plantations in the sharpness of the boundaries between household and market. But the internal principles of households engaged in petty commodity production differ significantly from those of the slave plantation. Nothing better reveals the extent and nature of this difference than the problematic household membership of the slaves themselves.

Recent debates over the nature and strength of the slave community have been largely cast with specific reference to the family rather than the household, in accordance with twentieth-century preoccupations with the vitality or pathology of the family as a bedrock of social order and labor discipline. Yet the choice of family as the appropriate prism through which to assess the effects of slavery on Afro-Americans has prejudiced the formulation of the issues from the start. The issue is not so much whether enslaved men and women loved each other and their offspring and remained as loyal to each other as extraordinary circumstances permitted—whether an impressive family life arose in the quarters—but whether they chose, or circumstances encouraged them to do so exclusively or even predominantly, through the forms propounded by whites for themselves.

The useful but frequently ill-formulated debates suggest how much can be clarified by adopting household rather than family as the appropriate unit of analysis. Considering slave experience from the perspective of households does not necessarily yield intrinsically more optimistic or pessimistic conclusions than does considering that experience with primary reference to the family. But it assuredly calls attention to the specific forms of oppression implied by enslavement. And, as a by-product, it suggests both the extraordinary accomplishments represented by the emergence of a distinct Afro-American culture and some possible explanations for the importance of non-household based ties such as extended kin and religious networks in the articulation and transmission of that culture.

The definition of households as income-pooling units in particular—as the use of households as a unit of analysis in general—underscores the interdependence of slave and master households. Whether from the perspective of income or from that of power—understood as the minimal ability to make the important decisions that affect one's life—slaves belonged to the households of their masters. Such truncated households as slaves managed to form were formed largely at the pleasure or with the sufferance of the master. They had no independent economic bases worthy of the name, and they could not withstand the exercise of the master's will or the fluctuations of the economic fortunes of his household. This estimate of the respective abilities of masters and slaves to form viable households does not imply an acceptance of the Elkins thesis or its variants (Elkins, 1959). Rather, it compels attention to the economic conditions of slave life and the development of Afro-American culture in what, after all, was essentially a labor system.

Slaves resisted the implications of those conditions in innumerable ways and adjusted to them in ways that reflected not passive acquiescence, but active struggles to shape their own lives as much as the conditions permitted. To the extent that the conditions were established by the attitudes of individual masters as well as dominant legal forms and prevailing economic exigencies, they varied among plantations and farms of different size (Genovese, 1975). For example, the literary evidence suggests that slaves of small planters who held less than ten slaves would be directly assimilated to the patterns of domestic labor of the white family, much in the manner of indentured servants. Even with the small farms, however, the lines are hard to draw, for an overseer could be employed for as few as five to seven slaves. But it was not uncommon in these small households for the male slave to work alongside the master and his sons at a variety of tasks, and for a female slave to work alongside the mistress and her daughters in the house, or alongside the mistress or the master in the fields. This pattern could yield either especially harsh or especially pleasant working conditions in accordance with the personality of the master and his family and the character of the particular slaves (Drake, 1948). A small slaveholder might own several slaves, all of whom belonged to a single family, and he might provide them with a cabin. On this basis of kin and co-residence, the slaves might also share domestic functions, establish their own gender and generational division of labor, and pool their minimal bits of income. But the independent character of such a household, even under the most favorable circumstances, remained narrowly circumscribed. Food, clothing, and other goods the slaves received normally were apportioned as shares of the stock of the master's own family, although the quality and variety of food and clothing might be somewhat or considerably lower than that allotted to whites. But slaves on such small farms also might not receive independent housing, but instead sleep as they could in the kitchen or other outbuildings. And slaves on most farms probably did not live with any of their own kin (Kulikoff, 1977).

Larger plantations were much more likely to provide more space for an independent slave community and thus for the formation of facsimiles of slave households. Planters who owned ten or more slaves, especially those who owned fifty or more, would invariably provide independent living units for their slaves. Larger plantations increased the likelihood that slaves would have husband, wife, or other family members on the same plantations. Larger plantations could also permit greater independence for slaves in the preparation of food, the supplementing of diet, and even the pursuit of extra "income". But recent studies of individual plantations in different parts of the South, during different decades of the nineteenth century, present a less than rosy picture of the possibilities for independent slave household formation (Dunn, 1977; Faust, 1980; Jordan, 1948; Mathis, 1979).

As the debate over the capitalist or precapitalist character of southern slave society testifies, there remain divergent interpretations of the available evidence. In this respect, there is also likely to be difference of opinion about the correct interpretation of southern households, especially the problematical status of slave households. But it is striking that similar pictures of the large plantation emerge from the writings of those who differ sharply over the interpretation of the nature of southern slavery. Fogel and Engerman (1974), for example, do not pose the question of the slave household. They do insist upon the integrity of the slave family and its Victorian mores, just as they celebarate the independent accomplishments of the slave community. But when they turn to describing the daily workings of the large plantation they emphasize, intentionally or not, the slaveholder's direction of a complex inter-related household. They supplement their picture of the master's leadership with emphasis upon slave cabins, supplemental activities to generate extra food, and strong family ties among slaves. But they never assess the nature of the slave household, much less its possible changing status and composition over time within a specific plantation. And their general description presents the master rather than the slaves as determining the allocation of income.

How far do we wish to stretch the evidence? Even Fogel and Engerman, with their strong views upon the capitalist nature of the system, do not describe the sustenance of the slave as a wage. Three can be no doubt that the slave's sustenance could be described as income in the most general sense, but that description contributes little to an analysis that seeks to expose the specific character of slavery as a system of labor relations. The labor of the slaves generated income for the master, not for the slaves. In particular instances, individual slaves might generate bits of income for themselves through their "rights" to retain a portion of their hire or through the sale of commodities that they had cultivated or produced on their own time. But, even in most of these cases, the hire of slaves, certainly of rural slaves, was negotiated by masters, and their commodities were sold to masters who discouragead independent marketing or peddling by slaves. In short, in the vast majority of cases, masters mediated the slaves' income-yielding labor.

When we consider the various categories of income—wages, household susbsistence activities, marketing, rent, and transfer payments—it becomes clear that slaves rarely, if ever, determined their own relation to income, and, as a rule, assuredly did not do so as members of households. All the recent studies of individual plantations suggest that masters actively sought the maximum control of their slaves' lives. And, although masters might emerge less than victorious from struggles with individual slaves or with their slave force as a whole, they were reasonably successful in their attempts to forestall the formation of independent slave households. Such households did exist—although a determination of their character and frequency would require fresh study—but they existed on the sufferance of the master, even when, as Gutman (1976) so forcefully argues, they did not conform to white models.

The customary distribution of food and clothing, which constituted the essential elements of slave sustenance, reveals much about the relation between slave "income" and slave "households". Most masters, as Drew Faust's fine study of John Henry Hammond illustrates anew, sought to highlight their own roles as providers through ceremonious distribution of rations (Faust, 1982). Planters used the occasion of food distribution to remind their slaves of the masters' roles as providers for their people. Scholars have called attention to this behavior as an important indication of the masters' cultivation of paternalistic, or even patriarchal, relations with their slaves. While the importance of the symbolic nature of this weekly ceremony is not in doubt, it is well not to neglect its practical implications. The rations were often allocated to individuals, although they could also be allocated to household groups whose existence the master might recognize. Following allocation, the rations could be pooled and supplemented within households, or cooked communally for larger units. Probably both masters and slaves contributed to the decisions about the units in which food would be prepared and eaten. Masters like John Horry Dent might also attempt to control the rhythm of their slaves' consumption. Dent, like many others, shifted the day of food distribution from Saturday until Monday in order to prevent his slaves from feasting over the weekend and running short of rations by the end of the week (Mathis, 1979).

Just as masters controlled the distribution of slave rations, so did they allocate living space to slaves. On a large, well-established plantation, slaves might share cabins on the basis of family membership. But, under frontier conditions, they might temporarily be housed with another family or simply assigned to a cabin as part of a large random group. The fragmentary evidence suggests that cabin assignments could change frequently according to changing determinations of the master or changing relations among the slaves. Masters could differ significantly in the importance they attached to stable relations ("marriages") among slave men and women. Even those masters who apparently valued such stable relations often destroyed them through the sale of one or both partners. Typically, masters sought, like Hugh Davis, to maintain equal numbers of men and women among their slaves, even when the men and women were not married (Jordan, 1948). But Davis also occasionally made special efforts to purchase or hire spouses or other family members for his slaves. Evidence from individual plantations also suggests that there was a higher incidence of promiscuity, polygamy, and matrilfocality than the currently popular image of the Black family would lead us to believe. In fact, the slight opportunity for slaves to form households on the basis on income-pooling probably encouraged "promiscuity", which, in turn contributed to the Malthusian childbearing of slaves. The master's control over household formation thus, intentionally or not, reinforced the master's determination to have his female slaves bear the maximum number of children. Since there is no special reason to believe that Black slaves should have chosen to form households according to White models or to observe White sexual norms, the varieties of slave sexual behavior and household forms does not prove anything about the health or pathology of the life of the slave community. But the variety and instability of forms does suggest that slaves enjoyed only minimal control over the formation and duration of their own households.[9]

Slave households cannot profitably be studied without reference to the condition of chattel slavery. Slaves—even more than serfs, peasants, or proletarians—lacked that margin of autonomy or choice that would permit them to constitute anything but fragmentary or truncated households. If income-pooling was problematical among slaves who lived on the same plantations, it was next to impossible for slaves who lived on different plantations. Studying the behavior of the members of

9. Despite Gutman's substantial contribution (1976), we are still far from understanding enough about the conditions under which the family life of slaves unfolded or the balance among African survivals, Afro-American adaptations, and White norms in the development of the slaves' attitudes towards marriage and family. The evidence of forcible separation of families is mounting and will be reinforced by Allan Kulikoff's study on migration (forthcoming), the preliminary findings of which indicate that, at the very least, migrating planters wrenched children of seven to seventeen years from their families of origin. Specific attention is finally being devoted to the experience to Black women under slavery, but has yet to yield clear and uncontested results. Deborah G. White (1979) presses the case for African survivals beyond plausibility. White's view that female slaves were more "liberated" under slavery than were contemporaneous White women simply fails to take adequate account of the brutalization of slavery on men as well as women and the attendant constraints on relations between them; but scholars will have to come to terms with White's insistence on the importance of the divergence between African and White American patterns. The recent overview by Jacqueline Jones (1982) does not fill the gap. For a suggestive discussion of marital patterns in West Africa, see Paulme (1971), especially the introduction. For a Caribbean comparison, see Clarke (1957). For a view of rural ex-slave women immediately following emancipation, see Frankel (1982).

the slave community as an indication of the specific preference of and bonds between slaves retains inestimable value. Our understanding of slavery and of the Black experience has advanced far through careful studies of the struggles between slaves and their master and through full appreciation of the heroic, if not always openly rebellious, determination of slaves to shape their own lives, relations, and culture (Aptheker, 1943; Genovese, 1975; 1979; Harding, 1981; Levine, 1977). But, adopting the household as a unit of analysis for the life of North American slaves sharply underscores the constraints under which that life developed and therefore helps measure the long odds the slaves always faced.

It is more appropriate to regard slaves as members of the household of their master, defined as the plantation or farm, than to regard them primarily as members of distinct slave households. Themselves defined as property, slaves could not legally own property. Although they could occasionally shape the composition of the sub-households to which they belonged, they had no right to do so. Only at the margin could they affect the nature of the income they received, or even its disposition. It is possible to consider the basic support allocated to slaves as the maintenance of working capital from the perspective of the masters, rather than as wages from the perspective of the slaves. Neither description is entirely satisfactory.

Slaves normally received all of their basic support in kind: their rations, their clothing, their lodging. Frequently, the slaves contributed to the production of these goods through their own subsistence activities: Many farms and plantations produced their own basic food supply; most were likely to buy shoes and clothing, although many bought cloth and made clothing from it, and some even produced cloth; slave cabins were constructed by slaves, normally from logs cleared from plantation land. But all of the goods belonged to the master and, to the extent that the slaves participated in their production, they did so under the direction of the master. The master would also require the slaves to clean their cabins thoroughly one to four times a year. The cleaning, and sometimes whitewashing and resetting or reliming of floors, would be undertaken by all members of the plantation household on the same day. The master also provided the slaves with health care. With professional medical care inspiring something less than total confidence, it is no wonder that frequently the planter, his wife, a slave mid-wife, or a slave healer would supply additional medical assistance.

Slaves could contest their master's control in innumerable ways, and most masters, even the most authoritarian, learned to be somewhat flexible in their management of their "troublesome property". A wise master might well tolerate a slave's malingering in the infirmary for a few days, might fail to punish a chronic, temporary runaway severely, and might tolerate a considerable amount of pilfering (Genovese, 1975; Faust, 1980). Never the total institution that some have claimed it to be, southern slavery always permitted some flexibility on the margin. On some plantations, slaves might well cultivate their own garden plots to supplement their diets, or even raise a few eggs for sale. Slave men often hunted small game to add a variety to the basic rations. These additional forms of income, like the pork stolen from the master, would be shared with other members of the slave community, especially the members of one's family or household. But, to the extent that the slave—and his or her time—belonged to the master, these forms can best be understood as redistributions of the income of the plantation household as a whole.

All slaves contributed to the income of the plantation through their labor, although the extent of their contributions varied over the life cycle of the individual. Slave children under ten performed little or no labor, although they might be set to an occasional odd job. Slightly older children participated in trash gangs, watched smaller children, or performed small tasks. The labor of older slaves much resembled that of children. Adult slaves, from fifteen to fifty or a bit more, provided the basic labor for the plantation and normally ensured the reproduction or extension of the slave population. The records suggest that there were few immutable rules of task allocation according to gender. Women worked in the fields, including the plow gangs, which historians once thought a male preserve. Women frequently served as plantation cooks, although on any specific plantation a man might be assigned that responsibility. House slaves in general were more likely to be women, but men also served in the house. In peak seasons, the maximum number of slaves were set to work in the fields. In slack seasons, slaves participated in a variety of household tasks, from clearing fields, to cleaning cabins, to repairing fences and equipment. But most masters—and perhaps some slaves—retained a preference for gender-specific allocation of tasks when conditions permitted. The most dramatic example of this preference was the general tendency to reserve artisanal crafts for males.

The slaves who performed highly specialized crafts and trades were especially valued. Planters set great store by a good cook. Slave carpenters and blacksmiths frequently received special consideration. There was normally some relation between the ability to perform highly specialized labor and rewards for that labor. Cooks, blacksmiths, and carpenters were in good positions to supplement their basic ration with special perquisites. A carpenter or blacksmith might be hired out on a regular basis, might retain a share of his hire, and might enjoy greater freedom of movement. A cook would have access to better food than the normal slave allotment and would be able to share some of it with members of her family or sub-household. But the more specialized slaves, especially cooks, nurses, or house servants, might also be more closely identified with the white family and household. Some of the more intimate house slaves would frequently sleep in the big house, stretched outside the door of the bedroom—or within it—in case something was needed during the night.

For specialized slaves, as for ordinary slaves, the basic component of "income" consisted in the subsistence provided by the master. The level of that basic income depended upon the success of the plantation as a whole. If it was unlikely to fall to deprivation levels—a master would be obliged to sell some slaves rather than to endanger the minimal well-being of the rest—it could rise with a planter's growing prosperity (Mathis, 1979). A successful planter might well increase the level of rations of food and clothing as well as build additional cabins. Although some slaves were able to increase this basic "income" through special talents, supplementary activities, or theft, the basic standard of living remained reasonably constant within the plantation.

Because of its special character as a domestic formation within a capitalist world market, southern slavery had special characteristics. It was not a wage relation, a customary lord-peasant relation, or a landlord-tenant relation. Some are apt to consider the support of the slaves as the maintenance of the master's working capital. This interpretation woefully ignores the complexity of the master-slave relation in practice, but its distortions call attention to the ways in which slaves were indeed primarily members of the farm or plantation household. Slaves did constitute sub-households, but their composition, like the income on which their members survived, remained decisively subject to the control of the master. Whatever the importance of those sub-households in the daily lives of slaves, they did not provide stable units of production or reproduction: They were not essential units of income-pooling, and they did not anchor the development of Afro-American culture.

The special hybrid character of the internal and external relations of the southern plantation household had distinct consequences for the character, culture, and politics of the southern slaveholding class as for the South as a whole, but that is another story. Adopting the household as a basic unit of historical analysis assuredly sharpens our understanding of the life of the White southern community; calls attention to the special context of the lives and culture of southern women; demonstrates the unusually centralized character of the income of southern plantations; and calls attention to the special character of southern society as primarily a network of households rather than cities or capitalist enterprises. It does not fundamentally revise the Marxist analysis of the antebellum South, but it casts a fresh perspective on familar questions.

With respect to the Black slave members of southern households in particular, and the slave community in general, adopting the household as basic unit of historical analysis may have rather more dramatic implications for familiar debates. For exploring the nature of slave household membership unequivocally demonstrates how misguided it has been to attempt to understand the strength and vitality of the slave community as a function of slave family life. The power of the master as the director of income-pooling made nuclear slave families—the middle-class White model of the healthy family—hostage to the master's whim and economic needs. There is no need to rehearse the formidable resistance of slaves to a system whose logic of would reduce them to things; but it is essential to recognize that the power of the master over the household in which slaves worked, lived, and reproduced influenced the specific form and content of slave resistance. The fragility of nuclear family relations resulted in no small measure from the conditions of slaves' membership in larger plantation households. The kin, co-residence, and domestic function components of household life were never entirely within the slaves' control. Under these conditions, the family life of slaves lacked the material foundations of household membership. The role of the master in assigning slave membership in sub-households and preventing a presumptive tie between family and sub-household membership meant that such sub-household membership, like nuclear family membership, could not provide slaves with reliable bases of resistance. Under these conditions, extended kin, fictive kin, and religious affiliation provided far more flexible and reliable sources of slave identity and resistance. Scholars, rather than continuing to exaggerate stable slave nuclear families as if the dignity of the Black experience in slavery depended upon it, should accept the lesson of the plantation as household. They should, that is, seek the vital sources of Afro-American culture in the ties and institutions that could provide the maximum support for individuals who could rely neither on independent household nor on family membership for constant identification.

References

Aptheker, Herbert (1943). *American Negro Slave Revolts.* New York: Columbia Univ. Press.

Bateman, Fred & Weiss, Thomas (1981). *A Deplorable Scarcity: the Failure of Industrialization in the Slave Economy.* Chapel Hill: Univ. of North Carolina Press.

Bender, Donald R. (1967). "A Refinement of the Concept of Household: Families, Co-residence, and Domestic Functions," American Anthropologist, LXIX, 5, Oct., 493-504.

Bleser, Carol, ed. (1981). *The Hammonds of Redcliffe.* New York: Oxford Univ. Press.

Bradford, M. E. (1979). *A Better Guide Than Reason: Studies in the American Revolution.* La Salle, IL: Sherwood Sugden & Company.

Bradford, M. E. (1982). *A Worthy Company. Brief Lives of the Framers of the United States Constitution.* Marlborough, NH: Plymouth Rock Foundation.

Chayanov, A. V. (1966). *The Theory of Peasant Economy.* Homewood, IL: Dorsey.

Clark, Blanche (1942). *The Tennessee Yeomen, 1840-1860.* Nashville: Vanderbilt Univ. Press.

Clark, Christopher (1979). "The Household Economy, Market Exchange and the Rise of Capitalism in the Connecticut Valley, 1800-1860," *Journal of Social History*, XIII, 2, Win., 169-90.

Clarke, Edith (1957). *My Mother Who Fathered Me: A Study of the Family in Three Selected Communities in Jamaica.* London: Allen & Unwin.

Drake, Daniel, M. D. (1948). *Pioneer Life in Kentucky 1785-1800,* Emmet Field Horine, M.D., ed. New York: Henry Schuman.

Dunn, Richard S. (1977) "A Tale of Two Plantations: Slave Life at Mesopotamia in Jamaica and Mount Airy in Virginia, 1799-1828," *William and Mary Quarterly*, 3rd. Series, XXXIV, 1, Jan., 32-59.

Eaton, Clement (1964). *The Freedom of Thought Struggle in the Old South.* New York: Harper & Row.

Elkins, Stanley (1959). *Slavery: A Problem in American Institutional and Intellectual Life.* Chicago: Univ. of Chicago Press.

Faust, Drew Gilpin (1980). "Culture, Conflict and Community: The Meaning of Power on an Ante-Bellum Plantation," *Journal of Social History,* XIV, 1, Fall, 83-98.

Faust, Drew Gilpin, ed. (1981). *The Ideology of Slavery: Proslavery in the Antebellum South, 1830-1860.* Baton Rouge: Louisiana State Univ. Press.

Faust, Drew Gilpin (1982). *James Henry Hammond and the Old South: A Design for Masters.* Baton Rouge: Louisiana State Univ. Press.

Finley, M. I. (1980). *Ancient Slavery and Modern Ideology.* New York: Viking.

Fithian, Philip Vickers (1957). *Journal and Letters of Philip Vickers Fithian 1773-1774: A Plantation Tutor of the Old Dominion,* Hunter Dickinson Farish, ed. Charlottesville: University Press of Virginia.

Fogel, Robert William & Engerman, Stanley L. (1974). *Time of the Cross.* Boston Little, Brown.

Fox-Genovese, Elizabeth (1975). "Poor Richard at Work in the Cotton Fields: Psychological and Ideological Presuppositions of Time on the Cross," *Review of Radical Political Economy,* VII, 3, Fall, 67-83.

Fox-Genovese, Elizabeth & Genovese, Eugene D. (1983). *Fruits of Merchant Capital.* New York: Oxford Univ. Press.

Frankel, Noralee (1982). "Workers, Wives, and Mothers: Black Women in Mississippi, 1860-1870," unpubl. Ph.D. diss., George Washington Univ.

Freehling, William (1965). *Prelude to Civil War*. New York: Harper & Row.

Friedmann, Harriet (1980). "Household Production and the National Economy: Concepts for the Analysis of Agrarian Functions," *The Journal of Peasant Studies*, VII, 2, Jan., 158-84.

Genovese, Eugene D. (1965). *The Political Economy of Slavery*. New York: Pantheon.

Genovese, Eugene D. (1975). *Roll, Jordan, Roll: The World the Slaves Made*. New York: Pantheon.

Genovese, Eugene D. (1979). *From Rebelllion to Revolution: Afro-American Slave Revolts in the Making of the Modern World*. Baton Rouge: Louisiana State Univ. Press.

Gonzalez, Nancie L. Lolien (1969). *Black Carib Household Structure: A Study of Migration and Modernization*. Seattle: Univ. of Washington Press.

Gray, Lewis C. (1958). *History of Agriculture in the Southern United States to 1860*. Gloucester, MA: Peter Smith.

Gutman, Herbert G. (1976). *The Black Family in Slavery and Freedom 1750-1925*. New York: Pantheon.

Hahn, Steven Howard (1979). "The Roots of Southern Populism: Yeomen Farmers and the Transformation of Georgia's Upper Piedmont, 1850-1890," unpubl. Ph.D. diss., Yale.

Harding, Vincent (1981). *There Is a River: The Black Struggle for Freedom in America*. New York: Harcourt, Brace, Jovanovich.

Henretta, James A. (1978). "Families and Farms: *Mentalité* in Pre-Industrial America," *William and Mary Quarterly*, 3rd series, XXXV, 1, Jan, 3-32.

Hilliard, Sam Bowers (1972). *Hog Meat and Hoecake: Food Supply in the Old South*. Carbondale: Southern Illinois Univ. Press.

House, Albert Virgil, ed. (1954). *Planter Management and Captialism in Ante-Bellum Georgia: The Journal of Hugh Fraser Grant, Ricegrower*. New York: Columbia Univ. Press.

Isaac, Rhys (1982). *The Transformation of Virginia, 1740-1790*. Chapel Hill: Univ. of North Carolina Press.

Jones, Jacqueline (1982). " 'My Mother was Much of a Woman': Black Women, Work and the Family Under Slavery," *Feminist Studies*, VIII, 2, Sum., 235-70.

Jordan, Weymouth T. (1948). *Hugh Davis and His Alabama Plantation*. University, AL: Univ. of Alabama Press.

Kaufman, Allen (1982). *On the Nature of Antebellum Political Economy*. Austin: Univ. of Texas Press.

Kemble, Frances Anne (1975). *Journal of a Residence on a Georgian Plantation in 1838-1839*, J.A. Scott, ed. New York: Knopf.

Kulikoff, Allan (1977). "The Beginnings of the Afro-American Family in Maryland," in Aubrey C. Land, Lois Green Carr & Edward C. Papenfuse, eds. *Law, Society and Politics in Early Maryland*. Baltimore: The Johns Hopkins Univ. Press.

Kulikoff, Allan (forthcoming). *Tobacco and Slaves: The Development of Southern Cultures in the Chesapeake Colonies, 1680-1780*. Chapel Hill: Univ. of North Carolina Press.

Land, Aubrey C., Carr, Lois Green, & Papenfuse, Edward C. (1977). *Law Society and Politics in Early Maryland*. Baltimore: The Johns Hopkins Univ. Press.

Levine, Lawrence W. (1977) *Black Culture and Black Consciousness: Afro-American Folk Thought From Slavery To Freedom*. New York: Oxford Univ. Press.

Loveland, Anne C. (1980). *Southern Evangelicals and the Social Order, 1800-1860.* Baton Rouge: Louisiana State Univ. Press.

Lumpkin, Katharine du Pre (1971). *The Making of a Southerner.* Westport, CT: Greenwood Press.

Marx, Karl (1964). *Pre-Capitalist Economic Formations,* E. J. Hobsbawm, ed. New York: International Publishers.

Mathews, Donald G. (1977). *Religion and the Old South.* Chicago: Univ. of Chicago Press.

Mathis, Ray (1979). *John Horry Dent: South Carolina Aristocrat on the Alabama Frontier.* University, AL: Univ. of Alabama Press.

Medick, Hans (1976) "The Proto-Industrial Family Economy: The Structural Function of Household and Family during the Transition from Peasant Society to Industrial Capitalism," *Social History,* No. 3, Oct., 291-315.

Menard, Russell (1980). "Why African Slavery? Free Land, Plantation Agriculture, and the Supply of Labor in the Growth of British-American Slave Societies," unpubl. paper delivered at the conference on New World Slavery, Rutgers Univ. at Newark.

Merrill, Michael (1977). "Cash Is Good to Eat: Self-Sufficiency and Exchange in the Rural Economy of the United States," *Radical History Review,* IV, 1, Win., 42-71.

Morgan, Edmund W. (1975). *American Slavery, American Freedom: The Ordeal of Colonial Virginia.* New York: Norton.

Mullin, Gerald (1972). *Flight and Rebellion: Slave Resistance in Eighteenth-Century Virginia.* New York: Oxford Univ. Press.

Oakes, James (1982). *The Ruling Race: A History of American Salveholders.* New York: Knopf.

Owsley, Frank L. (1949). *Plain Folk of the Old South.* Baton Rouge: Louisiana State Univ. Press.

Paulme, Denise, ed. (1971). *Women of Tropical Africa.* Berkeley: Univ. of California Press.

Phillips, Ulrich B. (1929). *Life and Labor in the Old South.* Boston: Little, Brown.

Phillips, Ulrich B. (1969). *The Slave Economy of the Old South,* E. D. Genovese, ed., Baton Rouge: Louisiana State Univ. Press.

Price, Jacob (1973). *France and the Chesapeake: A History of the Tobacco Monopoly, 1694-1791, and its Relationship to the British and American Tobacco Trades.* Ann Arbor: Univ. of Michigan Press.

Shammas, Carole (1982). "How Self-Sufficient Was Early America?" *The Journal of Interdisciplinary History,* XIII, 2, Aut., 247-72.

Stampp, Kenneth (1956). *The Peculiar Institution: Slavery in the Antebellum South.* New York: Knopf.

Tate, Thad W. & Ammerman, David, eds. (1977) *The Chesapeake in the Seventeenth Century: Essays on Anglo-American Society and Politics.* Chapel Hill: Univ. of North Carolina Press.

Tryon, Rolla Milton (1966). *Household Manfactures in the United States, 1640-1860.* New York: Augustus Kelley.

Tushnet, Mark V. (1981). *The American Law of Slavery 1810-1860. Considerations of Humanity and Interest.* Princeton, NJ: Princeton Univ. Press.

Verlinden, Charles (1970). *The Beginnings of Modern Colonization.* Ithaca, NY: Cornell Univ. Press.

Waters, John J. (1976). "The Traditional World of the New England Peasants: A View from Seventennth-Century Barnstable," *The New England Historical and Genealogical Register,* Vol. CXXX, Jan., 3-22.

Weaver, Herbert (1945). *Mississippi Farmers, 1850-1860.* Nashville: Vanderbilt Univ. Press.

White, Deborah S. (1979) "Ain't I a Woman? Female Slaves in the Antebellum South," unpubl. PhD. diss., Univ. of Illinois at Chicago Circle.

Wood, Peter (1974). *Black Majority: Negroes in Colonial South Carolina from 1670 through the Stono Rebellion.* New York: Knopf.

Woodman, Harold D. (1968). *King Cotton and His Retainers: Financing and Marketing the Cotton Crop of the South, 1800-1925.* Lexington: Univ. of Kentucky Press.

Woodman, Harold D.(1972). "Economic History and Economic Theory: The New Economic History in America," *The Journal of Interdisciplinary History,* III, 2 Aut., 323-50.

Wright, Gavin (1978). *The Political Economy of the Cotton South: Households, Markets, and Wealth in the Nineteenth Century.* New York: Norton.

FEMALE SLAVES: SEX ROLES AND STATUS IN THE ANTEBELLUM PLANTATION SOUTH

Deborah G. White*

Abstract: This paper analyzes female slave life in the context of female slave interaction and familial roles. It looks at the bonded woman's work, her control of particular resources, her contribution to slave households, and her ability to cooperate with other women on a daily basis. It suggests that in relation to the slave family, too much emphasis has been placed on what men could not do rather than on what women could do and did. It finds that the bonded female made significant "economic" contributions to the slave family, that the slave's world was sex stratified so that the female slave world existed quite independently of the male slave world, and that slave families were matrifocal.

In his 1939 study of the black family in America, sociologist E. Franklin Frazier theorized that in slave family and marriage relations, women played the dominant role. Specifically, Frazier wrote that "the Negro woman as wife or mother was the mistress of her cabin, and, save for the interference of master and overseer, her wishes in regard to mating and family matters were paramount." He also insisted that slavery had schooled the black woman in self-reliance and self-sufficiency and that "neither economic necessity nor tradition had instilled in her the spirit of subordination to masculine authority" (1939:125). The Frazier thesis received support from other social scientists, including historians Kenneth Stampp (1956:344) and Stanley Elkins (1959:130), both of whom held that slave men had been emasculated and stripped of their paternity rights by slave masters who left control of slave households to slave women. In his infamous 1965 national report, Daniel Patrick Moynihan (1965: 31) lent further confirmation to the Frazier thesis when he alleged that the fundamental problem with the modern black family was the "often reversed roles of husband and wife," and then traced the origin of the "problem" back to slavery.

Partly in response to the criticism spawned by the Moynihan Report, historians reanalyzed antebellum source material, and the matriarchy thesis was debunked. For better or worse, said historians Robert Fogel and Stanley Engerman (1974:141), the "dominant" role in slave society was played by men. Men were dominant, they said, because men occupied all managerial and artisan slots, and because masters recognized the male head of the family group. From historian John Blassingame we learned that by building furnishings and providing extra food for their families, men found indirect ways of gaining status. If a garden plot was to be cultivated, the husband

*Deborah G. White is Assistant Professor of History at the University of Wisconsin, Milwaukee.

"led" his wife in the family undertaking (1972:92). After a very thoughtful appraisal of male slave activities, historian Eugene Genovese concluded that "slaves from their own experience had come to value a two-parent, male-centered household, no matter how much difficulty they had in realizing the ideal" (1974:491-492). Further tipping the scales toward partiarchal slave households, historian Herbert Gutman argued that the belief that matrifocal households prevailed among slaves was a misconception. He demonstrated that children were more likely to be named after their fathers than mothers, and that during the Civil War slave men acted like fathers and husbands by fighting for their freedom and by protecting their wives and children when they were threatened by Union troops or angry slaveholders (1976:188-191, 369-386).

With the reinterpretation of male roles came a revision of female roles. Once considered dominant, slave women were now characterized as subordinated and sometimes submissive. Fogel and Engerman found proof of their subordinated status in the fact that they were excluded from working in plow gangs and did all of the household chores (1974:141-142). Genovese maintained that slave women's "attitude toward housework, especially cooking, and toward their own femininity," belied the conventional wisdom "according to which women unwittingly helped ruin their men by asserting themselves in the home, protecting their children, and assuming other normally masculine responsibilities (1974:500). Gutman found one Sea Island slave community where the black church imposed a submissive role upon married slave women (1976:72).

In current interpretations of the contemporary black family the woman's role has not been "feminized" as much as it has been "deemphasized." The stress in studies like those done by Carol Stack (1974) and Theodore Kennedy (1980), is not on roles per se but on the black family's ability to survive in flexible kinship networks that are viable bulwarks against discrimination and racism. These interpretations also make the point that black kinship patterns are not based exclusively on consanguineous relationships but are also determined by social contacts that sometimes have their basis in economic support.

Clearly then, the pendulum has swung away from the idea that women ruled slave households, and that their dominance during the slave era formed the foundation of the modern day matriarchal black family. But how far should that pendulum swing? This paper suggests that we should tread the road that leads to the patriarchal slave household and the contemporary amorphous black family with great caution. It suggests that, at least in relation to the slave family, too much emphasis has been placed on what men could not do rather than on what women could do and did. What follows is not a comprehensive study of female slavery, but an attempt to reassess Frazier's claim that slave women were self-reliant and self-sufficient through an examination of some of their activities, specifically their work, their control of particular resources, their contribution to their households and their ability to cooperate with each other on a daily basis. Further, this paper will examine some of the implications of these activities, and their probable impact on the slave woman's status in slave society, and the black family.

At the outset a few points must be made about the subject matter and the source material used to research it. Obviously, a study that concentrates solely on females runs the risk of overstating woman's roles and their importance in society. One must therefore keep in mind that this is only one aspect, although a very critical one, of slave family and community life. In addition, what follows is a synthesis of the probable sex role of the average slave woman on plantations with at least twenty slaves.[1] In the process of constructing this synthesis I have taken into account such variables as plantation size, crop, region of the South, and the personal idosyncrasies of slave masters. Finally, in drawing conclusions about the sex role and status of slave women, I have detailed their activities and analyzed them in terms of what anthropologists know about women who do similar things in analogous settings. I took this approach for two reasons. First, information about female slaves cannot be garnered from sources left by slave women because they left few narratives, diaries or letters. The dearth of source material makes it impossible to draw conclusions about the slave woman's feelings. Second, even given the ex-slave interviews, a rich source material for this subject, it is almost impossible to draw conclusions about female slave status from an analysis of their individual personalities. Comments such as that made by the slave woman, Fannie, to her husband Bob, "I don't want no sorry nigger around me," perhaps says something about Fannie, but not about all slave women (Egypt et al., 1945:184). Similarly, for every mother who grieved over the sale of her children there was probably a father whose heart was also broken. Here, only the activities of the slave woman will be examined in an effort to discern her status in black society.

Turning first to the work done by slave women, it appears that they did a variety of heavy and dirty labor, work which was also done by men. In 1853, Frederick Olmsted saw South Carolina slaves of both sexes carting manure on their heads to the cotton field where they spread it with their hands between the ridges in which cotton was planted. In Fayetteville, North Carolina, he noticed that women not only hoed and shovelled but they also cut down trees and drew wood (Olmsted, 1971:67, 81). The use of women as lumberjacks occurred quite frequently, especially in the lower South and Southwest, areas which retained a frontier quality during the antebellum era. Solomon Northup, a kidnapped slave, knew women who wielded the ax so perfectly that the largest oak or sycamore fell before their well-directed blows. An Arkansas ex-slave remembered that her mother used to carry logs (Osofsky, 1969:308-309; Rawick, 1972, vol. 10, pt. 5:54). On Southwestern plantations women did all kinds of work. In the region of the Bayou Boeuf women were expected to "plough, drag, drive team, clear wild lands, work on the highway," and do any other type of work required of them (Osofsky, 1969:313). In short, full female hands frequently did the same kind of work as male hands.

It is difficult, however, to say how often they did the same kind of field work, and it would be mistake to say that there was no differentiation of field labor on Southern farms and plantations. The most common form of differentiation was that women hoed while men plowed. Yet, the exceptions to the rule were so numerous as to make a mockery of it. Many men hoed on a regular basis. Similarly, if a field had to be plowed and there were not enough male hands to do it, then it was not unusual for an overseer to command a strong woman to plow. This could happen

[1]The majority of the available source material seems to be from plantations or farms with more than one or two slave families. Relatively few ex-slave interviewees admit to being one of only three or four slaves. If Genovese is right and at least half of the slaves in the South lived on units of twenty slaves or more, this synthesis probably describes the life of a majority of slave women (Genovese, 1974:7).

on a plantation of twenty slaves or a farm of five.[2]

It is likely, however, that women were more often called to do the heavy labor usually assigned to men after their child-bearing years. Pregnant women, and sometimes women breastfeeding infants, were usually given less physically demanding work.[3] If, as recent studies indicate (see Dunn, 1977:58; Gutman, 1976:50, 74, 124, 171; Trussell, 1978:504), slave women began childbearing when about twenty years of age and had children at approximately two and a half year intervals, at least until age thirty-five, slave women probably spent a considerable amount of time doing tasks which men did not do.[4] Pregnant and nursing women were classified as half-hands or three-quarter hands and such workers did only some of the work that was also done by full hands. For instance, it was not unusual for them to pick cotton or even hoe, work done on a regular basis by both sexes. But frequently, they were assigned to "light work" like raking stubble or pulling weeds, which was often given to children and the elderly.[5]

Slave women might have preferred to be exempt from such labor, but they might also have gained some intangibles from doing the same work as men. Anthropologists (Mullings, 1976:243-244; Sacks, 1974:213-222) have demonstrated that in societies where men and women are engaged in the production of the same kinds of goods and where widespread private property is not a factor, participation in production gives women freedom and independence. Since neither slave men nor women had access to, or control over, the products of their labor, parity in the field may have encouraged equalitarianism in the slave quarters. In Southern Togo, for instance, where women work alongside their husbands in the field because men do not alone produce goods which are highly valued, democracy prevails in relationships between men and women (Rocher et al., 1962:151-152).

But bondswomen did do a lot of traditional "female work" and one has to wonder whether this work, as well as the work done as a "half-hand" tallied on the side of female subordination. In the case of the female slave, domestic work was not always confined to the home, and often "woman's work" required skills that were highly valued and even coveted because of the place it could purchase in the higher social echelons of the slave world. For example, cooking was definitely "female work" but it was also a skilled occupation. Good cooks were highly respected by both blacks and whites, and their occupation was raised in status because the masses of slave women did not cook on a regular basis. Since field work occupied the time of most women, meals were often served communally. Female slaves therefore,

[2]For other examples of work done by female slaves and indications that they did the same work required of men, see Nairne, 1732:60; Kemble, 1961:65; Olmsted, 1971:67-81; Olmsted, 1907:81; Drew, 1969:92; Rawick, 1972, vol. 13, pt. 4:357; vol. 6:46, 151, 158, 270, 338.

[3]See Rawick, 1972, vol. 4, pt. 3:160; Hughes, 1897:22, 41; Rawick, 1972, vol. 10, pt. 7:255; Olmsted, 1856:430; SHC, Plantation Instructions; Olmsted, 1971:78, 175; Kemble, 1961:87, 179; Drew, 1969:128; Davis, 1943:127.

[4]Although Fogel and Engerman cite the slave woman's age at first birth as 22.5, other historians, including Gutman and Dunn, found that age to be substantially lower—Gutman a range from 17 to 19, and Dunn (average age at first birth on the Mount Airy, Virginia Plantation) 19.22 years. More recently, economists Trussell and Steckel have found the age to be 20.6 years (Fogel and Engerman, 1974:137-138; Dunn, 1977:58; Gutman, 1976:50, 75, 124, 171; Trussell and Steckel, 1978:504.

[5]For examples, see n. 3.

were, for the most part, relieved of this traditional chore, and the occupation of "cook" became specialized.[6]

Sewing too was often raised above the level of inferior "woman's work." All females at one time or another had to spin and weave. Occasionally each woman was given cloth and told to make her family's clothes, but this was unusual and more likely to happen on small farms than on plantations. During slack seasons women probably did more sewing than during planting and harvesting seasons, and pregnant women were often put to work spinning, weaving and sewing. Nevertheless, sewing could be raised to the level of a skilled art, especially if a woman sewed well enough to make the white family's clothes. Such women were sometimes hired out and allowed to keep a portion of the profit they brought their master and mistress (Rawick, 1972, vol. 17, 158; SHC, White Hill Plantation Books:13; Rawick, 1972, vol. 2, pt. 2:114).

Other occupations which were solidly anchored in the female domain, and which increased a woman's prestige, were midwifery and doctoring. The length of time and extent of training it took to become a midwife is indicated by the testimony of Clara Walker, a former slave interviewed in Arkansas, who remembered that she trained for five years under a doctor who became so lazy after she had mastered the job that he would sit down and let her do all the work. After her "apprenticeship" ended she delivered babies for both slave and free, black and white (Rawick, 1972, vol. 10, pt. 5:21).[7] Other midwives learned the trade from a female relative, often their mother, and they in turn passed the skill on to another female relative.

A midwife's duty often extended beyond delivering babies, and they sometimes became known as "doctor women." In this capacity they cared for men, women, and children. Old women, some with a history of midwifery and some without, also gained respect as "doctor women." They "knowed a heap about yarbs [herbs]," recalled a Georgia ex-slave (Rawick, 1972, vol. 2, pt. 2:112).[8] Old women had innumerable cures, especially for children's diseases, and since plantation "nurseries" were usually under their supervision, they had ample opportunity to practice their art. In sum, a good portion of the slave's medical care, particularly that of women and children, was supervised by slave women.

Of course, not all women were hired-out seamstresses, cooks, or midwives; a good deal of "female work" was laborious and mundane. An important aspect of this work, as well as of the field work done by women, was that is was frequently done in female groups. As previously noted, women often hoed while men plowed. In addition, when women sewed they usually did so with other women. Quilts were made by women at gatherings called, naturally enough, "quiltins." Such gatherings were attended only by women and many former slaves had vivid recollections of them. The "quiltin's and spinnin' frolics dat de women folks had" were the most outstanding remembrances of Hattie Anne Nettles, an Alabama ex-slave (Rawick, 1972, vol. 6:297, 360). Women also gathered, independent of male slaves,

[6]For an example of the privileges this occupation *could* involve, see Chesnut, 1905:24.

[7]For other examples of midwives see Rawick, vol. 6:256, 318; vol. 16:90-91; vol. 10, pt. 5:125. The job status of the midwife needs to be examined more closely than is possible here. Midwives were curers whose duty usually extended beyond delivering babies. Occasionally their cures spilled over into witchcraft or voodoo, and slaves who practiced these arts were often feared.

[8]See also Rawick, 1972, vol. 2, pt. 2:55; vol. 17:174; Olmsted, 1907:76.

on Saturday afternoons to do washing. Said one ex-slave, "they all had a regular picnic of it as they would work and spread the clothes on the bushes and low branches of the tree to dry. They would get to spend the day together" (Rawick, 1972, vol. 7:315).

In addition, when pregnant women did field work they sometimes did it together. On large plantations the group they worked in was sometimes known as the "trash gang." This gang, made up of pregnant women, women with nursing infants, children and old slaves, was primarily a female work gang.[9] Since it was the group that young girls worked with when just being initiated into the work world of the plantation, one must assume that it served some kind of socialization function. Most likely, many lessons about life were learned by twelve-year-old girls from this group of women who were either pregnant or breastfeeding, or who were grandmothers many times over.

It has been noted that women frequently depended on slave midwives to bring children into the world; their dependence on other slave women did not end with childbirth but continued through the early life of their children. Sometimes women with infants took their children to the fields with them. Some worked with their children wrapped to their backs, others laid them under a tree. Frequently, however, an elderly woman watched slave children during the day while their mothers worked in the field. Sometimes the cook supervised young children at the master's house.[10] Mothers who were absent from their children most of the day, indeed most of the week, depended on these surrogate mothers to assist them in child socialization. Many ex-slaves remember these women affectionately. Said one South Carolinian: "De old lady, she looked after every blessed thing for us all day long en cooked for us right along wid de mindin' " (Rawick, 1972, vol. 2, pt. 1:99).

Looking at the work done by female slaves in the antebellum South, therefore, we find that sex role differentiation in field labor was not absolute but that there was differentiation in other kinds of work. Domestic chores were usually done exclusively by women, and certain "professional" occupations were reserved for females. It would be a mistake to infer from this differentiation that it was the basis of male dominance. A less culturally biased conclusion would be that women's roles were different or complementary. For example, in her overview of African societies, Denise Paulme notes that in almost all African societies, women do most of the domestic chores, yet they lead lives that are quite independent of men. Indeed, according to Paulme, in Africa, "a wife's contribution to the needs of the household is direct and indispensable, and her husband is just as much in need of her as she of him" (1963:4). Other anthropologists have suggested that we should not evaluate women's roles in terms of men's roles because in a given society, women may not perceive the world in the same way that men do (Rogers, 1978:152-162). In other words, men and women may share a common culture but on different terms, and when this is the case, questions of dominance and subservience are irrelevant. The degree to which male and female ideologies are different is often suggested by the degree to which men and women are independently able to rank and order themselves and cooperate with members of their sex in the performance of

[9]Somtimes pregnant women were made to weave, spin, or sew, in which case they usually did it with other women. The term "trash gang" was probably used only on very large plantations, but units of pregnant women, girls, elderly females, as well as boys and elderly men, probably worked together on a farm with twenty slaves. See n. 2.

[10]See, for instance, Olmsted, 1856:423 and Phillips, 1909:I, 127.

their duties. In societies where women are not isolated from one another and placed under a man's authority, where women cooperate in the performance of household tasks, where women form groups or associations, women's roles are usually complementary to those of men, and the female world exists independently of the male world. Because women control what goes on in their world, they rank and order themselves vis à vis other women, not men, and they are able to influence decisions made by their society because they exert pressure as a group. Ethnographic studies of the Igbo women of Eastern Nigeria (Tanner, 1974:146-150), the Ga women of Central Accra in Ghana (Robertson, 1976:115-132), and the Patani of Southern Nigeria (Leis, 1974, 221-242) confirm these generalizations. Elements of female slave society—the chores done in and by groups, the intrasex cooperation and dependency in the areas of child care and medical care, the existence of high echelon female slave occupations—may be an indication, not that slave women were inferior to slave men, but that the roles were complementary and that the female slave world allowed women the opportunity to rank and order themselves and obtain a sense of self which was quite apart from the men of their race and even the men of the master class.

That bondswomen were able to rank and order themselves is further suggested by evidence indicating that in the community of the slave quarters certain women were looked to for leadership. Leadership was based on either one or a combination of factors, including occupation, association with the master class, age, or number of children. It was manifested in all aspects of female slave life. For instance, Louis Hughes, an escaped slave, noted that each plantation had a "forewoman who . . . had charge of the female slaves and also the boys and girls from twelve to sixteen years of age, and all the old people that were feeble" (Hughes, 1897:22). Bennett H. Barrow repeatedly lamented the fact that Big Lucy, one of his oldest slaves, had more control over his female slaves then he did: "Anica, Center, Cook Jane, the better you treat them the worse they are. Big Lucy, the Leader, corrupts every young negro in her power" (Davis, 1943:191).[11] When Elizabeth Botume went to the Sea Islands after the Civil War, she had a house servant a young woman named Amy who performed her tasks slowly and sullenly until Aunt Mary arrived from Beaufort. In Aunt Mary's presence the obstreperous Amy was "quiet, orderly, helpful and painstaking" (Botume, 1893:132).[12]

Another important feature of female life, bearing on the ability of women to rank and order themselves independently of men, was the control women exercised over each other by quarreling. In all kinds of sources there are indications that women were given to fighting and irritating each other. From Jesse Belflowers, the overseer of the Allston rice plantation in South Carolina, Adele Petigru Allston learned that "mostly mongst the Woman," there was "goodeal of quarling and disputing and telling lies" (Easterby, 1945:291). Harriet Ware, a northern missionary, writing from the Sea Islands in 1863 blamed the turmoil she found in black community life on the "tongues of the women" (Pearson,

[11]Big Lucy thwarted all of Barrow's instructions and her influence extended to the men also; see Davis, 1943:168, 173.

[12]On a given plantation there could be a number of slave women recognized by other slave women as leaders. For instance, when Frances Kemble first toured Butler Island she found that the cook's position went to the oldest wife in the settlement.

1906:210).[13] The evidence of excessive quarreling among women hints at the existence of a gossip network among female slaves. Anthropologists (Rosaldo, 1974:10-11, 38; Stack, 1974:109-115; Wolfe, 1974:162) have found gossip to be a principal strategy used by women to control other women as well as men. Significantly, the female gossip network, the means by which community members are praised, shamed, and coerced, is usually found in societies where women are highly dependent on each other and where women work in groups or form female associations.[14]

In summary, when the activities of female slaves are compared to those of women in other societies a clearer picture of the female slave sex role emerges. It seems that slave women were schooled in self-reliance and self-sufficiency but the "self" was more likely the female slave collective than the individual slave woman. On the other hand, if the female world was highly stratified and if women cooperated with each other to a great extent, odds are that the same can be said of men, in which case neither sex can be said to have been dominant or subordinate.

There are other aspects of the female slave's life that suggest that her world was independent of the male slave's and that slave women were rather self-reliant. It has long been recognized (Blassingame, 1972: 77-103) that slave women did not derive traditional benefits from the marriage relationship, that there was no property to share and essential needs like food, clothing, and shelter were not provided by slave men. Since in almost all societies where men consistently control women, that control is based on male ownership and distribution of property and/or control of certain culturally valued subsistence goods, these realities of slave life had to contribute to female slave self-sufficiency and independence from slave men. The practice of "marrying abroad," having a spouse on a different plantation, could only have reinforced this tendency, for as ethnographers (Noon, 1949:30-31; Rosaldo, 1974:36, 39) have found, when men live apart from women, they cannot control them.[15] We have yet to learn what kind of obligations brothers, uncles, and male cousins fulfilled for their female kin, but is it improbable that wives were controlled by husbands whom they saw only once or twice a week. Indeed, "abroad marriages" may have intensified female intradependency.

The fact that marriage did not yield traditional benefits for women, and that "abroad marriages" existed, does not mean that women did not depend on slave men for foodstuffs beyond the weekly rations, but since additional food was not guaranteed, it probably meant that women along with men had to take initiatives in supplementing slave diets. So much has been made of the activities of slave men in

[13]Additional evidence that women quarreled can be found in a pamphlet stating the terms of an overseer's contract: "Fighting, particularly amongst the women . . . is to be always rigorously punished." Similarly, an ex-slave interviewed in Georgia noted that "sometimes de women uster git whuppins for fightin." See Bassett, 1925:32 and Rawick, 1972, vol. 12, pt. 2:57.

[14]Gossip is one of many means by which women influence political decisions and interpersonal relationships. In Taiwan, for instance, women gather in the village square and whisper to each other. In other places, such as among the Marina of Madagascar, women gather and shout loud insults at men or other women. In still other societies, such as the black ghetto area studied by Carol Stack, the gossip network takes the form of a grapevine. See Rosaldo 1974:10-11; Wolf, 1974:162; and Stack, 1974:109-115.

[15]For instance, it is thought that Iroquois women obtained a high degree of political and economic power partly because of the prolonged absences of males due to trading and warfare (Noon, 1949:30-31).

this sphere (Blassingame, 1972:92; Genovese, 1974:486) that the role of slave women has been overlooked.[16] Female house slaves, in particular, were especially able to supplement their family's diet. Mary Chesnut's maid Molly, made no secret of the fact that she fed her offspring and other slave children in the Confederate politician's house. "Dey gets a little of all dat's going," she once told Chesnut (Chesnut, 1905:348). Frederick Douglass remembered that his grandmother was not only a good nurse but a "capitol hand at catching fish and making the nets she caught them in" (1855:27). Eliza Overton, an ex-slave, remembered how her mother stole, slaughtered, and cooked one of her master's hogs. Another ex-slave was not too bashful to admit that her mother "could hunt good ez any man." (Rawick, 1972, vol. 11:53, 267.)[17] Women, as well as men, were sometimes given the opportunity to earn money. Women often sold baskets they had woven, but they also earned money by burning charcoal for blacksmiths and cutting cordwood (Olmsted, 1971:26; Rawick, 1972, vol. 7; 23). Thus, procuring extra provisions for the family was sometimes a male and sometimes a female responsibility, one that probably fostered a self-reliant and independent spirit.

The high degree of female cooperation, the ability of slave women to rank and order themselves, the independence women derived from the absence of property considerations in the conjugal relationship, "abroad marriages," and the female slave's ability to provide supplementary foodstuffs are factors which should not be ignored in considerations of the character of the slave family. In fact, they conform to the criteria most anthropologists (Gonzalez, 1970:231-243; Smith, 1956:257-260, 1973:125; Tanner, 1974: 129-156) list for that most misunderstood concept—matrifocality. Matrifocality is a term used to convey the fact that women *in their role as mothers* are the focus of familial relationships. It does not mean that fathers are absent; indeed two-parent households can be matrifocal. Nor does it stress a power relationship where women rule men. When *mothers* become the focal point of family activity, they are just more central than are fathers to a family's continuity and survival as a unit. While there is no set model for matrifocality, Smith (1973:125) has noted that in societies as diverse as Java, Jamaica, and the Igbo of eastern Nigeria, societies recognized as matrifocal, certain elements are constant.[18] Among these elements are female solidarity, particularly in regard to their cooperation within the domestic sphere. Another factor is the economic activity of women which enables them to support their children independent of fathers *if they desire to do so or are forced to do so.* The most important factor is the supremacy of the mother-child bond over all other relationships (Smith, 1973:139-142).

Female solidarity and the "economic" contribution of bondswomen in the form of medical care, foodstuffs, and money has already been discussed; what can be said of the mother-child bond? We know from previous works on slavery (Bassett, 1925:

[16]Of male slaves who provided extra food, John Blassingame wrote: "The slave who did such things for his family gained not only the approbation of his wife, but he also gained status in the quarters." According to Genovese, "the slaves would have suffered much more than many in fact did from malnutrition and the hidden hungers of nutritional deficiencies if men had not taken the initiative to hunt and trap animals."

[17]For other examples of women who managed to provide extra food for their families see Rawick, 1972, vol. 16:16; Brent, 1816:9.

[18]See also Smith, 1956:257-260; Tanner, 1974:129-156.

31, 139, 141; Kemble, 1961:95, 127, 179; Phillips, 1909:I, 109, 312) that certain slaveholder practices encouraged the primacy of the mother-child relationship. These included the tendency to sell mothers and small children as family units, and to accord special treatment to pregnant and nursing women and women who were exceptionally prolific. We also know (Gutman, 1976:76) that a husband and wife secured themselves somewhat from sale and separation when they had children. Perhaps what has not been emphasized enough is the fact that it was the wife's childbearing and her ability to keep a child alive that were the crucial factors in the security achieved in this way. As such, the insurance against sale which husbands and wives received once women had borne and nurtured children heads the list of female contributions to slave households.

In addition to slaveowner encouragement of close mother-child bonds there are indications that slave women themselves considered this their most important relationship.[19] Much has been made of the fact that slave women were not ostracized by slave society when they had children out of "wedlock" (Genovese, 1974:465-466; Gutman, 1976:74, 117-118). Historians have usually explained this aspect of slave life in the context of slave sexual norms which allowed a good deal of freedom to young unmarried slave women. However, the slave attitude concerning "illegitimacy" might also reveal the importance that women, and slave society as a whole, placed on the mother role and the mother-child dyad. For instance, in the Alabama community studied by Charles S. Johnson (1934:29, 66-70) in the 1930s, most black women felt no guilt and suffered no loss of status when they bore children out of wedlock. This was also a community in which, according to Johnson, the role of the mother was "of much greater importance than in the more familiar American family group." Similarly, in his 1956 study of the black family in British Guyana, Smith (1956:109, 158, 250-251) found the mother-child bond to be the strongest in the whole matrix of social relationships, and it was manifested in a lack of condemnation of women who bore children out of legal marriage. If slave women were not ostracized for having children without husbands, it could mean that the mother-child relationship took precedence over the husband-wife relationships.

The mystique which shrouded conception and childbirth is perhaps another indication of the high value slave women placed on motherhood and childbirth. Many female slaves claimed that they were kept ignorant of the details of conception and childbirth. For instance, a female slave interviewed in Nashville, noted that at age twelve or thirteen, she and an older girl went around to parsley beds and hollow logs looking for newborn babies. "They didn't tell you a thing," she said (Egypt et al., 1945:10; Rawick, 1972, vol. 16:15). Another ex-slave testified that her mother told her that doctors brought babies, and another Virginia ex-slave remembered that "people was very particular in them days. They wouldn't let children know anything:" (Egypt et al.,

[19]Gutman suggests that the husband-wife and father-child dyad were as strong as the mother-child bond. I think not. It has been demonstrated that in most Western Hemisphere black societies as well as in Africa, the mother-child bond is the strongest and most enduring bond. This does not mean that fathers have no relationship with their children or that they are absent. The father-child relationship is of a more formal nature than the mother-child relationship. Moreover, the conjugal relationship appears, on the surface, to be similar to the Western norm in that two-parent households prevail, but, when competing with consanguineous relationships, conjugal affiliations usually lose. See Gutman, 1976:79; Smith, 1970:62-70; Smith, 1973:129; Stack, 1974:102-105.

1945:8; Rawick, 1972, vol. 16:25. See also Rawick, 1972, vol. 7:3-24 and vol. 2:51-52). This alleged naiveté can perhaps be understood if examined in the context of motherhood as a *rite de passage.* Sociologist Joyce Ladner (1971:177-263) found that many black girls growing up in a ghetto area of St. Louis in the late 1960s were equally ignorant of the facts concerning conception and childbirth. Their mothers had related only "old wives tales" about sex and childbirth even though the community was one where the mother-child bond took precedence over both the husband-wife bond and the father-child bond. In this St. Louis area, having a child was considered the most important turning point in a black girl's life, a more important *rite de passage* than marriage. Once a female had a child all sorts of privileges were bestowed upon her. That conception and childbirth were cloaked in mystery in antebellum slave society is perhaps an indication of the sacredness of motherhood. When considered in tandem with the slave attitude toward "illegitimacy," the mother-child relationship emerges as the most important familial relationship in the slave family.

Finally, any consideration of the slave's attitude about motherhood and the expectations which the slave community had of childbearing women must consider the slave's African heritage. In many West African tribes the mother-child relationship is and has always been the most important of all human relationships.[20] To cite one of many possible examples, while studying the role of women in Ibo society, Sylvia Leith-Ross (1939:127) asked an Ibo woman how many of ten husbands would love their wives and how many of ten sons would love their mothers. The answer she received demonstrated the precedence which the mother-child tie took: "Three husbands would love their wives but seven sons would love their mothers."

When E. Franklin Frazier (1939:125) wrote that slave women were self-reliant and that they were strangers to male slave authority he evoked an image of an overbearing, even brawny woman. In all probability visions of Sapphire danced in our heads as we learned from Frazier that the female slave played the dominant role in courtship, marriage and family relationships, and later from Elkins (1959: 130) that male slaves were reduced to childlike dependency on the slave master. Both the Frazier and Elkins theses have been overturned by historians who have found that male slaves were more than just visitors to their wive's cabins, and women something other than unwitting allies in the degradation of their men. Sambo and Sapphire may continue to find refuge in American folklore but they will never again be legitimized by social scientists.

However, beyond the image evoked by Frazier is the stark reality that slave women did not play the traditional female role as it was defined in nineteenth-century America, and regardless of how hard we try to cast her in a subordinate or submissive role in relation to slave men, we will have difficulty reconciling that role with the plantation realities. When we consider the work done by women in groups, the existence of upper echelon female slave jobs, the intradependence of women in childcare and medical care; if we presume that the quarreling or "fighting and disputing" among slave women is evidence of a gossip network and that certain women were elevated by their peers to positions of respect, then what we are confronted with are slave women who are able, within the limits set by slaveowners, to rank and order their female world, women who identified and co-

[20]See Paulme, 1963:14; Tanner, 1974:147; Fortes, 1939:127.

operated more with other slave women than with slave men. There is nothing abnormal about this. It is a feature of many societies around the world, especially where strict sex role differentiation is the rule.

Added to these elements of female interdependence and cooperation were the realities of chattel slavery that decreased the bondsman's leverage over the bondswoman, made female self-reliance a necessity, and encouraged the retention of the African tradition which made the mother-child bond more sacred than the husband-wife bond. To say that this amounted to a matrifocal family is not to say a bad word. It is not to say that it precluded male-female cooperation, or mutual respect, or traditional romance and courtship. It does, however, help to explain how African-American men and women survived chattel slavery.

BIBLIOGRAPHY

Bassett, John Spencer
1925 The Southern Plantation Overseer, As Revealed in his Letters. Northhampton, Massachusetts: Southworth Press.

Bibb, Henry
1969 Narrative of the Life and Adventures of Henry Bibb. In Gilbert Osofsky, ed., Puttin on Ole Massa, 51-171. New York: Harper and Row Publishers.

Blassingame, John W.
1972 The Slave Community: Plantation Life in the Antebellum South. New York: Oxford University Press.

Botume, Elizabeth Hyde
1893 First Days Amongst the Contrabands. Boston: Lee and Shepard Publishers.

Brent, Linda
1816 Incidents in the Life of a Slave Girl. Ed. Lydia Maria Child, Boston: by the author.

Brown, William Wells
1969 Narrative of William Wells Brown. In Osofsky, 1969: 173-223.

Chesnut, Mary Bokin
1905 A Diary From Dixie. Ed. Ben Ames Williams. New York: D. Appleton and Company.

Davis, Adwon Adams
1943 Plantation Life in the Florida Parishes of Louisiana 1836-1846 as Reflected in the Diary of Bennet H. Barrow. New York: Columbia University Press.

Drew Benjamin
1969 The Refugee: A North Side View of Slavery. Boston: Addison Wesley.

Dunn, Richard
1977 "The Tale of Two Plantations: Slave Life at Mesopotamia in Jamaica and Mount Airy in Virginia, 1799-1828." William and Mary Quarterly 34:32-65.

Easterby, J. E., ed.
1945 The South Carolina Rice Plantations as Revealed in the Papers of Robert W. Allston. Chicago: University of Chicago Press.

Egypt, Ophelia S., J. Masuoka and Charles S. Johnson, eds.
1945 Unwritten History of Slavery: Autobiographical Accounts of Negro Ex-slaves. Nashville: Fisk University Press.

Elkins, Stanley M.
1959 Slavery; A Problem in American Institutional and Intellectual Life. 2nd ed. Chicago: University of Chicago Press.

Fogel, Robert William and Stanley Engerman
1974 Time on the Cross: The Economics of American Negro Slavery. Boston: Little, Brown.

Fortes, Mayer
1939 "Kinship and Marriage among the Ashanti." In A. R. Radcliffe-Brown and Daryll Forde, eds. African Systems of Kinship and Marriage, 252-284. London: Routledge and Kegan Paul.

Frazier, E. Franklin
1939 The Negro Family in the United States. Chicago: University of Chicago Press.

Genovese, Eugene
1974 Roll, Jordan, Roll: The World the Slaves Made. New York: Vintage Books.

Gutman, Herbert
1976 The Black Family in Slavery and Freedom, 1750-1925. New York: Pantheon Books.

Gonzalez, Nancie
1970 "Toward a Definition of Matrifocality." In Norman E. Whitten, Jr. and John F. Szwed, eds. Afro-American Anthropology: Contemporary Perspectives, 231-243. New York: The Free Press.

Hakfin, Nancy J. and Edna G. Bay
1976 Women in Africa: Studies in Social and Economic Change. Stanford: Stanford University Press.
Hughes, Louis
1897 Thirty Years a Slave. Milwaukee: South Side Printing.
Johnson, Charles S.
1934 Shadow of the Plantation. Chicago: University of Chicago Press.
Kemble, Frances Anne
1961 Journal of a Residence on a Georgian Plantation. Ed. John A. Scott. New York: Alfred Knopf.
Kennedy, Theodore R.
1980 You Gotta Deal With It: Black Family Relations in a Southern Community. New York: Oxford University Press.
Ladner, Joyce
1971 Tomorrow's Tomorrow: The Black Woman. New York: Doubleday.
Leis, Nancy B.
1974 "Women in Groups: Ijaw Women's Associations." In Rosaldo and Lamphere, 1974:223-242.
Leith-Ross, Sylvia
1939 African Women: A Study of the Ibo of Nigeria. London: Routledge and Kegan Paul.
Moynihan, Daniel Patrick
1965 The Negro Family: The Case for National Action. Washington, D.C.: Government Printing Office.
Mullings, Leith
1976 "Women and Economic Change in Africa," In Hafkin, 1976:239-264.
Nairne, Thomas
1732 A Letter from South Carolina. London: J. Clark.
Noon, John A.
1949 Law and Government of the Grand River Iroquois. New York: Viking.
Northup, Solomon
1969 Twelve Years a Slave: Narrative of Solomon Northup. In Osofsky, 1969:225-406.
Olmsted, Frederick L.
1856 A Journey in the Seaboard Slave States. New York: Dix and Edwards.
1907 A Journey in the Back Country. New York: G. P. Putnam's Sons.
1971 The Cotton Kingdom. Ed. David Freeman Hawke. New York: Bobbs-Merrill.
Osofsky, Gilbert, ed.
1969 Puttin' on Ole Massa. New York: Harper and Row.
Paulme, Denise, ed.
1963 Women of Tropical Africa. Berkeley: University of California Press.
Pearson, Elizabeth Ware, ed.
1906 Letters from Port Royal Written at the Time of the Civil War. Boston: W. B. Clarke.
Phillips, Ulrich B.
1909 Plantation and Frontier Documents 1649-1863. 2 vols. Cleveland: Arthur H. Clarke.
Rawick, George, ed.
1972 The American Slave: A Composite Autobiography. 19 vols. Westport, Connecticut: Greenwood Press.
Robertson, Claire
1976 "Ga Women and Socioeconomic Change in Accra, Ghana." In Hafkin, 1976:111-134.
Rocher, Guy, R. Clignet, and F. N. N'sougan Agblemagon
1962 "Three Preliminary Studies: Canada, Ivory Coast, Togo." International Social Science Journal 14:130-156.
Rogers, Susan Carol
1978 "Woman's Place: A Critical Review of Anthropological Theory." Comparative Studies in Society and History. 20:123-162.
Rosaldo, Michelle
1974 "Woman, Culture and Society: A Theoretical Overview." In Rosaldo and Lamphere, 1974:17-42.
Rosaldo, Michelle and Louise Lamphere, eds.
1974 Woman, Culture and Society. Stanford: Stanford University Press.
Sacks, Karen
1974 "Engels Revisted: Women, the Organization of Production, and Private Property." In Rosaldo and Lamphere, 1974:207-222.
Smith, Raymond T.
1956 The Negro Family in British Guiana: Family Structure and Social Status in the Villages. London: Routledge and Kegan Paul.
1970 "The Nuclear Family in Afro-American Kinship." Journal of Comparative Family Studies 1:55-70.
1973 "The Matrifocal Family." In Jack Goody, ed., The Character of Kinship, 121-144. London: Cambridge University Press.
Southern Historical Collection [SHC]
Bayside Plantation Records (1846-1852)
Plantation Instructions (undated)
White Hill Plantation Books (1817-1860)
Stack, Carol
1974 All Our Kin: Strategies for Survival in a Black Community. New York: Harper and Row.

Stampp, Kenneth
1956 The Peculiar Institution: Slavery in the Ante-Bellum South. New York: Vintage Books.

Tanner, Nancy
1974 "Matrifocality in Indonesia and Africa and Among Black Americans." In Rosaldo and Lamphere, 1974:129-156.

Trussell, James and Richard Steckel
1978 "Age of Slaves at Menarche and Their First Birth." Journal of Interdisciplinary History 8:477-505.

Wolf, Margery
1974 "Chinese Women: Old Skill in a New Context." In Rosaldo and Lamphere, 1974: 157-172.

Mother Love and Infant Death, 1750–1920

Nancy Schrom Dye and Daniel Blake Smith

American motherhood has only recently begun to acquire a past. Mothering is far more than a biological constant; it is an activity whose meaning has altered considerably over time. Changes in cultural values, maternal self-perceptions, and attitudes toward children—all these factors underscore the historical dimensions of motherhood. Indeed, the shifting status of women and the changing nature of the family in history cannot be fully understood without close study of the experience of mothering.

Yet despite all the valuable work on women and the family in recent years, this central dimension in women's past has remained largely unexamined. Almost all previous research has either examined parental roles through the prescriptive lens of sermons and childrearing manuals, or it has addressed the question of how changing childrearing styles affected children's personality development.[1] As a result a good deal is known about normative ideals of motherhood, particularly in the antebellum period, but comparatively little is known about women's own emotions and experiences of mothering.

This essay suggests elements of both change and continuity in the history of American motherhood by addressing two related questions. First, what were American women's experiences and perceptions as mothers, and how did maternal feelings and perceptions change over time? Second, how did the persistent reality of high infant mortality affect mothers and the relationships they established with their children? How did mothers come to terms with the ever-present reality that their children might die? These questions are explored primarily by examining women's personal writings—diaries, journals, and letters—to illuminate maternal experience.

Women's writings suggest that the experience of infant death formed a constant

Nancy Schrom Dye and Daniel Blake Smith are associate professors of history at the University of Kentucky.

[1] For an interpretive discussion of prescriptive maternal values, see Ruth H. Bloch, "American Feminine Ideals in Transition: The Rise of the Moral Mother, 1785–1815," *Feminist Studies*, 4 (June 1978), 101–26; Nancy Cott, "Notes toward an Interpretation of Antebellum Childrearing," *Psychohistory Review*, 6 (Spring 1978), 4–20; Mary P. Ryan, *Womanhood in America: From Colonial Times to the Present* (New York, 1975), esp. 45–49, 106–14, 140–48, 150–72, 180–91; Mary P. Ryan, *The Empire of the Mother: American Writing about Domesticity, 1830–1860* (New York, 1982), esp. 19–70, 97–114. The best historical analysis of the effects of childrearing patterns on personality development is Philip J. Greven, *The Protestant Temperament: Patterns of Childrearing, Religious Experience, and the Self in Early America* (New York, 1977).

backdrop against which mothers' experiences and emotions must be set. Infant mortality remained high throughout the entire period under consideration. During the nineteenth century as much as 40 percent of the total death rate was comprised of the deaths of children under the age of five. Not until near the turn of the twentieth century, with improvements in public health, nutrition, and general standard of living, was there a dramatic downturn in the infant death rate.[2] Despite the continuous reality of infant death, mothers' responses to sickness and death in their families changed significantly over time as cultural explanations for infant death and definitions of maternal roles changed. Women's personal reflections on and descriptions of day-to-day mothering — fragmentary as they sometimes are — point to three central modes in mothering during the American past.

Throughout the colonial period, as Laurel Thatcher Ulrich and others have suggested, mothering was "extensive" in nature.[3] The experience of motherhood was shaped largely by the permeable household structure of colonial America, in which neighbors, friends, and kin played significant caretaking roles, and by a general dependence on Divine Providence for interpreting maternal experience, especially in times of infant death or illness.

During the second half of the eighteenth century, Americans began to move away from the well-ordered, father-dominated family of early America, with its emphasis on paternal control, obedience, and emotional restraint, toward a strikingly affectionate, self-consciously private family environment in which children gradually became the focus of indulgent attention and mothers emerged as guardians of their moral and physical well-being.[4] By 1800, and even earlier in some instances, one can trace an increasing focus on the individual mother as the most influential force in shaping and preserving a child's life. Reliance on God gradually gave way to a more secular belief that a child's welfare lay primarily in the hands of loving, watchful mothers. The belief in the centrality of mothers to infant well-being has,

[2] R. S. Meindl and A. C. Swedlund, "Secular Trends in Mortality in the Connecticut Valley, 1700–1850," *Human Biology*, 49 (Sept. 1977), 389–414; Maris A. Vinovskis, "Mortality Rates and Trends in Massachusetts before 1860," *Journal of Economic History*, 32 (March 1972), 195–201; Henry H. Hibbs, Jr., *Infant Mortality: Its Relation to Social and Industrial Conditions* (New York, 1916), 3–16; C.-E. A. Winslow and Dorothy Holland, "The Influence of Certain Public Health Procedures upon Infant Mortality," *Human Biology*, 9 (May 1937), 133–74. For contemporary documentation compiled from bills of mortality, see Gouverneur Emerson, "Vital Statistics of Philadelphia, for the Decennial Period from 1830 to 1840," *American Journal of Medical Sciences*, 16 (July 1848), 13–32; Lemuel Shattuck, "On the Vital Statistics of Boston," *ibid.*, 17 (April 1841), 369–99; Gouverneur Emerson, "Observations upon the Mortality of Philadelphia Under the Age of Puberty," *ibid.*, 17 (Nov. 1835), 56–59; and Charles A. Lee, "Medical Statistics; Comprising a Series of Calculations and Tables Showing the Mortality in New York and Its Immediate Causes, During a Period of Sixteen Years," *ibid.*, 18 (Nov. 1836), 25–51.

[3] Laurel Thatcher Ulrich, *Good Wives: Image and Reality in the Lives of Women in Northern New England, 1650–1750* (New York, 1982), 146–63; Michael Zuckerman, "William Byrd's Family," *Perspectives in American History*, 12 (1979), 255–311.

[4] Carl N. Degler, *At Odds: Women and the Family in America from the Revolution to the Present* (New York, 1980), 8–25; John Demos, "The American Family in Past Time," *American Scholar*, 43 (Summer 1974), 422–46; Joan Hoff Wilson, "The Illusion of Change: Women and the American Revolution," in *The American Revolution: Explorations in the History of American Radicalism*, ed. Alfred F. Young (Dekalb, Ill., 1976), 383–445; Mary Beth Norton, *Liberty's Daughters: The Revolutionary Experience of American Women, 1750–1800* (Boston, 1980), 92–105, 243–50; Daniel Scott Smith, "Parental Power and Marriage Patterns: An Analysis of Historical Trends in Hingham, Massachusetts," *Journal of Marriage and the Family*, 35 (Aug. 1973), 419–28; Daniel Blake Smith, *Inside the Great House: Planter Family Life in Eighteenth-Century Chesapeake Society* (Ithaca, 1980), 285–99.

of course, persisted to the present day. It carried particular force, however, throughout the nineteenth century.

By the turn of the twentieth century, women, working through women's clubs, municipal reform groups, and social welfare organizations, began to give public voice to their concerns about the deaths of so many children and to turn infant death—once seen solely as a private tragedy—into a major social and political issue. The first decades of the twentieth century, then, witnessed a movement away from the confined, privatized mother-child relationship of nineteenth-century America toward a more broadly based "social motherhood" in which mothers shared responsibility for child welfare with public health officials, the medical profession, and ultimately the state.

Such a general overview drawn from women's personal documents requires certain caveats. By virtue of their literacy, the eighteenth- and nineteenth-century mothers studied here belonged to middle- and upper-class families; their relatively privileged status may well have colored their maternal experiences and social values. No claim is made, therefore, that working-class women shared their particular perspective on motherhood.[5] In addition, the changes in women's maternal values discussed here, like much else in family history, are gradual and complex, rarely displaying dichotomous shifts. They reflect not so much abrupt transformations at certain specific times as blends of changing experiences and attitudes. Finally, the almost complete absence of female diaries and letters before 1750 severely hinders historians' understanding of motherhood in the colonial era. Despite such limitations, focusing on the writings of mothers themselves highlights central threads in the changing fabric of American family life and illustrates the nature and direction of change in American mothering.

Colonial Americans inhabited an uncertain world. Periodic epidemics of diphtheria, smallpox, scarlet fever, measles, whooping cough, and a host of other infectious diseases swept through early American communities, striking babies and young children with special ferocity. Given the dearth of writings by women, it is necessary to turn to men's writings to gain some sense of how seventeenth- and early eighteenth-century women experienced motherhood in the midst of almost continuous disease and death.

The diary of Massachusetts clergyman Ebenezer Parkman provides a vivid picture of the high child mortality that was central to mothers' experience. In early 1739 Parkman recorded the death of his own infant dauther. "A Morning of great Trouble!" he wrote. ". . . About nine o'Clock I was called down from my study with

[5] On the experiences and perceptions of working-class women, see esp. Mary Christine Stansell, "Women of the Laboring Poor in New York City, 1820–1860" (Ph.D. diss., Yale University, 1979); Sharon Ann Burnston, "Babies in the Well: An Underground Insight into Deviant Behavior in Eighteenth-Century Philadelphia," *Pennsylvania Magazine of History and Biography*, 106 (April 1982), 151–86; and Lois Green Carr and Lorena S. Walsh, "The Planter's Wife: The Experience of White Women in Seventeenth-Century Maryland," *William and Mary Quarterly*, 34 (Oct. 1977), 542–71.

the Alarm that the Child was dying! About 10 She ceas'd to breathe. The will of the Lord be done! . . . O that we might have a due sense of the Divine Mind concerning us!" On February 5 he noted the death of another baby: "Mrs. Samuel Fay junior Infant Child bury'd which bled to death at Naval." And on May 18 there was yet another infant death to record: "Molly Hicks (infant) dyed—My wife there all night." In the first months of 1740, the "throat distemper"—a virulent strain of diphtheria that killed as many as half the children in some New England communities—appeared in Parkman's community of Marlborough. Parkman noted the mounting death toll among infants and children. In a typical entry he wrote, "A.M. I went over to the Funeral of widow Tomlin's Child and P.M. to the Funeral of Deacon Newton's Child both of which Dy'd of the Throat Distemper. A Third Grave was open'd this Day . . . for a Stillborn Infant of Daniel Stone."[6]

An incident Cotton Mather recorded in his diary suggests the parental response to such continuous illness and death among children. "Alas, for *my Sin*," Mather wrote after his daughter was badly burned in a household accident, "the just God throwes *my Child* into the *Fire!*"[7] Mather's comment reveals the inescapable power attributed to Divine Providence, especially in determining the fate of infants and children. It is one of the paradoxes of colonial family life that parents cared deeply for their children and yet expected neither conscientious care nor the best medical attention to cure their children's illnesses, prevent dangerous accidents, or forestall death. Children were God's temporary gift to parents; what He had freely given, He could just as freely—and suddenly—take away.[8]

The belief that the ultimate responsibility for a child's welfare lay in the hands of God is one of the cultural norms that must have shaped women's experiences as mothers. Ebenezer Parkman, for example, gives this description of a mother's response to her newborn's dangerously ill condition: "As to her dear Infant She had given it to God before it was born; She gave it up to him when it was born and I give it up to him now, Said She, and Shd be glad to do it in . . . Baptism." Reflecting on the loss of eight out of eleven children born to her between 1717 and 1736, a New England mother observed, "[S]o it pleased God to take away one after another of my dear children, I hope, to himself."[9]

By the mid-eighteenth century the beginning of a major transformation in American family values was underway through which mothers assumed increasingly important responsibilities for the nurturance and moral development of children.

[6] Francis G. Walett, ed., "The Diary of Ebenezer Parkman," *Proceedings of the American Antiquarian Society*, 72 (part 1, 1962), 31, 33, 36, 50. See also, Anne Bradstreet, "In Memory of My Dear Grandchild Anne Bradstreet Who Deceased June 20, 1669, Being Three Years and Seven Months Old," in *The Works of Anne Bradstreet*, ed. Jeannine Hensely (Cambridge, Mass., 1967), 236.

[7] "Diary of Cotton Mather, 1681–1708," *Massachusetts Historical Society Collections*, 7th series, vol. 7 (Boston, 1911), 283. See also Peter G. Slater, "'From the *Cradle* to the *Coffin*': Parental Bereavement and the Shadow of Infant Damnation in Puritan Society," *Psychohistory Review*, 6 (Fall-Winter 1977–78), 4–24.

[8] Peter Gregg Slater, *Children in the New England Mind: In Life and in Death* (Hamden, Conn., 1977); David E. Stannard, *The Puritan Way of Death: A Study in Religion, Culture, and Social Change* (New York, 1977), 57–71.

[9] Walett, ed., "Diary of Ebenezer Parkman," 101; Ulrich, *Good Wives*, 161. See also Joy Day Buel and Richard Buel, Jr., *The Way of Duty: A Woman and Her Family in Revolutionary America* (New York, 1984), 30–32, 39, 61–64.

Consequently, the women who left maternal diaries during the late eighteenth century were transitional figures in the history of American mothering, sharing some of the values and attitudes typically associated with the colonial and the antebellum eras. Their accounts reflect a growing affection and concern for children alongside a continued reliance on Divine Providence.

Despite the growth of increasingly private, child-centered families beginning in the revolutionary era, child care remained essentially a cooperative venture in many late eighteenth-century households, involving not only parents but servants, relatives, and friends as well. Children were born into large and busy households with continually changing casts of characters. Abigail Adams, for example, referred to her "constant family" of eighteen, "ten of which make my own family." Elizabeth Porter Phelps and Mary Vial Holyoke, far from remaining closeted at home with their children, thrust themselves into rounds of visiting, attending births, baptisms, and funerals, and running errands in their Massachusetts communities. A typical entry from Phelps's diary in the 1780s: "Monday I a visit at Mr. Hop[kins] took the two Little girls. Left them at Mr. Gaylords. Tuesday I down again—Mrs. Gaylord and I a visit at Mrs. Colts, the widow Warner went with us—at night we brought home Betty—left Thankful to go do school. Thursday Mrs. Crouch a visit here, the Majors wife and her new Daughter Eleazers wife a visit here. Fryday Mother up to see Rosel Smiths wife and her mother Prat is there too."[10]

Elizabeth Cranch Norton, of Weymouth, Massachusetts, likewise raised her children in an open, inclusive household. Norton and her husband were usually in residence, although they frequently traveled to visit relatives elsewhere in Massachusetts and Rhode Island. In turn, relatives and friends—and their children—came for lengthy visits. Servants, whose ranks included children, also came and went. For example, in January 1795, "Solomon Porter, a boy about 12 years old came to live with us." The following year, "Mrs. Bates came and brought her daughter Nancy to spend some time with us—to be instructed in needle work, reading, writing, etc." In April of the same year, "Becca Clevely came to live with me . . . aged 13 years . . . am to cloathe her if she continues with me till she is 18."[11]

Such continuous coming and going did not slow down while women were pregnant, nursing, or caring for infants. On December 1, 1799, shortly before the birth of her fifth child, Elizabeth Norton recorded that "Mrs. Bicknell came and spent the evening and night." On December 11 Norton took her oldest son to her parents' home in Quincy, Massachusetts, while "Mrs. Bicknell staid and took care of my baby

[10] Stewart Mitchell, ed., *New Letters of Abigail Adams, 1788–1801* (Boston, 1947), 33; Thomas Eliot Andrews, ed., "The Diary of Elizabeth (Porter) Phelps," *New England Historical and Genealogical Register*, 119 (April 1965), 136; "Diary of Mary (Vial) Holyoke, 1760–1800," in *The Holyoke Diaries, 1709–1865*, ed. George Francis Dow (Salem, Mass., 1911), 58, 59, 60, 69, 70, 75. See also Buel and Buel, *Way of Duty*, 42.

[11] Elizabeth Cranch Norton Diary, Jan. 2, 1795, Aug. 22, April 19, 1796, Norton Family Papers (Massachusetts Historical Society, Boston). The practice of taking in children is amply documented in eighteenth-century diaries and journals. See, for example, Thomas Eliot Andrews, ed., "The Diary of Elizabeth (Porter) Phelps," *New England Historical and Genealogical Register*, 118 (April 1964), 119; *ibid.*, 118 (Oct. 1964), 300, 305; *ibid.*, 119 (Jan. 1965), 43; *ibid.*, 119 (April 1965), 135, 137, 140; *ibid.*, 119 (July 1965), 208, 212, 215, 221; *ibid.*, 119 (Oct. 1965), 289, 304; and Elizabeth Drinker's diary excerpted in Cecil K. Drinker, *Not So Long Ago: A Chronicle of Medicine and Doctors in Colonial Philadelphia* (New York, 1937), 37–39, 63–64.

for me." Three days later Elizabeth visited "young Mr. Tufts. Betty Burrell took care of my baby." On Christmas day the Nortons left for Quincy. Once again their servant Betty Burrell took care of baby Thomas, then ten months old. With all this bustling movement in and out of the Norton home, Elizabeth Norton was rarely alone. Indeed, a day such as December 25, 1794, about which she wrote "Staid at home with children all day—had to do all my housework—no help," stands out amid constant travel and visiting.[12]

Children in such households, even when very young, also seem to have spent considerable time elsewhere. Elizabeth Phelps's diary indicates that she frequently left her daughters, Betty and Thankful, with friends and relatives, and Mary Vial Holyoke often transported her children from Salem, Massachusetts, to Cambridge, where they stayed with her parents. All of Elizabeth Norton's children, beginning in infancy, stayed for extended periods in their grandparents' home in Quincy, a two-hour journey from Weymouth. This practice may have served several purposes. The timing of children's visits sometimes coincided with a particularly difficult pregnancy or illness. Children sometimes left their own households to go to school elsewhere. And their lengthy stays in the households of relatives may have served to foster close ties with members of an extended-kin network.[13] The frequent movement of both parents and children in and out of households contributed to the permeable quality of late eighteenth-century family life and suggests that mothers' relationships with their children formed part of a larger, continuously changing tapestry of multiple personal ties.

Given that extensive mothering style, it is perhaps not surprising that children—especially infants and toddlers—rarely figured in mothers' daily accounts of their own activities. When children were mentioned the notations were spare and brief, often related to matters of birth and death. Between 1760 and 1782, for instance, Mary Vial Holyoke bore twelve children, eight of whom died in infancy. In the following entries she describes the birth and death of a daughter:

> Sept. 5, 1767. I was brought to bed about 2 o'clock AM of a daughter.
> Sept. 6. The Child Baptized Mary.
> Sept. 7. The Baby very well till ten o'clock in the evening & then taken with fits.
> Sept. 8. The Baby remained ill all day.
> Sept. 9. It died about 8 o'clock in the morning.
> Sept. 10. Was buried.

The diary of Sarah Snell Bryant also reflects this cryptic style. The wife of a Massachusetts physician, Bryant bore her third child on July 12, 1798. "A son born a little before sun set. Mrs. White and [Mrs.] Otis here." There were only two brief, indirect references to the baby until September 17, 1798: "babe sick—very rainy

[12] Norton Diary, Dec. 2, 3, 11, 14, 1799, Dec. 25, 1794.

[13] Andrews, ed., "Diary of Elizabeth (Porter) Phelps," *New England Historical and Genealogical Register,* 119 (Jan. 1965), 51; *ibid.,* 119 (April 1965), 128; "Diary of Mary (Vial) Holyoke, 1760–1800," 67–68; Norton Diary, Aug. 5, Nov. 11, Dec. 30, 1794, March 2, 1795, Sept. 5, Dec. 16, 1796, Dec. 15, 1797, Feb. 9, March 29, 1799, Aug. 20, Sept. 13, 1800, Jan. 26, May 28, 1802.

night—kept on [illegible] with the babe." Bryant did not refer to the infant by his name, Cyrus, until the following March, when he was eight months old.[14]

The late eighteenth-century maternal diaries tell little about how children looked or behaved. Although a child's teething and walking experiences were sometimes mentioned, most diarists did not reflect on developmental milestones. More important, the diaries do not reveal children's individual personalities. Some journals provide considerable detail about mothers' household work—when and how much they spun, wove, sewed, and ironed—and their daily social life—with whom they dined and visited, who stayed with them and how long—but their children, particularly infants, remain obscure. One wonders whether this silence testifies to something more significant—not to maternal indifference but to an unspoken acknowledgment that until infants had grown into children (and perhaps hearty ones at that) they remained something less than complete persons and their well-being remained beyond a mother's control.[15]

This absence of maternal control is suggested in the accounts of the numerous home accidents that appear in diaries and letters. While few late eighteenth-century mothers expressed the divine determinism so evident in Puritan parents such as Cotton Mather, they nonetheless displayed a similar feeling of powerlessness. Consider Elizabeth Phelps's description of a toddler's accident in 1773: "Thursday morning our babe was left alone in the Room, crept to a tea-kettle of scalding water—turned it over scalded one hand very bad, the other a little. Lord what a great mercy twas no worse. thou are our constant benefactor, O may this providence serve to put me upon consideration that the Child is thine. Let me never forget it." When one of Elizabeth Norton's children was bitten by a dog, she responded with characteristic passivity: "Richard was a little bitten by a Dog which gave me some anxiety, as many dogs lately run mad and occasioned the deaths of several persons—in God's hands is his life—let him do as it seemeth to him good!"[16]

In many respects Elizabeth Norton's experiences were emblematic of the complex, sometimes contradictory attitudes of mothers in the late eighteenth century. Although her prose is spare, even cryptic, Norton's diary and letters reveal a mother who was warm and affectionate, who worried over her children's physical and spiritual welfare, and who missed them when they were away. "I long to get my little Thomas home," she wrote her mother in 1801. "I must have him (upon trial at least) a week or a fortnight. I think of him a great deal and have lived hoping every week I should find it convenient to go for him." As her children grew older, she wrote of them more frequently and with more description, perhaps indicative of her growing expectations for them. And yet she stood ready to surrender her children

[14] "Diary of Mary (Vial) Holyoke," 67; Sarah Snell Bryant Diary, July 12–Sept. 17, 1798, Bryant Family Papers (Houghton Library, Harvard University, Cambridge, Mass.).

[15] John F. Walzer, "A Period of Ambivalence: Eighteenth-Century American Childhood," in *The History of Childhood*, ed. Lloyd deMause (New York, 1974), 380n100; Norton, *Liberty's Daughters*, 85–86; Daniel Scott Smith, "Child-Naming Practices, Kinship Ties, and Changes in Family Attitudes in Hingham, Massachusetts, 1641 to 1880," *Journal of Social History*, 18 (Summer 1985), 541–66.

[16] Andrews, ed., "Diary of Elizabeth (Porter) Phelps," *New England Historical and Genealogical Register*, 118 (April 1964), 125; Norton Diary, April 10, 1798. For a discussion of the relationship between frequent accidents and extensive mothering, see Ulrich, *Good Wives*, 157–58.

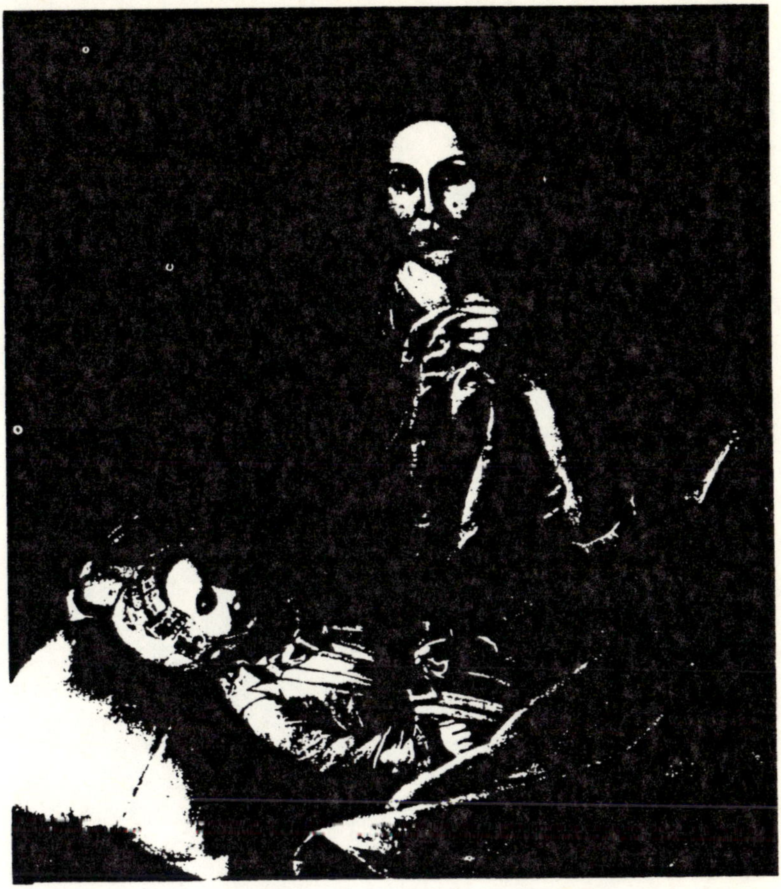

Rachel Weeping, by Charles Wilson Peale, 1772–1776.
Gift of Barra Foundation, Inc. Barra Foundation Collection.
Philadelphia Museum of Art.

to God. On her son William's seventh birthday, she noted: "May he be made a good and useful member of society if he should be continued to years of manhood—but may I be prepared to part with him, if so infinite wisdom should determine."[17]

Few maternal writings equal Louisa Park's sad account of her son Warren's death. Unlike many eighteenth-century women's personal writings, Louisa Park's diary effusively detailed the development and death of her child. Park's husband, a Newburyport, Massachusetts, physician, was away on shipboard throughout the period from Warren's birth in 1800 until his death one year later. Perhaps the father's absence drew mother and child unusally close together; indeed, Park seemed to luxu-

[17] Elizabeth Cranch Norton to Mary Cranch, Jan. 7, 1800, Norton Family Papers; Norton Diary, Dec. 29, 1798.

riate in caring for Warren—nursing him, playing with him, watching his growth, giving him medicine during his several bouts with influenza and other illnesses. "Stayed at home all day with my babe," she wrote in December 1800, "reading, writing, playing with my little innocent." One senses both the quiet pleasure and the tedium of Park's daily life as a mother: "My days have become so regular that when I have told the business of one, I have for the week. I rise at eight—eat breakfast at nine—then sew, what time I have besides the care of Warren, 'till after dinner. If no company presents, writing and reading in the afternoon. In the evening, knitting, if circumstances permit."[18]

In the midst of a virulent influenza epidemic, Park began to worry openly about Warren, even though he was not yet ill. On January 29, 1801, when Warren was nine months old, she declared in her diary, "I hope Warren is not going to be sick. I begin to love him much." By March her son was dangerously ill and despite numerous consultations with physicians and heroic efforts to save him, he died on April 25. A week after Warren's death (there are no entries during the final stages of the boy's illness), Park began to reflect on her loss. "Until today, I found it impossible to compose myself sufficiently to make the attempt [to write]. At bedtime, instead of my charming boy, my lovely babe . . . instead of my laughing cherub to receive the caresses of a tender mother—I found a lifeless corps—laid out in the white robes of innocence and death. Though I wept and pressed him, he could not look at me. How could I endure it—much less compose myself—but by believing him gone to perfect rest and happiness—there to wait for his father and mother." Her son's death, without the consoling presence of her husband, left Louisa Park desperately alone. "I know not what to do with myself, now I have no Warren to care for, attend to, caress and love." By the next day, though, she was able to let go of her child. In a single sentence she gave voice to a range of powerful emotions and values, touching on both her love for Warren and her religious resignation: "Yet I do not wish thee back again, my lovely innocent. No—I will bless my God who has taken thee to Himself before thou couldst offend him, and has saved thee from a life of sickness, sorrow, and woe, although it has been at the expense of my health and happiness."[19]

Louisa Park's account of her emotions and experiences suggests that by the turn of the nineteenth century, American concepts of mothering were changing. In her detailed description of her son's life, Park seems to have developed a richer, more intense relationship with her child than was characteristic of earlier generations of American mothers. As the nineteenth century progressed, such mother-child bonds became the norm. Over the same years ministers, educators, physicians, and social commentators produced a flood of childrearing literature advising women that motherhood was a full-time responsibility for which they were fitted by natural instinct and inclination. Central to that emerging concept of maternity was the belief

[18] Louisa Park Diary, Dec. 14, Dec. 24, 1800 (American Antiquarian Society, Worcester, Mass.).
[19] *Ibid.*, Jan. 29, May 2–May 4, 1801.

that women stood as guardians of traditional moral values in an increasingly secular, commercialized society.[20]

Other social and cultural developments over the course of the century influenced women's perceptions of themselves as mothers and of the relationships they established with their children. The increasingly private and isolated nature of the family in nineteenth-century America seems to have encouraged the establishment of intense mother-infant bonds. And in all but the most evangelical of families, Americans gradually supplemented reliance on Divine Providence with faith in the power of human agency. To be sure, mothers continued to turn to God in times of sickness and death and tried to resign themselves to God's will when children died. But increasingly they took active and sustained measures to ensure their children's health and well-being. Despite a continuously high infant death rate—indeed, the mortality rate may have risen in the first half of the nineteenth century as a result of urbanization—reactions to infant death gradually changed.[21] Individual mothers slowly came to replace God as the most important guarantors of their children's welfare—a role that created great anxiety for many nineteenth-century American women.

Women's accounts of mothering reflect a sense of high purpose and responsibility so characteristic of antebellem advice literature on maternity. "I will be obliged to consider his wants first, dear husband," Bessie Huntting Rudd wrote in 1860, shortly after giving birth to her first child. "How strange it seems to think of a *pet* coming into our thoughts requiring the *first* care and attention." For some women childrearing seems to have been more than a full-time commitment; it meant assuming a new identity altogether. As Elizabeth Sedgwick wrote after the birth of her first child, "At 6 o'clock on the 7th of January 1824 I was a *mother* and experienced that delightful transition from suffering, danger, and anxiety to happiness and that intense delight, that unspeakable sentiment which pervades the heart at its first maternal throb." For Fanny Appleton Longfellow the transformation from young wife to mother was signaled by her decision to give up the diary she had kept since she was a young girl. "With this day my Journal ends," she noted a few months after her first child's birth, "for I now have a living one to keep faithfully, more faithfully than this."[22]

Middle-class mothers in the nineteenth century cared for their children in relative isolation, compared with the large sociable households of early America. Left alone for the greater part of each day with their babies, mothers assumed primary responsibility for their care. Servants and nurses, although often present, were relegated

[20] Barbara Welter, "The Cult of True Womanhood: 1820–1860," *American Quarterly*, 18 (Summer 1966), 151–74; Bernard Wishy, *The Child and the Republic: The Dawn of Modern American Child Nurture* (Philadelphia, 1968), esp. 22–66.

[21] Meindl and Swedlund, "Secular Trends in Mortality in the Connecticut Valley," 389–96; Vinovskis, "Mortality Rates and Trends in Massachusetts before 1860," 195–201.

[22] Bessie Huntting Rudd to Edward Rudd, n.d. [summer 1860], Bessie Huntting Rudd Correspondence, Huntting-Rudd Papers (Schlesinger Library, Radcliffe College, Cambridge, Mass.); Elizabeth Dana Ellery Sedgwick Journal, 1824 (Houghton Library); Fanny Longfellow Diary, July 13, 1844, Fanny Appleton Longfellow Papers (Longfellow Historical Site, Cambridge, Mass.).

to secondary roles. "I have been employed, and very happily so, with the child all day," Mary Lee noted in her journal in 1813. In the first months of their babies' lives, many mothers rarely left home. Her firstborn was nearly three months old before Caroline White ventured out for an evening band concert. "It was a much longer time to leave baby than I have ever done before," White noted in her journal. Elizabeth Sedgwick found fulfillment in her hours of solitude with her children. Writing in 1827, when she was the mother of three children under three years old, Sedgwick declared, "My situation this winter confining me wholly to the House, excepting a daily walk for exercise, enabled me to devote myself very much to my children. Indeed my home was so happy a one that I found my Interest in general society constantly lessening."[23]

The secluded nature of the middle-class household and the amount of time that mothers spent in the company of their babies encouraged intense attachments between mothers and infants.[24] There is much evidence of such early attachment. Writing in 1810, Mary Lee declared that she had "passed a most delightful day in tending my child; she has been unusually pleasant and I have enjoyed the true comfort of a *little* baby." Writing several generations later, in 1863, Elizabeth Child described her first sight of her baby daughter: "I remember that while I looked you opened your eyes . . . and as they met mine I thought they mutely recognized the new tie." "The dear little fellow," Caroline White wrote of her newborn in 1856, "I did not think I should love him so well so soon."[25].

Some mothers devoted their journals exclusively to detailed accounts of their children's development. Elizabeth Sedgwick, for instance, kept a daily account of her daughter's life. "Long has been my intention to keep a journal of my child's life extending even to the minutest action and the slightest unfolding of her character," she noted in the first entry. "The smallest events of her life have had their peculiar interest for us, who have been watching her as parents always watch their heart's treasure." When the child Lizzie Sedgwick herself became a mother, she continued the tradition. Fanny Longfellow was the mother of three children when she resumed a journal of 1847. In place of the introspective musings and accounts of social activities that had filled her earlier journals, her new diary, aptly titled "Chronicle of the Children of Craigie Castle," was given over to the unfolding of her children's personalities and to notes on their activities and behavior.[26]

Infants and toddlers appear in nineteenth-century journals as full-fledged, albeit

[23] Frank Rollins Morse, ed., *Henry and Mary Lee: Letters and Journals, with Other Family Papers, 1802–1860* (Boston, 1926), 178–79; Caroline White Diary, Aug. 1, 1856, White Family Papers (American Antiquarian Society, Worcester, Mass.); Sedgwick Journal, n.d. [winter 1827].

[24] For a discussion of the privatization of the household, see Mary P. Ryan, *Cradle of the Middle Class: The Family in Oneida County, New York, 1790–1865* (Cambridge, Eng., 1981); Kirk Jeffrey, "The Family as a Utopian Retreat from the City: The Nineteenth Century," *Soundings*, 55 (Spring 1972), 24–41; Edward Shorter, *The Making of the Modern Family* (New York, 1975), 168–204, 242, 250; and Robert V. Wells, "Family History and Demographic Transition," *Journal of Social History*, 9 (Fall 1975), 1–19.

[25] Morse, ed., *Henry and Mary Lee*, 91; Elizabeth Sedgwick Child Journal, n.d. [1865] (Houghton Library); White Diary, June 12, 1856.

[26] Sedgwick Journal, n.d. [1824]; Child Journal, 1865–1874; Longfellow Diary, 1848. Most other nineteenth-century maternal diaries examined contained daily comments on children.

physically fragile, individuals. Children are almost always referred to by name or, commonly, by affectionate nicknames: They are "birdies," "chicks," "kitties," "pets." Mothers also adopted as nicknames the names children called themselves. Thus Mary Lee's daughter Betty is "Beppa" in her writings; Caroline White's son Charlie is "Larlie"; Fanny Longfellow's daughter is "Sipsie."

Children's distinct personalities and physical characteristics emerge clearly. Fanny Longfellow's four-year-old son Charley was a "Man of action" who "promises to have a rich and noble nature." Erny, at two, was "an angelic little child" who "loves to nestle in one's lap with his thumb in his mouth . . . as timid and tender as a young bird. He promises to be the poet." And "Little Fan, not a year old, is only a round rosy merry plaything with dark blue eyes, a cunning little mouth and a very intelligent eager air." Calista Hall presents a similarly lively description of her baby daughter, "Little Frances grows more interesting every day. She will try to say everything you tell her too. Ask her whose baby she is, she will say Pa and Ma. . . . She is a little rogue. She will pull of her shoes and stokings as fast as I can put them on."[27]

Nineteenth-century mothers carefully recorded developmental milestones. On January 9, 1848, for instance, Fanny Longfellow noted that her daughter had "learned to creep." By February 3, "Little Fan has a tooth and climbs by chairs upon her feet." On March 8, "Baby . . . looked at me and smiling said, 'Mama' then put her finger in my mouth." Elizabeth Sedgwick gave a precise description of her daughter's walking: "[At] 14 months and 6 days old, you rose from your chair with great deliberation and walked across the nursery. . . . You seemed neither pleased nor surprised."[28].

Such detailed description of children's behavior and the many expressions of affection that fill these writings attest to the richly textured emotional bonds between middle-class women and their children. Mothers clearly delighted in their children. "Took Charley to village," Fanny Longfellow noted in a typical entry. "Love to feel his hand in mine for a walk and he is so glad to go with me." Or as Bessie Rudd wrote about her infant son, "He grows into our hearts every day, . . . he is becoming an idol with me, and his sweet face, as he looks up so innocently, seems to steal your heart immediately." But beneath this delight lay the ever-present fear that their children might die. In the first days and weeks after giving birth, many mothers appear to have been frightened by the intensity of their feelings for infants whose lives seemed so fragile. "He is so tender," Caroline White wrote of her son in 1856, "I feel as though a very slight injury or sickness could carry him off—and I do not feel ready to part with him—short time as our relation to each other has existed."[29]

As their infants grew, mothers became more anxious and appear to have regarded serious illness as inevitable. Accounts of children's illnesses and their treatment consume a significant part of nineteenth-century maternal writings. "Edwin was quite

[27] Longfellow Diary, Jan. 1848; Carol Kammen, ed., "The Letters of Calista Hall," *New York History*, 63 (April 1982), 218.

[28] Longfellow Diary, Jan. 9, Feb. 3, March 8, 1848; Sedgwick Journal, March 13, 1826.

[29] Longfellow Diary, June 14, 1848; Bessie Huntting Rudd to Edward Rudd, n.d. [summer 1860], Bessie Huntting Rudd Correspondence, Huntting-Rudd Papers; White Diary, June 13, 1856.

Fanny Longfellow with sons Charles and Ernest. Daguerreotype portrait by Lucius H. Cathan, c. 1849.
Courtesy United States Department of the Interior, National Park Service, Longfellow National Historic Site.

sick Sunday night," Calista Hall wrote in 1849 in a typical description. "He could not keep any thing down and had a high fever. I set holding him. . . . I was afraid he would die, he seemed so sick." Elizabeth Cleveland's detailed record of her baby daughter's fatal illness is also characteristic of such accounts. In the spring of 1848, Cleveland wrote, "my dear little Lucretia had her first sickness. I was very anxious—as the Dr. considered it a bad state of the digestive organs—cankered bowels." The little girl improved temporarily, but became seriously ill in July. For more than a month, Cleveland's journal was given over to daily entries describing her daughter's symptoms and the medical efforts made to cure her. Late in August, despite Cleveland's increasingly frantic efforts to save her daughter, the child died. Only then did Cleveland invoke God: "I must show my love in my resignation that she has gone to God," she wrote some days after Lucretia died.[30]

Infancy and early childhood emerge as periods of successive physical crises. Feeding, teething, weaning, and walking all possessed their peculiar dangers. Feeding crises were particularly common. A breast infection and phlebitis forced Caroline White to wean her first child prematurely, and "the poor little fellow has

[30] Kammen, ed., "Letters of Calista Hall," 226; Elizabeth Cleveland Journal, May–August 1848 (Essex Institute, Salem, Mass.).

pained and been ailing ever since." Mothers who weaned their infants early or who bottlefed them had good reason to be apprehensive, for at a time when water and milk supplies could not be counted on to be clean, babies brought up "by hand" were at far greater risk of disease. For months after she weaned her son in 1856, White devoted her journal to the daily fluctuations in her son's weight and health. A gain in weight, however slight, was cause for rejoicing. But there were frequent setbacks. "Called on friend with six-week old baby bigger than mine of sixteen weeks. Poor little thing—he now weighs ten pounds—six weeks ago he weighed thirteen." Charlie White survived and developed into a healthy, thriving child, but his mother dreaded the possibility of raising another baby "by hand." She anxiously kept track of each infant's weight and despaired of her ability to nurse them successfully. "I am not strong—I feel quite discouraged about having nourishment enough for baby," she wrote shortly after the birth of her daughter in 1863. "I have to feed her considerably now—am hoping for a better state of things. She does not grow as well as she ought."[31]

Children's teething, long regarded as a critical period in infants' lives, was also a time of apprehension for mothers. Both mothers and physicians believed that dentition was a major cause of infant death. "The period of teething is filled with terror to a mother's imagination and I had looked forward to it with unceasing anxiety," Elizabeth Sedgwick wrote. "Poor little Erny was found . . . in his crib in convulsions from teeth," Fanny Longfellow noted in early 1848. "Little fragile flower. I tremble as I look at him and am devoured by anxiety." Longfellow believed that teething caused her daughter's fatal illness later that year. When little Fanny was eighteen months old, her mother noted that the child was "having a hard time teething." Less than a week after the first symptoms appeared, what had seemingly begun as difficult teething had developed into a life-threatening illness. "A very anxious day," Fanny Longfellow wrote on September 6. "Poor little baby seemed to have much trouble in her head and the Doctor feared congestion of the brain." Heroic medical measures, including large doses of mercury, were employed in a futile attempt to save her life. On September 11, Fanny died. "Sinking, sinking away from us," Longfellow wrote on the day of her daughter's death. "Felt a terrible desire to seize her in my arms and warm her to life again at my breast. Oh for one look of love, one mood or smile. . . . Heard her breathing shorten, then cease, without a flutter."[32]

Fanny Longfellow's profound grief over the death of her daughter plunged her into a lengthy depression. "I seem to have lost all interest in the future and can enjoy my children only from hour to hour. I feel as if my lost darling were drawing me to her—as I controlled her life before birth so does she me now." Almost all of Longfellow's diary notations for the next year dwelt on little Fanny's death and the fear that her remaining children would die. She could not look at them, she wrote, without imagining them in their own small graves. And for months after her loss,

[31] White Diary, Sept. 14, Sept. 15, 1856, June 30, 1863.

[32] Sedgwick Journal, n.d. [1825]; Longfellow Diary, Feb. 18, Aug. 18, Sept. 6, Sept. 11, 1848.

Longfellow found herself reliving the final days of her daughter's life, "haunted by thoughts of what might have been avoided, the most pitiless of all."[33]

The child's death was a tragedy from which Fanny Longfellow never fully recovered. In 1850, she bore a second daughter, Alice, who seemed "an especial grace of God." But Alice's birth coincided with her son Erny's serious bout with pleurisy. "We were terribly anxious," Fanny wrote in the same entry in which she recorded Alice's birth. "I felt as if a great stone were hurled back upon my heart from which I had just been relieved. I have never been without anxiety for him but now it will be increased tenfold." Her daughter's death remained the central event in Fanny Longfellow's life.[34]

Why did nineteenth-century mothers appear to fear child illness and death so much more intensely than parents in early America? What factors account for growing intimacy between mother and child? To be sure, early American parents feared death, too, and grieved over the loss of loved ones.[35] But one detects in those parents a more passive attitude of Christian resignation. By the early decades of the nineteenth century, except among evangelical families, Divine Providence was giving way to exalted motherhood in the care and protection of children.[36] Parents, as always, tried to submit to God's will in the face of infant illness and death, but it was an effort increasingly undermined by the growing belief that a child's health depended mainly on maternal dedication and appropriate medical treatment. Mothers may well have worried so incessantly about the health of their children because they were coming to believe—despite persistently high infant death rates—that good mothering could somehow ensure a baby's survival.

That gradual shift in the locus of control reflected new assumptions about the mother's centrality in the family and her principal responsibility for child nurture. At a deeper level, however, it seems closely linked to the growing belief that human agency could shape and control the natural order. Just as Americans were beginning to reject pain and death as necessary concomitants of childbearing—as the growing popularity of ether and chloroform in childbirth attest—they embraced the idea of maternal efficacy in overseeing the health of their infants.[37] As the author of one popular home medical guide stated, "No one can for a moment believe that the excessive and increasing infant mortality among us, is part of the established order of nature, or of the systematic arrangements of Divine Providence." Or as another

[33] Longfellow Diary, Oct. 14, Sept. 13, 1848.

[34] *Ibid.*, n.d. [1850], Feb. 22, 1851. For a discussion of death in nineteenth-century families, see Lewis Saum, "Death in the Popular Mind of Pre-Civil War America," *American Quarterly*, 26 (Dec. 1974), 477–95; and Jan Lewis, *The Pursuit of Happiness: Family and Values in Jefferson's Virginia* (New York, 1983), 98–102.

[35] See, for example, David Stannard, "Death and the Puritan Child," *American Quarterly*, 26 (Dec. 1974), 456–76; Smith, *Inside the Great House*, 249–80; and Lewis, *Pursuit of Happiness*, 72–76.

[36] On evangelical childrearing see William G. McLoughlin, "Evangelical Childrearing in the Age of Jackson: Francis Wayland's Views on When and How to Subdue the Willfulness of Children," *Journal of Social History*, 9 (Fall 1975), 21–43; and Greven, *Protestant Temperament*, 21-61.

[37] Judith Walzer Leavitt, "'Science' Enters the Birthing Room: Obstetrics in America since the Eighteenth Century," *Journal of American History*, 70 (Sept. 1983), 281–304. Historians have just begun to examine fathers' responses to these developments. For a good example of a father whose attitudes toward parenting reflected changes in thinking about human agency, see Carol E. Hoffecker, ed., "The Diaries of Edmund Canby, A Quaker Miller, 1822-1848," *Delaware History*, 16 (Oct. 1974), 79–121; *ibid.*, 16 (Spring-Summer 1975), 184–243.

leading maternal advisor observed in 1844, "The first and most important truth . . . to be impressed on mothers, is, that the constitution of their offspring depends on natural consequences, many of which are under their own control.[38]

Physicians were concerned about good mothering but paid little attention to infant mortality. Many doctors were well aware of the fact that infant deaths constituted a very large percentage of total mortality, but medical literature throughout the century devoted strikingly little attention to this problem. Specialized medical interest in pediatrics was just emerging in the 1830s and 1840s. The few physicans who wrote on children's diseases believed that infancy was a period of extreme physical debility and weakness; inevitably, given infants' natural susceptibility to disease, many would perish. As D. Francis Condie, one of the first writers on pediatrics, explained, "During infancy and childhood, there exists a very strong predisposition to disease. . . . During the first few weeks of existence, the imperfect organization of the body, and the deficiency in vigour of most of its functions, render it particularly liable to the actions of various agents, the impression of which . . . produces in the delicate organs of the infant, the most serious disturbance, resulting in the greater number of cases, in a rapid extinction of life."[39] Infancy, like old age, was a time to die.

Significantly, doctors and other writers of medical guides did not recognize the social and economic dimensions of infant diseases and their prevention. Concerns about health lay entirely within individual mothers' domain. As one physician declared, the chief cause of infant death was the "ignorance and false pride of the mothers. Children are killed by the manner in which they are dressed, and by the food that is given them, as much as any other cause." Doctors agreed that there was much individual mothers could do to ensure their children's well-being. Mothers could excercise constant vigilance over their children's day-to-day care – bathing, dressing, playing, and ministering to them during illness. Most important, mothers had a duty to nurse their own infants. A mother "must not delegate to any being the sacred and delightful task of suckling her child." Mothers could school themselves in the symptoms and etiology of childhood diseases and the essentials of child hygiene. They could learn to distinguish between ordinary innocuous "snuffles" and the "morbid snuffles" that portended serious illness or death. And they could treat their vulnerable infants gently by refraining from cold baths and harsh purgatives and medications, and by sheltering their delicate nervous systems from bright lights, extreme temperatures, and loud noises.[40] Just as Americans assigned mothers

[38] An American Matron [pseud.], *The Maternal Physician: A Treatise on the Nurture and Management of Infants, From the Birth Until Two Years Old, Being the Result of Sixteen Years' Experience in the Nursery* (Philadelphia, 1810), 7; Mrs. [Louisa Mary Bacon] Barwell, *Infant Treatment: With Directions to Mothers for Self-Management Before, During, and After Pregnancy* (New York, 1844), 15.

[39] D. Francis Condie, *A Practical Treatise on the Diseases of Children* (Philadelphia, 1844), 85–86.

[40] "Infant Mortality and Fashionable Dress," *New York Medical Journal*, 10 (Jan. 1870), 424–25; John W. Thrailkill, *An Essay on the Causes of Infant Mortality; Being a Brief Account of the Origins of the Feebleness and Diseases Which Afflict and Destroy So Many Children Under Five Years of Age* (St. Louis, 1869), 6–7; William P. Dewees, *A Treatise on the Physical and Medical Treatment of Children* (Philadelphia, 1836), 48, 72, 108; W. M. Ireland, *Advice to Mothers on the Management of Infants and Young Children, with Directions on How to Distinguish and Prevent Their Complaints* (New York, 1820), esp. 5–38; American Matron [pseud.], *Maternal Physician*, 60–61.

Mother bathing baby. Photograph c. 1890–1910, Charles Van Schaick Collection. *Courtesy State Historical Society of Wisconsin.*

the responsibility for their children's moral welfare, so too did they vouchsafe to them their babies' very survival.

American culture, then, as reflected in both professional and popular medical literature, sent mothers a mixed message. On the one hand, death in infancy was recognized as commonplace, even expected. On the other, "good" mothers were encouraged to believe that careful nurturing could ensure the well-being of their offspring. It is not known how many mothers read such medical guides or how they interpreted them. Still, the perception of infancy as a time of extreme physical vulnerability and the belief that only mothers could provide proper care help explain maternal anxiety. Certainly women looked on infancy and early childhood as precarious times. Given the limited knowledge of infectious disease, it was impossible for a mother to gauge the severity of a child's illness. Thus any illness appeared potentially fatal. Alone at home with children whose fragile health they believed lay largely in their own hands, mothers fell prey to anxiety and fear.

The private agonies of watchful and worried mothers bear witness to the special intimacies of their increasingly separate sphere at home. While no doubt mothers could share some of their fears with caring husbands, for the most part their strong maternal feelings found expression in sentimental literature, maternal associations, and women's networks of friends and relatives.[41] In this context the idea of the family as a calm and soothing refuge from a busy world takes on a peculiarly patriarchal cast. For men away at work, hearth and home may have seemed like a place of repose and comfort; for many women, the family was the seat of apprehension and turmoil.[42]

Children in early nineteenth-century America were gradually slipping out of the hands of God and into their mothers' warm, if nervous, embrace. And infant death, like so much else in the increasingly intimate world of the family, became a private tragedy. Whereas the world beyond the household paid little notice to infant mortality, for mothers the lives and deaths of their infants were matters that took a powerful emotional toll. Living beyond the time of unquestioned confidence in the providential power of an omnipotent God and before that of public health advances and reliable medical help, women experienced motherhood in solitude—sole possessors of all the delights and fears that come with raising children.

When it came time to have her baby in Madison, Wisconsin, in 1906, Dorothy Reed Mendenhall expected a safe and normal delivery. A physician herself, she had been well trained in obstetrics at Johns Hopkins University Medical School in the 1890s and, thanks to several years at New York's Babies' Hospital, she had unusually thorough grounding in pediatrics as well. As soon as she learned she was pregnant, Mendenhall placed herself in the care of the surgeon reputed to be the best in the city. What followed was a disaster. Her physician proved careless and incompetent. After two days of lingering labor, the doctor manually turned the baby and delivered it feet first, a hazardous obstetrical procedure. "All I remember was turning my head into the pillow and thinking this will be the end; I shall die, he doesn't know what to do." A few hours later, Mendenhall became aware of her baby's labored and abnormal breathing. She tried to resuscitate her daughter with artificial respiration, but a few hours later "Margaret, my firstborn and only girl, died of cerebral hemorrhage and bad obstetrics."[43]

Mendenhall had three other children (the second of whom also died in early childhood) and for several years devoted herself to childrearing rather than to her career as a physician. But in 1914, on the urging of a home economist at the University of Wisconsin, she began to travel to small Wisconsin towns to lecture to women on maternal and infant welfare. What she found—women desperately looking for medical assistance and information on baby care—launched Mendenhall on a long public career as a maternal and infant health reformer.[44]

[41] See, for example, Welter, "Cult of True Womanhood"; and Carroll Smith-Rosenberg, "The Female World of Love and Ritual: Relations between Women in Nineteenth Century America," *Signs*, 1 (Autumn 1975), 1–30. For a different interpretation of early nineteenth-century maternal values that is based on literary sources, see Ann Douglas, *The Feminization of American Culture* (New York, 1977), esp. 1–13, 50–93, 240–72.

[42] For the view of the early nineteenth-century family as refuge, see Jeffrey, "Family as a Utopian Retreat from the City"; and Ryan, *Cradle of the Middle Class*, 146–55, 191–98.

[43] Dorothy Reed Mendenhall, unpublished autobiography, section H, p. 13, Dorothy Reed Mendenhall Papers, Sophia Smith Collection (Smith College, North Hampton, Mass.).

[44] *Ibid.*, section I, p. 2.

Mendenhall's medical training enabled her, unlike nineteenth-century mothers, to translate her private grief into public action. "My own part in [maternal and infant welfare] work is a great satisfaction to me," she reflected some years later. "It, in a way, was a compensation reaction to help me bear the bitter frustration that the deaths of my babies gave me. Helping another mother have her child safely and advising countless mothers how to care for their babies was a real outlet for my grief."[45]

Mendenhall's experience reflects a new development in the history of American mothering: By the first decades of the twentieth century, mothers' attitudes toward infant death had undergone a seachange. No longer was the loss of a child to be viewed passively as the will of God or to be endured silently in the privacy of the home. Instead, women in communities throughout the United States made the nation's high infant mortality a matter of serious public, political concern and called on doctors, public health officials, and the state to take action to reduce the number of infant deaths. Social reformer Florence Kelley articulated the new consciousness: "So long as mothers did not know that children need not die. . . . [W]e strove for resignation, not intelligence. A generation ago we could only vainly mourn. Today we now know that every dying child accuses the community. For knowledge is available for keeping alive and well so nearly all, that we may justly be said to sin in the light of the new day when we let any die."[46]

Such a dramatic change in attitude was due, in part, to the new views of infancy reflected in the child-study movement so popular with American mothers at the turn of the century. More important, however, during the Progressive Era women worked in a variety of ways to make visible and public concerns that had in earlier generations been private and to document connections between the quality of life in the home and the social and political institutions of the larger community. At the same time, Americans continued to identify mothers as the primary guarantors of children's well-being and to emphasize the crucial importance of mother-infant bonds. Thus both change and continuity—the new emphasis on the social and public aspects of mothering and the traditional belief in the sanctity of the mother-infant bond and maternal responsibility—characterize the history of American mothering in the modern period.

The child-study movement illustrates how nineteenth-century concepts of intensive mothering continued to influence twentieth-century mothers' perceptions of their roles and responsibilities. The movement, a coalition of psychologists interested in defining and charting infancy as a critical, distinct stage in human development and mothers anxious to raise their children according to scientific principles and to enhance the status of motherhood, produced a unique literature aptly called "baby biography."[47] Purportedly scientific in method and intent, baby biographies

[45] *Ibid.*

[46] Florence Kelley, "Children in the Cities," *National Municipal Review*, 4 (April 1915), 199.

[47] On the child-study movement, see Steven L. Schlossman, "Before Home Start: Notes toward a History of Parent Education in America, 1897–1929," *Harvard Educational Review*, 46 (Aug. 1976), 436–67; Sheila M. Rothman, *Woman's Proper Place: A History of Changing Ideals and Practices, 1870 to the Present* (New York,

were meticulously detailed accounts, usually kept by mothers, of the day-to-day development of individual infants. For example, Louise E. Hogan, who published her journal of her son's development, *A Study of a Child*, in 1898, made careful daily observations of her baby's behavior. A typical entry reads: "He began to build with blocks to-day, placing five or six on top of each other with great care and precision. The words he has learned since November, when he was nine months old, are as follows, given in the order of acquirement: 'Oh, mammam,' 'hab'em,' 'gib'em,' 'ups-a-dada,' 'wow wow,' 'bow wow,' 'ba' and 'baba' for papa (he generally says 'ba'), 'by-bye.'" Such works attested to the primacy of individual mothers in guiding infant development: Because infancy was a crucial time on which future emotional and intellectual growth depended, mothers' close relationships with their infants were critical. As Elizabeth Harrison explained in *A Study of Child-Nature from the Kindergarten Standpoint* (1907), "One of the greatest lines of the world's work lies here before us: the understanding of little children, in order that they may be properly trained. Correctly understood, it demands of woman her highest endeavor, the broadest culture, the most complete command of herself, and the understanding of her resources and environments. It demands of her that she become a physician, an artist, a teacher, a poet, a philosopher, a priest." Authors of baby biographies exhorted other mothers to keep systematic records of their own children's development, either by following the general outlines of published studies or by making notations in one of the commercially marketed, highly detailed "baby books" that appeared in the United States by the 1880s.[48]

By 1910 child study had lost its momentum as a social movement, but its popularity, however brief, provides insight into the ways that mothers, educators, and behavioral scientists placed new emphasis on the importance of infancy as a developmental stage and simultaneously reaffirmed traditional concepts of motherhood: Much as antebellum Americans entrusted mothers with the responsibility of imbuing children with sound moral values and republican ideals, Americans at the turn of the twentieth century assigned to mothers the responsibility of overseeing their children's cognitive and emotional development.

During the same years a generation of women progressive reformers also played a central role in reshaping American views of childhood and in making the issue of infant welfare the focus of social concern. Women such as Julia Lathrop and Grace Abbott, both of whom headed the federal Children's Bureau; Florence Kelley; Dorothy Mendenhall; S. Josephine Baker, who headed New York's Bureau of Child Hygiene; and Elizabeth Putnam, who pioneered in the development of prenatal care, made common cause with public health officials and physicians to create

---

1978), 97–106; and Joseph F. Kett, *Rites of Passage: Adolescence in America, 1790 to the Present* (New York, 1977), 228–30.

[48] Louise E. Hogan, *A Study of a Child* (New York, 1898), 1–14, 30–31; Elizabeth Harrison, *A Study of Child-Nature from the Kindergarten Standpoint* (Chicago, 1907), 11; Milicent Washburn Shinn, *The Biography of a Baby* (Boston, 1900), esp. 1–6, 10–19; Jessie Chase Fenton, *Practical Psychology of Babyhood: The Mental Development and Mental Hygiene of the First Two Years of Life* (Boston, 1925), esp. 315–41. See also Winifred S. Hall, "The First 500 Days of a Child's Life," *Child-Study Monthly*, 2 (Nov. 1896), 330–42; *ibid.*, 2 (Dec. 1896), 394–407; *ibid.*, 2 (Jan. 1897), 458–73; *ibid.*, 2 (Feb. 1897), 522–37.

influential maternal- and child-welfare movements. Equally important, women in communities throughout the United States acted through women's clubs, mothers' associations, and civic-reform organizations to link child health to municipal politics.

Women active in the infant-welfare movement differed among themselves as to the most efficacious solutions to the problem of an infant death rate that in 1900 remained as high as 159 per 1000 population under one year old and soared to as high as 235 per 1000 infant population in some industrial cities.[49] Some reformers stressed overarching social and economic problems such as poverty; others emphasized the importance of individual solutions such as maternal education and breast-feeding. Many women believed that both municipal reform and maternal education were necessary.[50] Collectively, however, women's groups and organizations such as the American Association for the Study and Prevention of Infant Mortality, established in 1909, made infant mortality a highly visible public issue. In cities and towns all over the country, women's clubs organized "baby weeks," "baby-saving campaigns," and child-welfare exhibits. Those who visited the exhibits viewed graphic displays of the ways poverty, overcrowding, inadequate municipal services, substandard housing, and impure milk supplies affected the infant death rate.[51]

At one level, the child-welfare activities were designed to reach individual mothers, particularly working-class, immigrant, and rural women, to teach them about infant feeding and child care. But at a deeper level, the intentions of reformers cut across class lines, for their activities were meant to serve a broad educational function: The dedication of individual mothers, the reformers stressed, was futile in communities that failed to provide adequate sanitation, clean water, or pure milk. Nor could maternal efforts alone succeed in a society that paid lip service to the importance of mothering and the family but did not actually value children sufficiently to commit resources to try to keep them alive. Physician Emma DeVries put the matter bluntly in a letter to Julia Lathrop: "Here's to the future day when

[49] Hibbs, *Infant Mortality*, 12. As late as the first decades of the twentieth century, neither the federal government nor most state governments provided for complete and accurate registration of births. The lack of such vital statistics renders infant mortality figures imprecise. See James H. Cassedy, "The Registration Area and American Vital Statistics: Development of a Health Research Resource, 1885–1915," *Bulletin of the History of Medicine*, 39 (May-June 1965), 221–32.

[50] Harvey Levenstein, "'Best for Babies' or 'Preventable Infanticide'? The Controversy over Artificial Feeding of Infants in America, 1880–1920," *Journal of American History*, 70 (June 1983), 75–94; J. Stanley Lemons, "The Sheppard-Towner Act: Progressivism in the 1920s," *ibid.*, 55 (March 1969), 776–86; Judith Walzer Leavitt, *The Healthiest City: Milwaukee and the Politics of Health Reform* (Princeton, 1982), 156–89; Constance D. Leupp, "Campaigning for Babies' Lives," *McClure's Magazine*, 38 (Aug. 1912), 361–73; "For the Babies of Philadelphia," *Survey*, July 10, 1909, p. 533; "Survey of Sickness," *ibid.*, Oct. 16, 1915, pp. 65–69; Helen Worthington Rogers, "A Modest Experiment in Foster-Motherhood; The Work of the Pure Milk Commission of the Children's Aid Association of Indianapolis," *ibid.*, May 1, 1909, pp. 176–83; Wilbur C. Phillips, "The Mother and the Baby," *ibid.*, Aug. 7, 1909, pp. 623–31; "Coordinated Child-Saving," *Charities and The Commons*, Feb. 20, 1909, p. 1010; "The Right View of the Child," *ibid.*, April 25, 1908, pp. 123–25; "To Reduce Infant Mortality," *ibid.*, May 30, 1908, p. 285; S. Josephine Baker, "The Value of Municipal Control of Child Hygiene," *American Journal of Obstetrics and the Diseases of Women and Children*, 65 (June 1912), 1061–68; Mrs. William Lowell Putnam, "The Importance of Prenatal Care," *ibid.*, 78 (July 1918), 103–107.

[51] Mary Ritter Beard, *Woman's Work in Municipalities* (New York, 1915), 56–68; Anna Louise Strong, "Child Welfare Exhibits," *National Municipal Review*, 1 (April 1912), 248–52; S. Josephine Baker, *Fighting for Life* (New York, 1939).

The "$acred Motherhood" postcard, 1911, widely distributed by the Women's Trade Union League. The postcard was reproduced from the original drawing by William H. Bradley. *Courtesy State Historical Society of Wisconsin.*

our dear old Uncle Sam will enable the Children's Bureau to do as much for the babies as has been done for the pigs."[52]

Women's growing conviction that mothers alone could not reduce infant mor-

[52] Emma DeVries to Julia Lathrop, March 6, 1916, Records of the U.S. Department of Labor Children's Bureau, RG 102 (National Archives).

tality and that increased medical help and government involvement were necessary to preserve the well-being of their babies is illustrated most vividly in the hundreds of thousands of letters mothers wrote to the federal Children's Bureau after its establishment in 1912. Women from every region of the country and every social class wrote to the bureau, pouring out details of their mothering experiences.[53] Their letters provide graphic, often eloquent testimony to mothers' search for knowledge and assistance.

Many letters reflect both mothers' frustration at knowing so little about childbirth and infant care and their anger at the lack of available medical expertise and social support. After losing her four-month-old son, for example, an Illinois woman wrote the bureau that "it was then that I knew how helpless I was when it came to knowing what a mother should know. My baby was sacrificed thru mere ignorance. . . . I felt my own baby had every chance. Our home was clean and sanitary and far more luxurious than lots of children. But when I had to stand by and see my baby slowly starve I made up my mind I'd fight the world but what I'd find out some way to teach people more about babies." The angry mother, writing two years after her child's death, was now living in Boston and had just attended a lecture series on baby welfare. She was trying to "study every word I [can] find" on baby care, for she was convinced that it was neither God nor bad mothering, but the "lack of proper care" that had killed her son. "I soon found that not only mothers of large families knew nothing about the scientific care of babies but the best doctors of the city knew less."[54]

An Alabama woman who had been isolated from reliable medical help when her twin sons, born prematurely, died at the age of thirteen days wrote to the bureau for information when she became pregnant again. "I want to find out the reason and how to prevent anything like that this time. . . . What could have been done during those thirteen days and what was possibly done that should not have been done? It there any reason why the next child will be born before the full term on account of the twins coming too soon? is there anything that can be done to prevent it? . . . We are reading and trying to prepare but as this is such a poor place to get help of the right sort I am afraid that we still will know too little to handle a similar situation should we be placed that way again. My doctor seems to know nothing about premature births and I want some information there."[55] Such urgent requests for information reflect mothers' continued belief that they were responsible for their children's welfare and a strong conviction that, through knowledge and proper care, infants deaths could be prevented.

Many mothers who wrote to the bureau criticized what they perceived as widespread public indifference to children's well-being. "With the Baby Week Campaign in progress and knowing the importance of taking good care of babies," a

[53] Nancy Weiss, "Mother, the Invention of Necessity: Dr. Benjamin Spock's *Baby and Child Care*," *American Quarterly*, 29 (Winter 1977), 519–46.

[54] Mrs. WRD, Cambridge, Mass., to Children's Bureau, June 22, 1918, Records of the U.S. Department of Labor Children's Bureau.

[55] MH, Bladon Springs, Alabama, to Children's Bureau, July 8, 1919, *ibid.*

Maryland woman wrote, "I cannot help making a few remarks." Neither pasteurized milk nor ice was available in her community, she continued, although "we are right close to the Naval Academy Dairy where they pasteurize milk and make ice every day, still the Government refuses to sell either article. If babies are to be saved these things are necessary." "I write to see if the US Department [Children's Bureau] will see that a pregnant women gets medical attention when needed," a Virginia woman stated. "Will not our government soon do something for the poor mothers of America to help her raise her babies? Now that I am soon to become a mother again will I have to see my child pass out of my arms to the Great beyond or will the Government help us poor mothers by just seeing we get physicians at the time of birth?" Or as an Ohio woman declared in 1920, "it seems to me that the progress in the treatment of obstetrical care is almost inexcusably slow or treated with remarkable indifference. Could not this matter be more seriously stressed by the government?" The federal government ought to hire physicians "to doctor these women and babies," a South Dakota woman wrote. "When that is done, the efforts of the government to save the mothers and babies will be partly accomplished."[56]

Perhaps no mother expressed so well the modern frustration and impatience with needless infant deaths as a Mississippi woman. "Here in Jackson we have been recently having such sad deaths," she wrote to the bureau in 1915. "I have just come from a funeral this afternoon, the baby was buried two or three days ago, the Mother to-day. . . ." She demanded to know what was responsible for such deaths. "Is it the corsets we wear? Is it the food we eat? Is it the strain we live under? What is it? It makes me mad to hear the preachers say 'It's God's will' 'She has fulfilled her mission,' etc. Something's got to be done—and done quickly."[57]

For mothers who wrote to the Children's Bureau, both maternal education, which would enable individual mothers to carry out their responsibilities more effectively, and social reform were essential. Underlying those maternal concerns were two assumptions that distinguished mothering in the twentieth century from that of previous generations. First, infant deaths were preventable. And second, society at large—rather than Divine Providence or individual mothers alone—must assume responsibility for children's survival and well-being.

For the first three centuries of American history, infant death was the central reality of maternal experience. Although mothers' interpretations of and responses to the ever-present possibility that their children might die changed considerably—from the seventeenth- and eighteenth-century conviction that God alone determined the fate of infants to the Progressive Era belief that civic reform and public health measures could ensure babies' survival—women's writings attest to the importance of infant death in shaping maternal experience and consciousness. Only as infant

[56] Mrs. IL, Annapolis, to Children's Bureau, May 12, 1915, *ibid.*; Mrs. DEH, Staunton, Va., to Children's Bureau, July 3, 1920, *ibid.*; Mrs. HBC, Steubenville, Ohio, to Children's Bureau, Feb. 10, 1920, *ibid.*; Mrs. RN, South Dakota, to Children's Bureau, Aug. 12, 1919, *ibid.*

[57] Mrs. CFH, Jackson, Miss., to Children's Bureau, April 28, 1915, *ibid.*

mortality began to decline significantly after 1900 did the deaths of infants and young children cease to be common events in middle-class families. By the 1920s maternal consciousness was no longer shaped primarily by incessant anxiety that babies might die. In this crucial respect the first decades of the twentieth century are a watershed in the history of mothering and of the family.

In another important respect, however, maternal experience has shown greater continuity than change. Since the turn of the nineteenth century, women's perceptions of themselves as mothers have been influenced by a cultural definition of motherhood that stresses the intense, essentially private nature of the mother-child bond and the primary responsibility of mothers for the well-being of their children. Americans redefined specific maternal responsibilities over time, but the new definitions supplemented traditional beliefs rather than supplanted them. In those beliefs the essential continuity in definitions of motherhood can be traced from the early nineteenth century to the present day. Early twentieth-century women articulated a new, public dimension to motherhood that became institutionalized in the acceptance of some degree of government responsibility for child welfare. American society, however, has continued to define mothering almost entirely as an individual, private experience and to assign to individual mothers the primary responsibility for their children's care and welfare.

Wife Beating in Nineteenth-Century America

ELIZABETH PLECK
University of Michigan

A reanalysis of appellate court decisions, state statutes, and autobiographies indicates that wife-beating was illegal in most states by 1870 and considered illegitimate by many American men as well as women. The manner of punishing wifebeaters, far different from our own, however, depended mostly on the sanctions of neighbors and churches. Battered wives found some protection from violent husbands as long as they fitted the Victorian definition of woman as weak and defenseless, but those who stepped out of the traditional female role were largely unprotected and excoriated. Nonetheless the nineteenth-century system seems to have worked about as well as our own in protecting the morally upright, physically abused wife.

An upstate New York Methodist exhorter in the 1840s beat his wife every other week and believed he had the right to do so (Blackwell, 1930:4). Several decades later, Santino, a Sicilian immigrant at a Missouri mining camp constantly struck his young wife, Rosa, and his infant son, one time in front of a group of Sicilian men. These boarders did not intervene when the violence occurred, but a few days later they took Rosa and the infant to the railroad station and waited there—with stones in their hands—until the train arrived (Ets, 1970:183). A drunken husband in late-nineteenth century Boston flung his wife from a window, knocking out her teeth and breaking her jaw. A few minutes later a neighborhood constable arrested him (Associated Charities, 1881:24). All of these nineteenth-century American husbands beat their wives, but punishment they received differed. The Methodist exhorter was never punished; neither was Santino, but the Italian miners were ready to stone him if he appeared; and the drunken husband was arrested by the Boston police. Wifebeaters today are disciplined largely by formal methods—by the police, courts, and social agencies. But what of the past? What were the legal and social means of punishing wifebeaters in nineteenth-century America?

It has often been claimed that wife-beating in nineteenth-century America was legal. Robert Calvert writes, "There is no specific time when the husband lost his authority to beat his wife" (1974:89). Actually, though, several states passed statutes legally prohibiting wifebeating; and at least one statute even predates the American Revolution. The Massachusetts Bay Colony prohibited wife beating as early as 1655. The edict states: "No man shall strike his wife nor any woman her husband on penalty of such fine not exceeding ten pounds for one offense, or such corporal punishment as the County shall determine" (Sprague, 1884:12–13). It is unclear whether this law still obtained after the Revolution, although by 1879 a Massachusetts statute stiffened the penalties for wifebeaters arrested on charges of assault and battery (Massachusetts, 1879:444). Between 1853 and 1903 anti-wifebeating statutes were passed by seven other states: Tennessee, Nebraska, Georgia, Maryland, New Mexico, Delaware, and Arkansas (Arkansas, 1947:271; Nebraska, 1974:101; Tennessee, 1955:88; Maryland, 1882:172; Park, Skillman, and Strozier, 1933:198; Delaware, 1901:493; New Mexico, 1887:46). The Pennsylvania and Massachusetts legislatures, influenced by the passage of the Maryland law, considered but did not pass statutes which punished wifebeaters with floggings. Apparently, legislators in both states failed to pass these bills because they did not want to reintroduce the whipping post as a form of punishment (Adams, 1886). It is much more difficult to discover municipal ordinances about wifebeating. Del Martin refers to a Pennsylvania town ordinance, dating from the 1780s, which prohibited a husband from beating his wife after 10 o'clock at night or on Sundays, but the author has been unable to locate this ordinance (1978:113). It is possible that cities treated wifebeaters differently from the way states did, but that seems unlikely.

Punishment of wifebeaters in the states with statutory prohibitions was relatively severe. A wifebeater, according to the Maryland law of 1882, could receive forty lashes or one year in prison (Maryland, 1882:172). In Delaware he was punished with five to thirty lashes at the whipping post, and in New Mexico with a fine of $255 to $1000 or one to five years in prison (Delaware, 1901:493; New Mexico, 1887:46). American missionaries even tried to discipline wifebeaters in foreign countries. Protestant clergy in Hawaii, for example, established rules governing the behavior of native laborers. They fined Hawaiian husbands who whipped their wives a dollar for each offense, probably a month's pay at that time (Damon, 1927:188).

The law elsewhere was vague. In Nebraska, Arkansas, and Georgia, statutes seem to have been deliberately vague as to punishment. Blackstone decried the old common-law doctrine that a husband had the right to beat his wife with a whip no bigger than his thumb. Many observers have quoted from nineteenth-century judicial opinions which upheld this right of chastisement. But selective quotation from nineteenth-century judicial opinions and a failure to examine both the reasoning in the opinions as well as the actual decisions has led to oversimplified conclusions. Table 1 identifies twelve appellate court decisions between 1824 and 1893 which involved a husband charged with assault and battery on his wife. As Table 1 indicates, only three decisions (one in Mississippi, two in North Carolina) approved the old doctrine of moderate chastisement, three

Table 1

State Appellate Court Decisions Involving a Husband's Assault and Battery on His Wife, 1824–1893

Case, State and Year	Approves Husband's Right of Chastisement	Definition of Assault & Battery	Lower Court Ruling	Appellate Court Ruling
Bradley v. State, 1 Miss. 157, 1824	yes	beatings & bruises	husband guilty	husband guilty
State v. Buckley, 2 Del. 69, 1838	no		husband guilty	husband guilty
State v. Hussey, 44 N.C. 123, 1852			husband guilty	husband not guilty
State v. Black, 60 N.C. 262, 1864	yes	permanent injury and/or malicious intent	husband guilty	new trial
State v. Rhodes, 61 N.C. 453, 1868	yes	permanent injury	husband not guilty	husband not guilty
State v. Mabrey, 64 N.C. 503, 1870		threatened use of a weapon and/or permanent injury	husband not guilty	husband guilty
Commonwealth v. McAfee, 102 Mass. 458, 1871	no	beating or striking	husband guilty	husband guilty
Fulgham v. State, 46 Ala. 143, 1874	no		husband guilty	husband guilty
State v. Oliver, 70 N.C. 44, 1874	no	permanent injury	husband guilty	husband guilty
Gorman v. State, 42 Tex. 221, 1875			husband guilty	husband not guilty*
Turner v. State, 60 Neb. 351, 1882	no		husband guilty	husband guilty
Carpenter v. Commonwealth, 92 Ky. 452, 1883	no	malicious intent and/or permanent injury	husband guilty	husband guilty

* This husband was held "not guilty" on the basis of a legal technicality. The wrong name was used in the indictment.

did not rule on it, and six denounced it. Moreover, in eight out of the twelve cases, the appellate justices found the abusive husband guilty.

The three appellate court cases which upheld the right of chastisement represent the most extreme nineteenth-century judicial opinion. In Bradley v. State (1824), the Mississippi Supreme Court upheld the right of moderate chastisement, but it also found Calvin Bradley guilty of assault and battery on his wife Lydia. In State v. Black (1864) a lower court in North Carolina found Jesse Black guilty of assault and battery on his wife Tamsey, but the State Supreme Court overturned the ruling and ordered a new trial. In this case the North Carolina Supreme Court upheld the right of a husband "to use towards his wife such a degree of force as is necessary." Jesse Black's actions, they argued, did not constitute assault and battery. After his wife, Tamsey, had taunted him (accusing him of visiting Sal Daly, a prostitute, and calling him a hog thief) he had seized her by the hair and pulled her to the floor and held her there. Since he did not hit or choke her, the court decided he had not committed assault and battery. In State v. Rhodes (1868), A. B. Rhodes gave his wife, Elizabeth, three licks with a stick the size of one of his fingers. A lower court held that Rhodes was not guilty, and upon appeal the North Carolina Supreme Court upheld that ruling. Even so, the North Carolina Supreme Court did not claim "that the husband has the right to whip his wife much or little" but enunciated a different standard of judgment. The ruling read: "We will not interfere with family government in trifling cases." A trifling case, the court indicated, was one where no permanent injury had been inflicted. State v. Rhodes has been widely quoted, probably because the North Carolina justices went to great lengths in explaining their ruling, but their decision does not represent typical judicial opinion, even for its time. The North Carolina Court obviously felt the need to justify its lengthy ruling as is evident in this passage: "Our opinion is not in unison with the decision of some of the sister States, or with the philosophy of some very respectable law writers, and could not be in unison with all, because of their contrariety—a decent respect for the opinions of others has induced us to be very full in stating the reasons for our conclusion."

Wives did not receive justice in Mississippi or North Carolina; but even at the time, these two states were regarded as exceptions. Wifebeating was prohibited by statute in eight states and by judicial decision in five others (New York, Texas, Delaware, Alabama, and Kentucky). Nor does the absence of a specific statutory prohibition prove that wifebeating was legal. Prior to the passage of the Maryland law of 1882, wifebeaters in that state were arrested for assault and battery. Similarly, although no judicial decisions were issued about the right of chastisement in Pennsylvania and South Carolina and neither state had a statute prohibiting wifebeating, it was nonetheless the case that violent husbands in both states were arrested on charges of assault and battery.

A more general claim is that wifebeating, even if a criminal offense, was nonetheless considered appropriate behavior for nineteenth-century American husbands. To be sure, numerous Victorian jokes, limericks, and drawings lampooned violent family disputes; and some proverbs appear to have sanctioned wifebeating (e.g., "A wife is like an egg; the more she is beaten, the better she is.") But for every proverb that legitimated wifebeating, another excoriated it. Two other proverbs extant were, "A husband's wrath spoils the best broth," and "What is there that beats a good wife? A bad husband." These contrary examples demonstrate simply that aggression in families has been—and is—a source of tension often released in laughter; they do not constitute proof that Americans approved of wifebeating.

It goes without saying that some American husbands a century ago did believe they possessed the right to beat their wives. At an Irish wedding in late nineteenth-century Philadelphia, a drunken male guest told an equally inebriated bridegroom, "Don't let her answer you back; start your marriage right." So the drunken husband punched his bride in the mouth and knocked her to the floor (Gluck, 1976:131). But it also appears that other Irish wives were far from passive; they hit back or they tried to get their brothers or fathers to protect them.

Other Americans disapproved of wifebeating. Nineteenth-century feminists, of course, considered wifebeating an instance of male brutality. The abolitionist and suffragist Sarah Grimke, for example, pointed to the many poverty-stricken wives who died from their husbands' beatings (Grimke, 1838). Women volunteers in antebellum city missions decried the tyrannical American husband who ruled "his trembling subjects with a rod of iron" (Rosenberg, 1971:122), and health reformers, such as Mary Gove Nichols and her husband, R. L. Nichols, openly wondered, "Is there any sanctity [to the marriage contract] where there is force on one side and fear on the other?" (Nichols and Nichols, 1854). But the idea that wifebeating was illegitimate was more widely shared. The chief of the Boston police testified on the many cases of brutal wifebeating in Boston (Gage, 1893:334). Disapproval of wifebeating easily fitted with beliefs about male strength and female weakness. The prevailing view of women as the "weaker sex" was inadvertently made clear by the authors of an American Bar Association resolution in 1886, favoring the use of the whipping post for wifebeaters: "Resolved, that in the opinion of the Association, the interests of society would be promoted by the general use of the whipping post as a mode of punishment for wifebeating and other assaults on the weak and defenseless . . ." (1886:293). Even men closer to the bottom of the social scale were opposed to wifebeating. A black Alabama sharecropper hated his father for beating his mother. He recalled years later," I didn't see no cause for it . . . that was a poor example to stamp and beat up children's mothers right before them" (Rosengarten, 1974:197). Miners in Cripple Creek, Colorado at the turn of the century resented the popular stereotype of the miner as "an inferior sort of animal, ignorant and brutal, drinking up his wages and beating his wife and living in dirt and squalor" (Jameson, 1977:175).

Despite the legal sanctions for police arrest of abusive husbands and the belief of many Americans that wifebeating was illegitimate, American legal justice in the Victorian age was mostly ineffectual. The most common remedy for abused wives today, divorce, was relatively rare a century ago and highly stigmatized. The abused wife seeking a divorce on grounds of cruelty had to offer proof of her husband's assault (in most states, a single act of violence was accepted) and also had to show that she had not provoked him or continued to live with him thereafter. If the abused wife seeking a divorce appeared to the judges "a chaste, industrious, economical, faithful, useful, and obedient wife," she could expect fair treatment (Turner v. Turner, 44 Ala. 437, 1870). She had shown "patient endurance, then forebearance, even martyrdom, in the face of her husband's violent acts" (Reese v. Reese, 23 Ala. 437, 1870). She needed protection because she could not protect herself. But the unruly wife deserved no divorce. If she had acted disobediently or countered violence with violence, she had willed her fate. In such cases, it was generally ruled, "The ill treatment she has received has been owing mainly to her own misconduct," as the Alabama Supreme Court decreed in a divorce case in 1855 (David v. David, 30 Ala. 322). In 1871 the Iowa Supreme Court boldly defined this double standard of justice: "The gentle, fragile, submissive woman might be entitled to a divorce for causes which would scarcely furnish the amazon just cause of complaint" (Knight v. Knight, 1 Iowa 452).

Criminal rather than civil action was the legal remedy for most nineteenth-century battered wives. Wifebeaters received such a wide range of sentences that it is very difficult to make any definitive conclusions about criminal penalties. The Woman's Journal, a suffragist newspaper in Boston, complained about the drunken San Francisco wifebeater who had to pay a fine but was not sentenced to jail (March 13, 1880). Penalties in Boston in the late nineteenth century appear to have been stiffer. One wifebeater there served a month in prison for his first offense and four months for his second. The best evidence about penalties comes from a unique study of 211 wifebeaters in Pennsylvania during the 1880's. These men served an average sentence of three months for assault and battery on their wives (Adams, 1886:8–9).

The wifebeater, according to police records, was generally an immigrant or a black. In Pennsylvania most of the men arrested for wifebeating were immigrants: Germans, Irish, English, Hungarians, and Italians (Adams, 1886:8–9). Between 1889 and 1894, fifty-eight out of sixty men arrested for wifebeating in Charleston, South Carolina were black (Hoffman, 1898:227). There is no way of knowing whether these patterns of arrest reflected a higher incidence of wifebeating in these groups of men or simply the heightened visibility of violence in immigrant and black neighborhoods. Nonetheless, it seems likely that some white as well as black husbands were beating their wives in Charleston and that the racial differential in arrests there reflected the unwillingness of the police to arrest white wifebeaters. At the same time, it also appears that black (and immigrant) wives were more likely to complain to the police than other abused wives. In fact, black newspapers of that period chided black wives for their willingness to have their husbands arrested: "Stay out of the Police court with your petty quarrels," urged the Richmond Planet (April 9, 1890). And the Savannah Colored Tribune was just as explicit—and insulting: "The habit of these dirty colored women of arresting their husbands every time they have a family quarrel is becoming intolerable and should be either stopped or colored men should stop marrying. White families quarrel and disagree as much as colored do but you never hear of white women however low they may be running to the magistrate to have their husbands jailed" (April 22, 1876).

Very little is known about police patterns of arresting wifebeaters. The number of arrests of wifebeaters in Baltimore between 1882 and 1886 was compiled because of the interest in the effectiveness of the state's anti-wifebeating law, passed in 1882 (see Table 2). It might seem that the enactment of the criminal statute increased the number of wifebeaters arrested, but in fact the opposite occurred. In 1882, before the law took effect, 156 wifebeaters were arrested; the next year the police arrested 115 abusive husbands, and in 1884 they arrested 131. By 1885 the number of arrests had fallen to sixty-seven. The proponents of the law suggested that the single stiff sentence prescribed for a wifebeater (whipping and a year in prison) deterred violent husbands and led to a decline in incidence. But it is doubtful that one severe law had such a widespread effect. It seems more likely that the greater difficulty in securing convictions under the new law deterred police from making arrests. The number of abusive husbands convicted before the law was passed is unknown; but after its enactment, only one wifebeater was indicted in Baltimore in 1883, none in 1884, and only one more husband in 1885. Another comparison, of convictions in Baltimore and Philadelphia in 1884, also suggests that the possibility of a higher rate of conviction of wifebeaters increased the likelihood of arrest. Philadelphia's police

Table 2

Arrests, Complaints, and Convictions of Husbands for Assault and Battery on Their Wives in American and British Cities, 1874–1975

City and Year	Arrests	Complaints Filed	Convictions	Source
London, 1874				Adams, 1886
Charleston, S.C., 1889–1894	60			Hoffman, 1898
Baltimore, 1882	156			ABA, 1886
1883	115		1	ABA, 1886
1884	131	0	0	ABA, 1886
1885	67	1	1	ABA, 1886
Philadelphia, 1883		308	182	Adams, 1886
1900		184		Lane, 1978
Detroit, 1972		4900		Martin, 1976
Washtenaw County, Michigan, 1974	740			Fojtik, 1976
New York City, 1975		7237		Novak and Meismer, 1977–78
Edinburgh & Glasgow, 1978	791			Dobash and Dobash, 1977–78

arrested four times as many wifebeaters as their counterparts in Baltimore, yet Philadelphia was only two and a half times larger than Baltimore. Furthermore, eighty Philadelphia wifebeaters were convicted in 1884, whereas in Baltimore only one man was convicted that year. Therefore, it seems likely that Philadelphia's police were simply more interested in arresting wifebeaters because they believed conviction would more often result from their efforts.

The problems of criminal justice appear, nonetheless, to have rested less with the police than with the victims themselves and the prosecuting attorneys. In an ordinary assault and battery case, the wife filed a complaint against her husband before a justice of the peace. But many abused wives, once they reached the courtroom, pleaded for their husbands' release. The District Attorney of Schuylkill County, Pennsylvania in 1884 regretted that "there were about forty cases in which there was no trial, from the fact the wives asked the court to withdraw the prosecution. To imprison the defendant would only leave the families in want" (Adams, 1886:9). The District Attorney in Pittsburgh reached the same conclusion: "In most cases the wives come into court and beg for the release of their husbands" (Adams, 1886:10). But these district attorneys were avoiding their own responsibility: many of them regarded wifebeating as petty crime which did not warrant prosecution. Prosecution of all Philadelphia assault and battery cases (which included wifebeatings) fell dramatically in the 1890s simply because Philadelphia district attorneys lost interest in taking these cases.

As little as the modern system of legal regulation aids abused wives, it still appears that police and district attorneys today are more likely to regulate wifebeating than their counterparts one hundred years ago. Figures on arrests and prosecution of wifebeaters charged with assault and battery in English and American cities are presented in Table 2. Even in proportion to the population, the number of arrests has increased dramatically between 1883 and 1975. It is possible that these figures reflect higher incidence of wifebeating today than in the past, but that seems unlikely, since many of the precipitating social factors behind violence—unemployment, poor housing, drunkenness, lack of economic opportunities for married women—have declined drastically in the last century. It seems more likely, then, that the increase in arrests and prosecutions reflects a more vigorous modern American as well as British interest in the eradication of wifebeating.

Punishment of wifebeaters by legal methods was only one means of discipline. All societies regulate behavior. But some use rewards and punishment, others use flogging or torture; some rely on psychiatrists and social workers, others on witch doctors or ministers. A culture's view of punishment is deeply connected with its attitudes toward pain and torture as well as its ideas about rehabilitation. There is much truth in the notion that law is necessary only when other forms of social control are weak.

One means of informal regulation was the intervention of friends and relatives of the wife, who tried to stop an abusive husband and punished him for attacking his wife. When James Gahn, a Louisiana clerk, tried to strike his wife, his father-in-law stopped him. A South Dakota man, in bed with his wife, started shouting at her, "Where is the razor? I will get the razor and I will kill you and myself, too." As he moved toward the drawer where the razor was kept, his mother grabbed him and forced him to leave the room (Gahn v. Darby, 36 La. 70, 1885). But concerned relatives were often unable to prevent injury to the wife. One drunken Kentucky husband began raining verbal abuse on his wife and sister. He took his wife aside, pleaded with her, thrust his left hand on her forehead, pushed her back against the wall, and deliberately cut her throat from ear to ear. Only the appearance of his sister, who had heard the screams, stopped him from plunging the knife a second time (Carpenter v. Commonwealth, 92 Ky. 422, 1892). Boarders also came to the aid of abused wives. One male roomer in an Alabama household kept the husband from throwing his wife out of doors in the middle of the night (Moyler v. Moyler, 11 Ala. 620, 1847).

These intervenors often tried to get the husband to reform and fulfill his responsibilities. The adult sons of an abusive Polish father in Chicago ordered him to contribute $3 a week to the support of his young children (Znaniecki and Thomas, 1918–1920, 1813). Some of these protectors simply wanted to make threats in order to extract a promise of good behavior. A Chicago airshaft carried nightly the screeches of a musician's wife. Finally a male neighbor confronted the man. He knocked at the apartment door, threatened to call the police, but ended up pleading, "Will you be good?" (Dreiser, 1931: 176).

Women often helped "runaway wives" to flee their homes. The most dramatic example was the protection a battered wife and her daughter received from Susan B. Anthony and another feminist, Lydia Mott. The battered wife, a mother of three, was the sister of a U.S. Senator and the wife of a Massachusetts legislator; she had written several books and had operated an academy. When she discovered that her husband had committed adultery, she confronted him; but he became consumed with anger, kicked her down the stairs, abused her, and even had her committed to an insane asylum for a year and a half. Finally, after her release, she stayed at her brother's house; but her husband kept the children. When one of her daughters came for a visit, this mother decided to take her and flee. A Quaker family, which took in the refugees, asked Susan B. Anthony to help them escape. Anthony accompanied the wife and her daughter to New York City, where they were aided by another suffragist, who found them a place to live and secured a job for the mother sewing shirts. The woman's brother secretly sent money through Lydia Mott. This mother and her daughter successfully hid for about a year, until one day the daughter was snatched up on her way to Sunday School and returned to the custody of her father. Anthony, an abolitionist as well as a feminist, likened her actions to aiding a runaway slave. When William Lloyd Garrison and Wendell Phillips heard about Anthony's rescue efforts, they asked her to surrender the child to her father. Anthony, who refused, told them, "You would die before you would deliver a slave to his master, and I will die before I will give up that child to this father" (Harper, 1898:204).

The Protestant church, the most important moral force in frontier and rural areas, also tried to regulate the moral behavior of its members: clergymen classed wifebeating with the "sins" of gambling, drinking, dancing, and horseracing. The Baptists, who believed God wanted them to chastise sinners, urged members to settle disputes in church courts rather than by legal action. A Baptist wifebeater who confessed his misdeed was restored to good standing. If he refused, he was prohibited from taking communion. A repeated offender was excommunicated. Baptists in Elkhorn, Kentucky expelled Brother Baker Erving for "intoxication, for misusing his wife and disobeying the call of the church" (Sweet, 1931:304).

Black Baptists in antebellum Virginia used similar methods of discipline. The African Baptist church in antebellum Richmond was comprised of slave and free black members presided over by a white minister. The black deacons of the church heard complaints about the moral laxity of church members. They tried to stop violent husbands and fathers from administering beatings; if that failed, they expelled them from the congregation. Religious group members with the most rigorous method of regulation were probably the Quakers. A Friend who beat his wife or child could be expelled from membership, although this action was rarely taken. Friends developed elaborate mechanisms of surveillance and discipline; each Quaker was expected to call attention to the moral failings of other Quakers (Frost, 1973:56). Yet even among the Quakers, women's separate meetings did not determine disciplinary actions, only the yearly men's meetings had the power of disownment. Deacons of the African Baptist Church and white Baptist congregations made the regulations and decided whom to punish. The power of church regulation, then, derived from male dominance of social institutions; it was the power of senior male members to discipline aggressive and disobedient men and unchaste women.

Aside from the moral regulation exercised by organized religion, men often took the law into their own hands. Many of America's most famous vigilante groups—the Regulators of South Carolina, the White Caps, and the Ku Klux Klan—punished wifebeaters and child abusers. In the 1750s a group of Elizabethtown, New Jersey men calling themselves Regulators dressed in women's clothes and painted their faces and flogged local men who reportedly beat their wives (Davis, 1975:315). More is known about the manner of moral regulation on the nineteenth-century American frontier. After their beginning in southern Indiana, the White Caps gained adherents in Ohio, Texas, New Mexico, and Tennessee. White Caps were men who wanted to rid their communities of wifebeaters and child abusers as well as lazy and drunken men, adulterers, prostitutes, and mothers of illegitimate children. In the late nineteenth century, newspapers in Southern Indiana drew a profile of the typical White Cap: he was a solid citizen and a stock trader, a salesman of McCormick reapers, or a farmer; he was a church-going Methodist who believed in the frontier tradition of settling disputes. On Saturday night patrols the White Caps, wearing white hoods to cover their faces and necks, delivered notes to the doorsteps of offenders: stop the mistreatment, these warned, or receive a whipping. Among the eighty targets of White Caps in Harrison County, Indiana, nine were violent husbands or fathers (Noble, 1973:70–71).

The Ku Klux Klan flourished in the devastated South of the 1870s and reemerged in the South and Southwest and in Northern cities in the 1920s. After the Civil War, white-robed Klansmen threatened to whip Southern freedmen who beat their wives, but most of the targets of the Ku Klux Klan were poor white men (Calhoun, 1919:16). To these vigilantes the wifebeater could be a vagrant, like Jack Morgan, who, after his release by the Shreveport police late one evening in May of 1921, was taken to an isolated spot on a dirt road, stripped naked, and coated with tar and feathers by a Klansman (Alexander, 1965:43). Or he could be morally suspect, like the Enid, Oklahoma theater owner who was whipped one night by the Klan (Alexander, 1965:45). But he was always a wayward male who could be punished by "true" men. Klansmen in Texarkana, Arkansas and Houston, Texas carried signs reading: "Wife-beaters, Family-deserters, Home-wreckers, We have no room for you" and "Wife beaters beware" (Alexander, 1965:42). Klan broadsides explicitly connected wifebeating to moral impurity:

> Every criminal, every gambler, every thug, every libertine, every girl ruiner, every home wrecker, every wifebeater, every dope peddler, every moonshiner, every crooked politician, every pagan Papist priest, every shyster lawyer, every K. of C., every white slaver, every brothel madam, every Rome-controlled newspaper, every black spider is fighting the Klan. Think it over. Which side are you on? (Jackson, 1967:19).

The Regulators, the White Caps, and the Klan were among America's well-known vigilante groups, but moral regulators also included ordinary farmers and townsmen without elaborate insignia and paraphernalia. Farmers in rural Ontario heard about the abusive immigrant farmer who beat his wife with a fence rail. They visited his farm, dragged him from hiding, and warned him that if he failed to reform, "treatment more drastic would be meted out" to him (MacDougall, 1913:46). The male prerogative to discipline other men appears to have been uppermost among another group of farmers in rural Idaho during the 1920s who visited the farm of a neighbor:

> They presented themselves gravely, and asked him to promise them that the wife beatings would stop. The wife-beater told them to mind their own business. The spokesman for the group said that they were not prepared to accept that. Human decency required that they insist on his promise the beatings would stop. The wife-beater sneered and asked if any one of them was "man enough" to try to make him stop. The spokesman for the delegation stepped forward and said, "I will try." The powerful wife-

> beater quickly injured him so badly that he could not continue. The bully then sneeringly asked if any of the rest wanted what the first one had gotten.
>
> At this point, the five remaining men formed a line, a queue. The first stepped forward and combat ensued. . . . After a severe, battering struggle, the bully surrendered. The men gathered around him and the spokesman said, "We want your promise that your wife will be treated well." The pale husband said, "I promise." At this each man shook hands with him and congratulated him. The spokesman said, "You should know we will watch, and if necessary, we'll be back." The ex-wifebeater said, very seriously, "It won't be necessary." At this point, each of the men shook his hand again. After some hesitation, one said, "We'd be proud to have your family over for dinner Sunday. Can you make it?" Looking him in the eye, the other said, "I'm sure we'd like to come" (Jackins, 1976:6).

It has been claimed that society has made progress in its punishment of wifebeaters: at one time physical chastisement of a wife was legal and appropriate behavior, and now it is illegal and considered by most Americans to be inappropriate. It has been argued here that wifebeating was illegal in most states by 1870 and considered by many nineteenth-century Americans as inappropriate. The difference between the past and the present was not a modern intention to prohibit wife-beating but a change in the manner of regulation. A century ago the system of formal regulation against wifebeaters was relatively weak and cumbersome whereas the mechanisms for informal regulation were relatively vigorous and extensive; today the opposite is more nearly the case. The shift has many sources: rural communities have been absorbed by towns and cities; the moral force of religion has waned; the family has less responsibility for the provision of social welfare to its members; and, at the same time, the bureaucratic control of the family so evident in the rise of divorce (itself a product of a more bureaucratic and legal method for dissolving marriages), has resulted in the growth of modern police forces, social agencies, and family courts and an increase in the power of the state as against the power of the individual family.

The very qualities that appear so distasteful in the system of informal regulation—its intense scrutiny of behavior, its almost Biblical method for punishing transgressors—represented its great strengths as well as its weaknesses. Informal regulation did not have to depend on the complaint of the victim; third parties were watching a husband's behavior and reporting his misdeeds to a policing group. The sanctions relied on in informal regulation—swift physical punishment, public shaming, extreme community disapproval—probably were far more powerful deterrents to continued wrongdoing than a suspended sentence from a judge or a stern lecture from a policeman. Nonetheless, the regulation of wifebeaters by the White Caps or the Baptists in the past cannot be construed to constitute some golden age of the past, a time of vigilance and justice for American wives. Past societies with a great deal of informal regulation of violent members were also sexually repressive communities, which punished the adulteress, the illegitimate mother, and the prostitute just as severely as the physically abusive husband. Such a tightly controlled moral world should remain a thing of the past, not a blueprint for the future. While it seems likely that a more bureaucratized, formal system of courts, agencies, and police probably offers less physical protection for abused wives, it probably extends another form of protection—that provided by a relatively orderly process for securing justice, a system of procedures by which the regulators and the physically violent must be held accountable.

But in the final analysis, the abusive husband in both the past and the present has been largely deterred, punished, and judged by males acting in the name of the community, who have set the standards for proper behavior and determined the kinds of sanctions to be used. Our modern-day regulators, like those of the nineteenth century, are mostly men, whose standards of justice are embedded in notions about proper definitions of manhood and womanhood and concepts of moral purity. Men, acting for the community, whether they be judges, churchmen, or vigilantes, have reserved the right to regulate the behavior of other men. The author of Maryland's anti-wifebeating law of 1882, (Baldwin, 1899:4) nicely summed up the viewpoint so often behind the regulation of wifebeaters in nineteenth-century America: "The man who beats his wife and is cowhided for it by her father and brother is thought by all to have received his just reward."

REFERENCES

Adams, Robert
1886 Wife Beating as a Crime and Its Relation to Taxation. Philadelphia: Social Science Association.

Alexander, Charles C.
1965 The Ku Klux Klan in the Southwest. Lexington: University of Kentucky Press.

American Bar Association
1886 Annual Report. Philadelphia: Dando Printing and Publishing.

Associated Charities of Boston
1881 Second Annual Report. Boston: Tolman and White.

Baldwin, Simeon E.
1899 "Whipping and Castration as Punishments for Crime." Yale Law Journal 8:1–16.

Blackwell, Alice Stone
1930 Lucy Stone: Pioneer of Woman's Rights. Boston: Little, Brown.

Commonwealth of Massachusetts
1879 Acts and Resolves Passed by the General Court of Massachusetts. Boston: Wright and Potter.

Calvert, Robert
1974 "Criminal and Civil Liability in Husband-Wife Assaults." Pp. 88–91 in Suzanne K. Steinmetz and Murry A. Straus (eds.), Violence in the Family. New York: Dodd, Mead.

Damon, Ethel M.
1927 Father Bond of Kohala: A Chronicle of Pioneer Life. Honolulu: The Friend.

Davis, Natalie Zemon
1975 Society and Culture in Early Modern France. Stanford: Stanford.

Dobash, Rebecca E. and Russell P. Dobash
1977–8 "Wives: The 'Appropriate' Victims of Marital Violence. Victimology 2:426–442.

Dreiser, Theodore
1931 Dawn. New York: H. Liveright.

Ets, Marie Hall
1970 Rosa: the Life of an Italian Immigrant. Minneapolis: University of Minnesota.

Fojtik, Kathleen M.
1976 Wife Beating. Ann Arbor MI: Ann Arbor National Organization of Women.

Frost, J. William
1973 The Quaker Family in Colonial America. New York: St. Martin's.

Gage, Matilda
1893 Woman, Church and State. New York: Truth Seeker.

Gluck, Sherna (ed.)
1976 From Parlor to Prison: Five American Suffragists Talk About their Lives. New York: Vintage.

Grimke, Sarah
1838 Letters on the Equality of the Sexes and the Condition of Women. Boston: I. Knapp.

Harper, Ida Husted
1898 The Life and Work of Susan B. Anthony, Vol. I. Indianapolis: Hollenbeck.

Hoffman, Frederick L.
1898 Race Traits and Tendencies in the American Negro. Boston: American Economic Association.

Jackins, Harvey
1976 "Being a Man." The Re-evaluation Counseling Teacher 6:1976.

Jackson, Kenneth T.
1967 The Ku Klux Klan in the City, 1915–1930. New York: Oxford.

Jameson, Elizabeth
1977 "Imperfect Unions: Class and Gender in Cripple Creek, 1884–1904." Pp. 166–202 in Milton Cantor and Bruce Laurie (eds.), Class, Sex, and the Woman Worker. Westport CT: Greenwood Press.

Lane, Roger
1978 Crime in Philadelphia. Unpublished manuscript.

MacDougall, John
1913 Rural Life in Canada. Toronto: Westminster.

Martin, Del
1978 "Battered Women: Society's Problem." Pp. 111–114 in Jane Roberts Chapman and Margaret Gates (eds.), The Victimization of Women. Beverly Hills and London: Sage Publications.

Nichols, T. L. and Mary S. Gove Nichols
1854 "Marriage: Its History, Character and Results: Its Sanctities and its Profanities, its Science and its Facts." P. 286 in Nancy F. Cott (ed.), Roots of Bitterness: Documents in the Social History of American Women. New York: Dutton.

Noble, Madeleine M.
1973 The White Caps of Harrison and Crawford County, Indiana: A Study in the Violent Enforcement of Morality. Unpublished Ph.D. Dissertation: University of Michigan.

Novak, Deborah G. and Deborah Tucker Meismer
1977–78 "A Plea for Help." Victimology 2:647–652.

O'Brien, John Thomas
1975 From Bondage to Citizenship: the Richmond Black Community, 1865–1867, Unpublished Ph.D. dissertation, University of Rochester.

Park, Orville A., Harry B. Skillman, and Harry S. Strozier
1933 Code of Georgia Annotated. Atlanta: Byrd.

Richmond Planet
April 9, 1890.

Rosenberg, Carroll Smith
1971 Religion and the Rise of the American City: The New York City Mission Movement, 1812–1870. Ithaca: Cornell.

Rosengarten, Theodore
1974 All God's Dangers: The Life of Nate Shaw. New York: Avon.

Savannah Colored Tribune
April 22, 1876.

Sprague, Henry H.
1884 Women under the Law of Massachusetts. Boston: W. B. Clarke and Carruth.

State of Arkansas
1947 Statutes. Indianapolis: Bobbs-Merrill.

State of Delaware
1901 Laws. Milford DE: Milford Chronicle.

State of Maryland
1882 Laws. Baltimore: J. D. Toy.

State of Nebraska
1974 Laws, Statutes, Revised Statutes of Nebraska. Lincoln: J. North.

State of Tennessee
1955 Code Annotated. Indianapolis: Bobbs-Merrill.

Sweet, William Warren
1931 Religion on the American Frontier: The Baptist, 1783–1830. New York: Henry Holt and Company.

Territory of New Mexico
1887 Acts of the Legislative Assembly. Las Vegas NM: Imprenta del Rio Grande.

Thomas, William I. and Florian Znaniecki
1918–1920 The Polish Peasant in Europe and America. Vol. I. Chicago IL: University of Chicago.

Woman's Journal
March 13, 1880.

Cases on Criminal Liability for Assault and Battery:
Bradley v. State, 1 Miss. 157, 1824; State v. Buckley, 2 Del. 69, 1838; State v. Hussey, 44 N.C. 123, 1852; State v. Black, 60 N.C. 262, 1864; State v. Rhodes, 61 N.C. 453, 1868; State v. Mabrey, 64 N.C. 503, 1870; Commonwealth v. McAfee, 102 Mass. 458, 1871; Fulgham v. State, 46 Ala. 143, 1871; State v. Oliver, 70 N.C. 44, 1874; Gorman v. State, 42 Tex. 221, 1875; Turner v. State, 60 Neb. 351, 1882; Carpenter v. Commonwealth, 92 Ky. 452, 1893.

Divorce Cases:
Reese v. Reese, 23 Ala. 437, 1870; Turner v. Turner, 44 Ala. 437, 1870; Moyler v. Moyler, 11 Ala. 620, 1847; David v. David, 30 Ala. 322, 1855; Gahn v. Darby, 36 La. 70, 1885.

About the Author

Elizabeth H. Pleck is an assistant professor of history at the University of Michigan, where she teaches American social and urban history. The research reported here is part of a book-length study of the history of wife and child abuse in the American family. Beginning stages of the research were aided by a Ford Foundation Faculty Fellowship for Research on Women in Society, 1975–1976.

For further information or for reprints of the article contact the author at 25 Trowbridge St., Newton Centre MA 02159.

FAMILY LIMITATION, SEXUAL CONTROL, AND DOMESTIC FEMINISM IN VICTORIAN AMERICA

Daniel Scott Smith

The history of women is inextricably connected with the social evolution of the family. The revitalization of the American feminist movement and the surge of interest in social history among professional historians during the past decade have combined to make the study of women in the family a crucial concern. The central insight of the new feminism—the critical relationship of family structure and roles to the possibilities for full participation by women in the larger society—provides an immediate impetus to the historical study of that relationship. To isolate a central historical question conceptually, however, is far easier than to examine it empirically. Women in the family do not generate written documents describing their ordinary life experiences. It is easier, for example, to describe historical attitudes toward women's proper role than to determine what the roles actually were at any given time. Only painstaking research into local history, a systematic study of personal documents describing ordinary behavior, and tracing life histories of women through manuscript lists can bridge this major gap in the historiography of American women.[1] At this point, then, a different approach seems necessary and useful.

An examination of three rather well-established quantitative indicators showing the relationship of the entire population of American women to the family suggests the hypothesis that over the course of the nineteenth century the average woman experienced a great increase in power and autonomy *within* the family. The important contribution women made to the radical decline in nineteenth-century marital fertility provides the central evidence for this hypothesis. Empirical data on the details of family limitation and the control of sexuality in the nineteenth century unfortunately are limited. However, an analysis of nineteenth century sexual ideology supports the theory that women

I wish to thank Carl Degler, A. William Hoglund, Peter Stearns, and especially Ellen Dubois for their comments and suggestions on an earlier version of this analysis; none of the above should be held responsible for its flaws and errors.

acquired an increasing power over sex and reproduction within marriage. The hypothesis that women's power increased within the nineteenth-century family also accords well with such important themes as the narrow social base of the women's movement in America before the late nineteenth century, the flourishing of women's groups opposed to female suffrage, and the centrality of the attack on aspects of male culture in such movements as temperance. A long-term perspective is essential for understanding the history of women in the family. I shall suggest how the situation of women varied in three periods: the pre-industrial (seventeenth and eighteenth century); industrial (nineteenth century); and the post-industrial (recent) phases of American society.

From the colonial period to the present, *an overwhelming majority*—from 89 to 96 percent—*of American women surviving past the age of forty-five have married* (Table 1). The proportion who never married was highest for those born in the last four decades of the nineteenth century. Small percentage changes represent, of course, thousands of women. While marriage was overwhelmingly the typical experience for American women, before the present century roughly a third of all females did not survive long enough to be eligible for marriage.[2] In addition, the numerically tiny minority who remained single had a far larger historical importance than their percentage would suggest. For example, 30.1 percent of 45-49-year-old native-white female college graduates in 1940 were unmarried.[3] Before the marked increase in life-expectancy in the late nineteenth and early twentieth century, the average American woman married in her early-to-mid-twenties, survived with her husband for some three decades, and, if widowed, spent an additional decade or so in widowhood.[4]

The implications of these figures for historians of women are obvious but must still be emphasized. Labor historians now realize that most workers historically did not belong to unions, black historians have been conscious that most Negroes were not in civil-rights organizations, and urban historians have discovered that groups other than politicians and elites dwell in cities. The search for the history of "anonymous Americans" has generally focused on population elements that in one sense or another have been defined as "social problems." For these groups there exists at least some information imbedded in contemporary myths and prejudices. It will be more difficult to write the history of the average or model American woman, a person substantively akin to William Graham Sumner's Forgotten Man. She was, in 1880, for example, a 38-year-old white wife of a farmer living eight miles west-by-south of Cincinnati and the mother eventually of five or six children.[5] Intensive study of local records may reveal a surprising degree of social participation in church and voluntary associations and perhaps performance in other roles as well. Yet the primary statuses of the modal woman were those of wife and mother.

While nearly all American women have married, *married American women did not work outside the home until the twentieth century,* with the major increase coming in the last three decades (Table 2). Only one white married woman in forty was classified in the labor force in 1890 and only one in seven in 1940; today two-fifths of all married women are working according to official

TABLE 1
Percentage of American Women Who Never Married

Census or survey, and	birth cohort	Age at enumeration	Percentage never-married
1910	1835-38	70-74	7.3
	1840-44	65-69	7.1
	1845-49	60-64	8.0
	1850-54	55-59	7.7
	1855-59	50-54	8.9
	1860-64	45-49	10.0
1940	1865-69	70-74	11.1
	1870-74	65-69	10.9
	1875-79	60-64	10.4
	1880-84	55-59	8.7
	1885-89	50-54	8.8
	1890-94	45-49	8.6
1950	1895-99	50-54	7.7
	1900-04	45-49	8.0
1960	1905-09	50-54	7.6
	1910-14	45-49	6.5
1965	1915-19	45-49	4.8
1969	1921-25	45-49	4.5
	1926-30	40-44	5.0

SOURCE: Calculated from Irene B. Taeuber, "Growth of the population of the United States in the Twentieth Century," Table 11, p. 40 in *Demographic and Social Aspects of Population Growth*, eds., Charles F. Westoff and Robert Parke, Jr., vol. 1, U.S. Commission on Population Growth and the American Future (Washington: Government Printing Office, 1972).

definition.[6] The increase in labor-force participation for single women in the twentieth century has been less dramatic. More generally, many indicators (an increase in single-person households for the young and widowed, the disappearance of boarders and lodgers from family units, the decline in the age at marriage, an increase in premarital intercourse, and the legalization of abortion and no-fault divorce) point to an emerging post-industrial family pattern in the post-World-War-II period. This major shift in the family has important implications for the periodization of women's history.

The statistical trend presents an interesting historical problem. During the nineteenth century, some ninety percent of women got married, over ninety-five

TABLE 2
Female Participation in the Labor Force (in percentage)

Year	Total	White only		Native-white, age 35-44	
		Single	Married	Single	Married
1830[a]	(7)	—	—	—	—
1890[a]	12.1	35.2	2.5	39.3	2.3
1940[a]	26.9	47.9	14.6	73.6	17.9
1960[a]	34.1	45.5	29.6	76.5	29.9

	All Women			Age 35-44		
	Single	Married, husband present	Widowed, divorced, separated	Single	Married, husband present	Widowed, divorced, separated
1950[b]	50.5	23.8	37.8	83.6	28.5	65.4
1960[b]	44.1	30.5	40.0	79.7	36.2	67.4
1972[b]	54.9	41.5	40.1	71.5	48.6	71.7

[a] Stanley Lebergott, *Manpower in Economic Growth* (New York: McGraw Hill, 1964), Table A-10, p. 519.

[b] Bureau of Labor Statistics, summarized in *The New York Times*, January 31, 1973, pp. 20.

percent of the married were not employed outside the home, yet *women progressively bore fewer and fewer children*. The average number born to a white woman surviving to menopause fell from 7.04 in 1800 to 6.14 in 1840, to 4.24 in 1880, and finally to 3.56 in 1900 (Table 3). The same decline is also apparent in U.S. census data on completed fertility.[7] Between 1800 and 1900 the total fertility rate decreased by half. By the late nineteenth century, France was the only European country whose fertility rate was lower than America's.[8] Despite the demographic effects of a later marriage age and of more women remaining permanently single, from one-half to three-fourths of the nineteenth-century decline in fertility may be attributed to the reduction of fertility within marriage.[9]

The decline in marital fertility is of critical importance in structuring the possibilities open to the average woman. A fifteen-to-twenty-year cycle of conception-birth-nursing-weaning-conception (broken not infrequently by

TABLE 3

Total Fertility Rates (TFR) for Whites, 1800-1968

Year	TFR	Year	TFR	Year	TFR
1800	7.04	1860	5.21	1920	3.17
1810	6.92	1870	4.55	1930	2.45
1820	6.73	1880	4.24	1940	2.19
1830	6.55	1890	3.87	1950	3.00
1840	6.14	1900	3.56	1960	3.52
1850	5.42	1910	3.42	1968	2.36

SOURCES: For 1800-1960, Ansley J. Coale and Melvin Zelnik, *New Estimates of Fertility and Population in the United States* (Princeton: Princeton University Press, 1963), Table 2, p. 36; 1968 calculated from Irene B. Taueber, "Growth of the Population of the United States in the Twentieth Century," in *Demographic and Social Aspects of Population Growth*, eds. Charles F. Westoff and Robert Parke, Jr., U.S. Commission on Population Growth and the American Future, vol. 1 (Washington, D.C.: Government Printing Office, 1972), Table 7, p. 33.

spontaneous abortions) at the height of active adulthood obviously limits chances for social and economic participation as well as for individual development. Child-rearing must be added to this onerous cycle. The great transition in fertility is a central event in the history of woman. A dominant theme in the history is that women have not shaped their own lives. Things are done to women, not by them. Thus it is important to examine the extent to which nineteenth-century women did gain control over their reproductive lives.

Many forces, to be mentioned later, were clearly at work in curbing fertility, but the power of the wife to persuade or coerce her husband into practicing birth control deserves examination. While women did employ contraceptive methods in the nineteenth century (principally douching and the sponge), the major practices involved the control of male sexuality—*coitus interruptus* (withdrawal) and abstinence.[10] Following Kraditor's excellent definition of the essence of feminism as the demand for autonomy, sexual control of the husband by the wife can easily be subsumed under the label of "domestic feminism."[11]

Before marshalling empirical data showing the strengthening of the position of women within the nineteenth-century American family, it is first necessary to consider certain misconceptions about women's place in the industrial and pre-industrial periods. Many of the recent interpretations of the history of American women have been devoted to an autopsy of the "failure" of women's suffrage. According to Kraditor, late nineteenth-and early-twentieth-century American women became conservative and were co-opted into the general progressive movement.[12] In Degler's view, women lacked an ideology that could properly guide them to full status as human beings.[13] For O'Neill, the "failure" lay in the refusal of the movement to assult the ideology and reality of the conjugal family structure that sustained women's inferior position.[14] This "what-went-wrong" approach implicitly assumes the constancy of woman's role within the family, and, more damagingly, interprets the behavior and responses of women as deviations from a preconceived standard rather than as responses to their actual situations. The turn toward conservatism in the leadership of active American women, for example, is seen as a tactical mistake rather than as the result of interaction between the leaders and their female constituency.

The extremely low percentage of married women in the nineteenth-century labor force suggests that the domestic-sphere versus social-participation dichotomy is not appropriate for the interpretation of women's history during the industrial period. If the average woman in the last century failed to perceive her situation through the modern feminist insight, this did not mean she was not increasing her autonomy, exercising more power, or even achieving happiness within the domestic sphere. Rather than examining Victorian culture and especially the Victorian family at its heart through a twentieth-century perspective, it is more useful and revealing to contrast nineteenth-century values and institutions with their pre-industrial antecedents.

Misconceptions about women in the pre-industrial family fit integrally into the pessimistic view of the Victorian era derived from the modern feminist perspective. Having portrayed the nineteenth century as something of a nadir for women, by implication, all other eras must be favorable by comparison. In order to show that women are not inevitably entrapped by the family, it has seemed important to emphasize that somewhere or sometime the status and role of women were quite different. While cross-culture evidence supports this argument adequately, more compelling are conclusions drawn from as little as two centuries ago in American or Western culture. Historians, however, have been properly cautious about more than hinting at a Golden Age for the pre-industrial American woman. There is, to be sure, a sharp difference between the pre-industrial and industrial family and the corresponding position of women in each. A conjugal family system, in the sense of the centrality of the married pair, in contrast to the dominance of the family line, did emerge in the United States during the early nineteenth century.[15]

The effects of this shift for women are complex. The conventional belief in the more favorable position of the average woman in pre-industrial society rests on three arguments: the intimacy and complementary nature of sex roles in an undifferentiated economy; Aries' thesis that the boundary between the pre-industrial family and society was very permeable; and finally, in the American case, the favorable implications for women of the relative female and labor scarcity on the frontier. The first argument may be compared to George Fitzhugh's defense of slavery, but extreme subordination and superordination do not require a highly differentiated economy and society. The very absence of complexity in the pre-industrial family doubtless contributed to the subordination of women. While the identity of the place of work and residence in an agricultural economy inevitably meant some sharing of productive tasks by husband and wife, the husband's presence, given the prevailing ideological and cultural values, deterred the wife from gaining a sense of autonomy. Just as the gender stereotypes of masculine and feminine were not as rigidly defined as in the Victorian period, the prestige attached to the status of wife and mother was less than in the nineteenth century. Social prestige depended on the position of the woman's family in the hierarchical structure of pre-industrial society. Daughters and wives shared in the deference paid to important families. When this system collapsed in the nineteenth century, women of high-status families experienced considerable deprivation compared to their high-ranking colonial counterparts. Women born to more modest circumstances, however, derived enhanced status from the shift away from deference and ascription.

Although Aries has little to say about women, his thesis that the line between the Western pre-industrial family and community was not sharply delineated is of considerable importance here.[16] There does exist scattered evidence of women's nonfamilial activity, e.g., voting, operating businesses, etc., in the pre-industrial period. The incidence of women's nonfamilial activity over time, its relationship to family and conventional sex roles, and finally, its importance in the social structure as a whole have not been explored. The existing social history of colonial women has successfully demonstrated that wider participation was not unknown.[17] The details of such nonfamilial participation have been much more fully researched for the colonial period than for the nineteenth century. Spinsters almost certainly were more marginal and deviant in pre-industrial American society than during the nineteenth century. Only widows who controlled property may have been in a more favorable position. While changes in colonial America law permitted a married woman to exercise certain rights, these innovations related mainly to acting as a stand-in for a husband.[18] By negating the impact of male absence because of travel and death, these modifications in colonial law made the family a more efficient economic unit; historians should not confuse a response to high mortality and slow transportation with normative support for women's being outside the family. In fact, nonfamilial participation by pre-industrial women must generally be viewed as a substitution for the activities of absent husbands. In effect, a woman's activity outside the pre-industrial family was a *familial* responsibility.

Systematic evidence comparing the position of women in the pre-industrial and industrial phases of American society is scarce; what exists points to the comparatively unfavorable place of women in the earlier stage. In most populations, for example, women live considerably longer than men. Yet this was not the case in four (Andover, Higham, Plymouth and Salem) of the five seventeenth-century New England communities studied to date. Only in seventeenth-century Ipswich did the typical pattern of longer survival for adult females exist.[19] In Hingham, furthermore, an inverse relationship between family wealth and mortality is apparent only for eighteenth-century married women, not for their husbands or children.[20] Literacy is a good index of the potential to perform complex tasks. The scattered published data on the frequency of signatures on documents suggest that there may have been some narrowing of the historic differential between male and female literacy during the eighteenth century. The gap, however, was not fully closed until the nineteenth century.[21] The sex differential in literacy is, of course, also a class differential. Compared to those of pre-industrial men, the burdens of life were harsh for women, particularly those of low status. Finally, the resemblance in that era of the sexual act itself to the Hobbesian state of nature is revealing. Marital sex, succinctly summarized by Shorter as "simple up-and-down, man on top, woman on bottom, little foreplay, rapid ejaculation, masculine unconcern with femine orgasm,"[22] perhaps mirrored the broader social relationship men and women.

It may be argued that America was not Europe and that the relative strength of the woman's movement in nineteenth-century America can be attributed to a decline from a more favorable situation during the colonial period. The existence of protest, however, is not an index of oppression, but rather a measure of the ambiguities and weaknesses of the system of control. It is ironic that the Turnerian frontier theory, implicitly biased by its emphasis on male experience, survives most strongly in the field of women's history.[23] As Domar has shown, however, labor scarcity and free land are intimately related to the institutions of slavery and serfdom.[24] The economic factor associated with the exceptional freedom of white American males was a precondition of the equally exceptional degree of suppression of blacks. For a group to gain from favorable economic conditions, it must be able to benefit from the operation of the market. While this was true for single women in the nineteenth century (but not in the pre-industrial period), it decidedly was not true for married women. Wives were not free to strike a better bargain with a new mate. What appears to be crucial in determining the turn toward freedom or suppresion of the vulnerable group are the ideology and values of the dominant group.[25] Neither the position of the labor force nor of women can be mechanistically reduced to simple economic factors.[26]

The empirical basis for the importance of the frontier in the history of women is not impressive. On the nineteenth-century frontier at least, the high male-to-female sex ratio was a transitory phenomenon.[27] For the entire American population, the high rate of natural increase during the colonial period quickly narrowed the differential in the sex ratio created by immigration.[28] The truth left in the frontier argument is also ironic. Women's suffrage undeniably came earlier in the West. That development, as Grimes has argued, reflected the potential usefulness of women as voters along the conservative wife-mother line rather than a recognition of Western women as citizens per se.[29] Farber's interesting analysis of the East-Midwest variation in marriage prohibition statutes points to a relative emphasis on the conjugal family in the newer areas of the country. Midwestern states tend to prohibit marriages of cousins while certain affinal marriages are illegal in the East and South.[30] In summary, then, the frontier and the general newness of social institutions in America benefitted women chiefly as part of the elevation of conjugality in family structure.

The majority of women in nineteenth-century families had good reason to perceive themselves as better off than their pre-industrial forebearers. This shift involved not merely the level of material comfort but, more importantly, the quality of social and familial relationships. Since being a wife and mother was now evaluated more positively, women recognized an improvement within their "sphere" and thus channelled their efforts within and not beyond the family unit. It is not surprising that contemporary and later critics of the Victorian family referred to it as patriarchal, since that was the older form being superseded. If a descriptive label with a Latin root is wanted, however, "matriarchal" would be more suitable for the nineteenth-century family. Men had inordinate power within the Victorian family, but it was as husbands—not as fathers. The conservative conception of woman's role focused, after all, on the submissive wife rather than the submissive daughter.[31] Nineteenth-century women, once married, did not retain crucial ties to their family of birth; marriage joined individuals and not their families.[32]

While the interpretation being advanced here stresses the significance of the new autonomy of women within the family as an explanation of the decline of fertility during the nineteenth century, this is not to deny the importance of economic, instrumental, or "male" considerations. The shift from agriculture, the separation of production from the family, the urbanization of the population, and the loss of child labor through compulsory education doubtless also contributed. Indeed, the wife's demand for a smaller family may have been so successful precisely because it was not contrary to the rational calculations of her husband. Since the fertility decline was nationwide and affected urban and rural areas simultaneously, attitudes and values as well as structural factors are obviously of relevance.[33] The romantic cult of childhood, for example, may have induced a change from quantitative to qualitative fertility goals on the part of parents.

The social correlates of lower fertility found in modern populations are relevant to this discussion of the history of American fertility. A common finding of cross-national studies, for example, is a strong negative relationship between fertility and female participation in the labor force.[34] The American historical record, however, does not provide much support for this theory. During the 1830-1890 period, there was probably only a slight increase in the labor-force participation of married women and yet marital fertility continuously declined.[35] During both the post-World-War-II baby boom and the fertility decline since 1957, labor-force activity of married women increased.[36] For lower fertility, what is important is the meaning women assign to themselves and their work, either in or out of the home.[37] Since work is compatible with a traditional orientation for women,[38] the converse may also be true. Finally, the strong relationship between lower fertility and the educational attainment of a woman may involve more than a response to the higher financial return of nonfamilial activity for the better educated.[39] Education may be a proxy variable for the degree to which a woman defines her life in terms of self rather than others.

Some quantitative support for the hypothesis that the wife significantly controlled family planning in the nineteenth century derives from a comparison of sex ratios of last children in small and large families, and an analysis of the sex composition of very small families in Hingham, Massachusetts. Most studies indicate that men and women equally prefer boys to girls.[40] Given a residue of patriarchal bias in nineteenth-century values, it is not an unlikely assumption that women would be more satisfied than men with girl children. A suggestive psychological study supports this notion. In a sample of Swedish women expecting their first child, those preferring a boy were found to have less of a sense of personal autonomy. Of the eleven of the eighty-one women in the sample who considered themselves dominant in their marriages, only two wanted sons. The "no-preference" women were better adjusted psychologically and scored higher on intelligence tests.[41] In short, the less autonomous and adjusted the woman, the more likely she is to want her first child to be a boy.

In Hingham marriages formed between 1821 and 1860, the last child was more likely to be a girl in small families and a boy in the larger families (see Table 4). The difference between the sex ratios of the final child in families with one to four children as compared to those with five and more is statistically significant only at the 0.1 level. Given the complexity of the argument here, this is not impressive. Small families, however, tended to contain only girls. Sixty percent of only children were girls (21 of 35); 27 percent and 17 percent of two-child families were both girls (14) and boys (9) respectively; and 14 percent and 6 percent of three-child families were all girls (9) and all boys (4) respectively. The independent probability of these differences is less than one in ten, one in four, and one in twenty respectively. With a slight biological tendency toward males in births to young women, these figures suggest that differing sex-preferences of husbands and wives may explain the pattern. On the other hand, twentieth-century sex-ratio samples show either no difference or a bias toward males in the sex ratio of the last-born child.[42] In the absence of very marked differences in the preference of husband and wives and with less than perfect contraceptive methods available to nineteenth-century couples, no extreme relationship should appear. This quantitative pattern does suggest that the Victorian family had a domestic-feminist rather than a patriarchal orientation.

TABLE 4

Sex ratio of last versus other children of stated parity and the probability of having another child according to sex of the last child: Hingham women in complete families marrying before age twenty-five between 1821 and 1860.

	Sex ratio		Parity progression ratios		
Parity	Last	Not last	Male last	Female last	Difference
1	57(22)	124(242)	.944	.885	+.059
2	113(32)	82(211)	.848	.855	—.037
3	69(49)	83(165)	.789	.756	+.033
4	83(42)	114(124)	.776	.716	+.060
5	107(31)	114(94)	.758	.746	+.012
6	237(22)	74(66)	.596	.826	—.230
7	150(20)	77(46)	.625	.764	—.139
8&+	124(47)	105(86)	.628	.667	—.039

NOTE: Sample sizes in parentheses. Chi-Square (1-4) vs. (5 and more) 2.882, significant at 0.1 level.
SOURCE: Daniel Scott Smith,"Population, Family and Society in Hingham, Massachusetts, 1635-1880," (unpublished Ph.D. dissertation, University of California, Berkeley, 1973), p. 360.

Recognition of the desirability and even the existence of female control of marital sexual intercourse may be found in nineteenth-century marital advice literature. In these manuals, "marital excess," i.e., too-frequent coitus, was a pervasive theme. Although conservative writers, such as William Alcott, proclaimed that "the submissive wife should do everything for your husband which your strength and a due regard to your health would admit,"[43] women rejected submission. In fact, Dio Lewis claimed that marital excess was the topic best received by his female audience during his lecture tours of the 1850s. The Moral Education Society, according to Lewis, asserted the right "of a wife to be her own person, and her sacred right to deny her husband if need be; and to decide how often and when she should become a mother."[44] The theme of the wife's right to control her body and her fertility was not uncommon. "It is a woman's right, not her privilege, to control the surrender of her person; she should have pleasure or not allow access unless she wanted a child.[45]

It should be emphasized that both the husband and the wife had good (albeit different) reasons for limiting the size of their family. In most marriages, perhaps, these decisions were made jointly by the couple. Nor is it necessarily true that the wife imposed abstinence on her husband. While *coitus interruptus* is the male contraceptive par excellence, the wife could assist "with voluntary [though unspecified] effort."[46] Withdrawal was, according to one physician, "so universal it may be called a national vice, so common that it is unblushingly acknowledged by its perpetrators, *for the commission of which the husband is even eulogized by his wife and applauded by her friends* [italics added]."[47] In the marriage manuals, withdrawal was the most denounced means of marital contraception and, it may be inferred, the most common method in actual practice.

There are serious questions about the applicability of this literary evidence to actual behavior. Even among the urban middle classes (presumably the consumers of these manuals and tracts) reality and ideology probably diverged considerably. Historical variation in sexual ideology doubtless is much greater than change in actual sexual behavior.[48] The anti-sexual themes of the nineteenth century should not, however, be ignored. One may view this ideology as the product of underlying social circumstances—the conscious tip, so to speak, of the submerged iceberg of sexual conflict. While the influence of this literature is difficult to assess, its functions can be examined. It can be argued that anti-sexual themes had little to do with family limitation. Nor was contraception universally condemned by respectable opinion. The *Nation* in June 1869 called family limitation "not the noblest motive of action, of course; but there is something finely human about it."[49] Male sexual self-control was necessary, it has been suggested, to produce ordered, disciplined personalities who could focus relentlessly on success in the marketplace.[50] The conventional interpretation of these anti-sexual themes, of course, is that Victorian morality was but another means for suppressing women. The trouble with these arguments is that men more than women should be expected to favor, support, and extend the operation of this morality.

To understand the function of this ideology we must examine the market system involving the exchange of services between women and men. In historical, pre-industrial, hierarchical society, male control and suppression of female sexuality focused especially on the paternal control of daughters. This system of control existed for the establishment of marriage alliances and for the protection of one's females from the intrusions of social inferiors. Sexual restrictiveness need not, however, imply direct male domination. In a system of equality between males in which females are denied access to other resources, a sexually restrictive ideology is predictable. Nineteenth-century mate-choice was more or less an autonomous process uncontrolled by elders. American women, as Tocqueville and others noted, had considerable freedom before marriage. Lacking economic resources, however, they could bargain with their only available good—sex. The price of sex, as of other commodities, varies inversely with the supply. Since husbands were limited by the autonomy of single women in finding sexual gratification elsewhere, sexual restrictiveness also served the interests of married women. Furthermore, in a democratic society, men could not easily violate the prerogatives of their male equals by seducing their wives. Thus Victorian morality functioned in the interest of both single and married women.[51] By having an effective monopoly on the supply of sexual gratification, married women could increase the "price" since their husbands still generally expressed a traditional uncontrolled demand for sex. Instead of being "possessed," women could now bargain. Respectable sexual ideology argued, it is true, that men should substitute work for sex. This would reduce the price that wives could exact. At the same time, according to the prevailing sexual ideology, marital sex was the least dangerous kind. In contrast to masturbation or prostitution, marital intercourse was evaluated positively. But, contrary to these ideological trends, prostitution appears to have increased during the nineteenth century. Whether or not prostitution was a substitute for marital sex or merely a reflection of the relative increase in the proportion of unattached males created by late marriage and high geographical mobility is uncertain. This brief economic analysis of the supply and demand of sex at least suggests the possibility that Victorian morality had distinctly feminist overtones.

In principle, Victorian sexual ideology did advance the interest of individual women. Whether or not this represented a genuine feminist ideology depends to some extent on the behavior of women as a group. The evidence seems to be fairly clear on this point. If women as individuals had wished to maximize their advantage, they could have furthered the devaluation of non-marital sex for men by drawing more firmly the line between "good" and "bad" women, between the lady and the whore. While mothers may have done this on an individual basis, for example, by threatening their daughters with the dishonor of being a fallen woman, collectively they tended to sympathize with the prostitute or fallen woman and condemn the male exploiter or seducer.[52] The activity of the New York Female Moral Reform Society is an instructive case in point.[53]

Historians have had some difficulty in interpreting the anti-sexual theme in nineteenth-century women's history. Although Rosenberg recognizes the implicit radicalness of the assault on the double standard and the demand for a reformation in male sexual behavior, she tends to apologize for the failure of sexual reformers to link up with the "real" feminism represented by Sarah Grimke's feminist manifesto.[54] More serious is the distortion of the central question of the periodization of women's history. Cott's labeling of the first half of the nineteenth century as a question of "the cult of domesticity vs. social change," Kraditor's similar choice of "the family vs. autonomy," and Lerner's dichotomy of "the lady and the mill girl" all perpetuate the half-truth that the family served only as a source of social stability and change for women occurred only outside of the family.[55] I am arguing here, however, that the domestic roles of women and the perceptions that developed out of these roles were not an alternative to social change but presented a significant and positive development for nineteenth-century women.

Linking the decline of marital fertility to women's increasing autonomy within the family—the concept of "domestic feminism"—conflicts with several other theories held by scholars. To stress the failure of the woman's movement to support family limitation, as the Bankses do in their analyses for England, ignores the possibility of a parallel domestic feminist movement. It may be more to the point that anti-feminists blamed the revolt against maternity and marital sexual intercourse on the public feminists.[56] The Bankses suggest that individual feminists may have fought a battle to gain control over their own reproduction.[57] The nineteenth-century neo-Malthusians and the woman's movement had different purposes; the former attempted to control the fertility of "others," i.e., the working classes, while the latter sought reforms in its own interest. Since mechanical means of contraception were associated with non-marital sex of a kind exploitative of women, the opposition of women to these devices was an expression of the deeper hostility to the double standard.

A more serious objection to identifying the increasing power and autonomy of women within the family as feminism is, of course, the existence of the parallel tradition of "real" or "public" feminism. This tradition—linking Wollstonecraft, Seneca Falls, Stanton, Anthony, and Gilman—at least partially recognized the centrality of the role and position of women in the family to the general subjugation of women in society. In contrast, the goals of domestic feminism, at least in its initial stage, were situated entirely within marriage. Clearly some explanation is needed of why both strands of feminism existed. A possible answer relates to the evolution of the family in the process of modernization. With the democratization of American society, prestige ascribed by birth declined. Women born into familes of high social status could not obtain deference if they remained single; even if a woman married a man of equally high status, his position would not assure her prestige; his status depended on his achievement. The satisfactory and valued performance in the roles of wife and mother could not compensate for the loss of status associated with the family line in preindustrial society. Thus public feminism would be most attractive to women of high social origin.[58] This conception of the woman as an atomistic person and citizen naturally drew on the Enlightenment attack on traditional social ties. The modeling of the Seneca Falls manifesto on the Declaration of Independence is suggestive in this regard.[59]

The liberal origins of public feminism were both its strength and its weakness. Because it emphasized a clear standard of justice and stressed the importance of human individuality, it was consistent with the most fundamental values in American political history. But it was also limiting as a political ideology in that it cast its rhetoric against nearly obsolete social forms that had little relevance in the experience of the average American woman, i.e., patriarchalism and arbitrary male authority. Paradoxically, public feminism was simultaneously behind and ahead of the times. Resting on eighteenth-century notions, it clashed with the romantic and sentimental mood of the nineteenth century. The social basis of the appeal of public feminism—the opportunity for married women to assume both family and social roles—would not be created for the average woman until the post-industrial period.

Domestic feminism, on the other hand, was a nineteenth-century creation, born out of the emerging conjugal family and the social stresses accompanying modern economic growth. Instead of postulating woman as an atom in competitive society, domestic feminism viewed woman as a person in the context of relationships with others. By defining the family as a community, this ideology allowed women to engage in something of a critique of male, materialistic, market society and simultaneously proceed to seize power within the family. Women asserted themselves within the family much as their husbands were attempting to assert themselves outside the home. Critics such as de Tocqueville concluded that the Victorian conjugal family was really a manifestation of selfishness and a retreat from the older conception of community as place. As one utopian-communitarian put it, the basic social question of the day was "whether the existence of the marital family is compatible with that of the universal family which the term 'Community' signifies."[60]

Community—"that mythical state of social wholeness in which each member has his place and in which life is regulated by cooperation rather than by competition and conflict,"[61]—is not fixed historically in one social institution. Rather, as Kirk Jeffrey has argued, the nineteenth-century home was conceived of as a utopian community—at once a retreat, refuge and critique of the city.[62] Jeffrey, however, does not fully realize the implications of his insight. He admits that the literature of the utopian home demanded that husbands consult their wives, avoid sexual assault on them, and even consciously structure their own behavior on the model of their spouses. Yet he still concludes that "there seems little doubt that they (women) suffered a notable decline in autonomy and morale during the three-quarters of a century following the founding of the American republic."[63] He suggests that women who engaged in writing, social activities, political reform, drug use, and sickliness were "dropping out" of domesticity. On the contrary, these responses reflect both the time and autonomy newly available to women. The romantic ideal of woman as wife and mother in contrast to the Enlightenment model of woman as person and citizen did not have entirely negative consequences—particularly for the vast majority of American women who did not benefit from the position of their family in society.

The perspective suggested above helps to explain why the history of the suffrage movement involved a shift from the woman-as-atomistic-person notion toward the ideology of woman as wife-and-mother. Drawing on the perceptions gained from their rise within the family, women finally entered politics in large numbers at the turn of the twentieth century. Given the importance of family limitation and sexual control in domestic feminism, it is not surprising that women were involved in and strongly supported the temperance and social purity movements—reform attempts implicitly attacking male culture. Since these anti-male responses and attitudes were based on the familial and social experience of women, it seems beside the point to infer psychological abnormality from this emphasis.[64]

In an important sense, the traditions of domestic and public feminism merged in the fight for suffrage in the early twentieth century. In a study of "elite" women surveyed in 1913, Jensen found that mothers of completed fertility actually exhibited more support for suffrage than childless married women.[65] Women in careers involving more social interaction, for example, medicine, law, administration, tended to favor suffrage more strongly than women in more privatistic occupations, for example, teaching, writing, art.[66] In short, the dichotomy between women trapped or suppressed within marriage and women seeking to gain freedom through social participation does not accurately represent the history of American women in the nineteenth century.

It has been argued that historians must take seriously the changing roles and behavior of women within the Victorian conjugal family. That women eventually attained a larger arena of activity was not so much an alternative to the woman-as-wife-and-mother as an extension of the progress made within the family itself. Future research doubtless will qualify, if not completely obviate, the arguments presented in this essay. Although power relationships within contemporary marriages are poorly understood by social scientists, this critical area very much needs a historical dimension.[67] The history of women must take into account major changes in the structure of society and the family. During the pre-industrial period, women (mainly widows) exercised power as replacements for men. In the industrializing phase of the last century, married women gained power and a sense of autonomy within the family. In the post-industrial era, the potentiality for full social participation of women clearly exists. The construction of these historical stages inevitably involves over-simplification. Drawing these sharp contrasts, however, permits the historian to escape from the present-day definition of the situation. Once it is clear just what the long-run course of change actually was, more subtlety and attention to the mechanism of change will be possible in the analysis of women's history.

FOOTNOTES

1 The attempt to examine systematically the lives of ordinary women is well under way; for example, see Theodore Hershberg, "A Method for the Computerized Study of Family and Household Structure Using the Manuscript Schedules of the U.S. Census of Population," *Family in Historical Perspective Newsletter* 3 (Spring 1973): 6-20.

2 For a suggestive illustration of the impact of changing mortality on the average female, see Peter R. Uhlenberg, "A Study of Cohort Life Cycles: Cohorts of Native-Born Massachusetts Women, 1830-1920," *Population Studies* 23 (November 1969): 407-420.

3 Wilson H. Grabill, Clyde V. Kiser, and Pascal K. Whelpton, *The Fertility of American Women* (New York: John Wiley & Sons, Inc., 1958), Table 67, p. 145.

4 Robert V. Wells, "Demographic Change and the Life Cycle of American Families," *Journal of Interdisciplinary History* 2 (Autumn 1971): Table 2, p. 282.

5 This modal woman was constructed from the median age of household heads (less four years) from U.S. Bureau of the Census, *Historical Statistics of the United States, Colonial Times to 1957* (Washington, D.C.: Government Printing Office, 1960), Series A-263, p. 16; from the center of population gravity, from *U.S. Statistical Abstract* (87th ed., 1966), Table 11; from the mean number (5.6) of children born to rural-farm women in the north-central region born between 1835 and 1844 and married only once, U.S. Bureau of the Census, Sixteenth Census., *Population: Differential Fertility 1940 and 1910, Women by Number of Children ever Born* (Washington: Government Printing Office, 1945), Table 81, p. 237; and from the fact that 51.3 percent of the workforce in 1880 was employed in agriculture, Stanley Lebergott, *Manpower in Economic Growth* (New York: McGraw Hill, 1964), Table A-1, p. 510.

6 Some working women may have been counted as housewives by the census takers. Lebergott, *Manpower*, pp. 70-73, however, makes a cogent case for accepting the census figures.

7 Grabill *et al., Fertility*, Table 9, p. 22.

8 Ansley J. Coale and Melvin Zelnik, *New Estimates of Fertility and Population in the United States* (Princeton: Princeton University Press, 1963), p. 41.

9 Yasukichi Yasuba, *Birth Rates of the White Population in the United States, 1800-1860* (Baltimore: Johns Hopkins Press, 1961), Table IV-9, p. 119, attributes 64.3 percent of the Connecticut fertility decline between 1774 and 1890 and 74.3 percent of the New Hampshire decline between 1774 and 1890 to change in marital fertility. Longer birth intervals and an earlier age at the termination of childbearing contributed nearly equally to the decrease in marital fertility. See Daniel Scott Smith, "Change in American Family Structure before the Demographic Transition: The Case of Hingham, Massachusetts," (unpublished paper presented to the American Society for Ethnohistory, October 1972), p. 3.

10 For a summary of the importance of withdrawal in the history of European contraception, see D. V. Glass, *Population: Policies and Movements in Europe* (New York: Augustus M. Kelley, Booksellers, 1967), p. 46-50.

11 For this definition, see Aileen S. Kraditor, *Up from the Pedestal* (Chicago: Quadrangle Books, 1968), p. 5.

12 Aileen S. Kraditor, *The Ideas of the Woman Suffrage Movement* (New York: Anchor Books, 1971).

13 Carl N. Degler, "Revolution without Ideology: The Changing Place of Women in America," *Daedalus* 93 (Spring 1964): 653-670.

14 William L. O'Neill, *Everyone was Brave* (Chicago: Quadrangle Books, 1969).

15 My use of the term conjugal is intended to be much broader than the strict application to household composition. On the relatively unchanging conjugal (or nuclear) structure of the household see Peter Laslett, ed., *Household and Family in Past Time* (Cambridge: Cambridge University Press, 1972). For an empirical demonstration of the types of changes involved see my article, "Parental Power and Mariage Patterns: An Analysis of Historical Trends in Hingham, Massachusetts," in the special historical issue of *Journal of Marriage and the Family* 35 (August 1973).

16 Phillipe Aries, *Centuries of Childhood: A Social History of Family Life*, trans. Robert Baldick (New York: Vintage Books, 1962).

17 Julia Cherry Spruill, *Women's Life and Work in the Southern Colonies* (Chapel Hill: University of North Carolina Press, 1938) and Elisabeth Anthony Dexter, *Colonial Women of Affairs* (Boston: Houghton Mifflin Company, 1924).

18 Richard B. Morris, *Studies in the History of American Law*, 2nd ed. (Philadelphia: Joseph M. Mitchell Co., 1959), pp. 126-200.

19 Maris Vinovskis, "Mortality Rates and Trends in Massachusetts before 1860," *Journal of Economic History* 32 (March 1972): 198-199. In the eighteenth century women began to live longer than men with the exception again of Ipswich.

20 Daniel Scott Smith, "Population, Family and Society in Hingham, Massachusetts, 1635-1880," (unpublished Ph.D. dissertation, University of California, Berkeley, 1973), pp. 225-227.

21 Scattered American data are available in Lawrence A. Cremin, *American Education: The Colonial Experience, 1607-1783* (New York: Harper Torchbooks, 1970), pp. 526, 533, 540. Also see Carlo M. Cipolla, *Literacy and Development in the West* (Baltimore: Penguin Books, 1969), Table 1, p. 14. Professor Kenneth Lockridge of the University of Michigan, who is undertaking a major study of literacy in early America has written me, however, that women using a mark may have been able to read.

22 Edward Shorter, "Capitalism, Culture and Sexuality: Some Competing Models," *Social Science Quarterly* 53 (September 1972): 339.

23 David M. Potter, "American Women and the American Character," in *History and American Society: Essays of David M. Potter*, ed. Don E. Fehrenbacher (New York: Oxford University Press, 1973), pp. 227-303.

24 Evsey D. Domar, "The Causes of Slavery or Serfdom: A Hypothesis," *Journal of Economic History* 30 (March 1970): 18-32.

25 See Edmund S. Morgan, "Slavery and Freedom: An American Paradox," *Journal of American History* 59 (June 1972): 3-29.

26 Stanley Engerman, "Some Considerations Relating to Property Rights in Man," *Journal of Economic History* 33 (March 1973): 56-65.

27 Jack E. Eblen, "An Analysis of Nineteenth Century Frontier Populations," *Demography* 2 (1965): 399-413.

28 See Herbert Moller, "Sex Composition and Correlated Culture Patterns of Colonial America," *William and Mary Quarterly* 2 (April 1945): 113-153 for data on sex ratios.

29 Alan P. Grimes, *The Puritan Ethic and Woman Suffrage* (New York: Oxford University Press, 1967).

30 Bernard Farber, *Comparative Kinship Systems* (New York: John Wiley & Sons, Inc., 1968), pp. 23-46.

31 Walter E. Houghton, *The Victorian Frame of Mind* (New Haven: Yale University Press, 1957), pp. 348-353.

32 See Smith, "Parental Power and Marriage Patterns . . ." *Journal of Marriage and the Family* (August 1973).

33 Grabill *et al., Fertility*, pp. 16-19. For insights based on differentials in census child-woman ratios see Yasuba, *Birth Rates*, as well as Colin Forster and G. S. L. Tucker, *Economic Opportunity and White American Fertility Ratios, 1800-1860* (New Haven: Yale University Press, 1972). For a brief statement of the structural argument see Richard Easterlin, "Does Fertility Adjust to the Environment?" *American Economic Review* 61 (1971): 394-407.

34 John D. Kasarda, "Economic Structure and Fertility: A Comparative Analysis," *Demography* 8 (August 1971): 307-317.

35 Lebergott, *Manpower*, p. 63.

36 Kingsley Davis, "The American Family in Relation to Demographic Change," in *Demographic and Social Aspects of Population Growth*, eds. Charles F. Westoff and Robert Parke, Jr. (Washington, D.C.: Government Printing Office, 1972), p. 245.

37 One study involving seven Latin American cities has suggestively concluded that the "wife's motivation for employment, her education, and her preferred role seem to exert greater influence on her fertility than her actual role of employee or homemaker." Paula H. Hass, "Maternal Role Incompatability and Fertility in Urban Latin America," *Journal of Social Issues* 28 (1972): 111-127.

38 Virginia Yans McLaughlin, "Patterns of Work and Family Organization: Buffalo's Italians," *Journal of Interdisciplinary History* 2 (Autumn 1971): 299-314.

39 For the relationship between fertility and individual characteristics see the special issue of the *Journal of Political Economy* 81, pt. 2 (March/April 1973) on "new economic approaches to fertility."

40 See the summary by Gerald E. Markle and Charles B. Nam, "Sex Determination: Its Impact on Fertility," *Social Biology* 18 (March 1971): 73-82.

41 N. Uddenberg, P. E. Almgren and A. Nilsson, "Preference for Sex of Child among Pregnant Women," *Journal of Biosocial Science* 3 (July 1971): 267-280.

42 In a study of early twentieth century *Who's Who*, cited by Markle and Nam, the sex ratio of the last child was 117.4 in 5,466 families, No differences appear in Harriet L. Fancher, "The

Relationship between the Occupational Status of Individuals and the Sex Ratio of their Offspring," *Human Biology* 28 (September 1966): 316-322.

43 William A. Alcott, *The Young Man's Wife, or Duties of Women in the Marriage Role* (Boston: George W. Light, 1837), p. 176.

44 Dio Lewis, *Chastity, or our Secret Sins* (New York: Canfield Publishing Company, 1888), p. 18.

45 Henry C. Wright, *Marriage and Parentage* (Boston: Bela Marsh, 1853), pp. 242-255.

46 Anon, *Satan in Society* (Cincinnati: C. V. Vent, 1875), p. 153.

47 Ibid., p. 152.

48 For a discussion of the gradualness of change in sexual behavior see Daniel Scott Smith, "The Dating of the American Sexual Revolution: Evidence and Interpretation," in *The American Family in Social-Historical Perspective*, ed., Michael Gordon (New York: St. Martin's Press, 1973), pp. 321-335.

49 Quoted by George Humphrey Napheys, *The Physical Life of Women* (Philadelphia: H. C. Watts Co., 1882), p. 119.

50 Peter C. Cominos, "Late Victorian Sexual Respectability and the Social System," *International Review of Social History* 8 (1963): 18-48, 216-250.

51 Although the basic argument here was formulated independently, Randall Collins, "A Conflict Theory of Sexual Stratification," *Social Problems* 19 (Summer 1971): 3-21; and David G. Berger and Morton C. Wenger, "The Ideology of Virginity," (paper read at the 1972 meeting of the National Council on Family Relations) were very helpful in developing this theme.

52 On attitudes toward prostitution, see Margaret Wyman, "The Rise of the Fallen Woman," *American Quarterly* 3 (Summer 1951): 167-177; and Robert E. Riegel, "Changing American Attitudes Toward Prostitution," *Journal of the History of Ideas* 29 (July-September 1968): 437-452.

53 Carroll Smith-Rosenberg, "Beauty, the Beast and the Militant Woman: a Case Study in Sex Roles in Jacksonian America," *American Quarterly* 23 (October 1971): 562-584.

54 Ibid.

55 Nancy F. Cott, *Root of Bitterness* (New York: E. P. Dutton & Co., Inc., 1972): 11-14; Kraditor, *Up from the Pedestal*, p. 21; Gerda Lerner, "The Lady and the Mill Girl: Changes in the Status of Women in the Age of Jackson," *Midcontinent American Studies Journal* 10 (Spring 1969): 5-14.

56 J. A. and Olive Banks, *Feminism and Family Planning in Victorian England* (Liverpool: Liverpool University Press, 1964); esp. pp. 53-57.

57 Ibid., p. 125.

58 In his book, *Daughters of the Promised Land* (Boston: Little, Brown, 1970), Page Smith argues that many prominent feminists had strong fathers. It might be that the true relationship, if any in fact exists, is between public feminism and high status fathers.

59 Robert A. Nisbet, *The Sociological Tradition* (New York: Basic Books, 1966), ch. 3, esp. pp. 47-51.

60 Quoted by John L. Thomas, "Romantic Reform in America, 1815-1865," *American Quarterly* 17 (Winter 1965): p. 677.

61 Charles Abrams, *The Language of Cities* (New York: Viking Press, 1971), p. 60.

62 Kirk Jeffrey effectively develops this theme in "The Family as Utopian Retreat from the City: The Nineteenth Century Contribution" in *The Family, Communes and Utopian Societies*, ed. Sallie Teselle (New York: Harper Torchbooks, 1972), pp. 21-41.

63 Ibid., p. 30.

64 For a psychological emphasis see James R. McGovern, "Anna Howard Shaw: New Approaches to Feminism," *Journal of Social History* 3 (Winter 1969-70): 135-153.

65 Richard Jensen, "Family, Career, and Reform: Women Leaders of the Progressive Era," in *The American Family in Social-Historical Perspective*, Table 7, p. 277.

66 Ibid., Table 2, p. 273.

67 An analysis of recent literature of this important topic is presented by Constantina Safilios-Rothschild, "The Study of Family Power Structure: A Review 1960-1969," *Journal of Marriage and the Family* 32 (November 1970): 539-552.

Frank F. Furstenberg, Jr.,
Theodore Hershberg, and John Modell

The Origins of the Female-Headed Black Family: The Impact of the Urban Experience

The link between family structure and social mobility has been a topic of considerable sociological speculation. For some years now, there has been a running controversy among scholars working in the area of the family as to whether certain kinship arrangements are especially conducive to success in an industrial society. Specifically, a general proposition was set forth, principally by Parsons, that the most prevalent family form in this society—the nuclear household—emerged at about the time of industrialization in response to demands of the economy for a highly flexible, mobile, emotionally bonded, small kin unit. Parsons contends that extended family forms restrict social mobility by subordinating immediate economic motives to longer range familial interests. Strong commitment to kin, according to this line of reasoning, detracts from unqualified commitment to economic achievement, for it fosters a sense of collectivity rather than individualism, an emphasis on personal qualities rather than on general performance.[1]

Frank F. Furstenberg, Jr., is Associate Professor of Sociology at the University of Pennsylvania. Theodore Hershberg is Associate Professor of History at the University of Pennsylvania. John Modell is Associate Professor of History at the University of Minnesota.

The authors wish to express their appreciation to the Center for the Study of Metropolitan Problems, National Institute of Mental Health, the financial support of which (MH16621) has made this research possible. An earlier version of this paper was presented at the 1973 annual meeting of the American Sociological Association.

The data presented here were collected by the Philadelphia Social History Project, directed by Theodore Hershberg. They are part of a larger study of the impact of urbanization, industrialization, and immigration on social and family structure, the formation and transformation of neighborhoods, the organization of and journey to work, the development of an intra-urban transportation network, and patterns of migration and social mobility. To study these topics, a massive machine-readable data base has been created describing individual persons, families, businesses, manufacturing firms, and transportation facilities. See Theodore Hershberg, "The Philadelphia Social History Project: A Methodological History," unpub. Ph.D. diss. (Stanford, 1973). The authors are indebted to the critical readings of Etienne van de Walle and John Durand.

1 Talcott Parsons, "Age and Sex in the Structure of the United States," *American Sociological Review*, VII (1942), 604–616; Parsons and Robert F. Bales, *Family, Socialization and the Interaction Process* (New York, 1965), ch 1.

Although the functional explanation for the family in contemporary Western society has a plausible ring, empirical support has been conspicuously absent. Indeed, many of the studies on the relationship of the economy, family forms, and social mobility have failed to confirm even basic assumptions underlying the evolution of the contemporary Western family: (1) several historical studies have cast doubt on the proposition that the traditional family in Western society was extended and non-nuclear in form in preindustrial society; (2) cross-cultural comparisons suggest that although the form of the family is changing in many societies in response to economic conditions, various family forms can co-exist with industrialized economies; (3) relations with extended kin abound in contemporary society, indicating that the family is not so nuclear or isolated as was supposed in the classic formulation; (4) extensive kinship relations may promote social mobility by providing economic resources and social support not available in a small family unit.[2]

The evidence which runs counter to the classic formulation of the functional relationship between industrialization and social mobility is still inconclusive; nevertheless, it suggests that it is a sociological problem that bears further consideration. Until further historical data are assembled, there is little basis to select among the conflicting interpretations or to develop a more integrative theory.

In recent years, however, another even more compelling reason for gathering further information on this problem has arisen. As attention shifted in the 1960s from an undifferentiated examination of the experience of the "American family" to a more detailed inspection of the subcultural variations in family form, a bitter debate erupted on one aspect of the broad question of the articulation of economy, family, and social mobility. At the locus of this disagreement was the question of whether "structural defects" in the black family accounted for the economically disadvantaged position of blacks in American society.

2 Ethel Shanas and Gordon F. Streib (eds.), *Social Structure and the Family: Generational Relations* (Englewood Cliffs, N.J., 1965); Marvin B. Sussman, "The Isolated Nuclear Family: Fact or Fiction?" *Social Problems*, VI (1959), 333–340; Sussman and Lee Burchinal, "Kin Family Network: Unheralded Structure in Current Conceptualizations of Family Functioning," *Marriage and Family Living*, XXIV (1962), 221–240; Eugene Litwack, "Occupational Mobility and Extended Family Cohesion," *American Sociological Review*, XXV (1960), 9–21; Elizabeth Bott, *Family and Social Network* (London, 1957); William J. Goode, *World Revolution and Family Patterns* (New York, 1963). See also Michael Gordon and Tamara K. Hareven (eds.), "New Social History of the Family," special issue of *Journal of Marriage and the Family*, XXXV (1973).

Even before and especially since the earlier writings of Frazier, the sociological writings on the black family were heavily laced with references to the destructive legacy of slavery, the missing male, and the matrifocal character of black family life.[3] However, Frazier's observations were amplified and extended in the early 1960s in Nathan Glazer and Daniel P. Moynihan's widely acclaimed book, *Beyond the Melting Pot* (Cambridge, Mass., 1964). While acknowledging the impact of prejudice and economic discrimination, Glazer and Moynihan, following Frazier, traced the current position of blacks in America back to slavery. They contended that the black family, weakened by slavery, could not withstand the pressures of urban life.

In reviewing the Glazer/Moynihan section on the condition of the black family in the nineteenth century, it is impossible not to be impressed by the absence of supporting data. Both the propositions that slavery resulted in a permanent deterioration of the black family structure and that family structure accounts for economic disadvantage are accepted uncritically. Several years later, the Glazer/Moynihan thesis was restated in the report on the black family that Moynihan prepared for the Johnson administration. In this later document, the argument is further amplified and family structure is accorded even greater importance in accounting for the current fate of black Americans:

> Obviously, not every instance of social pathology afflicting the Negro community can be traced to the weakness of family structure. . . . Nonetheless, at the center of the tangle of pathology is the weakness of the family structure. . . . It was by destroying the Negro family under slavery that white Americans broke the will of the Negro people. Although that will has reasserted itself in our time, it is a resurgence doomed to frustration unless the viability of the Negro family is restored.[4]

Needless to say, the Moynihan report has engendered a heated discussion of a number of crucial issues: What was the impact of slavery on the family structure of Afro-Americans? How does family structure shape prospects of economic success in American society? How do the answers to these questions contribute to our understanding of the potential effect of various strategies for ameliorating economic disadvantage? In a very real sense, these questions raised by the Moynihan

3 E. Franklin Frazier, *The Negro Family in the United States* (Chicago, 1939).
4 Lee Rainwater and William Yancey (eds.), *The Moynihan Report and the Politics of Controversy* (Cambridge, Mass., 1967), 76.

thesis are specifications of the general problem of how family structure is linked to economic success in American society. Are certain forms of the family more or less conducive to social mobility in an industrialized economy? Specifically, is there reason to believe that the couple-headed nuclear family is better equipped to utilize economic resources and confer special advantages on their offspring than a non-couple-headed or non-nuclear family structure?

A few contemporary studies have explored the link between family structure and social mobility with largely inconclusive results.[5] The most penetrating historical studies have so far concentrated on questioning the link between slavery and black family structure.[6] As yet, little historical information has been brought to bear on the status of the black family relative to other ethnic groups and the economic consequences of family structure for people of different ethnic backgrounds. Thus, it is not even known whether sizable variations existed in the structure of families among various ethnic groups prior to this century, much less whether such variations influenced the mobility patterns of these different populations.

This paper examines how family structure and family composition varied by ethnic group in the second half of the nineteenth century in Philadelphia, the nation's second largest city. Our analysis is based on samples drawn from the decennial Federal population manuscript schedules for 1850 through 1880. The black sample consists of all black households; the white ethnic samples are drawn systematically from the whole number of households headed by immigrants from Ireland and Germany, and by native white Americans. None includes fewer than 2,000 households for each census year.[7]

THE STRUCTURE OF THE HOUSEHOLD Although our information does not reach back into the early nineteenth century, it does lend

5 O. D. Duncan and Beverly Duncan, "Family Stability and Occupational Success," *Social Problems*, XVI (1969), 273–285.

6 Herbert Gutman, "Persistent Myths about the Afro-American Family," above, 181–210. See also Theodore Hershberg, "Free Blacks in Antebellum Philadelphia: A Study of Ex-slaves, Freeborn and Socioeconomic Decline," *Journal of Social History*, V (1971), 183–209; Elizabeth Pleck, "The Two-Parent Household: Black Family Structure in Late Nineteenth-Century Boston," *Ibid.* VI (1972), 3–31.

7 About 4 percent of the city's population were neither black, Irish, German, nor native white. For a detailed description of how the samples were drawn, see Hershberg, "Philadelphia Social History Project," ch. 2.

further support to the position that complex households were less common than simple nuclear structures, at least in one major urban area.[8] When we examined the 1880 data from Philadelphia, several interesting observations came to light. First, considering only those families in which a child was present, more than three-fourths of the households in Philadelphia consisted of nuclear families, that is families comprised of parents and children with no other relatives present in the home. Of greatest significance is our finding that only minor variations exist among the four ethnic groups (Table 1). Blacks and native whites were slightly less likely to reside in nuclear households than the Irish and German, probably in large measure because the latter groups —more recent immigrants to Philadelphia—had less time for extended kin to develop in this country.

Table 1 Household Structure by Ethnicity, 1880[a]

	BLACK	IRISH	GERMAN	NWA
Nuclear	75.2%	82.2%	84.5%	73.1%
Extended	17.3	10.6	10.2	17.0
Expanded	7.5	7.3	5.3	9.9
	N=2,949	*N*=1,637	*N*=1,766	*N*=1,730

a The figures in this and the following tables refer only to households with children. Here and throughout tables, decimals in total percentage are due to rounding.

Extended families were the second most common household arrangement. Approximately 14 percent of the sample resided in three-generation families, a figure somewhat greater than the proportion in the current census of Philadelphia. Again we find little variation among the different ethnic groups in the proportion of extended households. Blacks had the highest proportion (17.3 percent); the lowest were German immigrants, of whom 10.2 percent were residing in three-generation families. Expanded families made up only 7 percent of the households. Again, no conspicuous differences appear among ethnic

8 For purposes of this analysis, a detailed code of family forms was developed. Families are classified into nuclear, extended (households of three or more generations), and expanded (households with additional relatives but which do not extend generationally). These family types are further subdivided into couple-headed, male-headed, and female-headed. This distinction allows us to look at the family composition within the three different structural forms. For each of these nine types, a further breakdown is made between those families with and without children.

groups. In particular, blacks were about as likely as other ethnic groups to be organized in complex households, and the patterns between the blacks and native white Americans are almost identical. Thus, whatever the benefits or liabilities of the nuclear family in promoting economic mobility, the household structure cannot explain the differential patterns of social mobility which emerge in the latter part of the nineteenth century.

CHANGES IN HOUSEHOLD STRUCTURE OVER TIME Of course, it is possible that, by 1880, many changes had already taken place in the structure of the family, that our snapshot was taken after the action occurred. In particular, one might speculate that it was too late to detect the damage done to the black family by slavery. Even if this were the case, it would represent a finding of great worth, suggesting that the presumed effects of slavery were quickly erased and that the structure of the contemporary black family could hardly be traced in an unbroken line back to slavery. Our evidence, however, casts doubt even on this hypothesis. When the household composition of the black family in 1880 is compared with the structure of the black household in the antebellum period in 1850, we discover a remarkable degree of continuity. Virtually the same proportion of blacks were living in nuclear households in 1850 as in 1880. Indeed, if anything, there had been a slight decrease in nuclear households.

Other ethnic groups revealed a slight trend toward nuclearity; however, the increase in each case was only a few percentage points (Table 2). Apart from the information that these figures provide about the black family, the comparisons of household structure over time are significant in another respect. They offer little support for the proposition that household structure was changing, at least within the urban areas, as a result of increasing industrialization. This finding, again, seems to run counter to the widely held view that the American family evolved from an extended family to a nuclear family in response to changing industrial conditions. Of course, the findings here are limited, not only in time, but, more significantly, to an urban population. Quite possibly the impact of industrialization on family structure was accomplished by migration from rural America to the rapidly growing cities.

Our data do not permit a direct test of the effects of industrialization on the family. In subsequent analyses, however, we shall be able to examine the link between the occupational and family structure within the city of Philadelphia during the middle and latter part of the

Table 2 Household Structure by Ethnicity, 1850 and 1880

	INFERRED RELATIONSHIPS, 1850[a]			
	BLACK	IRISH	GERMAN	NWA
Nuclear	60.6%	60.6%	61.4%	45.6%
Extended	6.6	4.4	3.5	4.7
Expanded	32.8	35.0	35.0	49.7
	N=1,739	*N*=1,844	*N*=1,564	*N*=1,648
	INFERRED RELATIONSHIPS, 1880			
	BLACK	IRISH	GERMAN	NWA
Nuclear	57.6%	67.1%	65.5%	52.4%
Extended	4.9	5.6	4.3	5.3
Expanded	37.6	27.2	30.2	42.3
	N=3,206	*N*=1,637	*N*=1,726	*N*=1,680

a The Federal population manuscript schedules of the United States Census became for the first time in 1850 an enumeration of every inhabitant of the nation, and recorded important information describing each individual within each household unit; but it was not until 1880 that the relationship of each member of the household to the household head was recorded. Researchers using the schedules for 1850, 1860, and 1870, therefore, must *infer* these relationships from the information which was included, such as surname, age, sex, position of listing in the household, etc. The PSHP has developed a computer program to make these inferences; see Theodore Hershberg, "A Method for the Computerized Study of Family and Household Structure Using the Manuscript Schedules of the U.S. Census of Population, 1850–1880," *The Family in Historical Perspective, An International Newsletter*, I (1973), 6–20; Buffington Clay Miller, "A Computerized Method of Determining Family Structure from Mid-Nineteenth Century Census Data," unpub. M.S. diss. (Moore School of Electrical Engineering, University of Pennsylvania, 1972). For the analysis of the 1880 data presented in this paper, however, we have used the given relationships, as recorded in the 1880 manuscript census. In the 1850 and 1880 "inferred" tables, individual relationships which cannot be determined by the computer program (such as "Servant," "Brother-in-Law") are categorized as "Others." The computer program assigns households with "Others" to the expanded category (households with relatives), thus considering all "Others" as relatives. The expanded category, therefore, is inflated by the number of households with only non-relative "Others" (boarders and servants). This can be seen by comparing Table 2 for 1880 based on "inferred" relationships with Table 1 based on "given" relationships.

nineteenth century. Although not definitive, this forthcoming analysis should provide some clue to the effect of industrialization on the American family in urban areas of the country.

ETHNICITY AND FAMILY COMPOSITION Earlier we drew a distinction between household structure and family composition (referring to the membership of the family unit). Most contemporary research on the black family has been concerned, not with the issue of household structure, but with that of family membership. In particular, researchers have been preoccupied with the question of who heads the family unit. As we noted earlier, there is reason to wonder whether this question deserves the prominence that it has received. Reserving our judgment on this issue, we shall in this section examine whether the family composition of blacks differs significantly from other ethnic groups before the turn of the century.

Households were divided into three categories: couple-headed households in which a male was head and in which his wife was listed as present in the home; male-headed households in which the wife was not listed as present in the home; female-headed households. This basic division does not take into account whether the households were nuclear or some complex unit. Furthermore, we again considered only those households in which children were present.[9]

Using this simple classification scheme, there is a noticeable relationship between family composition and ethnicity in the 1850 and 1880 census data (Table 3). German Americans are most likely to be living in couple-headed households, followed by native whites, closely in 1880 but less so in 1850. Irish households were somewhat less likely to be couple-headed and blacks had the lowest proportion of families in which both parents were present. Thus, the contemporary pattern of a high prevalence of matrifocal households among blacks is visible before the turn of the century and before the arrival in the city of numbers of freedmen.

It is one thing to demonstrate the existence of this pattern and quite another to interpret its significance. In the first place, the magnitude of

9 In two recent studies on black family structure (Gutman, "Persistent Myths"; Pleck, "Two-Parent Household"), the proportion of female-headed households is misrepresented because the calculations include couple-headed households *without* children. We disagree with this procedure for three reasons. First, to include childless couples but not households with a single member biases the proportion of female heads substantially downward. Second, the assumption that underlies the association of the female-headed household with a set of negative social consequences is that the absence of a father adversely affects the socialization of the young. To include childless families, therefore, introduces an irrelevant component. Third, this irrelevant component has a downward bias because childless families tend to be younger and less likely to have experienced family dissolution. A further refinement might have been to remove from consideration those families where the youngest child in the household was presumably beyond the age of childhood socialization. Among the 1880 blacks, applying age 20 as the cutoff point would have removed almost 15 percent of the families from consideration. Such a procedure, however, would have affected almost exclusively the oldest categories of families, and would leave untouched the distinctions and trends treated in this paper.

Table 3 Family Composition by Ethnicity, 1850 and 1880

	INFERRED HEADSHIP, 1850[a]			
	BLACK	IRISH	GERMAN	NWA
Female Head	22.5%	13.4%	3.3%	13.3%
Male Head	6.0	7.2	3.2	4.0
Couple Head	71.5	79.4	93.5	82.6
	$N=1,739$	$N=1,844$	$N=1,564$	$N=1,648$
	GIVEN HEADSHIP, 1880			
	BLACK	IRISH	GERMAN	NWA
Female Head	25.3%	12.7%	8.3%	13.6%
Male Head	5.9	7.5	5.3	6.2
Couple Head	68.8	79.8	86.5	80.2
	$N=2,949$	$N=1,637$	$N=1,766$	$N=1,730$

a Although inferring household *structure* by computer is difficult, inferring household *headship* is simple and certain. Results derived by such an inference are almost exactly those found from "given" relationships. Were we to use "inferred" figures for headship in 1880, the percentage of female heads would be 24.5, 12.6, 8.5, and 11.5 for the blacks, Irish, Germans, and native whites, respectively.

the difference can be seen in two quite separate lights. We could say that blacks are more than twice as likely as foreign and native-born white Americans to live in households headed by a female. Such a statement emphasizes the differential. Alternatively, we could point out that the great majority of all ethnic groups live in couple-headed households. Even among blacks, only one-fourth of the households were headed by a female. Moreover, among the various ethnic groups there is a difference of only 17 percentage points between the group with the lowest proportion of female-headed households—the German Americans—and that with the highest, black Americans. Obviously, this characterization tends to minimize the differences by underscoring the similarities. The only reasonable way of resolving this issue of interpretation is to delve further into the source of these differences. To us, their significance is to be found more in how they came about than in their magnitude.

Contemporary research on female-headed families has demonstrated the existence of a strong link between economic status and family composition. Male absence is far more prevalent in the lower class than in the middle class. Accordingly, differences in female-headedness between blacks and whites diminish sharply under conditions of economic parity. This finding has caused many to question the position that variations in family composition can be traced to divergent subcultural standards. In many respects the argument that the roots of the black matrifocal family are to be found in slavery represents an extension of the subcultural argument, and the same criticisms that pertain to the subcultural explanation can be applied historically.

New historical studies provide compelling reason to question the destructive impact which slavery allegedly had on the black family. One of the major conclusions reached by econometric historians Fogel and Engerman is that the slave family was considerably stronger than has been believed. Further evidence which challenges the standing interpretation comes from research conducted by Gutman, whose data are consistent with conclusions reached by Fogel and Engerman. In groundbreaking essays, Gutman examined "the family patterns of those Negroes closest in time to actual chattel slavery," and did not find "instability," "chaos," or "disorder." Instead, in fourteen varied Southern cities and counties between 1865 and 1880, Gutman found viable two-parent households ranging from 70 to 90 percent. The empirical picture presented here is staggering. Gutman's data make clear that the vast majority of black families were headed by both parents, and they convincingly contradict the view that slavery "destroyed" the black family.[10]

The data for Philadelphia, moreover, are consistent with the findings of Gutman, and Fogel and Engerman. We know from unique information on status-at-birth reported in a Quaker census of Philadelphia blacks in 1847 that only 10 percent of all of the city blacks had been born slaves. More importantly, however, these ex-slaves were *more* likely than than the freeborn to have two-parent households. However unrepresentative of all slaves the ex-slaves in Philadelphia's population may have been, direct contact with slavery cannot explain the degree of matrifocality which existed at mid-century.[11] In 1880, one out of every two Philadelphia blacks had been born in the South. Although it is impossible to know with absolute certainty who among these immigrants had been freeborn or slaveborn, place of birth constitutes a plausible proxy for ex-slave status, especially when considered in conjunction with illiteracy.[12]

10 Robert William Fogel and Stanley L. Engerman, *Time on the Cross: The Economics of American Negro Slavery* (Boston, 1974), I, 5, 126–144; Gutman, "Persistent Myths."

11 Hershberg, "Free Blacks," 192–204.

12 See Pleck, "Two-Parent Household," 18–19; note 3, above. Although there are problems in this approach, combining the variables of place of birth and illiteracy brings us closer to identifying accurately those blacks most likely to have been slave-born. There were slightly more female illiterates among both northern-born and southern-born black Philadelphians, but this difference was not at all of a magnitude to suggest that the relationships shown in Table 4 are spurious.

Therefore, if the slavery argument is valid, this segment of the population should account for a disproportionate share of the female-headed households. Yet this, in fact, was *not* the case: southern-born illiterate blacks were *less* likely than their northern-born counterparts to have female-headed families (Table 4).

Table 4 Black Family Composition by Literacy and Place of Birth, 1880[a]

	LITERATE			ILLITERATE		
		OTHER			OTHER	
	PA.	NORTH	SOUTH	PA.	NORTH	SOUTH
Female Head	25.8%	23.4%	18.3%	46.9%	47.9%	31.9%
Male Head	6.6	4.4	5.3	3.5	4.2	6.6
Couple Head	67.5	72.2	76.4	49.7	47.9	61.5
	$N=798$	$N=158$	$N=1{,}103$	$N=143$	$N=48$	$N=636$

a Literacy and place of birth refer to the household head.

FAMILY COMPOSITION AND ECONOMIC CONDITION In place of the subcultural "legacy of slavery" explanation for disorganization in the black family, we wish to argue for the primacy of urban economic and demographic factors. The vast majority of Philadelphia's blacks faced a life of abject poverty. Job discrimination was ubiquitous in the economy. Of every ten black males in the labor force, eight worked at unskilled jobs; the comparable figure for the Irish was five, and for the Germans and native whites fewer than two (see Table 5). When converted to wages and yearly income, these figures bear stark testimony to the difficulty black men faced in attempting to raise and provide for their families. Although there is some disagreement over the amount of a subsistence income for families in 1880, it is quite clear that unskilled laborers were faced with a serious shortfall.[13] In such grim economic

13 Eudice Glassberg calculates the subsistence income for a family of five in "Philadelphia's Poverty Line, 1860 and 1880: A Comparison of Earnings and Minimum Standard of Living," unpub. paper, PSHP (Oct. 1973). Unskilled workers rarely made as much as $400 a year. Using Glassberg's figures, the shortfall is about 40 percent. Most families were able to compensate in a variety of ways, which included working wives and children, the pooling of income in expanded and extended families, the taking in of boarders, etc.

Table 5 Occupational Structure by Ethnicity, 1880

	(FOR MALES 18 YEARS AND OLDER)			
	BLACK	IRISH	GERMAN	NWA
Professional High White Collar	1.1%	1.6%	1.6%	5.1%
Proprietary[a] Low White Collar	4.4	13.4	17.5	27.8
Skilled	13.7	31.5	59.7	45.3
Unskilled	79.2	50.1	15.3	17.2
	N=8,700	*N*=36,333	*N*=25,172	*N*=90,756

a Percentages do not add up to 100; the missing percentages—1.6, 3.5, 5.9, and 4.6—for the four groups, respectively, represent a category of ambiguous occupational designation such as "liquor store." Based on other characteristics of this category, we suspect that such individuals were in fact proprietors and should be added to the "proprietary" category.

circumstances, the conditions for the maintenance of stable family life were at best precarious.

These economic circumstances bear a direct and powerful relationship to the incidence of female-headed families. This can be seen in Table 6A, which relates wealth (real and personal property holdings) to family composition. Wealth data are not reported in the manuscript schedules for 1880, but they are for 1870. In that year, as in 1880, a greater percentage of black families with children were headed by females (27.1) than for the Irish (16.9), Germans (5.9), and native whites (14.3). Female-headedness varies inversely with wealth. They were found far less often among families with property valued at more than $500 than among propertyless families: half as often for the blacks and Irish; two-thirds as often for the native whites; and one-third as often for the Germans. Table 6B focuses on a special group of household heads, those 30–39 years of age. By examining this group, we eliminate variations which arise from different age structures among the four ethnic groups—an important control because age structure is strongly related both to mortality and to the acquisition of wealth. The same inverse relationship between female-headedness and wealth is found in the 30–39 age group, but the strength of the relationship is far more pronounced.

Table 7 presents these same data in a different form, as the percent differences in female-headedness between blacks and each of the three white groups. Using different wealth categories Table 7B shows that the original variation observed between all black and Irish families with

Table 6 Proportion of Household Heads Female, by Ethnicity and Wealth, 1870[a]

WEALTH $	BLACK		IRISH		GERMAN		NWA	
A. ALL HOUSEHOLDS WITH CHILDREN								
0	31.2	(1,414)	21.3	(889)	9.6	(616)	18.8	(674)
100–199	20.2	(129)	15.9	(113)	8.3	(96)	16.7	(96)
200–299	18.7	(91)	12.9	(101)	4.5	(132)	8.3	(157)
300–499	14.6	(48)	10.7	(75)	3.2	(156)	10.6	(179)
500–999	8.3	(72)	9.3	(75)	3.7	(189)	10.5	(143)
1,000 +	17.0	(206)	10.6	(378)	3.5	(633)	12.8	(695)
All	27.1	(1,962)	16.9	(1,636)	5.9	(1,825)	14.3	(1,946)
B. HOUSEHOLDS WITH CHILDREN HEADED BY 30–39 YEAR OLDS								
0	25.8	(395)	18.1	(282)	6.1	(212)	14.2	(211)
100–199	11.1	(36)	5.7	(35)	5.4	(37)	9.1	(33)
200–299	8.0	(25)	7.9	(38)	0	(54)	6.9	(58)
300–499	7.1	(14)	4.8	(21)	0	(43)	3.4	(58)
500–999	15.0	(20)	0	(22)	1.5	(65)	8.1	(62)
1,000 +	6.3	(32)	2.3	(86)	3.5	(172)	10.1	(178)
All	21.8	(522)	12.5	(488)	3.8	(583)	10.3	(600)

a Wealth consists of all real and personal property holding reported in the census manuscripts. Figures shown are percentages of all households in a particular ethnic wealth category headed by women; the figures in parentheses are the *N*s for these classes.

children—9.3 percent—is reduced: to 4.5 percent among holders of "any wealth" and yet further to 4.0 percent among holders of "wealth greater than $1,000." The same is true for the variation observed between blacks and Germans: the 18 percent separating them is reduced to 7.0 among holders of "any" wealth and 2.8 percent among holders of "wealth greater than $1,000." Most striking, however, is the reduction of the variation between blacks and native whites. The observed variation for all families is reduced to 1.2 percent among holders of "any" wealth, and for those owning more than $1,000 the relationship is reversed: native whites in this category were more likely than blacks to have female-headed families. Among the propertied across the entire ethnic spectrum, then, most of the variation in female-headedness is eliminated.

Although the economic data presented in Tables 6 and 7 describe the dramatic reduction of observed variation in female-headedness among holders of property, among the propertyless little or none of the variation is eliminated. There remains, in other words, a variation of 11.5 percent between blacks and native whites, and 9.3 and 18.0 percent

Table 7 Percentage Difference in Female-Headedness by Property Holdings between Blacks and the White Ethnic Groups, 1870

	ALL HOUSEHOLDS	WITHOUT ANY WEALTH	WITH ANY WEALTH	WITH WEALTH GREATER THAN $1,000
A. ALL HOUSEHOLDS WITH CHILDREN				
Black-Irish	10.2	9.9	4.8	6.4
Black-German	21.2	21.6	12.5	13.5
Black-Native White	12.8	12.4	4.7	4.2
B. HOUSEHOLDS WITH CHILDREN HEADED BY 30–39 YEAR OLDS				
Black-Irish	9.3	7.7	4.5	4.0
Black-German	18.0	19.7	7.0	2.8
Black-Native White	11.5	11.6	1.2	−3.8

respectively, between blacks and the Irish and Germans. There are two reasons for this residual variation. The substantial portion is accounted for by differential mortality which we discuss in detail below. The remainder is at least in part an artifact of the way property holding was reported in the Federal population manuscript schedules. Census marshals were instructed not to record property holding in amounts less than $100. When we observe the category "without property," we are in fact looking at *two* groups: those with some property worth less than $100 and those without any property at all. This distinction is an important one to bear in mind. Table 8 displays data describing all black families with children in Philadelphia, collected in 1838 by the Pennsylvania Abolition Society and in 1847 by the Society of Friends.[14] Unlike the Federal population manuscript schedules, these forms report property holding down to amounts of $5, and permit the study of variation in female-headedness along a rank order of wealth which includes 95 percent of all black families.

As with the 1870 Federal census, female-headedness and property holding are negatively related (see Table 8). Significantly, this negative relationship is visible for sums of less than $100, so that in 1838, for example, black families with $50–$99 of property were only about three-

14 See Hershberg, "Free Blacks," 184–185; *idem*, "Free-Born and Slave-Born Blacks in Antebellum Philadelphia," in Eugene D. Genovese and Stanley L. Engerman (eds). *Race and Slavery in the Western Hemisphere: Quantitative Studies* (Princeton, 1975), 395–426.

Table 8 Proportion of Black Household Heads Female by Wealth, 1838 and 1847

WEALTH FAMILIES WITH	1838 ALL CHILDREN	1847 CHILDREN 0–4	1847 CHILDREN 5–14
0–50	31.4 (570)	27.8 (298)	37.9 (610)
50–99	24.2 (241)	12.0 (150)	22.3 (350)
100–499	13.3 (420)	6.1 (181)	17.3 (567)
500 . .	8.5 (216)	16.3 (49)	10.6 (254)

SOURCES: 1838: Manuscript Census, Pennsylvania Abolition Society.
1847: Manuscript Census, Society of Friends.

fourths as likely to be female-headed as families with less than $50. If, as we have good reason to suppose in light of the occupational distributions of the several groups, whites in the 1870 "less than $100" category clustered at its higher reaches, while blacks were far more prevalent at the bottom, then an unknown but sizable proportion of the black-white variation among the 1870 "propertyless" can be understood.

FAMILY COMPOSITION AND MORTALITY Differential wealth thus accounts for the observed disparity between Philadelphia's blacks and whites in family composition. Contemporary studies of family life among the poor tend to stress illegitimacy, desertion, and divorce in understanding female headship, but in the nineteenth century a different consideration was the major link between female headship and the poverty cycle: mortality.[15] Today, family instability can be traced to the limited economic prospects that the poor recognize for themselves; in the last century sickness and death played the more important part.[16] Those most ravaged were the urban poor blacks, irregularly employed, segregated, and neglected in matters of public health.

15 For evidence of the extraordinary mortality differentials by race (esp. in infant mortality), see the 1879 life tables for Baltimore and Washington (which had more blacks than Philadelphia, but similar mortality experiences) in U.S. Census Office, *Census of 1880*, XII: *Mortality and Vital Statistics* (Washington, 1883), pt. 2, 773–777. See also W. E. B. DuBois' excellent discussion of health and mortality differentials in Philadelphia, in which he lays the blame immediately on the ignorance of hygiene among the victims and on the uneven distribution of public-health effort (*The Philadelphia Negro: A Social Study* [New York, 1967], ch. 10).

16 See Frank F. Furstenberg, "Work Experience and Family Life," in James O'Toole (ed.), *Work and the Quality of Life* (Cambridge, Mass., 1974), 341–360; Reynolds Farley, *Growth of the Black Population* (Chicago, 1973).

Table 9 Reported Marital Status of Female Household Heads, Households with Children, by Ethnicity, 1880

	BLACK	IRISH	GERMAN	NWA
Widowed	74.3%	79.5%	77.8%	75.0%
Single	5.0	1.4	3.3	2.5
Divorced	1.1	0.9	0.7	1.0
Married	19.7	18.3	18.3	21.5
	N=747	*N*=219	*N*=153	*N*=200

Table 9 seeks to elucidate the contribution of widowhood to female-headedness among black families in Philadelphia in 1880 by examining the reported marital status of each female-headed household (for families with children). Though, as we have seen, females constituted a larger minority of all household heads among blacks than in other ethnic groups, Table 9 shows that for blacks as for the others, widowhood overwhelmingly predominates among female household heads. In each ethnic group, most of the remaining female heads are married women whose spouses are absent—presumably deserted in some cases, with husbands temporarily away at work in others. When we combine the separated, divorced, and single mothers, they constitute only one-fourth of all female heads. It is to widowhood, therefore, that we must attribute the excess of female-headedness among black families with children. This stands in stark contrast with today, when among blacks widowhood is overshadowed by separation and single parenthood as a source of family breakup.

Mortality, of course, increases sharply with age. Had the black population been notably older than other groups, their age distribution might account for the prevalence of widowhood. But this is not the case. Table 10 presents the composition of families by age, measuring age according to the female's age when she is present, and according to the male's age when she is not.[17] At every age, the composition of black families is different, with an increasing excess of widows. So fierce was the mortality among Philadelphia's blacks that at least a quarter of the married Negro women in families with children were widowed by their 40s.[18]

17 The same finding appears when, to avoid the clumsiness of measuring "age" of the family sometimes by the woman, sometimes by the man, we measure it by the age of the oldest child, as a proxy of how long the marriage has been established.

18 When all households, and not just those with children, are examined, quite the same white/black pattern of differences obtains.

Table 10, however, goes beyond the obvious and the awful. We note, for instance, that despite the extraordinarily high incidence of widowhood among blacks, *widowerhood* is rarer among them than in the other groups. This requires explanation. The figures presented are on reported marital status at a given moment in time. Thus, the number of widows counted would (under ideal census conditions) be equal to the

Table 10 Sex and Marital Status of Heads of Households (with Children) by Age of Head and Ethnicity, 1880[a]

	AGE OF HEAD				
HEADED BY:	LESS THAN 30	30–39	40–49	50–59	60+
Couples					
Black	84.5	77.2	62.0	44.8	31.0
Irish	90.7	93.5	83.5	75.5	39.5
German	93.4	90.4	82.9	71.2	45.0
NWA	93.8	92.5	84.3	73.5	44.2
Widows					
Black	4.2	11.4	20.8	29.1	35.5
Irish	1.1	3.2	8.6	10.3	16.8
German	2.0	5.4	9.9	11.4	19.3
NWA	0.6	4.4	8.8	10.7	25.1
Other Females					
Black	6.7	5.3	6.1	5.7	4.7
Irish	2.3	1.0	1.4	1.8	0.8
German	1.6	1.2	2.7	3.2	4.2
NWA	0.9	1.4	1.8	2.7	2.5
Widowers					
Black	0.1	0.8	2.7	4.6	12.5
Irish	0.4	1.3	3.0	7.3	26.6
German	0.4	1.3	1.3	7.1	15.8
NWA	0	1.4	2.8	5.3	15.0
Other Males					
Black	3.9	3.6	4.2	5.0	6.0
Irish	5.2	1.7	1.9	5.0	4.8
German	2.7	1.9	2.1	3.2	5.0
NWA	4.8	1.2	1.3	5.3	6.7
Ns					
Black	899	887	526	281	168
Irish	265	418	369	220	124
German	256	470	374	253	120
NWA	336	517	394	226	120

a Female's age for couples, widows, and other female heads; male's age for widowers and other male heads. Figures shown are percentages.

number of persons ever widowed, less the number who had remarried; likewise for widowers. Sex differentials in black mortality cannot account for so large a difference. One implication of these statistics is that black men could remarry with relative ease, but black women could not. Another is that a larger proportion of black men than black women who were left with children by the deaths of their spouses found it impossible or inadvisable to raise the children while unmarried, and left them with relatives or others.

Data on marital status by age strongly bear this out, and point as well to a sex ratio considerably favoring the marriage and remarriage chances of males. These imbalances can be seen in Table 11. Taking all

Table 11 Marital Status by Age and Sex, Blacks, 1880

	MARRIED		ALL UNMARRIED		WIDOWED ONLY	
	MALES	FEMALES	MALES	FEMALES	MALES	FEMALES
15–19	13	143	925	1,434	1	9
20–24	426	986	1,147	1,574	8	79
25–29	929	1,206	806	947	44	158
30–34	939	937	464	577	41	207
35–39	970	839	333	549	52	288
40–44	641	513	211	486	62	293
45–49	425	325	124	397	47	285
50–54	376	257	114	453	48	338
55–59	196	144	78	251	45	207
60–64	184	74	70	275	43	229
65–69	101	45	36	174	27	147
70+	114	43	91	397	70	340
TOTAL	5,314	5,512	4,399	7,514	488	2,580

blacks in Philadelphia as our base, and not just those living in families with children (for the former constitute the marriage pool), we find that by ages 35–39, more than one-fifth of all black women were living as widows. Overall in this age group, four in ten black women were, for one reason or another, not currently married; this is so for only a quarter of the men.[19] Black women generally married men older than themselves by an average of about three years; therefore, we should treat the next older age category as the most likely remarriage pool for widowed black women. By this reasoning, 35–39 year-old widows

19 This argument rests on the fact that the effective marriage pool for blacks was other blacks. See Theodore Hershberg, "Mulattoes and Blacks: Intra-Group Color Differences and Social Stratification in Nineteenth-Century Philadelphia," *Journal of American History* (forthcoming, 1976).

looked to remarry 40–44 year-old men. This group, however, was smaller to begin with because of differential inmigration by sex. Because they were older, because males generally suffer higher mortality, and because of the physically taxing nature of "nigger work," the pool experienced still further attrition. Very nearly half of Philadelphia's large number of widows, then, can be "explained" by their inability to find suitably aged mates.

Aggravating the situation even more is the fact that black males may have had more reason to leave the city than females when their spouses died, or to have placed their children with friends or relatives, rather than raise them alone on a scant and uncertain income. Women more easily than men could find jobs and at the same time support their children. (It is also possible that Philadelphia attracted an inmigration of widowed women. A detailed analysis of the widowed black population of Philadelphia, however, indicates that unlike native whites, black inmigrants who were widowed were, if anything, *less* likely at given ages than those born in Pennsylvania to be household heads, and among those who were household heads, less likely to have children.) Many of the female heads of families were employed as seamstresses and domestics, or were able to take in boarders, thus making it possible for them not to remarry. Unless female kin were available to serve as parent surrogates, men undoubtedly found it more difficult to remain unmarried, especially with young children. Finally, men had a further advantage in the remarriage market because they could more actively initiate a marriage contract. Women without means commanded little bargaining power and therefore were in an especially weak position to attract a mate.

We have chosen to accept as *prima facie* evidence the marital status recorded by census marshals a hundred years ago. We have not done so naively. We recognize the likelihood that at least some black female respondents may have told the census marshals what they thought they wanted to hear, explaining by "widowhood" the absence of a male household head, whatever the real reason.[20] But we can validate the

20 We would expect that among female heads with children, the proportion of widows would increase with the age of the youngest child of the female head, since (assuming no illegitimacy) the younger the child, the fewer the elapsed years since the female head's husband surely was alive. Trends along these lines are present but quite weak and irregular; they are, however, virtually identical for each of the four ethnic groups. If we have not in this fashion gained greater confidence in the literal meaning of census "widowhood," we have discovered that its meaning seems to have been similar across ethnic lines.

plausibility of the claims of widowhood by reference to death statistics contained in other documents and to known patterns of mortality by age. Our procedure has been to construct estimates of joint survival probabilities for a hypothetical population of black couples, which will allow us to suggest, at appropriate levels of mortality, the likely, or "expected" proportion of widows among the once-married female population, assuming for the moment that remarriage is negligible.[21] Table 12 compares the "expected" proportions of widows at this level of mortality with that measured for the whole black female population of Philadelphia in 1880; we have also prepared a slightly more severe mortality schedule displayed in the same Table.

The findings are unequivocal. By far the greatest part of reported "widowhood" can readily be explained by the level of mortality among black Philadelphians. To be sure, there was some remarriage of widows, which would suggest a somewhat greater discrepancy between stated "widows" and the proportion expected by mortality alone. Table 12 shows a close fit at all ages between expected and observed widowhood, suggesting that a fraction of declared widows were not so, but rather were unmarried or deserted women hiding their actual condition from the census taker.

21 Mortality for "colored" persons (including negligible numbers of Chinese, Japanese, and Indians) for Philadelphia in 1890 and for the six years preceding 1890 are derived from registration materials tabulated in U.S. Census Office, *Eleventh Census, 1890* (Washington, 1895), IV: *Mortality*, 662, 1046–1047. John S. Billings, who supervised the 1890 vital statistics volumes, noted that, as in the other 27 cities to which he devoted a volume, registration of deaths was "based upon certificates of deaths by physicians, [collected] under a compulsory registration law." The crude colored death rate in Philadelphia, 30.1, can be compared with the rate there for whites, 23.0, and with colored death rates of 32.9 in Baltimore, 34.0 in Washington, 34.6 in New York, and 30.9 for all 28 cities studied (U.S. Census Office, *Report on Vital and Social Statistics of the United States at the Eleventh Census: 1890, Part II—Vital Statistics. Cities of 100,000 Population and Upward* [Washington, 1892], 1–5). The age-specific figures, distributing the unknown ages, and taking the average one-year level from the figures for the six-year period, were then compared with linearly interpolated estimates for 1887 of the Philadelphia black population by age and sex, based on PSHP grid-square tallies for 1880 and U.S. Census Office, *Population, 1890*, II, 127. The age-specific mortality rates were matched with model life tables in Ansley J. Coale and Paul Demeny, *Regional Model Life Tables and Stable Populations* (Princeton, 1966), and a good match was found on ages 20–50 at South Level 3, a severe mortality regime where the high rate of infant and child mortality proved closer to the observed Philadelphia black mortality than did the West series tables, more often applied to American populations. Good matches were also found between South Level 3 and the black life tables centering on 1879 for Baltimore and Washington, cited above, note 15. South Level 3 implies an expectation of life at birth of 25 years; Level 2 implies 22.5 years.

Table 12 "Expected" Proportion of Widows Among Ever-Married Black Women, 1887, at Two Levels of Mortality, Compared with Proportion Recorded in the 1880 Census, by Age[a]

AGE	"EXPECTED" AT SOUTH LEVEL 3 MORTALITY	"EXPECTED" AT SOUTH LEVEL 2 MORTALITY	"MEASURED," 1880 CENSUS
25–29	7.2	14.8	11.5
30–34	14.1	21.6	18.1
35–39	21.3	28.7	25.4
40–44	29.1	36.5	36.1
45–49	37.5	45.6	46.6
50–54	47.0	53.4	56.5
55–59	57.8	63.5	59.0
60–64	69.9	74.6	75.3
65–69	81.8	84.3	76.2

a Figures shown are percentages.

VARIANT PATTERNS IN FAMILY COMPOSITION In bringing out the excess of widowed female heads among blacks, the data presented in Table 10 also reveal a persistent difference in headship by "other females," most of whom are married without spouse (Table 9). The proportion of "other female" headship for blacks is about 5 or 6 percent, unvarying with age. We have here what might be considered a variant pattern.

In our attempt to probe the source of this variant pattern, we examined marital status by age of non-widowed female heads. Divorcées at every age represent an insignificant proportion of this group. Unmarried mothers, although constituting almost a quarter of all female heads less than 30, virtually disappear at older ages. Separated women are at every age the largest proportion of non-widowed female heads, but their numbers, too, decline with age. This decline cannot be explained by mortality alone. These patterns are identical across ethnic groups.

Had there been cultural support within the black community for female-headed families (whatever the reason), we should have found a growing number of families of this type with advancing age. Instead, they decline, doing so in the face of a remarriage market that offered them extremely limited prospects. In summary, the data provide no evidence for believing that Philadelphia's blacks valued anything distinct from what poverty and death often denied them: to raise their children in stable and continuous families.

Much of the speculation about the origins of the matrifocal black family has been uninformed by systematic historical data. In recent years, historians have begun to correct this situation. It is becoming increasingly clear with each new study that misconceptions about the past have resulted in certain erroneous interpretations of the present. The PSHP data indicate that the household structure in 1850, 1870, and 1880 was highly similar among each of the ethnic groups. Black families were just as likely to be organized in nuclear households, and, hence, were not more or less able to adapt to conditions created by industrialization than other ethnic groups. A somewhat higher proportion of black families were headed by a female than was true for other ethnic groups. However, we argue that a cultural explanation cannot account for this disparity.

In the first place, the great majority of black families were couple-headed. Second, ex-slaves were more likely to reside in couple-headed households. Third, when property holding among the different ethnic grouping was held constant, variations in family composition largely disappeared. Finally, we were able to show that economic status had a powerful effect on the structure of the black family because blacks suffered extremely high mortality and females with children faced difficulties in remarrying. To the extent that the female-headed family appeared during this period, it emerged, not as a legacy of slavery, but as a result of the destructive conditions of northern urban life.[22]

With a few important exceptions, students of black history have not adequately appreciated the impact of the urban experience. In part, this is because the institution of slavery has so dominated the history of Afro-Americans. Ever since the 1920s when justification for the low status of black Americans shifted from a genetic to an environmental interpretation, scholars have for the most part accepted without question

22 This interpretation finds support in the statistics offered by Gutman, "Persistent Myths," above. Of all of the urban and rural communities that he studied, those with the highest percentages of female-headed households were cities: Natchez (30%), Beaufort (30%), Richmond (27%), and Mobile (26%), although the percentages for rural areas were all below 19%. These percentages, moreover, if re-calculated after childless households are removed (see note 9 above), may increase as much as 8 percentage points. The cities varied widely in their size, type of economy, and rate of growth, to be sure; nonetheless, some differential process must have been operating to generate these statistics.

the slavery hypothesis. After all, it followed logically that any institution as morally reprehensible as slavery also had to be destructive.

We do not wish to imply that the institution of slavery was *not* brutalizing and dehumanizing. Yet, one must not convert a sense of moral outrage into a monolithic interpretation of the black experience. Once we recognize that the matrifocal black family is a product of economic discrimination, poverty, and disease we cease to blame the distant past for problems which have their origins in more recent times. It was, and still is, much easier to lament the sins of one's forefathers than to confront the injustices of more contemporary socioeconomic systems.

FEMINIST IMPLICATIONS OF MORMON POLYGYNY

JOAN IVERSEN

One of the interesting anomalies of nineteenth-century women's history is the fact that one of its most vocal feminist groups comprised the Mormon women of Utah defending their territorial right to vote and their religious practice of polygyny, called "plural," or "patriarchal" marriage.[1] Utah was the second territory in the United States to grant female suffrage. Although there was no feminist agitation leading to the granting of the franchise, and there is question as to the actual motives of the Mormon leadership in granting suffrage, Utah women were the first to vote in the country. Ironically, the opponents of the Latter-day Saints had been the first to propose enfranchising Mormon women, arguing that the women would then cast off the marriage system which had scandalized "Gentile," that is, non-Mormon, America since its acknowledgment in 1852. From the Mormon point of view the suggestion was a direct challenge, and by giving their women the vote, Mormon men reasoned they could both increase Mormon influence and "vindicate the polygamic system." Thus, Marilyn Warenski concluded that "suffrage came to Utah more because of polygamy than in spite of it."[2]

Within two years of obtaining the franchise, Mormon women began publication of a staunchly feminist periodical entitled the *Woman's Exponent.* Woman managed, supported, and produced, the *Woman's Exponent* was the second women's periodical in the trans-Mississippi West. Its masthead declared for "The Rights of Women of Zion, and the Rights of Women of All Nations," and its pages discussed women's rights issues throughout the nation while defending Mormon women from increasing numbers of detractors.

The Mormon woman was viewed by critics as the degraded, depraved, and debased victim of the Mormon priesthood, her situation equated with that of women in the Turkish harem and

Feminist Studies 10, no. 3 (Fall 1984).

under slavery.[3] An antipolygamy crusade rose to a peak in the 1880s, culminating in federal legislation which removed the vote from Utah women and criminalized polygamy (Edmunds-Tucker Act, 1887). In the course of the struggle, leading Utah women became prominent suffragists, joining the National Woman Suffrage Association (NWSA) in 1879 and working through the Utah Woman Suffrage Assocation for the restoration of the vote, which was granted with Utah's statehood in 1895.

Unquestionably, Mormon women presented a dilemma for the feminist of the time. As early as 1856 the Republican national party had condemned Mormon polygamy as one of the "twin relics of barbarism" along with slavery. Prominent women like Harriet Beecher Stowe and Frances Willard had joined the antipolygamy ranks as part of the entire thrust of the "purity crusade" following the Civil War. Probably because of this, one Mormon historian inaccurately wrote that eastern feminists had "joined forces" to repeal woman suffrage in Utah. Although the full story of the relationship of the Mormon women with eastern feminists has never been told, the record shows that the leaders of the NWSA had testified on behalf of Mormon women in the legislature in 1876 and 1879 and had also accompanied the Mormon women to visit the White House.[4] These actions evoked criticism of NWSA leaders but they persisted in their support, demonstrating their sensitivity to the plight of the Mormon plural wives and children. Matilda Joslyn Gage and Sara Spencer, in pleading the cause of the Mormon women at the White House, indicated their opposition to a law which "would make 50 thousand women outcasts and their children illegitimate."[5] When the Edmunds-Tucker Act eventually disfranchised the Utah women and punished them for polygamy, Lucy Stone also condemned the action. Although there is no evidence that these leaders endorsed plural marriage, their broader perspective kept them from joining the ranks of those attacking Mormon women. In fact, one Mormon of the period credited them with preventing the disfranchisement of Utah's women earlier.[6]

Mormon suffragists saw their feminism and plural marriage as firmly linked. Although the antipolygamy crusade argued against the Mormon marriage system in the name of women's rights, the Latter-day Saints employed the rhetoric of women's rights to defend plural marriage. The paradox was noted at the time. "But even more staggering is the fact that Mormon women base their indignation against their persecuting saviours in women's rights, the very ground upon which their saviours have based their crusade."[7]

The Utah women's defense of polygamy, rooted both in Mormon theology and the ideals of the larger society's view of Victorian womanhood, was mounted in the face of a strident antipolygamy attack. Consequently, their feminist claims are, at first glance, characterized by considerable defensiveness and are barely credible. Credibility is further strained when one examines the theological basis for polygyny. At the root of plural marriage was a patriarchal concept of society and of afterlife in which women and children were the appendages of the Mormon males who all held priesthood. Wives gained their status in the afterlife through their husbands. This patriarchal theology and the antifeminist record of the contemporary Mormon hierarchy predisposes a modern observer to dismiss the nineteenth-century Mormon suffragist as simply the pawn of a monolithic culture and history. However, the relationship of polygyny, patriarchy, and feminism are more complex.

This article explores the relationship between the Mormon marriage system and Mormon feminism through an examination of the arguments offered by Utah's spokeswomen in the *Woman's Exponent,* through some of the observations made by Utah's plural wives, and through the writings of the antipolygamy critics, all scrutinized from the perspective of modern feminism. Re-examining this literature from a contemporary vantage point suggests surprising implications—that plural marriage, a practice based upon patriarchal power and privilege, resulted in an assault upon the ideology of romantic love which produced unplanned outcomes.

Historians of Mormon society have richly documented the complexities of Mormon women's lives.[8] However, the recent feminist movement, in its assault on the ideology of domesticity, has left us a perspective which permits us to question the value of romantic love, monogamy, and the nuclear family and which brings a new appreciation for the strengths needed by divorced mothers.[9] Such a framework, brought to the literature left by Mormons and their Gentile critics, reveals that plural marriage, primarily through its assault on the ideology of romantic love, produced outcomes such as intense female bonding, increased female independence, and closer mother/child bonds. Although it would be questionable to call these outcomes "feminist" in twentieth-century terms, they do suggest surprising implications for a patriarchal society. At the very least, an examination of these implications increases our understanding of the nineteenth-century Mormon suffrage leadership.

The Mormons regarded plural marriage as a reform that offered all women the opportunity to become honored wives and mothers with homes of their own and social position. Utah women were self-consciously aware of themselves as part of an important Utopian reform. Susa Young Gates, for example, argued that "Mormon women are working grandly at the sex problem of the nineteenth century" and furthermore, that their marital practice would "be a grand factor in bringing to pass a millenium."[10] And yet, despite this brave declaration, the factual evidence reveals that Mormons showed a remarkable resistance to plural marriage. In the face of strong theological pressure for its adoption, at its height only a maximum of 20 percent of Mormon families were polygamous and 90 percent of the Mormons did not enter polygamy.[11] While polygamists were in the minority, however, all the central church leaders were involved, and there is strong reason to believe that the practice was an effective device for assuring loyalty.[12]

Mormon women also faced compelling reasons for defending plural marriage. Because Mormon religious beliefs held that a woman without a husband in the afterlife would have a less desirable place, marriage was therefore even more important to Latter-day Saint women than to other nineteenth-century women. Women were allowed only one husband, although a liberal divorce law in Utah may have provided an escape route for some women from unhappy marriages. Through polygamy, Mormon women argued, all women had an opportunity to have a home and family. Mormon men, it was believed, would, through the practice of plural marriage, be kept from licentiousness and adultery, and women would be better able to achieve a spacing of pregnancies. Thus, Mormons viewed plural marriage in eugenic and utopian terms. Plural marriage also had to be preserved because its removal would leave the families of these marriages in the unenviable position of illegitimacy. All these reasons led one writer to observe, "When you consider what Mormon women had at stake in the Celestial marriage plan, it is easy to understand why they rose up to defend it."[13]

In addition to the practical and theological stake that Mormon women had in polygamy, there was a resultant defensiveness in their position which came from the intensity of the attacks upon them by the antipolygamy crusade. Critics habitually wrote of the coarseness, indelicacy, and absence of virtue among Mormon women and attributed the worst of character faults to the progeny of plural homes.[14] These attacks were so unfair that the apostate, T.B.H. Stenhouse, felt called upon to defend the women of Utah from this injustice. Although both of the Stenhouses abandoned the church and the practice of plural marriage, they found it necessary to defend plural wives as cultured and refined to non-Mormons.

The stridency of the antipolygamy crusade had the further effect of creating a situation where any open rejection of polygamy was tantamount to rejecting the church itself. For this reason, undoubtedly, monogamous Mormons did not openly criticize the doctrine. This silence frustrates our inquiry into the full effects of the system on women. We can only speculate on the way in which the threat to women of the taking of another wife may have operated to the advantage of patriarchal control. Mormon women alluded to this worry. Writing to a Mormon woman friend in California, a plural wife suggests that the Californian might be hesitating to return to Utah because of fear of the "plurality of the wife System."[16]

The fact that Mormon polygyny was practiced in the face of the organized hostility of an antipolygamy crusade, during a time of very restricted views of domesticity, was significant. Although some cultures have established norms for polygynous living patterns and interactions, Mormon polygyny was practiced in its brief sixty-five-year period against the backdrop of Victorian domesticity and romanticism. Not surprisingly, Mormon women based their defense of plural marriage firmly upon the arguments of Victorian ideals of womanhood, family, and purity.

Their arguments mirrored the mainstream Victorian ideal of motherhood with its concomitant ambivalence toward sexuality. Polygamy, they argued, gave women freedom from some sexual obligations and the benefits of continence during periods of pregnancy and lactation. It would appear that these arguments had certain validity. While Mormon women had considerably higher birthrates than the rest of American women in this period, recent research has found that polygamous Mormon women had a lower birthrate than monogamous Mormon women.[17]

Utah's feminists completely accepted the traditional role of woman as wife and mother held by nineteenth-century mainstream culture and, in their arguments for polygamy, they attempted to stand on an even higher moral ground. In arguing for the benefits of plural marriage over monogamy, for example, Mormon apologists inextricably linked the latter to prostitution and adultery. Patriarchal marriage, they believed, was suited to man's natural sexual drives and therefore would increase his purity. Whereas mainstream Victorian womanhood sought to end the double standard by improving the virtue of males, Mormon women argued that their divinely ordained marital system insured this virtue. The undesirable by-products of Gentile society such as infanticide and "white slavery" would be eliminated by the practice of polygamy.[17] With this perspective on Victorian monogamous marriage and within this framework of Victorian morality, Mormons could claim to be in the feminist vanguard. As one enthusiastic male Mormon proclaimed: "the women of Mormondom and the women of America have a common cause, in this all-vital marriage question, which is destined . . . [for] solution before the end of the century."[18]

Mormon feminists argued for an enlarged sphere of usefulness for women. In this view, however, they were following the direction of the male hierarchy as Brigham Young had urged Utah's women to enlarge their activities in 1869. Dictated no doubt in part by the labor needs of a pioneer society, Latter-day Saint women were encouraged to work in nontraditional jobs. By 1874, Utah had developed a "respectable class of professional and highly literate women" and a visitor marveled that "they close no career on a woman in Utah."[19] Mormons were proud of the experimental role they were providing for their women and argued for women's increased responsibility. The *Woman's Exponent* strongly opposed the concept of women as passive ornaments and urged the education of girls for self-sufficiency. In a strong feminist editorial, the *Woman's Exponent* urged that women be allowed the choice of all branches of knowledge. Refuting the Victorian concept of female delicacy, the writer urged that women could decide themselves what was "improper" for they "will know it a thousand times better than men."[20]

Susa Young Gates, plural wife and friend of Charlotte Perkins Gilman, urged that Mormon wives have time for self-development. Polygamy offered obvious advantages in providing women with assistance. "Woman will always be the head and genius of the home but whether it is a corollary that she shall forever wash dishes and scrub floors has become a grave question." Yet in a myriad of practical ways, polygamy demanded increased responsibility of women. Polygamy often required the assistance of women to support plural families. When separate dwellings were maintained, women sometimes had to fend for themselves and be self-sufficient. On occasion, a wife was given capital and full managerial responsibility for land or farm, and significant indication of this can be found in the early Utah census reports which listed plural wives as "heads of households." It was a rare plural wife that had no activity in addition to the home. Women cultivated skills like sewing and millinery to augment a family's income. One plural wife went to school at age forty-nine to become a midwife. She delivered 700 babies thereafter and took the little gold pieces that she received as payment for her services to share with all of the plural family.[21]

Recent research indicates that plural wives on farms did much of the same hard, traditional women's work as non-Mormon frontier women. Nonetheless, there was a definite pattern within polygamy of requiring women to be resourceful and to contribute to the family's support. A comparative study of the polygamous and monogamous wives found that the former participated more in the economic support of families, many with outside occupations.[22] Such patterns challenged the nineteenth-century stereotypes of dependent womanhood and breadwinner male.

It was this violation of the traditional stereotype as housekeeper that apparently aroused a great deal of the antipolygamy criticism. Gentile critics often pointed to the unseemly and indelicate lives of Utah's women, calling them slaves and drudges. Often these critics revealed an urban and upper-class bias in their disdain for the Utah frontier society. Their attacks on polygamy were highly revealing and often unintentionally documented the strengths of polygamy. For example, one of the prominent leaders of the Anti-Polygamy Society, Mrs. Froiseth, in expressing her outrage at a marital system in which plural wives helped with their own support, urged that Utah law be changed to prohibit plural wives claiming land as head of the family. How dare Mormons allow "surplus" wives to own land when legal wives in the larger society were not allowed such ownership! Although she argued in the name of women's rights, Froiseth advocated a narrower view of woman's sphere than the "degraded" Mormons.[23]

One of the most prominent critics of polygamy was Brigham Young's runaway wife who joined the lecture circuit and also wrote a popular expose of the marital system. A careful reading of Ann Eliza's brief against Brigham Young, however, reveals that her primary grievance with the man and the system was economic. Her long litany of persecution dealt with not being kept in adequate style, and her final break with the Mormon leader occurred when he refused to buy her a larger stove to ease her burden in running a boardinghouse. She demanded a divorce settlement of $200,000 as well as $1,000 a month for support.[24]

When the women of the *Woman's Exponent* defended plural marriage, they challenged the contemporary view of dependent womanhood, urging a vision of more competent womanhood: "We have left the petted slave in the Greek household, to go onward and foreward. We have left the idle toy and the painted doll . . . God lead us to find the true Woman in the free American home."[25]

But was Mormon polygamy such an unmixed blessing for Utah's women? The evidence is clearly negative. Mormon literature abounds with descriptions of the hardships, bitterness, and heartbreaks of plural marriage. Even contemporary Mormon writers caution that some of the reports of the harmony and idyllic nature of plural marriage are of a "saccharine sweetness" and, in retrospect, "a little too good to be true." And one writer asserts that some of these plural wives were nothing less than "true religious martyrs."[26]

In the face of these facts, should we discount the feminist arguments of the Mormon polygamists as merely so much defensiveness? Must we concur with one assessment that Utah's women, arguing for the advantages of polygamy, were "the ultimate example of how women have been coerced 'in the name of God' to participate in their own oppression?"[27] Or is it possible that the insistence of Utah's feminists upon the relationship of their marriage system to their liberation has some underlying validity?

Verification for this thesis calls for a perspective not available to the nineteenth-century Mormon woman. Although a plural wife could stoutly maintain that polygamy had "done the most towards making me a free woman in every sense of the word," she could not always articulate the ways in which that was so.[28] The major difficulty that Utah's feminists faced in attempting to describe the relationship between their marital system and their feminism was the fact that they so completely accepted the larger society's view of womanhood and marriage. In the sixty-five years that polygamy was practiced, the only model that was understood was that of monogamy. Despite brave declarations for marital reform, the Mormon family was essentially Victorian and accepted the tacit assumption that romantic love was an ideal. Additionally, the Mormon apologists held as an ideal patriarchal dominance within the family. Consequently, the aspects of polygamy that link it to modern feminism were not acknowledged as positive characteristics in the Mormon and non-Mormon literature, up to the present.

Contemporary feminism suggests a new perspective from which to examine the effects of polygamy upon the development of women. It is a perspective shaped by a consideration of monogamy, romantic love, and the nuclear family as impediments to woman's autonomy. It is a perspective that has rejected the desirability of the competition among women for sexual fulfillment, and, one that has developed a sensitivity to the problems of divorced mothers.

Without the contemporary value placed upon woman's competence and independence, nineteenth-century Mormon feminists had difficulty in communicating to their Gentile sisters the independence that they knew to have come to them from polygamy. One Mormon wife attempted to describe the advantage of plural marriage by stating that the Mormon wife was "not so much a slave as a single girl," while another reported that plural marriage had helped her to become less "bound" to her husband and that she had become "freer" and able to "work out her individual character as separate from her husband."[29]

Because the quality of independence and the role of the single woman contradicted the Victorian concept of role of wife and mother, Utah's feminists found it difficult to describe the benefits of polygamy. They frequently relied on the term "character-building," which would evoke less opprobrium in nineteenth-century language. Hence an 1894 *Woman's Exponent* editorial which summarized the outcomes of polygamy: "Whatever other qualities it may engender, it develops strength in character. Women are left to depend more upon their own judgment and to take more full charge of their own home and affairs. It brings out latent and dormant powers. *A wife becomes literally the head of her household.*"[30]

Mormon women did not always acknowledge this independence as a positive development because it clearly conflicted with their earlier religious training. Thus, Annie Clark Tanner is almost apologetic that she had to abandon her girlhood ideals when faced with the realities of polygamy. "The plural wife . . .

becomes conscious of her own power to make decisions . . . it takes more than the authority of the leader in a patriarchal marriage to make a successful home."[31]

Further evidence of the role of polygamy in providing independence for women comes from one of the leading critics of plural marriage. Apostate Fanny Stenhouse recalls the social independence of Mormon women when she describes the balls held in Salt Lake City where women frequently arrived and left on their own. "No observation is made if a lady there enters the ballroom alone," she wrote disapprovingly.[32]

Closely related to the independence produced by polygamy was the development of a strong mother/child bond and increasing power of the mother in the home. "No matter how much the patriarchal order might put the husband and father in the top place, in actual fact, the women had a great deal of control over the family."[33] This outcome was understandable when women were left in separate households.

Nineteenth-century Mormon feminists, accepting the ideal of Mormon marriage as the husband/father patriarch, do not stress the close ties between mother and children in polygyny. Recent scholars note the phenomenon.[34] The literature supports this conclusion, documenting a record of conflicts with husbands over the children. One mother, for example, explained that she refused to move with her husband and plural family because she wanted her children educated in a certain community. After all, she commented, "A man doesn't come first when there are children."[35] This same mother explained that her husband believed in corporal punishment but that she did not permit him to beat their children.

Similarly, Annie Clark Tanner described conflicts with her husband over the children which arose because of, in her words, his "Prussianlike" views of discipline. "He was a dictator and he expected to be obeyed." Later she is unequivocal in stating the relationship of her independence to this closeness with her children. "I had the attitude of many Mormon women in polygamy. I felt the responsibility of my family, and I developed an independence that women in monogamy never know. A woman in polygamy is compelled by her lone position to make a confidant of her children."[36] This remarkable woman reared six children alone during the period when polygamy was most beleaguered. She revealed an enlightened interest in the findings of child psychology, and her memoirs attested to her children's intense loyalty and devotion to her.

Further evidence of the bond between children of plural homes and their mothers may be glimpsed through critics of the system. Writers alluded to the intense hatred of polygamous children toward the system, because of their loyalties to their mothers, sometimes seen as hostility to the father. In her first published attack on polygamy, Fanny Stenhouse described proof of the failure of polygamy to be found in the fact that children in plural homes preferred their mothers. Fathers, she explained, were regarded by the children with the same indifference that the plural wife/mothers had to assume toward their husbands in order to bear the trials of polygamy.[37]

Annie Clark Tanner believed that the close relationship that she had with her daughter was due to the absence of the polygamist father. Her husband could not be her confidant, Annie explained, therefore Jennie and I "were more like sisters than mother and daughter." Regardless of why, the outcome seems evident and is confirmed by a survey of the descendants of plural families: mothers often held dominant positions, a finding that one researcher admits was "a remarkable modification" in a society committed to "the patriarchal, authoritarian pattern."[38]

The critics of polygamy attacked plural marriage from their certainty of the ideal of romantic love. Thus, Fanny Stenhouse warned the male polygamist that the acquiescence of his wife often meant that she had become indifferent. Plural marriage must of necessity mean the loss of "true love," she observed, because "where there is no jealousy there is very little love." One of the memories that especially irritated Fanny Stenhouse was that of attending the Salt Lake City theater to see stage tales of true love, of the comingling of two souls. Indignantly, she recalled that these stories did not represent the "cruelties of polygamy."[39]

The apologists for polygamy frequently shared this assumption that romantic love was the ideal and hesitated to remark on its loss. Therefore, one plural wife hastened to report that although she had experienced a "loss of enthusiasm" when her new husband failed to keep his first assignation with her, she "learned to love" him dearly and doubted if "anyone was a more ardent lover" than she.[40]

But running as a thread throughout the success stories of Mormon plural marriage is evidence that it inherently assaulted the ideology of romantic love. Courtship was described in one instance as riding in a buggy with a man and his first wife. A daughter from a polygynist home reported that she didn't think "those polygamists knew what romantic love means."[42] Perhaps, as one historian observed, romantic love was a "salient feature of monogamy" and therefore not adaptable to polygamy.[42] Clearly, romantic love as the monogamous, exclusive, sexual relatioship of a man and a woman could not be incorporated in plural marriage. Nor could romantic love as evidenced by jealousy and competition between and within the sexes be comfortably absorbed into polygamy.

The arrangements required for the successful functioning of polygyny undercut romantic love, but were often characterized by remarkable examples of female cooperation and unselfishness. If feminism can be defined in any way by a community of women, the presence of sisterhood, cooperation and woman bonding, then this can be amply found in the story of Mormon polygyny. One historian has suggested that the ties of sisterhood among plural wives was a "compensatory emotional function of this loss of romantic love." Whether this sense of sisterhood was emotional compensation or rather, as one plural wife explained, a blessing that resulted from the elimination of jealousy, is open for speculation. Yet throughout the polygamy literature, one finds extraordinary stories and examples of cooperation among women.[43]

Annie Clark Tanner was a second wife who considered herself unsuccessful as a polygamist, yet left us several positive descriptions of the friendship and relationship of sister/wives. When she was newly married, Annie visited the first Mrs. Tanner and left with gifts of fruit and money toward the purchase of a new stove. This first wife was childless and Annie named her first baby after her and described how "Aunt Jennie," eyes filled with tears, first viewed the baby girl. Despite these ties to the first wife, Annie confessed that she felt closer to the third wife, Josephine, because she felt "more like an equal" with her. They had much in common, Annie reported, and "enjoyed each other's company." An interesting footnote to the story of the loyalty of the plural wives in the Tanner family emerged in later years when Annie was estranged from her husband and her son was visiting his father and the plural wives in Canada. Annie recorded in her memoirs that when the boy became ill during his visit her sister/wives insisted that the money be provided to give the young man adequate medical care.[44]

Polygamy offered obvious opportunities for women to share work and offer other types of assistance. In cases of death and illness, women took care of the children of sister/wives. One correspondent to the *Woman's Exponent* wrote in 1873 to explain that she had been silent for some time because she had been to another town to assist a sick sister/wife. While there she had, she reported, made twelve dresses for the little girls of the family.[45]

Sometimes women remembered these early years of polygamy with what seems to be a fond nostalgia. "We acted as nurses for each other during confinement, we were too poor to hire nurses. One suit or outfit for new babies and confinement did for us all, and when one piece wore out, it was supplied by another. For many years we lived thus, working together."[46]

Such cooperation sometimes worked to the disadvantage of the polygamist/husband. Women often found strength in numbers and joined in their efforts to influence a husband's decisions or actions. Mormon family histories record this dynamic and many of the horror stories of the antipolygamy crusade unwittingly document the bonding of plural wives. Fanny Stenhouse scathingly warned the polygamist not to "allow his wives to become too intimate" because "they will certainly plot mischief and destroy his power and peace."[47]

Fanny Stenhouse believed that women became friendly in this way only because they had ceased to care for the husband. And yet she presents one of the most dramatic and poignant examples of woman friendship in polygamy when she describes the deathbed scene of Carrie, a young woman friend, who had refused to become Mr. Stenhouse's plural wife. Facing imminent death, the young woman confesses to Fanny and asks that, after death, Fanny and husband marry her by proxy: "When I am gone, will you kneel by your husband's side in the Endowment House, and be married to him for me? . . . We shall then be together in eternity, and I am happy at the thought of that, for I think I love you even better than I love him."[48]

Leaving aside the melodrama of the preceeding deathbed description, it is recorded that some plural wives chose a family through affection for a previous wife. The biographers of Emmeline B. Wells, editor of the *Woman's Exponent,* speculate that her first plural marriage was made in part because of her admiration for the first wife, Elizabeth Whitney. Emmeline and Elizabeth remained close friends throughout "Mother" Whitney's life. A visitor to Utah left a description of a similar sister/wife friendship.

Observing the first and second wife in earnest conversation, the visitor was told by the daughter of the first wife that her mother loved the sister/wife "better than any of us."[49]

Another account of the support network provided by sister/wives comes to us through the story of the well-known Mormon plural wife and medical doctor, Ellis Shipp. This remarkable woman had gone to finish medical school in Philadelphia while pregnant and with little money. She found herself left on New Year's day with one dollar. The mail, however, brought her fifty dollars from her sister/wife Lizzie who sent money again in a few months to help Ellis successfully complete her studies.[50]

How can we explain these close relationships? It is important to remember that these women shared deeply held religious beliefs. Moreover, their story closely resembles the nineteenth-century world of women's "love and ritual" found by Carroll Smith-Rosenberg in her study of thirty-five families. Her research suggested that this intense female bonding characterized the period and could be explained as the outcome of the separate female/male spheres which marked the era. If so, Mormon patriarchal marriage, which one historian believed created even more distinct female/male spheres, could be seen as contributing to these similar intense woman friendships.[51]

It is not completely clear how this relationship of the Mormon sister/wives related to the practice of polygyny itself, to shared religious convictions, or to the emotional bonding created by shared suffering. Perhaps the answer will be found in further study of how the sisterhood of plural wives differed from the closeness of Mormon women in other relationships.

In the last analysis, however, Mormon women proclaimed that their marital system was directly linked to their feminism and in certain ways they were correct. One cannot truly apply the term "feminist" to the Mormon plural wives because feminism and patriarchal religion are incompatible. However, because of polygamy, the Mormon women were thrust into the late nineteenth-century suffrage movement and thereafter became active in promoting an enlarged sphere for women. A leadership group emerged around the *Woman's Exponent* which joined in the struggle of eastern suffragists. When the vote was removed from Utah women, this group did not retreat, but worked to restore it. This leadership group demonstrated, in the terms of one historian, an "almost feminist awareness," in the course of this antipolygamy and suffrage struggle.[52] It would appear that the controversial nature of their marital system politicized these women. While plural marriage did not bring the Mormon woman into conflict with the patriarchal hierarchy of the church, it did bring them to an apparent increase in independence and an openness to more radical social experiments. Thus, Charlotte Perkins Gilman found a receptive audience for some of her theories in Salt Lake City among the Mormons in 1899, nearly a decade after plural marriage had been renounced.[53]

When plural marriage was later abandoned, following a brutal attack by outside society, Mormon women became even more intensely loyal to their beliefs. This loyalty persevered as Mormon society led them away from frontier activism and daring utopianism toward a growing sense of Victorian gentility. These changes led to increasing restrictions on women, and the past century has seen their role in Mormon society become more narrowly defined.

A reader must speculate on whether the system of plural marriage, left in place, might have changed these developments. In later years, Martha Cannon, plural wife, doctor, and legislator, told Beatrice Webb, English Fabian socialist, that if plural marriage had been allowed to continue, practiced freely, it would have given women an independent life. A plural wife, she explained, was not as "completely absorbed as one wife is in her husband."[54] Polygamy, based upon a most patriarchal theology, contained elements that contradicted Victorian domesticity. Some Mormon women had found through plural marriage greater autonomy, some economic self-sufficiency, and a community of women. These outcomes were, if not the result of, then accompanied by, the breaking with an ideal of romantic love and monogamy. Mormon polygamy led, in this way, to a path of less male-identified womanhood alluded to by the Mormon woman who posed the question: "Is there then nothing worth living for, but to be petted, humored, and caressed, by a man?"[55]

NOTES

This paper has been significantly revised from its earlier presentation at the Female Sphere Conference, New Harmony, Indiana (October 1981). I wish to express my appreciation to the readers for *Feminist Studies* who have helped in this revision.

1. The correct anthropological term for Mormon marriage is polygyny; however, nineteenth-century usage referred to Mormon marriage as polygamy. Both terms are used interchangeably in this paper. Latter-day Saints also referred to their practice as

plural marriage, or the Principle. The system was also sometimes referred to as the patriarchal order of matrimony or "celestial marriage." Actually celestial marriage is not a synonym for plural marriage as it refers to the eternal status of the highest type of marriage which could also be accorded monogamous Mormon marriage.

2. Thomas G. Alexander, "An Experiment in Progressive Legislation: The Granting of Woman Suffrage in Utah in 1870," *Utah Historical Quarterly* 38 (Winter 1970): 27. See also Louis J. Kern, *An Ordered Love: Sex Roles and Sexuality in Victorian Utopias—The Shakers, the Mormons, and the Oneida Community* (Chapel Hill: University of North Carolina Press, 1981), 192; and Marilyn Warenski, *Patriarchs and Politics: The Plight of the Mormon Woman* (New York: McGraw-Hill, 1978): 144.

3. Gail Farr Casterline, "'In the Toils' or 'Onward for Zion': Images of the Mormon Woman" (masters thesis, Utah State University, 1974), 129.

4. Thomas F. O'Dea, *The Mormons* (Chicago: University of Chicago Press, 1957), 249; Warenski, 179; and "Matilda Joslyn Gage Scrapbooks," Rare Books Division, Library of Congress, Washington, D.C.

5. "Matilda Joslyn Gage Scrapbooks."

6. See Robert J. Dwyer, *The Gentile Comes to Utah* (Washington, D.C.: Catholic University Press, 1941), 201, n; and Edward W. Tullidge, *The Women of Mormondom* (New York, 1877; reprint, Salt Lake City, 1957), 511-15.

7. Gustive O. Larsen, *The Americanization of Utah for Statehood* (San Marino, Calif.: Huntington Library, 1971), 57. Quote by Philip Robinson, 1883.

8. Laurence Foster, *Religion and Sexuality: Three American Communal Experiments of the Nineteenth Century* (New York: Oxford University Press, 1981); Julie Roy Jeffrey, *Frontier Women: The Trans-Mississippi West, 1840-1880* (New York: Hill & Wang, 1979). Both Foster and Jeffrey astutely analyze the positive aspects for women of polygamy. Jeffrey also suggests that Mormon women gained a perspective of themselves as women through their defense of polygamy, 176.

9. Although single-parent households headed by women often account for today's "feminization of poverty," research has shown that the divorced woman is often found to be more self-assertive, indicating that the forced independence of divorce can be a transforming experience. See Jessie Barnard, *The Female World* (New York: Free Press, 1981), 176 n.

10. Susa Young Gates, "Family Life Among the Mormons," *North American Review* (March 1890): 349.

11. Stanley S. Ivins, "Notes on Mormon Polygamy," *Western Humanities Review* 10 (Summer 1956): 232; and Leonard J. Arrington and David Bitton, *The Mormon Experience* (New York: Alfred A. Knopf, 1979), 203. A nineteenth-century source reported that 7,000 women in Utah were living in polygamous marriage according to James E. Smith and Phillip R. Kunz, "Polygyny and Fertility in Nineteenth-Century America," *Population Studies* 30 (1976): 471.

12. Arrington and Bitton, 204.

13. Laurence Foster, "Between Two Worlds: The Origins of Shaker Celibacy, Oneida Community Complex Marriage, and Mormon Polygamy" (Ph.D. diss., University of Chicago, 1976), 399-400; Kern, 168-69; and Warenski, 231.

14. Particularly outrageous examples of this can be found throughout Jennie A. Froiseth, *The Women of Mormonism* (Detroit: C.G.G. Paine, 1882) and in the introduction of Walter M. Gallihan's *Women under Polygamy* (New York: Dodd, Mead & Co., 1915).

15. Samuel George Ellsworth, ed., *Dear Ellen: Two Mormon Women and Their Letters* (Salt Lake City: Tanner Trust Fund, 1974), 23.

16. Kathleen Marquis, "Diamond Cut Diamond: Mormon Women and the Cult of Domesticity in the Nineteenth Century," *University of Michigan Papers in Women's Studies* 2 (1976), 105; Casterline, 103; Kern, 183; Smith and Kunz, 465-80.

17. Helen Mar Whitney, *Why We Practice Plural Marriage* (Salt Lake City: Juvenile Instructor Office, 1884), 25-27; 29-32.
18. Tullidge, 515.
19. Casterline, 76-77.
20. *Woman's Exponent* 1 (1 April 1873), 163.
21. Gates, 349; Kern, 186-87; Kimball Young, *Isn't One Wife Enough?* (New York: Henry Holt & Company, 1954), 167; Vicky Burgess-Olson, "Family Structures and Dynamics in Early Utah Mormon Families, 1847-1885" (Ph.D. diss., Northwestern University, 1975), 87 (Burgess-Olson found that of the families studied 80 percent maintained separate households for some of the time.) Foster, "Between Two Worlds," 392; Burgess-Olson, "Family Structures and Dynamics," 67; and Juliaetta B. Jensen, *Little Gold Pieces* (Salt Lake City: Stanway, 1948), 88.
22. Jessie L. Embry, "Master or Slave: The Economic Role of Mormon Polygamous Wives" (unpublished manuscript): 13; Burgess-Olson, "Family Structures and Dynamics," 112; Claudia L. Bushman, ed., *Mormon Sisters: Women in Early Utah* (Cambridge, Mass.: Emmeline Press, 1976), 104-5.
23. Marquis, 115; Froiseth, 324, 360.
24. Ann Eliza Young, *Wife No. 19* (1875; reprint, New York: Arno Press, 1972), 532-37; 554-55.
25. *Woman's Exponent* 1 (1 Apr. 1873), 163.
26. Bushman, 101; Warenski, 158-59.
27. Warenski, 156.
28. Kimball Young, 52.
29. Marquis, 112; and Arrington & Bitton, 230.
30. Quoted in Leonard Arrington, "Blessed Damozels: Women in Mormon History," *Dialogue* 6 (Summer 1971): 30 (Italics not in original).
31. Annie Clark Tanner, *A Mormon Mother* (Salt Lake City: Tanner Trust, University of Utah, 1969), 116, 270.
32. Mrs. T.B.H. Stenhouse, *Exposé of Polygamy in Utah: A Lady's Life Among the Mormons,* 2d ed. (New York: American News Company, 1872), 91.
33. Kimball Young, 450.
34. Foster, "Between Two Worlds," 389; Kimball Young, 251.
35. Kimball Young, 69.
36. Tanner, 267-69.
37. Kimball Young, 404; Stenhouse, *Exposé of Polygamy in Utah,* 75.
38. Tanner, 185, 298; Kimball Young, 251.
39. Stenhouse, *Exposé of Polygamy in Utah,* 75, 123; Mrs. T.B.H. Stenhouse, *Tell It All: The Tyranny of Mormonism, or, An Englishwoman in Utah* (Reprint, New York: Praeger, 1971), 213.
40. Kimball Young, 183.
41. Bushman, 89; Kimball Young, 117.
42. Raymond Lee Muncy, *Sex and Marriage in Utopian Communities,* (Bloomington: Indiana University Press, 1973), 158-59.
43. Foster, "Between Two Worlds," 390; Whitney, 5.
44. Tanner, 106 ff.; 131-32; 150 ff.
45. *Woman's Exponent* 2 (15 Aug. 1873), 47.
46. Kimball Young, 217.
47. Froiseth, 74-89; Stenhouse, *Exposé of Polygamy in Utah,* 76.
48. Stenhouse, *Tell It All,* 290.
49. Vicky Burgess-Olson, *Sister Saints,* vol. 5 of *Studies in Mormon History,* ed. James B. Allen (Provo, Utah: Brigham Young University Press, 1978), 463; William Mulder and A. Russell Mortensen, eds. *Among the Mormons: Historic Accounts by Contemporary Observers* (New York: Alfred A. Knopf, 1958), 402-3.

50. Arrington, "Blessed Damozels," 29.
51. Carroll Smith-Rosenberg, "The Female World of Love and Ritual: Relations between Women in Nineteenth-Century America," *Signs* 1 (Autumn 1975): 1-29; Kern, 179.
52. Laurence Foster, "From Frontier Activism to Neo-Victorian Domesticity: Mormon Women in the Nineteenth and Twentieth Centuries," *Journal of Mormon History* 6 (1979): 11. The circulation of the *Woman's Exponent* was never over 1,000, according to Burgess-Olson, *Sister Saints,* 149.
53. This trip was called to my attention by Mary A. Hill, the biographer of Charlotte Perkins Gilman.
54. Quoted in Burgess-Olson, *Sister Saints,* 391.
55. *Woman's Exponent* 3 (30 Sept. 1874): 67.

Jane Snyder Richards described life under polygamy. USHS collections.

Polygamy and the Frontier: Mormon Women in Early Utah

BY LAWRENCE FOSTER

THE MORMON ATTEMPT TO ESTABLISH POLYGAMY in Utah and adjacent areas in the Intermountain West during the last half of the nineteenth century constitutes the largest, best organized, and most contro-

Dr. Foster is associate professor in the School of Social Sciences, Georgia Institute of Technology.

versial effort to radically restructure marriage and family life in nineteenth-century America. While other alternatives to monogamy in this period, such as the systems of the celibate Shakers and the free-love Oneida Perfectionists, directly affected only a few thousand individuals at most, polygamy ultimately became the family ideal for more than one hundred thousand Latter-day Saints who placed their indelible cultural imprint on much of the American West. In setting up their Great Basin kingdom the Mormons skillfully and systematically sought to create an autonomous religious and cultural order based on American and biblical models. Polygamy became an integral part of that larger effort between 1852, when the Mormons in Utah first publicly announced that they were practicing it, and 1890, when, under intense federal pressure, they began to give up the practice.[1]

Few aspects of Mormon polygamy have been more controversial than its impact on women. During the nineteenth century hostile external observers attacked the practice as a "relic of barbarism," a system of institutionalized lust that degraded women, destroyed the unity of the family, and led inevitably to unhappiness, debaucheries, and excesses of all kinds. Nineteenth-century Latter-day Saints were equally vigorous in defending their marital practices, arguing that plural marriage and the Old Testament patriarchal model on which it was based actually strengthened family and kinship ties, led to the rearing of righteous children in the best families, and allowed women greater freedom in choosing the men they really wanted to marry. More recently, both Mormon and non-Mormon scholars have attempted to treat polygamy with greater objectivity, to show how it functioned in pioneer Utah and what it meant to the people who participated in it. Through the use of demographic studies, literary analyses, oral histories, group biographies, and a variety of other methods, these writers have highlighted key questions raised by this extraordinary effort to introduce new forms of marriage and family relations in nineteenth-century America.[2]

[1] For a treatment of the process by which the Mormon form of polygamy was conceived, introduced, and institutionalized, see Lawrence Foster, *Religion and Sexuality: Three American Communal Experiments of the Nineteenth Century* (New York: Oxford University Press, 1981). Portions of that study have been used here by arrangement. A contrasting perspective on the theory and practice of polygamy, unfortunately based on limited primary research, is presented in Louis J. Kern, *An Ordered Love: Sex Roles and Sexuality in Victorian Utopias—the Shakers, the Mormons, and the Oneida Community* (Chapel Hill: University of North Carolina Press, 1981).

[2] Among the historically important treatments of Mormon polygamy by apostates, see John C. Bennett, *The History of the Saints* (Boston, 1842); John Hyde, Jr., *Mormonism: Its Leaders and Designs* (New York, 1857); T. B. H. Stenhouse, *The Rocky Mountain Saints* (New York, 1873); Fanny Stenhouse, *"Tell It All"* (Hartford, Conn., 1874); and John D. Lee, *Mormonism*

Based on current research and available manuscript materials, it is now possible to move beyond simple polemics and begin to understand the complex ways in which polygamy affected relationships between men and women in the Great Basin region. Although polygamy had been secretly taught and practiced by Mormons at least as early as 1841 in Nauvoo, Illinois,[3] not until the difficult exodus to the relative isolation of the Intermountain West were the Latter-day Saints free to set up their unorthodox marriage system without constant external interference. During the years between 1847, when the Mormons first arrived in Utah, and 1877, when Brigham Young died, polygamy became an integral part of Mormon life in the Great Basin region and profoundly influenced the experiences and activity of women there.

The problems and challenges of life under polygamy in Utah are described in numerous diaries, journals, letters, and other first-hand accounts by Mormon women.[4] Perhaps the finest presentation of the range of women's experiences under polygamy is found in the reflections of Jane Snyder Richards, first wife of the Mormon apostle Franklin D. Richards and herself active in many capacities on behalf of her family and the women of Utah. In 1880 in an interview entitled "The Inner Facts of Social Life in Utah," Mrs. Richards spoke candidly about her experiences and feelings with the non-Mormon Mrs. Hubert Howe Bancroft who was helping her husband collect information for his monumental history of Utah. Although Mrs. Richards was far from a typical Mormon wife and mother, her interview and other writings sensitively portray many of the characteristic features of early polygamy as well as the complex adjustments necessary to make polygamy work, even in an

Unveiled, ed. W. W. Bishop (Saint Louis, 1877). Semi-novelistic attacks on Mormon polygamy are surveyed in Leonard J. Arrington and Jon Haupt, "Intolerable Zion: The Image of Mormonism in Nineteenth Century American Literature," *Western Humanities Review* 22 (1968): 243–60. Mormon defenses of polygamy are presented in Orson Pratt's periodical, *The Seer* (Liverpool, 1853–54); Helen Mar Kimball Whitney, *Why We Practice Plural Marriage* (Salt Lake City, 1884); and periodical publications such as the *Journal of Discourses*, the *Deseret News*, and the *Woman's Exponent*. A bibliographic essay analyzing scholarly treatments of polygamy is Davis Bitton, "Mormon Polygamy: A Review Article," *Journal of Mormon History* 4 (1977): 101–18.

[3] Documentation of the Mormon efforts to set up polygamy prior to Utah is provided in Foster, *Religion and Sexuality*, pp. 123–80; Danel W. Bachman, "A Study of the Mormon Practice of Plural Marriage before the Death of Joseph Smith" (M.A. thesis, Purdue University, 1975); and Charles W. Shook, *The True Origin of Mormon Polygamy* (Cincinnati: Standard Publishing Co., 1914).

[4] A comprehensive survey of the major collections of Mormon manuscript writings is Davis Bitton, *Guide to Mormon Diaries and Autobiographies* (Provo: Brigham Young University Press, 1977). Also see Stanley Snow Ivins's notebooks and transcripts, Utah State Historical Society Library, Salt Lake City, and the Kimball Young Papers, Huntington Library in San Marino, Calif., and the Garrett Theological Seminary Library in Evanston, Ill.

unusually good relationship. Observing Mr. and Mrs. Richards together, Mrs. Bancroft wrote:

> He seems remarkably considerate and kind and speaks of her with gratitude and pride, and that he wanted her to enjoy this little visit to California for she has suffered so much affliction and so many hardships. . . . his attentions and kind consideration for her are very marked. She is certainly very devoted to him, and I am imagining this trip and the one they have just returned from in the East, as a sort of honey-moon in middle life.[5]

Before abstracting out some of the characteristic aspects of polygamy illustrated by the Richards case, a brief look at their relationship and experience is in order. Jane Snyder was born on January 31, 1823, in Pamelia, New York, one of the youngest of eleven children of a prosperous farmer and stock raiser. Her father had not belonged to any church before joining the Mormons, while her mother had been a devout Methodist. Jane showed her strength of will at age seventeen when, upon deciding to join the Mormon church in midwinter, she insisted on undergoing a proper baptism by immersion out-of-doors in a lake near her home in La Porte, Illinois.[6]

Franklin D. Richards was born in Richmond, Massachusetts, on April 2, 1821. The fourth of nine children, he grew up accustomed to hard manual labor on his father's farm, but in his spare time he loved to read and discuss issues of the day. At age ten Franklin left home and traveled about as an itinerant worker until he joined the Mormon church in 1838. He rose rapidly in the hierarchy as he demonstrated his remarkable organizational and proselytizing skills.

Jane Snyder and Franklin Richards met through their mutual involvement in the Mormon church. Robert Snyder, Jane's father, was one of Franklin's traveling missionary companions. When Franklin became seriously ill on one occasion, Jane nursed him back to health in the Snyder family home in La Porte. Thereafter, he became a frequent

[5] Interview of Mrs. Hubert Howe Bancroft with Mrs. F. D. Richards, "The Inner Facts of Social Life in Utah," p. 11, Hubert Howe Bancroft Collection of Mormon Manuscripts, Bancroft Library, University of California at Berkeley. Unless otherwise indicated, most of the evidence about Jane and Franklin Richards comes from this source and from "Reminiscences of Mrs. Franklin D. Richards" and "Narrative of Franklin Dewey Richards," both manuscripts in the Bancroft Collection. See also Andrew Jenson, comp., *Latter-day Saint Biographical Encyclopedia*, 4 vols. (Salt Lake City: Andrew Jenson History Co., 1901–36), 2:115–21; D. Michael Quinn, "Organizational Development and Social Organization of the Mormon Hierarchy, 1832–1932: A Prosopographical Study" (M.A. thesis, University of Utah, 1973), p. 271; and Connie Duncan Cannon, "Jane Snyder Richards: The Blue-White Diamond," in Vicky Burgess-Olson, ed., *Sister Saints: Women in Early Utah* (Provo: Brigham Young University Press, 1978), pp. 173–98.

[6] Cannon, "Jane Synder Richards," pp. 175–77.

visitor to La Porte, eventually marrying Jane in December 1842. Their first child was born in November 1843, and in the spring of the following year Franklin was called on a mission to England.

As an increasingly prominent member of the Mormon church, Franklin soon learned of the new belief in polygamous marriage as a necessity for the highest exaltation in the afterlife. About eight months after their marriage, when Jane was in the advanced stages of pregnancy, he approached her about the possibility of taking another wife. She was deeply hurt at this suggestion, and her opposition may have been largely responsible for his waiting nearly three years before finally taking the seventeen-year-old Elizabeth McFate as a plural wife in January 1846, eight days after he and Jane had been sealed together for "time and eternity" in the new temple.

Although Jane Richards had severe misgivings about polygamy, she found that she and Elizabeth could get on well together. Aware of the awkwardness of the situation, Elizabeth was deferential to Jane and tried to be especially kind and considerate. Jane lived in the lower half of the house, while Elizabeth was assigned to the upper story. They divided the labor between them. If Elizabeth did the cooking, for instance, Jane did the washing, and vice versa. To those who knew that the Mormons were practicing polygamy, Jane Richards spoke of Elizabeth as Mrs. Elizabeth Richards.

In May 1846 the Richardses reluctantly sold for a mere pittance the house that they had sacrificed to build. Along with the other Mormons who were fleeing the anti-Mormon mobs in Illinois, Jane and Elizabeth Richards began an incredibly difficult journey west. The two women had to take almost complete responsibility for the difficult move, since Mr. Richards was called away on another mission at the time of their departure from Illinois. During the trip west, Jane gave birth to a second child, who promptly died. She also lost her first daughter. Elizabeth, whose health had never been robust, died of "consumption" en route. During the trip Jane was so sick at times that, in her own words, "I only lived because I could not die." Seeing her pitiable state when the Mormons stopped for the winter in Nebraska, Brigham Young expressed special concern for her, saying that if he had known her situation, he would not have required her husband to go on a mission at that time.

Conditions improved somewhat after Jane's arrival in Salt Lake, but life was still exceptionally difficult for her. In 1849, after Franklin had been back only a short time, he was appointed one of Brigham Young's twelve apostles and shortly thereafter was called to undertake yet another mission to England. There he was playing an increasingly important role in originating and developing the remarkable Mormon emigration system. Before he left, he was married to Sarah Snyder, a sister of his wife Jane. Sarah had been deserted by her first husband while she was coming west, and she was having considerable difficulty managing alone with five small children. Also in 1849, Franklin took Charlotte Fox as a plural wife.

The succeeding fifteen years were marked by Franklin's repeated missionary and church appointments and by his resulting long absences from home. Following a highly successful term as president of the British Mission from 1850 to 1852, during which time 16,000 people joined the Mormon church, Franklin Richards returned home to the Great Basin, taking three additional wives, Susan S. Pierson in 1853, Laura A. Snyder in 1854, and Josephine de la Harpe in 1857. After Willard Richards died in 1854, Franklin was counseled by Brigham Young—following the Mormon variant on the Mosaic practice of the levirate—to marry his uncle's widows. As a result, four more women, Nancy Longstroth, Mary Thompson, Susannah Bayliss, and Rodah H. Foss, were sealed to him by Brigham Young in March 1857.[7]

Living conditions for the various wives differed greatly during the course of their marriages to Franklin Richards. The early years were the hardest. When Franklin was called to go to England in October 1849, for instance, Jane Richards was left temporarily in a one-room, floorless, and almost roofless house. As soon as possible, she and the other women who married Franklin took steps to improve their condition. To a considerable extent they were on their own resources, at least until 1869 when Franklin finally came back permanently to live in the Great Basin region after the last of his four major missionary trips to England. Jane Richards eventually established a house in Ogden, while the other wives lived in different cities in Utah. During this period Jane played an active role in the Relief Society, the women's organization in the church, as well as in national women's organizations, while Franklin

[7] In levirate marriage as described in Deuteronomy 25:5–10 it was the duty of the brother of a man who died without leaving any male heir to take the dead man's wife as his own and sire children by her to perpetuate the dead brother's name and family line. In the Mormon system, as practiced in this instance, women who had been sealed to Willard Richards for "time and eternity" were remarried following his death "for time only" to Franklin D. Richards. Children born to that union were considered to belong to the Willard Richards family in the afterlife, according to Mormon marital theory.

served variously as judge, church historian, and president of the Council of the Twelve Apostles, one of the highest positions in the church. Though his work still called him away from home much of the time, many of the greatest pressures from the early period were gone after he had finally completed his missionary activities abroad.

Underlying the entire interview between Mrs. Bancroft and Mrs. Richards was an awareness of the intense personal commitment and the difficult personal renunciations involved in the practice of polygamy, especially for women and, most especially, for the first wife. Romantic love was sharply undercut by the new arrangements. Jane Richards spoke of her initial "repugnance" when she first learned of polygamy in Illinois; how "crushed" she felt when her husband first approached her about the possibility of taking another wife; and of her unhappiness when he married three new wives in Utah after he had returned from an extended mission to England. Like many other Mormon women, Mrs. Richards was only able to accept polygamy because she convinced herself that it was essential to her salvation and to that of her husband. She found that in practice polygamy "was not such a trial as she had feared" and that she and the other wives were able to cooperate effectively. On several occasions during the interview Mrs. Richards appeared to be trying to reassure herself that her husband was motivated by a sense of religious duty and not by any lustful desires. Mrs. Bancroft concluded her record of the interview by observing that on the whole it seemed to her that Mormon women considered polygamy

> . . . as a religious duty and schooled themselves to bear its discomforts as a sort of religious penance, and that it was a matter of pride to make everybody believe they lived happily and to persuade themselves and others that was not a trial; and that a long life of such discipline makes the trial lighter.[8]

Other diary and journal accounts, interviews with individuals who lived in polygamous families, and recent quantitative analyses show that religious commitment was, indeed, the primary reason that most Mormon women—and most men as well—gave for entering into plural marriage. Only a sense of the cosmic importance of their endeavor was enough to convince thousands of individuals to accept or adopt practices radically at variance with all that they had ever been taught. As the

[8] "Social Life in Utah," p. 18.

Mormon mother Annie Clark Tanner, who grew up in a polygamous household and became a plural wife herself, declared:

> I am sure that women would never have accepted polygamy had it not been for their religion. No woman ever consented to its practice without great sacrifice on her part. There is something so sacred about the relationship of husband and wife that a third party in the family is sure to disturb the confidence and security that formerly existed.
>
> The principle of Celestial Marriage was considered the capstone of the Mormon religion. Only by practicing it would the highest exaltation in the Celestial Kingdom of God be obtained. According to the founders of the Mormon Church, the great purpose of this life is to prepare for the Celestial Kingdom in the world to come. The tremendous sacrifices of the Mormon people can only be understood if one keeps in mind this basic otherworld philosophy.[9]

Although polygamy was especially difficult for women, it also required significant renunciations from the men who took on the responsibility of marrying plural wives. Since polygamists such as Franklin Richards were typically of a higher religious and economic status than the average member, they were frequently called away from home on church business for extended periods of time so that they had relatively little opportunity to be with their families. Furthermore, even when such Mormon polygamists were at home, they faced complex problems of family management that made significant expression of romantic love difficult. Like other serious polygamists, Franklin Richards had to try to avoid favoritism toward his plural wives if he were to maintain family harmony; he had to try to make an equitable distribution of his time, money, and affections when he was not away on church business. Jane Richards remembered how even her husband's most sincere efforts to treat his wives equally led to frustration and heartache.[10] Even with the best of will, individuals who had been socialized into monogamous norms found the necessary transition to the new patterns of relationships in polygamy difficult.

Given the complexities of polygamy and the renunciations that it entailed, it is not surprising to find that plural marriage was far from

[9] Annie Clark Tanner, *A Mormon Mother: An Autobiography* (Salt Lake City: University of Utah Press, 1969), pp. 116, 1. Also see Whitney, *Why We Practice Plural Marriage*, pp. 23–24; James E. Hulett, Jr., "The Sociological and Social Psychological Aspects of the Mormon Polygamous Family" (Ph.D. diss., University of Wisconsin, 1939); and Vicky Burgess-Olson, "Family Structure and Dynamics in Early Utah Mormon Families, 1847–1885" (Ph.D. diss., Northwestern University, 1975), pp. 69–82.

[10] "Social Life in Utah," p. 6.

universally practiced in the Great Basin. Using a sample of more than 6,000 prominent Mormon families, Stanley Snow Ivins estimated that at most only 15 to 20 percent were polygamous. Using a subsample of 1,784 polygamous men, Ivins found that a large majority, 66.3 percent, married only the one extra wife considered necessary for the highest exaltation in the celestial kingdom. Another 21.2 percent married three wives, and 6.7 percent went so far as to take four wives. The remaining group of less than 6 percent married five or more women. The limited incidence of polygamy may also have been due in part to the limited number of available women. At no time during Utah territorial history did the total number of women outnumber the men. Finally, according to Ivins's figures, the rate at which new polygamous marriages were established was always in an overall decline after the early 1856–57 peak. Sporadic increases in the rate of entry into polygamous marriages occurred during times of internal or external crisis, when polygamy served as a rallying point through which Mormons could prove their loyalty to the church, but continued exhortation and group pressure appear to have been necessary to sustain the practice.[11]

Although plural marriage may well have been less than appealing to many men and women, such arrangements can be viewed in context as part of the necessary subordination of individual desires to long-term group goals that underlay Mormon success in the rapid settlement and development of the Intermountain West. Sexual impulses were sublimated into the arduous group enterprise of settling Utah and building up a Zion in the wilderness. As the historian Leonard Arrington has observed—"Only a high degree of religious devotion and discipline, superb organization and planning, made survival possible" in early Utah.[12] Mormon men, particularly the leading Mormon men who were most often polygamists, had to be willing to move flexibly on church assignments as the demands of the group required. By partially breaking down exclusive bonds between a husband and wife, and by undercutting direct emotional involvement in family affairs in favor of church business, polyg-

[11] Stanley Snow Ivins, "Notes on Mormon Polygamy," *Western Humanities Review* 10 (1956): 229–39. Ivins's interpretation is elaborated and qualified in James E. Smith and Philip R. Kunz, "Polygyny and Fertility in Nineteenth century America," *Population Studies* 30 (1976): 465–80. United States census figures for Utah Territory prior to 1890 show an approximately equal balance between men and women, always with a slightly higher number of men.

[12] Leonard J. Arrington, *Great Basin Kingdom: An Economic History of the Latter-day Saints, 1830–1900* (Cambridge, Mass.: Harvard University Press, 1958), p. 38. See also Dean L. May, "The Making of Saints: The Mormon Town as a Setting for the Study of Cultural Change," *Utah Historical Quarterly* 45 (1977): 75–92.

amy may well have contributed significantly to the long-range demands of centralized planning and the rapid establishment of a new religious and communal order.

II

Polygamy obviously required difficult renunciations and tended to undercut, though by no means to eliminate, emotional attachments based on romantic love. Yet polygamy also had certain positive features that gave it staying power. In a rather impressionistic survey of 110 plural marriages, the sociologist Kimball Young concluded that 53 percent were highly or reasonably successful, 25 percent were of moderate to doubtful success, and 23 percent were unsuccessful.[13] Other evidence, which will be indicated below, also suggests positive features that could be present in polygamous marriages. What were some of the possible compensatory aspects of plural marriage for women, and how did they adapt to the demands of the new arrangements? How did polygamy in some instances encourage women to develop self-reliance and independence?

The status advantages of being a plural wife have seldom been seriously considered. Non-Mormon critics of polygamy have almost invariably assumed that since they would have felt degraded under plural marriage, plural wives must also have felt degraded. Plausible though this might seem, little internal Mormon evidence supports such a view. Life certainly did hold special trials for plural wives, but at least until the 1880s, being a plural wife brought higher status through association with the most influential men and through a sense of serving as a religious and social model for others. First wives such as Jane Richards who married under monogamous expectations often had considerable difficulty in adjusting, but many plural wives had other reactions. In some cases, first wives actively encouraged a reluctant husband to take a plural wife so that they could both reach the highest state of exaltation in the afterlife or for other more pragmatic economic or personal considerations. Viewed as an honorable and desirable practice, plural marriage could give women a sense of pride and significance within the Mormon community.[14]

The almost cosmic importance attached to home and family life was a major factor determining woman's status in the Great Basin

[13] Kimball Young, *Isn't One Wife Enough?* (New York: Henry Holt, 1954), pp. 56–57.

[14] Both Kimball Young and James E. Hulett, Jr., stress the extraordinary range of personal reactions possible to polygamy. For additional evidence, see Quinn, "The Mormon Hierarchy," pp. 177–245.

region. Children were highly valued by Mormons. Like outside converts, children provided an essential work force to help in settling the new land and in building up an essentially agrarian economy in Utah. One polygamous wife emphasized the extreme importance that Mormons placed on childbearing and child rearing:

> Our children are considered stars in a mother's crown, and the more there are, if righteous, the more glory they will add to her and their father's eternal kingdom, for their parents on earth, if they continue righteous, will eventually become as Gods to reign in glory. Nothing but this, and a desire to please our Father in heaven, could tempt the majority of Mormon men or women either, to take upon themselves the burdens and responsibilities of plural marriage.[15]

In terms strikingly familiar to those used by their Victorian contemporaries, Mormons stressed the positive and vital social role that women could play in the family and, by extension, in the larger community, which in the Mormon case was generally coterminous with the family. As one observer has noted, "Polygamy seemed to introduce no outstanding change in how Mormon women viewed themselves in their home role; the family was often treated in the same sentimental tones used by those who lauded the monogamous family."[16]

The Mormon emphasis on the mother-child relationship served compensatory emotional functions for women whose husbands were often absent. Jane Richards, like many other plural wives, indicated that her primary emotional involvement was with her children, rather than with her husband. Similarly, Mrs. S. A. Cooks, who became a Mormon despite her aversion to polygamy, described how Heber C. Kimball's first wife, Vilate, had advised an unhappy plural wife that "her comfort must be wholly in her children; that she must lay aside wholly all interest or thought in what her husband was doing while he was away from her" and simply be as "pleased to see him when he came in as she was pleased to see any friend." In short, the woman was advised to maintain an emotional distance from her husband in order to avoid psychic hurt.

[15] Whitney, *Why We Practice Plural Marriage*, p. 53. Of course, children were stars in the crown of the monogamous mother as well. Although plural families of three or more wives appear to have had fewer children per wife than monogamous wives did on the average, the objective was not producing the largest number of children per wife but rather the largest total number of children in the families of the best men where, presumably, they would be reared under the most advantageous circumstances. See Ivins, "Notes on Mormon Polygamy," pp. 236–37; Quinn, "The Mormon Hierarchy," pp. 246–91; Burgess-Olson, "Early Utah Mormon Families," pp. 100–104; and Smith and Kunz, "Polygyny and Fertility," p. 471.

[16] Gail Casterline, "'In the Toils' or 'Onward for Zion': Images of the Mormon Woman, 1852–1890" (M.A. thesis, Utah State University, 1974), p. 71.

Vilate Kimball,
first wife of Heber C. Kimball.
USHS collections.

Mrs. Cooks concluded: "Mrs. Kimball interested herself very much in the welfare of other's wives and their children to see that there was plenty of homespun clothing etc. for all; and set a noble example to others situated as she was."[17]

The strong stress on ties of sisterhood between plural wives also served an important compensatory emotional function when the husband was absent. Informal female support networks and cooperation among women developed, especially during crisis periods such as those associated with childbirth, economic hardship, and bereavement. Mormon "sister-wives," as they were sometimes called, often literally were blood sisters. Of Vicky Burgess-Olson's sample, for instance, 31.2 percent of the plural marriages included at least one pair of sisters. Although such sororal polygamy was a departure from Old Testament standards and led to erroneous allegations that the Mormons practiced "incest," such arrangements made much practical sense. If two sisters were married to the same man, they could more easily adjust to each other in the marriage than total strangers could.[18]

[17] Mrs. S. A. Cooks, "Theatrical and Social Affairs in Utah" (Salt Lake City, 1884), pp. 5–6, in Bancroft Collection.

[18] Female support networks in nineteenth-century America are analyzed in Carroll Smith Rosenberg, "The Female World of Love and Ritual: Relations between Women in Nineteenth

The popular semi-novelistic American stereotype of the plural wife as living in a Mormon "harem" had almost no basis in fact. Far from secluding women from the world, polygamy and the cohesive Mormon village community with which it was associated could lead some women to participate actively in the larger society. The non-Mormon historian Gail Casterline has noted:

> As in New England colonial families, the Mormon wife seemed to move with relative ease and frequency between home, neighborhood, and church; the Mormon village plan of settlement allowed a variety of social contacts outside the immediate family. Wives were not cloistered or excluded from the larger society as in a harem, although husbands did seem to have a possessive attitude on the issue of their womenfolk associating with Gentiles.[19]

Women's independence was stimulated in a variety of ways by the social conditions of frontier Utah and by the practice of polygamy. With husbands frequently away on church missions, wives and their children tended to be thrown back on their own resources and on those of their immediate relatives and friends. Jane Richards said that her husband

> . . . was away so much she learned to live comfortably without him, as she would tell him to tease him sometimes; and even now he is away two thirds of the time as she is the only wife in Ogden, so that she often forgets when he is home, and has even sat down at meals forgetting to call him. She says she always feels very badly about it when it happens, but that he was more necessary to her in her early life.

Mrs. Bancroft added: "And yet she is a very devoted wife, and he is remarkably attentive to her. To see them together I would never imagine either had a thought but the other shared."[20]

Other accounts also stressed this same tendency of polygamy practice to encourage women's independence. After stating that "Plural marriage destroys the oneness of course" and that it "is a great trial of feelings," Mary Horne noted that the practice got her away from being "so bound and so united to her husband that she could do nothing without him." She became "freer and can do herself individually things she

Century America," *Signs: Journal of Women in Society and Culture* 1 (Autumn 1975): 1–29. A Mormon analysis from a similar perspective is Maureen Ursenbach Beecher, "Sisters, Sister Wives, and Sisters in the Faith: Support Systems among Nineteenth Century Mormon Women," paper presented at the Conference on the History of Women, Saint Paul, Minn., October 22, 1977. Also see Burgess-Olson, "Early Utah Mormon Families," pp. 87–90. Ivins, "Notes on Mormon Polygamy," p. 234, observes that of a sample of 1,642 polygamists, 10 percent married one or more pairs of sisters.

[19] Casterline, "Images of the Mormon Woman," p. 71.

[20] "Social Life in Utah," pp. 13–14.

never could have attempted before; and work out her individual character as separate from her husband."[21] Evidently in some cases women also were grateful for the possibility polygamy offered for freedom from male sexual demands; as Mary J. Tanner noted: "It is a physical blessing to weakly women."[22] And the feisty Martha Hughes Cannon, who was the first woman state senator in the United States and the fourth wife of a polygamist, argued that a plural wife was in a better position than a single wife: "If her husband has four wives, she had three weeks of freedom every single month."[23]

While this might be the kind of "freedom" that some wives would wish to be freed *from*, it does suggest how polygamy and the exigencies of life in the Great Basin region could force women into new roles and break down certain sex stereotypes, at least temporarily. In the absence of their husbands, women and their children ran farms and businesses. Some early census reports even went so far as to identify plural wives as "heads of households." Burgess-Olson's sample showed that in polygamous marriages, husbands and wives exercised approximately equal responsibilities in financial management, while in her monogomous sample, men held greater control. By the late nineteenth century a relatively large class of professional women, many of them plural wives, had developed in Utah. Women dominated the medical profession, for instance, and a sizeable number worked as teachers and writers.[24]

Brigham Young and other early church leaders recognized the necessity of making use of female talent in establishing and maintaining the group in the sometimes hostile environment of the Great Basin. Mormon leaders encouraged education for women from the very early

[21] Mrs. Joseph Horne, "Migration and Settlement of the Latter Day Saints" (Salt Lake City, 1884), pp. 34–35, in Bancroft Collection. Mary Isabella Horne was Relief Society president of the Salt Lake Stake and a prominent woman in her own right.

[22] Letter of Mrs. Mary J. Tanner, Provo, Utah, 1880, pp. 5–6, in Bancroft Collection. Casterline, "Images of the Mormon Woman," p. 103, discusses the argument of Mormon women that polygamy freed them from masculine demands and allowed for a healthy continence. It also made possible continence during pregnancy and lactation, as recommended by nineteenth-century medical theory, and therefore was seen as making for healthier, better-spaced babies.

[23] *San Francisco Examiner*, November 8, 1896, as quoted in Charles A. Cannon, "The Awesome Power of Sex: The Polemical Campaign against Mormon Polygamy," *Pacific Historical Review* 43 (1974): 76n. For accounts of this remarkable woman, see Jean Bickmore White, "Dr. Martha Hughes Cannon: Doctor, Wife, Legislator, Exile," in Burgess-Olson, ed., *Sister Saints*, pp. 383–97, and Barbara Hayward, "Teaching the Slavish Virtues: The Public Life of Martha Hughes Cannon," *Century 2: A Brigham Young University Student Journal* 2 (1978): 1–15.

[24] Burgess-Olson, "Early Utah Mormon Families," p. 135; Casterline, "Images of the Mormon Woman," p. 77; Keith Calvin Terry, "The Contribution of Medical Women during the First Fifty Years in Utah" (M.A. thesis, Brigham Young University, 1964); and Leonard J. Arrington, "Women as a Force in the History of Utah," *Utah Historical Quarterly* 38 (1970): 3–6.

settlement period, as indicated by the establishment of the University of Deseret as a coeducational institution in 1850. Women voted earlier in Utah than in any other state or territory in the United States, including Wyoming. And, somewhat ironically in view of the non-Mormon attacks on the degradation polygamy supposedly caused women, the efforts of Mormon women in the 1870s and 1880s to organize themselves to support plural marriage against external attacks served as a significant means of increasing their political awareness and involvement.[25]

One major forum for women's expression in the church was the Relief Society. Originally founded in 1842, the Relief Society was organized "under the priesthood after a pattern of the priesthood" to support a variety of activities, including the building of a temple, charitable work, and cultural betterment. During the troubled period that followed Joseph Smith's death, the Relief Society became largely inactive, but with the reestablishment of the society in the mid-1850s under the leadership of Eliza R. Snow, it went on to play an important role in Utah economic, social, and cultural life.[26]

Perhaps the most impressive achievement of the women of Utah in the late nineteenth century was the publication of the *Woman's Exponent*. Although it was not officially sponsored or financed by the church, this largely woman-managed, -supported, and -produced newspaper served as the major voice for Mormon women's concerns during its publication between 1872 and 1914. The *Exponent* was the second periodical expressly for women to appear in the trans–Mississippi West. A respectable and well-produced periodical by any standards, the *Exponent* spoke highly for the literacy and intelligence of its women contributors and designers. The wide-ranging historical and literary concerns of this publication were by no means limited to sectarian matters.[27]

[25] See Jill Mulvay Derr, "Woman's Place in Brigham Young's World," *BYU Studies* 18 (1978): 377–95, and Shauna Adix, "Education for Women: The Utah Legacy," *Boston University Journal of Education* 159 (August 1977): 38–49. Although Wyoming in 1869 was the first territory to pass a bill granting woman suffrage, women in Utah actually went to the polls in 1870 under a similar bill passed that year and cast their votes before women in Wyoming did. Articles on this topic include Thomas G. Alexander, "An Experiment in Progressive Legislation: The Granting of Woman Suffrage in Utah in 1870," *Utah Historical Quarterly* 38 (1970): 20–30; Beverly Beeton, "Woman Suffrage in Territorial Utah," *Utah Historical Quarterly* 46 (1978): 100–120; and T. A. Larson, "Woman Suffrage in Western America," *Utah Historical Quarterly* 38 (1970): 7–19. The campaign by Mormon women in support of polygamy is discussed in Casterline, "Images of the Mormon Woman," pp. 94–100.

[26] General Board of the Relief Society, *History of the Relief Society, 1842–1966* (Salt Lake City: General Board of the Relief Society, 1966), p. 18. Also see Leonard J. Arrington, "The Economic Role of Pioneer Mormon Women," *Western Humanities Review* 9 (1955): 145–64.

[27] Casterline, "Images of the Mormon Woman," pp. 83–94; Sherilyn Cox Bennion, "The *Woman's Exponent*: Forty-two Years of Speaking for Women," *Utah Historical Quarterly* 44

As suggested by its masthead slogan: "The Rights of the Women of Zion, The Rights of the Women of All Nations," the *Woman's Exponent* provided an important forum for the discussion of many problems of "woman's sphere." Expressing an almost feminist awareness at times, the *Exponent* devoted much attention to the universally inequitable position of women in politics, education, and the professions. Even marriage was not put forward as an absolute imperative for women. In the *Exponent*'s wide-ranging discussion of issues, only polygamy, then one of the key elements of Mormon self-definition as a group, failed to receive a critique. Overall, the *Woman's Exponent* portrayed Mormon women as individuals of character, intelligence, and high aspirations. It served an important identity-building function and helped to reinforce pride and unity among the women of the church.

As Casterline observed:

> The reinstitution of the ancient custom of polygamy may have in its own subtle ways served as a liberating force for women. This may have occurred by default, with restless or dissatisfied plural wives looking for places to direct their energies, or it may have occurred through the necessity of a wife's suporting her family. Some women may have welcomed polygamy as a great boon, as it decreased some of the demands and divided the duties of the wife role, allowing them more time to develop personal talents. By these quirks in its machinery, plural marriage did in some cases provide a working method for women to achieve independence from men.[28]

III

Despite certain positive or at least mitigating features such as those mentioned above, polygamy was obviously a more demanding way to organize marriage than monogamy. Even under the best of circumstances, developing and sustaining an optimal relationship among husband, wives, and children in polygamous families was difficult. How did Mormon families deal with the inevitable tensions that arose in plural marriages? Although the studies of James E. Hulett, Jr., Kimball Young, and Vicky Burgess-Olson reveal great differences in the ways conflict situations were managed in both monogamous and polygamous families, the general rule was to try to deal with problems within the home as much as possible.[29] As Jane Richards noted: "It is making confidants

(1976): 222–39; and Carol Cornwall Madsen, "'Remember the Women of Zion': A Study of the Editorial Content of the *Woman's Exponent*, A Mormon Woman's Journal" (M.A. thesis, University of Utah, 1977).

[28] Casterline, "Images of the Mormon Woman," pp. 80–81.

[29] Hulett, "The Mormon Polygamous Family," pp. 308–403; Young, *Isn't One Wife Enough?*, pp. 191–225; and Burgess-Olson, "Early Utah Mormon Families," pp. 117–19.

of other women in their domestic disturbances that has brought about most of the trouble in polygamy, and the less people gossip, the better off they are."[30] In the practice of polygamy, as in other aspects of social life in Utah, great stress was placed on unity and consensus, on the avoidance of public expressions of hostility. This emphasis may well help account for the impressive degree of external order and social harmony described by many of the more open-minded visitors to Utah in the nineteenth century.[31]

Even with good will and sincere effort, attempts to salvage a relationship could fail. In such cases the possibility of separation or divorce always remained. Jane Richards was quite frank in noting, for instance, that when her husband first talked with her in Illinois about the possibility of taking another wife, she told him that he should do what he felt he had to do and that "if she found they [she and the new wife] could not live without quarreling, she should leave him." This never became necessary for her, but she noted that others had taken such steps: "If a marriage is unhappy, the parties can go to any of the council and present their difficulties and are readily granted a divorce."[32]

How representative were Jane Richards's informal observations on nineteenth-century Mormon attitudes toward divorce? This topic has only recently begun to be investigated, but a few preliminary observations may be made. One initial point of reference is Utah territorial divorce policy. The Utah divorce law of February 4, 1852, was one of the most liberal in the country. For instance, a divorce could be granted not only to a person who "is a resident of the Territory" but also to a person who "wishes to become one." Presumably this proviso allowed the Mormon church flexibility in dealing rapidly with converts who had separated from an unbelieving spouse and who needed to be reintegrated as quickly as possible into the new Mormon society. In addition to the usual causes, a divorce could be granted to the plaintiff in cases in which the defendant was guilty of "absenting himself without reasonable cause for more than one year." If liberally applied, such a provision could be used to terminate unsatisfactory relationships in which missionaries were gone for extended periods of time. Finally, the territorial law contained an omnibus clause allowing divorce "when it shall be made to appear

[30] "Reminiscences of Mrs. F. D. Richards," p. 47.

[31] See especially J. W. Gunnison, *The Mormons* (Philadelphia, 1852), and Richard F. Burton, *City of the Saints* (London, 1861).

[32] "Social Life in Utah," p. 1, and "Reminiscences of Mrs. F. D. Richards," p. 55.

to the satisfaction of the court, that the parties cannot live in peace and union together, and that their welfare requires a separation."[33]

The Utah divorce law cannot necessarily be assumed to represent Mormon church policy, since marriage and divorce—particularly polygamous marriage and divorce, which were not directly recognized in territorial law—were handled primarily through church courts and procedures. Instead, the primary function of the divorce law probably was to provide maximum flexibility for Mormons in handling their own unorthodox arrangements. What, then, was the Mormon church's policy on divorce? The official stand was a highly complex one. In theory, divorce was strongly discouraged. Marriage was viewed in the light of eternity as a vital part of life that brought out the finest aspects of human relationships. Brigham Young and other early leaders repeatedly inveighed against divorce, particularly when requested by the man. Using rather salty language, Young could suggest, for example, that one man had made his bed and would have to lie in it. Declarations such as the following were typical: "It is not right for men to divorce their wives the way they do. I am determined that if men do not stop divorcing their wives, I will stop sealing."[34]

Yet, if men were discouraged from divorcing their wives, women were given remarkable freedom in seeking a divorce for themselves in unsatisfactory situations. Young himself once publicly offered to give a divorce to any of his wives who did not want to live with him any longer. He could declare that "he liked a woman to live with her husband as long as she could bear with him and if her life became too burdensome then leave and get a divorce." In an important sermon in the Salt Lake Tabernacle on October 8, 1861, Brigham Young further developed the argument about when a women could leave a man lawfully. He said that if a woman became alienated in her feelings and affections from her husband, then it was his duty to give her a bill of divorce and set her free. Men must not have sexual relations with their wives when they were thus alienated. Children born of such alienated unions were properly seen as "bastards," not the product of a full marriage relationship.[35]

[33] The law is printed in *Acts, Resolutions and Memorials, Passed at the Several Annual Sessions of the Legislative Assembly of the Territory of Utah* (Great Salt Lake City, 1855), pp. 162–64.

[34] Brigham Young's statements appear in Historian's Office Journal, 1858–1859 Book, p. 11 (December 15, 1858), and p. 15 (December 17, 1858), Archives Division, Historical Department, Church of Jesus Christ of Latter-day Saints, Salt Lake City, hereafter referred to as LDS Archives. These statements were called to my attention by D. Michael Quinn.

[35] See *Journal of Discourses*, 26 vols. (Liverpool, 1854–86), 4:55–56, and Brigham Young's Office Journal, 1858–1863, p. 300 (October 8, 1861), LDS Archives. The latter statement was

This line of argument is strikingly similar to the 1842 argument put out in Illinois in *The Peace Maker*, the first defense of polygamy ever printed under Mormon auspices. According to that pamphlet, whose authorship and significance have been hotly debated, the only "biblical" (i.e., legitimate) grounds for divorce was the alienation of a wife's affections from her husband. If a man became dissatisfied with his wife he could not legitimately divorce her if she remained loyal to him, since that would be an irresponsible shirking of family duties. Instead, his option in such a case was to take additional wives, while maintaining the first and her children. This approach is essentially the same as early Utah practice. Women had the primary initiative in determining when to terminate a relationship, while the husband could not easily divorce his wife if she were opposed. No stigma was attached to the remarriage of a divorced woman; indeed, such remarriage was normally assumed. Thus, in Utah, women could find through easy divorce and remarriage the opportunity for what amounted to a sort of de facto serial polygamy (though Mormon writings never spoke in such terms), while their husbands were allowed to take additional wives if they wished.[36]

The relationship of polygamy and divorce in early Utah may also be easier to understand as a result of the recent recovery of records of 1,645 divorces granted during the Brigham Young period (1847–77). Although these records have not yet been thoroughly analyzed, the bulk of the cases appear to have involved plural marriages. Since the entire population of Utah numbered only 86,786 in 1870 (with a high percentage of the population consisting of unmarried children and youths), the divorce rate might appear rather high. Support for such a conclusion is also suggested by D. Michael Quinn's listing of Mormon church leaders and their wives between 1832 and 1932. A simple analysis of his data shows that the 72 church leaders who practiced plural marriage had a total of 391 wives, with 54 divorces, 26 separations, and 1 annulment. For perspective, one should note that at least some of these divorces were those of apparently nonconjugal wives whose marital ties were only symbolic. The extent to which the divorce situation in Utah and

called to my attention by David J. Whittaker. A summary of Brigham Young's speech of October 8, 1861, is found in the entry for that date in James Beck's Notebook I, 1859–1865, LDS Archives. The original speech, recorded stenographically by G. D. Watt, is in LDS Archives and has been reproduced in an unauthorized transcription in Dennis R. Short, *For WoMen Only: The Lord's Law of Obedience* (Salt Lake City: Dennis R. Short, 1977), pp. 85–90.

[36] For a discussion of the pamphlet, its argument, and its significance, see Lawrence Foster, "A Little-known Defense of Polygamy from the Mormon Press in 1842," *Dialogue: A Journal of Mormon Thought* 9 (1974): 21–34.

surrounding areas of Mormon settlement differed from that of other frontier areas also needs to be investigated.[37]

To understand the significance of this data on divorce, it must be placed within the larger context of the development of plural marriage and other early Mormon social institutions. Plural marriage appears never to have become fully institutionalized during the relatively brief period when it was publicly practiced in Utah. Joseph Smith's revelatory mandate promulgating polygamy in 1843 had required that polygamy be introduced, but it did not specify exactly how it was to be practiced after it was introduced. Later Mormon leaders apparently also claimed no special inspiration on exactly how the system was to be regulated, except to continue to insist, as Joseph Smith had, that all plural marriages must be sanctioned and sealed by the central church authorities.

The wide variation in polygamy practice has been noted by scholars. James E. Hulett, Jr., one of the earliest serious students of Mormon polygamy, observed that he had "expected to find a variety of behavior but not so great a variety." No fully standardized patterns of handling the needs of polygamous families for things such as shelter, food, clothing, and amusement appear to have developed, although there were tendencies toward such standardization. For example, plural wives sometimes lived together under one roof, sometimes had separate houses adjoining each other, and sometimes lived in entirely different locations. Hulett argued that Mormon society of the period continued to remain basically monogamous in its norms and that "except for the broad outlines, the local culture provided no efficient and detailed techniques for control of the polygamous family; each family in a sense had to develop its own culture." Although Hulett's sample was primarily taken from the period of extreme stress in the late nineteenth century when polygamy was under heavy attack, scholars who have focused on the period when polygamy was more openly practiced have also found significant variation in the ways polygamous families were organized.[38]

[37] The existence and whereabouts of the divorce records, which have now been microfilmed, are reported in Eugene E. Campbell and Bruce L. Campbell, "Divorce among Mormon Polygamists: Extent and Explanations," *Utah Historical Quarterly* 46 (1978): 4–23. Ibid., p. 6, bases its figures on Quinn, "The Mormon Hierarchy," pp. 248–91. Quinn, pp. 154–56, provides information on some of Brigham Young's wives who were not publicly acknowledged and bore him no children.

[38] Hulett, "The Mormon Polygamous Family," pp. 11, 406, and Burgess-Olson, "Early Utah Mormon Families," pp. 59–68. Housing patterns of leaders ran the gamut from Brigham Young, second president of the church, who set up most of his wives and children in two large houses, to John Taylor, third president of the church, who eventually established all his wives in separate houses. For a discussion of Brigham Young's remarkable household, see Clarissa Young Spencer

The primary reason that polygamy never became fully standardized in Utah was the short period of time that it existed before the intense antipolygamy persecution of the late nineteenth century led the Mormon church to discontinue the practice. Had there been greater time for the new cultural patterns to develop free of external pressure, plural marriage probably would have continued to adapt itself to the changing conditions of the Great Basin region. Just how the new marriage practices would eventually have stabilized will now never be known, however. After the mainstream of the Mormon church broke decisively with polygamy practice at the turn of the century, a small number of dissidents did continue to practice polygamy, but the church as a whole moved on to find new ways of expressing its underlying family ideals through monogamous marriage. Today, somewhat paradoxically, Mormons are among the most "traditional" of any group in their attitudes toward family life and the role of women.[39]

IV

What is the significance of this extraordinary nineteenth-century Mormon experiment with plural marriage? Was the effort simply a freakish American sideshow, a rather unpleasant and unappealing aberration, or does it raise larger issues that are of concern today?

As the largest and best sustained attempt in nineteenth-century America to create an alternative to monogamous marriage and family life, Mormon polygamy does suggest larger issues worthy of further exploration. At the most basic level, investigations such as those of Ivins, Burgess-Olson, Smith and Kunz, and others are needed to show how monogamous and polygamous Mormon marriages in early Utah differed from each other. To what extent were the distinctive features of nineteenth-century Mormon family life due to the existence of polygamy and to what extent were they a product of the broader Mormon drive

and Mabel Harmer, *Brigham Young at Home* (Salt Lake City: Deseret News Press, 1947), especially pp. 15–80.

[39] For bibliographic introductions to the extensive literature on the political campaign against Mormon polygamy, see James B. Allen and Glen M. Leonard, *The Story of the Latter-day Saints* (Salt Lake City: Deseret Book Co., 1976), pp. 681–87, and Bitton, "Mormon Polygamy: A Review Article," pp. 106–11. The best book-length treatment is Gustive O. Larson, *The "Americanization" of Utah for Statehood* (San Marino, Calif.: Huntington Library, 1971). A convincing scholarly analysis of the persistence and recurrence of splinter Mormon polygamous groups since the Manifesto of 1890 remains to be written. A study of the relationship of such groups to the emotional and intellectual upheavals caused when the main body of Latter-day Saints gave up the practice of polygamy could shed much light on the development of modern Mormonism. For an analysis with implications for such an investigation, see Lawrence Foster, "From Frontier Activism to Neo-Victorian Domesticity: Mormon Women in the Nineteenth and Twentieth Centuries," *Journal of Mormon History* 6 (1979): 3–21.

for cultural and religious autonomy? How did the life experiences of monogamous wives differ from those of first wives or of subsequent wives in polygamous families?

A second area worthy of further investigation is a comparison of the experiences of Mormon plural wives with the experiences of other women on the frontier or in the larger Victorian society. Recent research by Maureen Ursenbach Beecher, for instance, suggests that at least in the economic sphere, Mormon women were largely indistinguishable from other women in the frontier West.[40] Similarly, Mormon women appear to have been remarkably closely in touch with general currents of thought and practice in Victorian society. At times, in fact, they seem to have been in advance of popular trends. In what ways were Mormon women in contact with the larger society, and what role did polygamy play in that contact?

Finally, Mormon polygamy of the nineteenth century raises comparative and cross-cultural questions of much significance for the present. The problems of women acting as heads of single-parent families, for example, bear much resemblance to the problems of women in some polygamous families. The issue of easy divorce and its effect on family life are also worthy of comparison. And, of course, the Mormon experience provides an American example of polygamy that could be compared with polygamy as it functions in non-Western societies today, as studied by anthropologists such as Remi Clignet.[41]

These and other questions may fruitfully be investigated by using the nineteenth-century Mormon experience as a reference point. Perry Miller could as easily have been speaking of the Mormons as of the New England Puritans when he wrote of their experiment as an "ideal laboratory": "It was relatively isolated, the people were comparatively homogenous and the forces of history played upon it in ways that can more satisfactorily be traced than in more complex societies. Here is an opportunity, as nearly perfect as the student is apt to find, for extracting certain generalizations about the relationship of thought or ideas to communal experience."[42] Scholars have only begun to make use of the rich Mormon experience to understand the nature and significance of women's varied experiences in nineteenth-century America.

[40] Maureen Ursenbach Beecher, "Women's Work on the Mormon Frontier," *Utah Historical Quarterly* 49 (1981): 276–90.

[41] Remi Clignet, *Many Wives, Many Powers: Authority and Power in Polygamous Families* (Evanston, Ill.: Northwestern University Press, 1970).

[42] Perry Miller, *The New England Mind: From Colony to Province* (Cambridge, Mass.: Harvard University Press, 1953), foreword.

SONIA S. SUNOO

Korean Women Pioneers of The Pacific Northwest

THE USUAL thought of pioneer women in the Pacific Northwest brings to mind women in long dresses and sunbonnets who crossed the Plains in covered wagons, or perhaps native American Indian women. But there were others at later times, like the first Korean women in the region. What were these later pioneers like, and why did they leave the security of their families and homes? When did they come, and what were their experiences?

The earliest group of Koreans emigrated to the Hawaiian sugar plantations as laborers between 1903 and 1905. Compared to other Asian groups, their numbers were small—only 7,226.[1] The next group came between 1910-1924, the period covering Japan's annexation of Korea and the signing of the Oriental Exclusion Act of 1924. From a total of 60 persons contacted by the author for the purpose of preparing a history of the early Korean immigrants in the United States, 32 were in this group: 10 men and 22 women. Six of the women stated that they had spent a major portion of their lives on farms in Oregon and Montana. Their stories are presented here; though they were few, these Korean women contributed constructively to the history of the Pacific Northwest.

Following Japan's annexation of Korea, anti-Japanese activities grew among Korean immigrants in Hawaii and the United States. This development was a grave concern to the Japanese, who decided to grant exit permits to young Korean women willing to go abroad under marriage contracts—a measure intended to calm political passions among overseas Koreans. Subsequently this decision to issue exit permits to Korean women resulted in over a thousand marriages between 1910 and 1924. Many came under the "picture bride" system, used also by Chinese and Japanese.[2]

1. For background, see Lee Houchins and Chang-su Houchins, "The Korean Experience in America, 1903-1924," *Pacific Historical Review*, XLIII (November 1974), 548-75.

2. *Ibid.* The "picture bride" system is described on pp. 559-60.

All six of the women whose experiences are described came as picture brides during the 1910-1924 period. Five were from Kyungsan-do (Kyongsan), in southern Korea, and the one who came from Pyongan-do (Pyonggang) in central Korea proved to be the only childless woman. The others gave birth to a total of 34 children. All the women were widowed, and in 1976 their average age was slightly more than 77 years.

In-Sook's Story

In-Sook is one example of a young girl who was adventurous and eager for change. When she was 14, she became very restless in her highly protected village and home environment. Even at 10 years she had yearned to leave home but knew it was forbidden at her age. She longed to discover the meaning of her scholarly older brother's comment that "Our young Korean women are content like frogs croaking deep down inside a well, knowing only that the heavens are high, without any concept of the breadth of society." Through the whispered grapevine, she heard of a couple in Pusan City who were engaged in making arrangements for young maidens interested in finding husbands in America. In-Sook had also heard that America was a land where the streets were paved with gold. So she dreamed of being married to a man in America, of an independent life offering her freedom, ease, and luxury—a dream she was determined to make come true before her 15th birthday.

She gathered as much information as she possibly could from other girls in the village whenever she was permitted to go to market with one of the family's servant girls. She found out precisely where to go and whom to see. Over and over she planned how to get away. Finally she managed to sneak away from her closely guarded home and get to the matchmaker Sonam, in Pusan.

At first In-Sook was bewildered by the hustle and bustle of the busy city, but soon mustered enough courage to find her way to Sonam to find out how she, too, could qualify for a husband in America. She was told: "First, you must have your picture taken." In-Sook had no idea how to go about that, so Sonam took her to be photographed. She was to return when notified that the men's photographs had arrived from America, and to pick a husband among them. In-Sook's heart thumped wildly at the enormity of her commitment, but she managed to sneak back to her home.

Some time later, she got word that the young men's photographs had arrived. She was beside herself with excitement, and filled with terror lest her family discover her doings. Once again she managed to sneak away undetected, reached her destination, and boldly pointed to the photo of the man she prefered. Sonam assured her that he would be receiving her photo and some information about her. Then if he found her satisfactory, he would send for her. In-Sook doesn't remember how she ever managed to regain her composure after she stole back into her room. She recalled that she fairly collapsed. Imagine! Choosing her own husband! She was only 15 years old.

All did not go smoothly and circumstances were such that the facts had to be revealed to her family. There were tears and loud wailing at the shocking news. In-Sook was accused of selling herself for prostitution, of having disgraced the family. It was tearfully impressed upon her that no member of their clan would ever be able to face the community or hold up their heads as long as they lived. In-Sook expected this reaction, and waited for the day when she would be released from this turmoil and be established in the world paved with gold and live in the security of her chosen husband. That dream sustained her through the months of daily mounting mental and physical revilement and condemnation.

One day, In-Sook received the bitter news that it would be a while before her chosen husband could send for her, "perhaps a couple of years." In-Sook knew for certain that her family would condemn her to "the lake of fire and brimstone" the moment they found out about the delay. In those days, it was believed that any girl with an ounce of decency would not have dared even to dream of the things that In-Sook had already done, and now her chosen man's inability to send for her would be equated to a breach of promise. In-Sook felt she could take no more abuse and humiliation from her own family, and so in deep desperation, the teenager committed another most brazen and unheard of action for a girl of her era. She secretly wrote to her prospective "father-in-law" that she was "ready and determined" to live with them. The anticipation of escaping to her "in-laws" occupied her thoughts and gave her the strength to bear the daily scoldings that grew more and more intense and harsh. One day, a servant announced the name of a guest. Her father-in-law came calling! Though she recognized his name and immediately knew his mission, her family was completely taken by surprise when she calmly appeared at the gate with her personal belongings neatly tied in a cloth bundle, and left with her father-in-law without so much as a goodbye.

Little did In-Sook know what was in store for her. She was to have joined her "husband" after three years, but her ailing father-in-law passed away just before the end of the third year, and because of the strict mourning custom of those feudalistic days, she as the eldest daughter-in-law, in the absence of the eldest son, was forced to remain and mourn the father-in-law for a minimum of three years. Her strict mother-in-law absolutely refused to release her from her traditional duties.

After six years of "marriage" in which In-Sook had only given her photograph and exchanged a few letters and had been a dutiful daughter-in-law, she was finally freed to join her "husband" at age 20. As the ship headed for the United States and sounded its deafening horn, In-Sook felt delicious relief when she pulled off the white mourning ribbon from her hair and cast it into the Pacific Ocean—the last reminder of her bondage to the traditional feudalistic society of Korea.

Her dream of a life of ease and luxury in a world paved with gold was completely shattered the moment she set foot in Seattle. Her husband immediately brought her to his sugar beet farm in Montana, her home for the next 20 years. She toiled and labored beside him whenever she found time between the births of their ten children and the household chores. Her tenth child was but a month old when her husband passed away. In-Sook's life has been exceptionally difficult, but it is shared in other ways with other courageous and strong women of her days. Today she is able to boast that she raised the ten children alone and "asked not for even one slice of stale bread from anyone."

Ok-Ja's Story

Ok-Ja had a burning desire to travel and study. She, too, could not bear to live under the yoke of the existing feudalistic society in Korea. She was 17 and the youngest of three children when she decided to leave home and go to Japan to see for herself "that other world" that the girls in the dormitory dared only to whisper about. Her father was a traditional conservative feudalist and told her that once she left, she was never to set foot in his home again. It was unheard of that a girl in her generation should step out of her home's gates once she reached the age of ten, and inconceivable that she should think of traveling to a foreign land. But Ok-Ja's mind was made up and she left her family and home forever in 1917.

While in Japan, she learned that she could get to America only as a picture bride. Ok-Ja was desperate and agreed; in her heart, she was only going to "borrow" someone's name to gain legitimate entry to America, and then pursue her own goal to study. When she arrived in Honolulu, she was immediately deported to Japan by the immigration authorities because of an eye condition that needed medical correction. She returned and was deported a second time, then detained for another three months at the immigration station until her eye disease was cleared. All the expenses incurred were being borne by her husband-to-be. Sensing her coolness towards him, he asked, "Do you wish to marry me or do you have other ideas?"

She answered, "If you wish marriage, I'll marry you."

He said, "Yes, I do wish marriage."

So they were married, but not happily. Together they had five children, but one day he packed and left. Ok-Ja never remarried, but was determined to raise the young ones and give them the education she had missed. She was a skilled seamstress, a talent which helped support her family until her sons were old enough to supplement her earnings. Meanwhile, they moved to a large city in California where she continued as a seamstress until she fell in love with Oregon while spending a vacation there. She found the natural beauty of the mountains and the ocean overwhelming. It was winter, and all the young farming families were enjoying a leisurely time together. Ok-Ja had missed the close fellowship of her own family, and was convinced that she had found a satisfactory substitute here. Now that her sons were old enough to help on a farm, they decided to leave the city and move to Oregon to farm—really a romantic venture in which they had no experience.

Their first year was the most difficult. Little did they know of the physical hardships involved or the expenses in even renting farm machinery. They had to learn from friends and hired hands. Ok-Ja recalled that she didn't know the meaning of work when she lived in Korea. The initial shock of arriving in Hawaii and having to struggle in dire poverty and hardship is still vivid in her memory. She recalls that her first stove was a tin can with a hold cut out for the pot, and her home was constructed of wooden slats which offered no privacy at night when the lights were on. "One advantage, though, of the loosely constructed house was that the tradewinds breezed freely across the room," Ok-Ja added with a soft laugh. And she asked, "Can you imagine men working 10 hours a day for 77 cents? Rice was $10 a sack, soy sauce $2.00 a gallon. Even with close management, there was barely enough for the family of seven to survive."

Life in Oregon was difficult, but gradually she was able to adapt herself to it and later leased land through her American-born son, eventually purchasing their farmland. Despite the fact that Ok-Ja's ambition to study in America didn't materialize, she did not wish to return to the Korea she had left or to visit the home from which she had been banished. The price of freedom was high, but she cherishes it and today she is a completely liberated woman accountable only to herself. She is content at having been able to travel and to have had experiences in "that other world."

Myong-Soon's Story

Myong-Soon is another picture bride who came to America when she was only 17. Her husband, 20 years old, farmed in Montana and thus was entitled to bring in a wife from Korea. Her decision to become a picture bride to a man the family had never met was cause for family friction and dissension, but her decision to marry and leave Korea was stronger than anyone's argument. She left to meet her husband in Seattle in December of 1914. A wedding reception was given to them by a group of 30 Koreans who were already residents there. Most of them were bachelors who were on vacation from the Alaskan canneries. They were not entitled by law to bring in wives as they only worked six months out of the year, and their jobs were not considered steady enough to support a wife.

Myong-Soon's husband had arrived in Honolulu as a young teenager and found working as a laborer on a sugar plantation unbearably humiliating and difficult. Upon the advice of a Chinese friend, he left the Islands with four other young men. Together they leased land in Montana and farmed. When Myong-Soon arrived, she found quite a Korean community there—about 400 people. During the planting and harvesting period, everyone was busily occupied. The mothers felt a need for a Korean language school but attempts to get one organized were unsuccessful; during the busy season even the children's help was needed on the farm. It was also difficult to secure teachers.

The Korean people yearned for and needed a feeling for unity in this strange environment. Although there already was a Korean National Association, not all the residents were included and there was divisiveness concerning the organization. The women eventually formed the Chinmock-hoe (Friendship Club). This group met socially to celebrate traditional holidays. During the long winter periods they mostly met at each other's homes. Half-a-dozen families and their bachelor workhands would easily make a group of 50 to 60, or even a hundred persons. Often the entire weekend would be spent together. The men would occupy themselves with card games, limiting the bets to 25 cents "to make the game more fun." The winner would give the group some kind of special treat. Myong-Soon remembers that the women used to make beer for the men until they felt it was too much work, and the men took to drinking stronger liquor. The women spent most of their time in the kitchen and enjoyed the company, including their cooking and eating. Usually the children were taken care of separately and they, too, had fun playing together. They all slept on the floor in one room. Myong-Soon says it is hard to believe that such a harmonious group had existed for years until a shooting incident brought it to an end.

Despite the full life Myong-Soon had on the Montana farm, she became terribly homesick for her aging mother in Korea. Her husband made arrangements for her to visit her with their five children. She was pregnant with a sixth child. Once there, Myong-Soon found it more and more difficult to leave her aged and ailing mother, and her visit was prolonged for three years.

Myong-Soon's friend wrote that her husband was in urgent need of her and that he wept and called the names of each of the children every night. She returned to find her husband had become a hopeless alcoholic, hiding bottles of liquor everywhere, and "more beast than human." At first, she did not realize that her husband was a sick man. She blamed only herself for his condition and did all in her power to appease him, and also to keep the family together as a unit. Myong-Soon sadly recalls the numerous times when her husband would drive into town for groceries, then would spend the rest of the day and night getting drunk in a saloon while vandals looted the truck-load of groceries, and how their children had gone hungry for days.

In a few years' time, their family increased to ten children but her husband's condition remained unchanged. Myong-Soon continued the farm work with the help of a hired hand until her husband died. Gradually, the sons entered the services; four of her daughters married until there were but three of the younger ones left on the farm. At this point, she had no alternative but to sell out. She moved to southern California where friends told her jobs on the farms were plentiful. She and the children labored until she could no longer work due to physical pain. But did she complain? Hardly. If she did, it was only because her arthritis prevented her from working.

What she regrets most is that the three years in Korea had such a negative effect upon her older children's education. In Korea they were put into classes with children several years younger than themselves because of a lack of the Korean language. In the United States, they were chronologically older than the rest of the children in their classes because of the loss suffered during their three years in Korea. At present, Myong-Soon is satisfied that all her ten children are either well married or gainfully employed.

Soon-Hi's Story

Soon-Hi came as a picture bride in 1916, also anticipating a "Golden World" in which she would live in luxury. However, she met with a life so shockingly different and wretched that she commented: "Even the life of a butcher in Korea would have been better!" (Butchers are considered to be the lowliest of workers and are looked upon with contempt.) Her father was a farmer in southern Korea. She was 18 when she came to America, and first met her husband in Seattle. After a series of short moves, they settled in Montana, and for 24 years raised vegetables and did trucking. The winters were hard and long, and she had seven children to raise. Soon-Hi's first two were sons and the last five were a consecutive row of daughters, but she says her husband was happy it was that way for he had always envied those of his friends who had sisters.

Soon-Hi's husband passed away while she was eight months pregnant with the last daughter, and the oldest son was 18 years old. She and her sons continued on the farm with the help of hired hands until her older son left to learn welding in an Oregon shipyard that was busy just before World War II. While there he convinced his mother that she should leave Montana for Oregon.

The following year Soon-Hi packed most of the family's worldly belongings into a truck which her older son drove. The children and the remainder of her belongings were put into a passenger car driven by a younger son. She remembers that they had been driving since dawn; the baby had been held for the entire trip, and everyone else was exhausted. It was 1941, shortly after Pearl Harbor, and there were many inspections along the way. When they stopped at a hotel, the manager refused them rooms fearing that they were Japanese. Soon-Hi was furious at his attitude, and in her broken English, sought the aid of a night policeman. The officer immediately honored the identification badge issued by the Korean National Association and ordered the hotel manager to put them up for the night. They occupied three rooms. In the morning, they encountered similar problems with service at a restaurant. Again, Soon-Hi appealed to an officer who ordered that these Koreans be served.

Life in Oregon was no less difficult than in Montana, though the winters were not as severe. Soon-Hi has vivid recollections of the chilly early mornings when they worked in the vegetable fields and the hot summer days of backbreaking labor picking strawberries. She is especially saddened by memories of how her sons struggled following their father's untimely death. Before going to school, they would have to get up before dawn to truck the vegetables to the markets; then go to a barber shop in town to change into their school clothes; then try to stay awake during the class hours. She recalls how she herself would get all bundled up at dawn to pick broccoli and hear the ice crackle under her heavy boots as she trudged between the rows. The broccoli was so cold and icy that it had to be thawed in the shed before it could be tied into bunches for marketing. With a sigh of relief she said, "Our one world of living was on the farm and our existence was just like that. We knew no other way."

Today she lives alone by choice and enjoys her freedom and independence, and the proximity to her children, friends and relatives.

Bokki's Story

In 1924 Bokki arrived in the United States as a picture bride. She insists that she enjoyed a life of ease. Did she really? Her case is different from any of the others interviewed in that her "Old Man," as she affectionately refers to her husband, traveled to Korea to marry his picture bride, then requested she remain with his aged parents for three years before joining him. After three years, she reminded him it was time that he come for her, which he eventually did. Moreover, he bought a first class passage ticket for her. He had heard that those holding first class passage tickets were rarely detained at the immigration office. For himself he purchased a third class ticket, as he knew he would have no problems with the immigration people. Ironically, when the ship arrived in Canada, all passengers were detained and examined. Bokki was among those quarantined in Seattle and was held for 23 days for medical reasons. Strong medication was impossible, she said, as she was in early pregnancy. She recalls her Old Man getting most impatient with the unanticipated delay that caused his "pocket cash" to dwindle away while he waited for her at the hotel and had to buy all his meals. He was also due back at his Montana farm.

Eventually they arrived at their destination. After nine years of farming, her Old Man had saved enough money to set up a corporation with four others. He worked in Chicago while she remained in Montana with their two children. The farming enterprise did not go too well and the corporation was dissolved.

Bokki's husband returned to Montana in order to move his family to Chicago. She took in the two bachelors who had been farming with her Old Man and treated them as members of the family during the winter. Bokki, in her calm and matter-of-fact way, explained: "There was room in the house; food enough to share; and we'd probably need them as farm hands in the spring." Though her Old Man owned a truck, he did not know how to drive, and the younger bachelor did. In the spring, one of the bachelors found employment with a restaurant, and the one who knew how to drive tossed the keys to the truck to Bokki's 19-year-old, having decided that he no longer wanted to work on the farm.

Since there was nothing that could prevent the men from leaving, Bokki took it all in stride and calmly set up a roadside stand. At first her Old Man scoffed at the idea, but eventually success was far beyond their expectations. Soon they set up a regular highway market. They were doing so well that it became necessary for their customers to put in advance orders for their vegetables. Even the retail produce markets were ordering directly from them. Bokki added: "They found our produce to be cleaner, fresher, and more attractive than the wholesalers'." Bokki and her Old Man bought out the vegetables from the neighboring farms to supplement their own produce, and continued in this fashion for nine years. Bokki's husband was 24 years her senior and he began to feel concern for her and their children should anything happen to him. In 1943 they left Chicago for Oregon in order to be near her widowed sister and her seven children.

At the ripe old age of "almost 93" Bokki's husband passed away in 1972. "He was never a burden to me—always so gentle and affectionate. Even in dying he slipped quietly away after a brief stay in the hospital. My life was easy and we always worked together from seven in the morning until midnight. Every night we sat together and my Old Man read from the Bible, then sang a verse of hymn, and prayed for all His goodness and blessings. That was my life with him."

Bong-Nim's Story

Bong-Nim came from Pyongyang as a picture bride when she was 19. Most of her married life was spent farming near Salem,

Oregon. She had not known the meaning of work until she joined her husband. Her dreams of going to school vanished when she found herself on the farm. She toiled side by side with her husband and did all the household chores and cooked all the meals for the farm help as well.

Their chief concern was over the labor shortage after the bombing of Pearl Harbor. Most of the able-bodied men had been drafted or had left the farm for more lucrative jobs in defense plants and cities. It was most frustrating at that time when their Filipino helpers took over the Japanese farms for practically nothing after the Japanese farmers were relocated. Bong-Nim and her husband were left with only one farm hand to do the work of 18 men! She said that was an experience so overwhelming that she'll never forget it.

After four more years, they finally retired. Bong-Nim recalls the good days when they were able to help many of the new immigrants, especially the Korean students, who were provided with jobs on their farm during the summer vacations. Since they had no children of their own, they also gave much financial and physical aid to their relatives and friends in need.

The experiences of these six Korean pioneer women of the Pacific Northwest are only a sample of what they and other Korean immigrants faced. There is no written history of the personal lives of these heroic women, and what has been presented has been obtained through taped interviews of the few who are still with us. The common struggles of all pioneer women in a new and hostile environment are present. There are similarities in their determined and courageous search for a better world in which to plant their roots and rear their families, and in their deeply felt need for freedom from injustices inflicted upon them.

The early Korean women who settled in the Pacific Northwest all came as picture brides, and all had romantic dreams of a life of luxury in a golden world of opportunities. Not one of them had such dreams realized. Rather, they met extremes of work, suffering and disappointment. For the most part, they were greeted by husbands who were from eight to 24 years older, and they found themselves immediately placed on primitive farms. What must have run through their young heads? The naive picture brides were but teenagers who had never experienced life outside of their own protected feudal society—young women who probably never saw a man other than their brothers; even they were separated before they reached puberty.

As a group, the Korean pioneer women of the Pacific Northwest were not only courageous and determined, but precocious. Early in their teens they felt and recognized the stifling effect of the traditional feudalistic society, and decided they could not tolerate such restriction of their basic human rights. They knew that drastic action would be their only salvation. They were more than romantic picture brides seeking a "Golden World"; basically, they were willing to stake everything to be liberated—marriage to a man they had never known, travel to an unknown region of the world and departure from everything that had been familiar to them.

An outstanding and admirable feature of the early Korean pioneer women is their deep loyalty as picture brides; they were true to the men they got to know only after meeting them for the first time in America. Their love of family and devotion to children is a heritage to be cherished. The Myong-Soons, Soon-His, In-Sooks and other Korean pioneer women courageously continued the farm life alone in order to rear and educate their children after the death of their husbands, teaching the children Koreanness as well as good citizenship. No known major crimes have ever been committed by their offspring. The ingenuity and the adaptability to sudden crisis as evidenced by Bokki are further strengths displayed. These women claim that their lives have indeed strengthened them. Granted that they had little other choice, throughout the interviews the message comes loud and clear that these young women were going to lay the foundations to create that better world they did not find; they were determined that their children would find themselves in a better world. Perhaps it was this ray of hope that sustained them through all their years of struggles and humiliations. The strengths and lessons we can draw through the experiences of the Korean women of the Pacific Northwest are indeed inspirational.

SONDRA R. HERMAN
De Anza College

Loving Courtship or the Marriage Market? The Ideal and Its Critics 1871–1911*

DURING THE LAST THREE DECADES OF THE 19TH CENTURY AND THE FIRST OF the 20th, American feminists generally avoided discussion of marital and sexual issues. Fearful of disgracing the movement with scandal, particularly after the Victoria Woodhull affair, and sharing the sexually repressive standards of the age, feminists increasingly turned their attention to the suffrage and the supposed benefits it would bring all of society.

Yet in these same decades of repression a debate *did* arise over marital questions. If the implications of sexuality could not be considered freely, neither could the subject of marriage be avoided. More women were going to work; more were seeking a college education, particularly after the 1890s. More couples were moving to the city. Defenders of traditional marriage promulgated the old ideals of female domesticity, submissiveness and sexual purity in the face of what they thought were some dangerous trends. Critics of American marriage found that male domination, female uselessness and economic dependency had distorted marital happiness. Both groups concentrated their attention on the processes of courtship, for here they perceived the sex roles they were either defending or challenging took on most obvious forms.

The debate centered on a peculiar question: Was American courtship a process of practical love-seeking or was it a marriage market? Since we have no evidence that American marriages were in fact marriages of convenience in the 1880s and 1890s any more than earlier, the critics' charge of

*A revised version of a paper presented at the meeting of the Organization of American Historians, Apr. 1972.

materialism seemed in large measure a weapon in the battle for female independence. The defense of courtship as love-seeking similarly was part of an effort to keep women at home in an age known for the restlessness of its females.

Both defenders and critics realized that their evaluation of marriage was connected to their evaluations of the whole social order. In general the defenders of traditional marriage implied that America offered opportunity enough for men and contentment for wives if they would only be supportive. The critics of American marriage, at least the five treated here: Edward Bellamy, Lester Frank Ward, Charlotte Perkins Gilman, Thorstein Veblen and Theodore Dreiser attacked traditional marriage as part of the general injustice of American society. Thus while the debate could not before 1910 take direct sexual terms, it took a social form—defense of or attack upon the social status quo.

The defenders of the status quo were most often Protestant, especially evangelical clergy, conservative women, and doctors who wrote books offering the most traditional marital advice. The critics were intellectuals who refused to acknowledge religious authority and who openly challenged the ideal of fixed sex roles contained in such works. Only toward the end of the era, after 1910 or so, did an actual rebellion against repressive notions of sexuality begin. The debate in the eighties and nineties, while occasionally hinting at discontent with sexual standards, focused on proper sex roles and on woman's economic dependency.

Writers of the marriage manuals frequently asserted that indissoluble matrimony was the foundation of the whole social order. It was a "duty binding upon all well-equipped people who cannot show some larger obligation that is inconsistent with this."[1] It was, first, essential to complete the humanity of each man and woman. The two sexes, more different from one another than alike, needed to enter a human trinity—man, woman, child, so that each could become more truly a self. Celibacy not only meant incompletion, it threatened a sinful life, especially for men. Marriage was essential, secondly, to fulfill the social obligation of parenthood.[2] Sex was an expression of love but essential for reproduction only.

[1]Delos S. Wilcox, *Ethical Marriage: A Discussion of the Relation of Sex from the Standpoint of Social Duty* (Ann Arbor: Wood-Allen, 1900), p. 10; see also John L. Brandt, *Marriage and the Home* (Chicago: Laird & Lee, 1892), pp. 21–22, 57.

[2]Caroline Corbin, *A Woman's Philosophy of Love* (Boston: Lee, Shepard, 1893), p. 13; Minot Judson Savage, *Man, Woman, and Child* (Boston: George Ellis, 1884), pp. 64, 136–37; George McLean, *The Curtain Lifted: Hidden Secrets Revealed* (Chicago: Lewis, 1887), pp. 165–67; James Reed, *Man and Woman: Equal but Unlike* (Boston: Nichols & Noyes, 1870), *passim;* Samuel R. Wells, *Wedlock* (New York: S. R. Wells, 1871), pp. 24–25; William H. Holcombe, *The Sexes Here and Hereafter* (Philadelphia: Lippincott, 1869), p. 166; and George H. Napheys, M.D., *The Physical Life of Woman* (Philadelphia: David McKay, 1888), pp. 57–58.

Like the Puritan clergy generations earlier, the marital advisers of the late 19th century assumed that it was completely within the partners' capabilities to make or unmake their marriage. Marital happiness became a duty to be performed not only for the husband and wife's own benefit, but for the sake of the children and society.

Critics of American marriage, on the other hand, believed that marital happiness was deeply influenced by social conditions outside of marriage. They implied by the term "marriage market" that materialistic motives were necessarily present in most marriage choices. Young ladies presented themselves as merchandise for eager young men to marry. The girls, being dependent, had to do so in order to survive. Secondly, the term "market" suggested a terrible impersonality in the exchange of love for support. The harshness of the business world was invading the home itself. Home was no longer a refuge from the cold world, but rather its extension. To correct these conditions, the critics argued, a new social ethic was needed—more independence for women, more freedom to marry outside of one's class, more freedom to reject marriage altogether.

The audience for these strictures was an urban middle class who may have found marital choice freer and more difficult than ever before.[3] The sheer population of neighborhoods, the increasing opportunities for men and women to meet at work, made it virtually impossible for parents to know all the eligibles from whom a son or daughter would make a choice. Some resource had to replace the valuable gossip of the small town. The marriage advice books flowed into the gap. Some of these works, particularly those of doctors promising postnuptial sexual advice, as well as advice as to marital choice, were quite popular. *The Physical Life of Woman* by Dr. George Napheys sold 150,000 copies in its original 1869 edition and was reprinted in 1888. Others appeared to be collections of sermons circulating little further than the clergyman's parish, but clerical works sometimes ran to later editions as well.[4]

[3]The author is indebted to Prof. Samuel Haber of the University of California, Berkeley for this observation and for pointing out that the very existence of many choices may have popularized the phrase "marriage market."

[4]Napheys, *Physical Life*, preface, p. vii. Other doctor works include Henry Hanchett, *Sexual Health* (New York: Charles Harlburt, 1887); Henry Guernsey, *Plain Talks on Avoided Subjects* (Philadelphia: F. A. Davis, 1882); and H. S. Pomeroy, *The Ethics of Marriage* (New York: Funk & Wagnalls, 1888), commended as an anti-birth-control work in Brevard Sinclair, *The Crowning Sin of the Age* (Boston: H. L. Hastings, 1892), p. 15, and in *Journal of the American Medical Association*, 2 (1888), 309–11. Clerical works or limited edition collections of sermons used as brides' books include: S. D. & Mary Kilgore Gordon, *Quiet Talks on Home Ideals* (New York: Fleming Revell, 1909); Robert F. Horton, *On the Art of Living Together* (New York: Dodd Mead, 1896); and F. B. Meyer, *Lovers Always* (New York: Fleming Revell, 1899). Examples of second editions in marital guidebooks are: Wells, *Wedlock* (c. 1869, 1871 ed.); Mrs. E. B. Duffy, *The Relations of the Sexes* (New York: M. L. Holbrook, c. 1876, 1889 ed.); and James R. Miller, D.D., *The Wedded Life* (Presbyterian Board of Publication of Philadelphia, c. 1886, 1894 ed.).

The marital advice books attempted to erect barriers against changing values. They cautioned against neglect of the church and against extravagant, worldly women. They upheld static definitions of role, relating these to the protection of the American home from declining moral standards. The major responsibility for creating a moral society, by building the foundations at home, lay with the wife. Unlike the critics, the nuptial guides viewed woman as relatively influential because they valued her role as moral guardian. Home was to provide a haven of tenderness in the cold world, and woman, by nature more emotional than man, was the source of that warmth. Her husband's success and therefore the economic well-being of the family, her children's character, and therefore the moral future of the republic, depended critically upon her patient strength. She, more than anyone else, upheld the ideals of sexual purity and family devotion.[5]

Given such conditions the ministers and doctors wrote fairly uniform descriptions of the good wife, and they castigated behavior that did not conform with their ideals. Men were advised to seek both character and performance in a wife. The prospective bride had to show she could become a thrifty, meticulous housekeeper. But prevalent female extravagance in dress made this requirement difficult to meet. The writers feared that idle wives who ministered only to their husbands' sensual needs were on the increase. Their families were not large enough to occupy them.[6] A wife, secondly, had to identify her future with her husband's completely, listen sympathetically to his plans and comfort him when they failed. And sympathy was needed by the husband. "I counsel the wife to remember in what a severe and terrific battle of life her husband is engaged," preached the Reverend DeWitt Talmage in 1886.[7] The independent college graduate

[5]Brandt, *Marriage and Home*, pp. 51, 210; Wells, *Wedlock*, p. 173; and Savage, *Man, Woman, and Child*, pp. 33, 37. The same assumptions cropped up in personal correspondence concerning courtships and betrothal. For example, when Austin Baldwin of Savannah became engaged to Louise Maynard of Massachusetts, Baldwin's brother wrote: "It is . . . not the man that makes his wife, but the wife that more often makes the man and I hope my new sister will prove a good advisor and helpmate. . . . If Lou is as good as she is handsome . . . you may date your success in life from the time you were married." T. J. Baldwin to A. Baldwin, May 15, 1872, Baldwin Family Papers, Schlesinger Archives, Radcliffe College. Similarly, Emily Blackwell wrote her sister Elizabeth: "I felt a great deal depended upon the woman he married. If she had been a girl whose ambition was for society . . . it would have spoiled him. Frances will be ambitious for him to choose a worthwhile career, and will support him in any serious work. I believe she will be an excellent influence in his life." Nov. 6, 1904, Blackwell Family Papers, Schlesinger Archives, Radcliffe College.

[6]Cortland Myers, *The Lost Wedding Ring* (New York: Funk & Wagnalls, 1902), pp. 100–2; Elizabeth Blackwell, *Counsel to Parents on the Moral Education of their Children* (New York: Brentano, 1883), p. 75; Charles Frederick Goss, *Husband, Wife and Home* (Philadelphia: Vir Publishing, 1905), pp. 33–34; Brandt, *Marriage*, pp. 70–71, 81–85, 85–88; and Miller, *Wedded Life*, pp. 65–67.

[7]*The Marriage Ring: A Series of Discourses in Brooklyn Tabernacle* (New York: Funk & Wagnalls, 1886), p. 62. See also Savage, *Man, Woman, and Child*, p. 38; and Miller, *Wedded Life*, pp. 20–21.

more in evidence in the next decade evidently had to learn this submissive, traditional role. Above all, the wife had to be trustworthy, which meant both that she could be her husband's confidante, and that she was sexually pure. No hint of sexual interest should ever touch her manner or conversation. Her reputation, more than her husband's, became the reputation of the entire family. For the most part, the marriage advisers believed that this requirement would be easier to meet than the others. Most asserted or implied that woman's sexual drive was much weaker than man's, although some doctors emphasized that it was not absent altogether.[8] The fulfillment of these feminine ideals—tenderness, chastity, homemaking skills—came with maternity. The requirements of motherhood pervaded the advice literature which was often anti-birth-control literature as well.

Similarly, the prospective husband was regarded in his role as paterfamilias. If a woman's duty was to comfort and serve, a man's was to love and protect. Assuming that man's "animal nature" was much stronger than woman's (yet necessary for the propagation of the race), the doctors and clergy issued stern warnings about the average masculine morality. Women might exercise a softening influence, but they could never reform fundamental wrongs. The girls should avoid men much older than themselves, licentious men, drunkards, gamblers, cold-hearted tyrants, those whose work took them away from home frequently and "despisers of the Christian religion."[9] Of all the postnuptial failings, man's overabsorption in his business and in the attractions of hotel life were believed most common. Marriage advisers warned wives to stay neat and attractive.[10]

The wife's choice of a husband (but interestingly, not the husband's choice of a wife) was deemed fatal. Presumably the clergy's opposition to divorce would equalize the seriousness of choosing. It did not. Some writers acknowledged that a man could always escape to his club, but a woman had no escape. Was this an implied acknowledgment of the double standard? It is hard to say, for other advisers cautioned men against "lascivious actions which are a drain upon the whole system" and asked them to come to the marriage bed as virginal as their brides.[11]

One factor that increased the dangers of poor choice by the woman, her economic dependence, a major concern of the critics, was rarely mentioned by the guides. They may have taken the husband's provider role for

[8]Napheys, *Physical Life*, pp. 96, 102; Hanchett, *Sexual Health*, p. 37; Brandt, *Marriage*, pp. 80–81.

[9]Talmage, *Marriage Ring*, pp. 24–25, 28–29; M. Salmonsen, *From the Marriage License Window* (Chicago: John Anderson, 1887), pp. 100, 103; Savage, *Man, Woman, and Child*, pp. 13–21; and Miller, *Wedded Life*, pp. 31–39, 42–49, 52–54 detail the masculine ideal.

[10]Goss, *Husband, Wife, Home*, pp. 50, 66–68; and Talmage, *Marriage Ring*, pp. 62–64, 66.

[11]Guernsey, *Plain Talks*, p. 36; Brandt, *Marriage*, p. 111; Talmage, *Marriage Ring*, pp. 24–25; Myers, *Wedding Ring*, p. 84.

granted. Yet this avoidance of any discussion of money appeared to be related to the estimate of woman's weaker sex drive. When a man sought a girl he was following a powerful instinct. The girl, on the other hand, could judge a suitor more rationally.[12] Thus the clergymen avoided any statement implying ecclesiastical approval of women coldly evaluating prospective husbands in terms of earning power.

Having presented marriage as a sacred institution, and home as a refuge from the world's commercialism, the advisers could hardly allow commercial standards of judgment about marriage. To have acknowledged materialistic motives on a general scale would have been to admit precisely what the critics implied—the obligation to Christianize the social order, an order that had so corrupted matrimony. The marital advisers acted on the contrary assumption: the traditional marital relationship was pure. It did not need woman's economic independence to cure its materialism. On the contrary, when marriage was delayed in order to acquire the money for a respectable "establishment," it was the sinner's corruption not society's. Woman's worship of fashion, man's "absurd social ambition," were individual evils, not symptoms of social disorder.[13]

After cautioning their readers about financial extravagance, the preachers presumed to tell lovers how to judge love. Their intentions were clear—to discourage matches of sudden passion and deceptive romance. Sudden falling in love they believed a myth fostered by too much novel reading. A marriage based upon passion was as dangerous as an overcalculating one. Instead, men and women should grow in love, that is, make reasonable and practical choices based upon secure knowledge of one another's characters. Above all, it was important to distinguish passion from love. The first was easily satiated and carnal, but love was at least partially spiritual and entirely unselfish, reasonable and tender. It could pass certain tests which lovers should make before they married. It had the constancy required for indissoluble marriage and responsible parenthood.[14] By emphasizing love's reasonableness, the nuptial counselors gave hardly any hint of the mysterious process by which men and women discovered their mutuality, nor of the possibilities of tragic choices. If one was sensible,

[12] Frank N. Hagar, *The American Family: A Sociological Problem* (New York: University Publishing Soc., 1905), pp. 44–45.

[13] McLean, *Curtain Lifted*, pp. 161–62; Kate Gannett Wells, "Why More Men Do Not Marry," *North American Review*, 165 (July 1897), 124; George Shinn, *Friendly Talks About Marriage* (Boston: Jos. Knight, c. 1897), pp. 56–57.

[14] Anthony W. Thorald, *On Marriage* (New York: Dodd Mead, 1896), p. 16; Pomeroy, *Ethics of Marriage*, p. 51; Sarah Grand, "Marriage Questions in Fiction; The Standpoint of a Typical Modern Woman," *Living Age*, 217 (Apr. 1898), 73; Corbin, *Woman's Philosophy*, pp. 38–41; Mary Wood-Allen, M.D., *What a Young Woman Ought to Know* (Philadelphia: Vir Publishing, 1893), pp. 200–4; Brandt, *Marriage*, pp. 41–42; and Wells, *Wedlock*, pp. 51–52.

the endings were happy. Love, true tender love, was essential to marriage. It was the greatest guarantee of marital and social stability.

Frequently, objections to romantic love merged with objections to marriage across class lines. Harmonious differences in temperament were considered healthy, but not marked differences in status. Cultural incompatibility would destroy such a marriage which might have been motivated by social climbing on the part of the poorer partner. As they feared such class mixtures (and certainly racial and religious mixtures were beyond the pale), so the advisers feared the drowning of an educated, Protestant, older American population in a sea of ignorant, immigrant poor. The urging of practical, compatible marriages sometimes took place in this context.[15]

In spite of the pleas for class compatibility, the Cinderella ideal remained as popular as ever in short stories and plays. Writers usually sought a formula to prove that Cinderella was not a fortune-hunter. In one of the longest-run productions on the New York stage and on the road, Steel McKaye's *Hazel Kirke* (1880), the lovely, submissive miller's daughter fell in love with a titled Englishman, quite unaware of his position. When the inevitable obstacles arose in the form of previously promised marriages of convenience, the hero sacrificed fortune and position to keep Hazel—thereby equalizing their social positions. In most short stories, however, in the women's mass circulation magazines of the first decade of the 20th century, the fortune, hidden during courtship, was revealed and kept at the end as a reward for true love.[16] Although the fiction upheld the Cinderella ideal and the marriage manuals cautioned against it, together they constituted a success literature. Both declared that chastity and virtuous courtship would win rewards—both spiritual and practical.

It is difficult to know just how seriously readers took the advice to marry within their class. Some middle-class families, perhaps chiefly those in the upper middle class, found that neighborhood acquaintance alone was not enough to maintain the lines. When Ethel Sturgis, daughter of the President of the Chicago, Northwestern Bank, became engaged to Francis Dummer, Vice President of the same bank in 1888, she wrote, "I almost tremble to think if love and duty had not coincided, what a struggle our two lives would have been." Ethel's father and Francis' sister had, however, pointed out the

[15]Wilcox, *Ethical Marriage*, pp. 25-28; Thorold, *Marriage*, p. 25; Myers, *Wedding Ring*, p. 7; McLean, *Curtain Lifted*, pp. 161-62; Shinn, *Friendly Talks About Marriage*, pp. 31-32; Hagar, *American Family*, pp. 73-74; Sinclair, *Crowning Sin*, pp. 13, 17-18; and Wells, *Wedlock*, pp. 45, 47, 49.

[16]Arthur Hobson Quinn, ed., *Representative American Plays* (New York: Appleton-Century, 1930) pp. 435-36, 439-40, 451, 453, 457, 465, 470; and Donald Makosky, "The Portrayal of Women in Wide Circulation Magazine Short Stories, 1905-1955," Diss. University of Pennsylvania 1966, pp. 139-40.

virtues of Ethel and Francis to each other.[17] In contrast, when a niece of the famous Doctors Blackwell, Elizabeth and Emily, pursued a young farmer in Martha's Vineyard, the family placed every possible obstacle in the way of this "common" marriage. In spite of their niece's behavior the aunts assumed a lower moral standard went with the lower class.[18]

In this assumption, the Blackwells reflected an undercurrent of anxiety that ran through some of the purity campaigns of the 1890s and 1900s. The purity crusaders were a diverse group of women, doctors, prohibitionists, later progressives who launched a series of campaigns against prostitution and lax age-of-consent laws. They certainly wanted a single standard of sexual morality—but not only for both sexes, but for all classes as well. They resented society's "heartless discriminations in favor of the rich and the influential."[19] As Benjamin Flower, editor of the *Arena*, a vehicle for the movement, observed: "The immorality and degradation of rapid life among the mushroom aristocracy is matched by the grosser manifestations of immorality in the social cellar . . . [and] the great middle class absorbs the contagion from above and below."[20]

The purity advocates warned against social climbing in marriage, believing that ambitious marriages increased extramarital temptations. Avaricious parents led innocent sons and daughters into such marriages while corrupt churchmen ignored the social consequences.[21] As Nathan G. Hale has pointed out, the purity campaigns for sex education, their muckraking against white slavery, the whole drive for a break in the wall of silence they claimed protected vice, had very different results than they envisioned. The campaigns undermined the old repressive standards.[22] In spite of this contrast in effects, the campaigners upheld the same values as those of the churchmen whose protection of virtue they considered so inadequate. Their ideals remained: chastity, female domesticity, rational love and class compatibility.

[17] Ethel Sturgis to Francis Dummer, June 11, 1888. See also Dummer to Sturgis, Mar. 6, 1888; Mrs. Sturgis to F. Dummer, June 12, 1888; Katherine Dummer to Ethel Sturgis, June 12, 1888; and Katherine Dummer to Francis Dummer, June 12, 1888, Sturgis-Dummer Family Papers, Schlesinger Archives, Radcliffe College.

[18] Emily Blackwell to Elizabeth Blackwell, Aug. 13, 1881, Oct. 2, 1881. For a contrasting view within the family see Alice Stone Blackwell to Kitty Barry Blackwell, July 23, 1882, Aug. 27, 1882, Blackwell Family Papers, Schlesinger Archives, Radcliffe College. The marriage took place nevertheless.

[19] J. Bellanger, "Sexual Purity and the Double Standard," *Arena*, 11 (Feb. 1895), 373.

[20] "Social Conditions as Feeders of Immorality," *Arena*, 11 (Feb. 1895), 410-11. For the way in which the purity movement shifted from an ecclesiastical to a scientific rationale for its positions, see David J. Pivar, "The New Abolitionism: The Quest for Social Purity, 1876-1900," Diss. University of Pennsylvania 1965.

[21] Helen Gardiner, *Is This Your Son My Lord?* (Boston: Arena Publishing, 1890), *passim*.

[22] *Freud and the Americans: The Beginnings of Psychoanalysis in the United States, 1876-1917* (New York: Oxford Univ. Press, 1971), pp. 252-54.

The purity campaigners' emphasis upon the social injustices which they thought imperiled the home was one indication among many that Americans were, by the 1880s, more receptive to more radical analyses of their society. No stronger weapon existed in the radical armory than the charge that even the home, the supposed haven of warmth and love, was corrupted by materialism. All of the five critics: Bellamy, Ward, Gilman, Veblen and Dreiser had reason to challenge the alliance of church, home and business. Edward Bellamy and Lester Frank Ward, for example, had early experienced crises of belief which left them with the idea that the church's repressive sexual standards and the guilt they induced were themselves a source of evil.[23] Economic insecurity had scarred the childhoods of Charlotte Perkins Gilman and Theodore Dreiser. Mrs. Gilman's father had deserted a family of four, offering only occasional financial, and no psychological support. Charlotte, seeing her mother's submissive suffering, could never play the traditional female role. Theodore Dreiser's family disintegrated altogether under the combined disasters of his father's obsessive moralism and frequent unemployment. Thorstein Veblen appeared to have learned his skepticism early by contrasting the life of the hard-working Norwegian American farmers with that of the Yankee middle class. By the time he attended Carleton College, he was a full-fledged rebel.[24] In various ways, then, these critics' early experiences led them to reject the conservative success ethos that shaped traditional marital standards.

Edward Bellamy, whose utopian novel, *Looking Backward* (1888) appealed both to intellectuals and to the general public as a solution to the ills of monopolistic capitalism, did not revolt against his own closely knit family, but first against the remnants of Calvinist dogma which crushed the individual conscience. The destructive sense of guilt, the haunting Nemesis of an evil fate, he considered more psychologically damaging than any evil deed. By the 1870s his vaguely transcendental Religion of Solidarity replaced the old religion and provided the philosophical ground of his utopia, being at once impersonal and social.[25]

[23]Joseph Schiffman, "Editor's Introduction," *Edward Bellamy: Selected Writings on Religion and Society* (New York: Liberal Arts Press, 1955), pp. xii–iii; Bellamy, *Dr. Heidenhoff's Process* (New York: c. 1880, Ams. Press, 1969), pp. 119–20, 138–39; Ward, "Revealed Religion and Human Progress," from *Iconoclast*, 1 (Nov. 1, 1870); *Glimpses of the Cosmos* (New York: Putnam, 1918), 1: 91–95; and "The Social Evil," *Iconoclast*, 2 (Aug. 1871), *Glimpses*, 1: 238–41.

[24]Carl N. Degler, "Introduction to the Torchbook Edition," Gilman, *Woman and Economics* (New York: Harper & Row, 1966), pp. ix–x; Robert H. Elias, *Theodore Dreiser, Apostle of Nature* (Ithaca: Cornell Univ. Press, 1970), pp. 6, 11–13; and Henry Steele Commager, *The American Mind: An Interpretation of American Thought and Character Since the 1880's* (New Haven: Yale Univ. Press, 1959), pp. 238–39.

[25]"The Religion of Solidarity" (1874) in Schiffman, *Bellamy. Religion and Society*, pp. 15–17; Arthur E. Morgan, *Edward Bellamy* (New York: Columbia Univ. Press, 1955), p. 138.

While he was in his twenties, in the midst of this religious crisis, Bellamy *had* entertained profound doubts about marriage. Avoiding it himself, he argued that marriage became the grave of the creative man who had to prostitute his talents in order to support dependents. In an unpublished novel, *Eliot Carson,* he toyed with the monastic solution for artists. This could hardly answer for all of society. Bellamy himself finally found it unsatisfactory and married late in his thirties.[26] Yet the question remained: How could men have love and a home without the imprisoning economic dependency of women?

Only when Bellamy turned from his fiction of individual psychological transformation to his utopia of revolutionary social transformation did he find the answer. In *Looking Backward,* the hero Julian awoke in the year 2000 to find a society in which both men and women worked for the state until their forties, and all received state support throughout their lifetimes. Men had the delights of domesticity without its restrictive burdens; women, having simpler homes (and with much of the traditional domestic labor performed publicly), had the interest of working in the world. The price, unfortunately, was considerable regimentation, but Bellamy did not think this an obstacle.[27] Society was rid of inhumane poverty and inequality.

The economic equality of the year 2000 utterly destroyed the marriage market. Men and women married for love alone; there could be no other reasons. Class distinctions in marriage were gone as were the classes themselves. Bellamy believed that such a free marriage system had tremendous genetic implications: "For the first time in human history, the principle of sexual selection with the tendency to preserve and transmit the better types of the race . . . has unhindered operation. The necessity of poverty, the need of having a home, no longer tempt women to accept as fathers of their children men whom they can neither love nor respect. . . . The gifts of the person, mind, and disposition . . . are sure of transmission to posterity."[28]

Thus did Bellamy affirm one of the strongest values of the radical critics of American marriage—the goal of an improved future generation. This goal, which was also implicit in the marital guidebooks' concern for proper parenthood, took a different form in the critics' analysis. They thought about the development of future generations more in post-Darwinian terms. Bellamy had even for a time entertained the idea of stirpiculture.[29] The

[26]Sylvia E. Bowman, *The Year 2000: A Critical Biography of Edward Bellamy* (New York: Bookman Associates, 1959), pp. 69–70, 279; and Morgan, *Edward Bellamy,* p. 55.

[27]*New Nation,* I (Mar. 14, 1891), 110; (Apr. 4, 1891), 159.

[28]*Looking Backward 2000–1887* (New York: Random House, n.d.), p. 218.

[29]"Stirpiculture," *Springfield Daily Union* (Oct. 2, 1875), p. 4. The term, used by John

guides believed that a marriage system which preserved class divisions, and in which the educated produced more children than the poor and uneducated, promised the best future. The critics believed that a class society, and a society of economically dependent women, harmed the future generation. They valued instead what Veblen called the parental bent—concern not just for one's own children, but for all children and for their future.

Bellamy relied upon "nationalism" to destroy the marriage market and he claimed it would end such accompanying evils as female triviality, hypocrisy (induced by 19th century courtship) and the double standard. This last reflected sexual economics more than sexual morality. It protected the purity of dependent married women at a horrible cost in prostitution. Since true ethical behavior could originate only with free choice, and since neither prostitutes nor chaste women were free, true sexual morality could begin only when women were economically independent of men. Such free women could frankly confess their love to men. No longer compelled to please the average man, in order to catch a husband, each woman could develop her own interests and talents. Women would no longer pass on their "mental and moral slavery" to their offspring.[30]

In thus simplifying the problem in economic terms, Bellamy was deferring to the popular, sexually repressive opinion of his day. His brother Charles had offered in a utopian novel, *An Experiment in Marriage* (1889), solutions Edward eschewed—virtually complete communal living, easy divorce and frequent remarriage. Only this system preserved the freshness of love.[31] With his brother's ideals of frank courtship and female equality Edward agreed. But divorce he could not endorse publicly, and he certainly had reservations about the sensuality favored in *An Experiment in Marriage.* Under "nationalism" he suggested the sexual drive would be not more intense but more diffuse, "like light that passes through a prism . . . refracted into many shades and hues."[32] In place of the free divorce system he created in the story "To Whom This May Come" a society of mind readers who recognized their true loves at once (vitiating the need for

---

Humphrey Noyes of the Oneida Community and briefly practiced there, meant arranged marriages to bring out the genetic strengths of the partners—the breeding of children. At the same time Bellamy was supporting "common-sense" in marriage which he occasionally identified with "like marrying like" in terms somewhat similar to those of the guides. He thought that marked class differences were accompanied by cultural differences, but he did not raise the objections of fortune hunting, etc. See "Literary Notices," *Springfield Daily Union* (Jan. 30, 1875), p. 6; and (Feb. 6, 1875), p. 6. *Looking Backward* then meant a considerable change in outlook.

[30] *Equality*, 10th ed. (New York: Appleton, 1909), pp. 135–38, 140–41.

[31] *An Experiment in Marriage: A Romance* (Albany: Albany Book, 1889), pp. 17, 24–25, 96–102, 116–17.

[32] *New Nation*, I (1891), 298.

sensual experimentation). And these mind readers' unions were, of course, more spiritual than passionate, affirming the Bellamy ideal of love—moderate rapture. Since men would not have to support women in the socialist state, intense passion would not be needed to induce marriage. As family relationships declined in intensity, everyone would be "a thousand-fold more than now occupied with nature and the next steps of the race."[33]

Like Bellamy, Lester Frank Ward and Charlotte Perkins Gilman attacked the exaggerated sexual differentiation of lives in late 19th century America. While Ward deplored sexual repression, Mrs. Gilman, who had paid the high price of nervous depression, divorce and separation from her daughter to attain autonomy, felt that American marriages *over-emphasized* sensuality. She was never able to accept the freer standards of the war years. In the early seventies Ward launched attacks upon the church, whose doctrines of female submission and indissoluble marriage he held directly responsible for prostitution.[34] Yet he left off his attack as he turned his attention to evolutionary theory and only took up the defense of freer sexual expression in 1903. In the 1890s then both Ward and Gilman criticized American marriage in the only "acceptable" way it could be criticized—by challenging traditional notions of the female role.

Both asserted that female inferiority was not inherent, but developed in the processes of the marriage market. Both extended the discussion to include a naturalistic consideration of the mate-selection process. Ward outlined a woman-centered theory of evolution indicating how the female of the species had abandoned an initially superior status. In all subhuman species, he noted, it was the female, not the male, who transmitted the characteristics of the race. She selected the males with whom to mate. Eventually, however, the females began to select not only the strongest, but the most intelligent mates. At that point, just as primitive man evolved, a crucial transformation took place. The men perceived that it was easier to seize females for mating than to contest for their favors with stronger males, allowing the female to choose the victor. This seizure and rape process, male-dominated mate selection, was the germ of marriage. And men continued to dominate the marriage market until modern times.[35]

Charlotte Perkins Gilman added that this male domination of the market

[33] *The Blindman's World and Other Stories* (New York: Garrett, 1968), pp. 405–6, 408–9; papers B 2-7-10,11 quoted in Arthur E. Morgan, *The Philosophy of Edward Bellamy* (New York: Kings Crown, 1945), pp. 76–77. Bellamy's distrust of passion came early and remained with him; see Morgan, *Bellamy* (biography), p. 81.

[34] "Revealed Religion and Human Progress" and "The Social Evil."

[35] "Our Better Halves," *Forum*, 6 (Nov. 1888), 266–75; Speech Before the Six O'Clock Club, May 24, 1888, *Glimpses*, 4: 129; and *Dynamic Sociology* (New York: Appleton, 1883), 1: 617, 648.

bred a race of frail, backward women. Men chose such women for wives, so the smarter, stronger ones did not reproduce their own kind. But there was an even more crucial reason for female inferiority. Once man had conquered woman and enslaved her, she could no longer hunt for her own food, or provide for her own young as female animals did. Man stood between woman and the challenging environment of the economic world. Women, thus, developed largely through their relationships with men. They developed those traits needed to catch a husband: conformity, flirtatiousness, sexual exaggeration and passivity.[36] Marriageable women, as much as prostitutes, were utterly dependent upon men and in essence sold themselves. "When we confront this fact boldly . . . in the open market of vice, we are sick with horror. When we see the same economic relation made permanent, established by law . . . sanctified by religion, covered with flowers and accumulated sentiment, we think it innocent, lovely, and right. The transient trade we think evil, the bargain for life we think good."[37]

Both Ward and Gilman saw signs, however, that the age of the marriage market was passing. As societies became more complex and more highly civilized, the most fastidious individuals, Ward believed, had difficulty choosing a mate, and tended to decline marriage altogether. This, and the burden of economically unproductive women, made the goal of one indissoluble marriage for each impossible of realization.[38]

Ward asserted that by the end of the 19th century male-dominated selection was fortunately declining. If men continued to select women for their frail, ephemeral beauty, the race would eventually be extinct. But modern men were selecting women for their mental and moral strengths as well as for beauty. By this process they happily increased female influence. More and more *mutual* selection took place. Ward identified this mutual selection with romantic love. Unlike most nuptial guides, he cherished and celebrated romance as not only beautiful for individuals, but beneficial for society. It was the highest form of man's noblest natural instinct—sexual love. When men and women fell in love, they advanced both the race and the civilization. By choosing mates of contrasting temperament and build, they acted out of a natural wisdom to produce well-balanced offspring. Thus the only sound eugenics was obedience to the law of love.[39] Ward, arguing in

[36] *Our Androcentric Culture or the Man-Made World*, as serialized in *Forerunner*, 1 (Nov. 1909), 23-25; *Women and Economics*, pp. 61-63, 86-88.

[37] *Women and Economics*, pp. 63-64.

[38] *Dynamic Sociology*, 1: 624-26.

[39] *Pure Sociology* (New York: Macmillan, 1903), pp. 381, 384, 398-99. In spite of Ward's appreciation for the importance of the sexual drive, Harriet Stanton Blatch thought he underestimated female sexuality, and even the "pretty clear physiological aim" of those mothers whom the world thought mercenary in pushing their daughters into the marriage market. Blatch to Ward, June 31, 1903, Sept. 2, 1903, Ward Collection, Brown University.

evolutionary terms, was using a powerful weapon against "practical" marriage advice.

Moreover, romantic love aided civilization just because it rarely ran smooth. For each couple it meant working, struggling, long denial. Out of this yearning struggle came man's deepest inspirations to create in the arts and sciences. And the struggle, unstable in itself, ended in fulfillment, with the onset of calm conjugal love. Society's standards, therefore, should not be sexually repressive. Love was a "higher law" that should prevail over social conventions. Free divorce should be allowed so that marriages contracted out of unromantic motives, loveless, practical marriages could be ended for the sake of romance and the next generation.[40] This combination of romantic idealism and evolutionary science constituted Ward's plea for greater sexual freedom.

Mrs. Gilman was distinctly less enthusiastic about sexual freedom, although she too wanted love unshackled from economic marriage. Her own experiences, her early allegiance to Bellamy's socialism, led her to emphasize the collective life of modern society which she wished women to enter. In her famous *Women and Economics* (1898) she demonstrated that the individualism of the marital relation contradicted and distorted economic relations which tended to collectivity as industries modernized. Man's selfishness for "the sake of the family" was no more reasonable in a cooperative world than woman's isolation at home or overspecialization as to sex. The traditional roles had to and would decay for the world's benefit. Already a complex economy was drawing women out of the home, ending their alienation from creative labor. Primitive household labor was becoming obsolete. Woman's very restlessness in the domestic role indicated a new social consciousness.[41]

Woman's economic independence would not threaten marriage itself, but would end the male-dominated marriage market. Marriage would no longer be a "sexuo-economic" relationship. Women would choose husbands, sublimating immediate sexual attractiveness to the demands of "right parentage." At the same time, female influence would counteract the aggressive tendencies of the man-made world with the values of "peaceful, helpful interservice." A new social environment, reinforcing industrial efficiency, would prevail, making the egalitarian changes in the marriage relationship permanent.[42]

Although he was less hopeful than Mrs. Gilman, Thorstein Veblen made

[40] *Pure Sociology*, p. 398 n.; pp. 401–3.

[41] *Woman and Economics*, pp. 105–7, 143, 154–57, 160; see also "All the World to Her," *Independent*, 55 (July 9, 1903), 1614 for the effects of woman receiving the world through her husband, and her overconcentration upon him.

[42] "Man Made World," *Forerunner*, 1 (Dec. 1910), 22–24; (Dec. 1909), 14.

a very similar identification between the peaceful primitive matriarchy of the past and a possible future industrial republic. Like Ward and Gilman he looked backward in order to criticize the present and reconstruct the future. His anthropological economics was so implicitly subversive that readers could only regard their own mores as vestiges of barbarism. In all the Veblenian lexicon the most barbaric institution of all was the patriarchal marriage.

The patriarchy originated when primitive tribes acquired an excess of goods and encountered hostile tribes. Seizing the conquered tribes' goods and women, they eventually made war a way of life. In the transformation into a barbaric society, private ownership, slavery and patriarchal marriage originated. Because only wives and slaves worked, labor was judged irksome. The patriarch displayed his wives as possessions, and he owned the products of their labor. Riches and status came together. "The ownership and control of women is gratifying evidence of prowess and high standing."[43]

When Veblen extended this argument into a work both popular and scholarly, *The Theory of the Leisure Class* (1899), he forged a weapon of considerable power against traditional sex roles. For in stating that the middle-class wife functioned only to display luxury and idleness as proof of her husband's social standing, he touched an area as sensitive with the conservative preachers as with the radical critics. America's traditional values could not encompass idleness or uselessness and Veblen knew this. Moreover, he answered a hopeful strain of the 1890s by stating that in spite of the interference of barbaric capitalism, the processes of modern technology would destroy the patriarchal marriage and allow a reemergence of "the most ancient habits of thought of the race."[44]

Veblen's economics implied goals very similar to those of Bellamy's utopia, Gilman's feminist analysis and Ward's naturalistic sociology. All viewed marriage as an institution distorted by late 19th century capitalistic culture. In its distorted form, in its competitive materialism, it was an impediment to a cooperative future. While the writers of marriage manuals viewed marriage as a sacred absolute, the critics thought it had the tinges of a modern slavery. Nevertheless, they too suggested an ideal marriage at the end of evolutionary change—a relationship personal yet more responsive to community needs, romantic because freed from the man's one-sided economic dominance and responsibilities. In place of the guides' values—home,

[43]"The Barbarian Status of Women," *American Journal of Sociology*, 4 (Jan. 1899), 510; see also pp. 503-4 and "The Beginnings of Ownership" (Nov. 1898), pp. 364-65.

[44]"Barbarian Status," p. 514. For Veblen's discussion of feminine beauty and dress in this regard see *The Theory of the Leisure Class* (New York: Modern Library, 1934), pp. 146-48, 179-82.

purity, social order—they cherished woman's economic independence, creative and cooperative labor, romantic love and the parental bent. They grounded these values in a naturalistic Weltanschauung rather than in a traditionally Protestant one.

Only when the repressive sexual ethic met a direct challenge, however, would the revolt against the older morality be launched. Of course, changing behavior itself was such a challenge. But ideologically the challenge, out of a naturalistic framework, was issued by a "new man" with no loyalty to the older, small-town America, to its code or its optimism. Theodore Dreiser confronted the sexual code by depicting directly its everyday violations. His first two novels, *Sister Carrie* (1900) and *Jennie Gerhardt* (1911) grew out of his sister's experiences with the civilized morality. In those works, as in his others, Dreiser painted Americans as they actually stood—unprotected in the lonely urban world. His newspaper experience had told him a great deal about the city's real values in contrast to the small-town pieties.[45] But Dreiser's first lessons began at home.

After witnessing repeated contradictions between the standard 19th century moral conventions and his sisters' escape from poverty through illicit affairs, between his father's gloomy prudery and the life of pleasure his brother, songwriter Paul Dresser, led, Theodore compounded his own naturalistic religion to replace his father's Catholicism. He came to believe that sexual love, infused with the love of natural beauty, was *the* experience initiating men and women into nature's truth. Change was the law of life, and any static institutions or ideals of respectability had to be cast aside if they stood in the way of sheer survival.[46]

In *Sister Carrie* the heroine adapted to the urban world, first by a simple, hardly considered abandonment of virginity, then by a determined struggle and finally by developing into an actress. In choosing to become Drouet's mistress, rather than remain a cold, poorly paid, worn factory-hand, Carrie was taking the first step toward survival and success, rather than toward the traditional downfall and ruin. Her second lover, Hurstwood, destroyed himself not by stealing money or committing adultery, but in a futile effort to retain his middle-class respectability.[47] Carrie knew how to fight; Hurstwood gave up. That was all. Their sexual behavior brought neither

[45] Dreiser, *Dawn* (New York: Liveright, 1931), pp. 173, 264; *A Book About Myself* (London: Constable, 1939), pp. 65-67, 70, 480, 488-89; Malcolm Cowley, "Sister Carrie Her Fall and Rise," *The Stature of Theodore Dreiser*, eds. Alfred Kazin and Charles Shapiro (Bloomington: Indiana Univ. Press, 1965), p. 174.

[46] Maxwell Geismar, *Rebels and Ancestors: The American Novel, 1890-1915* (Boston: Houghton Mifflin, 1953), p. 291; John McAleer, *Theodore Dreiser: An Introduction and an Interpretation* (New York: Holt, Rinehart & Winston, 1968), pp. 34-35.

[47] *Sister Carrie* (New York: New American Library, 1961), pp. 56, 61-62, 75-76, 84-88, 258, 267, 270-72, 315, 330-31, 421-22, 462.

punishment nor reward. That was what was most devastating about Dreiser's portraits—his refusal to pass any condemning judgments. Carrie trading her body outside of marriage appeared not a whit more materialistic than Hurstwood's wife trading within marriage, and offering her daughter Jessica in the marriage market.

In *Jennie Gerhardt* (1911) Dreiser drew the contrast between "the grasping legality of established matrimony" and the free flow of love most clearly. Jennie was that most ancient of literary heroines, the woman in love. Full of passionate tenderness, she seemed at one with nature itself. Lester Kane, her lover, heir to a manufacturing fortune, shared a passionate communion with Jennie. But he knew he need never marry her. She was a lower-class girl and marriage was a very practical arrangement. He had hoped to escape it altogether. When business interests and his family dictated otherwise, Kane left Jennie to marry an attractive, rich widow with whom he shared social and intellectual interests. Thus Dreiser portrayed man in the natural world of feeling, a world of great depth, and yet bound to the world of convention, if unable to pay the price of defiance. The conventional world upheld that static institution—marriage—and reversed the natural value of passionate love. That was reason enough for Dreiser's contempt for convention. Jennie, alone, having lost social acceptance, her love and her child, triumphed by sheer affirmation of natural love.[48]

By the time Dreiser wrote this defiance of the marriage market, the age of new sexual standards was beginning. *Jennie Gerhardt* was a critical and popular success. Although his subsequent struggle with *The Genius* (1915) indicated that Comstockery did not die all at once, the tide had turned. Perhaps for this very reason the revolt of the 1880s and 1890s seemed excessive to the new age. Dreiser's attack upon marriage, and especially upon the class divisions marriage upheld, was not repeated, although studies confirmed that Americans continued to marry those of similar wealth and status.[49] To the postwar generation there would be something anachronistic about Gilman's feminism, although American women had not achieved anything approaching her ideal of economic independence.

Above all, the critics' implicit association between marital discontent and the inequalities of late 19th century society seemed too radical for the war and postwar generations. Did social institutions require a thoroughgoing

[48] *Jennie Gerhardt: A Novel* (New York: Harper, 1911), pp. 18, 128, 130, 215, 238, 313, 317, 322.

[49] August Hollingshead, "Cultural Factors in Selection of Marriage Mates," in Marvin Sussman, ed., *Sourcebook in Marriage and the Family* (Cambridge: Riverside Press, 1955), pp. 43-50; and Richard Centers, "Occupational Endogamy in Marital Selection," ibid., pp. 56-61.

transformation for men and women to enjoy a healthier, franker relationship? In the age of Freud the younger generation doubted it. The double standard was withering, but women were receptive to a new ideology of domesticity. Yet the radicals of the 1880s and 1890s *did* connect social transformation with true freedom for romantic love. The sexually repressive standards of Gilman and Bellamy were distinctly Victorian. But in their attacks upon the home, upon women's economic dependency and upon exaggerated sexual differentiation of roles, the critics appear to speak more to our own generation than they did to the generations that directly succeeded them.[50]

[50]The author would like to thank all of the following individuals for helpful comments on an earlier version of this paper although none should be associated with the positions I have taken in it: Carl N. Degler, Samuel Haber, Anne Sherrill, Carroll Smith-Rosenberg, Warren I. Susman.

WOMEN AND MIGRATION
Autonomous Female Migrants to Chicago, 1880-1930

JOANNE MEYEROWITZ
University of Cincinnati

On a cold Saturday morning in the spring of 1916, an eighteen-year-old white woman arrived in Chicago from Joliet, Illinois. Her aunt had bought her a railroad ticket, given her one dollar, and told her to find a job in the city.[1] Over a year later, in the summer of 1917, a fifteen-year-old black woman wrote to Chicago from New Orleans:

> I wont to come there and work i have ben looking for work here for three month and cand find any . . . the only help i have is my mother . . . and she have four children young then me . . . and she have such a hard time tell she is willing for me to go.[2]

In the late nineteenth and early twentieth centuries, thousands of women migrated to Chicago autonomously. That is, they did not move with families or relatives; instead, they came alone and boarded or lodged in the city. The largest group of autonomous female migrants were young, unmarried women who came to Chicago from villages, towns, and cities as well as from rural regions.[3] They included native-born white women who migrated from the Northeast and increasingly from Chicago's midwestern hinterlands, and black women who migrated from Kentucky, Tennessee, Missouri, and, increasingly in the twentieth century, from the Deep South. In addition, some foreign-born women migrated alone to Chicago, especially Scandinavian, Polish, Canadian, and Irish women.[4]

While the exact numbers of autonomous female migrants to Chicago are lost to us, the number of boarders and lodgers in the city offers a rough approximation. In 1900, over 22,000 women, or over one-fifth of the Chicago female labor force, boarded or lodged apart from family and relatives.[5] (These figures exclude domestic servants, many of whom were autonomous migrants living in the homes of their employers.) The Chicago figures reflect national trends. In 1900, nineteen percent of the nonservant urban female labor force boarded or lodged apart from family. The results of a number of surveys conducted in Chicago and other cities between 1880 and 1925 suggest that the number of female boarders and lodgers grew about as rapidly as the number of jobs for women increased, ranging roughly between one-fifth and one-sixth of the nonservant female labor force.[6]

The large-scale migration of women is not a new discovery for historians and demographers. In fact, for at least a century now, social scientists have suggested that, in some historical contexts, more women migrated than men. In 1885, E. G. Ravenstein wrote in his well-known laws of migration: "Females are more migratory than males."[7] In the one hundred years since Ravenstein first set out this dictum, numerous demographers, geographers, sociologists, and anthropologists have reiterated his findings. In early twentieth-century France and recently in Latin America, the Caribbean, the Philippines and other parts of Asia, women predominated in certain streams of internal migration, especially in shorter distance migrations from country to city.[8] In the nineteenth- and early twentieth-century United States as well, historians and sociologists have suggested that more women migrated to cities than did men. We find evidence of female-dominated migrations among young, native-born whites in New England in the 1830s, among free blacks in the antebellum and postwar South, among nineteenth-century Irish immigrants, and among the sons and daughters of farmers in Iowa, Minnesota, Illinois, Michigan, Kentucky, and New York in the late nineteenth and early twentieth centuries.[9] In a national study of the farm population in 1920, the U.S. Bureau of the Census concluded: "The farmer's daughter is more likely to leave the farm and go to the city than is the farmer's son."[10]

Despite this evidence of large-scale female migration to cities, few American historians have investigated autonomous female migration in any detail.[11] Much of the historical literature on American migration and geographic mobility focuses primarily on the migration of men or on the migration of families and kin networks.[12] Many studies assume either that women migrated to cities by association only, joining or following male relatives who searched for urban work, or that the migration of women differed little in motive and outcome from the migration of men.

Granted, the quantitative dimensions of autonomous female migration are particularly elusive. We have few records of internal migration. Furthermore, we cannot accurately determine female persistence rates in the city because women changed their names after marriage. Nevertheless, a wide range of nonquantitative sources makes possible a preliminary investigation of the motives for female migration and the experiences of autonomous female migrants in the city.

Why did women migrate to Chicago? The most obvious reason and the reason most often cited by historians is the need for work. According to many demographers as well, the primary "push" for migration during industrialization was economic hardship at home and the primary "pull" was the availability of work in the city.[13] Especially in working-class, tenant farm, and small farm families, the income of the father often did not suffice to support the entire family. In the eighteenth century, many daughters contributed to the economic well-being of their families by sewing, baking, spinning, and performing other domestic chores. By the end of the nineteenth century, factory production had replaced much of this home manufacture. An unemployed daughter who lived at home drew on the family resources for food, clothing, and shelter, and offered little in return. For example, a black woman, seventeen years old, wrote to the black newspaper *The Chicago Defender* from Alexandria, Louisiana. She hoped to migrate to Chicago:

> I have a mother and father my father do all he can for me but it is so hard. A child with any respect about herself or hisself wouldn't like to see there mother and father work so hard and earn nothing. I feel it my duty to help.[14]

In short, unless she worked for wages, a daughter burdened her family. Accordingly, by 1890, forty percent of all single women in the United States worked for wages.[15] By 1930, over half had joined the paid labor force.[16]

Some women migrated after death, divorce, or desertion disrupted the family economy. In some cases, the death of a primary breadwinner, a relatively common occurrence, threw women wholly on their own resources. Orphans and widows who did not live in large cities often migrated in search of work.[17] In some fatherless families, daughters came to support their mothers or their siblings. Mary Kenney, later a labor leader, supported her invalid, widowed mother. She moved to Chicago in the late nineteenth century when she lost her job in a bindery in Hannibal, Missouri. "I was told there was plenty of business in Chicago," she wrote later. "If I could not get work in a bindery, I'd work at anything, even at washing dishes in a hotel."[18] A smaller group of women migrated when desertion or divorce removed their customary male source of support.[19]

While some women migrated when their families could not support them, other women migrated when their families would not support them. In some cases, daughters left home when parents or guardians chose to terminate their economic obligations. In one such case, a woman from a troubled home in a city in Indiana migrated to Chicago. Her mother was dead; her father drank and gambled; her stepmother disliked her. When she was seventeen, "her father refused to clothe her and in an awful fit of anger swore that he would do nothing more for her."[20] In times of need, other adult daughters returned to their parents' homes only to find their parents unwilling to care for them. When her husband died in 1916, Philiminia P., a twenty-two-year-old black woman, returned to her parents' home in Colorado. "They treated me so rotten," she said, "I come back [to Chicago]. . . . My family put me and my three brothers out. . . . I couldn't live there."[21] The family economy did not always provide adult daughters with cushions in times of crisis.

Other women had jobs or economic support at home but came to Chicago in search of better-paying or more rewarding work. Black women (and men) from the South expected to find higher-paying jobs and less overt employment discrimination in northern cities. One black woman from New Orleans wrote: "I read and hear daly of the great chance that a colored parson has in Chicago of making a living with all the privileg that the whites have."[22] Other women who desired careers sometimes came to the city with hopes of finding greater opportunities for upward mobility. One white office worker, for example, left a dead-end job in her home town when a friend told her of better opportunities in Chicago.[23] Another woman ran away from her home to pursue a career on the stage.[24] Like men, these women saw the city, especially an expanding city like Chicago, as a place of opportunity.

At first glance, then, it appears that women migrated, as men did, in search of work: they came from families that could not or would not support them, and they came with high ambition to pursue careers. A closer observation, however, reveals that women had, in addition, specifically "female" reasons for migrating.

For one, the distinctive features of the female labor market often governed migrations. That is, the structure of the female labor market compelled many women who needed work to go to a large city like Chicago to find it. Aside from a limited number of positions as servants and a handful of jobs as teachers, job-seeking women found few occupations open to them in rural areas and small towns. As one student of migration wrote in 1924:

> Fewer women than men are needed on needed on the farm. One woman, ordinarily, does the work of the family. . . . Not only are fewer women needed, but the occupations open to them in the country are fewer. Practically the only alternatives to marriage for country girls are teaching school and leaving home to go to the city.[25]

Similarly, some smaller industrial cities had few job openings for women. In cities like Gary, Indiana, and Youngstown, Ohio, where traditionally male heavy industries such as steel predominated, jobs for women were scarce.[26]

In several large northern cities, however, the demand for female workers skyrocketed in the late nineteenth and early twentieth centuries. From 1870 to 1930, the female labor force in Chicago grew from 18,300 to 407,600, or by over 2,000 percent.[27] The rate of increase of the female labor force in Chicago was over four times as great as the rate of increase of the female labor force for the nation as a whole. These figures reflect more general urban trends. In 1900, twenty-three percent of adult women in larger cities worked in the wage labor force; only eighteen percent worked for wages in the rest of the nation.[28] By 1920, the gap had widened. Thirty-three percent of adult women worked for wages in larger cities while only twenty-one percent worked for wages in smaller cities, towns, and rural areas.[29] In both years, this rural-urban gap in jobs per capita was larger for women (more than twice as large) than it was for men.[30] Given the dearth of wage work for women outside of large cities and the plethora of jobs within them, it is not surprising that women sometimes migrated to cities in greater numbers than men. Stated simply, the geography of the female labor market differed from the geography of the male labor market.

Still, the search for employment and the structure of the labor market do not explain fully why many women left their homes. In the personal accounts of migrants and in the case records of social investigators, other explanations appear with frequency. Several of these explanations point to noneconomic female concerns. It is impossible to quantify these motives, and it is equally difficult to assign priorities when women listed several different reasons for leaving home. Nonetheless, the existence of these additional motives points to a private side of the female migration experience often neglected by demographers and historians.[31]

For example, some women left their homes to escape the stigma attached by family and community to an unmarried woman suspected of being sexually active. Raped or pregnant women sought the anonymity of life in a city where no one knew them. One such woman came to Chicago in 1888 after she had been seduced and impregnated by a farmer in a nearby county.[32] Another woman worked as a live-in domestic servant until she met a young man who "ruined and deserted" her. After an attempted suicide, she too fled to Chicago.[33]

In other cases, parents and guardians expelled daughters from their homes for sexual behavior deemed unacceptable. An investigator of prostitution in 1911 found a woman whose parents "made her leave home because she went out at night." She told the investigator that she was " 'going to hell proper' now."[34]

Just as blacks and Jews often migrated in family groups to escape racial oppression and religious persecution, so many women who lived in patriarchal families moved out on their own to escape oppressive male relatives. Some women left home because fathers, stepfathers, uncles, or husbands abused them physically. In one such case, a twenty-year-old women "had lived with an uncle in Pennsylvania, who demanded her wages, and upon her refusal beat her." According to the charity worker who interviewed her, "She arrived at our terminal still carrying the bruises."[35] In another case, a Hungarian immigrant came to Chicago from New York to escape her violent and alcoholic husband.[36]

Several cases of incest and attempted incest appeared in the records of social and charity workers. The Travelers' Aid Society of the Young Women's Christian Association reported one such case in 1912:

> The girl arrived in the city at midnight without hat or coat, seeking protection. Her stepfather had been making improper advances toward her for some time, but so far she had been able to resist them. Her life was threatened if she told her mother.
>
> But the importunities of the man had become so insistent that the girl was afraid·to remain longer and she fled.[37]

Women were not only expelled from their homes by stigmatization or by abuse of patriarchal authority. Increasingly in the early twentieth century, women, especially young women, chose to migrate to escape the restrictions routinely imposed upon daughters in the family economy. Parents, fearful for their daughters' chastity, often restricted their daughters' nightlife, and, in addition, parents often required daughters (and less often required sons) to turn their entire wage into the common family fund.[38] Daughters protested.

Some left home when parents or guardians refused to let them spend their evenings as they chose. One woman ran away from home after her parents threatened to send her away for "go[ing] out with fellows."[39] In the early 1920s, another woman came to Chicago from a town in Michigan after her stepfather attempted to whip her for staying out late on a date. She explained:

> We kept having fights back and forth about the boys I went out with and the hours that I kept. He even accused me of wanting to do things which I'd not even thought of doing up to that time. One night the auto I was in broke down—it really did—and I didn't get in until after one o'clock. We had a big fight at home and he even tried to whip me. I told him I wouldn't stand for that and would leave home. . . . I was always willing to stand up for my rights.[40]

Other daughters migrated because they resented their lack of economic independence. One seventeen-year-old woman ran away from home because her father, an alcoholic, demanded her wages.[41] In a letter to the *Farmer's Voice*, Miss Alta Hooper warned farm parents that their daughters would leave home unless accorded greater economic freedom: "She isn't going to 'stay put,' but will get out where she can earn some money of her very own, to buy the little things so dear to the hearts of girls; and she will not be questioned and scolded over every little expenditure."[42]

Some of these women were probably drawn to the city by the new possibilities for urban consumer pleasure. By the early twentieth century, new urban nightlife—movies, dance halls, cabarets—offered women entertainment and the chance to mingle freely with their peers. And advertising broadcast the possibility for consumerism in department and other retail stores.

Some women seemed especially eager to have their own money to spend on attractive clothing. An eighteen-year-old Danish woman from Michigan, for example, migrated to Chicago in part "because she could not have the clothes she wanted."[43]

Recent writings in European women's history tend to depict a woman's decision to migrate as part of a "family strategy," an economic calculation based on the needs and decisions of the entire family unit.[44] In this study of migration to Chicago, however, the "family strategy" approach provides only partial explanation and, in some cases, obscures the conflicting interests of individual family members.[45] Within the family, stigmatization and abuse sometimes overshadowed cooperation, and, outside the family, increasing urban opportunities for self-indulgence sometimes appealed to women weary of self-abnegation in the family interest.

This is not to imply (as does Edward Shorter) that migration liberated oppressed women to lives of self-seeking and self-satisfied individualism.[46] Once in the city, a self-supporting female migrant learned that she faced obstacles that a self-supporting man did not. She learned to mistrust strangers who might see her as an especially easy mark for exploitation, and she learned too that strangers often mistrusted her, reading her lone status as a badge of sexual misbehavior. Most important, she discovered that employers paid her the low wages of a dependent daughter or wife.

For some women, the harsh lesson began when they first stepped off the train into the city. Criminals sometimes chose railroad stations as the most likely locations in which to find vulnerable female victims. For example, a newcomer from Cleveland "was taken" from the railroad station to a hotel where "her money $2.00 . . . her satchel and her bag were taken from her."[47] The Travelers' Aid Society of Chicago, the Immigrants' Protective League of Chicago, the National League for the Protection of Colored Women, and other similar organizations were founded specifically to protect the female migrant from those who marked her as their prey.[48]

Criminals may well have cheated and robbed naive male migrants just as often as they cheated and robbed naive female migrants. Criminals, panderers, and mashers, however, chose women newcomers as their primary targets for sexual exploitation. Women newcomers who trusted strangers were vulnerable to sexual crimes such as rape. In one such case, a migrant, in search of a hotel room, accepted the help of a man she met outside the Dearborn Street railway station. He took her to a nearby hotel "where she was outraged and detained for weeks."[49] Other women newcomers encountered procurers who attempted to entice them with offers of high pay for work in brothels. More often perhaps, migrants encountered city slickers who simply hoped to seduce them. The annual reports of the Travelers' Aid Society of Chicago include numerous such cases.

The woman migrant who made her way safely through the depot often faced other obstacles when she searched for housing. In many neighborhoods—immigrant, black, and native-born white—landladies expressed clear preference for male boarders and lodgers whom they considered less demanding. They complained that female lodgers were too fussy, that they used the bathroom too often, and that they broke house rules that prohibited cooking and laundering in the rooms.[50] In addition, landladies and neighbors sometimes suspected lone women of what they considered immoral sexual behavior. Recalling her youth in Chicago, one wage-earning woman who lived in her parents' home said, "If a girl didn't live at home, we thought she was bad."[51] In contrast, men who lived on their own usually found their independent status accepted without suspicion.

Women migrants may also have had greater difficulty finding work than male migrants because employers sometimes discriminated against lone women in hiring. Like landladies and neighbors, some employers suspected the working woman who lived away from family of immoral behavior. Others knew that the wages they paid did not suffice for independent living. In 1894, Edward Hillman of the Boston Store, an employer of about 1,900 women in Chicago, said, "A girl who boards out cannot support herself on a low wage. We have to enforce the rule as to living with the family or with friends to insure the moral character of our employe[e]s."[52] Similarly, in the 1920s, the American Telephone and Telegraph Company had a hiring policy that favored "girls who live at home, who are American, and who are 'respectable.' "[53]

The most important constraint faced by a woman migrant was undoubtedly poverty. In almost all of the jobs an unskilled migrant might obtain, she could expect low, and sometimes below-subsistence, wages. Employers and others assumed that working women lived in families in which working males provided partial support. They conceded readily that they did not expect women workers to live solely on their wages. The wages they paid women workers were intended as supplemental; the wages they paid male workers were intended for self and sometimes family support.[54] A survey of store and factory workers, conducted by the federal government in 1908, found that over half of the self-supporting women in Chicago earned less than eight dollars a week, the widely acknowledged subsistence wage.[55] Nationwide, in 1914, women in twenty-four manufacturing industries earned on average $7.75 per week; in the same industries, men earned on average $13.92.[56]

The poverty, the potential victimization, the stigmatization, and the discrimination in housing and hiring did not produce a class of passive victims. Instead, migrants found and created settings that offered substitutes for family support and companionship. Many women rented rooms in private families where they might be treated as if they were daughters. Some lived in subsidized boarding homes managed by churches or by middle-class women's reform organizations such as the YMCA and the Phyllis Wheatley Home Association. Others shared rooms with roommates and cooperated in other ways with their peers, pooling their resources for rent, food, and entertainment. Still others reentered family life by returning home or marrying as quickly as possible.[57] Living in private families or in organized homes, cooperating with peers, returning home, and marriage were options chosen by male migrants as well as female. Women migrants, however, participated in additional substitutes for family support that were available primarily to women. Two such female options were live-in domestic service and dependence on higher-paid men.

At the turn of the century, probably about half of the lone female migrants to Chicago chose to relinquish their independent status and reenter the family's boundaries as hired household workers. Because the demand often outreached the supply, jobs as live-in servants were readily available to female migrants. The room and board offered to live-in servants appealed to some migrants, especially penniless migrants who needed immediate room and board but could not afford to buy them. In addition, the supposed protection of a family setting attracted women who were afraid of the city. A black woman from New Orleans, for example, tried to arrange a live-in position in Chicago in a "good home with good people" because, she wrote, "its very trying for a good girl to be out in a large city by self among strangers."[58]

Still, as David Katzman has written, the long hours, restricted independence, and personal subservience of domestic work repelled many women. Those women who had other work options avoided domestic service. By 1900, white women, who might find work in offices, stores, and factories, often considered domestic service degrading. And black women, who were excluded from most nonservice occupations, increasingly chose to work as day-working servants rather than live in the homes of their employers.[59] The proportion of wage-earning women in Chicago who worked as live-in servants dropped steadily in the last decades of the nineteenth century and continued to drop in the twentieth.[60]

Another primarily female substitute for family support was dependence on higher-paid men. Although quantitative data are not available, it seems that this option became more widespread or, at least, more visible in the early twentieth-century city. Especially in the furnished-room districts of Chicago, social investigators noted that boarders and lodgers entered unsupervised relationships that offered unmarried women opportunities for male support. At one extreme, women exchanged sexual intercourse for money on a full-time basis. Prostitution, however, was only one of several types of heterosexual relationships that lone female migrants entered with the expectation of financial reward. Other women accepted sexual service jobs that did not require the selling of intercourse. In the new urban commercialized recreation industries, women earned relatively high salaries and tips as chorus girls, masseuses, cabaret dancers, taxi-dancers, and cocktail waitresses.[61]

More women undoubtedly relied less formally on their sexual allure. In the late nineteenth and early twentieth centuries, women depended on men customarily for economic support in marriage. Among autonomous female migrants and other women who lived apart from family, this kind of dependence began to appear outside of marriage in a less permanent, more contractual and partial support. This dependence covered a range of behavior from respectable dating to cynical gold digging to "occasional prostitution." Higher-paid men paid for entertainment, luxuries, gifts, and sometimes necessities. Women, in return, gave limited sexual favors, perhaps charming companionship, a good-night kiss, heavy petting, or maybe sexual intercourse.

At its simplest, a self-supporting woman who could not afford to pay for her own amusements could accept a date with a man who, by convention, paid for the evening's entertainment. A federal report on self-supporting women, published in 1910, stated:

> Even if most of the girls do not spend money for amusements, it is no proof that they go without them. Many of the girls have "gentlemen friends" who take them out. "Sure I go out all the time, but it doesn't cost me anything; my gentleman friend takes me," was the type of remark heard again and again.

The report went further. It suggested that women who wore attractive clothing could meet men on the streets who would pay for their entertainment:

> The majority, even if they have no money to spend or no one to take them out, as long as they have clothes that are presentable, can have some entertainment. They can "take a walk" on the street, go

> into the free dance halls, where they meet men who will treat them to the entertainment the place affords. . . . Or they will take a car to some amusement park where they often make acquaintances who take them the rounds of the resort.[62]

As this report indicates, commercialized recreation industries promoted this kind of dependence. The new movies, restaurants, cabarets, dance halls, and amusement parks catered to a sexually integrated leisure-time subculture in which men paid for the entertainment, food, and drink of women.[63]

Women were aware of the economics of dating. A waitress said: "If I did not have a man, I could not get along on my wages."[64] A saleswoman in a department store explained why she powdered her face: "I might get invited out to supper and save twenty cents."[65] And a chambermaid in a hotel said: "If the girls are good and refuse invitations to go out, they simply have no pleasure."[66]

This dependence of women on men did not always end with entertainment and meals in restaurants. Some women, like Theodore Dreiser's fictional Sister Carrie, also depended on men for money, clothes, or housing. Some of these women worked in stores, offices, factories, and restaurants during the day and sold their sexual services on occasional nights for extra money. For example, a nineteen-year-old migrant from Indiana worked in a restaurant and lodged in a rooming house on Michigan Avenue. A vice report stated: "Is not a regular prostitute, goes out with men for presents or money. Is poorly paid at restaurant."[67] Other women, "kept" women, moved into homes with the men who supported them, living out of wedlock as if they were married.[68]

These economic relationships sometimes led to devious and dishonest behavior by men and women both. Some men tried to get sexual favors from low-income women by bribing them or hounding them with false promises of material comforts.[69] And some women in turn tried to sucker men into giving them gifts and money. These women were known in stereotype as "gold diggers." One streetwise gold digger described her attitude toward men: "What I earn is mine. And what they have is mine, too, if I am smart enough to get it. . . . I'll show you how to take their socks away."[70]

In the mid-1920s, a sixteen-year-old migrant from Wisconsin, Alma, gave an especially detailed account of one of her gold-digging scams. "The first impression a girl has to make," she said, "is that she is a good girl under hard circumstances." When a man asked her for a date, Alma would first have him pay the wages she would earn if she stayed at the dance hall where she worked: "When he ask[s] how much that is, I make it seven or eight dollars rather than four dollars which it usually is." She would let her date treat her to a meal in a nice cafe or restaurant. Then she might excuse herself for a moment and leave through the back door. Or she might telephone an older woman friend "to come right down to where I am, to walk in and claim me as her niece and to threaten to make a scene." Alma and her friend would leave together; the friend would get half of the "rake-off."[71] Most likely, only a few women engaged in such elaborate and conscious gold digging.

The autonomous female migrant, however, was probably more likely to enter some form of informal dependent relationship than was the woman who lived with family. A lone migrant often lacked the funds for comfortable self-support, and she also often lacked the cushion that family might provide in times of unemployment. Equally important, the woman who lived apart from family escaped the watchful eyes of parental authorities.

Not surprisingly, the possibility of dependence on men outside of marriage disturbed middle-class observers. In the late nineteenth century, the more conservative writers simply vilified women who lived outside of families. In their view, if a female migrant, an orphan, or any woman without kin nearby avoided her proper place as a live-in servant, she was likely a promiscuous gad-about who refused her womanly calling. One particularly vehement observer wrote in response to an expose of Chicago sweatshops in 1888:

> But let me ask who is to blame if they work for two to four dollars per week, which every rational mind knows will not support them? But have we not seen these very girls in their finery and gay toggery on Saturday nights in the streets and on Sundays at the parks better dressed than many virtuous wives and daughters? Your

> sympathies are misplaced. . . . Today there are thousands of families in this county who would gladly employ these girls as domestics in their homes at two, three, or four dollars per week and board. But these would-be ladies of pants and shirt manufactories prefer this life to home comforts and home influences of good, respectable people. I argue these "poor girls" are themselves to blame if they seek the filth of life instead of the purity of it.[72]

Most writers were more sympathetic. They worried about the chastity of female migrants and sought to protect them in surrogate families. The label "woman adrift" captures this image. A woman without family nearby was thought to be drifting helplessly, buffeted hither and yon by forces beyond her control, specifically buffeted by the ruthless economic competition in the city and by the predatory urban men who skulked in railroad stations, parks, and other public places. One especially effusive writer used the "adrift" metaphor as follows: "There are thousands of homeless women . . . who are like flotsam and jetsam on the ocean of life. They have been cast onto the sea of misfortune and are like shipwrecked beings not knowing how to save themselves."[73] Using a different metaphor, another writer drew a more dismal picture: "Whether foreign born or native the girls all come to the city seeking fame or fortune, burning with high hope and filled with great resolves, but the remorseless city takes them, grinds them crushes them, and at last deposits them in unknown graves."[74] In the view of these reformers, the family, the haven of love, had failed to protect its daughters, and the cruel city threatened to ruin them. The "woman adrift" symbolized the victimization of the innocent and weak in an urban world without moral standards.

Whether they vilified the migrant or sympathized with her, the concern of these writers demonstrates that contemporaries distinguished the female migrant from her male counterpart. In the late nineteenth and early twentieth centuries, observers rarely focused so keenly on the experience and behavior of male migrants to Chicago.

This preliminary investigation focuses on the more obvious ways in which autonomous female migration to cities in the late nineteenth and early twentieth centuries differed from male migration. A lengthier study would undoubtedly reveal ethnic and racial differences among female migrants. A black laundress, a Polish peasant, and a native-born white typist would all come to the city, of course, with different expectations and would certainly have diverse urban experiences. This study emphasizes those features of female migration that cut across these ethnic and racial barriers.

The women who came alone to Chicago sometimes had distinctly "female" reasons for leaving home. Once in the city, they encountered certain obstacles that male migrants rarely encountered, and some of them found substitutes for family support on avenues open only to women. The female labor market (including the often-neglected sexual service sector), the sexual double standard, women's roles in the traditional family economy, and women's emerging roles in an expanding consumer society influenced women's motives for migration, the constraints they faced as migrants, and the responses they forged in the urban environment. Although they moved beyond the walls of the home, the women migrants to Chicago in the late nineteenth and early twentieth centuries did not escape the institutions and ideologies that shaped American womanhood.

NOTES

1. An earlier version of this article was presented at the Organization of American Historians' Convention, April 1985. I am grateful to John Alexander, Estelle Freedman, Laurence Glasco, Lois Helmbold, Richard Hopkins, Elizabeth Pleck, and Leila Rupp for their helpful comments. The Travelers' Aid Society of Chicago and Illinois, *Second Annual Report*, April 1, 1916.

2. Emmett J. Scott, "Letters of Negro Migrants of 1916-1918," *Journal of Negro History* (July 1919), 316.

3. Throughout this article, I use the term "autonomous" to refer to self-supporting migrants who came to Chicago alone and who did not live with family or relatives in the city. I use the word migrant to include both internal migrants and immigrants.

4. This brief description of the places of origin of female migrants is drawn from the federal manuscript censuses of 1880 and 1910. I drew two systematic samples of working women who did not live with family, relatives, or employers: 957 women from the 1880 census schedules for Chicago and 905 women from the 1910 census schedules for Chicago.

Most of these women were boarders and roomers. In 1880, five-sixths and, in 1910, four-fifths of the working women sampled listed birthplaces outside of the state of Illinois. In addition, many of the boarders and lodgers born in Illinois had undoubtedly migrated from Joliet, Peoria, Rockford, and other small cities, towns, and rural regions within the state. Because I sampled only women who lived apart from family and relatives, many samples are composed of women unlikely to be involved in chain migrations. While the census data provide place of birth, age, race, marital status, and so on, they do not give the year of migration to Chicago. The young average age of the single women sampled (late twenties) and the fact that few were under the age of sixteen suggest that most migrants arrived in Chicago in their late teens and twenties. Census data from 1910 provide more detailed information on the age of arrival of foreign-born women. In 1910, census takers asked immigrants in what year they had arrived in the United States. Ninety percent of the foreign-born women who had lived in the United States for less than five years were single, and eighty-five percent were under the age of thirty. This evidence corroborates the findings of demographers: Migration is usually most prevalent among young adults. Compared to the population of the city of Chicago, black women and white native-born women with native-born parents were overrepresented among the self supporting women sampled. Least represented were the native-born daughters of foreign-born parent(s). Because their families often lived in the city, these women had less reason to leave home in order to find work. And those who did migrate often had urban kin with whom to live. For the most part, black and white native-born female migrants came from the same states as all migrants to Chicago. Certain immigrant groups, however, were overrepresented. In 1880, the proportion of foreign-born women sampled who came from Norway, Sweden, and Canada exceeded the proportions of Norwegians, Swedes, and Canadians in the foreign-born population of Chicago as a whole. In 1910, Polish women were highly overrepresented. Twenty-nine percent of foreign-born women sampled were native Polish speakers; only sixteen percent of the Chicago foreign-born population, however, listed Polish as their mother tongue. To a lesser extent, Norwegian, Swedish, Canadian, Irish, and Lithuanian women were also overrepresented in 1910. German women, Italian women, and to a lesser extent, Russian Jewish women were underrepresented.

5. U.S. Bureau of the Census, *Statistics of Women at Work* (Washington, DC, 1907), 29.

6. Ibid. This estimate is derived from my samples from 1880 to 1910 as well as from such surveys as Commissioner of Labor, *Fourth Annual Report, 1888: Working Women in Large Cities* (Washington, DC, 1889); Illinois Bureau of Labor Statistics, *Seventh Biennial Report, 1892, Part 1: Working Women in Chicago* (Springfield, 1893); Illinois Bureau of Labor Statistics, *Fifteenth Biennial Report, 1908, Part 3: Women Employed in Department Stores* (Springfield, 1910); Charles P. Neill, *Wage-Earning Women in Stores and Factories, Vol. 5, Report on Condition of Woman and Child Wage-Earners in the United States* (Washington, DC, 1910); Joseph A. Hill, *Women in Gainful Occupations, 1870-1920* (Washington, DC, 1921); U.S. Women's Bureau, *Women Workers in Flint, Michigan*, Bulletin 67 (Washington, DC, 1929).

7. E. G. Ravenstein, "The Laws of Migration," *Journal of the Statistical Society* (June 1885), 199.

8. See Leslie Page Moch, "Adolescence and Migration: Nimes, France, 1906," *Social Science History* (February 1981), 25-51; Ester Boserup, *Women's Role in Economic Development* (New York, 1970), 186-187; Elizabeth Jelin, "Migration and Labor Force Participation of Latin American Women: The Domestic Servants in the Cities," *Signs:*

Journal of Women in Culture and Society (Fall 1977), 129-141; Orlando Patterson, "Migration of Caribbean Societies: Socioeconomic and Symbolic Resource," in William H. McNeill and Ruth S. Adams, eds., *Human Migration: Patterns and Policies* (Bloomington, 1978), 115; James T. Fawcett, Siew-Ean Khoo, and Peter C. Smith, eds., *Women in the Cities of Asia: Migration and Urban Adaptation* (Boulder, 1984).

9. Most of this evidence comes from sex ratios of urban and rural populations. Joseph F. Kett, *Rites of Passage: Adolescence in America, 1790 to the Present* (New York, 1977), 96; Jane Riblett Wilkie, "The Black Urban Population of the Pre-Civil War South," *Phylon* (September 1976), 257, 260; Suzanne Lebsock, *The Free Women of Petersburg: Status and Culture in a Southern Town, 1784-1860* (New York, 1983), 99; Zane Miller, "Urban Blacks in the South, 1865-1920: The Richmond, Savannah, New Orleans, Louisville, and Birmingham Experience," in Leo Schnore, ed., *The New Urban History* (Princeton, 1975); Hasia R. Diner, *Erin's Daughters in America: Irish Immigrant Women in the Nineteenth Century* (Baltimore, 1983), 31; Bengt Ankarloo, "Agriculture and Women's Work: Directions of Change in the West, 1700-1900," *Journal of Family History* (Summer 1979), 118; Carle C. Zimmerman, "The Migration to Towns and Cities," *American Journal of Sociology* (November 1926), 450-455; C. Warren Thornthwaite, *Internal Migration in the United States* (Philadelphia, 1934), 32; E. C. Young, *The Movement of Farm Population* (Ithaca, 1924), 16, 20.

10. U.S. Bureau of the Census, *Farm Population of the United States, 1920* (Washington, DC, 1926), 62.

11. There are exceptional works that include discussions of women and migration. See, for example, Thomas Dublin, *Women at Work: The Transformation of Work and Community in Lowell, Massachusetts, 1826-1860* (New York, 1979); Diner, *Erin's Daughters in America*; Laurence A. Glasco, "The Life Cycles and Household Structures of American Ethnic Groups: Irish, Germans, and Native-born Whites in Buffalo, New York, 1855," in Nancy F. Cott and Elizabeth H. Pleck, eds., *A Heritage of Her Own: Toward a New Social History of Women* (New York, 1979), 268-289; Janice L. Reiff, Michel R. Dahlin, and Daniel Scott Smith, "Rural Push and Urban Pull: Work and Family Experiences of Older Black Women in Southern Cities, 1880-1900," *Journal of Social History* (Summer 1983), 39-48.

12. For studies that focus on men, see Peter R. Knights, *The Plain People of Boston, 1830-1860: A Study in City Growth* (New York, 1971); Howard Chudacoff, *Mobile Americans: Residential and Social Mobility in Omaha, 1880-1920* (New York, 1972; Stephan Thernstrom, *The Other Bostonians: Poverty and Progress in the American Metropolis, 1880-1970* (Cambridge, 1973); Dean R. Esslinger, *Immigrants and the City: Ethnicity and Mobility in a Nineteenth-Century Midwestern Community* (Port Washington, 1975); Robert Doherty, *Society and Power: Five New England Towns, 1800-1860* (Amherst, 1977). For studies that focus on family and kin, see Tamara K. Hareven, *Family Time and Industrial Time: The Relationship Between the Family and Work in a New England Industrial Community* (Cambridge, 1982); David Paul Davenport, "Tracing Rural New York's Out-Migrants, 1855-1860," *Historical Methods Newsletter* (Spring 1984), 59-67.

13. See, for example, Peter A. Morrison, "The Functions and Dynamics of the Migration Process," in Alan A. Brown and Egon Neuberger, ed., *Internal Migration: A Comparative Perspective* (New York, 1977), 63.

14. Emmett J. Scott, "Additional Letters of Negro Migrants of 1916-1918" *Journal of Negro History* (October 1919), 413.

15. *Statistics of Women at Work*, 16.

16. U.S. Bureau of the Census, *Fifteenth Census, 1930, Population*, vol. 4, 42.

17. See, for example, Louise DeKoven Bowen, *The Department Store Girl* (Chicago, 1911), 11.

18. Mary Kenney O'Sullivan (typewritten autobiography, Schlesinger Library, Radcliffe College), 27.

19. See, for example, "Alma N. Z________r," Paul Cressey notes, ca. 1926, *Ernest Burgess Papers*, 129, 6, University of Chicago Manuscript Collections.

20. Seth Cook Rees, *Miracles in the Slums, or Thrilling Stories of Those Rescued from the Cesspools of Iniquity, and Touching Incidents in the Lives of the Unfortunate* (Chicago, 1905), 120.

21. Interview with Philiminia P., conducted by author, October 24, 1980.

22. Scott, "Additional Letters of Negro Migrants," 426.

23. Ruth Shonle Cavan, *Business Girls: A Study of Their Interests and Problems* (n.p., 1929), 1.

24. Vice Commission of Chicago, *The Social Evil in Chicago: A Study of Existing Conditions with Recommendations by the Vice Commission of Chicago* (Chicago, 1922), 132.

25. Young, *The Movement of Farm Population*, 20, 23, 24.

26. For example, in 1900, only 16.6 percent of adult women worked for wages in Youngstown while 23.2 percent worked for wages in Chicago. U.S. Bureau of the Census, *Twelfth Census, 1900, Population*, vol. 2, cliii, clv.

27. U.S. Bureau of the Census, *Ninth Census, 1870, Population*, 768; U.S. Bureau of the Census, *Fifteenth Census, 1930, Population*, vol 4, 440. In the same period, the total population of Chicago grew half as rapidly, from 299,000 to 3,376,400, or by over 1000 percent.

28. U.S. Bureau of the Census, *Twelfth Census, 1900, Population*, vol. 2, 550-601. The large cities considered here are those with populations greater than or equal to 100,000.

29. Joseph A. Hill, *Women in Gainful Occupations, 1870-1920* (Washington, DC, 1921), 9.

30. U.S. Bureau of the Census, *Twelfth Census, 1900, Population*, vol. 2, 550-601; U.S. Bureau of the Census, *Fourteenth Census, 1920, Population*, vol. 4, 33, 128.

31. These noneconomic "push" and "pull" factors influenced the migrations of women from larger cities as well as from small cities, towns, and rural regions. Some readers might question the veracity of explanation women migrants gave to charity workers and social investigators. To screen out unreliable accounts, I have not included any "stories" that seemed inconsistent, overly self-serving, or especially maudlin. The accounts of pregnancy, rape, seduction, prostitution, and incest included here seem to me at least as honest or sincere as the accounts that focus on economic motives for migration. In an era that placed high value on female chastity, most women would probably not fabricate such potentially embarrassing reasons for leaving home.

32. Case record, 1/7/88, *Illinois Humane Society Papers* 3, University of Illinois at Chicago Manuscript Collections.

33. Rees, *Miracles in the Slums*, 120.

33. *The Social Evil in Chicago*, 95. I have not found evidence of this kind of expulsion from family among black women. Further research is needed on the impact of the sexual double standard in black communities.

35. Travelers' Aid Society of Chicago, *Report of the General Secretary for the Year Ending March 31, 1919.*

36. Walter C. Reckless, *Vice in Chicago* (Chicago, 1933), 46.

37. Young Women's Christian Association of Chicago, *36th Annual Report* (1912), 29.

38. See Louise Montgomery, *The American Girl in the Stockyards District* (Chicago, 1913), 57, 58.

39. *The Social Evil in Chicago*, 189.

40. "Lillian S. W. ______n," Paul Cressey notes, ca. 1926, *Ernest Burgess Papers*, 129, 6, University of Chicago Manuscript Collections.

41. Young Women's Christian Association of Chicago, *38th Annual Report* (1914).

42. William A. McKeever, *Farm Boys and Girls* (New York, 1912), 238. John Mack Faragher has argued that farm daughters also migrated to escape drudgery that befell farm wives; see John Mack Faragher, "Sister Carrie's Sisters: White Country Girls in the City of Chicago, 1880-1930," (unpublished paper, 1983).

43. Ruth Shonle Cavan, "Suicide: A Study of Personal Disorganization" (M.A. thesis, University of Chicago, 1926), 66.

44. See especially Louise A. Tilly and Joan W. Scott, *Women, Work, and Family* (New York, 1978), 121.

45. On the family as a "locus of struggle," see Heidi I. Hartmann, "The Family as the Locus of Gender, Class, and Political Struggle: The Example of Housework," *Signs* (Spring 1981), 368.

46. Edward Shorter, *The Making of the Modern Family* (New York, 1975), 260.

47. Case record, 6/25/91, *Illinois Humane Society Papers* 5, University of Illinois at Chicago Manuscript Collections.

48. The records of the Travelers' Aid Society of Chicago and the Immigrants' Protective League of Chicago are in the University of Illinois at Chicago Manuscript Collections. Initially, the TAS was under the auspices of the YWCA, and the IPL was under the auspices of the Women's Trade Union League of Chicago. On the National League for the Protection of Colored Women, see Nancy J. Weiss, *The National Urban League, 1910-1940* (New York, 1974), 18, 19.

49. Jean Turner-Zimmerman, *Chicago's Black Traffic in White Girls* (n.p., 1912), 37.

50. See Chicago Commission on Race Relations, *The Negro in Chicago* (Chicago, 1922), 16; Franklin Kline Fretz, *The Furnished Room Problem in Phildelphia* (n.p., 1912), 59. For a fictional account, see Anzia Yezierska, *Bread Givers* (New York, 1975, originally 1925), 157.

51. Group interview at Amalgamated Clothing and Textile Workers Union Retirement Center in Chicago, conducted by author, August 27, 1980; see also Theresa Wolfson, *The Woman Worker and the Trade Unions* (New York, 1926), 43.

52. William T. Stead, *If Christ Came to Chicago! A Plea for the Union of All Who Love in the Service of All Who Suffer* (London, 1894), 245.

53. Wolfson, *The Woman Worker and the Trade Unions*, 115. For a fictional account, see Theodore Dreiser, *An American Tragedy* (New York, 1964, originally 1925), 240.

54. For a more extended treatment of women's wages, see Leslie Woodcock Tentler, *Wage-Earning Women: Industrial Work and Family Life in the United States, 1900-1930* (New York, 1979).

55. Charles P. Neill, *Wage-Earning Women in Stores and Factories, Vol. V, Report on Condition of Woman and Child Wage-Earners in the United States* (Washington, DC, 1910), 106, 113, 118.

56. National Industrial Conference Board, *Wages in the United States, 1914-1930* (New York, 1931), 52. Foreign-born women and black women often earned especially low wages. One study of a Chicago employment agency found that black cooks and servants frequently received one dollar less per week than white cooks and servants. See "Employment of Colored Women in Chicago," *The Crisis* (January 1911), 24-25.

57. For a discussion of the options available to migrants, see Joanne Meyerowitz, "Holding Their Own: Working Women Apart from Family in Chicago, 1880-1930" (Ph.D. dissertation, Stanford University, 1983), ch. 3 and 4.

58. "Letters of Negro Migrants," 317.

59. David M. Katzman, *Seven Days a Week: Women and Domestic Service in Industrializing America* (New York, 1978).

60. The proportion of wage-earning women in Chicago who worked as servants dropped from thirty-eight percent in 1880 to fifteen percent in 1910 to twelve percent in 1930. U.S. Bureau of the Census, *Tenth Census, 1880, Population*, vol. 1, 870; U.S. Bureau of the Census, *Thirteenth Census, 1880, Population*, vol. 4, 546, 547; U.S. Bureau of the Census, *Fifteenth Census, 1930, Population*, vol. 3, 652; Estelle Hill Scott, *Occupational Changes Among Negroes in Chicago* (Chicago, 1939), 236. On the shift from live-in service to day work, see Joseph A. Hill, *Women in Gainful Occupations*, 138, and Katzman, *Seven Days a Week*.

61. On sexual service work, see Meyerowitz, "Holding Their Own," 53-55.

62. Neill, *Wage-Earning Women in Stores and Factories*, 75.

63. On this leisure-time subculture, see Kathy Peiss, " 'Charity Girls' and City Pleasures: Historical Notes on Working-Class Sexuality, 1880-1920," in Ann Snitow et al., *Powers of Desire: The Politics of Sexuality* (New York, 1983).

64. Louise DeKoven Bowen, *The Girl Employed in Hotels and Restaurants* (Chicago, 1912).

65. Chicago *Record-Herald*, December 25, 1911.

66. "Summary of the Report on Hotels," ca. 1910, *Juvenile Protective Association of Chicago Papers*, 16, University of Illinois Chicago Manuscript Collections.

67. *The Social Evil in Chicago*, 95.

68. See *The Social Evil in Chicago*, 188, 191.

69. See, Thomas H. Russell, The Girl's Fight for a Living: How to Protect Working Women from Dangers Due to Low Wages (Chicago, 1913), 12, 13, 166.

70. Chicago *Daily News*, January 31, 1930; see also *The Social Evil in Chicago*, 189.

71. Life story of Alma N. Z________r, Paul Cressey notes, ca. 1926, *Ernest Burgess Papers*, 129, 6, University of Chicago Manuscript Collections.

72. Chicago *Times*, August 5, 1888.

73. Bertha A. Loeb, "A Refuge for Homeless Women," Chicago *Record-Herald*, January 29, 1911.

74. Leona Prall Groetziner, *The City's Perils* (n.p., ca. 1910), 13.

Amerika Nadeshiko: Japanese Immigrant Women In the United States, 1900–1924

Yuji Ichioka

The author is a research associate in the Asian American Studies Center, University of California, Los Angeles

DESPITE PLAYING A CRUCIAL role in the growth of Japanese immigrant society, Japanese immigrant women are absent from most historical accounts of Japanese immigration. Race, sex, and class factors account for this glaring omission. Apart from works covering the internment of Japanese during World War II, the existing literature in English is mainly devoted to the origins, causes, and development of the anti-Japanese exclusion movement in the first quarter of this century and the adverse repercussions it had on Japanese-American relations.[1] High-

---

In 1978 I conducted a series of group discussions with retired Issei women living in the Japanese Retirement Home located in East Los Angeles. The discussions consisted of weekly sessions of two-hour duration held over a period of two months. I used the opportunity to confirm or revise interpretations about Japanese immigrant women at which I had arrived through readings of the immigrant press and other sources. Because of the personal nature of aspects of the discussions, the participants will remain anonymous. Here I would like to express my sincere gratitude to all those who participated. I would also like to thank Toshiko Sugiyama and Tazuko Shibuzawa of the retirement home, who rendered invaluable assistance, and Emma Gee, who critically read a draft version of this essay.

[1]Yuji Ichioka *et al.*, *A Buried Past: An Annotated Bibliography of the Japanese American Research Project Collection* (Berkeley and Los Angeles, 1974), 3–11; Roger Daniels, "American Historians and East Asian Immigrants," *Pacific Historical Review*, XLIII (1974), 449–472.

lighting the *excluders* rather than the *excluded*, the literature seldom examines how Japanese immigrants thought about and reacted to being excluded. Until recently, what was done to the immigrants has been considered more important than the immigrants themselves. Except for notable upperclass women, historians have seldom bothered to study women, especially working-class immigrant women. This sex and class bias has also contributed to the paucity of research on Japanese immigrant women. A few recent studies explore aspects of the life and role of women in Japanese immigrant society, marking a small beginning in incorporating them fully into the history of Japanese immigration.[2] Based upon immigrant language sources and interviews, this essay will examine the immigration of Japanese women to the United States from 1900 to 1924 and its effect on Japanese immigrant society.

Few Japanese women immigrated to the United States until the early twentieth century. The earliest Japanese immigrants were indigent male students who began to arrive in the mid-1880s. Male laborers followed closely on their heels after 1890, and soon formed the largest group in Japanese immigrant society. Initially, these men dreamed of returning to Japan as soon as they had earned enough money. Between 1905 and 1920, however, many of them left the ranks of common laborers to become small farmers and small businessmen, thereby transforming themselves from sojourners into permanent settlers. An economic stake in farms and businesses persuaded them to cast off the old ideal of returning to Japan and enabled them to summon wives from Japan which reinforced the economic underpinning of permanent residency. At the turn of the century, according to census data, there were only

[2]Emma Gee, "Issei: The First Women," in *Asian Women* (Berkeley, 1971), 8–15; Yuji Ichioka, "Ameyuki-san: Japanese Prostitutes in Nineteenth Century America," *Amerasia Journal*, IV:1 (1977), 1–21; Susan M. Kataoka, "Issei Women: A Study in Subordinate Status" (Ph.D. dissertation, University of California, Los Angeles, 1977); and Akemi Kikumura, "The Life History of an Issei Woman: Conflicts and Strain in the Process of Acculturation" (Ph.D. dissertation, University of California, Los Angeles, 1979). Issei Oral History Project, *Issei Christians* (Sacramento, 1977) includes biographies of two Issei women. Shindō Kaneto, *Matsuri no Koe* (Tokyo, 1977) and Yamazaki Tomoko, *Ameyuki-san no Uta* (Tokyo, 1978) are two additional biographical studies in Japanese. Itō Kazuo, *Hokubei Hyakunen Sakura* (Seattle, 1969), 311–357, has an excellent chapter on women. This work has been translated; see Shin'ichiro Nakamura and Jean S. Gerard, trans., *Issei: A History of Japanese Immigrants in North America* (Seattle, 1973), 247–287.

985 Japanese females in the continental United States. The increasing number of married women relative to the total Japanese population in 1900, 1910, 1920, and 1930 reflects the arrival of Japanese women after the turn of the century:[3]

Year	Japanese Population	Married Women
1900	24,326	410
1910	72,157	5,581
1920	111,010	22,193
1930	138,834	23,930

The arrival of married women at this time, particularly between 1910 and 1920, was not by happenstance. After the turn of the century immigrant leaders began exhorting their countrymen to set new goals for themselves in American society. The foremost advocate of permanent settlement was Abiko Kyūtarō, publisher of the largest and most influential immigrant daily, the *Nichibei Shimbun* of San Francisco. Beginning in 1905 he argued that the dream of returning to Japan was an obstacle to the development of a stable, prosperous immigrant society. In his judgment, if the foundations of immigrant society were ever to rest on firm ground, the dream had to be discarded. Accordingly, Abiko promoted long-term residency by urging laborers to take up farming and to summon wives from Japan. An economic interest in agriculture and settled family life, he believed, would change laborers from sojourners to permanent residents. In addition, family life would help to rid immigrant society of prostitution and gambling.[4]

Taking the advice to heart, many men secured wives who entered immigrant society in one of three ways. Among wives who had been left behind in Japan, some were summoned by their husbands. Other women married single men who returned

[3]Yamato Ichihashi, *Japanese in the United States* (Stanford, 1932), 291; U.S. Bureau of the Census, *Fifteenth Census of the United States, 1930: Population* (Washington, D.C., 1933), II, 845.

[4]For Abiko Kyūtarō's advocacy of permanent residency, see Okina Kyūin, *Okina Kyūin Zenshū* (Toyama, 1972), III, 78–81. See also Oka Shigeki Papers, box 133, folder 4, Japanese American Research Project Collection (hereafter cited as JARP), Special Collections, University of California, Los Angeles, which contains biographical material pertaining to Abiko.

to Japan to seek mates and then to bring them to the United States. The wife of Abiko Kyūtarō, Yonako, married her husband in 1909 when he himself returned. Two factors limited the number of bachelors who returned for this purpose. Few could afford the time and expense of such a trip, which included heavy outlays for marriage required by social custom in Japan. Some returnees, moreover, faced the possibility of being inducted into the military. All Japanese men living abroad enjoyed deferments, but lost their deferred status if they returned for more than thirty days. The time spent in finding an appropriate mate, in entering into a formal engagement, and in getting married often exceeded a month.

Thus many bachelors resorted to the so-called picture-bride practice, the third way by which women entered immigrant society.[5] The practice itself did not diverge sharply from traditional Japanese custom. In Japan, marriage was never an individual matter but always a family affair.[6] Heads of households selected marriage partners for family members through go-betweens. An exchange of photographs sometimes took place in the screening process, with family genealogy, wealth, education, and health figuring heavily in the selection criteria. Go-betweens arranged parleys between families at which heads of households discussed proposed unions. Although prospective spouses normally met each other for the first time at such meetings, they rarely if ever exchanged words. The meetings were for the benefit of heads of households; they were not intended for couples to become acquainted with each other. If families mutually consented, engagement and marriage ensued.

In general, the picture-bride practice conformed to this marriage custom. Single immigrant men had brides picked for them by their parents or relatives. Along with photographs of themselves, the men forwarded information about their lives in America, which go-betweens used in negotiations with parents of eligible daughters. The practice deviated in only one im-

[5]The English term "picture-bride" is somewhat misleading owing to the inaccurate translation of the Japanese term *shashin kekkon*, which literally means "photo-marriage." Japanese immigrants were not the only ones who engaged in this practice. Greek immigrants, for example, also engaged in it. See Theodore Saloutos, *The Greeks in the United States* (Cambridge, Mass., 1964), 85.

[6]Yanagida Kunio, *Meiji Bunkashi* (Tokyo, 1954), XIII, 227–256.

portant respect from conventional marriages: bridegrooms physically were absent at wedding ceremonies. Still, the practice satisfied all social and legal requirements governing marriage in Japan. Marriages were legal as long as husbands fulfilled a simple bureaucratic condition. They had to enter the names of their brides into their own family registries. By meeting this requirement, men were considered legally bethrothed no matter where they resided. That they never laid eyes upon their brides or were absent from their own wedding ceremonies was irrelevant.

Exactly how many married women landed as picture-brides is unknown. Neither the Japanese nor American government maintained precise statistics over the years. Yet there is little doubt that the number was sizable. By resorting to the picture-bride practice, single men were able to save the time and expense of going back to Japan and avoid the risk of being conscripted. Both considerations made the practice appealing to the average bachelor. In all probability, picture-brides comprised over half of all the married women who arrived between 1910 and 1920.[7]

The Japanese government regulated the passage of women across the Pacific. Concerned about the appearance of Japanese prostitutes on the Pacific Coast in the late nineteenth century, Japan first instituted strict control over the issuance of passports to women.[8] Events in the United States dictated even tighter controls. In 1900 agitation against Japanese immigration fully surfaced in San Francisco. In direct response to it, the Foreign Ministry, on August 2, 1900, ceased to issue passports to male or female laborers bound for the continental United States and Canada.[9] Two years later it slightly relaxed its restrictive policy

---

[7]Based upon incomplete United States immigration statistics, Kanzaki Kiichi, general secretary of the Japanese Association of America, testified before the House Committee on Immigration and Naturalization in 1920 that 6,321 picture-brides entered through Seattle and San Francisco between 1912 and 1919. See U.S. Congress, House Committee On Immigration and Naturalization, *Hearings on Japanese Immigration*, 66 Cong., 2 sess. (1921), pt. 2, p. 717. If the number of picture-brides who were admitted before 1912, in 1920, and through other ports of entry is added, the total figure would be much higher.

[8]Ichioka, "Ameyuki-san," 16.

[9]Aoki Shūzō to Takahira Kogorō, Aug. 2, 1900, in Nihon Gaimushō, *Nihon Gaikō Bunsho, 1900* (Tokyo, 1956), 461. See also Irie Toraji, *Hōjin Kaigai Hatten* (Tokyo, 1938), I, 315–317.

by issuing passports to returnees, including laborers, who applied for repassage to the United States. The Foreign Ministry also began issuing passports to the wives, children, and parents of Japanese residing in the United States.[10] After 1905 the clamor against Japanese immigration intensified, and the Japanese government voluntarily agreed to continue restricting labor immigration. Under the terms of the Gentlemen's Agreement, negotiated between the Japanese and American governments in the winter of 1907–1908, Japan reaffirmed its policy of not issuing passports to laborers.[11] Returnees continued to be eligible for passports, as did the wives, children, and parents of bonafide Japanese residents.

To control the passage of married women, Japanese consuls set rigid standards. The fundamental yardstick was economic. Only men who had proven means of supporting families were qualified to summon wives. All laborers were ineligible until 1915. Rare exceptions were made for those in urban occupations—for example, butlers, waiters, and cooks—if they commanded high wages and could provide proof of continuous employment and savings of at least a thousand dollars, an enormous sum for any laborer. Businessmen and farmers were eligible, but they had to meet specific criteria. A businessman had to have an annual gross income of twelve hundred dollars or more, a farmer had to have an annual profit of four to five hundred dollars, and both had to have savings of at least a thousand dollars as well.[12] In 1915 the Japanese government modified its requirements to make laborers eligible. Effective July 1, 1915, all male residents of the United States, including laborers, became eligible to summon wives, provided they had savings of eight hundred dollars.[13] To reduce the possibility of

---

[10] Komura [Jutarō] to Keishi Sōkan *et al.*, June 9, 1902, in Nihon Gaimushō, *Nihon Gaikō Bunsho, 1902* (Tokyo, 1957), 699.

[11] For the Gentlemen's Agreement, see Charles E. Neu, *An Uncertain Friendship: Theodore Roosevelt and Japan, 1906–1909* (Cambridge, Mass., 1967), 163–180; Raymond A. Esthus, *Theodore Roosevelt and Japan* (Seattle, 1966), 146–166, 196–228; and Nihon Gaimushō, *Nihon Gaikō Bunsho: Tai-Bei Imin Mondai Keika Gaiyō* (Tokyo, 1972), 243–334.

[12] Nagai Matsuzō to Chinda Sutemi, June 17, 1912, and enclosure, "Geisai no Shikaku," reel 3, Japanese Foreign Ministry Archival Documents, Asian American Studies Center, University of California, Los Angeles.

[13] *Shin Sekai*, July 8, 1915.

fraud, Japanese consuls required that applicants filing papers to bring over their wives submit bank deposit books as proof that this sum had been in their accounts for no less than five months preceding the date of application.

Women had to satisfy specific government regulations too. If they were picture-brides, their names had to be entered into their husbands' family registries six months prior to their applications for passports. This requirement, Japanese officials believed, impeded procurers from obtaining prostitutes disguised as picture-brides. After 1915 picture-brides also had to meet an age regulation. They could not be more than thirteen years younger than their spouses. This age limit was set on the premise that too wide a disparity was not conducive to harmonious marriages. If there were extenuating circumstances, however, the rule might be waived. All Japanese emigrants had to pass physical examinations at ports of embarkation. American immigration statutes barred the admission of immigrants bearing contagious diseases. Immigration inspectors were especially on the alert for those afflicted with trachoma and hookworm, two fairly common diseases in Japan. Aware of American regulations, the Japanese government administered physical examinations to all departing women to make sure that they had neither.

No single motive explains why women came to the United States. In the case of married women who had been left behind in Japan, they responded to their spouses' summons to join them. Most picture-brides no doubt simply obeyed parents. Bethrothed by parental arrangement, they too came to join their spouses. To refuse would have been an act of filial disobedience, a grave moral offense. One woman gave a down-to-earth account of her situation. A tall, robust female with broad shoulders and large feet, she agreed to her father's arrangement of marriage with an older man living in California. Her father was convinced that no male in Japan would marry his "ungainly" daughter, and she had accepted his bleak assessment of her marital prospects.[14] There were also economic motives. Some daughters became picture-brides to help their families

[14]Interview with Mrs. X, Feb. 10, 1978.

through hard times or to put a younger sibling through school.[15] By working in the United States, they expected to be able to remit money to their families. For women who found themselves in social predicaments, marriage with men abroad offered an avenue of escape.[16] For these women life in America held out hopes for a new beginning, a future in a country which evoked images of material comforts unimaginable at home. Some women came for even more fundamental economic reasons—they lacked sufficient food, clothing, and shelter.

Regardless of motives, all women were beset by common problems as soon as they landed. Their first encounter with America was the ordeal of passing through the labyrinth of the immigration station. Most women arrived as third-class steerage passengers for whom an inspection was a grim experience. Inspectors examined them more scrupulously than first- or second-class passengers. Advance briefings about what to expect did not allay anxieties. Many questions worried the women to no end. Were their papers in order? Each wife had to have a valid passport, a certified copy of her husband's family registry, and a health certificate. Would she pass the physical examination? That she had been found free of trachoma and hookworm in Japan was no guarantee she would. Would her husband be at the immigration station to welcome her? Some wives did not know. All husbands had to appear in person to receive wives. Picture-brides gazed upon their spouses for the first time in the station. Such anxieties were compounded by fear of the unknown and by lack of knowledge of English.

Wives were matched up with husbands in the immigration station. Immigration officials required husbands to present documents to avert mix-ups. First, they had to have certificates issued by the Japanese consul which attested to their identity and occupation. Second, they had to have additional proof of employment. Farmers had to show land titles or lease agreements, businessmen commercial licenses, and salaried workers letters signed by employers. Third, they had to have bank

---

[15]Shindō, *Matsuri no Koe*, 12–15.

[16]In her short story, "And the Soul Shall Dance," Wakako Yamauchi has captured this motive very well. See Frank Chin *et al.*, eds., *Aiiieeee!: An Anthology of Asian-American Writers* (Washington, D.C., 1974), 193–200.

deposit books as evidence of their ability to support wives. If everything was in order, officials released wives into the custody of husbands. Prior to 1917 the American government did not recognize photo-marriages, and this forced picture-brides and their spouses to be remarried in another ceremony in order to be considered legally married in the United States. Group ceremonies were conducted in the immigration station at the beginning; later they were held in hotel lobbies or churches by special arrangement with immigration authorities. In 1917 the State Department granted legal recognition to photo-marriages, allowing picture-brides and their spouses to dispense with the second wedding ceremony.[17]

Many picture-brides were genuinely shocked to see their husbands. Sometimes the person was much older than he appeared in his photograph. As a rule husbands were older than wives by ten to fifteen years, and occasionally more. Men often forwarded photographs taken in their youth or touched-up ones that concealed their real age. No wonder some picture-brides, upon sighting their spouses, lamented dejectedly that they had married an old man. Husbands appeared unexpectedly different in other ways. Some men had photographs touched up, not just to look youthful but to improve their overall appearance. They had all traces of facial blemishes and baldness removed. Picture-brides understandably were taken aback because such men did not physically correspond with their photographs at all. Suave, handsome appearing gentlemen proved to be pockmarked, country bumpkins. A few disillusioned picture-brides declined to join their husbands and asked to be sent back to Japan. Others who had married distant relatives or men they had known in their villages as young girls were disappointed, perhaps, but not crestfallen.

Almost all women landed wearing Japanese kimonos and sandals. As a part of their initiation into American society, it was common for husbands to take their wives to a clothing store to purchase a set of Western clothes.[18] Of all the strange items of

---

[17]This recognition was the result of negotiations conducted by the Japanese ambassador with the State Department. See U.S. Dept. of State, *Papers Relating to the Foreign Relations of the United States, 1917* (Washington, D.C., 1926), 848–876.

[18]Gee, "Issei: The First Women," 12.

apparel, corsets were the most uncomfortable. Newly outfitted women had trouble breathing wearing something so constricting. Western-style shoes were no less uncomfortable. The enclosed, pointed toe of shoes, particularly of fashionable, high lace boots, were not suited for Japanese women whose feet, shaped since childhood by open slippers and sandals, were wide and flat. Pointed shoes were painful to wear and impossible to walk in initially.

Other more serious problems lay in store. Besides sending touched-up photographs, Japanese immigrant men were sometimes disingenuous in other ways. To enable parents or relatives to find brides easily, they often exaggerated their own attractiveness as future husbands.[19] Keepers of small Japanese-style inns or boardinghouses referred to themselves as hotel operators. In Japan, the word "hotel" connoted something much larger than either, conjuring up images of modern, multistoried brick or concrete structures. Similarly, sharecroppers passed themselves off as landowning farmers, small shopkeepers as big merchants, hotel bellboys as elevator engineers, railroad section foremen as labor contractors. A female reader of the *Shin Sekai* of San Francisco once wrote that, if the newspaper ever printed the letters men forwarded to Japan in seeking picture-brides, the men would have to cringe in shame. She believed that these letters were devoid of sincerity.[20] A few men were culpable of more than hyperboles; they relayed utterly false information about themselves. A picture-bride in one case discovered that her husband was an itinerant gambler instead of being the landowning fruit grower he had claimed to be.[21] Picture-brides had no way of personally verifying information about their spouses. In general, they believed what they heard from go-betweens until they arrived and learned otherwise.

Women came into direct contact with American realities through work. The majority went into rural areas. Many entered labor camps operated by their husbands. Scattered

[19]The immigrant press is full of examples. For example, see "Asahaka na Kekkon," *Taihoku Nippō*, April 25, 26, 28–30, and May 1–3, 1913; and "Kiyū Komogomo Itaru Dōhō no Shashin Kekkon," *Nichibei Shimbun*, April 15–17, 1914.

[20]Fujita Kiyuko, " 'Zairyū Fujin ni Atau' wo Yomite," *Shin Sekai*, Sept. 8–10, 1912.

[21]"Watashi no Kokuhaku," *Shin Sekai*, April 9, 13, 16, 17, and 19, 1914; see also *Taihoku Nippō*, April 13, 16, 18, 22, and 23, 1914.

throughout the western United States, these camps provided laborers for such industries as railroads, coal mines in Wyoming, sugar beet fields in Utah and Idaho, lumber camps and mills in the Pacific Northwest, and salmon canneries in Alaska. Alternatively, women entered farmlands on which their husbands were tilling the soil as cash or share tenants. This practice was especially common in California where Japanese immigrant agriculture flourished the most. In urban areas women entered small businesses in which their husbands were engaged: laundries, bathhouses, bars, markets, restaurants, boardinghouses, and poolhalls. Or they became domestic servants, seamstresses, or cannery workers. But no matter where they ended up, an oppressive life of unending labor was their lot. Ideally, women were supposed to be confined to the home as "dutiful wives and intelligent mothers" (*ryōsai kenbo*). But very few women limited themselves to these two roles. Economic realities forced the majority to assume a third role as workers whose labor was indispensable in the operation of labor camps, farms, and small businesses.

Living and working conditions generally were primitive. In rural areas women had to draw water from wells for cooking, washing, and bathing. Kindling wood was the source of heat. Frequently women had to cook for large gangs of workers employed by their husbands. Makeshift wooden shacks on farms and small rented rooms in towns usually served as initial living quarters. Working from dawn to dusk left little time to socialize, even less to devote oneself to the leisure arts or to learn something about America besides labor. Women were compelled to work in order to survive, a reality which made them aware of hyperboles and falsehoods told by husbands before marriage, causing not a few to become severely disenchanted.

This harsh reality formed the background to marital scandals known as *kakeochi* or desertions of husbands by wives. How often desertion occurred is difficult to ascertain without statistics, but other evidence indicates that it happened with surprising regularity. The immigrant press is replete with kakeochi announcements. A typical notice claims that a married woman and a "scoundrel," both specifically named, had "disappeared," meaning that they had absconded together. The notice includes their physical description, place of origin in Japan, and even photographs of them. Husbands who had been abandoned or local immigrant organizations placed this type of announcement in the immigrant press and offered rewards for information leading to the discovery of the guilty parties. The *Shin Sekai* ran a typical notice in 1909, submitted by Kojima Aizō of Walnut Grove, announcing that his wife, Tsuta, had absconded with Miki Jōkichi.[22] A native of Wakayama Prefecture, Miki is described as thirty-three or thirty-four-years-old, 5 feet 2 inches, 115 pounds with dark complexion and a scar at the nape of his neck. A native of Yamaguchi Prefecture, Tsuta is described as twenty-eight-years old, 5 feet, 110 pounds with fair complexion. The notice states that they vanished together on December 12, 1909. Kojima offered a reward of twenty-five dollars to any party furnishing information on their whereabouts. The *Nichibei Shimbun* of San Francisco, the leading immigrant daily, printed many similar announcements. In September 1912, for example, it ran one by Ōshima Suematsu of Hanford who declared that his wife, Tora, had run off clandestinely with Ōno Ken'ichi.[23] Ōshima likewise offered a reward of twenty-five dollars. Immigrant newspapers in other locales also carried kakeochi announcements.[24]

In addition to announcements, the immigrant press featured kakeochi reportage as regular fare for its readers. Desertion stories appeared as often as kakeochi notices. As early as April 1908, the *Shin Sekai* reported the case of Odawara Toshiko, who had fled from Sacramento to Stockton with her paramour.[25] In June 1914, the *Taihoku Nippō* of Seattle carried a story about Nishizaki Juta who was depicted as a moral derelict.[26] He had seduced the wife of Hashimoto Yōshirō of Tacoma and harbored her secretly until the local Japanese association uncovered his hideaway and had them arrested. Legal charges were dropped once Nishizaki agreed to pay Hashimoto six hundred dollars. Stories normally preceded announcements. The *Shin Sekai* ran a

[22] *Shin Sekai*, Dec. 29, 1909.
[23] *Nichibei Shimbun*, Sept. 12, 1912.
[24] See the preserved issues of the *Rafu Shimpō* of Los Angeles, the *Ōfu Nippō* of Sacramento, and the *Kakushū Jiji* of Denver.
[25] *Shin Sekai*, April 17, 18, and May 3, 1908.
[26] *Taihoku Nippō*, June 16 and 17, 1914.

story on September 20, 1916, about Kimura Haru, wife of Kimura Masaki, who left Loomis with her two-and-a-half-year-old child. Having suffered a miscarriage, she reportedly went to Sacramento in order to regain her health. There, by prearrangement, she met Shimizu Fudeki, who had been employed by her husband on his fruit orchard. The two then disappeared. A notice of this desertion appeared on September 21. The *Nichibei Shimbun*, in another story, reported on February 14–15, 1916, that Yamaura Toshie, wife of Yamaura Chiyozō of Lodi, abandoned not only her husband but her child as well. An announcement of her kakeochi appeared on February 18.

All stories contained variations on the basic theme of desertion. The details differed depending upon the story. A picture-bride deserts just after arriving, while another deserts after living with her husband for a spell. An older married woman leaves her husband and children, while another takes her infant with her. A woman and her paramour plot to steal her husband's hidden money before absconding together. A woman is caught and sent back to Japan, while another is placed into a church-sponsored women's home. The men with whom women run off range from young laborers to roving city salesmen, partners in their husbands' farms or businesses, or professional gamblers. Most stories are written in a tragic vein; a few have an element of the comic. All have didactic overtones. Embellishments and distortions undoubtedly crept into many stories. Newspapers, after all, published kakeochi stories to attract readers so as to enlarge circulation. Yet the stories were not imagined by reporters. They were based upon actual incidents. Combined with the kakeochi announcements, they therefore provide abundant evidence of the regular occurrence of desertion, particularly after 1910 as the number of married women increased within immigrant society.[27]

---

[27] Other sources confirm what appeared in the immigrant press about desertion. Shimanuki Hyōdayū, *Shin To-Bei Hō* (Tokyo, 1911), a Japanese guide book to the United States, decried the prevalence of family problems and desertions within immigrant society. Attributing the blame in part to "false expectations," it warned young women who intended to cross the Pacific to be realistic about life in the United States (pp. 231–240). Uemura Tora, *Hokubei no Nihonjin* (Tokyo, 1912), a book on immigrant society, lamented the "laxity of morals between the sexes" as manifested by "inane marital fights" and "desertions" which had become "intolerable" (p. 350). Niisato

The publication of kakeochi announcements and stories by the immigrant press was also a means of social control. The publicity exposed persons who engaged in desertion to public shame. Branded as "adulteresses" or "immoral hussies," deserting women were ostracized and invariably forced to move to new locales.[28] The *Nichibei Shimbun* printed two notices in July 1913, one announcing that Ōmoto Mine had deserted her husband in Alameda and another that Furube Shizue had left her husband in Oxnard. Both women fled eastward with their paramours, Mine to Wyoming and Shizue to Utah.[29] Remote places, however, were not always safe havens. A Stockton man deserted his own wife and absconded with another man's spouse in yet another case. The man and woman were apprehended in Medford, Oregon, as they were heading for Seattle by Japanese residents who recognized them.[30]

Complementing the social control function of the immigrant press were the Japanese associations which acted as the moral watchdogs of Japanese communities. Wherever Japanese settled, whether in California, Oregon, Washington, or in adjacent western states, they organized associations with which all immigrants had to register in compliance with Japanese government regulations.[31] In 1916 association leaders became alarmed over the rate of desertion. As evidence of a rising rate, the *Nichibei Shimbun* reported that the local association of San Francisco had received an inordinate number of kakeochi notices from other associations.[32] In the spring, secretaries of local associations

---

Kan'ichi, *Iminchi Aiwa: Katei Higeki-hen* (Tokyo, 1933), an anthology of authentic tales of broken families, includes the desertion theme. The theme is also common in fiction produced by immigrant writers. Okina Kyūin, a leading Issei writer, adapted desertion tales he had read or heard into his literary works published during the peak of the picture-bride practice. See Okina, *Okina Kyūin Zenshū*, 35–37. Hosaka Kiichi, *Wagahai no Mitaru Amerika* (Tokyo, 1914), a satirical novel, interprets desertions as an inevitable by-product of the defects in the picture-bride practice (II, 168–177). Sakai Yoneo, *Nikkei Shimin: Yuki* (Tokyo, 1968), a recent novel about an Issei woman, depicts the arrival in America of a picture-bride who finds her husband repulsive and abruptly deserts him.

[28] These pejorative terms appeared in the immigrant press. Other stronger terms were slut (*futei kusare onna*) and bitch (*indara onna*).

[29] *Nichibei Shimbun*, July 2 and 15, 1913; *Shin Sekai*, July 19, 1913.

[30] *Nichibei Shimbun*, Feb. 17–19, 1916.

[31] Yuji Ichioka, "Japanese Associations and the Japanese Government: A Special Relationship, 1909–1926," *Pacific Historical Review*, XLVI (1977), 409–437.

[32] *Nichibei Shimbun*, Oct. 11, 1916.

affiliated with the Japanese Association of America deliberated on the problem of desertion at their annual meeting. Each secretary described the state of marriages within his jurisdiction, and to account for marital failures, enumerated such factors as the drinking and gambling habits of husbands, the disillusionment of picture-brides, and the gaps in age and education among spouses. To the horror of the assembled males, a few cases were cited in which picture-brides had had affairs with seamen or other men aboard ships while en route. This prompted the Japanese Association of America to issue immediately a guide to the United States for women and to have it distributed at ports of embarkation in Japan. First published in August 1916, it was reissued in 1919.[33] The guide instructed young women how to conduct themselves aboard ships, how to manage a household, and how to behave in general in American society. It insisted that the women had the "responsibility" of never revealing "domestic scandals" to white Americans, for such scandals were sources of "embarassment" to all Japanese. In October 1916, the Japanese Association of America asked the T.K.K. Line, a Japanese steamship company, to assign matrons to its ships to supervise young women en route to America and petitioned the Foreign Ministry to direct other Japanese shipping lines to follow suit.[34]

All Japanese associations treated absconding couples as outcasts. The Western Idaho Japanese Association is a case in point. In late September 1923 this association received a letter from the North American Japanese Association of Seattle notifying it that Araeda Asako had absconded with Amano Sanji.[35] She had left her sick husband, Araeda Aiji, and her child. Photographs of her and her paramour were enclosed. The Seattle association asked the Idaho association to be alert to their possible appearance in its jurisdiction. Three weeks later the Idaho association received another letter, this one from the Japanese Association of Watsonville, California, with photo-

[33] *Shin Sekai*, Aug. 15 and 16, 1916; Zaibei Nihonjinkai, *Shin To-Bei Fujin no Shiori* (San Francisco, 1919).

[34] Zaibei Nihonjinkai, *Zaibei Nihonjinkai Nenpō* (San Francisco, 1917), 5–6.

[35] Hokubei Nihonjinkai to Aidaho Nihonjinkai, Sept. 25, 1923, in Seibu Aidaho-shū Nihonjinkai Ta no Nihonjinkai Yori Juryō Shita Shinsho, Jan. 1921–Dec. 1928, JARP.

graphs attached.[36] The letter asserted that Kasamatsu Chika had deserted her husband and three children and had run off with Kuramoto Hikosuke. Japanese associations communicated in this manner with each other, and as a matter of common policy refused to have any dealings with absconding couples. The network of associations made it well-nigh impossible for such couples to escape detection, even when they left one state and settled down in a Japanese community in another. If they wished to elude social ostracism altogether, they had no choice but to resettle in a place with no Japanese.

Marital estrangement was at the bottom of desertion. No woman took these matters lightly. Living in an alien land reinforced the traditional subordinate role of Japanese women. With little or no knowledge of the English language and American society, wives had to depend upon their husbands for almost everything. This dependency, coupled with threat of public exposure, inhibited drastic behavior like desertion. As a general rule, therefore, women who deserted had to be those who were very desperate. Becoming a social outcast, to them, was better than enduring conjugal relations which had degenerated to an insufferable level. Kawai Michiko, a prominent Christian educator in Japan, observed the picture-bride practice at first hand in 1917. She felt that "an outdated attitude" exhibited by men in America was the main cause of marital conflicts. Despite changes in ideas and practices in Japan, the men clung to archaic notions they had learned from their fathers in the nineteenth century about the absolute subordinate role of wives.[37]

On the positive side, the majority of married women did not engage in kakeochi and thus enabled many Japanese to enjoy settled family life. Reflecting the emergence of the Japanese immigrant family unit was the dramatic increase in the number of American-born or Nisei children between 1900 and 1930. At the turn of the century, there were only 269 children; by 1910 the number had grown to 4,502; and by 1920 it had multiplied more than sixfold to 29,672. In 1930 Nisei numbered

[36] Japanese Association of Watsonville to Nihonjinkai, Oct. 12, 1923, in *ibid.*

[37] Kawai Michiko, "Fujin no Me ni Eizuru Tokō Fujin," *Nihon Imin Kyōkai Hōkoku*, No. 14 (Dec. 3, 1917), 31–50.

68,357 out of a total Japanese population of 138,834.[38] Most women gave birth to these children through midwifery. Nearly every Japanese settlement had midwives. If a settlement did not have any, women relied upon those who worked in neighboring communities. Many pregnant women in the Imperial Valley, for example, entered maternity clinics in Los Angeles which were staffed with midwives. In isolated rural areas husbands served as midwives or women gave birth completely unassisted, even cutting and tying the umbilical cord themselves.[39] Most women never had extensive prenatal or postnatal care. They worked until a few days before delivery and resumed work shortly after. The growth of Nisei children accelerated the transformation of the Japanese from sojourners to permanent settlers as the parent generation ultimately identified its own future with that of its children in America. In short, the entry of women into immigrant society was integral to the process by which Japanese immigrants sank roots in American soil.

For anti-Japanese agitators Japanese women were easy targets to attack. Exclusionists assailed the picture-bride practice as an uncivilized "Asiatic" custom, a throwback as it were to barbarism by which women were wed without regard to morality or love. They alleged that the practice violated the Gentlemen's Agreement of 1907–1908 designed to curtail all labor immigration from Japan. Female laborers disguised as brides, according to critics, entered the United States, thereby deviously undermining the intent of the agreement. To make matters worse, women produced children who in turn permitted the Japanese to circumvent the California Alien Land Law of 1913, which prohibited aliens ineligible to citizenship from purchasing agricultural land and limited the leasing of such land to three years. Exclusionists contended that the Japanese, who were ineligible to citizenship, were buying agricultural land in the name of their offspring who were American citizens. Finally, they argued that because the children could not be assimilated into American society, they were dangerous increments to the Japanese population. Senator James D. Phelan of California and others leveled

---

[38]Edward K. Strong, *The Second-Generation Japanese Problem* (Stanford, 1934), 160.
[39]Gee, "Issei: The First Women," 14–15.

these allegations as part of a campaign they launched in early 1919 against the picture-bride practice in particular and Japanese immigration in general.[40]

In response to the agitation, the Japanese government in December 1919 decided unilaterally to cease issuing passports to picture-brides.[41] The picture-bride practice had become a useful issue for exclusionists in generating virulent anti-Japanese sentiments. The Foreign Ministry abolished the practice to deprive them of the issue. Because this action meant that single men were almost certainly doomed to permanent bachelorhood, Japanese immigrants overwhelmingly denounced it. Of the adult male Japanese population in 1920, some 42.5% or 24,423 were still unmarried.[42] These men, for the most part, had remained single, not by personal choice but rather by their inability to meet the requirements for summoning picture-brides.

Abiko Kyūtarō, publisher of the *Nichibei Shimbun*, led the immigrant opposition to the Foreign Ministry's decision. In line with his advocacy of permanent residency, he had consistently urged single men to send for wives from Japan. Although he acknowledged shortcomings in the picture-bride practice, he had always defended it as the only means by which bachelors could afford to get married. In 1915 he had objected strenuously to the eight-hundred-dollar savings requirement in the belief that no laborer could meet it.[43] Abiko's criticism of the abolition of the picture-bride practice was so caustic that the Japanese consul of San Francisco denounced him for "playing on the ignorance of the masses" in drumming up wide community opposition.[44] At a San Francisco protest rally sponsored by the

[40] *San Francisco Examiner*, March 7–9, 1919; Ichihashi, *Japanese in the United States*, 295–296.

[41] Ichioka, "Japanese Associations and the Japanese Government," 431–433.

[42] U.S. Bureau of the Census, *Fourteenth Census of the United States, 1920: Population* (Washington, D.C., 1922), II, 388 and 390.

[43] *Nichibei Shimbun*, editorials, July 20, Aug. 8 and 14, 1915.

[44] Ōta Tamekichi to Uchida Yasuya, Nov. 20, 1919, in Nihon Gaimushō, *Nihon Gaikō Bunsho, 1919* (Tokyo, 1970), I, 78. For Abiko's opposition to the termination of the picture-bride practice, see Okina, *Okina Kyūin Zenshū*, 230–231; and Akashi Junzō, "Abiko-shi no Inshō: Shashin Kekkon Kinshi Jiken no Kioku," 1956, Oka Shigeki Papers, box 133, folder 4, JARP.

Nichibei Shimbun, the opposition even embraced a demand for the recall of Consul Ōta Tamekichi who had recommended to the Foreign Ministry the termination of the practice. But the Foreign Ministry ignored the hue and cry, for it considered the appeasement of exclusionists more important than the welfare of immigrant bachelors. Beginning on March 1, 1920, it issued passports only to wives who accompanied spouses to the United States.

Thus photo-marriages became a thing of the past. Bachelors had one option left open to them. They still could return to Japan, marry, and bring back their wives with them. Due to the expensive cost of travel, however, few were able to exercise this option, which itself was closed four years later. Exclusionists were never placated by the abolition of the picture-bride practice. Seeking nothing less than the termination of all Japanese immigration, they continued to lobby for congressional legislation and achieved their goal with the enactment of the Immigration Act of 1924, which barred the admission of any alien ineligible to citizenship. A few bachelors rushed to Japan to get married during the spring of 1924 and managed to return with their brides before July 1, the effective date of the act. These brides were the last Japanese women to immigrate to the United States until well after World War II.

Although the abolition of the picture-bride practice and the Immigration Act of 1924 prevented the sex ratio within immigrant society from balancing out, the women who arrived prior to 1924 were sufficient in number to alter the character of that society. Their presence and the birth of the American-born generation had the effect of socially reinforcing the transformation of Japanese immigrant men from sojourners to permanent settlers.

SINGLE MOTHERS AND CHILD NEGLECT, 1880–1920[1]

LINDA GORDON
University of Wisconsin, Madison

IN 1917 CORA SIMPSON, A TWENTY-FIVE-YEAR-OLD MOTHER OF GIRLS AGED THREE and one-and-a-half, came to the office of the Massachusetts Society for the Prevention of Cruelty to Children (MSPCC) seeking help.[2] She was penniless, she said, because her husband had deserted her. Some excerpts from her case record may be of interest, both as an introduction to the issues that will be discussed here and to the sources on which this essay is based:

> August 1917. Mo . . . is in great need as she has no . . . income. She has previously received temporary aid from A.C. [Associated Charities] . . . she had the fa. in ct. for n-s [non-support] in March 1916 . . . Rosemary [age 1½] is rickety as recorded by a Doctor . . . the chn. were about half-starved during the winter; the mo. was about ready to give the chn. up but she reconsidered this when Mrs. W. offered to take her into her home to board but the expense was too great . . . Mrs. W. felt the fam. would have to go. Mrs. S. . . . former landlady, reported that the chn. were really destitute when with her. . . . Miss C., A.C., states that . . . a recent rumor that mo. had been imml. [immoral] had not been substantiated . . . there were no relas. [relatives] to help mo.

In September 1918 Mrs. Simpson returned to the MSPCC asking for help with a new baby, illegitimate.

[1]Revised Jan. 1985. The material in this paper comes from a study of the history of family violence, supported by the National Institutes of Mental Health. I am also grateful to the John Simon Guggenheim Foundation for support, to the staff of the MSPCC and BCSA for their courtesy, and to Ros Baxandall, Wini Breines, Nancy Cott, Ellen DuBois, Allen Hunter, Elizabeth Pleck, and Pauline Terrelonge for helpful critical readings.

[2]Confidentiality requirements prevent the use of actual names in this paper. This case history is taken from case records of the Massachusetts Society for the Prevention of Cruelty to Children, now in the Univ. of Massachusetts/Boston Archives. The records are not open to the public except with the permission of the MSPCC.

> Mo. is weaning baby and thinks she might go to work and start a home for herself and chn. with aged colored woman to care for chn. during day. . . . Miss B., A.C., seemed to think that mo. was an immoral woman . . . does not feel like reestablishing fam. but will try to get rela. in NY to help or may place two of chn. . . . mo to go service with the third.

This history did not end happily. No relatives would agree to board the children for free. In May 1919 Cora Simpson was earning fifteen dollars a week as a seamstress and was paying over half of that to two different women for the board of her girls, keeping the baby with her in the tailor shop. In July of that year she was evicted, accused by her landlord of earning "by illeg. means." She left her three children with friends and disappeared. Her children became wards of the state and were placed in an orphanage.[3]

This case is one of approximately a thousand sampled in a study of family violence and its social control in Boston from 1880 to 1960.[4] As a case of child *neglect* it is far more typical than the fewer but more publicized cases of *abuse*. As a case involving a single mother, it is also typical, because single mothers are consistently overrepresented as neglectful parents.

This essay is a contribution to the historical understanding of two intersecting contemporary social problems, single motherhood and child neglect, neither of which has a significant written history. An attempt to understand why single mothers appeared so often negligent illuminates both the historical construction of modern single motherhood and the modern concept of child neglect. In fact, these two social problems were mutually constructed. The very definition of child neglect arose as part of an ideology about proper family life that automatically conceived of single mothers as inadequate parents. Even accepting, momentarily, the definitions of adequate parenting imposed by child protection agencies (and they will be subjected to criticism below), these agency responses to neglectful single mothers were circular, blaming the mothers for child neglect but declining to help them become adequate mothers.

This contradiction was not merely a "bias" of charity and social workers. It resulted from the newly anomalous *structural* position of single mothers in an urbanizing society. The many "Mrs. Simpsons" in agency case records faced economic and social difficulties different from those of previous, more rural generations of single mothers. These included both objective difficulties in managing the tasks of earning and childraising simultaneously, and a new lack of

[3]Case code number #2503. I cite references to the cases using a coding system devised during this research. A researcher with permission to use the records should consult me for a key to the code.

[4]Case records from three child welfare agencies were sampled for every tenth year from 1880 to 1960. Jan Lambertz, Paul O'Keefe, Anne Doyle Kenney, Nancy McKerrow, and Martha Coons contributed to this research and to my understanding of it, but I alone must remain responsible for the conclusions in this paper. Hence when I refer to research data, I consider the project collective and use the word "our"; when I refer to findings and arguments, I use "I" or "my."

sympathy for their strategies. The lapse in sympathy resulted from the fact that the single mothers often sought to establish themselves as heads of households, an aspiration that seemed reprehensible to those holding traditional views about normative family life, even though it was often the best and arguably the only means of preventing children's suffering.

In order to examine this double-bind in which so many single mothers found themselves, I will introduce, first, the MSPCC and similar child-saving agencies, second, the circumstances of the single mothers in this study, and third, definitions of child neglect at the turn of the century.

In the 1870s an organized campaign arose against cruel or inadequate parenting. The MSPCC, one of the vanguard organizations dedicated to "child protection," was established in 1878; by 1880 there were thirty-four such societies in the United States and fifteen elsewhere.[5] Childraising, of course, has never been a completely private activity, and the Massachusetts colony had regulated it by statute since at least 1642.[6] The 1870s, however, brought a marked increase in concern about child mistreatment, partly owing to the visibility and intensity of urban poverty. In Boston, large-scale immigration (particularly from Italy, Ireland, and Canada) meant that the harsh conditions experienced by poor children combined with the culturally different patterns of immigrant neighborhoods to convince a Protestant, English-American elite that there was a virtual epidemic of child abuse. Initiated by relatively conservative Boston feminists and male moral reformers, the MSPCC was simultaneously an upper-class charity and a paragovernmental enforcement agency. Its agents—all educated, Protestant, and male, expanding in number from about five in the 1880s to nearly twenty by the World War I era—investigated reports of cruelty to children, prosecuted parents, and seized children found in neglectful homes. Recognized statutorily as an appropriate temporary guardian for neglected or abused children, the MSPCC quickly became Boston's *de facto* arbiter of acceptable means of childraising, its recommendations virtually always accepted by the courts.

The concept of the "single mother" is a recent one and, in some respects, it

[5]On the "discovery" of child abuse, see Joyce Antler and Stephen Antler, "From Child Rescue to Family Protection: The Evolution of the Child Protective Movement in the United States," *Children and Youth Service Review*, 1 (1979), 177–204.

[6]Harriet M. Skillern, "A Socio-legal Analysis of the Massachusetts Stubborn Child Law," Diss. Brandeis Univ. 1977, 14. This point is important because some recent scholarship erroneously adopts a model in which state and private-charity intervention into family life is assumed to be a new and unprecented development of the late nineteenth century. See, for example, Christopher Lasch, *Haven in a Heartless World* (New York: Basic Books, 1977); and Lasch, *The Culture of Narcissism* (New York: Norton, 1979). For critiques, see Eli Zaretsky, "The Place of the Family in the Origins of the Welfare State," in *Rethinking the Family*, ed. Barrie Thorne (New York: Longman, 1982), 188–224; Nancy Chodorow and Susan Contratto, "The Fantasy of the Perfect Mother," in ibid., 54–75; Linda Gordon, "Child Abuse, Gender, and the Myth of Family Independence: Thoughts on the History of Family Violence and Its Social Control 1880–1920," *New York University Review of Law and Social Change*, 12 (1983–84), 523–37.

is inferior as a category to the more specific, earlier labels of widow, deserted wife, unmarried mother, and divorcee. These labels called attention to the mothers' histories and thus to the circumstances that brought them to single motherhood and influenced their subsequent behavior. Yet these labels were also moralistic: widows and deserted wives, it was assumed, claimed sympathy while unmarried and divorced mothers deserved condemnation. Such labels continued a tradition of distinguishing the deserving from the undeserving poor and, in the hands of the child-savers, they operated to determine how the behavior of the women would be evaluated morally and what sorts of help might be offered.

Specifically, who were these child-neglecting single mothers? Thirty-five percent of them were widows. These were not only more numerous proportionately than they are today, but they were also younger and more often had young children, because illness and industrial accidents killed relatively more young men than they do today.

Sixty-one percent were married women separated from their husbands. Of these, twenty-eight percent had been deserted (they were so labeled either by themselves or by MSPCC workers). The problem of defining desertion requires mention here. The high proportion of deserted women in this period, compared to twentieth-century figures, results both from different forms of marital separation and from different interpretations of separation. Women's economic dependence, both their actual helplessness and their sense of helplessness when left without husbands, made some wives call themselves deserted when a modern observer might describe them as separated. It was simultaneously true that more separations resulted from men's unilateral actions than is the case today, again because of women's economic dependence, but also because men, particularly the poor immigrants so often the MSPCC clients, were unaccustomed to the lone responsibility for support of their families and, when faced with failure, often ran from the obligation.

There was an equally indistinct boundary between deserters and those husbands who were present but nonsupporting. In fact, many separated couples in these case records colluded in presenting their story as one of desertion in the hopes of winning sympathy and material aid for the wife; many husbands dropped in and out of their families, appearing occasionally by the week, the month, or even the year.[7] Other husbands lived with their families but did not support them adequately.

Only ten percent of these separated mothers were legally divorced. The primary significance of divorce for these women was that it allowed legal remarriage. Many separated women in fact reconstituted marriage-like relations and often, moreover, claimed to be married when visited by social workers. (However, the child-saving agencies always traced marriage registrations, a boon to researchers if

[7] #2042, #2053, #3041, for examples.

hardly to clients.) Their children, nevertheless, were illegitimate. The proportion of never-married women was less than five percent, and the majority of illegitimate children in agency records were born to married women. (Indeed, the category "illegitimate" tells nothing about whether the children actually had fathers in their households or their lives.)

As a result of these definitional complexities, the boundaries between woman- and man-headed families were not fixed. Many women labeled single by the agency were in *de facto* common-law marriages;[8] and other women, considered married, ran their households and supported their children alone. Furthermore, these conditions were shifting and many mothers were only temporarily single.

* * *

Just as the definition of a single mother was complex, so was the definition of child neglect. Laws prescribed procedures and penalties in cases of child neglect (and all cruelty-to-children cases were brought under the neglect laws, even if they were cases of abuse), but offered no objective definition of the problem. The Massachusetts 1882 statute for instance, broadly defined a neglected child as one "growing up without education or salutary control, and in circumstances exposing him to lead an idle and dissolute life, or is dependent upon public charity."[9] Lacking statutory specificity, judges gave extraordinary power to the MSPCC to define standards of proper parenting. From the case records it is possible to identify five operative categories of what was actually considered children's maltreatment: (1) physical neglect, including malnutrition, poor clothing, poor housing, dirtiness; (2) medical neglect, i.e., the failure to maintain good health standards or to seek professional medical treatment for illness; (3) lack of supervision, including leaving children alone or not disciplining them; (4) overwork, i.e., demanding too much labor (paid or unpaid) of children and/or keeping them from school; and (5) moral neglect, the failure to provide suitable moral standards in environment and training, including exposure to illicit sex or excessive drinking, and failure to send them to church. (Emotional neglect would be added as a category in the mid-twentieth century.)

Neglect could not be identified without substantial class, cultural, religious, even personal bias. For example, immigrants from poor and rural backgrounds were not accustomed to seeking professional medical treatment. The poor also lacked access to many domestic standards considered minimal by social workers, such as separate beds and bedrooms, clean linen, and regular baths. MSPCC agents, all of them white, Anglo-Saxon Protestants, prosperous and well-educated,

[8]There was no legal recognition of common-law marriage in Massachusetts.
[9]Acts of 1882, ch. 181, Sec. 3.

often disdained and misinterpreted the cultural and parental views of their clients, most of them Catholic, poor, and ill-educated. For example, the MSPCC agents disliked wine drinking, garlicky food, and loud voices. They did not believe that children should be allowed to play outside on dirty city streets. They did not believe that young children should be in the care of other young children.

Bias against single mothers also influenced the definitions of neglect. Looking at the proportions of single mothers involved from several different angles, it appears that single mothers were always overrepresented. They were slightly overrepresented in cases of child abuse—that is, assault on children—and strongly overrepresented in neglect cases. Single mother households were involved in 28 percent of all MSPCC cases between 1880 and 1920, but in 52 percent of child neglect cases.[10] From a different perspective, considering single-parenthood as a "stress" factor (like unemployment or illness), single-parenthood occurred in 50.5 percent of child-neglect cases, 25 percent of child-abuse cases. By comparison, 19 percent of all Boston families were headed by women.[11] Nor can the overrepresentation of single mothers be reduced to the greater economic and social difficulties of immigrants. Although the proportion of foreign-born women who headed households was larger than the overall average—8 percent of all Boston women were family heads, 12 percent of foreign-born women—it would still not account for thc high proportion of single mothers among the neglect cases.

Comparison of the child-neglect cases involving single mothers to those involving two parents suggested that the former were more likely to be child neglecters for two kinds of reasons: because their social and economic circumstances made it harder for them to provide adequate parenting, and because the agencies involved in defining the problem of child neglect (and in attempting to cure it) were biased against single mothers.

One indicator of discrimination against single mothers was the use of pejorative labels. Such labeling can be measured in two ways: by comparing single mothers to other clients, and by comparing the labels to actual behavior; in both, one must be cautious in disentangling gender from class prejudices. Social workers of this era were likely to believe the worst of working-class men, quick to label them depraved or degenerate. By contrast, poor women benefited from assumptions of good intentions, moral purity, and blameless victimization, if one can benefit from such condescension. Women, however, could lose this high evaluation at any sign of

[10]This statistic figured from our sampling of records from every tenth year; the MSPCC in its statistical compilations did not use the category "single mother." These percentages are of verified allegations, the unconfirmed having been eliminated.

[11]Averaging the 1885, 1895, and 1905 censuses. Nineteen percent is probably an underestimate because many married women were single heads of household for substantial but nevertheless unrecorded periods of time. For example, in our case records, fifteen percent of individuals were classified as "married and living together off and on," but not counted as single household heads.

failing. Women were, for example, more than twice as likely as men to be labeled immoral by agency workers (this diagnosis was applied 68.9 percent of the time to women, 31.1 percent to men); yet men more often conducted extramarital sexual affairs. Single mothers were also more likely to be called immoral than other women. Naturally single mothers were more likely than married women to have nonmarital sexual relationships, but, as noted above, many of these relationships were *de facto* marriages. Here across-the-board application of standards of propriety came down harder on single mothers. In a similar pattern women were somewhat less likely than men to be labeled intemperate (43.9 percent women, 56.1 percent men), but qualitative reading of the case records suggested that women were less likely actually to drink heavily. Single mothers were more often called intemperate than other women, without evidence of indulging in heavier drinking.

Furthermore, the weight of these labels was heavier for mothers than for fathers, for single mothers than for other mothers. Sexual immorality or intemperance in a mother was in itself grounds for child-neglect charges; not so in a father. When a mother had adulterous relations with a boarder, she was immoral; when a father did so with a housekeeper, *she* was the menace to the household morality.[12] In two-parent neglect cases, the mother was more likely to be considered the culpable parent. This pattern was particularly strong in moral neglect cases. For example, even though mothers were less likely to be considered intemperate than fathers, they were more likely to be charged with child neglect due to intemperance. Of those charged with child neglect due to immorality, 77 percent were mothers and 23 percent fathers. The application of this double standard by child-protective agencies was justified by their conviction that mothers had the greater moral influence on children. The problem from the point of view of single mothers was that they had to take on the responsibilities of men with neither the privileges of men nor the leeway granted to male peccadillos. Police were more often involved in complaints against single mothers than in those concerning two-parent families: overall in this period police were drawn into 76.6 percent of all cases and into 87.4 percent of single-mother cases.

The best measurement of the MSPCC's attitudes towards single mothers was its actions, especially its most drastic—removing children from their parents. In cases of equal average severity, as defined by the agency social workers, children were removed from 75 percent of single-mother homes and 54 percent of two-parent

[12]For a spelling out of this double standard, see Anna Ely Moorehouse, "The Neglected Children of Widowers," in *Children in Need of Special Care: Studies Based on Two Thousand Case Records of Social Agencies*, ed. Lucile Eaves et al. (Boston, 1923), 55; or consider Mary Richmond's comment, "the danger of family disintegration is much greater where the mother, rather than the father, is the weak member," in her *The Long View*, ed. Joanna Colcord (New York: Russell Sage Foundation, 1930), 450–51.

homes. (There were very few single-father families, only 3.6 percent of the cases, and they were eliminated in this comparison.) Furthermore, controlling for situations in which parents themselves asked to have children removed,[13] children were even more likely to be taken against the wishes of a single mother than of two parents. In fact, single mothers were less likely to want the removal of their children in the first place: only 15 percent of child-removal requests came from single mothers, although they comprised 28 percent of all cases.[14] By contrast, where a male-headed family was neglectful, neglect charges were less likely to be brought. Rather, the agency's strategy was more often to get the father arrested, usually for drunkenness or nonsupport, with a short or suspended sentence, or alternatively to issue warnings; both strategies were intended to pressure the parents into providing better care for their children.[15]

Only one variable other than single motherhood was a better predictor of court-ordered child removal: poverty. Yet this was just another aspect of the same phenomenon, for single mothers were poorer than other parents. From 1880 to 1920, forty-four percent of single mothers were in economic deprivation,[16] as compared to twenty-six percent of two-parent families. Only ten percent of single-mother families reached the economic level defined as competence, as compared to thirty-one percent of two-parent families. Of course, most of the MSPCC's clients were poor, not because poor people treated their children worse, but because they were more likely to be caught, and because poverty accounted for a considerable proportion of what maltreatment of children *was*. The Society was

[13]Parents asked this in eighteen percent of all cases, often seeking temporary placements during an illness, until a job could be found, in order to get a rest, or until the children were old enough for school or work.

[14]I can suggest two hypotheses to explain why single mothers, despite their greater poverty, were more committed to keeping their children at all times: (1) single women gained in social status and self-respect from having children more than women in couples did; (2) single women knew that they were more likely to lose custody of their children permanently if they gave them up even temporarily.

[15]The legal procedure in neglect cases was to have the child adjudged neglected and given over into the custody of an agency, or returned to the parents with a continuance under the supervision of an agency. Parents were neither convicted nor sentenced for child neglect; their punishment was, de facto, the loss of the child. Parents prosecuted for drunkenness or nonsupport did not necessarily or even usually lose their children.

[16]Detailed information about family earnings and expenditures began to be available in child protection case records only at the very end of this study, so that these attempts to characterize the standard of living of the clients is approximate. Five categories were established in this coding and researchers reading the cases were asked to make a judgment on the basis of all available clues in the case record. The categories were: deprivation, including those who lacked necessities for health, e.g. shoes, fuel, food subsistence, including those who maintained life and health with chronic insecurity and uncertainty; competence, including those who did not exhibit insecurity or uncertainty about ability to keep family members adequately housed, warmed, clothed, and fed, and who could afford at least some items defined as nonnecessary, e.g. a watch; middle class, including those with standards, aspirations, or employment that set them above manual laborers; and prosperous, including those who could afford substantial luxuries.

sensitive to allegations that it kidnapped poor people's children, and its stated policy was that it never removed children from their homes for poverty alone. Yet poverty was never alone. The characteristic signs of child neglect in this period—dirty clothing, soiled linen, lice and worms, crowded sleeping conditions, lack of attention and supervision, untreated infections and running sores, rickets and other malformations, truancy, malnutrition, and overwork—were often the direct results of poverty.

Two excerpts from case notes may provide a glimpse of what the child-savers encountered in neglectful homes:

> 1904. In the kitchen . . . about a dozen empty beer bottles. Two whiskey bottles one partly full the other empty. A beef bone in a pan on the stove looked as if it was cooked a month ago. . . . dry bread crusts on the table and 3 or 4 dirty dishes. In the bed room was an old bedstead with two very filthy mattresses on it with what was once two pillows. But they were so dirty and greasy it would be impossible to tell what they were made of. At the head of the bed was a vessel full of filth which from its look had not been emptied for a month. . . . Two younger children in the kitchen nearly naked as dirty as they could well be and covered with vermin. [#1544A.]
>
> 1919. The odor in the house was very bad and the kitchen was very dirty. The chn.s' clothes were dirty and ragged and meant for much older chn. Mo. came down stairs wearing a loose kimono and carrying a thin frail looking 7 months old baby who was very dirty. . . . The house had no fire and the chn all seemed to have colds. Mo. seemed unconcerned. . . . Said the chn sleep in clean beds at night but seemed reluctant to show them. Hazel, Gladys, and Morris sleep in the bed which she showed agt. [These children are 7, 8 and 11.] There was a very dirty mattress and no clothing. The floor was littered with rubbish. Hazel had been sent home from sch. recently because teacher said she was dirty but mo. had washed the dress just the day before. The air in the front room was stifling, the floor was covered with rubbish and . . . filth. Marion . . . wore no underclothing was wearing a shoe on one foot and no shoe or stocking on the other. Alice . . . had no underclothing on . . . no stockings. [#3050A.]

In addition, cases abounded of children treated with apparent callousness. Small children were found wandering on the streets at midnight, abandoned in the winter, and left alone in dark and unheated tenements without food. Babies were found undiapered or with their diapers unchanged, unfed and sucking on wet rags, with intestinal worms crawling visibly on diapers and skin and maggots attacking open sores. Drunken or sick mothers were unable to get out of bed to tend to needy children.

Such cases require reconsideration of the distinction, made above, between agency bias and objective neglect. Actual neglect defies such neat categorization. The "bias" of social workers could be described as prediction based on experience of the objective difficulties. Furthermore, neither the social workers nor contemporary researchers studying the case records could easily distinguish children's deprivations caused by poverty from those caused by parental indifference or hostility; parental indifference and hostility were among the most common products of poverty, and in addition, parents' depression was implicated both as cause and effect of poverty. Further, the social workers' standards of what constituted deprivation were "biased." In the originating conception of child-saving work, the notion of children's "rights" to a certain standard of treatment was the product of specific class and cultural experience. The irony embedded in child-saving work was that the reformers wanted to guarantee children a living standard often better than that of their parents, yet they wanted to preserve parental independence in child-raising.

* * *

If social workers could not usually distinguish neglectful parenting from the nature of single motherhood itself, that coalescence of problems reflected historical change. In agrarian economies, first, there were fewer single mothers, due mainly to lower illegitimacy and desertion rates. Second, greater household flexibility, community responsibility, and variable labor requirements allowed single mothers and their children to be integrated into extended or augmented households, even among the poor. The conditions single mothers encountered in Boston were quite different. Very few of the mothers in these case records were able to live in other family households.[17] Sixty-nine percent of those in the MSPCC cases were dependent on their own earnings for their own and their children's survival. Before the development of state mothers' pensions in the decade from 1910 to 1920, these women faced alone the task of earning a living while maintaining homes and supervising children.

Yet jobs were scarce and wages low. Boston was not a mill town hungry for women's and children's labor power. There was some light-industry factory work—candy making, for example—and sweated garment work. (Clerical work had not yet expanded and was still primarily male.) The most common women's occupation was, of course, domestic service. Yet for all these jobs young unmarried women were preferred. The scarcity of employment, moreover, depressed female wages for jobs other than domestic service even lower than in more industrial cities.[18]

A second problem facing working mothers was the lack of child care. Day nurseries were rare. It should not be surprising that inadequate supervision of children was cited in eighteen percent of MSPCC cases overall but in forty-three percent of single-mother cases. Lack of child-care resources was the reason that

[17]Of course these case records capture the experience of the least fortunate, by definition; those with stronger social support networks were much less likely to come to the attention of social agencies. Yet our subject *is* the least fortunate.

[18]Carroll D. Wright, *The Working Girls of Boston* (Boston, 1889), 81 and passim.

mothers, unlike childless women, preferred home work to outside jobs. They took in boarders, or washing, and did babysitting for others. Limiting the availability and the income of such work was the fact that the poor could afford very little for these services, while the rich preferred to have them done in their own homes. Thus few women successfully earned a living in this way. Better pay could be gotten from manufacturing piece work, usually hand sewing or hand assembly in the garment or millinery industries, but the working conditions were worse. Piece rates were low and women worked twelve to sixteen hours a day, neglected housekeeping and child-care, and put young children to work with them in order to make a living wage. Few women managed on this basis. A 1913 study of working women in nine cities, including Boston, showed that only twenty-eight percent of widows lived on home work. In comparison to work outside the home, home work produced lower earnings, longer hours, more stress, and more health damage.[19]

Other kinds of home work led to "immorality." Taking in boarders was frowned upon by the MSPCC and most agencies as a source of immoral influences,[20] although boarders' payments were vital to a large proportion of households. In Boston the boarding clientele was predominantly male, and many mothers in the MSPCC cases did indeed appear to be having sexual relationships with "boarders"—such allegations were made against forty-one percent of single mothers—which offense automatically made them "unfit" mothers.[21] These "star boarders," as landladies' lovers were called, also figured prominently in MSPCC cases as abusers of children, another danger facing the mothers. Single mothers with abusive lovers or boarders faced a dilemma similar to that of wives with abusive husbands: their desire to keep their children and need for help in supporting them made them less able to protect themselves and their children from molestation or abuse.

Some of the most lucrative home work was illegal—notably prostitution and bootlegging, both common among single mothers; even before Prohibition many women manufactured and sold home brew. Both were virtually automatic grounds

[19]Mary E. Richmond and Fred S. Hall, *A Study of Nine Hundred and Eighty-five Widows Known to Certain Charity Organization Societies in 1910* (New York: Russell Sage Foundation, 1910), 22; Irene O. Andrews, *The Relation of Irregular Employment to the Living Wage for Women* (New York: New York State Factory Investigating Commission, 1915); Emily C. Brown, *Industrial Home Work* (Washington, D.C.: U.S. Women's Bureau Bulletin #79, 1930); Louise C. Odencrantz, *Italian Women in Industry* (New York: Russell Sage Foundation, 1919); Mary Van Kleeck, *Artificial Flower Makers* (New York: Survey Associates, 1913).

[20]Helen Glenn Tyson, "The Fatherless Family," in Frank D. Watson, ed., *Social Work with Families: Social Case Treatment*, Vol. 77 and Supplement of *Annals*, American Academy of Political and Social Science (Philadelphia) May 1918, 85.

[21]Included here are allegations made by MSPCC workers, relatives, or neighbors. One should not assume, however, that these were boarders who became lovers, thereby proving the moral dangers of taking boarders. They may as well have been lovers, or "common-law" husbands, whom the women were trying to disguise to social workers as boarders.

for child-neglect charges. In several MSPCC cases women turned parts of their flats into informal bars or speakeasies.[22] In other cases already crowded families gave up space to small-scale commercial operations in return for help with the rent.[23]

In seeking outside jobs the presence of relatives or friends to care for children was crucial to success. A deserted wife or a widow might manage if her parents or a sister would take her and her family in, and others might even manage to maintain their own household with babysitting help. Yet such solutions were usually unstable. Many mothers resented the indignity of becoming a dependent again, subject to another head of household; babysitters, even relatives, were themselves often unreliable and neglectful.

Most domestic servants were required to live in, and at best, in some cases, might be allowed to bring a nursing baby. Older children would have to be placed elsewhere. Employers sometimes "helped" their maids by applying to the Society for placement of older babies.[24] In these cases the mother's choice was to sign away her child or to lose her job. For such reasons mothers seized the opportunity to do nonresident house cleaning, or "day work," as it was called. One common form of day work was laundry. Several MSPCC cases offered the irony of filthy children in unwashed bedding whose mothers washed, bleached, and ironed for others. Day housecleaning work gradually increased in this period, not in private homes but in office buildings. This "day work," as it was called, was usually night work. (In a 1913 study, forty-eight percent of widows worked at night.)[25] Since arranging child care then was even harder than in the day, many children were left unattended, unless the mother also had boarders, lodgers, or relatives in her home. The MSPCC cases contain numerous examples of mothers trying to hide the fact that they worked nights so as not to have to answer questions about what they did with the children. Night cleaning furthermore deprived mothers of sleep and often meant that they worked around the clock.

In these circumstances mothers often leaned on their children to bring in income. This expectation continued traditional family economy patterns for many clients, but in their new urban situation, child labor was defined as neglect. Its frequency, nevertheless, was evidenced by the important role of the truant officer in referrals to the MSPCC. Other neglected children did illegal peddling or stealing (as, for example, from the coal scuttles of rich houses or railroad yards); these children's mothers were often even more "neglectful" than the authorities imagined, not only failing to prevent such mischief but actively encouraging it.

[22]That is, they sold liquor not only by the bottle but also by the drink.

[23]In one 1917 case, two rooms of a four-room tenement were sublet to a peddler who stored his fruits and vegetables there. Yet the two children were malnourished.

[24]#0814A.

[25]Richmond and Hall, *A Study of Nine Hundred and Eight-five Widows*, ch. 10.

In trying to provide adequate parenting, single mothers were often caught in a series of double binds. Their very attempts to nurture children could produce neglect. Doing home work led to overworking children, depriving them of attention and supervision, and overcrowding the apartment, with the likelihood of failing to provide adequately for children despite these hardships. Going out to work might require leaving children alone and vulnerable, or placing them with unloving and irresponsible babysitters. Looking for a male breadwinner might lead to immoral relations. Trying to protect children from the abuse of others might deprive the family of a breadwinner. Agency policies made it risky for single mothers to be honest, and they attempted to conceal their jobs, their babysitters, their lovers, their pregnancies, and even their illnesses for fear of losing their children.[26]

What might agencies such as the MSPCC have done to aid neglectful single mothers? It is important to remember the historical context in answering. Before 1920 not even the most radical reformers welcomed full-time employment for women or day care for children. In the last decade of this period mothers' pensions, sometimes called widows' pensions, were established by many states, representing the first large-scale charitable and governmental recognition that single mothers comprised a *category* of people needing help. The debate over mothers' pensions split the charities and correction establishment, many of its leading spokespeople, including MSPCC leaders, opposing this reform. Even its supporters expressed anxiety about woman-headed households. Still, the child-savers' opposition to mothers' pensions was not a simple product of concern about children's deprivations, and indeed it was in some aspects dissonant with the goal of protecting and nurturing children.

* * *

The anxiety about single mothers within the social work and especially the child-saving establishments could be seen in four related discourses: about desertion, illegitimacy, women's employment, and mothers' pensions. In confronting each issue, social workers aimed to punish and deter immorality, to protect children, and to encourage the construction of proper families. In practice, pursuing all these aims often produced contradictions, and this was particularly the case when woman-headed households were an option.

Desertion was perceived as an escalating and urgent social problem by the turn of the century and had been incorporated into the MSPCC program as ipso facto a

[26]E.g. #2001, #2500, #3302. See the excellent description of the worker-client relationship producing dishonesty in Jane Addams's *Democracy and Social Ethics* (New York: Macmillan, 1907), ch. 2.

major form of cruelty to children.[27] In practice, the case records show, the Society worried about desertion not only from the perspective of children's deprivations but also as a violation of the proper roles of men and women. Desertion was a result of a father's weak and cowardly evasion of masculine responsibility.[28] Therefore aid to wives and children of deserters had to meet the criterion that it did not further undermine the father's role as breadwinner, his duty to support, and his authority over his family. The Society's moralistic and punitive attitude towards deserters often required accepting, as a consequence, that the deserter's wife might have to suffer also. As Mary Richmond, influential spokesperson for the "scientific charity" tendency with which the MSPCC identified, argued, "It is absurd to go into a home and do for it what the legal and recognized head . . . has deliberately shirked . . . and then to suppose . . . that you have not interfered between man and wife."[29] Even blaming men unilaterally for their cowardly desertion did not benefit their wives: the most anti-male rhetoric, such as that of Ada Eliot, who considered the problem to result from men's "brute-like" nature, nevertheless argued against relief to support homes without men.[30]

MSPCC policy was to force deserters to pay rather than to seek aid for single mothers. In pursuing this policy it expanded its role and its control over its clients. Although it had declined to accept jurisdiction for arranging relief, it took responsibility for obtaining court orders requiring deserted or nonsupporting fathers to make support payments. Then, adding yet a new responsibility, the MSPCC arranged for fathers to turn over payments to the Society, which it then doled out to the mother, supervising her expenditures in the process.[31] The MSPCC became a virtual collection agency as its staff billed and dunned and tried to extradite deserters. It was influential in lobbying for legislation to increase the criminal penalties for nonsupport and desertion.[32] Since many deserters had not disappeared but were merely nonsupporters, the agency policies sometimes, ironically, increased an irresponsible husband's control over his family. For example, one estranged husband would make his payment to MSPCC, then force his wife to return the money to him so that he could circulate it back through the

[27]MSPCC, *Annual Report*, 1908, 17; Mary Conyngton, *How to Help: A Manual of Practical Charity* (New York: Macmillan, 1909), 150–51; Helen Foss, "The Genus Deserter: His Singularities and Their Social Consequences—A Study of Local Fact and Interstate Remedies," *Charities*, 10, 2 May 1903, 456–60.

[28]Zilpha D. Smith, *Deserted Wives and Deserting Husbands. A Study of 234 Families Based on the Experience of the District Committees and Agents* (Boston: Associated Charities, 1901), 9–13.

[29]Richmond, *The Long View*, 80, this essay orig. 1897.

[30]Eliot, "Deserted Wives," *Charities Review*, 10 (Oct. 1900), 347.

[31]The policy is explained in *Annual Report*, 1894; examples of actual agreements between the Society and fathers are in MSPCC, Early Correspondence, Univ. of Massachusetts Archives, e.g., agreement with Jeremiah Doherty, 25 Nov. 1892, folder 27.

[32]*Annual Reports*, 1894, 1908, 1911; State Rep. William T. Forbes to Theodore A. Lothrop, General Sec. of MSPCC, letter dated 12 Aug. 1930, MSPCC Archives, Boston, Massachusetts.

agency for his next payment.[33] Numerous estranged husbands offered to support their families if their wives would let them return to the household, although their wives had been requesting MSPCC aid precisely to get free of abusive husbands.[34]

Since the definition of desertion was elusive, and some deserted wives colluded with their husbands, hid their whereabouts, and/or let them return to the household periodically,[35] it was difficult to distinguish desertion, nonsupport, and unemployment. MSPCC policies punished all of these indiscriminately. Thus in a 1920 case a one-legged father, periodically unemployed, had broken his wooden leg and lost his job again. The social worker knew this but did not call on the family because "it is her intention to try and develop initiative in the family."[36] In a 1912 neglect case, children had been out begging and the agency threatened to remove them if they did not stop. The mother wanted to leave her good-for-nothing husband if there was a way she could do so without losing her children, but the agency recommended against aid to the family because it would encourage the father's laziness.[37]

Treating all these problems as somehow willful and unilateral on the husband's part brought further hardships. For example, the MSPCC often urged wives to prosecute husbands for nonsupport. Their success would bring a jail sentence, thus punishing the culprit and, it was argued, setting a deterrent example; but it also deprived the family of support. Many mothers lost their children because a jail sentence intended to reform the family took the father away.[38] Furthermore, prosecutions required wives to testify against their husbands, a procedure that could weaken the chances for future reconciliation, and that intimidated wives fearful of or ambivalent about their husbands.[39]

Another indicator of distrust of woman-headed families was the treatment of illegitimacy. If the illegitimate mother kept her child, she ran a risk of failing to provide good mothering because of her immorality. Yet if she were helped to get rid of her child, was not her immoral behavior being rewarded? Still, to force an unwilling girl to keep her child was not necessarily in the best interests of the child, and the child-savers believed that children ought not to be punished for the circumstances of their conception. Furthermore, most charity workers, even if they believed in punishment for sexual immorality, also perceived the unwed mother as herself a child in need of help and wanted to give girls-gone-wrong a chance to reclaim an honorable life.[40]

[33]#3401.

[34]#0305, #0314A, #1080.

[35]#2042, #2053, #3041, for examples.

[36]#2565, research by Nancy McKerrow.

[37]#2042.

[38]#3361, research by Nancy McKerrow.

[39]#0501, #0524, #0815A.

[40]A good view of this contradictory impulse in *The First Massachusetts Conference of Charities*, 1903, pamphlet, reprinted from *Charities*, 28 Nov. 1903, 8–11, 23–31; see also MSPCC, *Annual Report*, 1892.

Starting in the 1890s the MSPCC and other progressive agencies came to believe that, even without marriage, mother and child ought to be kept together.[41] This belief represented a victory for the sentimental cult of motherhood; charity workers believed that the experience of childbirth and the opportunity to be with the infant would create love and a sense of responsibility in the mother, and that this maternalism could in itself help to reform wayward girls.[42]

In practice, however, agency actions in response to unwed motherhood were divided and confused. The entire basis of the sentimental outlook rested on a view of these mothers as girls, and in the MSPCC cases they were rarely that: most were previously married women, and many were currently living in marriage-like relations. Thus the traditional first course of action—to arrange a marriage—was inappropriate; even if the mothers were girls, they would not usually have been at the agency had a marriage been possible.[43] The next best solution was to mobilize the mother's parents or other relatives to take her in with the child. Yet neither were these arrangements usually possible, often because the illegitimate mother had other children or because the relatives had poor and crowded households. A 1920 Boston survey showed that only twenty percent of illegitimate mothers aided by agencies were able to live with their parents, and of those only half did so with their child.[44] Another study showed that mother and child usually lived with her parents for a short time only.[45] Extended-family solutions did not resolve the long-range problem of single motherhood.

Grandparents failing, the MSPCC often tried placements in service positions.[46] Such placements were also temporary, limited to the child's infancy, and they often

[41]This reform over the earlier manner of dealing with illegitimacy represented a differential treatment for the poor, since prosperous girls who got "in trouble" continued to be moved away during the later stages of pregnancy, to deliver their babies in private homes, to surrender the babies, and return to normal life without damage to their futures. See Joan Brumberg, "'Ruined' Girls: Changing Community Responses to Illegitimacy in Upstate New York, 1890–1920," *Journal of Social History*, 18 (1985), 247–72.

[42]Boston Conference on Illegitimacy, untitled article, *Survey* 30, 13 Sept. 1913, 707–08; Anna T. Wilson, "Foundlings and Illegitimate Children," in International Congress of Charities, Corrections and Philanthropy, *The Care of Dependent, Neglected and Wayward Children*, ed. Anna Garlin Spencer and Charles Wesley Birtwell (Baltimore, 1894), 57–68; *First Massachusetts State Conference of Charities*, 11.

[43]Alberta S. B. Guibord and Ida R. Parker, *What Becomes of the Unmarried Mother? A Study of 82 Cases* (Boston, 1922), 37, for example.

[44]Ida R. Parker, *A Follow-up Study of 550 Illegitimacy Applications* (Boston: Research Bureau on Social Case Work, 1924). Of course this low figure reflects the fact that unmarried mothers who had supportive relatives were less likely to need agency help and would not appear in the records.

[45]The peak number of babies were with grandparents and illegitimate mothers at age nine months. Emma O. Lundberg and Katharine F. Lenroot, *Illegitimacy as a Child-Welfare Problem*, Report of the U.S. Department of Labor, Children's Bureau (Washington, D.C.: GPO, 1920), II, 144.

[46]Wilson, "Foundlings and Illegitimate Children"; David F. Tilley, [untitled statement], in *First Massachusetts Conference*, 9; George L. Jones, "How Does Our Treatment of the Unmarried Mother with the Second Child Differ from our Treatment of the Unmarried Mother with her First Child," National Conference of Charities and Corrections, *Procedures*, 1919, 81–85.

provoked great resistance on the part of the mother, owing to the lack of personal freedom she experienced as a live-in domestic.

Even when resident in other households, single mothers often needed to earn. Yet MSPCC workers were also critical of women's employment and of the nonmaternal child care it usually required. Many child-welfare workers believed there was no point in keeping mother and children together if someone else had to take care of the children. In practice MSPCC policy was all or nothing: it arranged placements in institutions or foster homes, not in day nurseries or with babysitters. Several MSPCC workers simply ordered women to stay home and look after their children, and women sometimes tried to hide their employment from agency visitors.[47]

Even social workers who wanted single mothers to become self-supporting expected women to remain economically dependent when living with husbands. Whenever a husband was in the home, no matter how poor, disabled, or irresponsible, charity workers were hostile to wives taking employment. This position did not always reflect the mother's judgment. One MSPCC record read:

> Mother . . . desiring to obtain elderly woman to come into her home and care for the chn as mo has to go out and do day work; sometimes earns as much as $18 a week. Fa has not had a steady position for quite a period of time, but is doing the best he can, and mo has no fault to find. . . . [I] made it quite evident to mo that the desirable thing was for her to stay at home and care for the chn and have fa obtain a steady position. [#3565A.]

Economic contributions from wives, they believed, would weaken a man's sense of his responsibility. Women who were wage earners before marriage tended to be "unfit for married life: [women] from the very fact of being economically independent may be led to assert her independence in ways which will in themselves be provocative of household friction."[48] Joanna Colcord, for the Russell Sage Foundation, wrote in 1919: "Many a non-supporter got his first

[47]E.g. #2024, #3041; MSPCC newsletter *The Square Deal* II, 1, Feb. 1919, 8. In one case of a nonsupporting husband, from an agency similar to the MSPCC, the record reads: "The woman was willing to work—had applied for day nursery care, but [the agency worker] had persuaded the nursery not to accept their children." Quoted approvingly by Joanna Colcord in her *Broken Homes: A Study of Desertion and its Social Treatment* (New York: Russell Sage Foundation, 1919). 189. The objections to women's employment stemmed from deep convictions about women's domesticity. This view was not a "sexist" attitude. Seeing women's employment as, at best, a misfortune was common among feminists as well, a result of the nearly universal understanding of motherhood as women's unique and essential calling. For example, Florence Kelly, "The Family and the Woman's Wage," National Conference of Charities and Corrections, *Proceedings*, 1909, 118–21; Jane Addams, Presidential Address, "Charity and Social Justice," in ibid., 1910, 6–7. George Mangold, a nonfeminist, makes exactly the same argument in his *Child Problems* (New York: Macmillan, 1910), 89–90, as does Conyngton, *How to Help*, 185.

[48]Colcord, *Broken Homes*, ch. 2; Conyngton, *How to Help*, 185; Earle Eubank, *A Study of Family Desertion* (Chicago: Dept. of Public Welfare, 1916), 13.

impulse in that direction when his wife became a wage-earner in some domestic crisis." Her advice to the wives of nonsupporting husbands: "If your husband comes home crying, and says he can't find any work, sit down . . . and cry until he does."[49]

Although mothers' pensions were a welfare provision specifically for single mothers, the controversy around this reform, oddly, disguised its gender and family implications. The social-work establishment debated the merits of public-versus-private responsibility for charity, and "outdoor" versus "indoor relief" (the traditional British terms for giving aid to people in their own homes versus institutionalization) as deterrents to pauperism.[50] Gender issues were obscured in this controversy relative to their explicitness in, say, arguments about protective legislation.

Nevertheless, a closer look at the debate, and at the practice of agencies like the MSPCC, reveals an anxiety about the potential effects of such pensions on gender roles. C.C.Carstens, General Agent of the MSPCC and at the time the most influential man in the United States' child-saving movement, was an opponent of aid to single mothers, and family-centered concerns were primary for him: his purpose was to abolish the class of single mothers, not establish it. "The enthusiast in favor of widows' pensions . . . is likely to hold lightly the ties of kinship."[51] Carstens's implicit definition of kinship here, one shared by many opponents, must have been marriage, for the very goal of mothers' pensions was to preserve filial ties. When Mary Wilcox Glenn argued that the pensions would "lessen the family's sense of responsibility for its own," by "family" she meant fathers.[52] Similarly ideological was Edward Devine's definition of "family" when he argued, "The breaking up of a family by an outside agency is justified only when it is merely the outward expression of a destruction which has already taken place . . . separation of husband and wife. . . ."[53] Only a definition that equated "family" with "married couple" could produce this conclu-

[49]Colcord, *Broken Homes*, 154.

[50]Many commentators have defined the mothers' pension controversy exclusively in these terms. See, for example, Mark H. Leff, "Consensus for Reform: The Mothers' Pension Movement in the Progressive Era," *Social Service Review*, 47 (1973), 397–417; James Leiby, *A History of Social Welfare and Social Work in the US* (New York: Columbia Univ. Press, 1978); Muriel W. Pumphrey and Ralph E. Pumphrey, "The Widows' Pension Movement, 1900–1930: Preventive Child-Saving or Social Control," in *Social Welfare or Social Control? Some Historical Reflections on "Regulating the Poor,"* ed. Walter I. Trattner (Knoxville: Univ. of Tennessee Press, 1983), 51–66. Only one previous work, to my knowledge, has noticed any of the gender dimensions of this controversy: Ann Vandepol, "Dependent Children, Child Custody, and the Mothers' Pensions: The Transformation of State-Family Relations in the Early 20th Century," *Social Problems*, 29 (1982), 221–35.

[51]C. C. Carstens, *Public Pensions to Widows with Children* (New York: Russell Sage Foundation, 1913), 28.

[52]National Conference of Charities and Corrections, *Proceedings*, 1914, 453. She added that pensions were not "virile!"

[53]Devine, "The Breaking Up of Families," *Charities Review*, 10 (1900), 461.

sion that mothers' pensions were "an insidious attack upon the family, inimical to the welfare of children. . . ."[54]

Mothers' pensions caught on widely and quickly, despite substantial social-work opposition, not only because they made sense for children, but also because agency clients were stubbornly demanding them. They did so not necessarily in those words or terms, but in searching for any aid that made it possible for them to keep and support their children. Thirty-four percent of single-mother cases were brought to the MSPCC by the mothers themselves asking for help. As reported above, they were less likely to ask for the placing out of their children than other parents. Their most common requests were for "separation and maintenance" orders, legal recognition as heads of family, child-support payments from fathers, regular relief payments, and, less commonly, help in finding daytime child care.

Yet the response of the MSPCC, a nationally leading agency in child protection, was disproportionately to deny material or counseling help to these mothers and to recommend the removal of children. This apparent discrimination against single mothers resulted simultaneously from observation of actual conditions making it difficult to combine breadwinning and childraising, from ideological anxieties about pauperization, and also from fear of destabilizing male and female roles. The bias against single mothers was a result not of malevolence but of fear and genuine concern for children. Nevertheless, the result was a contradiction: the failure of child-saving agencies to do the best they could to secure the welfare of neglected children. In an era of insistence on the vital importance of mothering, child-savers frequently recommended the institutionalization of children in preference to granting aid to their mothers. In 1900 the majority of children in institutions were only "half-orphans."[55] Between 1880 and 1920, seventy-four percent of the neglected children of single mothers were taken from those mothers by the MSPCC. Even assuming that a substantial proportion of these mothers would have remained permanently incompetent parents, many others were affected primarily by remediable problems such as poverty and overwork. Furthermore, mothers would have had to be extremely abusive to have done worse by their children than the usual institutions.[56]

At the same time, the rise of the child protective movement, in bringing out these contradictions, stimulated reform. Despite their intentions, child savers had

[54]Devine, "Pensions for Mothers," from *American Labor Legislation Review*, 3 (June 1913), reprinted in *Selected Articles on Mothers' Pensions*, comp. Edna D. Bullock (New York, n.p., 1915), 177.

[55]Homer Folks, *The Care of Destitute, Neglected and Delinquent Children* (New York: Macmillan, 1902), 134.

[56]Despite the enunciation of a policy of family placements for children, up through 1920 the majority was institutionalized; see Andrew Billingsley and Jeanne M. Giovannoni, *Children of the Storm: Black Children and American Child Welfare* (New York: Harcourt Brace Jovanovich, 1972), 69–70.

created agencies to which single mothers came pleading their desires and arguing their own proposals. One result of that pressure, both from the steady, stubborn, manipulative clients and from desperate, hysterical clients, both from "good" mothers and from "bad," was the rapid change of social-work opinion to favor mothers' pensions by 1920. In this way the MSPCCs, despite their highly ideological and culturally specific notions of good parenting, may in the long run have been beneficial even to parents of whom they disapproved.

My purpose in this article has not been to criticize child welfare work of the past, but to explore a previously unexamined aspect of the development of modern norms about proper family life. There has been a continuing tendency within both family scholarship and social welfare policy to treat single motherhood as aberrant, rather than common and "normal." Similarly, child neglect has been conceived as a product of parents' ill health, socio-economic stress, and defective family structure, rather than as in good measure a structural aspect of female poverty. Scholars and policy makers have assumed that stable families are economically independent, and that families needing "outside help" to support children could not be stable in the long run. The high incidence of urban woman-headed families for over a century, and the severe material problems that faced responsible and energetic as well as irresponsible and depressed single mothers, suggest the need to question whether economic independence should be the highest goal or even the desirable norm for good childraising.

Robert V. Wells

Demographic Change and the Life Cycle of American Families

Between the eighteenth and the twentieth centuries, major changes occurred in the patterns of birth and death of the American population. The birth rate declined by over 50 per cent, from around 50 per 1,000 in 1800 to less than 20 per 1,000 today.[1] Although the evidence on mortality is less clear, there can be no doubt that substantial improvements in life expectancy occurred during this period. The best estimates indicate that life expectancy at birth came close to doubling between about 1800 and 1970.[2] In view of the magnitude of these changes, it is surprising to find that so little is known of their impact on American social institutions.

How did these major demographic changes affect one of the fundamental parts of our society—the family? In particular, how did the decline in both fertility and mortality alter the life cycle of the American family in the two centuries since the American Revolution?[3]

Glick, who has played an important role in the study of American families in the twentieth century, has described the life cycle of the family:

> Between formation and dissolution, families go through a series of characteristic stages which lend themselves to demographic analysis. These stages include marriage, the establishment of a household, bearing and rearing children, marriage of the children, and the later years before the family is finally dissolved. Successive readjustments of behavior patterns are required as the adult members shift their roles from

Robert V. Wells is Assistant Professor of History at Union College. He is the author of "Family Size and Fertility Control in Eighteenth Century America: A Study of Quaker Families," *Population Studies*, XXV (1971). An earlier version of this paper was delivered at the 1971 meeting of the Population Association of America.

1 For estimates of the birth rate in 1800, see Ansley J. Coale and Melvin Zelnik, *New Estimates of Fertility and Population in the United States* (Princeton, 1963), 39; W. S. Thompson and P. K. Whelpton, *Population Trends in the United States* (New York, 1933), 263.

2 The standard estimate for life expectancy at birth for before 1800 is about 35 years; see Thompson and Whelpton, *Population Trends*, 239. My own work has indicated that this figure may be slightly low, but not by more than five years.

3 Compare the approach and findings of this study with Peter R. Uhlenberg, "A Study of Cohort Life Cycles: Cohorts of Native Born Massachusetts Women, 1830–1920," *Population Studies*, XXIII (1969), 407–420.

newly wedded persons to parents of small children, parents of older children, older couples without children at home, and surviving widows or widowers.[4]

By comparing the patterns of marriage, childbearing, and death of adults of the eighteenth and twentieth centuries, it should be possible to determine those aspects of family life which have remained relatively stable over time, as well as the ways in which the life of the family has changed in the last 200 years.

Two studies provide the basic evidence for this paper. My own work provides data on 276 Quaker families in which the wife was born before 1786. These families lived in New York, New Jersey, and Pennsylvania in the eighteenth and early nineteenth centuries. As most of the data come from before 1800, these will be referred to as eighteenth-century families. These Quakers cannot be assumed to represent the American population as a whole before 1800, but there is evidence to suggest that their life cycle was much the same as that of their contemporaries. Figures for American families in general in the nineteenth and twentieth centuries have been taken from the study by Glick and Parke, "New Approaches in Studying the Life Cycle of the Family."[5] This study was the first attempt to examine the family life cycle by cohort analysis, and, as such, is more comparable to the Quaker data than Glick's earlier work.[6] In all, Glick and Parke consider the family life cycle of six different cohorts of women (defined by the year of birth), but only two of these groups have been selected for consideration here. The first includes families in which the wives were born between 1880 and 1889; this is the earliest group for which the authors present data. The second group of families is defined by wives born between 1920 and 1929; they are selected for study here

4 Paul C. Glick, *American Families* (New York, 1957), 53.

5 See Paul C. Glick and Robert Parke, Jr., *Demography*, II (1965), 187–202; for a listing of Glick's earlier writings, see 187. It should be noted that, although the subjects of Glick's figures are still alive, he has predicted aggregate demographic characteristics on the basis of current mortality trends. Historians who wish to incorporate the family life cycle concept into their own work should consult the article by John B. Lansing and Leslie Kish, "Family Life Cycle as an Independent Variable," *American Sociological Review*, XXII (1957), 512–519. The importance of this study lies in the suggestion that behavior patterns of adults are likely to change as people move from one stage of the life cycle of the family to another.

6 Cohort analysis groups persons under study by events which they all experience at the same time. The two most common events used to define a group (i.e., a cohort) are the year of birth and the year of marriage. The cohorts are then followed over time, for as long as the study requires, to see when, or at what age, other events occur.

because they are the most recent group for which the figures are relatively complete.

Three other points need to be mentioned before proceeding to the analysis of change in family life cycles. First, the following information is for first marriages only. It raises several questions which will be considered at the end of the paper. Second, the discussion concentrates on the experience of the wives. In part this is because the data for the Quaker women of this study are better than that for their husbands, but it is also true that the figures for the men are virtually the same except for the fact that they married later than the women, and hence reached each successive stage of the family at a correspondingly older age. Third, this study concentrates on the experience of the adult members of a family. It would be of obvious interest to know how children were affected by changing fertility and mortality, but the lack of both data and space prevent an exploration of this subject here.

Since the life of a family begins with marriage, let us look first at the changes in the age at first marriage between the eighteenth and twentieth centuries. As seen in my study of the Quakers, the median age at first marriage was 20.5 for the women.[7] Studies of genealogies and New England town records suggest that, in this regard, they were much like other eighteenth-century Americans.[8] Among wives born between 1880 and 1889, however, families were formed somewhat later in the life of the bride as the median age at first marriage had increased to 21.6 among women. This increase is not surprising, for the age at first marriage among women appears to have been on the rise throughout the eighteenth century.[9] The twentieth century brought a reversal to this long-term trend, for women born between 1920 and 1929 were marrying at a median age of 20.8 years, much the same as in the colonial period. Certainly marriage patterns varied, but the difference between the highest and the lowest figures of just over one year among the women suggests that marriages were formed at much the same point in life throughout the last two centuries.

In most cases, marriage was followed within a year or two by a first child, whether the couple lived in the eighteenth or twentieth

7 These figures, and those which follow, have been summarized in Tables 1 and 2 in the Appendix. The sources for the data and the way in which the figures were calculated are described there.

8 This evidence has been collected in Robert V. Wells, "Quaker Marriage Patterns in a Colonial Perspective," unpublished paper.

9 *Ibid.*

centuries. But there the similarity in childbearing patterns ends. According to Glick and Parke, the median age of mothers at the birth of their last child was 30.5 for women born in the 1920s. Thus, for these wives, the median length of time spent between marriage and the end of the childbearing stage of life was only 9.7 years. This figure contrasts sharply with the 17.4 years which one of the Quaker women of the eighteenth century might expect to spend bearing children. Among the Friends studied here, the median age of mothers at the birth of the last child was 37.9 years.[10] I have suggested elsewhere that these Quakers were among the first Americans deliberately to limit the size of their families.[11] As a result, their families were, in all probability, smaller than the average for eighteenth-century America, and their childbearing presumably ended at an earlier age. Thus, if anything, the decline in length of the childbearing period between the late-eighteenth and the mid-twentieth centuries is understated. It is of interest to note that among wives born between 1880 and 1889, the median length of the childbearing period was 11.3 years, considerably shorter than that of the eighteenth-century families. Apparently, the decline in fertility was well underway by the end of the nineteenth century and, among groups like these Quakers, this trend may date back to the era of the American Revolution.

Because of the longer time spent in childbearing, parents of the eighteenth century also spent more of their life rearing their children than did parents in later years. Among the Quakers of this study, the last child married and left home when the mother was of a median age of 60.2. Wives born between 1880 and 1889 were of a median age of 56.2 when their last child left home. They were only slightly younger than the eighteenth-century women in this regard, because the rise in the age at marriage had partially offset the effects of the reduced childbearing period. But, by the mid-twentieth century, earlier marriages and a shorter time spent bearing children combined to free parents of their children at an earlier age. The median age among the last group of wives when their children were finally married and gone was 52.0, almost ten years less than the corresponding figure among the Quakers. Almost forty years passed between the formation of an eighteenth-century family and the time when child-rearing was finished. By the end of the nineteenth century, however, the effects of the

10 This figure is for all women married before the age of forty-five.

11 Robert V. Wells, "Family Size and Fertility Control in Eighteenth Century America: A Study of Quaker Families," *Population Studies*, XXV (1971), 173–182.

gradual decline in fertility were beginning to show. Families in which the wife was born between 1880 and 1889, and whose childbearing held to the average, were spending only thirty-five years in the child-rearing stage; among couples where the wife was born between 1920 and 1929, the median interval between the formation of a family and the departure of the last child was only thirty-one years.

In addition to spending less of their life rearing children, the evidence suggests that parents in the twentieth century experienced a more stable family situation. As Glick has pointed out, once modern parents stopped childbearing, their family was normally of a constant size until their children began to marry and leave home.[12] Families of the late eighteenth century, however, were subjected to growth for a much longer period and high mortality continually threatened the family with the death of parents and children. The stability of twentieth-century families is emphasized by the fact that only 31 per cent of the total time spent rearing children was devoted to childbearing by wives born between 1920 and 1929. The comparable figures are 33 per cent for wives born between 1880 and 1889, and 44 per cent for the wives born before 1786. Undoubtedly women benefited from this change, not only because they had fewer children to raise, but also because the burden of pregnancy less frequently interfered with their ability to rear their children.

In addition to the changes in the life cycle of the family introduced by the long-term decline in fertility, improving conditions of mortality also had a recognizable impact on the family. However, the effects of increased life expectancy were felt predominantly in the twentieth century, for, until about 1890, conditions of mortality improved slowly, if at all.

The most fundamental change wrought by the decline in mortality has been an increase in the length of marriage. Among the Quakers studied here, the median duration of marriage was 30.4 years. Although other information on mortality before 1800 is scarce, studies of Andover and Plymouth in Massachusetts suggest that the life chances of these Quakers were not unusually good in the context of the colonial period.[13] It is important to note, however, that the median duration of marriage is somewhat deceptive regarding mortality conditions. A

12 Glick, *American Families*, 67.

13 Philip J. Greven, Jr., *Four Generations: Population, Land, and Family in Colonial Andover, Massachusetts* (Ithaca, 1970), 192, 195; John Demos, *A Little Commonwealth: Family Life in Plymouth Colony* (New York, 1970), 192–193.

surprisingly high proportion of these Quaker unions ended relatively quickly. Although only 1.9 per cent of the marriages lasted less than a year, almost a fifth (18.8 per cent) had been dissolved by the death of one partner before the fifteenth anniversary had been reached; after twenty-five years, 38.4 per cent of the unions once formed no longer existed. Couples who lived at the end of the 1800s could hope for but a little more time together than had these Quakers. Wives born between 1880 and 1889 had a median duration of marriage of 35.4 years, an increase of just over five years in about a century. In the next forty years, however, medical and sanitary improvements had a striking effect on the family, the median length of married life increasing to 43.6 years among the last group of wives.[14]

The fact that husbands and wives could expect a longer life together after about 1900 is, in itself, important. It is especially important, however, when one recalls the reduction in the length of child-rearing which had occurred by that period. Couples who married in the twentieth century were among the first who could reasonably expect a life together after their children had left home. By subtracting the median figure for the length of the child-rearing stage of life from that of the duration of marriage, it is apparent that couples in which the wife was born between 1920 and 1929 could expect 12.4 years of married life after their children had left home. In contrast, half of the marriages involving a wife born between 1880 and 1889 were broken by the death of one partner less than a year after the last child departed. Even more startling is the situation among the families of the eighteenth century. Fully 69 per cent of all the Quaker marriages studied were of shorter duration than the median length of child-rearing among that group. In fact, a Quaker widow or widower, whose experience held to the median, could expect to have children to take care of for 9.3 years after the death of his or her first spouse. Thus, by the twentieth century, longer marriages combined with a continuing decline in fertility to produce a situation in which, for the first time, couples could *expect* a life together after their children were gone. Companionship was beginning to join reproduction as an important expectation of marriage.

The relative decrease in the importance of children in the life of twentieth-century families is further illustrated by the increased duration between the marriage of the last child and the death of the last

14 This figure is based on the estimates of mortality trends among the cohort born between 1920 and 1929 in Glick and Parke, "New Approaches," 194–195, and Table 1.

parent to die. Among the Quakers who lived in the late 1700s, marriage was virtually synonymous with children. We have already seen that one spouse could expect to die before the children were completely reared; of equal importance is the fact that the surviving partner could expect to die less than five years after the last child married. Old age, without family, was not common before 1800. This situation had clearly changed by the twentieth century, as the experience of the wives born from 1880 to 1889 indicates. Among this group of families, wives who outlived their husbands died almost twenty years after their last child had left home; among the men of this group who survived their wives, the corresponding figure was fifteen years. Obviously, similar figures for the families in which the wife was born between 1920 and 1929 are not available. But unless life chances are sharply reduced, the trend toward a longer life after the children have left home should continue. Apparently, old age with no children present is largely a phenomenon of the modern world; the nation's founders seldom had to face the problem.

The last stage of the life cycle of the family which concerns us here is the length of widowhood, that is, the time between the death of one spouse and the death of the second. Here, too, improvements in life expectancy have had their effects. The Quaker widows of the 1700s survived for an average of 13.7 years after the death of their husbands. This figure is considerably below the median length of widowhood of 18.7 years for the wives born between 1880 and 1889. The corresponding increase in the length of widowhood among the men was much less. While the Quaker widowers of this study lived for 12.5 years after their wives had died, the figure for men whose wives were born between 1880 and 1889 was 14.2, an increase of almost two years. In addition to living longer after their children have left home, parents of the twentieth century are faced with an increased amount of time in their old age with none of their family around. In a very real sense, the reductions in fertility and mortality have increased the possibility of loneliness in old age.

This analysis of changes in the life cycle of the family has been carried out on first marriages only. It is, therefore, desirable to examine how typical these patterns are of the experience of all families in the various periods under consideration. Among the Quakers studied here, fully 88 per cent of all marriages were the first for both partners. Furthermore, of the wives, 97.5 per cent had never been married before; among the husbands, the proportion marrying for the first time was 88.8 per cent. Remarriage among these Quakers was rare, and there is evidence to suggest that other eighteenth-century American populations shared this pattern of behavior.[15] While the proportion of first marriages to all marriages is rather high, a surprisingly large number of these Quakers never wed. Perhaps as many as half of the Quaker children born before 1800 never married at all. Of course, most of those who did not marry died before they had the opportunity to wed. But, between 12 and 15 per cent of these Quakers who lived to the age of fifty died without marrying.

Depending upon one's perspective, first marriages were both more and less typical in 1950 than they were before 1800. The proportion of marriages which were the first for both husband and wife had fallen from 88 per cent before 1800 to 67 per cent by 1950.[16] Likewise, while 97.5 per cent of the Quaker wives were marrying for the first time, only 74.4 per cent of the brides in 1950 had never been married before. The corresponding figures for the men show a decline in the proportion marrying for the first time from 88.8 per cent to 75.5 per cent. While first marriages were less typical of all marriages in the twentieth century than they had been earlier, there can be little doubt that a higher proportion of the population took a spouse at least once. The proportion never married in 1950 of 7 to 8 per cent was approximately half that found among the Quakers. The percentage of children who died before marrying was clearly less, too. Perhaps 80 to 85 per cent of all children born in the middle of the twentieth century could expect to marry, compared to about 50 per cent among these Quakers.[17]

One last difference between the Quaker families of the eighteenth century and those of Americans in the mid-twentieth century deserves mention. Once a Quaker couple married they remained united until one spouse died. Divorce was extremely rare among the Friends, and among their contemporaries as well.[18] Among Americans in 1950, however, about 16 per cent of all marriages involved one partner who had been married, but who had divorced his previous spouse.[19] In fact, much of the increase in remarriage between 1800 and 1950 may

15 See Wells, "Quaker Marriage Patterns."

16 Glick, *American Families*, 142.

17 *Ibid.*, 140.

18 George E. Howard, *A History of Matrimonial Institutions* (Chicago, 1904), II, last part.

19 Glick, *American Families*, 142.

be the result of a rising number of divorces which were followed by a new marriage for one or both partners. From the point of view of the children, the increased family stability which resulted from parents being assured of a longer life together has been offset, to some extent, by a willingness of couples voluntarily to end their unions.

When the life cycle of these Quaker families (who do not seem to have been greatly different from their contemporaries) is compared to that of modern families, it seems apparent that, in the course of the last two centuries, the life cycle of most American families has become significantly more complex. From an almost exclusive concern with childbearing and child-rearing before 1800, the emphasis within a family has gradually shifted until now the life of the parents after their children have left home has become a major part of family living. This change can only partially be explained by the improved mortality conditions in modern America. The long-term decline in fertility, which may have started about the time of the American Revolution, also reduced the emphasis on the childbearing aspects of marriage. Thus, the life cycle of the family in the mid-twentieth century reflects both an intimate relationship to the modern world, and has roots which extend back to the founding of the nation.

APPENDIX

Table 1 Median Age of Wives at Stages of the Life Cycle of the Family

STAGE OF THE LIFE CYCLE OF THE FAMILY	WIVES BORN		
	BEFORE 1786 (QUAKERS)	1880–1889	1920–1929
A. First marriage	20.5[a]	21.6	20.8
B. Birth of last child	37.9	32.9	30.5
C. Marriage of last child	60.2	56.2	52.0
D. Death of first spouse to die	50.9	57.0	64.4

a As measured by the interquartile range, the distribution around the median of the age at first marriage, the age of the mother at the birth of her last child, and the duration of marriage seem to have been much the same from one group to another.

Sources: The data for wives born before 1786 are my own. The information for the other wives is from Glick and Parke, "New Approaches", 190, Table 1.

Table 2 Median Length of Selected Stages of the Life Cycle of the Family (in Years)

STAGE OF THE LIFE CYCLE OF THE FAMILY	WIVES BORN		
	BEFORE 1786 (QUAKERS)	1880–1889	1920–1929
1. Childbearing	17.4	11.3	9.7
2. Child-rearing	39.7	34.6	31.2
3. Duration of Marriage	30.4	35.4	43.6
4. Old Age Together	− 9.3	0.8	12.4
5. Widowhood			
Female	13.7	18.7	—
Male	12.5	14.2	—
6. Marriage of last child to death of last spouse, when last is			
Female	4.4	19.5	—
Male	3.2	15.0	—

Source: The above table was derived as follows:

Table 2

Line 1 = Line B − Line A
Line 2 = Line C − Line A
Line 3 = Line D − Line A
Line 4 = Line D − Line C
} From Table 1

Line 5 = The figures for the husbands and wives born before 1786 were calculated directly from my data. For the others, see Glick and Parke, "New Approaches," 195.

Line 6 = Line 4 + Line 5

Updating the Life Cycle of the Family*

PAUL C. GLICK**
Population Division, Bureau of the Census

Changes from decade to decade in family life cycle patterns are analyzed for women who have married in the 20th Century. Longtime changes in the median age of women upon entering life cycle stages have occurred primarily because of fluctuations in birth rates and improvement in survival rates. A noteworthy recent development is the continuing postponement of marriage. Women entering marriage during the 1970's are expected to have between one and two fewer children, to end childbearing three years sooner, and to have 11 more years of married life after the last child marries than women who married during the first decade of the century.

The life cycle of the family is a term that has been used for many years in reference to the succession of critical stages through which the typical family passes during its life span.[1] This concept provides a highly meaningful framework for the analysis of data on conjugal families as they pass through such stages as marriage, birth of children, children leaving home, the "postchildren" or "empty nest" period, and ultimate dissolution of the marriage through death of one of the spouses.

The present study, as well as the one by Norton (1974), features the average ages at which married persons begin the several stages of the family life cycle. Other analyses of the family life cycle feature changes in the composition and economic characteristics of the family from its inception until its dissolution, as well as the range of variation in the ages of persons at the beginning of each stage of the cycle (Glick and Parke, 1965).

Some new types of information have been used in the preparation of this paper. The most relevant of these new materials is the series of reports which the Bureau of the Census has published on the number of children that women expect to have during their lifetime. The Bureau's staff has assembled data of this type for the period from 1967 to 1975, and has arrived at the cautious conclusion that the data provide reasonably reliable indications about the average size of completed family that women will have during the next decade or two. Building on the results obtained in the 1975 survey concerning birth expectations for women from 18 to 39 years of age (U.S. Bureau of the Census, 1976a), the present analysis has been extended forward by one more decade than the study made recently by Norton (1974) covering the cohorts of women who were born in the early 1900's through the 1940's. Thus, the present study shows the projected family life cycles of persons who were born as recently as the 1950's, most of whom have married or will marry in the 1970's.

Moreover, this study extends the analysis back in time by two more decades than Norton's study. The additional information presented for these earlier decades relates to women born in the 1880's and 1890's, most of whom had married for the first time between 1900 and 1920. The cycles shown here for these two decades constitute minor modifications of findings published earlier by Glick and Parke (1965). Therefore, the period of time covered in this study extends over eight decades. To the extent that available data permit, the findings relate to mothers who have been married only once. Corresponding results for men generally would be parallel to those for women, with the exception that the

[1] Among the early users of the concept were Loomis and Hamilton (1936) and Glick (1947). More recent users include Hill and Rodgers (1964), Duvall (1971), Norton (1974), and Spanier, Lewis and Cole (1975). Numerous other wordings for the concept that have been suggested include "lifetime family career" (Feldman and Feldman, 1975) and "life course of the family."

*Revision of a paper presented at the annual meeting of the Population Association of America in Montreal, Canada, on April 30, 1976. The tables and text were prepared from January to March 1976, but some of the numbers in the tables were compiled as long as twelve years ago.

**Population Division, Bureau of the Census, U.S. Department of Commerce, Washington, D.C. 20233.

TABLE 1. MEDIAN AGE OF MOTHERS AT SELECTED STAGES OF THE FAMILY LIFE CYCLE

Stage of the Family Life Cycle	80-Year Average	Period of Birth of Mother							
		1880's	1890's	1900's	1910's	1920's	1930's	1940's	1950's
		Approximate Period of First Marriage							
		1900's	1910's	1920's	1930's	1940's	1950's	1960's	1970's
Median age at:									
First marriage	20.9	21.4	21.2	21.0	21.4	20.7	20.0	20.5	21.2
Birth of first child	22.6	23.0	22.9	22.8	23.5	22.7	21.4	21.8	22.7
Birth of last child	31.3	32.9	32.0	31.0	32.0	31.5	31.2	30.1	29.6
Marriage of last child	53.5	55.4	54.8	53.0	53.2	53.2	53.6	52.7	52.3
Death of one spouse	62.8	57.0	59.6	62.3	63.7	64.4	65.1	65.1	65.2
Difference between age at first marriage and:									
Birth of first child	1.7	1.6	1.7	1.8	2.1	2.0	1.4	1.3	1.5
Birth of last child	10.4	11.5	10.8	10.0	10.6	10.8	11.2	9.6	8.4
Marriage of last child	32.6	34.0	33.6	32.0	31.8	32.5	33.6	32.2	31.1
Death of one spouse	41.9	35.6	38.4	41.3	42.3	43.7	45.1	44.6	44.0
Difference between:									
Age at birth of first and last children	8.7	9.9	9.1	8.2	8.5	8.8	9.8	8.3	6.9
Age at birth of and marriage of last child	22.2	22.5	22.8	22.0	21.2	21.7	22.4	22.6	22.7
Age at marriage of last child and death of one spouse (empty nest)	9.3	1.6	4.8	9.3	10.5	11.2	11.5	12.4	12.9

Source: U.S. Bureau of the Census Reports. See text.

longtime decline in age at marriage has been greater for men.[2]

STAGES OF THE FAMILY LIFE CYCLE

In this section, the median ages of women who are currently at the beginning of the several family life cycle stages are compared: (1) with the 80-year average of these ages and (2) with the range of variation in these ages from the highest to the lowest for the eight decades covered by the study. In both this section and the following section, some closely related measures of demographic changes that elucidate family life cycle changes are discussed. The final section deals with some of the implications of the underlying changes that have affected trends in family life cycle patterns.

The median age of women at first marriage has varied around the 80-year average of 20.9 years. The highest level was 21.4 years for women whose marriages occurred largely during the first decade of the 20th century and for those whose marriages occurred largely during the economic depression of the 1930's (Figure 1 and Table 1). The lowest level was 20.0 years for those who married in the 1950's. These women have had not only the youngest marriages but also the smallest proportion who never married—only 4

[2]The methodology followed in the preparation of the tables presented in this article is explained in considerable detail elsewhere (Shryock and Siegel, 1971:310-312; Glick and Parke, 1965). The values in the tables probably vary somewhat in degree of reliability, with those for the four central decades being based on the least estimation or projection.

percent—and the highest birth rate in many decades. Those women who are now in the main ages for entry into marriage will have an estimated median age at first marriage of 21.2 years. This is only slightly above the 80-year average but more than one year above the record low point that was reached in the 1950's.

Changes in the median age of *men* at first marriage are not featured here, but they have been more substantial than those of women.

FIGURE 1. MEDIAN AGE OF MOTHERS AT THE BEGINNING OF SELECTED STAGES OF THE FAMILY LIFE CYCLE

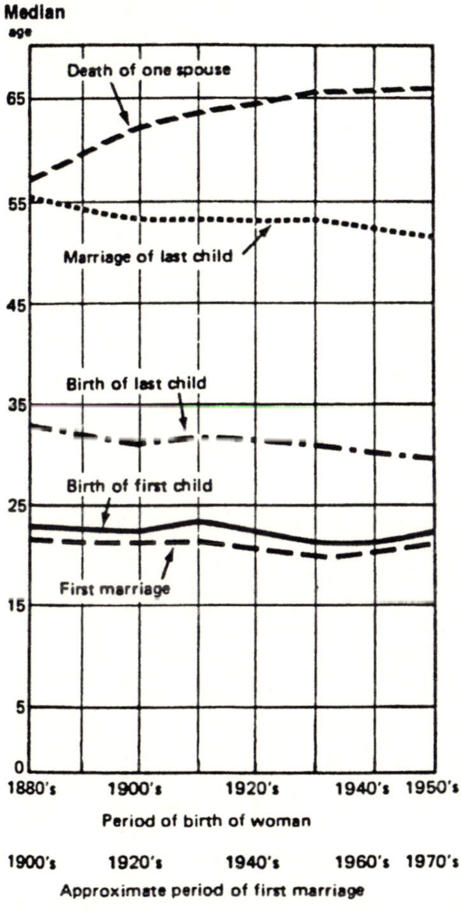

Source: Table 1.

Estimated median ages at first marriage for men who were born during the eight decades were as follows: 25.4 years for men born in the 1880's; 24.7 in the 1890's; 24.0 in the 1900's; 24.2 in the 1910's; 23.2 in the 1920's; 22.5 in the 1930's; 22.9 in the 1940's; and 23.6 in the 1950's. Of special interest is the fact that these estimates imply a decline of about three years in the median age at first marriage between the median age for those born in the earliest period and the one for those born 50 years later in the 1930's. Most of the men in the earlier group entered marriage during the first decade of the century and most of the later group entered during the period of high marriage rates after World War II. The corresponding decline for women was only about one-half as large. The time span between the early 1900's and the 1950's was marked by many changes including a gradual decline in the proportion of men in their twenties who consisted of relatively late-marrying persons of foreign birth.

The median age of mothers at the birth of their first child has ranged between 21.5 and 23.5 years. Women who marry in the 1970's are expected to be about 22.7 years old, on the average, at the birth of their first child. This is very near the 80-year average of 22.6 years. The highest median age at first childbirth was registered for women who married mostly during the 1930's. These women tended to marry late, to have a high rate of childlessness, and to have relatively few children, as is documented in Table 2. The lowest median age at first childbirth was that for women who married mostly during the 1950's, when women married early, when the interval between marriage and the birth of the first child was quite short, and when the number of children per mother reached a peak only a little lower than that for the oldest cohort covered in the study.

The median age of mothers at the birth of their last child has declined almost continuously from a high level of 32.9 years to an expected low level of 29.6 years. Women who married early in the century had the oldest age at the birth of the last child, consistent with their having the largest number of children (Table 2). By contrast, the youngest age at the completion of childbearing can be expected by women who are currently entering marriage. These women will proba-

TABLE 2. PERCENTAGE OF WOMEN IN THEIR FORTIES WHO NEVER MARRIED, PERCENTAGE WHO REMAINED CHILDLESS, AVERAGE NUMBER OF CHILDREN EVER BORN, AND AVERAGE INTERVAL PER CHILD BETWEEN MARRIAGE AND BIRTH OF LAST CHILD

SUBJECT	80-Year Average	Period of Birth of Woman							
		1880's	1890's	1900's	1910's	1920's	1930's	1940's	1950's
		Approximate Period of First Marriage							
		1900's	1910's	1920's	1930's	1940's	1950's	1960's	1970's
Marriage and Motherhood									
All women (thousands)	—	6,296	8,329	9,563	11,458	12,405	11,733	12,220	10,305
Percentage[a]	100.0	100.0	100.0	100.0	100.0	100.0	100.0	100.0	100.0
Ever married	93.2	91.2	90.9	91.9	93.7	94.6	95.9	94.0	93.0
Never married	6.9	8.8	9.1	8.1	6.3	5.4	4.1	6.0	7.0
Mothers	83.2	78.3	77.6	74.1	79.3	85.9	89.9	90.6	89.6
Ever married	82.3	77.4	76.7	73.3	78.6	85.3	89.1	89.6	88.6
Never married	0.8	0.9	0.9	0.8	0.6	0.5	0.8	1.0	1.0
Childless	16.8	21.7	22.4	25.9	20.7	14.1	10.1	9.4	10.4
Ever married	10.8	13.9	14.3	18.6	15.1	9.3	6.8	4.4	4.4
Never married	6.0	7.9	8.2	7.3	5.6	4.8	3.3	5.0	6.0
Number of Children									
Average number born:									
Per woman[a]	2.58	2.9	2.6	2.2	2.3	2.8	3.1	2.5	2.2
Per woman ever married	2.78	3.3	2.9	2.4	2.5	3.0	3.2	2.6	2.3
Per mother	3.18	3.9	3.4	3.1	2.9	3.3	3.5	2.8	2.5
Average number of years *per child* between first marriage and birth of the last child	3.3	2.9	3.2	3.2	3.7	3.3	3.2	3.4	3.4

Source: Several reports of the U.S. Bureau of the Census. See text.
[a] For women at or near the end of the reproductive period (in their forties).

bly have both a smaller number of children and a shorter period of childbearing than any other cohort of women who married during the 20th Century. The 80-year average age at the birth of the last child was 31.3 years.

The median age of mothers at the marriage of their last child has declined about three years, from 55.4 to 52.3 years, and has averaged 53.5 years.[3] When the last child leaves home, the "postchildren" or "empty nest" stage of the family life cycle begins. Among couples who reached this stage early in the 20th Century, the last child generally left home when he or she married and established a separate household. However, during more recent times an increasing proportion of young adults have been leaving home before they marry, but a long series of statistics to demonstrate this well-recognized fact is not available.[4] The end of childbearing is being reached at a younger age now than formerly, primarily because women are having fewer children and a decreasing proportion of their children are being born to them late in the reproductive period.

The estimated age of the last child at first marriage has changed very little over the last 80 years, as can be seen from the next to last

[3]The age of the last son or daughter at first marriage is assumed to be halfway between the ages at first marriage of men and women about three decades after their father and mother had married.

[4]Data from the U.S. Bureau of the Census (1973a: Tables 203 and 204) provide the basis for estimating that in 1970, one-half of the young women were no longer living in their parental home by the time they were about 18.8 years old, and nine-tenths had left by the age of 24.5 years. For young men, the corresponding ages were 19.2 years and 27.9 years.

line in Table 1. This finding is related to the more or less parallel decline (1) of the gap between the ages of husbands and wives and (2) of the age of the mother at the birth of her last child.

The median age at the death of one spouse increased sharply from 57.0 to 65.1 years and then leveled off. This eight-year increase in the joint survival of the married couple is largely a consequence of the lowering of mortality rates during the first half of the 20th century. Added to this eight-year longer survival is the three-year earlier age of the mother at the marriage of her last child. Thus, the period of the empty nest has been increased during the 80-year period by fully 11 years—from 1.6 years to 12.9 years—as the last line of Table 1 shows. Instead of the couple's marriage being dissolved through the death of one spouse (usually the husband) less than two years after the last child marries, as was the situation at the beginning of the period studied, the couple now entering marriage has the prospect of living together 13 years, or more than one-third of the 44 years of married life that lay ahead of them at the time of marriage.[5]

RELATED PATTERNS OF MARRIAGE AND MOTHERHOOD

As the foregoing discussion has pointed out, most of the fluctuations in the starting points of family life cycle stages have occurred when there were closely related changes in economic conditions (notably the economic depression of the 1930's and the decades of affluence after World War II) and longtime demographic changes. These demographic changes include a decline in the proportion of women who never marry, a decline in the rate of childlessness, a decline over much of the 80 years in the number of children per mother, a fluctuation of the intervals between children, and an improvement in the survival rates for adults. Documentation of most of these developments is found in the lower part of Table 1 and in Table 2 and is discussed in this section.

The proportion of women who never marry has averaged about 7 percent over the last 80 years. During the first three decades covered by this study, 8 or 9 percent of the women ended their reproductive period without having ever married. During the next three decades the proportion who never married declined to 6 percent, 5 percent, and 4 percent, respectively. The last figure, 4 percent, relates to women born during the low-birth-rate period of the economic depression but who married during the 1950's and who had both the lowest age at marriage and the highest birth rate per woman (but not per mother) of any cohort covered here. The two youngest cohorts have developed a pattern of postponing marriage and are assumed to be heading toward higher proportions of women who never marry before middle age—perhaps 6 or 7 percent. These young cohorts of women have faced the marital obstacle of their numbers during the main ages at first marriage being about 5 to 10 percent higher than the corresponding proportion for men—a phenomenon referred to for several years as the marriage squeeze (Carter and Glick, 1976:81). However, during the 1980's, the situation should be reversed, so that men, rather than women, of the most marriageable ages should be in excess supply.

During the last 80 years the proportion of women who have remained childless has averaged about 17 percent but has varied widely. The overall average includes 11 percent of all women who married but remained childless and 6 percent who never married and also remained childless. Between the first 40 years and the last 40 years covered by the study the rate of childlessness dropped very sharply—from a range of 21 to 26 percent for the first half to a range of only 9 to 14 percent for the second half. To what

[5]If the length of the empty nest period is measured from the time when the last child marries (rather than from the time of marriage), a very different perspective emerges. For the entire 80 years covered by the study, the average age at entering the empty nest period was 68.4 years. For successive birth cohorts the corresponding ages were: 69.2 for those born in the 1880's; 68.1 in the 1890's; 67.8 in the 1900's; 68.2 in the 1910's; 67.7 in the 1920's; 68.9 in the 1930's; 68.7 in the 1940's; and 68.6 for those born in the 1950's. This basis of measuring the empty nest period shows it to be 13.8 years for the oldest cohort (69.2 minus 55.4 years) as compared with 16.3 years for the youngest cohort (68.6 minus 52.3 years). Most of the 2.5-year increase in the period as determined by this approach is accounted for by the decrease in age at the marriage of the last child. Moreover, most of the difference between the measure of 11.3 years for the period by the first method and 2.5 years by the second method is attributable to the fact that nearly all of the improvement in sustaining the life of adults has been limited to the prolongation of life until persons are in their fifties.

extent this remarkable decline in childlessness is attributable to medical advances that produced changes in the level of diseases related to childbirth has not been examined by the author, but competent demographers, including Grabill, Kiser and Whelpton (1958:217) and Farley (1970:222-235), have been convinced that these factors are very important.

As a caution, the estimated proportion of ever-married women in the two youngest cohorts who remain childless (4.4 percent) is quite low but is based directly on the expectations of wives under 40 years old that were reported in the June 1975, Current Population Survey (adjusted to a base of *all* women). Likewise, the relatively large proportion of all women who will be childless never-married women in the two youngest cohorts is partly a consequence of an assumed upturn in singlehood among women who will be approaching middle age. Basic data used in arriving at this level were obtained from fertility data for single women in a 1970 census report (U.S. Bureau of the Census, 1973a: Table 65).

During the last 80 years the average ever-married mother had 3.2 children. The present study features averages for ever-married mothers and therefore removes from the coverage the widely variable proportions of women who remained unmarried and/or childless. The effect of basing the size of completed family on all women, all ever-married women, or ever-married mothers is substantial for the oldest cohort but minimal for the youngest cohort. The oldest cohort produced an average (mean) of 2.9 children per woman, 3.3 per ever-married woman, and 3.9 per ever-married mother. At the other extreme, the expected number of children to be produced by the youngest cohort is 2.2 per woman, 2.3 per ever-married woman, and 2.5 per ever-married mother. The swings in the average number of children per ever-married mother included a high level of 3.9 children for the oldest cohort, a gradual decline to a low level of 2.9 children for the cohort born in the 1910's (most of whom married during the depression years of the 1930's), a subsequent rise to a peak of 3.5 children during the 1950's (the main decade of the post-World War II baby boom), and a current phase of decline to an expected level of 2.5 children per ever-married mother.

During the last 80 years, the average period between first marriage and the birth of the first child was 1.7 years.[6] The longest interval between marriage and the birth of the first child occurred among women who were marrying in the 1930's and 1940's, when the interval was about 2 years. But the interval was as short as 1.6 years for women marrying in the early 1900's and as short as an estimated 1.3 years for those who married in the 1960's. The projected length of the interval for the youngest cohort is 1.5 years (18 months) between marriage and birth of the first child. The currently short interval between marriage and the birth of the first child results in part from the increase, during recent years, in the proportion of children who are born before their mothers marry. However, nearly all of these women eventually marry and therefore most of their children are included in the computations for ever-married mothers (that is, mothers who marry by the time they reach their forties).

During the last 80 years, the average period between first marriage and the birth of the last children was 10.4 years. The length of this period was highest, as expected, among mothers who married in the early 1900's and in the 1950's, when the average number of births was relatively high. During these decades, the childbearing interval exceeded 11 years. By contrast, the average interval is expected to be less than 10 years for those now entering marriage, because the age at first marriage is rising, the number of children is expected to be small, and the proportion of children who are born to women late in their reproductive period is continuing to decline. The growing proportion of women (or their husbands) who become voluntarily sterilized after they have all the children they want should reduce the possibility of a resurgence of the birth rate during the next decade or so (Presser and Bumpass, 1972).

In addition, if the median age at birth of last child seems to be higher than expected (30 years currently), and if the difference between the median age at birth of the first and last children seems too long (8 years currently), the reason may be that a child of a

[6]The intervals cited here and in the remainder of this section represent differences between the median ages of women at the time of two family life cycle events rather than direct measures of the intervals.

given order (second, third, etc.) tends to be spaced somewhat later in the life of the mother if it is her *last* child rather than a child of the same order that is born to a woman who subsequently has one or more additional children (U.S. Bureau of the Census, 1961: Table 11; Henry, 1954:760).

During the last 80 years, the average length of the interval per child between marriage and the birth of the last child was 3.3 years. Although the range of variation in this measure was relatively (and perhaps surprisingly) small, it did vary from 2.9 years per child for women who married in the early 1900's and who had the largest number of children to 3.7 years per child for women who married in the 1930's and who had the smallest number of children of any cohort before the recent decline to a new low level. This relatively small amount of variation in childspacing tends to reflect mainly an inverse relationship between the number of children and the length of the interval between children. If the projected size of completed family for the two youngest cohorts turns out to be as small as projected (2.8 and 2.5 children per mother, respectively), and if the interval between first marriage and the birth of the last child turns out to be as short as that projected (9.6 and 8.4 years, respectively), the average childspacing interval will be 3.4 years, or very near the 80-year average.

CONCLUSION

This study has featured an 80-year perspective on the average ages of mothers at the beginning of five stages in the life cycle, or life course, of the family. The most noteworthy *longtime* changes in the timing of the stages were shown to be traceable primarily to fluctuations in the birth rate and to improvements in survival rates among adults. The noteworthy *recent* changes include an increasing postponement of marriage on the part of women and a development not featured here, namely, the emergence of more single-parent families as a consequence of rising rates of separation, divorce, and premarital childbearing. Some implications of these changes will be discussed briefly.

The longtime decline in the birth rate was interrupted by the post-World War II baby boom which lasted about 15 years. The average family that was formed in the early years of the 20th century had four children, as compared with three children for the average family that was started during the depression years of the 1930's. The baby boom in the 1950's added about one child in every other family, whereas the recurrence of the historic decline in the birth rate during the last 15 years has once again reduced the average family size by one child. Consequently, the average mother who is forming her family during the present decade can expect to have somewhere between two and three children.

Growing up in a family of four children is quite different in many ways from growing up in one of two children. The larger the family the larger the proportion of time the children are likely to spend interacting with each other, whereas the smaller the family the greater the proportion of time the children are likely to spend interacting with their parents—whose views are likely to differ more widely from those of the child than the views of their brother(s) and/or sister(s). Moreover, the roles of the two parents in relation to each other undoubtedly tend to be affected by the fewer demands of two children rather than four children. The smaller family implies many other things, including the following: the period of family building tends to be shorter; the number and timing of the children's births are more likely to have been planned so as to minimize the negative effects of childbirth on the mother's health; the degree of need for the mother to devote full time for many years to childbearing is lessened; and the ability of the couple to provide adequately for the needs of their growing and maturing children is enhanced.

The much longer empty nest period now than formerly is perhaps the most dramatic change that has occurred in the pattern of the typical family life cycle. The increase from two years to 13 years for this stage, largely as a consequence of improving survival rates, has a multitude of social, economic, and psychological implications. These include a longer period during which husbands and their wives associate together in the absence of children—a situation that has the attendant potentiality of developing either more harmonious or more strained relations between the two. During this period, the average income per family member reaches a peak, in part, because many more wives seek employment at this time in order to fill their days with meaningful activity. At the same time, their earnings help to improve the living standard of their family, including their children who have established separate homes elsewhere. In addition, since this period is likely to last for a decade or more, a substantial number of postchildren couples find it worthwhile to move into smaller but more modern living quarters.

Other particularly noteworthy changes that are documented by this study include a recent trend toward a rising age at which women enter into first marriage and a projected decline in the average age at which the last child is born. These changes in marriage and childspacing have been developing during the last two decades in a period of declining fertility and a quite low level of childlessness. Among the consequences of these changes has been a more nearly universal sharing of the process of childrearing.

Finally, married couples are featured in this study, even though the current era is marked by increasing numbers of single-parent families and of couples living together informally. In this study, attention is called to the following observations about the continuing appeal of married life among most of the adults in this country who live through middle age (Uhlenberg, 1969):

(1) Eighty-four percent of all families in 1975 were husband-wife families, and in about seven of every eight of these families the husband was still in his first marriage (U.S. Bureau of the Census, 1973b, 1976b).
(2) Only a fraction of one percent of all couples have been identified as living together and maintaining a quasifamilial relationship outside of marriage (Carter and Glick, 1976: Chapter 13).
(3) Even if rising divorce rates eventually have the effect of dissolving one-third of all first marriages, as has been estimated (Norton and Glick, 1976; see also Preston, 1975), two of every three couples will have intact marriages throughout their joint survival.
(4) About three-fourths of the women and five-sixths of the men who become divorced eventually remarry (within an average interval of three years). Recently compiled figures indicate that it is likely that somewhere between one-half and two-thirds of those who remarry will remain married from that time forward as long as both partners survive (U.S. Bureau of the Census, 1976c).
(5) The eventual number of children per divorced woman who remarries and then remains married until the end of the reproductive period is quite similar to the number for women whose first marriage remains intact (U.S. Bureau of the Census, 1973a: Tables 22 and 23).

In view of the growing incidence of divorce in this country, a full analysis of the family life cycle for persons who divorce and remarry should be the subject of another study.

REFERENCES

Carter, Hugh, and Paul C. Glick
1976 Marriage and Divorce: A Social and Economic Study (2nd ed.). Cambridge, Massachusetts: Harvard University Press.

Duvall, Evelyn M.
1971 Family Development (4th ed.). Philadelphia: J. B. Lippincott.

Farley, Reynolds
1970 Growth of the Black Population: A Study of Demographic Trends. Chicago:Markham Publishing Co.

Feldman, Harold, and Margaret Feldman
1975 "The family life cycle: Some suggestions for recycling." Journal of Marriage and the Family 37 (May):277-284.

Glick, Paul C.
1947 "The family cycle." American Journal of Sociology 12 (April):164-174.

Glick, Paul C., and Robert Parke, Jr.
1965 "New approaches in studying the life cycle of the family." Demography 2:187-202.

Grabill, Wilson H., Clyde V. Kiser, and Pascal K. Whelpton
1958 The Fertility of American Women. New York: John Wiley and Sons.

Henry, Louis
1954 "Intervalles entre naissances." Population 9 (October-December):759-761.

Hill, Reuben, and Roy H. Rodgers
1964 "The developmental approach." Pp. 171-211 in Harold T. Christensen (Ed.), Handbook of Marriage and the Family. Chicago:Rand McNally.

Loomis, Charles P., and C. Horace Hamilton
1936 "Family life cycle analysis." Social Forces 15 (December):225-231.

Norton, Arthur J.
1974 "The family-life cycle updated: Components and uses." Pp. 162-170 in Robert F. Winch

and Graham B. Spanier (Eds.), Selected Studies in Marriage and the Family. New York: Holt, Rinehart, and Winston.

Norton, Arthur J., and Paul C. Glick
1976 "Marital instability: Past, present and future." Journal of Social Issues 32 (1):5-20.

Presser, Harriet B., and Larry L. Bumpass
1972 "The acceptability of contraceptive sterilization among U.S. couples: 1970." Family Planning Perspectives 4 (October):18-26.

Preston, Samuel H.
1975 "Estimating the proportion of American marriages that end in divorce." Sociological Methods and Research 3 (May):435-460.

Shryock, Henry S., and Jacob S. Siegel
1971 The Methods and Materials of Demography. Washington, D.C.:Superintendent of Documents.

Spanier, Graham B., and Robert A. Lewis, and Charles L. Cole
1975 "Marital adjustment over the family life cycle: The issue of curvilinearity." Journal of Marriage and the Family 37 (May):263-275.

Uhlenberg, Peter R.
1969 "A study of cohort life cycles: Cohorts of native born Massachusetts women, 1830-1920." Population Studies 23 (November):407-420.

U.S. Bureau of the Census
1961 "Marriage, fertility, and childspacing: August 1959." Current Population Reports (P-20, No. 108). Washington, D.C.:U.S. Government Printing Office.
1973a Women by Number of Children Ever Born. Subject Reports (PC2-3A). Washington, D.C.: U.S. Government Printing Office.
1973b Family Composition. Subject Reports (PC2-4A). Washington, D.C.:U.S. Government Printing Office.
1976a "Fertility history and prospects of American women: June 1975." Current Population Reports (P-20, No. 288). Washington, D.C.:U.S. Government Printing Office.
1976b "Household and family characteristics: March 1975." Current Population Reports (P-20, No. 291). Washington, D.C.:U.S. Government Printing Office.
1976c "Number, timing, and duration of marriages and divorces in the United States: June 1975." Current Population Reports (P-20, No. 297). Washington, D.C.:U.S. Government Printing Office.

Copyright Information

Demos, John. "The American Family in Past Time." *The American Scholar* 43:3 (Summer 1974): 422-446. "Reprinted from THE AMERICAN SCHOLAR, Volume 43, No. 3, Summer 1974. Copyright 1974 by the United Chapters of Phi Beta Kappa," Washington D.C., USA.

Smith, Daniel Scott. "Parental Power and Marriage Patterns: An Analysis of Historical Trends in Hingham, Massachusetts." *Journal of Marriage and the Family* 35:3 (August 1973): 419-428. "©Copyrighted 1973 by The National Council on Family Relations, 3989 Central Ave., N. E., Suite #550, Minneapolis, MN 55421 (USA) Reprinted by permission."

Wells, Robert V. "Family History and the Demographic Transition." *Journal of Social History* 9:1 (Fall 1975): 1-19. ©*Journal of Social History*, Carnegie-Mellon University Press, Pittsburgh, Pennsylvania, USA.

Cody, Cheryll Ann. "Naming, Kinship, and Estate Dispersal: Notes on Slave Family Life on a South Carolina Plantation, 1786 to 1833." *William and Mary Quarterly* 39:1 (January 1982): 192-211. ©Dr. Cheryll Ann Cody, University of Houston, Texas, USA.

Stowe, Steven M. "'The *Thing* Not Its Vision': A Woman's Courtship and Her Sphere in the Southern Planter Class." *Feminist Studies* 9:1 (Spring 1983): 113-30. ©by Feminist Studies, Inc., Women's Studies Program, University of Maryland, College Park, Maryland, USA.

Schweninger, Loren. "A Slave Family in the Ante Bellum South." *Journal of Negro History* 60:1 (January 1975): 29-44. "©1975 by Loren Schweninger in the *Journal of Negro History* published by the Association for the Study of Afro-American Life and History," Washington, DC, USA.

Fox-Genovese, Elizabeth. "Antebellum Southern Households: A New Perspective on a Familiar Question." *Review: a Journal of the Fernand Braudel Center* 7:2 (Fall 1983): 215-253. ©Fernand Braudel Center for the Study of Economics, Historical Systems, and Civilizations, State University of New York at Binghamton, Binghamton, New York, USA. Reprinted with permission of the Center and the author.

White, Deborah G. "Female Slaves: Sex Roles and Status in the Antebellum Plantation South." *Journal of Family History* 8:3 (Fall 1983): 248-61. ©JAI Press, Inc., Greenwich, CT, USA.

Dye, Nancy Schrom, and Daniel Blake Smith. "Mother Love and Infant Death, 1750-1920." *The Journal of American History* 73:2 (September 1986): 329-353. ©Organization of American Historians, 1986, Indiana University, Bloomington, Indiana, USA.

Pleck, Elizabeth. "Wife Beating in Nineteenth-Century America."*Victimology: An International Journal* 4:1 (1979): 60-74. "Reprinted by permission from *Victimology: An International Journal,* Volume 4, Number 1, pp. 60-74. ©1979, Victimology, Inc., All rights reserved." Arlington, Virginia, USA.

Smith, Daniel Scott. "Family Limitation, Sexual Control, and Domestic Feminism in Victorian America." *Feminist Studies* 1 (Winter-Spring 1973): 40-57. ©by Feminist Studies, Inc., Women's Studies Program, University of Maryland, College Park, Maryland, USA.

Furstenberg, Jr., Frank F., Theodore Hershberg, and John Modell. "The Origins of the Female-Headed Black Family: The Impact of the Urban Experience." *The Journal of Interdisciplinary History* 6:2 (Autumn 1975): 211-233. "Reprinted from *The Journal of Interdisciplinary History*, VI (1975), 211-233, with permission of the editors of *The Journal of Interdisciplinary History* and the MIT Press, Cambridge, Massachusetts. ©1975 by the Massachusetts Institute of Technology and the editors of *The Journal of Interdisiplinary History.*"

Iversen, Joan. "Feminist Implications of Mormon Polygyny." *Feminist Studies* 10:3 (Fall 1984): 505-522. ©by Feminist Studies, Inc., Women's Studies Program, University of Maryland, College Park, Maryland, USA.

Foster, Lawrence. "Polygamy and the Frontier: Mormon Women in Early Utah." *Utah Historical Quarterly* 50:3 (Summer 1982): 268-289. ©Utah State Historical Society, Salt Lake City, Utah, USA.

Sunoo, Sonia S. "Korean Women Pioneers of the Pacific Northwest." *Oregon Historical Quarterly* 79 (Spring 1978): 51-63. ©Oregon Historical Society, Portland, Oregon, USA.

Herman, Sondra R. "Loving Courtship or the Marriage Market? The Ideal and Its Critics, 1871-1911." *American Quarterly* 25:2 (May 1973), 235-52. "© 1973, 1985, 1986, 1965, 1966, 1981, 1982, 1980, 1979, 1967, 1974, American Studies Association, Washington, D. C., USA." Reprinted with permission of the Association and the author.

Meyerowitz, Joanne. "Women and Migration: Autonomous Female Migrants to Chicago, 1880-1930." *Journal of Urban History* 13:2 (February 1987): 147-168. "©1977 by Sage Publications, Inc. Reprinted by permission of Sage Publications, Inc., Newbury Park, California, USA."

Ichioka, Yuji. "*Amerika Nadeshiko*: Japanese Immigrant Women in the United States, 1900-1924." Pacific Historical Review 49:2 (May 1980), 339-357. "©1980 by The Pacific Coast Branch, American Historical Association. Reprinted from *Pacific Historical Review*, Vol. 48, No. 2, (May 1980), pp. 339-357 by permission" of the Association and the author.

Gordon, Linda. "Single Mothers and Child Neglect, 1880-1920." *American Quarterly* 37:2 (1985): 173-192. "© 1973, 1985, 1986, 1965, 1966, 1981, 1982, 1980, 1979, 1967, 1974, American Studies Association, Washington, D.C., USA." Reprinted with permission of the Association and the author.

Wells, Robert V. "Demographic Change and the Life Cycles of the American Families." *Journal of Interdisciplinary History* 2:2 (Autumn 1971): 273-282. "Reprinted from *The Journal of Interdisciplinary History*, II:2 (Autumn 1971), 211-233, with permission of the editors of *The Journal of Interdisciplinary History* and the MIT Press, Cambridge, Massachusetts. ©1971 by the Massachusetts Institute of Technology and the editors of *The Journal of Interdisiplinary History*."

Glick, Paul C. "Updating the Life Cycle of the Family." *Journal of Marriage and the Family* 39:1 (February 1977): 5-13. "©Copyrighted 1977 by The National Council on Family Relations, 3989 Central Ave., N. E., Suite #550, Minneapolis, MN 55421 (USA). Reprinted by permission."

Index